P9-DTM-187

COMMENTARY ON MARK

J. D. JONES

KREGEL PUBLICATIONS
Grand Rapids, Michigan 49501

Commentary on Mark by J. D. Jones © 1992 by Kregel
Publications, a division of Kregel Inc., P.O. Box 2607,
Grand Rapids, MI 49501. All rights reserved.

Cover & Book Design: Al Hartman

Library of Congress Cataloging-in-Publication Data

Jones, J. D. (John Daniel), 1865-1942.
  [Gospel according to St. Mark]
  Commentary on Mark / J. D. Jones.
    p. cm.
  Originally published: The Gospel according to St.
Mark. London: Religious Tract Society, 1914.
  1. Bible. N. T. Mark—Commentaries. I. Title.
BS2585.J58   1991   226.3'07—dc20   91-37165
                                                 CIP

ISBN 0-8254-2970-6

1 2 3 4 5 printing/year 96 95 94 93 92

Printed in the United States of America

126.307
718c

L. I. F. E Bible College
LIBRARY
1100 COVINA BLVD
SAN DIMAS, CA 91773

Contents

039228

5

6　　　　　　　　　　　　　　　　　　　　　　　　**Contents**

Contents

1
The Beginning of the Gospel

"The beginning of the Gospel of Jesus Christ, the Son of God." —Mark 1:1.

"The Gospel of Jesus Christ"
THE COMMENTATORS TELL us that the phrase "the Gospel of Jesus Christ" may mean one of two things. (a) It may mean the Gospel which Jesus Christ preached. (b) It may mean also the Gospel of which Jesus Christ is the subject.

The Gospel He Was
It is in this latter sense Mark uses the phrase here. He is thinking not so much of the Gospel Jesus preached, as of the Gospel He was. He is about to tell us the good news about Jesus, and—man of action as he is—he finds the "beginning" of it in our Lord's first public appearance and definite entrance upon the work of His ministry. And that, of course, was a very real beginning. As far as the great world was concerned, it was the beginning, for it knew nothing of the Gospel, the Gospel had no existence for it, until Jesus came teaching and preaching. But, as Dr. Morison says, "Mark might have gone further back, and found other fountains, the feeders of the fountains at which he pauses." That is to say, there are other "beginnings of the Gospel," carrying us further back than this "beginning" of St Mark. Let us think for a moment of some of these other "beginnings."

Other "Beginnings" of the Gospel: St. Matthew's and St. Luke's
(1) I turn to the Gospels by Matthew and Luke, and I find they "begin" with Bethlehem. The birth of the little Child "all amid the winter's snow" was to them the "beginning of the Gospel." That was how the angel announced His birth, "Behold, I bring you Gospel . . . there is born to you this day a Savior" (Luke 2:10, 11). And was it not true? Did not new hope and joy come into the world with the coming of that little Child? Trace back the pity and compassion and love that enrich the world today; you will find

9

they have their fountain in Bethlehem! Indeed, the world dates its life from the birthday of Jesus. We put A.D. on our letters, as if the years before Christ came were scarcely worth the counting, and could not be reckoned as true life at all. Yes, it was the "beginning of the Gospel" for the world, when the Son of God emptied Himself, "took upon Him the form of a servant, and was made in the likeness of men" (Phil. 2:7).

St. John's
(2) But I turn to the Gospel by St John, and I find that for his "beginning" he goes further back than Bethlehem. He travels beyond the region of time into the region of eternity. "In the beginning was the Word" (John 1:1), he writes, and at once transports us to the glory which the Son had with the Father before the world began. And back to that eternity where John starts from, we shall have to travel, if we want to discover the absolute "beginning of the Gospel."

So we are led ever further back in our search for "the beginning:" from the Baptism first of all to the Birth, and then from the Birth to the Promises, and then from the Promises to the Eternal Purpose of God. For Jesus was "the Lamb slain from the foundation of the world" (Rev. 13:8), or, as Peter states it still more strikingly, He was "pre-known from before the foundation of the world" (1 Peter 1:20). That is where the Gospel finds its real ultimate beginning, in "the determinate counsel and foreknowledge of God," and who shall attempt to fix a date for that?

In the Individual Soul
(3) And there is yet one other "beginning of the Gospel," i.e., the beginning it has in the individual soul. The Gospel has a new beginning when, as Paul would say, "Christ is formed" in a human heart. The Gospel began for Zacchaeus the day Christ lodged in his house. It began for Saul the day he heard the Lord's voice on the way to Damascus. It began for Augustine the day he heard the child sing, "Take and read, take and read." It began for John Wesley the day he felt his heart "strangely warmed " in the little meeting-house in Aldersgate Street.

Every time Christ is born in a man's heart, the Gospel has a new beginning. And every other beginning of the Gospel—its beginning in the eternal purpose of God, its beginning at Bethlehem, its beginning at the Baptism—will be of none effect, as far as you, my reader, and I are concerned, unless it has another "beginning" in you and me.

This is the "beginning" of the Gospel that saves a man—when the Christ of history becomes the Christ of the heart; when the infinite love of God to the world in His Son ceases to be a story, and becomes an experience.

2
The Forerunner

"As it is written in the Prophets, Behold, I send My messenger before Thy face, which shall prepare Thy way before Thee. The voice of one crying in the wilderness, Prepare ye the way of the Lord, make His paths straight. John did baptize in the wilderness, and preach the baptism of repentance for the remission of sins. And there went out unto him all the land of Judea, and they of Jerusalem, and were all baptized of him in the river of Jordan, confessing their sins. And John was clothed with camel's hair, and with a girdle of a skin about his loins; and he did eat locusts and wild honey; and preached, saying, There cometh One mightier than I after me, the latchet of whose shoes I am not worthy to stoop down and unloose. I indeed have baptized you with water: but He shall baptize you with the Holy Ghost."   —Mark 1:2-8.

THE PRECEDING CHAPTER dealt with "the beginning of the Gospel." Mark finds his "beginning" in our Lord's first public appearance at the baptism of John. It is quite natural therefore that he should begin the story of our Lord's life with a brief account of John and his work.

John the Baptist

Let us think together for a short time about that John of whom these verses speak. With his usual habit of going straight to the point, Mark omits what the other Evangelists have to say about John's birth and training, and introduces him to us actually engaged in that stupendous work to which God had called him from the womb.

His Work

And what was that work? It was the work of preparing the way for Jesus Christ. The commentators tell us that in the East the roads are usually so wretchedly kept that, whenever a royal personage wishes to visit any part of his dominions, a messenger must first of all be sent forward to make the road fit to travel on. And that is the function which Mark tells us (quoting the words of ancient prophecy) John fulfilled for Jesus. He went before Him to prepare the way. He traveled in advance to make things ready for the King's coming.

Other Preparers of the Way

We are not to suppose that John was the only one who prepared the way. In a very deep and real sense all history prepared the way for Jesus. The Jewish nation, with its unconquerable hope of a coming Redeemer; the Greek nation, with its incomparable language; the Roman nation, with its system of law and its unifying of the peoples— all prepared the way for Jesus. And the preparation that we see on the broad field of world history, we see still more clearly when we concentrate our attention on sacred history. What is the Old Testament? It is just a record of how God had been preparing the way. Begin in Genesis with the first promise of the "seed of the woman" who is to bruise the serpent's head, and read on till you come to Malachi with his announcement, "The Lord . . . shall suddenly come to His temple" (Mal. 3:1), and you will see how by means of prophet and psalmist and seer, God had been preparing the way. In this respect John only comes at the end of a long line.

John's Preeminence

And yet John was in a very special sense our Lord's forerunner. John's message was to the very same generation as that to which Christ preached. The men who flocked to John's baptism were the men who subsequently listened to Christ.

How He Prepared the Way

How did John prepare the way for Christ? By preaching the baptism of repentance. John's preaching was terrible preaching. Sin was his theme, and repentance his call. And by this terrible preaching he made straight the way of the Lord. It was sub-soil ploughing. He broke through the hard crust of conventionalism and self-righteousness, and made the ground of the heart soft and ready to receive the good seed of the Kingdom. And it is noticeable that it was from the ranks of those who had been baptized by John that our Lord gathered His first disciples. John had created within them a genuine sorrow for sin, an eager expectation of Messiah, and so when Jesus appeared they were ready to leave all and follow Him.

A Great Work, but Only Preparatory

It was a great work John did—but yet it was an imperfect work. It was a preparation, but it was only a preparation. John's call to repentance was no satisfaction to the craving of the soul. It needed the Gospel to perfect and complete it. John was himself conscious of the imperfection of his work, and always pointed on towards a great Another who was to come. "There cometh after me He that is mightier than I, the latchet of whose shoes I am not worthy to stoop down and unloose. . . . He shall baptize you with the Holy Ghost" (vv. 7, 8, R.V.). The utmost even the best of men can do is point to Jesus.

The Greater One and His Work

For there is only One who can really cleanse and regenerate the soul—"He shall baptize you with the Holy Ghost and with fire." "With the Holy Ghost"—and except a man be born of water and of the Spirit, he cannot enter the Kingdom of God. "And with fire"— to burn out all the dross and uncleanness of the heart and to inspire us with flaming zeal. Is not this the baptism we all want? For inward peace and efficiency in service, is not this the baptism we all want? This is the question of questions, Have ye received the Holy Ghost? For this gracious baptism we must look higher than man. We must look to the Greater One.

> "'Tis Thine to cleanse the heart,
>   To sanctify the soul—
> To pour fresh life in every part,
>   And new create the whole."

3
The Baptism

"And it came to pass in those days, that Jesus came from Nazareth of Galilee, and was baptized of John in Jordan. And straightway coming up out of the water, He saw the heavens opened, and the Spirit like a dove descending upon Him: And there came a voice from heaven, saying, Thou art My beloved Son, in whom I am well pleased." —Mark 1:9-11.

A Great Event Simply Told

How plain and simple and matter-of-fact the language of verse 9 is! And yet what a stupendous and altogether amazing event it chronicles! "And it came to pass in those days, that Jesus came from Nazareth of Galilee, and was baptized of John in Jordan" (v. 9). For what kind of a baptism was John's baptism? It was a baptism of repentance unto remission of sins. It was a baptism in which men made public confession of their sin, and cried to God to purge it away. But Jesus was "holy, harmless, undefiled, separate from sinners" (Heb. 7:26). He "did no sin, neither was guile found in His mouth" (1 Pet. 2:22).

What did Jesus want at a baptism of repentance? According to Matthew's account, John himself made protest against baptizing Jesus. We do not read that he hesitated to baptize anyone else. But when Jesus presented Himself he shrank from his office. His baptism was for the sinful, not for the sinless; for the vile, not for the holy. "I have need to be baptized of Thee," he cried, "and comest Thou to me?" (Matt. 3:14). But Jesus gently put John's objection aside, and the holy Lamb of God went down into the water and shared in the baptism of publicans and sinners.

The Meaning of Christ's Baptism

What is the meaning of our Lord's baptism? Perhaps the best commentary upon it is that deep word of St. Paul, "Him Who knew no sin He made to be sin on our behalf; that we might become the righteousness of God in Him" (2 Cor. 5:21, R.V.). For Jesus, as for all the rest, it was a "baptism of repentance."

But whose sin could He repent of? For He had no sin. No! He

15

had no sin of His own, but He had ours. He made confession in Jordan of your sin, my reader, and mine. For when Jesus entered our humanity, He so utterly and entirely identified Himself with us that He made our very sin His own. "Himself took our infirmities, and bare our sicknesses" (Matt. 8:17). He who knew no sin gathered upon His head and His heart all the sin and shame of His brothers and sisters; "He hath borne our griefs, and carried our sorrows. . . . And the Lord hath laid on Him the iniquity of us all" (Isa. 53:4, 6).

An Anticipation of Calvary

If we want to understand the full meaning of the baptism, we must see in it an anticipation of Calvary. The same boundless love which on the cross made our Lord offer sacrifice for sin, at the Jordan constrained Him to make confession of the sin of the race He had come to redeem. That was the central meaning of the baptism for Jesus.

The Descent of the Spirit

Mark proceeds to mention two significant events that accompanied it, viz., the descent of the Spirit and the Heavenly Voice.

"Straightway coming up out of the water, he saw the heavens rent asunder, and the Spirit as a dove descending upon Him" (v. 10, R.V.). The baptism marks our Lord's definite entrance upon His Messianic work; in the gift of the Spirit God furnishes Him with the equipment He needed for His high task. God never summons to a duty without supplying the necessary power.

It was so even with His Beloved Son. Up to now Jesus had lived a quiet, normal life at Nazareth; but after the baptism a change is to be noticed. He is equipped with the power of the Spirit. It was in the power of the Spirit He went into the wilderness to battle with Satan; it was in the power of the Spirit He came teaching and preaching in Galilee; it was in the power of the Spirit He healed the sick and cast out devils and did His many mighty works. God summoned Him to a stupendous task. But He also equipped Him for it; "God giveth not the Spirit by measure unto Him" (John 3:34).

"Like a Dove"

"Like a dove"; what an exquisite symbol! The action of the Spirit is compared in the Scriptures sometimes to the action of purifying and cleansing fire, sometimes to that of the mighty wind, blowing the chaff away. These are figures of violence. But the Spirit descended on Jesus "like a dove." What infinite gentleness and tenderness it suggests! Fit emblem for the Spirit of Him who never broke the bruised reed or quenched the smoking flax, and who was the "friend of publicans and sinners."

The Heavenly Voice

"And a voice came out of the heavens, Thou art my beloved Son, in Thee I am well pleased" (v. 11, R.V.). What was it evoked this expression of the Divine pleasure? The voluntary humiliation of our Lord. We sometimes make foolish antagonisms between God and Christ, as if wrath characterized the One and love the Other. But God and Christ are one in their passion for the redemption of men. And when Christ at the baptism stooped to bear human sin, God was well pleased.

"He that humbleth himself shall be exalted" (Luke 14:11), and it is then we are most truly God's sons, when we share in our Lord's baptism, and take upon our own hearts the burden and shame of human sin.

4
The Temptation

"And immediately the Spirit driveth Him into the wilderness. And He was there in the wilderness forty days, tempted of Satan; and was with the wild beasts; and the angels ministered unto Him."   —Mark 1:12, 13.

The Spirit's Compulsion

"AND STRAIGHTWAY THE Spirit driveth Him forth into the wilderness" (v. 12, R.V.). The Spirit did this! The Spirit which in Jordan had descended upon Him like a dove. The first thing the Spirit did was vehemently and violently to "cast Him forth" into the wilderness.

What strange work for the Spirit to do! It reminds us that there is an austere and bracing side to the Spirit's ministry. We sing, "Gracious Spirit, tender Spirit, dwell with me." But sometimes the Spirit comes as a "stern lawgiver." We read in Scripture of the Spirit hindering, forbidding, binding. It is this austere side of the Spirit's ministry we get here. The Spirit "driveth Him forth into the wilderness."

Its Meaning

"The Spirit driveth Him forth." What does this statement imply? Clearly this, there was a Divine necessity for the Temptation. This fierce struggle in the wilderness, just as certainly as the death on the cross, took place by the determinate counsel and foreknowledge of God. Can we discover wherein the "must needs" for this terrible experience lay? I think we may.

On the Side of God

(1) First there was a "must needs" from God's side. Jesus was God's chosen instrument for the redemption of the world and the establishment of His kingdom. But the redemption of the race was to be a costly business. It meant the bitter cross and everything that led up to it. And that was really the question that confronted our Lord in the wilderness. Was He ready to take God's path to the throne? The threefold temptation, as recorded by the other evan-

18

gelists, was really an appeal to Him to take a short cut to the throne, instead of traveling to it by the weary, rugged, blood-stained *via crucis*.

In vision it was revealed to our Lord what our redemption would cost. It was revealed to Him that it would mean rejection, scorn, Gethsemane, the cross. And the question was, whether Jesus was willing to do God's will at such a price. It was the Father's testing of the Son's obedience and faith. He showed Him the bitter cup the Redeemer of Souls would have to drink. Privations, sorrows, bitter scorn, the life of toil, the mean abode, the faithless kiss, the crown of thorns— these were all ingredients in that bitter cup. And the Father showed them all to His Son in the wilderness, and said, "Art Thou able to drink of the cup?" And our Lord, counting the bitternesses, every one, knowing all the pain and shame involved, answered His Father, "I am able."

On the Side of Man

(2) There was a further "must needs" in the Temptation from man's side. For Christ was to be not only God's Messiah, He was also to be our brother and friend. Now an untempted Christ could never be a friend for tempted folk. To be a true and helpful friend, it was necessary that He should be tempted in all points like as we are—for temptation plays a large part in every human life.

Queen Victoria, in a letter to Lord Tennyson after the death of his eldest son, wrote, "I say from the depth of a heart which has suffered cruelly and lost almost all it cared for and loved best, I feel for you; I know what you and your dear wife are suffering." The words that make that letter grateful and helpful are the words, "I know," "I feel." And Jesus passed through this struggle in the wilderness that He might be able to sympathize with us in our temptations. "I feel," Jesus cries to every struggling soul, "and I know."

Wild Beasts at Hand—and Angels

"And He was with the wild beasts; and the angels ministered unto Him" (v. 13, R:V.), "Wild beasts—angels"—what a startling contrast! "Wild beasts," eager to rend and tear and devour, and "angels," sent forth to minister for the sake of them that inherit salvation. They stand for the opposing forces at work in human souls, and in this great world of ours. There are wild beasts abroad. "My soul is among lions," cries the Psalmist (Psa. 57:4). "The devil, as a roaring lion, walketh about, seeking whom he may devour" (1 Pet. 5:8), says the apostle.

Here is an extract from a letter about one who had just made a start in the Christian life—"She has absolutely no help at home, as her mother will not allow the name of Jesus to be mentioned." Poor soul! She was among the "wild beasts."

But let us not forget that there are also angels about us, always eager to help and succor and save. And they come to us at our need, as they came to Jesus in the wilderness; as they came to Him again in the Garden; as they came to Peter on the eve of what was meant to be his execution; as they came to Paul when threatened with shipwreck. "He shall give His angels charge over thee" (Psa. 91:11). And after all the angels are mightier than the wild beasts. Where sin abounds, grace doth much more abound.

The Lord's Conflict and Ours

In the great conflict Jesus overcame. He "was in all points tempted like as we are, yet without sin" (Heb. 4:15). His victory is prophetic of ours. We too, in the strength of God, may "tread the powers of darkness down, and win the well-fought day."

5
John and Jesus

"Now, after that John was put in prison, Jesus came into Galilee, preaching the gospel of the kingdom of God, and saying, The time is fulfilled, and the kingdom of God is at hand: repent ye, and believe the gospel."

—Mark 1:14,15.

John and the Greater than John

The "delivering up" of John just when he was at the very height of his usefulness and power must have seemed to thousands in Palestine to be mere and sheer tragedy. But it often happens that "when the half gods go, the gods arrive," and so the imprisonment of John was but the signal for the appearance of Jesus.

When Herod shut up John in prison he probably thought he had silenced the one and only brave witness for purity and truth. When the people who loved John and believed in him heard that he had been so shut up, they probably thought that the great work he had begun was bound to come to an end. But Herod's hope and the people's fears were alike disappointed. Though John was silenced, God still had His witness. Though one worker was removed, God had Another ready to carry on the work. "Now after that John was delivered up, *Jesus came*" (v. 14, R.V.). The silencing of the Baptist opened the lips of Him who spake as never yet man spake.

The Futility of Resistance to God

How futile it is to try to stifle the truth and fight against the progress of the kingdom! God's work will never be allowed to come to a stand for lack of workers! The Sanhedrin stoned Stephen, but after Stephen came Paul. John Hus was burned in Constance, and Savonarola was gibbeted in Florence, but after Hus and Savonarola came Martin Luther. Mary kindled fires for Protestant confessors: she burned Latimer, Ridley, Hooper, Cranmer, in the hope of burning out Protestantism with them; but God raised one after another to continue their witness, and our free Protestant England is the result. It is ever so; God buries His workmen, but carries on His work. After John comes Jesus.

21

"Jesus came into Galilee, preaching the Gospel of God" (v. 14, R.V.). Jesus came to carry on John's work, and yet with a great difference.

The Two Messages

John's message was a stern one. It was his business to do what the old Scottish preachers called "law work," to beget conviction of sin; but the message of Jesus was a Gospel; it was glad tidings, it was good news. It was "the Gospel of God" He preached; the Gospel, that is, which originated with God, or which He received from God. It was a message of "pure mercy and of infinite love."

The Gospel of the Kingdom

And the mercy and love were specially revealed in the fact that the kingdom of God, long promised and long expected, was about to be established. But how different a kingdom it was from that which the Jews had looked for! "Jesus came preaching!" Preaching! What the Jews looked for was a prince who should come with a sword in his hand. Instead of that Jesus came preaching! He addressed Himself not to the political passions, but to the consciences of men. The kingdom He came to establish was not a kingdom of earthly majesty, it was a kingdom of souls.

Conditions of Entry into the Kingdom: Repentance

What are the conditions of entrance into this kingdom? "Repent ye," said Jesus, "and believe in the Gospel." "Repent"—that is John's call—taken up and repeated by Christ. And "repent" means more than being sorry for sin, it means the repudiation of it. "Lord, the half of my goods I give to the poor"—that is repenting. "What things were gain to me, these I counted loss for Christ"—that is repenting. "Burn them," said a convert in the Welsh Revival, handing to his minister three gambling-clubs' membership tickets—that is repenting. And let us settle it with our hearts, there is no entering the kingdom without repenting.

Faith

"Repent and believe." Repentance is incomplete without faith. John left it at "repent." Jesus added a new article, "and believe in the Gospel." John said, "Put your sin away." Jesus added, "and receive into your souls the love and mercy of God."

Believe in the Gospel! Believe in the goodness and the mercy of God. "The Son of God . . . loved me, and gave Himself for me " (Gal. 2:20)— believe in that.

The Case of Samuel Johnson

Do we believe in it? It is a simple and quiet faith in this Gospel that brings peace and joy. Dr. Johnson repented many a time, as his diaries bear witness. He was constantly bemoaning his sins. But it was not till he came to his dying bed that he really found peace. A clergyman wrote to him as he lay in his last illness to this effect: "I say to you, in the language of the Baptist, 'Behold the Lamb of God.'"

"Does it say so?" murmured Johnson. "Read it again."

And the word about Jesus, the Lamb of God, in love bearing the burden of human sin, brought quiet comfort to his heart; and as we believe in the same glorious Gospel we too shall enter into peace.

6
The Call of the First Disciples

"Now as He walked by the sea of Galilee, He saw Simon and Andrew his brother casting a net into the sea: for they were fishers. And Jesus said unto them, Come ye after Me, and I will make you to become fishers of men. And straightway they forsook their nets, and followed Him. And when He had gone a little farther thence, He saw James the son of Zebedee, and John his brother, who also were in the ship mending their nets. And straightway He called them: and they left their father Zebedee in the ship with the hired servants, and went after Him." —Mark 1:18-20.

The Master and the First Disciples

This was by no means the first meeting between Jesus and these two pairs of brothers. This is a case in which, to make the story rational, we must compare Scripture with Scripture. For we cannot conceive of these men leaving their boats and their nets, and in the case of two of them, their father and mother as well, had it been a complete and utter stranger who said to them, "Come ye after Me." Behind this call of Christ and the unhesitating obedience of the men called, there lies a whole history of the growth and maturing of faith.

The Way by Which They Were Led

To begin with, they had been disciples of the Baptist. To two of them John had pointed out Jesus as He walked and said, "Behold the Lamb of God," with the result that they followed Jesus, and the effect of their speech with Jesus was that they went in search of their nearest and best, saying, "We have found Messiah."

Then, in addition to the testimony of John, they had been eye-witnesses of some of Christ's wonderful works. The turning of the water into wine at Cana, the healing of the nobleman's son, the miraculous draught of fishes, are all probably to be dated before this incident. Faith had been for weeks and possibly months maturing in their hearts—first the blade, then the ear, then the full corn in the ear.

A Worthy Leader

These men followed Christ because they had already discovered that He was worth following. We often make an antithesis

24

between faith and reason, but the faith that makes a man follow Christ is the highest reason. For all the centuries combine to assert that Christ is worthy. The multitude of the redeemed in heaven sing, "Worthy is the Lamb that was slain!" They followed Him through great tribulation, through Gethsemanes and up Calvaries, but they never regretted their obedience. "He is worthy!" they cry.

Whom They Followed to the End

Peter and James and John and Andrew never repented their obedience to Christ's call. Following Christ's call brought James to the scaffold in Jerusalem, and John to exile in Patmos, and Peter to the cross in Rome. But though it entailed upon them a hard life and a bloody death, that is the word they cry to us—"He is worthy!" When Professor Elmslie lay a-dying he said to his wife, "Kate, God is love, all love. Kate, we will tell everybody that—but especially our own boy." What a testimony from a dying-bed! It was a modern Christian repeating the witness of prophets, saints, and martyrs, and saying, "Christ is worthy!"

Faith in Christ comes commended to us by the testimony of the centuries. He gives joy and peace in life; He gives triumph in death. And no one else and nothing else does. To leave all and follow Christ is not foolishness, it is the supremest reason.

Their New and Exalted Calling

"Come ye after me," said Jesus, "and I will make you to become fishers of men" (v. 17). What an exaltation this is! From fishers to fishers of men. But that is ever Christ's way. He dignifies and exalts our calling. Notice, Christ does not destroy, He converts. He does not destroy the qualities of watchfulness and alertness these men had gained by their business as fishermen. He turns them to higher uses, "Henceforth ye shall catch men."

And Ours

What is your gift—song? You shall sing for Him! Speech? You shall become a preacher of Salvation. Sympathy? You shall minister to His sick and poor. What are you—a builder? You shall help to build the temple of God. A soldier? You shall fight the good fight of the faith. A servant? You shall be a bond-servant of Christ. Our Lord never destroys a faculty. He consecrates and exalts it.

"Fishers of Men"

"Fishers of men!" And that is what we all ought to be; we are saved that we may become saviors. Notice how these men at once began to fish for others. Andrew went and called his own brother Simon; John went off and fetched James. Have we begun to fish for men? Have we ever laid hold of a soul for Christ? The joy of "catching a man alive" — there is nothing on earth to equal it.

How shall we become "fishers of men"? Not by our own cleverness or skill. "I will make you to become fishers of men," says our Lord. "I will make you"—that is the equipment. If we want to be successful fishers of men, we must go to Jesus Christ for the necessary qualifications. "Not by might, nor by power, but by My Spirit, saith the Lord of Hosts" (Zech. 4:6).

7

The Authority of Christ

"And they went into Capernaum; and straightway on the Sabbath day He entered into the synagogue, and taught. And they were astonished at His doctrine: for He taught them as one that had authority, and not as the scribes . . . And immediately His fame spread abroad throughout all the region round about Galilee." —Mark 1:21, 22, 28.

The Manner of Christ's Teaching: with Authority

THIS PARAGRAPH GIVES us an account of our Lord's first appearance as a preacher in the synagogue at Capernaum, and also of a mighty work He performed at the close of His sermon. Both the sermon and the miracle produced a profound impression upon the crowd; and the impression produced in each case was the impression of authority. At the close of the sermon "they were astonished," Mark tells us; "for He taught them as one having authority, and not as the scribes" (v. 22, R.V.). When they saw the demoniac restored to self-possession, "they were all amazed, . . . saying, What is this? a new teaching! With authority He commandeth even the unclean spirits, and they obey Him" (v. 27, R.V.).

His Authority of Character

Here, then, we get Jesus Christ as the Authoritative Teacher. What kind of an authority was it Jesus Christ possessed? (1) It was the authority of *character*. The scribes had the kind of authority that comes from office. But it was not that kind of authority Jesus wielded. He had no office. He had not, as we should say, been trained for the ministry. He had never been ordained. He came straight from the carpenter's shop. And yet when He spoke, men felt there was an authority about His words they never felt in the words of the scribes, their official teachers. It was the authority of character, of a pure and holy personality. In the presence of Jesus men felt themselves instinctively in the presence of a Holy Person. That was why the traffickers in the Temple tumbled out in disordered flight before Him. That was

27

why Pilate feared and trembled before Him. The human spirit is keenly sensitive to moral condition. And the people, as they listened, felt behind the words of Jesus all the tremendous force a holy character wields.

His Authority of Perfect Knowledge

(2) It was the authority of perfect *knowledge*. In a sense the scribes had authority, for they were the recognized masters of the Law, and the teachers of Divine truth. But Christ's authority was completely different.

"Not as the scribes." The scribes taught, shall we say, at second hand. They buttressed every statement by quoting the Law and tradition. But Jesus never quotes the Law and the Prophets in support of His statements. He abrogates, alters, amends, enlarges the law of Moses on the strength of His own *ipse dixit*. He lays down laws— declares truth with the assurance of intimate and first-hand knowledge. He speaks on the tremendous themes of God and the soul, of duty and destiny, with the authority of One who knew.

There is never a "perhaps" or "it may be"; there is never a guess or surmise in the speech of Christ. All is calm, authoritative, sure. He moves amongst the great problems of the soul as one who is perfectly at home. "I say unto you" —that is His formula. "He spoke as having authority" — it was the authority of perfect knowledge.

His Authority of Power

But it was not authoritative speech alone the people discovered in Jesus, but (3) authoritative *power* as well. At a word from Him "the unclean spirit, tearing him and crying with a loud voice, came out of him" (v. 26, R.V.). If the sermon revealed Him as the Authoritative Teacher, the miracle revealed Him as the Almighty Deliverer. He has authority over every evil spirit. He can break every chain of evil. He can release every prisoner in Satan's bondage held. This is a revelation every whit as welcome as the former. For man is not simply in the dark, and longs to see; he is bound, and wants to be freed.

A Provision for Our Needs

This double aspect of Christ's authority exactly meets our human need. Our two great desires are these: certitude in the realm of truth, and deliverance from the thraldom of evil. Men crave to know; they want certitude; they long to be sure. And to them Christ presents Himself as the Truth, God's Everlasting Yea, the answer to all their questioning. And they crave to be delivered. And to them Christ presents Himself as One who has authority over every unclean spirit. Does a man cry in his bitter bondage, "Who shall deliver me?" We can answer with the apostle, "Thanks be to God, which giveth us the victory through our Lord Jesus Christ" (1 Cor. 15:57).

8
Christ in the Home

"And forthwith, when they were come out of the synagogue, they entered into the house of Simon and Andrew, with James and John. But Simon's wife's mother lay sick of a fever, and anon they tell Him of her. And He came and took her by the hand, and lifted her up; and immediately the fever left her, and she ministered unto them." —Mark 1:29-31.

A Word of Significance
"AND STRAIGHTWAY"; SO our brief paragraph begins in the Revised Version. Look at that word "straightway" with me.

The commentators tell us the word is characteristic of St Mark's eager and vivid literary style. But it is really much more than an indication of St Mark's active and bustling mind; it is a revelation of the ceaseless activity of our Lord's life.

He had just been teaching in the synagogue, giving them an illustration of His power that left the people dumb with amazement; and "straightway" in Simon's house He performs another mighty deed, and gives another proof of His mercy and grace. In our Lord's life one miracle follows another; one great deed treads upon the heels of another.

The Master's Life
This word "straightway" illustrates, shall I say, the "pace" of our Lord's life. He had no slack time; He had no intervals of ease; He had no holidays from service. Our Lord had an abiding sense of the urgency and pressure of life. "I have a baptism to be baptized with," He said once, "and how am I straitened till it be accomplished" (Luke 12:50). "How am I straitened!"— what a tremendous urgency the phrase implies! And so He gave Himself to service with a devotion that filled all who beheld Him with wonder and awe.

Its Example to Us
What an example our Lord sets to us! We are slow, and slack, and listless. We sit at ease in Zion. We let opportunity slip, instead of buying it up. Here is the motto for the Christian— "straight-

way." John Ruskin had on his desk, confronting him whenever he stood by it, the words, "Do it now." The Christian might engrave this word "straightway" on the tables of his heart. Now is always the accepted time; now is always the day of salvation.

Christ in the Home

"And straightway, when they were come out of the synagogue, they came into the house of Simon and Andrew" (v. 29, R.V.). What a privilege was Simon's! How we envy the opportunities that fell to the lot of Simon and Zacchaeus and the sisters of Bethany! And yet why envy them? For the same happy privilege may be ours. "If a man love Me, he will keep My words: and My Father will love him, and We will come unto him, and make Our abode with him" (John 14:23). They came into Simon's house, and in Simon's house our Lord continued His ministry.

His Bounty There

"Now Simon's wife's mother lay sick of a fever; and straightway they tell Him of her: and He came and took her by the hand, and raised her up; and the fever left her" (vv. 30, 31, R.V.). It is Matthew Henry who says, commenting on this story, that, "Whenever Christ comes, He comes to do good, and will be sure to pay richly for His entertainment." And that is quite true. But never does He pay so richly as when a guest in a house of grief. Simon's house was such a house that day. And immediately upon our Lord's entry they tell Him their trouble. And they had no sooner told it to Him than He removed it—"He came and took her by the hand; and the fever left her."

Simon one day talked a little boastfully about the sacrifices he and his friends made when they followed Christ. And our Lord replied that there was no one who had left houses or mother or brethren or sisters or children or lands, who would not receive a hundredfold. Simon was receiving some of the hundredfold that day!

Christ in the Homes of Grief

All our homes at some time or another become homes of grief. But if Jesus is a guest, how richly He pays for His entertainment! For when we tell Him, somehow or other the burden is lifted. Not that the sickness, or whatever be the particular cause of anxiety, is at once removed, but the pain and grief are assuaged, and a blessed peace fills the soul.

How can the effect be better expressed than in the words the evangelist uses about Peter's wife's mother—"the fever left her"? That is exactly it! In the midst of our troubles and grief, when we feel the healing, cooling touch of Christ, the fever —the ache, the pain—passes out of our souls.

"Saved to Serve"

"The fever left her, and straightway she ministered unto them." The first use she made of her newly recovered strength was to minister to Jesus and His disciples. This is an illustration of what ought to be a universal rule. We are "saved to serve." Healing and life are given to us that we may use them in the holy service of Christ.

One commentator suggests that the serving on the part of Simon's wife's mother is the proof of the reality and completeness of the healing. If service is the proof evidence of healing, how does it stand with us? Are we serving? If not, is it certain that we have been healed? "We know," says St John, "that we have passed out of death into life, because we love the brethren" (1 John 3:14, R.V.).

9

The Balanced Life

"And at even, when the sun did set, they brought unto Him all that were diseased, and them that were possessed with devils. And all the city was gathered together at the door. And He healed many that were sick of divers diseases, and cast out many devils; and suffered not the devils to speak, because they knew Him. And in the morning, rising up a great while before day, He went out, and departed into a solitary place, and there prayed." — Mark 1:32-35.

Service and Supplication

ONE OF THE most difficult things in the religious life is to keep the balance true between service and devotion, between work and prayer. Instances of failure to preserve the true balance quickly suggest themselves. On the one hand there is the monk, who spends his days in the cloistered cell, who has sacrificed service to devotion. His is an ill-balanced life in the one direction. Then on the other hand there is the man who is so occupied with his manifold activities and philanthropies that he is too busy to pray. His is an ill-balanced life in the opposite direction.

The Balanced Life of Christ

But what a beautifully balanced life these verses reveal! Verses 32, 33 and 34 show Christ to us in the midst of His activities; verse 35 shows Him to us in the midst of His devotions. In the evening He is busy with the crowd; in the morning before the dawn He is alone with God. Christ's piety issued in practical service. His practical service was nourished and sustained by His piety. In our Lord's life, service and communion, work and prayer, each had its due and proper place. His was a perfectly "balanced" life.

A Crowded Day

Here we have, to begin with, a picture of Christ in the midst of His activities. What a Sabbath this was in the history of Christ! How crowded with work! First of all He preached in the synagogue; and let us never forget Christ's life blood was in every

33

sermon He preached. Then He cast the evil spirit out of the demoniac. Then after leaving the synagogue yet another call had been made on His compassion, and He had healed Simon's wife's mother. And let us never forget that what is true of Christ's sermons is also true of Christ's miracles—they cost. Power, one of the evangelists tells us, went forth from Him (Luke 8:46, R.V.). Every act of healing was a drain upon His vitality. It cost Him life to restore life to others.

A Wearied Toiler and New Labors

Now if that be so He must have been a tired Christ that Sabbath evening. The day had cost Him much in desire and compassion and sympathy, and He might fairly claim to have earned His rest. But it is not of rest we read, but of new and costly activities. "At even, when the sun did set, they brought unto Him all that were sick and them that were possessed with devils. And all the city was gathered together at the door" (vv. 32, 33, R.V.).

All the city at the door, and within a tired Christ! But He makes no mention of weariness. Out of Simon's house into the midst of that pathetic crowd He passes, carrying healing and blessing with Him. What tireless activity is this! Christ spent Himself in the service of men. He lived under the constraint of a great urgency. "We must work the works of Him that sent Me while it is day: the night cometh, when no man can work" (John 9:4, R.V.).

The Worker at Prayer

And side by side with this picture of Christ in the midst of His activities, we have a picture of Christ in the midst of His devotions. "In the morning, a great while before day, He rose up and went out, and departed into a desert place, and there prayed" (v. 35, R.V.). There is the most close and intimate connection between the one picture and the other.

I was once taken through the engineering shops in the Devonport dockyard. I saw innumerable machines busy at various kinds of work, most of them making considerable noise in the process. Then my conductor took me to a room which by contrast was almost silent, where a great engine was working smoothly and quietly.

"The Power-room"

"This," said he, "is the power-room." In that quiet room I found the secret of the multifarious activities of the machines in the various shops. In verses 32-34, Mark has been showing us our Lord's various activities. In verse 35 he takes us to the "power-room." Back of all the activities of the synagogue and the street lay a life of secret prayer. In communion with His Father, Jesus refreshed and renewed Himself for further labor and toil amongst men. "A great while before day"—Jesus made time for prayer! He snatched it from His sleep.

An Example for Us

What an object-lesson as to the indispensable necessity of prayer! We realize the obligation of service in these days, and consequently we have become very "busy." But are we neglecting the "power-room"? We must keep the balance true. We must never become too busy to pray.

"This kind," said our Lord, "can come out by nothing, save by prayer" (Mark 9:29, R.V.).

10
The Philanthropy of Jesus

"And Simon and they that were with him followed after Him. And when they had found Him, they said unto Him, All men seek for Thee. And He said unto them, Let us go into the next towns, that I may preach there also: for therefore came I forth. And He preached in their synagogues throughout all Galilee, and cast out devils." —Mark 1:38-39.

In Search of the Healer

OUR LORD HAD, according to verse 35, "risen up a great while before day," and had departed into a desert place to pray. He had stolen out while His disciples were asleep. It was only when, with the dawning of the day, those who had sick folk in the city, and who had not received Christ's healing grace on the previous evening, began to knock at the door and inquire for Him, that the disciples discovered He was not there. And then they pursued— that is the Greek word—in hot haste after Jesus.

Incidentally let us notice what a tribute there is here to the character of Jesus. These four disciples knew exactly where to look for Him. They had already become acquainted with His prayer habits. They knew His love for quiet and solitary communion. And so when He was missing, they went straight to the place of prayer to look for Him.

Retirement Hardly Found

"They pursued after Him." What an illustration this is of the difficulties of communion! "Scarcely can we turn aside," our hymn says, "for one brief hour of prayer." Jesus could "scarcely turn aside." It was with difficulty He found His "quiet time." Something or other—the clamor of the multitude, the cares of the world—was always following Him even into the desert place. We know this difficulty too. What between the claims of business and family, social and church duties, we have no leisure for the "quiet time." Every hour we are "pursued" by something or other. Nevertheless, we must make time for prayer. Meal times and prayer times, as the old saying puts it, are not lost times.

A Great Truth Expressed

"All men are seeking Thee," said Peter, half petulantly and reproachfully. And by that he meant that the people of Capernaum wanted to hear more of the wonderful Teacher, and to see more of the wonderful Healer who had so astonished them the day before. But Peter spoke better than he knew. "All men are seeking Thee." Does not this express the attitude of the wide world? Is it not Christ the world is wanting? Men are not always able to interpret their own needs, but is it not true that

"Far and wide, though all unknowing,
Pants for Thee each mortal breast;
Human tears for Thee are flowing,
Human hearts in Thee would rest"?

I read in John's Gospel of certain Greeks who came to Philip saying, "Sir, we would see Jesus" (John 12:21). I read in Henry Drummond's biography that the message the Japanese gave him to bring over to England was this, "Give us your Christ." "All men are seeking Thee." Christ is the common and universal need.

"All are seeking Thee," said Peter; but Jesus did not promptly return with them to Capernaum, all seething with expectancy and excitement.

Our Lord's Reply

"Let us go," was His reply, "elsewhere into the next towns, that I may preach there also" (v. 38, R.V.). "Behold," says one old commentator, remarking on this answer of our Lord, "the philanthropy of Christ."

The old commentator is quite right. That is what shines out of this answer, the philanthropy— the broad and all-embracing love for men—that filled Christ's heart. Peter's appeal was a selfish appeal. He would have confined Christ's ministrations to Capernaum. But Christ had a larger heart and a broader sympathy and a wider outlook than His disciple. "Let us go elsewhere," He said.

The Wider Fields

Our Lord was always thinking of the "elsewhere." When the minds of His disciples are full of Capernaum, He is thinking of the "elsewhere" of Galilee. When their minds are full of Judea, He is thinking of the "elsewhere" of Samaria. And when they have taken in the "elsewhere" of Samaria, He journeys with them to Tyre and

Sidon, to remind them of the "elsewhere" of the wide world. "Other sheep," He said, "I have, which are not of this fold: them I must bring" (John 10:16).

For Us Also

"Let us go elsewhere." In His larger sympathies the Master wants His disciples to share. A young missionary came home invalided. His friends thought that under the circumstances a home pastorate would be the best thing for him, but he himself longed and fretted to get back.

"Why do you wish to return?" said one of them to him.

"Because," was the reply, "I can't sleep for thinking of them." He felt the call and the pull and the appeal of the "elsewhere." Do we? Do we share in the philanthropy of Christ? Christ is ever on the march to the regions beyond, to the "elsewhere," and if we would enjoy His company we must keep step with Him.

11
The Healing of the Leper

"And there came a leper to Him, beseeching Him, and kneeling down to Him, and saying unto Him, If Thou wilt, Thou canst make me clean. And Jesus, moved with compassion, put forth His hand, and touched him, and saith unto him, I will; be thou clean. And as soon as He had spoken, immediately the leprosy departed from him, and he was cleansed. And He straitly charged him, and forthwith sent him away; And saith unto him, See thou say nothing to any man: but go thy way, show thyself to the priest, and offer for thy cleansing those things which Moses commanded, for a testimony unto them. But he went out, and began to publish it much, and to blaze abroad the matter, insomuch that Jesus could no more openly enter into the city, but was without in desert places: and they came to Him from every quarter."
—Mark 1:40-45.

A Manifestation of Power
WHAT A REVELATION, not simply of the power but of the exquisite tenderness of Christ, this story gives us! With a superb and daring faith the leper cried, "If Thou wilt (or willest), Thou canst make me clean," and in response our Lord said, "I will; be thou made clean" (vv. 40, 41, R.V.). But that was not all He did. It would have been sufficient, we know. Our Lord could with a word and at a distance have cleansed this man of his loathsome plague. That would have showed His power. But He did more than that. "Being moved with compassion, He stretched forth His hand, and touched him"; and that showed His love (v. 41, R.V.).

The Touch of Love
All the evangelists make special note of the "touch." It is in the "touch" that the real glory of Christ is seen. It is in the "touch" His compassion shines forth. Our Lord could have kept this man at a distance. He could have flung the gift of healing to him, as we fling a bone to a dog; and by so doing He might have hurt the man's soul while healing his body. But that is never Christ's way. "Moved with compassion, He stretched forth His hand, and touched him," and by that touch He brought healing to his soul as

39

well as cleansing to his body. It showed the leper that he had in Jesus not simply a Healer but a Lover of his soul.

Compassion Revealed

It is Dr. Dale who calls attention to this fact—that it is not in the words of Christ we find the fuller and deeper revelation of the divine compassion, but in His deeds. "I doubt," Dr. Dale says, "whether Christ ever said anything about the divine compassion more perfectly beautiful or more pathetic than had been said by the writer of the 103rd Psalm—'Like as a father pitieth his children, so the Lord pitieth them that fear Him.'" But new wonders of compassion, infinite reaches and depths of compassion, are revealed in our Lord's deeds. And amongst the actions of Christ that disclose the wealth of His compassion is this, "He stretched forth His hand, and touched him." Him! that poor, loathsome, abject creature, who had not felt the pressure of a clean hand upon him for years. Yet it was he whom Jesus stretched forth His hand and touched. It was not necessary for the healing of his body. This was love for the enriching and gladdening of his soul.

The One Undefiled

"He stretched forth His hand, and touched him." But did not the Law say that contact with a leper caused defilement? Yes, it did. But Jesus touches corruption, and yet contracts no taint. We have an old proverb to the effect that a man cannot touch pitch without being defiled. And Paul quotes a saying to much the same purpose, from an old Greek play when telling the Corinthians that "evil communications corrupt good manners" (1 Cor. 15:33). And yet Jesus was constantly touching what men would call "pitch" without defilement. Look at Him here. He lays His hand on the leper's loathsome flesh and contracts no taint; instead of that, the leper receives cleansing from His purity.

The Miracle an Acted Parable

Indeed, this is a parable of what Jesus was doing all through His life. He was continually "touching the leper." What was His Incarnation? It was a case of "touching the leper." He "took hold" upon the seed of Abraham. He was found in the likeness of sinful flesh. And yet He contracted no defilement. He dwelt amongst men, "holy, harmless, undefiled, separate from sinners." And all through His earthly career, was He not continually and deliberately "touching the leper"? He went and sat at meat with publicans and sinners; what is that but "touching the leper"?

"Zacchaeus, make haste and come down, for today I must abide at thy house"; what was that but "touching the leper"? And yet Jesus never brought a smudge or a stain upon His perfect purity. Instead of that His purity cleansed the sinners and lepers whom He touched.

The Master and the Servant

Can we not understand how it was Jesus was able not only to touch the sinner without defilement, but by His very purity uplifted and saved him? He came to be the Lamb without spot and without blemish; to live for, to die for others. God gave not the Spirit "by measure unto Him" (John 3:34). And we, too, if we be filled with the Spirit, may live even in Sardis and not "defile our garments."

12
The Healing of the Paralytic—I

"And again He entered into Capernaum after some days; and it was noised that He was in the house. And straightway many were gathered together, insomuch that there was no room to receive them, no, not so much as about the door: and He preached the word unto them. And they come unto Him, bringing one sick of the palsy, which was borne of four. And when they could not come nigh unto Him for the press, they uncovered the roof where He was: and when they had broken it up, they let down the bed wherein the sick of the palsy lay. When Jesus saw their faith, He said unto the sick of the palsy, Son, thy sins be forgiven thee." —Mark 2:1-5.

The Four Friends

It is a striking thing that in this story of the healing of the paralytic the sufferer himself plays a very small part. It would, perhaps, scarcely be true to say he was entirely passive; for Christ could not have spoken to him as He did had there not been some kind of faith and wistful longing in his soul. At the same time, it is quite obvious that the main interest of the story gathers, not around the paralytic, but around his four friends and our blessed Lord. The story is so replete with points that claim our notice, that we had better, in this chapter, confine ourselves to a study of the four friends and their action.

Their Character

1. What true and genuine friends these men were! Theirs was no fair-weather friendship. They stood by their friend in his hour of need and deep distress. That is the badge and sign of a true friendship—it bears the strain of misfortune and reverse. "I call you not servants . . . but . . . friends," said Jesus to His disciples (John 15:15). And in another verse we find the reason why our Lord bestowed this honorable title upon them. "Ye are they," He said, "which have continued with Me in My temptations" (Luke 22:28).

At the commencement of His career Christ had multitudes of admirers and followers. But as trials came thronging in, and as opposition deepened, these people turned their backs upon Him and deserted Him in shoals. But amid the wholesale desertion of the crowds the apostles remained staunch and true; and their loyalty to their Master in His day of trouble proved the genuineness of their friendship. For it was just on the eve of the Cross and Passion that Christ gave them that honorable name. "Ye are they which have continued with Me in My temptations. No longer do I call you servants, but I have called you friends." And these four men had the same claim to that honorable title. They continued with their friend in the time of his trouble and distress.

Their Action

Notice, too, how they fulfilled the highest office of friendship. They had heard of Christ's power, and they determined they would carry their friend to Him. They were ready to do anything to bring back health and vigor to his wasted and stricken frame. And that is again a mark of a genuine friendship—it always seeks the good of the loved one. It is always plotting and scheming for the well-being of the friend. That was how John Robinson, the beloved pastor of the Pilgrim Fathers, was described by one of his flock. "He ever sought our good, both body and soul." That was a true friendship.

And as man's good, both body and soul, is best secured by union with Christ, this follows, that the highest office of friendship is to do what these four men did, bring the friend to Jesus. When Andrew found Messiah, he hurried off to seek his brother Simon. "He brought him unto Jesus." What a friend he was to his brother that day! "Philip findeth Nathanael, and saith unto him, we have found Him" (John 1:45, R.V.). What a friend Philip was to Nathanael that day! Are we friends of that type?

Their Faith Undaunted by Difficulties

2. What magnificent faith these friends had! It was faith that was not daunted by difficulties. It was not an easy task to bring their friend to Jesus, but they persevered, in spite of all obstacles, and their faith won the blessing. "Jesus seeing their faith saith unto the sick of the palsy, Son, thy sins are forgiven" (2:5, R.V.). There are difficulties still in the way of bringing friends to Christ. The crowd of engagements and cares and pleasures, and the opposition of so-called society, they are all hindrances in the way—but a true faith perseveres. Monica wept and entreated and prayed for years, but at last she saw Augustine her son at the Savior's feet. "In due season we shall reap, if we faint not" (Gal. 6:9).

Exerted for Another

Theirs was a vicarious faith. "Jesus seeing their faith saith unto the sick of the palsy, Thy sins are forgiven." He blessed the sick man for the faith of the four devoted friends. We often talk of vicarious sacrifice. But here is vicarious faith! That people receive large and rich blessing on account of the faith of others, is not theory, but fact. The Bible is full of it. For the sake of ten righteous men God would have spared Sodom. The Lord blessed the house of Potiphar for Joseph's sake. God saved the whole ship-load of people because His servant Paul was on board. And so still, God blesses the world for the sake of His faithful servants who are in it. He blesses the house for the sake of a saintly mother. He blesses this man and that for the sake of a godly friend, just as He forgives and saves the world for the sake of a Holy Christ.

Here is encouragement to make our faith a real help to others. Are we doing this?

13

The Healing of the Paralytic—II

"When Jesus saw their faith, He said unto the sick of the palsy, Son, thy sins be forgiven thee. But there were certain of the scribes sitting there, and reasoning in their hearts, Why doth this man thus speak blasphemies? who can forgive sins but God only? And immediately when Jesus perceived in His spirit that they so reasoned within themselves, He said unto them, Why reason ye these things in your hearts? Whether is it easier to say to the sick of the palsy, Thy sins be forgiven thee; or to say, Arise, and take up thy bed, and walk? But that ye may know that the Son of man hath power on earth to forgive sins, (He saith to the sick of the palsy), I say unto thee, Arise, and take up thy bed, and go thy way into thine house. And immediately he arose, took up the bed, and went forth before them all; insomuch that they were all amazed, and glorified God, saying, We never saw it on this fashion."
— Mark 2:5-12.

IN THE LAST CHAPTER, we thought of the part played in this incident by the four faithful friends. Let us now study the action of our Lord. When the bed on which the sick of the palsy lay was lowered through the roof and let down just in front of Him, that was the first word He spoke to the sick man, "Son, thy sins are forgiven thee."

The Need and the Word
(1) What a strange and startling word it was! Sins? But who had said a word about sins? No one. What then was the meaning of our Lord's startling word? It was just a case of speaking to the young man's deepest and sorest need. The Gospels often remind us of Christ's wonderful power of insight. "He knew," John says, "what was in man" (2:25). And so He knew what was in this paralytic. He saw that he suffered from a sorer plague than the palsy. Probably his affliction was due to excess and sin; and it was the memory of the sin that was the intolerable burden. And Jesus speaks first to the most bitter and urgent need. He speaks to the guilt-laden soul. "Son," He said—and the tenderness of the

45

address is worthy of note, indicating as it did that prodigal though the paralytic had been, he was still beloved—"thy sins are forgiven thee." The four friends brought him to Jesus in order to get healing for his body; Jesus begins by healing the soul.

The Word and the Boon

(2) What a gracious word it was! If Jesus had done no more for this paralytic, I believe he would have gone back to his house a singing soul. If he had been carried home as physically helpless as he came, he would yet have possessed a joy beyond words. For Jesus had conferred upon him the boon he most urgently craved. He had delivered him from the burden and fear of his sin.

It was to give this supreme boon Jesus came to earth. "It is He," said the angel, "that shall save His people from their sins" (Matt. 1:21, R.V.). Sin is to this day the world's sorest plague. Sin is to this day the soul's deadliest hurt. Physical pain is nothing to the guilt and shame of sin. And it is from sin and its haunting dread that Jesus came to redeem us. He goes about our world, whispering to those who through fear of death have been all their lifetime subject to bondage, this gracious message: "Son, daughter, thy sins are forgiven thee."

The Boon and Its Giver

(3) But is it a true word? Can Jesus give the forgiveness of which He speaks? Or is He merely mocking men with a promise which He can never fulfil? That was the very point on which the scribes sitting by challenged Him. "He blasphemeth," they said; "who can forgive sins but one, even God"? (v. 7, R.V.). And Jesus promptly meets their challange, and gives evidence of His power to forgive. "Whether is easier," He asks them, "to say . . . Thy sins are forgiven; or to say, Arise,. . . and walk"? (v. 9, R.V.).

These scribes had been saying to themselves the offer of forgiveness was one the reality of which they could not test, and that Christ had spoken of forgiveness because He found Himself unable to heal. Our Lord proceeds at once to heal, in order to demonstrate His right to forgive—a demonstration all the more conclusive in the eyes of all present, inasmuch as they had a saying to this effect: "There is no sick man healed of his sickness until all his sins have been forgiven him." So, without waiting for a reply from the scribes, Jesus goes on to say, "But that ye may know that the Son of Man hath power [authority] on earth to forgive sins (He saith to the sick of the palsy) I say unto thee, Arise, take up thy bed, and go into thy house" (vv. 10, 11, R.V.).

The Giver and His Authority

Our Lord's strange but gracious word about forgiveness was also a true word. The healed man was the proof of the reality of forgiveness. The outward healing was the verification of the inward grace. The spiritual blessing manifested its reality in the sphere of the physical. We too have evidence in abundance to prove that the promise of forgiveness is no delusion. We know of people to whom Christ has spoken as He spoke to the sick of the palsy, and we can see the change. We know by their life, even by their very appearance that the burden of sin has been lifted and its haunting dread clean taken away. This word is a true word. Forgiveness is no word, no dream, no mere phrase. Men need never fear of being deceived in Christ. "He is a great forgiver," said a criminal on his way to execution. Yes, "a great forgiver!" He has authority to forgive, and however great our load and black our record we can yet say with humble confidence, in the familiar words of the creed, "I believe in the forgiveness of sins."

14

The Originality of Jesus Christ

"We never saw it on this fashion."   —Mark 2:12.

How Was Our Lord Original?

CHRIST'S MIRACLE UPON the paralytic left the crowd in a condition of excited and exultant amazement. And this was the comment they made upon it all, "We never saw it on this fashion." Christ was absolutely different from any other leader, healer, prophet they had either read about or seen. In His speech and action He was unique and unprecedented. The deepest impression made upon them was that of Christ's originality.

Now in what way was Christ original? Well, when we look at the story of the paralytic we find He was original in the Gospel He preached. When we look at verse thirteen we see He was original in His methods of preaching it. And when we look at the paragraph which tells us of the call of Levi, we find He was original in His choice of people to whom to preach it.

In His Gospel

(1) Our Lord was original in the Gospel He preached. The particular thing in Christ's treatment of the paralytic that most struck the crowd, the thing that was absolutely novel and unprecedented, was His first words to the sick man, "Son, thy sins be forgiven thee." It amounted to a declaration to the multitude that His mission was not to heal bodies, but to save souls; that His aims were not material but spiritual.

A Welcome Gospel

The Messianic Gospel, according to current Jewish expectation, spoke mainly if not exclusively of material benefits. The good news they expected to hear was the good news of national deliverance. Christ's good news spoke not of deliverance from the Roman yoke, but of deliverance from sin. It was thus an unexpected Gospel— but it was a most welcome Gospel, because it spoke to man's

48

deepest and sorest need. In verse 15 we read that the "Publicans and sinners sat down with" Christ; but the Greek word says they "kept following." It was this new Gospel of the forgiveness of sins that drew them.

A Universal Gospel

And it was not only a welcome Gospel, it was a universal Gospel. Had Jesus preached the kind of Gospel the Jews expected, it might have been good news to them—but to no one else. But His Gospel of forgiveness is a universal Gospel. For we have all sinned and come short of the glory of God, and the proclamation that the Son of Man hath power on earth to forgive sins is good news to the wide world.

The Method of Proclamation Original

(2) Our Lord was original in His method of preaching the Gospel. "He went forth again by the seaside, and all the multitude resorted unto Him, and He taught them" (v. 13, R.V.). "He taught them," not in any school or synagogue, but by the side of the blue sea and under God's broad skies. This was typical of Christ's methods. The Jew was scrupulous about sacred times and holy places. To Jesus every time was sacred and every place holy. Worship, to Jesus, did not depend upon questions of when or where; it was all a question of spirit. "Ye shall neither in this mountain nor yet at Jerusalem,'" He said to the Samaritan woman, "worship the Father. . . God is a Spirit: and they that worship Him must worship Him in Spirit and in truth" (John 4:21, 24).

And so the Lord broke through Jewish stiffness and narrowness. He refused to be tied down to sacred hours and dedicated buildings. The street, the seashore, the private house, the hillside, any place was acceptable to Him, because He knew, and wishes us to know that

"Where'er we seek Him God is found
And every spot is hallowed ground."

The Choice of Hearers Original

(3) Our Lord was original in His choice of people to whom to preach His Gospel. Verse 13 commences a paragraph which tells us how He called Levi from his toll-booth and then went and sat at meat with publicans and sinners. This was an absolutely unprecedented thing. All other teachers ask for the best people as their disciples. But Jesus deliberately cares for and befriends the worst. He was the "friend of publicans and sinners." He raked the gutter for His saints.

The exquisite India paper on which the Oxford Bibles are printed is made for the most part out of old sails—dirty, tattered, apparently worthless rags. And in much the same way out of the world's waste Jesus made some of the most shining of His saints. He made an apostle out of Levi; a theologian out of Augustine; a writer of holy books out of John Bunyan. He can save to the uttermost them that come to God through Him (Heb. 7:25).

15
The Call of Levi

"And as He passed by, He saw Levi the son of Alphaeus sitting at the receipt of custom, and said unto him, Follow Me. And he arose and followed Him. And it came to pass that, as Jesus sat at meat in his house, many publicans and sinners sat also together with Jesus and His disciples: for there were many, and they followed Him. And when the scribes and Pharisees saw Him eat with publicans and sinners, they said unto His disciples, How is it that He eateth and drinketh with publicans and sinners? When Jesus heard it, He saith unto them, They that are whole have no need of the physician, but they that are sick: I came not to call the righteous, but sinners to repentance."
—Mark 2:14-17.

The Man, the Call, and the Reason

LEVI—OR TO give him his more familiar name, Matthew—was a tax-gatherer, and to be a tax-gatherer in that country and at that time was almost equivalent to being a scoundrel and a thief. And yet this was the man Jesus called to be a disciple!

Why did Jesus call Levi? He called him because he was spiritually fit to be called. In this renegade publican's heart Jesus saw the hunger and thirst after righteousness! Scribes and Pharisees, judging by outward appearances, regarded him as outcast, vile beyond contempt, lost beyond hope. But Jesus, penetrating through the outward appearance, read his heart and knew him to be fit for the kingdom of God.

This is characteristic of Jesus. He saw good where no one else saw anything but evil. In publicans and sinners like Levi and Zacchaeus He saw that "feelings lay buried which grace could restore." And just because He saw good where no one else saw anything but evil, He hoped where everyone else despaired. "A dimly burning wick" (Isa. 42:3, R.V., margin), the prophet had said of Him, "He will not quench." He saw the "dimly burning wick" of a desire for holiness in Levi's heart, in the heart of the woman who was a sinner, in Zacchaeus' heart. He did not quench that flicker. He fanned it into a flame.

The Prompt Obedience

"Follow Me," said Jesus to Levi. And he arose and followed Him. Our Lord's confidence in Levi was justified by his prompt obedience. Of course we are not to suppose Jesus came to Levi that day as a perfect stranger. No one could live in Capernaum and not know about Jesus. The probability is that Levi had been one of those publicans who "kept following" Jesus. In view of Levi's action, we may well believe that, as he listened to Our Lord, he learned to loathe his life and to hate his sin and to long for holiness; and that it only needed this call to make him break away from his old associations and give his life and soul to holier and better things. "He arose and followed Him."

And Ready Sacrifice

What glorious and sacrificial obedience this was! Levi was not simply sorry for his life; he broke with it and left it, forever. As Dr. Salmond points out, it was a harder thing for Levi to rise up and follow Christ than it was for Peter and his comrades. Their occupation as fishermen was one to which they could easily return—as indeed they did return after the Resurrection. But there was no return to his toll-booth for Levi. When he left it, he left it altogether. Like St Paul, he suffered the loss of all things for Christ. And he did it without a moment's hesitation. "O my sweet Lord Jesus," he would say, with the seraphic Samuel Rutherford, "a smile from Thee is better than kingdoms."

The Token of Joy

He rose up and followed Christ, and then promptly made a feast, to which he invited all his old friends and associates. He did it in token of his joy. He had just made a stupendous sacrifice, for he had left all. But the thought of his sacrifice was swallowed up in the thought of his great gain. He had lost his toll-booth—he had gained the kingdom. And he did it in the second place, in order that he might share his joy. Joy is always communicative. When the woman found the lost piece of silver she sent for her friends and neighbors to rejoice with her. "Rejoice with me," she said, "for I have found the piece which I had lost" (Luke 15:9, R.V.). And that is what Levi was saying by this great feast of his, "Rejoice with me, for I have found the pearl of great price." Joy is always communicative, and especially the joy of a Savior found. The saved man at once turns missionary. The man who has once really experienced the redeeming love and grace of Christ wants to tell to all the world around him of the Savior he has found.

The Work of Grace

What great things Divine grace did for Levi! It found him a publican, it made him an apostle! It found him an outcast, it wrote his name on the foundations of the New Jerusalem! And notice how grace works. It always conserves a man's natural endowments. It destroys no power. It converts and consecrates it. Now Levi was clever with his pen. What grace did was to consecrate his natural gift. When Levi became a Christian, says Dr. Alexander Whyte, he took his pen and his ink-born with him, only now instead of using them for purposes of extortion, he used them to write the story of his Blessed Lord.

From a publican to an apostle—what cannot grace do? It can lay hold of us in our weakness and sin, set us among princes, and make us inherit a throne of glory.

16
The Law of Congruity

"And the disciples of John and of the Pharisees used to fast: and they come and say unto Him, Why do the disciples of John and of the Pharisees fast, but Thy disciples fast not? And Jesus said unto them, Can the children of the bridechamber fast, while the bridegroom is with them? as long as they have the bridegroom with them, they cannot fast. But the days will come, when the bridegroom shall be taken away from them, and then shall they fast in those days. No man also seweth a piece of new cloth on an old garment: else the new piece that filled it up taketh away from the old, and the rent is made worse. And no man putteth new wine into old bottles: else the new wine doth burst the bottles, and the wine is spilled, and the bottles will be marred: but new wine must be put into new bottles." —Mark 2:18-22.

Fasting—the Law and the Tradition

Our Lord's refusal to conform to the religious practices in vogue amongst the Jews often brought Him into collision with the rulers. This paragraph tells us of a controversy He had with the Pharisees and the disciples of John on the matter of fasting.

Fasting, by the law, was only prescribed for one day—the great Day of Atonement. But tradition had here, as in so many other things, added much to the written law, so that zealous Jews—like the Pharisee in Christ's parable—had come to fast on two days in the week. The disciples of John also seem to have had this much in common with the Pharisees, that they made much of this ascetic practice. Jesus, on the other hand, paid practically no attention to their fast days. And this nonconformity of His caused no little scandal to the Pharisees, and no little difficulty to the disciples of John.

The Appeal to Our Lord

Thus it was that on one of their fast days they came to Jesus— the disciples of John being put forward as spokesmen—and asked Him: "Why do John's disciples and the disciples of the Pharisees fast, but Thy disciples fast not"? (v. 18, R.V.). Jesus answers these puzzled men by an exquisite little illustration, justifying His own practice, while at the same time not condemning theirs. It was impossible, He said, for the sons of the bride-chamber to fast while the bridegroom was with them. But when the bridegroom was taken away, then would they fast in those days.

The Underlying Principle

Now, without pausing to note the tremendous claim Christ puts forward in applying the Divine name "bridegroom" to Himself, let us notice the principle that underlies our Lord's answer. It is the principle of appropriateness, the law of congruity. It was ridiculous, He said, to expect the sons of the bride-chamber to fast in the wedding week. The outward must always be the expression of the inward, and there is absolutely no merit in the outward form unless the inward feeling is congruous with it.

Now fasting was originally just the expression of penitence and sorrow and abasement for sin. But with the Pharisee, fasting had become, for the most part, a matter of rule, a mere bit of routine. All this was offensive to Jesus. He insists upon the law of congruity. It is the principle St James lays down when He says, "Is any among you suffering? Let him pray. Is any cheerful? Let him sing praise" (Jas. 5:13, R.V.). It is equivalent to saying that the religious life must be absolutely single and true and sincere; that there must be about it no trace of hypocrisy or deceit.

And Its Application

This is a very searching rule, which has its pertinent modern applications. The act of worship, for instance, according to this law, is of little or no value in God's sight, unless it is the expression of a worshipping spirit. "Saying one's prayers" is a barren and profitless exercise, unless behind the uttered words there is the praying soul. Even participation in the Holy Communion will profit us nothing, unless it be the expression of a lively faith in Christ, and an entire consecration of ourselves to His service. The inward feeling must accompany the outward form. "Let the words of my mouth, and the meditation of my heart, be acceptable in Thy sight, O Lord, my strength, and my Redeemer" (Psa. 19:14).

An Underlying Assurance

Notice, further, what our Lord's answer implies—that to possess Christ is to possess the secret of perpetual joy. "As long as they have the Bridegroom with them they cannot fast." The one real cause of grief and pain is the loss of Christ. "When the Bridegroom is taken away, then shall they fast." There is no sadness like that of those who are without the Bridegroom. But while the Bridegroom is with us we cannot fast. No matter what comes!

Heaven is associated not with fasting, but with feasting. We read of the marriage supper of the Lamb, and of ceaseless music and song; in a word, of perpetual joy. Do you know why the life of the world to come is not a fast, but a feast? It is because they have the Bridegroom there. "The Lamb is the light thereof."

17
The Sabbath

"And it came to pass, that He went through the corn fields on the Sabbath day; and His disciples began, as they went, to pluck the ears of corn. And the Pharisees said unto Him, Behold, why do they on the Sabbath day that which is not lawful? And He said unto them, Have ye never read what David did, when he had need, and was an hungered, he, and they that were with him? How he went into the house of God in the days of Abiathar the high priest, and did eat the shewbread, which is not lawful to eat but for the priests, and gave also to them which were with him? And He said unto them, The Sabbath was made for man, and not man for the Sabbath: Therefore the Son of man is Lord also of the Sabbath." —Mark 2:23-28.

Our Lord and Sabbath-breaking

WE SAW IN our last chapter how Jesus offended the Jews by His disregard of fast days. But He offended them deepest of all by His free treatment of the Sabbath. Dr. A.B. Bruce points out that we have in the Gospels no fewer than six instances recorded of offense given or taken on this account. In five of these Jesus Himself is the offender; in the other—the story of which is given at this point by Mark—it is the conduct of the disciples that comes in for censure.

All this seems to prove that Jesus deliberately intended to alter the entire spirit of Sabbath observance. The Jews, in consequence of our Lord's action, called Him a Sabbath-breaker. But He was no Sabbath-breaker. He was the true Sabbath-*keeper*. There is no hint or suggestion in any of these stories of His conflicts with the Pharisees of any repudiation of the Sabbatic law, of any intention to interfere with the day of rest. The hallowing of the Sabbath was one of those Divine commandments which our Lord bade others observe, and one which He observed Himself. What our Lord did protest against and fight against was the debasement of the Sabbath, that perversion of the commandment which had changed what God meant for a gracious boon into a most grievous burden.

57

The Charge of Sabbath-breaking

How far that perversion had gone is made abundantly clear by the two incidents which Mark here relates. In the first they bring a charge of Sabbath-breaking against the disciples because they plucked the ears of corn as they passed through the field.

In the other they bring a charge against our Lord Himself because He healed a man with a withered hand on the Sabbath day. Our Lord has His defense for each specific case. His answer to the charge against His disciples is that no ritual or ceremonial law is to stand in the way of urgent human need. His answer to the charge against Himself is that the Sabbath brings no holiday from beneficence; mercy is of universal and perpetual obligation.

Our Lord's Answer

But our Lord was not content simply to answer the narrow and pedantic accusations of the Pharisees. In one simple but profound sentence He set forth the real meaning, intention, and purpose of the Sabbath. "The Sabbath," He said, "was made for man, and not man for the Sabbath" (v. 27).

This answer of our Lord's is the key to a right conception of the Sabbath. The Pharisees had inverted the order. They had put the Sabbath first and man second, as if the whole duty of man was to observe a multitude of minute and detailed Sabbatic rules. Jesus restores the true order. He puts man first and the Sabbath second. Man was not made in order to keep the Sabbath; but the Sabbath was made in order to meet man's needs. The Sabbath, that is to say, is not something which God exacts from man, it is a grace that He confers upon him. It was meant not for a burden but for a boon.

"For Man"

That was not the Jews' thought of it, and perhaps that is not exactly how some modern Christians think of it. They think of the Sabbath only, as Mr. Latham says, as something done by men for God, and in so doing they make God a taskmaster like the gods of the pagans. But the Sabbath is really something done by God for men, and is a constantly recurring evidence of His pity and love and gracious care. And we do not think of the Sabbath rightly until we look at it, not as a burdensome obligation, but as a beautiful privilege and a great delight.

"The Sabbath was made for man." Notice the universal note. The Sabbath was not simply for the Jews; it was for man everywhere. It was a gift, not simply to the chosen people, but to all mankind. And the Sabbath was made for man, because man needed it. It was instituted for his convenience and benefit.

Within recent years the Sabbath has been spoken of as an "interruption in the week," and a strenuous effort has been made to do away with it, as if it were a hindrance and obstacle to human progress. But the Sabbath is no vexatious "interruption," it is a gracious ministry. The reason for the weekly rest day is lodged deep in human nature. Physically, mentally, spiritually man needs the Sabbath. And never was the Sabbath more needed than today, for never was the "pace" of life so fast.

What a boon our Lord's Day is, coming as it does week by week to tired men and women, with its opportunity of rest for mind, and body, and soul. Let us hold fast to it; let us thank God for it.

> "Accept, O God, our hymn of praise,
> That Thou this day hast given,
> Sweet foretaste of the endless day
> Of rest in heaven."

18
The Calling of the Twelve

"And He entered again into the synagogue; and there was a man there which had a withered hand. And they watched Him, whether He would heal him on the Sabbath day; that they might accuse Him. And He saith unto the man which had the withered hand, Stand forth. And He saith unto them, Is it lawful to do good on the Sabbath days, or to do evil? to save life, or to kill? But they held their peace. And when He had looked round about on them with anger, being grieved for the hardness of their hearts, He saith unto the man, Stretch forth thine hand. And he stretched it out: and his hand was restored whole as the other. And the Pharisees went forth, and straightway took counsel with the Herodians against Him, how they might destroy Him. But Jesus withdrew Himself with His disciples to the sea: and a great multitude from Galilee followed Him, and from Judaea, And from Jerusalem, and from Idumaea, and from beyond Jordan; and they about Tyre and Sidon, a great multitude, when they had heard what great things He did, came unto Him. And He spake to His disciples, that a small ship should wait on Him because of the multitude, lest they should throng Him. For He had healed many; insomuch that they pressed upon Him for to touch Him, as many as had plagues. And unclean spirits, when they saw Him, fell down before Him, and cried, saying, Thou art the Son of God. And He straitly charged them that they should not make Him known. And He goeth up into a mountain, and calleth unto him whom He would: and they came unto Him. And He ordained twelve, that they should be with Him, and that He might send them forth to preach, And to have power to heal sicknesses, and to cast out devils."
—Mark 3:1-15.

A Great Event

IT IS IMPOSSIBLE to exaggerate the importance of the calling of the Twelve Apostles. "The wall of the city," says John, in his Apocalypse, "had twelve foundations, and on them twelve names of the twelve Apostles of the Lamb" (Rev. 21:14, R.V.). That is only a parabolic way of saying that the whole fabric of the Christian Church bears forever upon it the stamp and impress of these men who laid its first foundations. Our Lord Himself realized that the choice of men to be His apostles was a critical choice, and, according to Luke's account, He prepared for it by a night of vigil and prayer.

The Hour

The opening verses of this chapter lead up to the account of the calling of the Twelve, and they help us to understand why it was just at this particular point in His career that our Lord felt the time had come to choose men who should be "with Him."

(1) The rulers had taken up an attitude of distinct hostility. In verse 6 we read: "The Pharisees went out, and straightway with the Herodians took counsel against Him, how they might destroy Him." Our Lord foresaw what this meant. He knew that in the long run it meant the Cross. And knowing that this death was to be His lot, He took forethought for the continuance of His work by the choice of the Twelve. (2) The work our Lord Himself had begun had so increased that more laborers were demanded in order to cope with it. Verses 7 and 8 speak of the ferment caused by the preaching and works of Jesus. Beyond the bounds of Palestine His fame had spread. The work had become too great for His single-handed efforts. And so Jesus called these twelve men to share with Him the work of preaching the good tidings of the Kingdom of God.

And the Men

"He appointed Twelve"; and the number twelve is significant. Jesus might have chosen more, had He so wished. A little later He did dispatch seventy disciples upon this same work of preaching. He chose twelve—so many and no more—as corresponding to the twelve tribes of Israel. It was a subtle way of suggesting to the Jews that He was founding a new theocracy—the newer and nobler theocracy that was to replace the old. There is thus implied in this choice of twelve our Lord's Messianic claim.

Their Work: in Relation to Christ

And what was the work of the apostles to be? It was to be a twofold work, (1) Christ called these twelve men, "that they might be with Him." Our Lord wanted friends. There is something inexpressibly touching in that little sentence. "He appointed twelve, that they might be with Him" (v. 14, R.V.). It brings our blessed Lord very near to us, for it reveals a soul on its human side hungry for sympathy. We know how the presence of a friend helps and cheers us in our hours of trial. Our Lord was like unto His brethren in this respect. With opposition and rejection and the bitter cross to face, He hungered for sympathy, He longed for friends; and so He called these twelve men, that they might be with Him.

In spite of their manifold blunderings, they did give Christ some of the sympathy and love He craved. By their loyalty and affection they made things easier for Him, they strengthened His hand in God, and it was with a full heart that Jesus said to them the night before He died, "Ye are they which have continued with Me in My temptations " (Luke 22:28, R.V.).

In Relation to the World

(2) He called these twelve men "that He might send them forth to preach." He called them not simply for His own sake, but even more for the work's sake. The calling was with a view to the sending. There are here implied two stages in the training of these men for their apostolic work. First of all, they were called that they might be with Him. They were to be Christ's companions, partly to help Him by their sympathy and love, but partly also that they might learn of Him. They were to be Christ's pupils and scholars. And then, having learned of Christ, they were to go forth and preach. The time of fellowship was meant to issue in service.

Privilege and Duty

You will see then, how privilege always "leads up to duty." The twelve were made disciples that they might become apostles. They were blessed that they might become a blessing. They were saved that they might become saviors. They were called that they might be sent.

The same duty follows privilege still. Have we been called to be "with Him"? It is in order that He may send us forth to preach. Experience ought to end in expression. "Oh, speak to me," we say in our hymn. What for? "That I may speak, In living echoes of Thy tone."

19
The Twelve:
The Men and Their Work

"And Simon He surnamed Peter: And James the son of Zebedee, and John the brother of James; and He surnamed them Boanerges, which is, The sons of thunder: And Andrew, and Philip, and Bartholomew, and Matthew, and Thomas, and James the son of Alphaeus, and Thaddaeus, and Simon the Canaanite, And Judas Iscariot, which also betrayed Him: and they went into an house." —Mark 3:16-19.

The Men Called

IN THE LAST chapter we made the calling of the Twelve the subject of meditation. Here let us think of the men called.

We speak of these twelve men as the "glorious company of the apostles." And a "glorious company" in the deepest and truest sense they were. But when Jesus summoned them to Him on the hill they did not appear a "glorious company" to the scribes and Pharisees. They could, indeed, scarcely have seemed more insignificant. For what were they? A band of poor and illiterate provincials—fishermen, for the most part. There does not appear to have been a single man of wealth or rank or culture amongst them. Judged by the ordinary standard of society the Twelve were amongst the "weak things," and the "base things," and the "despised things" of the world. But they were chosen of God (1 Cor. 1:27, 28).

Why These?

Why did Jesus choose fishermen and ex-publicans to be His first apostles? Probably, as Dr. A. B. Bruce suggests, for the prosaic reason that they were the best men that could be got. It was only amongst these humble provincials that Jesus could find the necessary love for Himself and faith in His mission. But while that may be true, it does not require any very great subtlety of thought to perceive that there must have been something in the social condition and personal character of these men that fitted them to become good apostles. (a) To begin with, they had unprejudiced minds, and were therefore far apter scholars in the school of Christ than scribes or rabbis could possibly have been. (b) Then, by the very fact that they were poor men, they belonged to what Mr. Latham calls "the stratum in which the center of gravity of humanity lay." (c) And again, as Mr. Latham points out, the plain, homely, matter-of-fact character of these men was in itself an excellent qualification for the apostolate.

An Apostle's Work

For what was the chief work and duty of the apostle? He was not primarily to be a theologian; his business was to be a witness, a witness to facts about Jesus, and especially to the great fact of the Resurrection. And when it comes to witnessing, the testimony of the plain, homely, unimaginative man is the most impressive of all. Now the apostles were men of that type. They were not subtle men, they were not imaginative or romantic men; they were not at all likely to confuse subjective experience and objective fact; they were men of a prosaic and literal type of mind, and therefore admirably fitted to be trustworthy and convincing witnesses.

Nevertheless, the striking fact remains that the Twelve chosen to be Christ's first apostles were humble men, poor men, socially insignificant men; and this fact suggests two thoughts:

The Secret of Their Success

(1) The very insignificance of the apostles makes it all the more evident that the success of their labors was not due to their own gifts, but to the power of God working with them. Had the twelve been men of genius, we might have been tempted to account for their success by the gifts they possessed. But they were just a handful of unlettered provincials! And yet they turned the world upside down. We look at the men, and then we see the work accomplished through them, and we say, "This is the power of God." The insignificance of the messenger throws into relief the Divinity of the message. The weakness of the instruments calls our attention to the real Worker. These base and weak things of the world were employed, in order that all might know that the excellency of the power was of God.

God and His Instruments

(2) This list reminds us of the great things God can do with feeble instruments. With these weak, and base and despised things of the world He put to shame the wise and strong, and brought to

nought things that are. God is continually putting His treasure into earthen vessels. He takes a Martin Luther, the son of a poor miner, a poverty- stricken student obliged to sing for his daily bread; He puts His truth in him, and then uses him to bring spiritual freedom to half Europe. He takes John Bunyan, a tinker—yes, and a profane and foolish tinker at that; He reveals His truth to him, and then sets him to write his Dream, that has helped thousands of pilgrims, in every part of the world, on their heavenward way. God can do wonders with poor tools and insignificant folk.

Shall we not put ourselves into God's hands and say, "Oh, use me, Lord, use even me"?

20
The Twelve: Their Diversity

"And Simon he surnamed Peter; And James the son of Zebedee, and John the brother of James; and he surnamed them Boanerges, which is, The sons of thunder: And Andrew, and Philip, and Bartholomew, and Matthew, and Thomas, and James the son of Alphaeus, and Thaddaeus, and Simon the Canaanite, And Judas Iscariot, which also betrayed him: and they went into an house."   —Mark 3:16-19.

IN THE LAST section we confined our attention to the social insignificance of the Twelve. But that is not the only notable thing about this list of the men whom Christ chose, to be His friends and apostles.

Diversity in Apostolic Temperament
I am greatly struck by the diversity and variety both of temperament and of gift that I find amongst them. Here you have, for instance, every diversity of temperament. The old physiologists used to talk of four temperaments—the Sanguine, the Choleric, the Phlegmatic, and the Melancholic. Each of these temperaments had its representative amongst the Twelve: the Sanguine in the impulsive Peter; the Choleric in the Sons of Thunder; the Phlegmatic in the slow and prosaic Philip; and the Melancholic in doubting Thomas.

In Gift
Here you have diversity of gifts—Peter the man of action; John the soaring mystic; Andrew the man of practical common sense; and Matthew the man of literary aptitudes.

In Political Feeling
Here, too, you find deep-seated difference of political feeling. In modern society somehow or other political differences beget extraordinary bitterness, and men who begin by being political opponents often end by becoming personal foes. But there were two men in the Apostolate between whom in the old days there existed a political hate, by the side of which modern political ran-

cors seem innocent and playful. These two men were Matthew and Simon the Zealot. Matthew had taken service with the hated Roman government; Simon had taken up arms against it. To Simon, Matthew was an apostate and a renegade and a traitor. And yet Matthew the publican and Simon the Zealot are in the Apostolate side by side. And from this diversity amongst the Twelve we may gather two or three lessons.

The Universality of the Savior's Love

To begin with, we may find a lesson as to the universality of the love of Jesus. What a Catholic, in the true sense of the term, the Lord Jesus was! Most men are partial in their likings. They give their affection only to people who are kindred spirits. If a man found Peter to his taste, I scarcely think he would have made a friend of Thomas. If he found Philip a kindred spirit, I scarcely think he could have made a friend of John. But Peter and Thomas, Philip and John, all found a place in the love of Christ.

The Unifying Power of the Savior's Love

Here also is a lesson as to the unifying power of the love of Jesus. Jesus loved these twelve men, different as they were, and by His love bound them all to Himself. But He did more than bind them to Himself; He bound them also to one another. A common love to Christ made even Matthew and Simon friends. "Beloved," the one said to the other, "if God so loved us, we ought also to love one another" (1 John 4:11). And so the fierce patriot and the man who had worn the livery of Rome clasped hands and greeted one another as brethren in Christ. The love of Christ is the great unifier. In His Church there is neither Greek nor Jew, circumcision nor uncircumcision, bond nor free—but all are one in Christ Jesus (Col. 3:11).

The Wide Opportunity of the Savior's Service

And here we may also discover a lesson about diversity of service. These men differed in gift as well as in temperament, but our Lord found room for them in His Apostolate and opportunity for the exercise of their varied gifts. It is not one type of worker Christ wants. He wants every type. There are diversities of operations. Every man has his proper gift; it may be a small gift, a one-talent gift, but Christ wants it and can use it.

The One Who Failed

There is one name in the list that always makes us wonder how it came to be there at all. It is the last name, "Judas Iscariot, which also betrayed Him" (v. 19). It is difficult—to us it is impossible—to explain why Jesus called Judas. But what an example of warning Judas is! If privilege could have saved a man, Judas ought to have had his name graven along with those of the eleven, upon the foundations of the New Jerusalem. But "there is a way to hell," as John Bunyan says, "even from the very gate of heaven." Cities and men, as a Greater than John Bunyan said, may be exalted to heaven in privilege, and yet thrust down to hell. That was the case with Judas Iscariot. And he stands upon the page of Scripture to warn us against trusting to religious privilege.

It is not outward connection with Christ that will save and keep us—but only living union with the Lord. "Let him that thinketh he standeth take heed lest he fall" (1 Cor. 10:12).

21
Christic and His Kinsfolk

"And the multitude cometh together again, so that they could not so much as eat bread. And when His friends heard of it, they went out to lay hold on Him: for they said, He is beside Himself. . . . There came then His brethren and His mother, and, standing without, sent unto Him, calling Him. And the multitude sat about Him, and they said unto Him, Behold, Thy mother and Thy brethren without seek for Thee. And He answered them, saying, Who is My mother, or My brethren! And He looked round about on them which sat about Him, and said, Behold My mother and My brethren! For whosoever shall do the will of God, the same is My brother, and My sister, and mother."
—Mark 3:20, 21, 31-35.

Our Lord and His Kinsfolk

The story of our Lord's relations and their well-meant but mistaken intervention is divided into two brief paragraphs by the interpolation of the account of our Lord's controversy with the Jerusalem scribes. Verses 20, 21 tell us how reports of Christ's doings reached them in Nazareth; how they concluded He was beside Himself, and resolved to go and lay hold on Him. Verses 31-35 tell us what was the upshot of the journey which they made to Capernaum in order to carry out their resolve. These separated verses clearly belong to one another, and between them tell us the story of the attempt our Lord's relations made to interfere with Him. We will think first of the interference and the charge brought against our Lord.

The Charge of Madness

Our Lord's kinsfolk, when reports of His tireless activities and sacrificial labors reached them in Nazareth, saw in them proof that His mind had lost its balance. "He is," they said, "beside Himself." Now it sounds a terrible thing that members of our Lord's own household should have thought Him mad, and should therefore have tried to put Him under restraint. But that was one of the sorrows Christ had to bear; He was misunderstood in His own home, for "neither did His brethren believe in Him" (John 7:5).

69

The Word and Its Enthusiasts

What we really get in their assertion that Christ was mad is often the world's verdict upon religious, and philanthropic enthusiasm. The world honors the man who for the sake of fame risks his life in battle; but if a man risks his life for souls for whom Christ died, it counts him a fool. The only kind of religion the world tolerates is religion of the tepid, Laodicean sort. But religion that breaks through the bonds of respectability and convention, religion that is earnest, red-hot, and means business, it calls "madness."

It has called it so all down the centuries. "Paul," cried Festus, "thou art mad; thy much learning doth turn thee to madness" (Acts 26:24, R.V.). "What crack-brained fanatics!" was the remark the gentlemen of the eighteenth century made about Wesley and Whitfield. When Christian and Faithful refused even to look at the wares of Vanity Fair, but turned their eyes to heaven, what could the dwellers in the Fair, who regarded these wares as the only things worth having, think of them but that they were Bedlams and outlandish men? And when men like Henry Martyn in recent times let themselves "burn out" for God, when they cheerfully sacrifice every hope of worldly wealth and fame, and think only of the soul and heaven and the unseen Christ, what can men who regard worldly wealth and pleasure and fame as the only things worth living for think of them, except that they are "beside themselves"? It is just the necessary and inevitable verdict of the world upon those who seek first the Kingdom of God and His righteousness.

What Is the Verdict on Ourselves?

Has the world ever said this about us? Is not this what is amiss with the Christian Church today? We lack zeal, enthusiasm, earnestness. We make compromises with the world. We are not out and out. The world sees nothing to be surprised at in us. And we are impotent as a result. Victory will come back only when we are willing to be counted fools for Christ's sake, and give ourselves ever, only, all to Him.

The Solitariness of Christ

"He is beside Himself"—it was just the verdict of the unspiritual person upon the zealous and sacrificial Christ. But it illustrates also the solitariness of Christ. How completely and utterly misunderstood He was! He was misunderstood even in His own home. Men can bear a great deal of opposition and misrepresentation from the world outside, if they find love and sympathy and appreciation waiting for them at home. But Jesus had none. He was the loneliest man who ever walked this earth; the loneliest just because He was the best. In the midst of the crowds that pressed upon Him and thronged Him, in the circle of the Twelve, at the family hearth, Jesus was a lonely man. There was none to understand or appreciate or sympathize. And this solitariness was part of the sore and heavy burden He took upon Himself when for us men and our salvation He consented to live His life of sacrifice and die His death of shame. "I have trodden the winepress alone; and of the peoples there was no man with Me" (Isa. 63:3, R.V.).

A Claim Resisted

Persuaded thus that Jesus was mad and needed to be put under restraint, His brethren, along with His mother Mary, make their way to Capernaum. They found Him engaged in preaching, with a great multitude listening to Him. For some time they seemed to have waited, and then, growing impatient, they send a message to Him—"Thy mother and Thy brethren without seek for Thee" (v. 32). Did Jesus know what they wanted Him for? I believe He did. He knew, at any rate, that there was no sympathy for Him amongst His kinsfolk. And so He declined to interrupt His work. "Who is My mother and My brethren"? was His reply to the message. "And looking round on them which sat round about Him, He saith, Behold, My mother and My brethren! For whosoever shall do the will of God, the same is My brother, and sister, and mother" (vv. 32, 33, R.V.).

The Cost of Resistance

What it must have cost Jesus to say this! For what does it mean? It means the setting of God's work above home-ties and family affection. A young fellow wanting to join the Church came to see his minister in trouble about that verse, "If any man cometh unto Me, and hateth not his own father, and mother, and wife, and children, and brethren, and sisters, yea, and his own life also, he cannot be My disciple" (Luke 14:26, R.V.). That seemed to him a harsh demand, and he did not know that he was equal to it. But it comes even to that sometimes. It comes to choosing between one's nearest and God. It came to that with Jesus Christ. He had to hate mother and sister and brethren for the Gospel's sake. "A sword shall pierce through thine own soul" (Luke 2:35), said Simeon to the exultant Mary when she presented her first-born in the Temple. Mary felt the stab of the sword that day; yes, and Jesus felt it too. He was pierced to the heart that day when He forsook mother and sisters and brethren for the Kingdom of God's sake.

The True Kinship

"Who is My mother and My brethren? . . . Whosoever shall do the will of God, the same is My brother, and sister, and mother" (vv. 33, 35, R.V.). There are affinities, our Lord says, more subtle and close and real than those of blood. The real kinship is a kinship of soul and spirit. Our Lord's one aim in life was to do God's will. It was for that He came into the world. And it was amongst those who cherished the like aim that He found His real kith and kin. The truth that spiritual kinship is the only real kinship is emphasized again and again in the New Testament. The true sons of Abraham are those who do the works of Abraham. The true circumcision is not the circumcision of the flesh, but of the spirit. The true sons of God are they that are led by the Spirit of God. So our Lord found His real kinsfolk, not in Joseph and Judah and James and Simon; He found His real kinsfolk in Peter and John and Nathanael and Matthew, and in that multitude of unnamed folk who heard the word of the Lord and received it.

In the Kingdom of God

This was a hard saying for Mary and her sons; but what a glorious word it has been for the world! It has enlarged the limits of Christ's family. It has multiplied the number of His brothers and sisters. Had kinship been a matter of blood, then you and I, my reader, had been forever excluded from Christ's family. But kinship is a matter of spirit, and so it becomes possible to you and me. One day, the Evangelist tells us, a woman in the crowd cried out, "Blessed is the womb that bare Thee" (Luke 11:27). There were many in Palestine who envied Mary the honor of being the mother of such a son. "Yea rather," was our Lord's reply, "blessed are they that hear the word of God, and keep it" (Luke 11:28). There is no need for any woman, as St Chrysostom says, to envy Mary. She can become as closely related to Jesus as His holy mother. "Whosoever shall do the will of God, the same is—My mother." So it becomes open to anyone to enter Christ's family, on condition they do the will of God.

The Family Speech

"To me to live is Christ" (Phil. 1:21), said Paul—that is the family speech. "I have but one passion, 'tis Jesus only," said Count Zinzendorf— that is the family speech. "I worship Thee, sweet Will of God," sang Faber—that is the family speech. Are we members of the family? How shall we know? Are we doing God's will? Notice, it is not mere outward connection with Christ's Church, nor the observance of the form of religion that gives us a place in the family, but only the doing of the will. Can Christ, as He looks upon us, say, "Behold My brother, My sister, My mother!"?

22
Christ and the Scribes

"And the scribes which came down from Jerusalem said, He hath Beelzebub, and by the prince of the devils casteth He out devils. And He called them unto Him, and said unto them in parables, How can Satan cast out Satan? And if a kingdom be divided against itself, that kingdom cannot stand. And if a house be divided against itself, that house cannot stand. And if Satan rise up against himself, and be divided, he cannot stand, but hath an end. No man can enter into a strong man's house, and spoil his goods, except he will first bind the strong man; and then he will spoil his house." —Mark 3:22-27.

Malice and Its Fruit

THE PRECEDING PARAGRAPH tells us of the way in which our Lord's own kinsfolk misunderstood Him. This paragraph tells us how utterly the religious leaders of Palestine misunderstood Him, and how cruelly they misrepresented Him. The misunderstanding of His brethren was born of ignorance and prejudice. The misunderstanding of the scribes was due to malice and wickedness. We may have pity for the one as a mistake, we can have nothing but indignation for the other as a sin.

The Miracle and the Blasphemy

These scribes had come down from Jerusalem on purpose to watch Christ and pick a quarrel with Him. An occasion soon presented itself. According to Matthew's account (Matt. 12:22), there was brought to Jesus one day a blind and dumb lunatic. And Jesus healed him, "insomuch that the dumb man spake and saw." It was, as all have agreed, a most striking miracle; and indeed may be regarded as three miracles in one. The multitudes who witnessed it were amazed, and the excited question began to pass from lip to lip, "Is it possible that this is the Son of David?" It was just at this point these scribes gave utterance to their terrible blasphemy. "He hath Beelzebub," they said, "and, By the prince of the devils casteth He out the devils" (v. 22, R.V.). They put down all Christ's deeds to Satanic agency. No doubt the slander was uttered in order to check the growing enthusiasm for Jesus; but it

74

illustrates to what lengths of wickedness malice and hate will carry men.

The Lord's Reply

Now let us look at the answer Christ makes to this wicked and slanderous charge. For the "meek and lowly in heart" condescends to reply to these men. Never had deadlier insult been flung at any man, and yet He does not retort with hot words. "Reviled, He reviled not again" (1 Peter 2:23). Instead of denouncing these scribes, He reasons with them.

The Folly of the Charge

"By the prince of the devils casteth He out the devils" was their account of His wonderful power. But, Jesus asks, "how can Satan cast out Satan?" Then, in two very brief seed-parables, He sets forth the consequences of disunion. "If a kingdom be divided against itself, that kingdom cannot stand. And if a house be divided against itself, that house will not be able to stand" (vv. 24, 25, R.V.). That is to say, disunion alike in states and houses ends in destruction. And so, our Lord adds, "if Satan hath risen up against himself and is divided, he cannot stand, but hath an end" (v. 26, R.V.). And that was exactly what their blasphemous assertion came to. For manifestly and undeniably, when Christ cast out evil spirits, and gave sight to the blind and speech to the dumb, and so on, He was destroying the works of the devil. But, according to the blasphemy of the scribes, He did it all "by the prince of the devils." So this was the absurdity to which the scribes had committed themselves—that the devil was busy destroying the works of the devil; in a word, that Satan was committing suicide!

The True Explanation

But if the "casting out" of these evil spirits was not Satan's voluntary act, if it was not suicide, what was it? There was only one answer—Satan had been conquered and overpowered. And in another brief parable our Lord gives the true explanation. Far from being Satan's ally, He was Satan's spoiler. "No one," He said, "can enter into the house of the strong man, and spoil his goods, except he first bind the strong man" (v. 27, R.V.). No one, He says in effect, can rescue the slaves and captives of Satan, unless he first overcome Satan himself. But the fact that Jesus had done it, that this man, afflicted with a blind and dumb spirit, had been rescued from the grip of Satan, and now both spoke and saw, was proof that Satan himself had been bound, that in Jesus he had more than met his match.

Christ the Mighty

That is the account Christ gives of this mighty deliverance; that is the great claim He makes for Himself. He is the "stronger than the strong." He has "bound the strong man." He has "cast out" Satan. He can "spoil his house." He can rob him of all his captives and slaves. And no as else can do it.

23
The Eternal Sin

"Verily I say unto you, All sins shall be forgiven unto the sons of men, and blasphemies wherewith soever they shall blaspheme: but he that shall blaspheme against the Holy Ghost hath never forgiveness, but is in danger of eternal damnation: because they said, He hath an unclean spirit."

—Mark 3:28-30.

IT BEHOVES ONE to walk warily and softly in discussing so solemn a passage as this; and yet perhaps there is in the whole of the New Testament no passage upon which we so imperatively need clear ideas, for mistaken interpretations of it have caused needless pain to thousands.

The Peril of the Scribes
Obviously it was addressed to those "scribes which came down from Jerusalem" (Mark 3:22). And the reason why it was addressed to them is plainly stated, "because they said, He hath an unclean spirit." There was something in that slander of theirs that told our Lord they were in peril of this eternal sin of "blaspheming against the Holy Spirit." Can we find what that something was? A glance at the terms of the warning will perhaps help us to our answer.

A Distinction Drawn
Our Lord draws a distinction between all other blasphemies and the blasphemy against the Holy Spirit. In Matthew's account (Matt. 12:31, 32) He says, for instance, that blasphemy against the Son of Man is forgivable, but blasphemy against the Holy Ghost is unforgivable. Why this distinction? Well, Jesus was so different from all the ideas of Messiah they had ever cherished that evil speech against Him need not indicate a "hopelessly evil nature," and so could be forgiven. But the ministry of the Holy Spirit is inward. It is the voice of God in a man's own soul. It is, as the Friends would say, "the inner light." A man might conceivably reject and denounce Christ in all good conscience, as Saul did. But when a

77

man sins against the Holy Spirit, he sins against his own conscience, against the light that is in him, and the man who enters
upon such a course is in danger of "eternal sin."

The Sin of the Scribes

Now that is exactly what these scribes had done. There was
some excuse for their doubt about the Messiahship of Jesus. There
was absolutely none for their wicked and monstrous charge that
by "Beelzebub the prince of devils casteth He out devils." They
knew that gracious miracle which they had witnessed was no
Satanic deed; they knew it was a work of God. But they hardened
their hearts, and deliberately put out the light that was in them,
and declared it was a work of the devil. And a person who does
that, says our Lord, is—not "in danger of eternal damnation" (as
the Authorized Version has it), nor even "is guilty of an eternal
sin" (as the Revised Version has it), but rather "is in the grip of, is
liable to, is involved in, eternal sin."

The Stifling of Conscience and Its Results

This is not a threat; this is simply the working out of one of the
great and austere laws of the spiritual world. No man can afford
to stifle his conscience. A neglected conscience becomes a seared
conscience. If a man ignores the light that is in him, the light itself
becomes darkness. That is to say, this sin against the inward light
tends to beget a permanent sinful state, an eternal sin. And these
scribes were in danger of it. They were busy putting out the light—
because they kept saying, "He hath an unclean spirit."

And so it brings a solemn warning to us as to the peril of persistent neglect of conscience and the testimony of the voice
within.

Unwarranted Inferences

Candor, however, compels me to add that multitudes have tor-
mented and still torment themselves needlessly on account of this
verse. They torture themselves with the thought that they have
committed some act of sin that has placed them beyond the reach
of the Divine forgiveness. This passage, however, solemn though
it is, warrants no such thought. It does not speak of any act of sin
as unpardonable. It does not speak of unpardonable sin at all.
What it speaks of is eternal sin. And that is the sin which cannot be
pardoned, the sin which is eternal. It cannot be pardoned, just
because it is eternal. A man may so harden himself in sin as to
become incapable of repenting, and because he cannot repent he

cannot be forgiven. This is not so much a case of unpardonable as of indomitable sin. It is not the grace of God that fails even here, but the man cannot be renewed unto repentance.

Does a man ever get into this awful state? I cannot tell; but at any rate those who go mourning because they think they have committed this sin, prove by their very broken-heartedness that they have not committed it. When a man gets into the grip of "eternal sin" he does not care—he is past feeling. The fact that men feel, is proof they are not in it. As Bishop Chadwick says, "No penitent has ever been rejected for this guilt, for no penitent has ever been thus guilty."

24
The Parables

"And He began again to teach by the sea side: and there was gathered unto Him a great multitude, so that He entered into a ship, and sat in the sea; and the whole multitude was by the sea on the land. And He taught them many things by parables, and said unto them in His doctrine, Hearken; Behold, there went out a sower to sow." —Mark 4:1-3.

The New Method
THIS CHAPTER BRINGS us to another clearly marked stage in the history of Christ, or at any rate to a new development of His ministry. From this point onward He taught the people "in parables." It is quite clear that He had not hitherto employed this method of teaching, from the surprise expressed by the disciples in verse 10. His preaching up to this time had been perfectly plain, simple and direct, as, for instance, in the great address known to us as the Sermon on the Mount. But from this point onward the "parable" was His favorite method of conveying truth to the multitude, and "without a parable spake He not unto them."

The Origin of the Parable
Now there must have been a reason for the adoption of the parabolic form of teaching at this particular time, and I want, if possible, to discover what that reason was. But before discussing the reasons why our Lord adopted the "parable" as His vehicle for conveying truth just at this juncture, we may profitably look at the facts which make the parable so useful. The Greek word literally means, "A placing of one thing beside another," with a view to comparison.

In the Correspondence between the Natural and the Spiritual
Now there is a deep correspondence between this natural world of ours and the spiritual world. "The world of nature and the world of spirit," as Archbishop Trench says, "proceed from the same hand and grow out of the same root." The things on earth are copies of the things in Heaven. The earthly tabernacle is made after

the fashion seen in the Mount. "The heavens declare the glory of God, and the firmament sheweth His handiwork." It is the same God who reigns in glory who has also made this earth of ours, and by understanding His laws in this lower realm we may gain glimpses into the laws of the realm of spirit and grace. For the invisible things of God are declared to us by the things that are made, and this earth is a ladder by which we can climb to heaven. "This entire moral and visible world," says Archbishop Trench, "from first to last, with its kings and its subjects, its parents and its children, its sun and its moon, its sowing and its harvest, its light and its darkness, its sleeping and its waking, its birth and its death, is from beginning to end a mighty parable, a great teacher of super-sensuous truth, a help at once to win faith and understanding."

This Harmony Perceived

This harmony and correspondence between the natural and the spiritual has been clearly discerned by the people of pure heart and open mind. Professor Henry Drummond—that man of stainless soul—that Bayard of the modern Christian Church—wrote his famous book *Natural Law and the Spiritual World* just to illustrate and prove this correspondence. But it had been observed long before Drummond's time. "Creation," Dr. Martineau had said, "is God thinking aloud." "I am thinking," said Kepler, as he traced the movement of the planets, "God's thoughts after Him." "Earth's crammed with heaven," wrote Mrs. Elizabeth Barrett Browning, "and every common bush's afire with God." "What if earth," writes Milton, "be but the shadow of heaven and things therein. Each to the other like more than on earth is taught."

And of Our Lord

But no one ever walked earth who had so pure a heart as Jesus. He did no sin, neither was guile found in His mouth, and consequently no one ever walked earth who had so clear an eye. He saw everywhere heavenly analogies, and the natural everywhere to Him shadowed forth the spiritual. You perhaps remember how Sir Edwin Arnold puts it:

> "The simplest sights we met—
> The Sower flinging seed on loam and rock,
> The darnel in the wheat; the mustard tree
> That hath its seed so little, and its boughs
> Wide-spreading; and the wandering sheep; and nets
> Shot in the wimpled waters, drawing forth

> Great fish and small; these and a hundred such
> Seen by us daily, never seen aright,
> Were pictures for Him from the page of life
> Teaching by parable."

And so He enriched the world forever with those exquisite parables of the Prodigal Son and the Lost Sheep and the Talents and the Sower in this Chapter, which have given us some of our most precious glimpses into the realm of spiritual truth.

The Purposes of the Parable

Now "speaking in parables" was by no means a new form of instruction. It was a popular method of teaching in the East. This teaching by story and picture was peculiarly adapted to the Eastern mind, and the Rabbis themselves were fond of beginning their lessons with the question, "What is the thing like?" It was an old enough method; the only thing peculiar about Christ's parables is that by their beauty, their naturalness, their depth, they make all other parables seem paltry and puerile.

Why was it that just at this juncture Jesus betook Himself to the parable? Perhaps we may get some help to our answer if we remember that as Bacon says, "Parables have a double use to veil and to illustrate, to teach and to conceal."

To Make Truth Plain

Now, I think we must start from this point—that Christ's primary object in teaching by parables was to make truth clearer. He used the parable as we use illustrations today—to light up His subject and to fasten it upon the minds of the hearers. The parable, as Mr. Latham says, enshrined an abstract truth in such a portable concrete form that it was made accessible to all men. It puts it into a shape familiar to orientals, a shape to which the Eastern tongue lent itself with ease, and which fitted readily into the minds of men.

Easily Understood

Or, to put the matter quite simply—the parable has two immense advantages for teaching purposes. (1) It made truth easily intelligible. Truth is never so easily grasped as when embodied in a tale. For instance, the story of the Pharisee and the Publican puts in a nutshell the distinction between true and false piety—and a long discourse could not have done it so well. The story of the Good Samaritan taught the meaning of neighborhood and the duty of love better than any abstract discussion could possibly have done.

And Easily Remembered

And (2) the parable made truth easily memorable. These exquisite stories never faded from the minds of those who heard them. They never fade from our mind. The parables are amongst the most familiar and cherished passages of Scripture. We might forget a discourse on the pity of God—but who can ever forget the moving story of the Prodigal Son? We might forget a sermon on Stewardship—but who can ever forget the Parable of the Pounds? We might forget a sermon on the duty of the rich to the poor—but who can ever forget the story of Dives and Lazarus? The parable was an excellent and indeed almost incomparable method of making truth easily understood and easily remembered. And, seeing that Christ knew that His time for preaching and teaching was short, I have no doubt these great advantages were in His mind when He began to speak unto them in parables.

But Also to Veil Truth

But that is not a complete account of the case. The parable veils as well as illustrates, it conceals as well as teaches. And I think that Christ had this effect of the parable also in His mind when He adopted the parabolic style of teaching. Remember that the parable is just an earthly illustration with a heavenly meaning. There was an outward and an inward aspect to it. There was a husk and a kernel, a body and a soul.

And so the parable, because of its dual nature might, and as a matter of fact did, have a double effect. As Matthew Henry puts it—"A parable is a shell that keeps good fruit for the diligent but keeps it from the slothful." The effect of the parable illustrated that great law that "to him that hath shall be given, but from him that hath not shall be taken away even that which he hath." For those who came with honest hearts and seeking souls and spiritual sympathy found wonderful revelations of truth in these exquisite parables. But the unspiritual, the worldly minded heard a pretty story, and nothing more.

The Result of Teaching of Parables

And so this method of teaching by parables became, shall I say, a kind of judgment. It sifted out the tares from the wheat, those who were genuinely spiritually minded from those whose thoughts were of the earth, earthy. For these latter, while they heard the story, missed entirely its heavenly meaning; hearing they heard, but did not understand; seeing they saw, but did not perceive. It was foolishness to them, for these things are spiritually discerned. "Whose fan is in His hand," John had said of Jesus, "and He will thoroughly cleanse His threshing-floor" (Matt. 3:12, R.V.). The parabolic method was part of Christ's plan. It purged the floor. It discovered the unworthy and casually minded. To some, as to the disciples, who never rested till they got to the inner meaning of the parable, it was the savour of life unto life; but to the unthinking, unreasoning crowd, who went away saying, "What a pretty tale," it was the savour of death unto death.

25
The Sower

"Hearken; Behold, there went out a sower to sow: And it came to pass, as he sowed, some fell by the way side, and the fowls of the air came and devoured it up. And some fell on stony ground, where it had not much earth; and immediatey it sprang up, because it had no depth of earth. But when the sun was up, it was scorched; and because it had no root, it withered away. And some fell among thorns, and the thorns grew up, and choked it, and it yielded no fruit. And other fell on good ground, and did yield fruit that sprang up and increased; and brought forth, some thirty, and some sixty and some an hundred. And He said unto them, He that hath ears to hear, let him hear. And when He was alone, they that were about Him with the twelve asked of Him the parable. And He said unto them, Unto you it is given to know the mystery of the kingdom of God: but unto them that are without, all these things are done in parables: That seeing they may see, and not perceive; and hearing they may hear, and not understand; lest at any time they should be converted, and their sins should be forgiven them. And He said unto them, Know ye not this parable? and how then will ye know all parables? The sower soweth the word. And these are they by the way side, where the word is sown; but when they have heard, Satan cometh immediately, and taketh away the word that was sown in their hearts. And these are they likewise which are sown on stony ground; who, when they have heard the word, immediately receive it with gladness; And have no root in themselves, and so endure but for a time: afterward, when affliction or persecution ariseth for the word's sake, immediately they are offended. And these are they which are sown among thorns; such as hear the word. And the cares of this world, and the deceitfulness of riches, and the lusts of other things entering in, choke the word, and it becometh unfruitful. And these are they which are sown on good ground; such as hear the word, and receive it, and bring forth fruit, some thirtyfold, some sixty, and some an hundred."
—Mark 4:3-20.

Turning to the first of the parables, we find it commonly spoken of as The Parable of the Sower. When we look closely at the parable, we shall probably think it might more properly have been called the Parable of the Soils; but the Sower shall claim all my attention now, the Soils being left over for the present.

Christ as the Sower

The Sower who went forth to sow His Seed is none other than our blessed Lord Himself. Yes, no doubt He stands also for every Christian minister, and every Christian teacher, and every Christian missionary, and, indeed, every one who in any way seeks to scatter the blessed seed of the Gospel. We are all of us, you may say, this Sower. But primarily and originally the Sower who went forth to sow was none other than Jesus Christ Himself.

Our Lord Describes His Own Ministry

Thus our Lord in this parable is describing the results of His own ministry. He was just at this time the object of much enthusiasm. The people were seriously inclined to believe that He was the Son of David. More than once they were tempted to take Him by force and make Him King. But all this excitement and enthusiasm did not deceive our Lord. He never for one moment imagined that all the people in the crowds that hung upon His words were His real and sincere followers. He knew theirs was but a surface enthusiasm. He looked forward, and He could see that in the near future these very people would go back, and follow no more after Him. He looked forward a little further, and He saw Himself a lonely and friendless prisoner, with the people—these people clamoring, "Crucify Him! Crucify Him !" No, our Lord was not deceived. He knew that out of the thousands who listened to Him there was only a tiny handful whose hearts were really touched. And the sight of a sower scattering his seed in the full sight of Him as He sat in the boat, dropping some of the seed on the wayside, and some on to the rocky ground, and some among the thorns, and some on the good ground, suggests to Him this parable. "Behold," He said, "a sower went forth to sow."

A Work of Faith

The work of the Sower is to plant, to sow the seed, to be in at the beginning of things. You and I, my brethren, can see some of the rich and glorious results of our Lord's sowing. It is partial harvest-time with us. He labored, and we have entered into His labors. But it was the day of beginnings with Him; it was a work of faith with Him. He was the Sower who went forth to sow; we have reaped where He sowed.

A Lonely Work

A Sower! As a rule the Sower works alone. The field at harvest-time is a very different place from the field at seed-time. At harvest-time there is company and gaiety. But there is neither company nor gaiety in seed-time. The sower goes on his way alone. And Christ knew Himself to be such a lonely Sower. I have referred already more than once to the loneliness of Christ. It was almost His sorest burden. It is true that He had the Twelve to be with Him; but even they did not understand Him, their aims were so very different from His. And thus it was that our Lord was solitary in His work. "I have trodden the winepress alone, and of the peoples there was no man with Me" (Isa. 63:3, R.V.).

A Cheerless Work

A Sower! Nature is almost at its dreariest when the sower is at his work. It is very different in harvest-time! Skies are blue then; suns are warm then; and all Nature seems to laugh and sing in the enjoyment of the brightness and the warmth. But Nature is sombre, stern, cheerless at seed-time. There is no foliage on the trees, there is no verdure in the field. Skies are gray and cloudy; and if the sun appears at all, it is only in fitful and watery gleams. There is nothing to make the heart cheerful at seed-time. And was it not like that with Jesus Christ? There was very little to cheer Him in His work. He lived His life beneath stormy skies. Even His kinsfolk, as we have seen, when they heard of His work, went out to lay hold on Him, for they said, "He is beside Himself." There were no encouraging conditions even in His own home. And the Scribes who came down from Jerusalem said, "He hath Beelzebub, and by the prince of the devils casteth He out the devils." He did His work in face of unceasing and bitter hostility on the part of the rulers. Our Lord was just a Sower, and it was cheerless winter weather for Him from the Baptism to the cross.

A Painful Work

A Sower! The very work of the sower is in a way painful work. I mean this, sowing is imparting, giving, flinging away. It is very different from harvesting. Harvesting is gathering, getting, receiving. No wonder there is joy at harvest; for the harvest means increase and enrichment. But sowing at the moment is sacrifice for improvement. The sower goes forth weeping, bearing his precious seed. He parts with a present good in the hope of a future reward. And Jesus was just a Sower. His whole life was a giving and an imparting, and it culminated in the sacrifice of the cross. It was hard work, it was sorrowful work, it was painful work. He went forth weeping, bearing His precious seed, but He looked for some far off interest for His tears. "Except a corn of wheat," He said—as

much to Himself as to the crowd—"fall into the ground and die, it
abideth alone; but if it die, it bringeth forth much fruit" (John 3:24).

A Work with Its Disappointments

A Sower! What disappointments the sower has to face! It is not
every seed that issues in harvest. "Out of a thousand seeds," says
Tennyson, "Nature brings but one to bear." This particular sower
dropped some seed by the way-side, and some on rocky ground,
and some among the thorns, and from these there was no fruit. So
the Lord Jesus was a sower, and similar disappointments attended Him. The way-side hearer and the rocky-ground hearer and the
thornpatch hearer—they were all in His congregation. From the
vast majority in the crowds that hung upon His words Jesus gathered no fruit.

Some of those who read this may at times feel almost broken-hearted by failure in Christian work. Men and women for whom we have
worked much, and from whom we hoped much, turn out such disappointments! I know how hard it is. I know something of the
heart-break of the sower who sows and reaps no harvest. But—Jesus
knew it too. What a sower He was! But for all His abundant sowing,
what scanty fruit He reaped! Yet He never murmured nor complained.
Let us go on with our sowing. It is sufficient for the disciple to be as
his Lord, and, if need be, we must be willing to be baptized into the
baptism of disappointment into which He was baptized.

And with Its Joys

"But some on good ground"—that is the saving clause. That is
the ray of glorious light in what might otherwise have been a
gloomy picture. "Some on good ground"—there was a Peter and
a John, and a Matthew and a Thomas among His hearers, and it
was worth while sowing the Word, if only for their sakes, for in
them it brought forth thirty, sixty, a hundredfold. "Some on good
ground"; it is not all disappointment. "Some on good ground,"
preachers of the Gospel, for one and another comes and asks the
way of Salvation. "Some on good ground," teachers, for this child
and that learns to love and obey Jesus. "Some on good ground,"
Christian worker, the faithful word, often seemingly spoken in
vain, sometimes finds a receptive soul. "Some on good ground"—
therein is the promise of the harvest. Let us not be weary in well-
doing. "He that goeth forth and weepeth, bearing precious seed,
shall doubtless come again with rejoicing bringing his sheaves
with him" (Psa. 126:6).

26
The Sower and the Soils

"And He began again to teach by the sea side: and there was gathered unto Him a great multitude, so that He entered into a ship, and sat in the sea; and the whole multitude was by the sea on the land. And He taught them many things by parables, and said unto them in His doctrine, Hearken; Behold, there went out a sower to sow: And it came to pass, as he sowed, some fell by the way side, and the fowls of the air came and devoured it up. And some fell on stony ground, where it had not much earth; and immediately it sprang up, because it had no depth of earth. But when the sun was up, it was scorched, and because it had no root it withered away. And some fell among thorns, and the thorns grew up, and choked it, and it yielded no fruit. And other fell on good ground, and did yield fruit that sprang up and increased; and brought forth, some thirty, and some sixty, and some an hundred. And He said unto them, He that hath ears to hear, let him hear. And when He was alone, they that were about Him with the twelve asked of Him the parable. And He said unto them, Unto you it is given to know the mystery of the kingdom of God: but unto them that are without, all these things are done in parables: That seeing they may see, and not perceive; and hearing they may hear, and not understand; lest at any time they should be converted, and their sins should be forgiven them. And He said unto them, Know ye not this parable? and how then will ye know all parables? The sower soweth the word. And these are they by the way side, where the word is sown; but when they have heard, Satan cometh immediately, and taketh away the word that was sown in their hearts. And these are they likewise which are sown on stony ground; who, when they have heard the word, immediately receive it with gladness; And have no root in themselves, and so endure but for a time: afterward, when affliction or persecution ariseth for the word's sake, immediately they are offended. And these are they which are sown among thorns; such as hear the word, And the cares of this world, and the deceitfulness of riches, and the lusts of other things entering in, choke the word, and it becometh unfruitful. And these are they which are sown on good ground; such as hear the word, and receive it, and bring forth fruit, some thirtyfold, some sixty, and some an hundred."
—Mark 4:1-20.

WE HAVE THOUGHT of the Sower. Let us now think of the Soils. Jesus Christ, as I said, was the Sower, and the seed which He sowed was the Word of the Kingdom. Roughly, we may say that the whole parable consists in an analogy drawn between the fortunes of a seed and the fortunes of the spoken Word.

The Seed and the Word Compared
Shall we dwell just for a moment on certain analogies between a seed and a word, which make the one an excellent type of the other?

In Reproductive Power
In the first place, there is immense reproductive power resident in each. A seed is not a dead thing. It contains vast potencies of life. It is a storehouse of energy. Waving fields of grain lie latent in the seed. And a word is like a seed in this respect. It is not a dead thing; not Luther's words alone, but all our words are living creatures. They are storehouses of energy. Dropped into a human heart, they may germinate and grow, and bring forth a harvest after their kind. And especially is this true of the Word of God. "The Word of God," says the writer of the Epistle to the Hebrews, "is living and active, and sharper than any two-edged sword . . . and quick to discern the thoughts and intents of the heart" (Heb. 4:12, R.V.).

In Need of Congenial Surroundings
There is a second point of resemblance in this that both the seed and the word need to find congenial surroundings before the life latent in each reveals itself. Before the seed multiplies into harvest, it needs to find suitable soil. Seed kept in the granary reveals no signs of life. It needs "the good ground" to develop the forces and potentialities that are in it. And in just the same way the Word, to reveal its life-giving power, must find the good heart. Even the living Word of God falls useless and profitless unless it is received with meekness into believing and obedient souls. Now, it is upon this latter fact, that the fortunes of both the seed and the word depend on the ground into which they fall, that the whole of this parable is built.

In Dependence on Soil Conditions
As Jesus sat in the boat teaching, He saw the sower going forth to sow. He saw some of the seed fall onto the trodden path and some on the ground through which here and there the rock peeped; and some into the corners of the field amongst the thorn bushes; and others into the soft, brown, fertile earth. And Jesus knew that though the seed that fell on the way-side and the rocky ground and amongst the thorns was itself every whit as good as

the seed that fell in the clear, rich soil; yet that the farmer would get no harvest from it, for the simple reason that it had not found favorable, suitable conditions. And all that reminded Him of His own experience as a preacher. If success depended upon the preacher, and upon the character of the word preached, what success ought to have fallen to Jesus, for His word was truth, and He Himself spake as never yet man spake!

The Word and the Hearer

But our Lord knew the success of the preaching depended not simply on the word and the preacher, but on the hearer too. And He knew perfectly well that though thousands followed Him, and though He taught them all, that it was only a comparative few who really received His word. In His case, as in the case of that sower before His eyes, some of the precious seed of the Gospel which He was scattering, was falling by the way-side, and some on rocky ground, and some among thorns, and from these He would never see a harvest. Yes, my brethren, the way-side hearer and the rocky-ground hearer, and the thorny-patch hearer, they were all in Christ's congregation, as they have been in every preacher's congregation since our Lord's day.

Now, let us see who the way-side hearer and the rocky-ground hearer and the thorny-ground hearer really are.

The Way-side Hearer

As the sower went on with his work, some seed fell on the way-side, on a beaten path that seems to have run across the field. Falling on that hard surface, the seed never got into the ground at all; and, lying there exposed to view, the birds soon espied it, and picked it up. Our Lord knew there were in His congregation that day some whose hearts were like that beaten track; they heard the Word of the Gospel, but it never got into them. A hard crust of insensibility kept the Gospel seed outside. That is the way-side hearer—the man on whom the Gospel takes no hold, into whose heart it does not penetrate at all.

How He Is Made Insensible

Half-a-dozen things may beget this insensibility. A person's training and upbringing may beget it. Some people are so trained or untrained as to be almost incapable of religion. The capacity for religion, as Bushnell would say, is almost extirpated by disuse. The Word of God, therefore, does not touch them. Theirs is a crust of insensibility, through which the seed of the Gospel does not penetrate. Then the incessant trampling through the heart of the world's business and pleasure and care may beget it. And sin may beget it. But, most terrible of all, as Dr. Maclaren points out, the very preaching of the Gospel may beget it. There are many ways in which the human heart may be beaten hard—but the most awful hardening takes place when a man becomes Gospel-hardened.

Whatever be the process by which the heart has arrived at that state, the result is still the same—the seed of the Gospel never gets a chance, for it never really penetrates at all. The Old Book is full of these men with the crust of insensibility: the Pharisees dismissing John's preaching with the remark, "He hath a devil"; Pilate, who set aside Christ's solemn words, asking that pitiful jest, "What is truth?"; the Athenians, who laughed when Paul made mention of the Resurrection; Festus, who cried out, "Paul, thou art mad." The Gospel really never got at these men. It lay outside of them, like the seed on the way-side. And then what happens? "Straightway cometh Satan, and taketh away the Word which hath been sown in them" (v. 15, R.V.). "Straightway"—the sermon is no sooner over than it is forgotten. It never really got into the mind or heart, and so the slightest thing is sufficient to sweep it all away. They are absolutely uninfluenced and unimpressed. It is a case of "Lost Seed."

The Rocky-ground Hearer

"Other fell on the rocky ground, where it had not much earth; and straightway it sprang up, because it had no deepness of earth: and when the sun was risen, it was scorched; and because it had no root, it withered away" (vv. 5, 6, R.V.). "And these," said our Lord in His interpretation of the parable, ". . . are they that are sown upon the rocky places, who, when they have heard the Word, straightway receive it with joy; and they have no root in themselves, but endure for a while; then, when tribulation or persecution ariseth because of the Word, straightway they stumble" (vv. 16, 17, R.V.). In the case of the way-side hearer the Word produced no effect; in the case of the rocky-ground hearer, it produces a temporary effect. In the former case the Gospel message took no hold; in this latter it takes only a superficial hold. They endure but for a time.

The rocky-ground hearer is really John Bunyan's Mr. Temporary. You perhaps remember the conversation between Christian and Hopeful with reference to him.

The Case of Mr. Temporary

"Well then," said Christian to his friend, as they walked on, "did you know about ten years ago one Temporary in your parts, who was a forward man in religion then?"

"Know him?" replied Hopeful, "Yes; he dwelt in Graceless, a town about two miles off of Honesty, and he dwelt next door to one Turn Back."

"Right," responded Christian, "he dwelt under the very same roof with him. Well, that man was much awakened once. I believe that he had some sight of his sins, and of the wages that was due thereto."

"I am of your mind," chimed in Hopeful, "for he would ofttimes come to me, and that with many tears. Truly I pitied the man, and was not altogether without hope of him; but one may see it is not every one that cries, Lord, Lord."

"He told me once," said Christian, "that he was resolved to go on Pilgrimage as we do now, but all of a sudden he grew acquainted with one Save-self, and then he became a stranger to me."

His Class

This Mr. Temporary, first cousin to Mr. Turn Back, living, indeed, under the same roof with Mr. Turn Back, is just the rocky-ground bearer. And our Lord knew Mr. Temporary right well. For there were people in His congregation who, when the Word was first preached, received it with all joy. They were full of enthusiasm. They wanted to take Him by force and make Him King. But when He talked strange words about eating His flesh and drinking His blood they turned their backs on Him in shoals. They had been charmed, not changed. The Gospel had touched their emotions, but had not penetrated to the heart. Paul knew Mr. Temporary. Listen, "Demas hath forsaken me, having loved this present world" (2 Tim. 4:10). Listen again. "Ye did run well; who did hinder you"? (Gal. 5:7). Every missioner knows Mr. Temporary, for in the excitement of the meetings numbers go into the enquiry rooms and fall away when faced by the stern realities of the Christian life. And every minister knows Mr. Temporary. For in every Church Year Book you will find a list of "Lapsed or Resigned "—a catalogue of men and women who endured for a time.

The Cause of Failure

Would you know what is amiss with the rocky ground hearer? "He had," Jesus says, "no root in himself." Fruitage is always a matter of rootage. You plant a tree by the river of water, and it will bring forth its fruit in its season, and its leaf will not wither. But this seed sown on the rocky ground had no root. It was not able to shoot its fibres down into the fat and nourishing soil, so, because it had no root, it withered away. And the rocky-ground hearer is a disappointment, an unfulfilled prophecy, for the very same reason. He has no root in himself. And what are we to understand by not having root in himself? This, I think. Religion had not penetrated deeply into him. It had touched him superficially, that was all. This is the account Hopeful gave of Temporary's defection. "Though the consciences of such men are awakened, yet their minds are not changed; therefore, when the power of guilt weareth away, that which provoketh them to be religious ceaseth." "You are pretty near the business," remarked Christian, "for the bottom of all is for want of a change in their mind and will." That is exactly it. The rocky-ground hearer has not been changed in mind and will. His religion has not gone deep. A religion based on sentiment, a religion that has its seat in the feelings, a religion that has not taken captive both mind and will, can never stand the shock of life's trials and temptations. The only religion that can last is the religion that has sent its roots deep down, that has laid hold of heart and soul, and mind and will. The man who is rooted and grounded and built up in Christ will stand four square to all the winds that blow.

The Thorny-ground Hearer

"And other," said our Lord, "fell among the thorns, and the thorns grew up, and choked it, and it yielded no fruit" (v. 7, R.V.). "And others," He said in His explanation, " are they that are sown among the thorns; these are they that have heard the Word, and the cares of the world, and the deceitfulness of riches, and the lusts of other things entering in, choke the Word, and it becometh unfruitful" (vv. 18, 19, R.V.). Now, if the way-side hearer stands for the man upon whom the Gospel takes no hold, and the rocky-ground hearer stands for the man of whom it only takes a superficial hold, the thorny-ground hearer stands for the man of whom the Gospel takes a disputed hold, whose heart is not wholly and entirely surrendered to the love of God. For by the thorny-ground of which our Lord here speaks we are not to understand those bushes into which some of the seed fell by accident. The thorns were not visible to the eye—they were buried underground. That is obvious from what our Lord says, "the thorns grew up." To all outward appearance this ground was clean and good. But beneath the surface of the soil, thorn roots and seeds lay hidden.

In other words, the fault of this soil was that it was impure. There were other things in possession. There were other seeds in it besides those which the sower scattered upon it, and the result was— two crops struggling for the mastery; and there was not nutriment enough for both. The bearing capacities of the soil are limited. It is equal to bearing one crop, but it is not equal to bearing two, or, at any rate, if two crops are sown in it, the growths from them are bound to be feeble and disappointing.

A Heart Weakness

Now in this respect the human heart is like the soil. The resources of the heart are limited, and a man is unequal to the task of serving Christ as He asks to be served, and serving somebody or something else at the same time. Listen to this; "Ye cannot serve God and mammon" (Matt 6:24). The heart may serve God, or it may serve gold, but no heart in the world is equal to the task of serving both. Listen again to this: "The friendship of the world is enmity with God" (Jas. 4:4), or as John puts it, "If any man love the world, the love of the Father is not in him" (1 John 2:15). Here are two things that cannot possibly coexist in the same soil. The growth of the one means inevitably the death of the other. It takes the whole heart to be a Christian. "Thou shalt love the Lord thy God with all thy heart, and with all thy soul, and with all thy mind, and with all thy strength" (Mark 12:30). "All!" No man can be a Christian with a divided heart. Now, the rocky-ground hearer is just a man who tries to do that impossible thing. He tries to be a Christian with a divided heart. He tries to serve God and the world at the same time. He cherishes other loves in his soul beside the love of Christ, and so his religion becomes a poor, sickly, stunted growth. These other things take all the sap and strength out of it, and "it becometh unfruitful."

Things That Produce it

Our Lord mentions specifically some of those thorn roots, which, if they are left in the heart, tend to choke the Word, and take all the strength out of a man's religion. Here they are—"The cares of the world and the deceitfulness of riches, and the lusts of other things entering in." "The cares of the world"—they can blight and destroy the spiritual life. "Be not anxious . . . what ye shall eat, or what ye shall drink" (Matt. 6:25, R.V.), said our Lord. He knew how easy it is for men to become engrossed in these mundane things, to the forgetting of the Kingdom of God and His righteousness, which is the one thing needful. Beware of this thorn. Forethought is right enough in its place, but absorption in the "cares of this world" may mean the starvation of the soul.

Riches

"The deceitfulness of riches!" The deceitfulness of riches, notice, i.e., the tendency of wealth to beget the passion for wealth; and also the tendency of wealth to beget the sense of sufficiency, so that a man no longer feels the need of treasure in heaven.

You must have seen the disastrous results of this thorn. I have known men who have grown poorer in soul as they have grown richer in purse. Their increase in wealth has been accompanied by a decrease in piety. Our Lord knew how deadly a thorn this was. "How hardly," He said, "shall they that have riches enter into the Kingdom of God" (Mark 10:23).

Pleasures

And "the lusts of other things entering in!" What are the lusts? According to Luke's account, they are "the pleasures of this life," and these pleasures, according to our Lord's statement, choke the Word. A man may smother his spiritual life by a passion for amusement. Indeed, we see this thing taking place. We see the strength and life being taken out of the religion of scores, and hundreds of young people by their devotion to pleasure. They promised well once upon a time. The seed gave good promise of a harvest; but this thorn was in the heart and it grew up and choked the Word, so that it became unfruitful.

The Fruitful Seed

"Some on good ground." And as I said before, this is the saving clause. The seed the farmer scattered was not all wasted. Some fell on the good ground, and there it yielded fruit, and brought forth thirty-fold, and sixty-fold, and a hundred-fold. And the harvest from the good ground compensated him for all his toil and labor. And so, too, some of the precious seed of the Gospel falls on hearts that are like the good-ground hearers who not only hear the Word but also accept it. They take it in. They "receive with meekness the implanted Word" (Jas. 1:21, R.V.) as the apostle says, and that implanted Word, received, is able to save their souls. They accept it. They take to themselves its promises; they receive its revelations and obey its precepts. And the Word thus received and accepted brings forth fruit in their lives.

The Necessary Conditions of True Holiness

The Word is a Word of life, but it profits us nothing unless we accept it. "The Word preached did not profit them, not being mixed with faith in them that heard" (Heb. 4:2). It was not accepted; it did not profit. But whenever it is accepted it brings forth fruit. It has its result in the life. "Beloved, if God so loved us, we ought also to love one another" (1 John 4:11). If we have honestly received that Word, we shall live the kindly and helpful life. "If any man would come after Me, let him deny himself and take up his cross, and follow Me" (Matt. 16:24, R.V.). If we have honestly received that Word, our lives will be marked by sacrifice. "Seek ye first the Kingdom of God, and His righteousness" (Matt. 6:33). If we have honestly received that Word, eternal things will be the first object of our seeking and our care.

Does the fruit show, in our case, that we have received the Word? Four classes of soils are spoken of in this parable, but really they reduce themselves to two—the soil that bears fruit, and the soil that does not. In the long run men are divided, not into four classes, but into just two—those who receive the Word, and those who do not. Those who show the results in life and character, and those who do not. In which class do we stand? "Take heed how ye hear."

27
The Responsibility of Hearing

"And He said unto them, Is a candle brought to be put under a bushel, or under a bed? and not to be set on a candlestick? For there is nothing hid, which shall not be manifested; neither was any thing kept secret, but that it should come abroad. If any man have ears to hear, let him hear. And He said unto them, Take heed what ye hear: with what measure ye mete, it shall be measured to you: and unto you that hear shall more be given. For he that hath, to him shall be given: and he that hath not, from him shall be taken even that which he hath." — Mark 4:21-25.

An Application
THE WORDS WE are now to consider are very closely connected with the preceding parable. They form, shall I say?—a kind of pendant to it. In part, they are meant to correct possible misconceptions that might arise from some of Christ's words, especially those in verses 11 and 12. In part they are designed to enforce and emphasize the teaching of the parable. If you like so to put it, they constitute the application of the sermon. The parable, as you may remember, sets forth the different kinds of reception the spoken Word meets with. The fate of the Word does not depend, says our Lord, simply upon the character of the Word itself, or upon the preacher; it depends also on the character of the hearer. These verses work upon that truth, and emphasize the responsibility of hearing.

And a Corrective
I think we can readily believe that the twelve had been congratulating themselves that they had privileges in this matter of hearing that were denied to the general multitude. The crowd had heard the story of the Sower, but the Twelve and a few other intimate disciples had heard its explanation as well. "Unto you," Jesus had said, "is given the mystery of the Kingdom of God: but unto them that are without, all things are done in parables" (v. 11, R.V.). Very likely they had been pluming themselves on the fact that secrets hidden from the ordinary hearer were revealed to them. This first word—if the disciples cherished any such feelings—must

have been a correction to them, for it asserts that privilege carries with it responsibility, and that light had been given to them simply in order that they might spread it.

The Duty of Sharing

"Is the lamp," said Jesus, using a homely but most suggestive figure, "brought to be put under the bushel, or under the bed, and not to be put on the stand?" (v. 21). The use of a light, Jesus said in effect, is to shine, and when men light a lamp they do not put it under a couch or under a measure, they put it where it will shine the best, they put it on the stand, in order that, as Matthew adds, it may give light unto all that are in the house. Light, Jesus says, is to be spread, diffused and shared. Now, we are back here at a principle which runs right through the New Testament, which is this, that every gift conferred upon us by God is conferred upon us for use; not for our own enjoyment or enrichment, but for service. God never blesses a man for his own sake; He blesses him that he may become a blessing. He never saves a man for his own sake; He saves him that he may become a savior. He never enriches a man for his own sake; He enriches him that he in his turn may become a source of enrichment to others.

A Corinthian Example

Paul mentions in 1 Corinthians 12 quite a long list of gifts enjoyed by the members of that quarrelsome but spiritually opulent Church. Some of them had the gift of knowledge, and others the gift of faith, and others the gift of healing, and others the gift of miracles, and others the gift of prophecy, and others the gift of tongues, and so on. But not one of these gifts was bestowed for private and personal gratification merely; each was bestowed upon the individual member for the benefit and profit of the whole body. The principle runs, indeed, through the entire ethical teaching of the New Testament. The individual exists not for himself alone, but for others. And this is specially true in regard to the Word of the Gospel. The Word of the Gospel is not a thing to be hoarded, it is a thing to be shared. We hear it in order that we may proclaim it. We listen to it in order that we may preach it. We receive it that we may spread it.

The Choice of the Illustration

Now let us look a little more closely at the figure our Lord uses to enforce this truth. "Is the lamp," He asks, "brought to be put under the bushel, or under the bed, and not to be put on the stand?" Now it is not by accident that our Lord used that figure. It is not a case of simply a pretty illustration.

The Word a Lamp

He uses it because the lamp sets forth certain qualities of the Word. The analogy is justified by a kinship. Just as the Word is like the seed, in that it contains within itself potentialities of life, so is it like the lamp, in that it is a source of knowledge and enlightenment. "Thy Word," says the psalmist, "is a lamp unto my feet, and a light unto my path" (Psa. 119:105). A lamp! And a lamp is only used when night falls. The lighted lamp implies the presence of darkness, and when the psalmist says, "Thy Word is a lamp," he implies a darkened world. A world in the dark about God, in the dark about duty, in the dark about the beyond. But "Thy Word is a lamp." "The entrance of thy Word giveth light." With the lamp of the Word in his hand, no man need stumble. He may walk safely and surely to his journey's end.

But Not for Private Use Only

But once again, the lamp is not for a man's private and personal use. "Let your light so shine before men," said Jesus, "that they may see your good works" (Matt. 5:16). That others may see! That was the purpose and end of our illumination—that others may see! For there are thousands and millions of our fellow creatures groping their way through the gloom, and we have to let our light so shine that these others may see. If we have a lamp, we must put it where it will best be seen. For the light was given to us that it might serve them too.

> "Heaven doth with us, as we with lighted torches do
> Not light them for themselves, for if our virtues
> Did not go forth from us, 'twere all alike
> As though we had them not."

This Word of the Gospel, this good tidings of God to which the disciples had been listening, they were to spread it, to diffuse it, to publish it. It was spoken to them just in order that they might proclaim it to others. The lamp was put into their hands just that they might put it on the stand and let it shine.

Have We Used It Aright?

Do you think that Christian people have learned this lesson, and recognized this obligation? Have we learned it? Have we recognized that the Word of the Gospel has been given to us that we might spread it? That we hold it in trust for others? That every hearer ought to be a preacher? "I have not hid Thy righteousness within my heart," says one of the psalmists; "I have declared Thy faithfulness and Thy salvation" (Psa. 40:10). Is that what we have done? Have we been intent upon spreading the good news? Have we taken every opportunity of telling others all around what a Savior we have found?

Or Have We Hidden It?

We rejoice—do we not?—in the possession of the lamp. Where, then, have we placed it? On the stand? Or is it hidden away under the bushel or the bed? For, as Dr. Glover says, there are all sorts of "bushels" under which we hide our lamp. There is the bushel of modesty, false modesty. "O Lord, I am not eloquent," said Moses; and we excuse ourselves today from bearing our testimony on the ground that we are not good enough or wise enough to speak, and so we turn the soul into a dark lantern. And then there is the bushel of selfishness. We do not trouble ourselves that other people are in the dark. Is not that the reason why people are so unconcerned in face of the paganism at home, and the vast stretches of heathenism abroad? We do not care enough for them to carry the light of our lamp to them. And then there is the bushel of timidity and cowardice. "I am not ashamed to own my Lord," we sing; but is it true? Do we not sometimes hide our faith? In certain society do we not keep silence about our Christian allegiance?

We are disciples, but secretly. We do not boldly announce it. We keep our lamp under the bushel—we do not put it on the stand. I am quite convinced there has been a great deal too much hiding of the light. We have not been as eager as we ought to have been to spread and preach the Word.

"Let the redeemed of the Lord say so" (Psa. 107:2). But we have kept quiet about it. We need to learn the principles of this passage. The light was given that it might be reflected, the Word was communicated that we might proclaim it. The good tidings have been announced to us that we might go and tell. The duty of evangelizing both at home and to the uttermost parts of the earth is wrapped up in this little sentence. Take your lamp from under whatever "bushel" may now be hiding it, and set it on the stand.

The Manifestation of the Hidden

"For," our Lord proceeds, "there is nothing hid, save that it should be manifested; neither was anything made secret, but that it should come to light" (v. 22). Our Lord assigns this as a reason for putting the lamp on the stand. The pertinency of the reasoning is not all at once apparent. But it becomes clear when we look at it more clearly. All this connects itself with that verse 11, to which I have already referred, in which Jesus said to His disciples, "Unto you is given the mystery of the Kingdom of God." The disciples may have thought that this was a kind of esoteric doctrine, which was to be kept secret from the crowds. No, says our Lord, whatever light is given to you is given that you may share it, for there is no one thing hidden unless that it may by and by be manifested. Nothing is to be hidden forever. There is always a final end to the hiding, and that is that it may be manifested.

The Method of Our Lord

Our Lord kept certain things back from His disciples, but He hid them for a time only, that He might manifest them when they were able to bear it. He kept certain things back from the crowd, and revealed them to the disciples, only in order that the disciples might reveal them to the crowd when they were spiritually fit to receive them. Jesus did not divide His disciples into two classes, as some of the Greek philosophers did, an outer and an inner circle; an outer circle, to whom He communicated elementary truth; an inner circle, to whom He communicated advanced truth. In Christianity, as Dr. Chadwick says, there is no privileged inner circle. There is no esoteric doctrine. All Christian knowledge is to be communicated and shared. If you have gained possession of any truth which is hidden from the average Christian, you are not to keep it hidden. There is nothing hidden, but that it may by and by be manifested; so set your lamp upon the stand.

Nothing hidden but that it may be manifested! Its primary reference is to Christian truth, but one cannot pass it by without a brief word about its broader application. Hiding, says Jesus, is not permanent; manifestation is the ultimate end. Now we see in a mirror darkly, but then face to face. "Now I know in part; but then shall I know even as also I am known" (1 Cor. 13:12).

The End-Manifestation

But this is not true of spiritual truth alone. It is true of all hidden and secret things. The final end is manifestation. Nothing is hidden save that it may be made manifest. The thoughts and intents of the heart, they shall all be made manifest. The desires and yearnings of our souls, they shall all be made manifest. The things we hide from our nearest and best, they shall all be made manifest. What we really are, not what we pretend to be, it shall be made manifest. What terror it would strike to our hearts if our hidden things were made manifest! And yet that manifestation is certainly coming. Concealment cannot last forever. There is nothing hidden, save that it should be made manifest. And that manifestation of our real selves, of our inmost hearts, will be the judgment. Every man shall go to his own place. To you who read this I say, have nothing hidden which you will be ashamed to have revealed. Keep a clean heart. And make this your daily prayer, "Let the words of my mouth, and the meditation of my heart be acceptable in Thy sight, O Lord, my Strength, and my Redeemer" (Psa 19:14).

How to Hear

And now our Lord, having spoken these words, perhaps for the warning of His disciples, returns to the broad and central lesson of the parable. "If any man hath ears to hear, let him hear" (v. 23). It is, as Dr. Morrison says, a proverbial and anecdotal saying, but its meaning is obvious enough. Hearing is not the simple matter some people think. It is not merely a case of possessing the physical faculty of hearing. For the way-side hearer heard, and the rocky-ground hearer heard, and the thorn-patch hearer heard. That is to say, they heard the words, but they profited nothing by them; for they did not hear with the soul, they did not understand, they did not accept the Word. Hearing, I repeat, demands more than the mere physical faculty. It demands the earnest attention of the mind, the prepared heart, the receptive soul. You would think it strange if your minister should come upon the Lord's day into the pulpit without having prepared himself to speak. It is, however, equally blameworthy to come and sit in the pews before him unless you have prepared yourselves to hear. "He that hath ears to hear, let him hear." So much depends upon the hearing. The Word will only profit us as we receive it with meekness into honest and good hearts.

What to Hear

Our Lord proceeds to add yet another counsel, "Take heed what ye hear" (v. 24). And what a necessary counsel it is! "Take heed what ye hear." Listen, said our Lord, with all earnestness. But be sure first of all that it is the kind of thing to which you ought to listen. There is to be election and selection in the case of the things to which we listen. I think our Lord had in view the fact that false teachers would come teaching pernicious and deadly heresies. It is not the Christian's business to listen to them. "Take heed what ye hear!"

A Modern Duty

Is not the counsel needed still? I am amazed at the absolutely gratuitous and irresponsible way in which Christian people will read books and listen to teachers whose whole aim is to undermine the Christian faith. Now do not misunderstand me. I am not for shutting Christian people upon a kind of glass case. I am not for having them close their eyes to all criticism of the truth. A faith that can only be preserved by refusing to listen to what can be said against it, is not worth very much. What I mean is that Christian people, not earnestly in search of truth and not intellectually fitted to be champions of the faith, will in sheer wantonness read any book and discuss any theme and listen to any teacher, and so imperil the faith of their souls. I know of people who have brought themselves into desolation and doubt through not taking heed what they hear. What wonder is it, Dr. Chadwick asks, that people who play with edged tools injure themselves, and become perverts and agnostics? When without possessing the intellectual equipment for discussing great religious problems, we read, for instance, skeptical books, we are deliberately rushing into temptation, we are deliberately playing with fire, and the penalty of playing with fire is that we get burnt.

The counsel admits of wider application. "Take heed what ye hear." There are certain books we had better never read, certain kinds of speech to which we had better never listen. Is it not a singular thing that we are more fastidious and nice with regard to all our other senses than we are with regard to our sense of hearing? How particular, for example, we are about our sense of taste! How nice we are about the matter of food! No one would dream of eating unclean, diseased or foul food; we shrink with disgust from the idea of feeding upon garbage. But we are not so particular about what we hear. We can listen to the diseased talk of the tattler and the scandal-monger. And we listen sometimes to foul and unclean talk. We are not afraid of garbage for the mind. And yet, what is the injury inflicted by diseased physical food, compared to the injury done by diseased and unclean mental food? The one taints the body, but the other defiles and debases the mind. What endless mischief and ruin would be saved, if only our boys and girls, our young men and young women, yes, and we older folk too, took heed what they hear!

Give and Take

"For with what measure ye mete," said Christ, "it shall be measured to you." He is back again at the subject of the responsibility of hearing. What you get, He says, depends upon what you give. What of profit you derive from any service depends upon what you bring to it. If you bring to it an indifferent mind and a distracted heart you will get no profit from it. But if you bring to it the eager mind, the receptive heart, the waiting soul, if you bring to it faith and expectancy and prayer, you shall receive the hundred fold. We complain sometimes that services are dry and barren and profitless. Whose fault is it? We are ready enough to say, the preacher's. But are we never to blame? Have we contributed our share? Have we come in the Spirit? Have we come up with prayer? Have we contributed the believing mind? What you get from a service depends upon what you bring to it. "For whosoever hath, to him shall be given . . . but whosoever hath not, from him shall be taken away even that he hath" (Matt. 13:12).

28

The Parable of the Fruit-Growing Earth

"And He said, So is the Kingdom of God, as if a man should cast seed into the ground; And should sleep, and rise night and day, and the seed should spring and grow up, he knoweth not how. For the earth bringeth forth fruit of herself; first the blade, then the ear, after that the full corn in the ear. But when the fruit is brought forth, immediately he putteth in the sickle, because the harvest is come." —Mark 4:28-29.

A Difficult Parable

THIS IS NOT a parable altogether easy of interpretation. In fact, scarcely two of the commentators I have consulted agree as to what is the real heart of the parable. And the difference between them becomes evident by the different titles they give to it. In our English Bible the parable is spoken of as the parable of the "Seed growing secretly," and in that description of it, apparently, Bishop Chadwick and Archbishop Trench agree. That places the center of gravity of the parable in verse 27, and makes the sentence "the seed should spring up and grow, he knoweth not how," the salient and all-important sentence. Dr. A.B. Bruce, on the other hand, calls the parable "The Blade, the Ear, the Full Corn," and he maintains that the chief lesson of the parable is that of the orderly development of the Kingdom of God. Dr. Salmond takes yet another point of view, and calls the parable the Parable of the Fruit-bearing Earth, and finds its central lesson in the statement, "The earth beareth fruit of itself"; and apparently Dr. Glover agrees with Dr. Salmond, for he says that the subject of the parable is the power of growth inherent in things divine.

A Parable of Encouragement

Now, when commentators differ so widely, it is perhaps presumption for an ordinary working minister to express an opinion. Especially, as all the truths which the different commentators maintain to be the central and primary truths are to be found in it. For the secret and mysterious growth of the seed is certainly here; and the orderly growth of the seed is also here; and the fruit-bearing power of the earth is also here. It is only a question, after all, of relative importance. It is only a question which of these various truths that are to be found in the parable is to be regarded as the central and primary one. On that question I side with Dr. Salmond and Dr. Glover, and believe that the lesson the parable is meant chiefly to emphasize is that there is a power of growth inherent in things Divine, "and that the Kingdom of God working, in quiet and without haste, through the moral forces deposited in human nature and society, is moving on to its assured end, by laws of its own." The parable is meant to be a parable of encouragement and in that respect is a complement to the Parable of the Sower.

Complementary to the Parable of the Sower

The Parable of the Sower, from one point of view, was a discouraging parable. For it spoke of the disappointments and failures that attend upon the work of the man who sows the Gospel seed. It mentions three cases of failure to one case of success. In the case of the way-side hearer and the rocky-ground hearer and the thornpatch hearer, the seed might just as well not have been sown, for it brought forth no fruit to perfection. Now, I say, that was a discouraging parable, enough almost to frighten anyone from work attended with so much disappointment. This parable is meant in a way to counteract any discouraging effect produced by the former parable. For this parable speaks, as Dr. Salmond says, of hidden forces beyond our knowledge or control, which secure the growth of the seed; it speaks of secret and prolonged processes, and tells us how seed which we have sown and almost forgotten, may at last issue in the full corn in the ear. This parable is the New Testament counterpart of that great Old Testament promise, "As the rain cometh down, and the snow from heaven, and returneth not thither, but watereth the earth and maketh it bring forth and bud, that it may give seed to the sower, and bread to the eater; so shall My word be that goeth forth out of My mouth; it shall not return unto Me void, but it shall accomplish that which I please, and it shall prosper in the thing whereto I sent it" (Isa. 55:10, 11).

The Limitation of Human Effort

Now let us turn to the parable itself. "So is the Kingdom of God," says our Lord, "as if a man should cast seed upon the earth; and should sleep and rise night and day" (vv. 26, 27, R.V.). What is the meaning of this sentence about "sleeping and rising night and day"? Does it signify indolence or carelessness, or indifference to the fate of the seed? Not at all, but rather the consciousness that the farmer had done all he could do, and that he must just leave the rest to Nature's processes. In connection with the seed and its growth, the farmer has something to do at the beginning, and he has something to do at the end. He has to do the sowing, and when the harvest is ripe he has to do the reaping. But all that lies between the sowing and the reaping is God's part, and not man's. No anxiety on the farmer's part will help the growth of the seed; it depends now on the sunshine and the dew and the rain—things in God's control, and not in his. There is a limit to what a man can do in the matter of preparing for a harvest. He can prepare the earth, and sow the seed in it. There is practically nothing else that he can do. Having done that, he may sleep and rise night and day, i.e., go about the ordinary duties of life, and pursue his varied avocations, for the future growth of the seed depends not upon him, but upon Nature and Nature's God.

The Spiritual Endeavor

And the Kingdom of God in its growth and development is much like that. There is a strict limit to what man can do. The growth of religion in the soul is not a human work, it is a Divine work. What can a man do? He can sow the seed. He can preach the Word. But having done that he has practically done all that he can do. Nothing that we can do can ensure that the seed shall take root and fructify. Nothing that we can do can ensure the thirty-fold and the sixty-fold and the hundred-fold. We have not the power to give a man a new heart, or to beget within him a new life. In a word, we have not the power to change and convert men. We can sow the seed, and we can take care it is good seed that we sow, but the question of fruitage and harvest we must leave entirely to God. The best and saintliest of men have to leave it there. Paul may plant, Apollos may water, but God giveth the increase. "Not by might, nor by power, but by My Spirit, saith the Lord of hosts" (Zech. 4:6).

A Fact to Be Recognized with Thankfulness

This is a fact to be recognized with humility and thankfulness, says Dr. Bruce. With thankfulness, for it relieves the heart of the too heavy burden of an unlimited responsibility. It would be more than flesh and blood could bear, to think that it depended upon us, and us alone, whether men were saved or not. But God relieves us of that heavy burden. We have to scatter the seed, to preach the Word, to declare the Gospel in all sincerity and earnestness. We must leave results and effects to God. Our business is to do the sowing; the harvest is God's care.

And with Humility

It is a fact to be recognized also with humility. For it teaches us that the real worker is God, and it drives us to a more humble dependence upon Him. We can oftentimes do more by prayer and humble waiting upon God than we can by fussy zeal. I am not sure whether we do not sometimes think we can manufacture a harvest of our own. I mean this; the tendency of our time is perhaps to multiply our forms of activity, and to neglect prayer. But the limits of the good that any activities of ours may do are very quickly reached. No amount of activity on our part can make religion take root and grow in the soul. That is God's work. And, if we want to see a harvest from the seed we scatter, it is to Him we should address ourselves. "My soul, wait thou only upon God, for my expectation is from Him" (Psa. 62:5).

The Quietness of Growth

The farmer flings his seed upon the ground, and leaves it there. He goes off to other work, to one or other of the varied duties of the farm. He sleeps and rises night and day; and what of the seed itself? The seed springs up and grows, he knoweth not how; quietly and silently. Here we are at that truth which our Authorized Version emphasizes as the central lesson of the parable— the lesson of the quiet and steady growth of the seed. You have noticed how silently the very mightiest forces work. The law of gravitation that holds the worlds in their places makes no noise. The light that transforms the entire face of nature comes without tumult. The sunshine and the dew that cause the earth to bring forth and bud, visit us with absolutely noiseless tread. But there is no process more wonderful than the death and resurrection process, that takes place in the history of every seed planted in the bosom of the brown earth. God has, as Dr. Raleigh used to say, His laboratory beneath the soil. He opens in every field ten thousand times ten thousand fountains of life. He kindles there ten thousand invisible fires; He never leaves the field. And by and by, for every seed he scattered, the farmer receives back thirty, sixty, and a hundred. This marvelous multiplying process has taken place in absolute silence and quietness. You can see and hear a building grow. You can mark its rise, brick by brick, storey by storey; but you cannot trace the growth of the seed beneath the soil. The child who plants the seed today, and then digs it up tomorrow, will not see the growth. It is a silent, quiet, unperceptible process, and it is like that, our Lord says, with the Kingdom of God.

The Growth within the Community

I think that possibly the original reference in the parable is not so much to the growth of religion, in the individual soul, as to the spread of religion in the community. The disciples were expecting an outward and visible Kingdom. They wanted it to come at once. You remember their question, "Lord, wilt Thou at this time restore again the Kingdom to Israel ?"(Acts 1:6). They did not see why it should not come suddenly, as the result of some great act of power. But "The Kingdom of God cometh not with observation" (Luke 17:20). Men can never say, "Lo, here! Lo, there!" And yet quietly it is growing, ceaselessly growing, and grow it will till the kingdoms of the world become the Kingdoms of our God and of His Christ.

The Growth in the Individual Soul

But though the primary reference may be to the Kingdom in its broadest sense, what our Lord says here is true of the growth of religion in the individual soul. Spiritual growth is mysterious in its beginning. "The wind bloweth where it listeth, and thou hearest the sound thereof, but canst not tell whence it cometh and whither it goeth: so is everyone that is born of the Spirit" (John 3:8). And it is quiet and imperceptible in its development. God is quietly at work in many hearts unknown to us. We can see no signs of life or change, perhaps; and yet the seed is springing and growing up.

Encouragement for Workers

There is infinite encouragement and hope in all this. We soon come to the end of our little resources, and we grieve that we see no visible results. But when that is so, remember that God never leaves the field. He never ceases His work, and under His fostering care the seed we scattered, unknown to us and unseen by us, is growing up. Where we never see it, faith is in existence. Where we never suspect it, it has often made considerable progress. Think of God's answer to Elijah, when he moaned out, that he alone in the whole of Israel was left to worship the living God. "Yet I have left Me seven thousand in Israel," was God's word to him, "all the knees which have not bowed unto Baal" (1 Kings 19:18). Think of God's message to Paul, when he was cast down and almost broken-hearted, at the seeming failure of his work at Corinth. Our Lord appeared to him in a vision by night, and told him, "I have much people in this city" (Acts 18:10). The seed that Paul thought had been scattered in vain had all the time been growing secretly. And so still in unsuspected places, and without any arresting sign, the truth takes effect. The minister sees nothing. Members of the family see nothing. Companions see nothing. Yet under God's fostering care the seed is growing up.

A Personal Reminiscence

Shall I tell you a personal incident? When I was at Lincoln I preached a sermon on "Friendship." It was addressed especially to young men. I remember feeling particularly discouraged after preaching that day. I kept company with Elijah under the juniper tree, and felt I had labored for naught and in vain. But since coming to Bournemouth I received a letter from Australia about that very sermon. And this was what it said. The writer was in Lincoln the Sunday I preached it. He was a complete stranger, and quite casually, or rather shall we say providentially, he turned into my old Church. He went out to Australia immediately afterwards, and lived rather a rough and careless life; but the sermon he heard at Lincoln clung to him. In his wildest days he said he kept hearing the appeal to make a Friend of Him who sticketh closer than a brother. And at last, six years after the sermon was preached, he gave himself body and soul to the Lord. Who would have thought of what was passing in the heart of that young fellow during these wild and careless years? Let us be of good cheer. Let us scatter the seed. In the most solitary places, in the most stubborn and obstinate hearts, it grows and springs up we know not how.

The Spontaneity of Growth

"For," says our Lord, "the earth beareth fruit of herself." This is not meant, of course, to exclude the Divine agency. What our Lord means to say is this; that when man has done with the seed, other forces begin to act upon it, forces inherent in the earth to which it is committed, forces of God's own providing in the way of fructifying sun and showers. Thus the truth Jesus wants us to remember is, that there are other forces besides our own human efforts which make for the growth and development of the seed.

From the Life in the Seed and the Possibilities of the Soil

First of all, there is an amazing life in the seed itself: "The Word is quick and powerful." By itself and of itself often the mere Word

seems to effect great spiritual changes. Then let us never forget that
the heart of man is made for the reception of the Divine Word. We
say that the heart of man is "desperately wicked" (Jer. 17:9), and
that is true. But we have to remember the truth expressed by
Augustine in that well-known saying, "O God, Thou hast made us
for Thyself, and our hearts are restless until they find rest in Thee."
There are hearts described by our Lord as "good ground," hearts
favorable to the growth of the Divine Word. Is not Augustine himself an illustration of this? His mother's prayers and teaching for
years seemed wasted upon him, while he plunged into folly and
excess and sin. But all the time the heart was retaining the
Word, and bringing it to fruition, and then one day, to his mother's
delighted surprise, Augustine gave himself in glad surrender to the
Lord. And then, in addition to the life in the seed and the capacity of the heart, there is the ceaseless ministry of the Spirit of God.
He is continually working upon the souls of men, and in the most
wonderful ways bringing the seed to harvest. And so we may venture to hope and trust. Though we may see no sign of harvest, yet
we may with patience wait for it.

The Orderliness of Growth

"The earth beareth fruit of herself; first the blade, then the ear,
then the full corn in the ear" (v. 28, R.V.). Notice the progression.
"First the blade, then the ear, then the full corn in the ear." This is
the orderliness of growth. Through all these stages the corn passes, and you must give it its time. You must not expect the full corn
in the ear in the springtime. It is the blade that you will see then.
The full corn in the ear belongs to the golden and mellow
autumn. There are similar stages in the development of the
good seed of the Kingdom. There are the feeble beginnings, the
enlarging strength, and the full maturity of Christian growth.
There are some Christians who are in the infant class, engaged
with the beggarly elements. There are some who are pressing on
to perfection. John in his Epistle seems to refer to three distinct
stages of Christian development. There are the little children who
have had their sins forgiven—the blade; there are the young men
who are strong and have overcome the evil one—the ear. There are
the fathers rich in experience, mature in knowledge, who have
known Him who is from the beginning (1 John 2:12-14)—the full
corn in the ear. The Christian life is a gradual and ordered
growth. Sanctification is a lifelong process. And this ought to teach
us patience and kindliness. You have no right to expect in the
young beginner the rich experience of an old disciple. However

crude the beginner's religion may be, hope the best, and believe the best. When Dr. Dale was a young man, many of the old saints in Carr's Lane shook their heads over him. I daresay his preaching then was a little violent and ill-balanced. "Let him alone," said John Angell James; "he'll come right." The blade with patience and kindly care will develop into the ear, and the full corn in the ear.

Questions for Ourselves

In what stage are we? Some of us have been Christians for many years. Is our sanctification making progress? Are we getting to that stage of Christian life when our Lord is getting a rich harvest in us? When He sends forth the sickle, because the harvest is come, will He find us with full corn in the ear?

29

The Parable of the Mustard Seed

"And He said, Whereunto shall we liken the kingdom of God? or with what comparison shall we compare it? It is like a grain of mustard seed, which, when it is sown in the earth, is less than all the seeds that be in the earth: But when it is sown, it groweth up, and becometh greater than all herbs, and shooteth out great branches; so that the fowls of the air may lodge under the shadow of it." —Mark 4:30-32.

Discouragement and Encouragement

THIS, LIKE THE Parable of The Seed Growing Secretly is a parable of encouragement and good hope. There had been in the Parable of the Sower, as I have already pointed out, a great deal to discourage and depress. It seemed to suggest that of the seed sown in men's hearts, three parts would be lost. For it records three cases of failure for one of success. And, according to Matthew's account, the parable of the Sower had been followed by a more discouraging parable still, i.e., the parable of the Tares. In addition to the perversity of the human heart, our Lord told His disciples that they had to reckon with an adversary who was just as tireless sowing the seeds of noxious weeds, as they were in sowing the good seed of the Kingdom. Between the parable of the Sower and the parable of the Tares I can well believe the disciples were sorely discouraged and depressed.

They may have wondered whether it was worth while to sow the seed of the Kingdom at all. And so our Lord followed up those two parables about the difficulties and discouragements of Christian work, with these two about the encouragements and glorious results of it. First, the parable of the fruit-bearing earth, and the seed growing secretly. And secondly, this parable of the mustard seed, which from tiny beginnings developed and grew until it became greater than all the herbs in the garden, and almost attained to the dimensions of a tree. Dr. J. A. Alexander says: "The truth taught is the expansive and diffusive nature of the true religion and the necessary growth of the Messiah's kingdom, both in society at large and in the hearts of individ-

114

uals from the most infinitesimal beginnings to the most immense results."

The Main Lesson of the Parable

The broad lesson of the parable is simple and obvious enough. It is that, as Dr. Hamilton puts it, of "a little germ and a large result, a small commencement and a conspicuous growth, an obscure and tiny granule followed by a vigorous vegetation, the least of all seeds becoming the greatest of all herbs." It was meant to teach the disciples not to despise the day of small things. The Kingdom of God, as they now saw it, was so unlike their anticipations, and so insignificant in its appearance; there was such a difference between their Master—a humble carpenter from Nazareth—and the conquering Prince of their dreams, that they may well have been filled with gloomy anticipations. It may have been the "mustard seed" appearance of the Kingdom that made Judas turn traitor. So this parable was spoken to correct any doubts in their minds, and to give them the assurance of a mighty future, in spite of the small and obscure beginnings.

The Tiny Seed

And now let us turn to the parable itself. Our Lord begins with fine oratorical tact, as Dr. Morison puts it, by asking a question. He invites His hearers to think of suitable similitudes. He invites them to let their minds play upon the subject. How shall we liken the Kingdom of God? He asked. Or in what parable shall we set it forth? And then, perhaps, He paused, as if waiting for a reply. I wonder what were the similitudes that suggested themselves to His hearers. If I had to guess, I should guess that they were all ambitious, grandiose, high-flown. For you must remember that these men had been brought up on the glowing imagery of the prophets. All their conceptions of the Kingdom they had derived from their impassioned pages. They would naturally and inevitably think, therefore, of those splendid pictures of Zion exalted on the tops of the mountains, and all the nations flowing into it (Isa 2:2); of that glorious city whose walls were Salvation and whose gates Praise, into which all nations poured their wealth, and to which the Kings of Sheba and Sheba offered gifts (Psa. 72).

It was some such majestic and ambitious picture as that, that presented itself to the disciples' minds. Judge, therefore, of their surprise, very likely of their disappointed surprise—when, after a gentle pause, Jesus answered His own question, and said, "It is like a grain of mustard seed." The disciples were thinking of something very great. Jesus Himself compared it to something very small. For the smallness of the mustard seed had passed into a proverb. It was indeed, as Jesus says Himself, "less than all the seeds," i.e., all the seeds in common use. And the Kingdom of God, Jesus says, is like that.

The Insignificant Beginnings of Christianity

Now, what our Lord has in mind here is the insignificance of the historic beginnings of Christianity. And what really could be more insignificant? Think of Jesus Christ Himself— since, as Archbishop Trench says, He Himself is really the Mustard Seed, for from Him all subsequent developments of Church and Kingdom have issued. What could be lowlier, humbler, more insignificant, judged by men's ordinary standards, than the career of Jesus? Growing up, as Trench says, in a distant and despised province; working in His town as an ordinary carpenter, He did not till His thirtieth year emerge from the bosom of His family. Then for two or three years He preached and taught in the neighboring towns and villages, with occasional visits to Jerusalem; gathered about Him a small band of disciples, for the most part fisherfolk; and at length, falling into the hands of His enemies, with no resistance on His part or on that of His followers, died a malefactor's death upon the Cross. What could have been more insignificant? The life and death of Jesus scarcely made a ripple in the life of the great world. Caesar in his palace never heard His name, and probably would not have given a second thought to it, if he had heard it.

The story of a Jewish provincial who had died a slave's death would be regarded as quite beneath notice. The insignificance and humbleness of the whole movement which Christ initiated were, indeed, cast up as a reproach against Him. "Have any of the rulers or of the Pharisees believed on Him?" (John 7:48) was the taunt flung at Him by unbelieving Jews. Here Christ quite freely and frankly admits that insignificance. There was nothing striking or obviously great about the Kingdom, as represented in Himself and His tiny band of disciples. "It is like a grain of mustard seed."

Other Characteristics of the Seed

Some commentators find a lesson in the fact that it is to the mustard seed Christ compares His Kingdom. Trench, for instance, thinks that our Lord chose the mustard seed not simply because of its tiny size, but also because of its heat and fiery vigor; and the fact that only through being bruised and broken does it give out its best virtues, all of which makes the mustard seed a fit type of the destinies of that Word of the Kingdom which centers in the preaching of Christ crucified —a Savior who gave His body to be broken and His blood to be shed for us—a preaching which seemed to the Greek foolishness, and was to the Jew a stumbling-block, but which, as a matter of fact, proved itself to be the power of God and the wisdom of God.

The Seed and Its Growth

But while such analogies may be true and helpful, I do not think they were in the mind of Christ when He uttered this parable. He had one single lesson which He wished to teach, and that was that very tiny beginnings might have great endings. Very likely the disciples were discouraged by the small show the Kingdom was making. They looked for thrones, and here they were a band of wandering preachers dependent on charity for support. Christ admits the insignificance; they were indeed but a "little flock," but He lifts their eyes to the great and glorious future. "It is like unto a grain of mustard seed," He said, but the mustard seed has this quality about it, that "when it is sown, it groweth up, and becometh greater than all the herbs, and putteth out great branches" (v. 32, R.V.). Some people have felt that the grown mustard herb was too insignificant a figure to describe the majestic growth of the Kingdom. The great oak or the cedar of Lebanon, they feel, would have been a more fitting simile. But it is not so much the majesty of the Kingdom that Christ is emphasizing here as the contrast between beginnings and endings, the difference between the seed and the product. And while the difference between the acorn and the oak is conspicuous enough, the difference between the mustard seed and the mustard herb is more striking still. For in the East, according to the testimony of travelers, the mustard will grow till it overtops a man on horseback. And that is the truth Christ wishes to drive home—great results may follow from tiny beginnings.

The Large Result

Christ never had any fears about the future. The fewness and the poverty of His disciples never dismayed or daunted Him. The fact that His career was to end upon a cross did not stagger Him. He looked away from the discouraging, depressing, insignificant present to the great and glorious future. He knew that, in spite of seeming weakness and defeat, the future was His. He knew His disciples were but a "little flock," few in numbers, almost beneath contempt in position and social influence, and yet He dared to say to them, "Fear not, little flock; for it is your Father's good pleasure to give you the kingdom" (Luke 12:32).

He knew that the cross was preparing for Himself, and yet, when thinking of it, it seemed to be transformed into a throne. "I, if I be lifted up from the earth, will draw all men unto Me" (John 12:32). And here He is bidding His disciples remember that from tiny and insignificant beginnings great results may flow; the seed, the least of seeds, may become a tree.

The "Great Tree" of Today

Has not our Lord's prophecy come true? No movement had any more insignificant beginning—no movement has ever had more stupendous results. It is the "great tree" Kingdom which began we see today. The Kingdom which began with Jesus and His handful of Galilean disciples, is now the mightiest force in the world. It has spread into every land. It numbers its subjects by the million. It differs from every earthly kingdom. They often make a great beginning, but come to a miserable and shameful end. Christ's Kingdom came without observation, but it is advancing by steady and persistent growth to its glorious consummation. The mustard seed has become greater than all herbs. That is always the way with the Kingdom of God. Its beginning is always insignificant, but none can compute its results.

The Growth in the Individual

It is so with the individual. The Word of the Kingdom drops into a man's heart. There is perhaps but little immediate and striking outward change. The Word is like a mustard seed, promising but little, but if allowed to grow, what mighty results it will produce! It will transform a man's whole life. It will affect all his activities. The Kingdom grows and grows until, body, soul and spirit, the man becomes the servant of King Jesus.

And in the Community

And as it is in the case of the individual so is it also in the case of communities, and perhaps it is this aspect of the growth of the Kingdom that is specially in Christ's mind. Numbers of illustrations of this rapid and striking growth of the Kingdom suggest themselves.

Fourteen hundred years ago Colomba and a dozen companions sailed from Ireland in a frail little skin-covered boat for Scotland. They landed in Iona, and built a tiny Christian temple there. That was the beginning of Christianity in Scotland. The Kingdom of God was a grain of mustard seed. But from Iona, Colomba and his companions went and preached to the dwellers on the mainland, to the Picts with their painted faces, to the Druids in their groves. And modern Scotland, with its innumerable houses of prayer and its widespread religion, is the result. The mustard seed has grown into the tree.

Five hundred years ago the seed of the Gospel found a lodging in the heart of Martin Luther. It was a case of the mustard seed in those days, when Luther, a humble and unknown monk, travailed in soul. But from Martin Luther and his spiritual conflicts the Protestantism of half Europe and America and Australia has sprung. The grain of mustard seed has become a great tree.

Two hundred and fifty years ago John Wesley's heart was "strangely warmed," in the little meeting-house in Aldersgate Street. The Kingdom of God in this case was like a grain of mustard seed. The great world never knew that anything extraordinary had happened. But from that experience sprang the great Evangelical Revival and the Methodist Church of today. The grain of mustard seed has become a great tree.

Two hundred years ago William Carey's soul was filled with concern about the heathen. He was a man of no great position and of little influence. Even his brother ministers pooh-poohed William Carey and his notion of converting the heathen. The Kingdom of God was like a grain of mustard seed. But from that passion in William Carey's heart the whole modern mission enterprise has sprung. The Northampton cobbler poring over his map of the world, that is the grain of mustard seed. The noble army of missionaries who have gone forth to plant in every land the banner of the Cross, the immense and incalculable work of missions in well nigh every quarter of the globe, that is the great tree. I need not multiply examples. The little one, as Dr. Glover says, when it is Divine, always becomes a thousand, and the small one a strong nation. "There shall be an handful of corn in the earth upon the top of the mountains; the fruit thereof shall shake like Lebanon" (Psa. 72:16).

A Message of Encouragement

What an encouragement all this is! We have our depressing and discouraging times. We are almost in despair at the weakness and insignificance of our efforts. But we may share our Lord's radiant faith. The future is ours! Despise not the day of small things. The Kingdom may be like the grain of mustard seed, but that tiny thing has life in it, indestructible life. The forces of evil cannot crush or destroy it. It will grow in spite of them. It will out-top and outlive them. "Of the increase of His government and peace there shall be no end" (Isa. 9:7).

The Shelter of the Kingdom

"And putteth out great branches; so that the birds of the heaven can lodge under the shadow thereof" (v. 32, R.V.). What are we to make of this sentence? Is it added merely for picturesque effect? Or did our Lord mean it to add something to our conception of the Kingdom? I believe He meant it to add something to our conception of the Kingdom. "It putteth out great branches," He says, and I think we may, without being fanciful, see here a reference, shall I say to the collateral blessings and benefits of the Christian faith? The prime business of the Church is to witness to the Unseen, the Spiritual; religion is its central concern. But the Church has continually put forth branches from the main stem; in addition to its purely religious function, the Church has started and still maintains all manner of philanthropic and social agencies. Very early it began to care for the sick, the poor and the orphan. A little later it made the education of the child its charge. Today it is providing for the pure and healthy recreation to our young people in the large cities. Our hospitals and infirmaries, they are just a branch; our orphanages and homes, they are just a branch; our institutions and schools, they are just a branch. Our Young Peoples' Clubs and Y.M.C.A.'s are just a branch. All kinds of ameliorative and redemptive agencies owe their very existence to the Christian Church. As it has grown, it has put forth "great branches."

And Its Rest

"So that the birds of the heavens can lodge under the shadow thereof." And that suggests to me the Kingdom, the Church of God as a place of rest. You remember that prophecy in Ezekiel about the tender twig which the Lord shall plant; it shall bring forth boughs, said the prophet, and bear fruit and be a goodly cedar and under it shall dwell all fowl of every wing. "In the shadow of the branches thereof they shall dwell." I think our Lord had a similar thought in His mind when He uttered these words. He thought of His Church as a shelter and rest. He thought of men flying to it for protection and peace. And such a shelter the Church has been.

Read the records of the past, and you will see how in the past the Church has been the great bulwark against tyranny and oppression, and that quite literally the poor and friendless fled to it for protection. But in a still deeper sense is the Church a shelter to men. It is a shelter to the man who is oppressed and harassed by temptation. Think what a difference it would make to many a tempted soul if all the holy and restraining influences of Christianity were removed. Men and women who are sorely tried out in the world yonder are strengthened for duty by communion with God's people. They find shelter in the tree. It is a shelter to men who are pursued by their sins They come up to God's house, they enter the fellowship of Christian people, and they hear of the cleansing blood of Christ, and their sins cease to pursue them. They are under the shelter of the Great Rock.

I saw men not long ago, weary men, asleep in St. Paul's Cathedral. They were evidently poor. They had probably been walking hither and thither looking for work, and there, tired out, they were asleep in the great cathedral. But there is a better rest than that, which men find in the Kingdom. "Come unto Me," says Jesus, "all ye that labor and are heavy laden, and I will give you rest" (Matt. 11:28). Rest to the soul, perfect satisfaction; and I can see men coming from every part of the world seeking it. "Who are these that fly as a cloud, and as the doves to their windows?" (Isa. 60:8). They are the many children of men seeking rest in the shadow of the tree. By her we shall be covered from the heat, and in her glory shall we dwell.

30
The Storm

"And the same day, when the even was come, He saith unto them, Let us pass over unto the other side. And when they had sent away the multitude, they took Him even as He was in the ship. And there were also with Him other little ships. And there arose a great storm of wind, and the waves beat into the ship, so that it was now full. And He was in the hinder part of the ship, asleep on a pillow: and they awake Him, and say unto Him, Master, carest thou not that we perish? And He arose, and rebuked the wind, and said unto the sea, Peace, be still. And the wind ceased, and there was a great calm. And He said unto them, Why are ye so fearful? how is it that ye have no faith? And they feared exceedingly, and said one to another, What manner of man is this, that even the wind and the sea obey Him?" —Mark 4:35-41.

THIS STORY OF the storm is, as Dr. Chadwick says, one of the most familiar narratives of the New Testament. It is a first favorite in our Sunday schools. It has formed the subject of many a picture, the theme of many a hymn. Looking back to the days of my own childhood, I believe that the first hymn I ever learned—and it has clung fast to my memory ever since—was that old hymn which begins:

> "A little ship was on the sea;
> It was a pretty sight,
> It sailed along so pleasantly,
> And all was calm and bright."

The Christ of the Story
But this incident of the storm is more than a pretty story. It is not only a charming narrative for children. It is pregnant with instruction for grown-up men and women. Indeed, my difficulty is not to know what to say, but to know what to leave out. But let us confine our attention here to the Christ this story reveals. There are many other things in the story. There is a whole sermon, for instance, in a study of the conduct of the disciples. Their considerateness, their panic-fear, their speechless wonder; but all these we must pass over, and be content to look simply at the Christ this narrative reveals.

The Weary Christ

And our first view of Him is a view of the weary Christ. Mark makes a special point of the day on which this incident took place. It was, he says, on "that day," that is, on the day on which He had preached these wonderful parables and several more besides, as we know from St Matthew's account. Apparently He had been preaching all the day long. It may have been one of those days when the multitude pressed upon Him to hear the Word of God, and He had not leisure so much as to eat. Anyhow, from morning till night He had been busy at His Holy work; and it was not till even was come that He suggested to His disciples that they should go over to the quiet and lonely shores on the other side of the lake.

A day's preaching in the hot and stifling atmosphere of the Galilean Sea, must, however, imply a tremendous strain. But the physical strain was not all; preaching was, with our Lord, no cheap and easy business. Indeed it is not a cheap and easy business to any preacher worth the name. To be an ambassador for Christ, beseeching men on Christ's behalf to be reconciled to God, this is no light or unimportant task. "Knowing . . . the terror of the Lord, we persuade men" (2 Cor. 5:11), that is no light responsibility. To warn men to flee from the wrath to come, that is not a thing a man can do with a glad and irresponsible heart. To watch for souls as those who shall give account, that is no pastime, that is not something a man can do with a laugh and a smile. Preaching, when it is worth the name, is a costly business. I know a great many folk think it is a very easy thing to preach, that the preacher has what is known as "a soft job." Possibly some who are themselves preachers find it such. But that is only because they have missed their vocation; for there is no work so burdensome, so toilsome, so exacting, so costly, as that of the true preacher. It puts a strain, not upon body and mind simply, but upon heart and spirit as well. It costs blood and sweat, and agony and tears; and of all preachers Jesus realized most vividly what preaching meant. His heart went out in a perfect passion of pity to the crowd to whom He spoke.

> "Oh, to save these—to perish for their saving,
> Die for their life, be offered for them all."

Preaching cost Him a great price. "Virtue went forth from Him." His pity, His passion for souls, drained Him of vital force. There was entreaty, there was desire, there was agony in the preaching of Jesus, and it left Him utterly exhausted and spent.

Asleep

How all this comes out in the narrative before us! It was the disciples who had to dismiss the crowd, and then they take Him, even as He was, and set sail for the other side. "Even as He was!" We have but to give play to our imagination and we may see a whole world of pathos in that little phrase, "Even as He was"—without stopping to furnish Him with another cloak for what might be a cold journey across the lake, without waiting even to refresh Him with food and drink—they take Him, "even as He was," weary, worn, faint and spent in the boat; and once in the boat Nature asserted her claim. On the hard boards of the fishing boat, our Lord fell asleep, with probably a bundle of nets for an extemporized pillow. He slept the deep and dreamless sleep of a worn-out and exhausted man. He slept on when the wind began to rise; He slept on through the roar of the waves; He slept on through all the excitement caused by the filling of the little boat. He was tired, weary, utterly spent. That is the Christ we see at the beginning of this incident, the worn and weary Christ.

The Lord Jesus as a Worker

What a worker Jesus was! He never spared Himself. He toiled till He dropped. We sing in our hymn, "Go, labor on, spend, and be spent." It is a fine sentiment with most of us, and little or nothing more. Who of us finds himself spent in the service of his fellows? Who of us finds himself utterly worn out and exhausted in the work of doing good? Spent! But it just describes our Lord's case. He spent Himself in ministering to men; comfort, ease, even time to eat—Christ cheerfully sacrificed them all. The zeal of God's house ate Him up. Here He is at the end of a day's work, and the disciples take Him with them, even as He was, a spent and weary Christ!

And for Us

What a hint we get here of the cost of our redemption! We are apt to confine our view to the cross when we think of the price paid for our redemption; but in a deep and true sense, Christ's whole life was a sacrifice, and long before He gave His blood, He lavished upon men sympathy and compassion and love at a cost beyond our computation. I look on this tired Christ, and I see all this was for me. It was part of the price He had to pay for our deliverance. And how near this brings our Lord to us! "He was touched with the feeling of all our infirmities." All? Yes, all! And among other things He knew what it was to be tired. There are a great many tired folk in the world. Well, Christ can sympathize, for

He was one Himself, a tired Christ. And there are some of us who get weary and worn in Christian work. We are in a glorious succession, for we are following in the steps of that weary Jesus, who fell asleep in the ship's stern and whom not even the hurtling storm could awake.

The Seemingly Heedless Christ

And there is another Christ we see in this story. We see the seemingly heedless Christ. It was fine when they started out on their sail across the lake. Under ordinary circumstances a sail of an hour and a half would have seen them across. But it was to be no swift and safe passage this time. The Lake of Galilee is notorious for its sudden and furious squalls. The commentators will tell you that its position in a kind of deep gorge, below the level of the sea, and with the snowy slopes of Hermon not very far away, accounts for the lake's bad reputation in this respect. And one of these sudden and furious squalls struck the lake on this particular night. There arose, says Mark, "a great storm of wind, and the waves beat into the boat, insomuch that the boat was now filling" (v. 37, R.V.). You may be sure the disciples did their best to keep their little boat afloat, for they were expert sailors. But, in spite of all their efforts, the storm was getting the better of them. "The boat was now filling." The furious waves dashed into their little craft, and a watery grave stared them in the face. And all the time while they were straining every nerve to ward off the threatening danger, all the time that they were fighting for dear life, Jesus was lying asleep in the stern, seemingly quite heedless of and indifferent to their trouble.

At last they awoke Him, and you can catch in their words the reproachfulness of the men who thought they had been neglected in their hour of need. "Master, carest Thou not that we perish?" (v. 38). The Master sleeping on, while His disciples were battling for dear life—here you have what to all appearance looks like a heedless Christ.

And there are times when it does seem as if Jesus did not care. Listen to this verse: "Behold, a Canaanitish woman came out from those borders, and cried, saying, Have mercy on me, O Lord, Thou son of David; my daughter is grievously vexed with a devil" (Matt. 15:22, R.V.). There you have a poor soul in sore trouble. Of course Jesus will give a swift and gracious answer. "But He answered her not a word" (v. 23). That looks like a heedless Christ. Listen to this other verse. "Now a certain man was sick, Lazarus of Bethany, of the village of Mary and her sister Martha . . . The sisters therefore sent unto Him, saying, Lord, behold, he whom Thou lovest is sick"

(John 11:1, 3, R.V.). Of course Jesus will hurry swiftly back to Bethany on the receipt of that news, for Jesus loved Martha, and her sister, and Lazarus (v. 5). But this is what I read: "When therefore He heard that he was sick, He abode at that time two days in the place where He was" (v. 6). What do you suppose the broken-hearted sisters thought of Him, when the days passed, and He did not come? Do you not think they must have thought Him a heedless Christ? And there come times to us when the storm of doubt and trouble and sorrow beats down upon us, and we are in sore and dire trouble, and Jesus makes no sign of coming to our help. We cry, and He does not seem to hear or answer us. We fight for very life, and He sleeps on, apparently indifferent to our fate, and we are tempted to think sometimes that He does not care.

Heedless in Appearance Only

But the heedlessness is never more than in seeming. "Master," said these panic-stricken disciples at the last, roughly perhaps awaking Him, "carest Thou not that we perish?" And Jesus was amazed at their panic. "Why are ye fearful?" He asked. "Have ye not yet faith"? (v. 40, R.V.). Not yet! They were slow scholars. The Master had given them proof after proof of His power. They had witnessed His authority over human disease and evil spirits. They had seen Him rescue this person and that from danger and death. The knowledge that Christ was with them in the boat ought to have been a sufficient safeguard against fear. They might have known no harm could befall them. Christ is not heedless. His presence, though He seems silent, is the pledge of our safety. Read the story of the Canaanitish woman to its close. This is how it ends: "O woman, great is thy faith; be it done unto thee even as thou wilt. And her daughter was healed from that hour" (Matt. 15:28, R.V.). She knew before she went home that Christ was not a heedless Christ.

Read the story of the sisters to its close, and this is how it ends: "When He had thus spoken, He cried with a loud voice, Lazarus, come forth. He that was dead came forth" (John 11:43, 44, R.V.). When they received their brother back again, alive and well, Martha and Mary would know that Christ was not a heedless Christ. Read this story to its close, and this is how it ends: "And the wind ceased, and there was a great calm" (v. 39). Before they reached the other side, these disciples knew that Jesus was not a heedless Christ. He is never a heedless Christ. He hears our sighs, He counts our tears. He may seem to be asleep sometimes, and to be indifferent to our distress; but He is watching all the time, and at the fitting moment He will come with help and succor. Be quite sure of this, my brethren, that to have Christ with us is a pledge and absolute assurance of safety. "No one shall snatch them out of My hand" (John 10:28, R.V.). Have Him in your life's vessel, and the storm is yet to be born that can overwhelm your little bark. "Row on! row on!" cried Caesar to his boatmen, as they were crossing the Adriatic in the teeth of a furious storm; "you are bearing Caesar and his fortunes." Well, I do not know that "bearing Caesar and his fortunes" was any guarantee of safety. But if we are bearing Christ, we need not fear.

"With Christ in the vessel, I smile at the storm."

The Mighty Christ

Now let me pass on to speak of another view of Christ I get in the narrative. I see Him not simply as the weary Christ, as the seemingly heedless Christ, but I see Him also as the mighty Christ. When His disciples awakened Him with their faithless cry, He arose and rebuked the wind, and said unto the sea, "Peace be still." "Be muzzled," He said, as if it were a raging, roaring beast. And both wind and sea heard His voice, and obeyed it, for "the wind ceased, and there was a great calm." Usually, long after the storm has blown itself out, the sea, by its heave and swell continues to show the results of it. But at the bidding of Jesus, as Dr. Salmond says, "the lake sank back, like an exhausted creature, into motionless repose." What power is this! Incidentally, notice how swift Christ is to answer human appeals, even when they are faulty and faithless. The cry of the disciples was scarcely a cry of faith. And yet Jesus responded to it. He deals gently and tenderly with the feeblest and most imperfect kind of faith. When a man can get no further than, "Lord, I believe, help Thou mine unbelief!", He hears and answers. It is a great encouragement to us. Cry to Him, even when faith falters and fails. He will never turn a deaf ear. "Him that cometh to Me, I will in no wise cast out"(John 6:37).

Still Mighty

It is a strong Deliverer whom this story reveals to us. He maketh the storm a calm, so that the waves thereof are still. He can hush the storm even now. What are some of the storms that break upon our heads as we pass through this mortal life? Well, there is the storm of trouble. It presses heavily upon us sometimes. We can say with the Psalmist sometimes, "All Thy waves and Thy billows are gone over me" (Psa. 42:7). And yet, even such a storm as that our mighty Lord can still. "Thou wilt keep Him in perfect peace, whose mind is stayed on Thee" (Isa. 26:3). "Rejoicing," says St Paul, "in tribulation." There you have the storm stilled. And there is the storm of guilt and shame. How men are tempest-tossed by the consciousness of sin! "Wretched man that I am! who shall deliver me from the body of this death?" (Rom. 7:24); that is a man out in the fierce storm. "Thanks be to God . . . through our Lord Jesus Christ" (1 Cor. 4:57); that is the storm stilled. In what a tempest of shame and sorrow the sinful woman knelt at Jesus' feet in Simon's house! But Jesus stilled the storm, "Go in peace," He said (Luke 7:50). And in that troubled soul there was great and holy calm.

Then there is the storm of death. How that shakes and terrifies the soul! And yet Jesus can still even that storm. "I am now ready to be offered," cries Paul." . . . Henceforth there is laid up for me a crown of righteousness, which the Lord, the righteous Judge, shall give me at that day" (2 Tim. 4:6, 8). That is the storm stilled. "Yea, though I walk through the valley of the shadow of death, I will fear no evil: for Thou art with me; Thy rod and Thy staff they comfort me" (Psa. 23:4). That is the storm stilled.

31
The Gadarene Demoniac

"And they came over unto the other side of the sea, into the country of the Gadarenes. And when He was come out of the ship, immediately there met Him out of the tombs a man with an unclean spirit, Who had his dwelling among the tombs; and no man could bind him, no, not with chains: Because that he had been often bound with fetters and chains, and the chains had been plucked asunder by him, and the fetters broken in pieces: neither could any man tame him. And always, night and day, he was in the mountains, and in the tombs, crying, and cutting himself with stones. But when he saw Jesus afar off, he ran and worshipped Him, And cried with a loud voice, and said, What have I to do with Thee, Jesus, thou Son of the most high God? I adjure Thee by God, that thou torment me not. For He said unto him, Come out of the man, thou unclean spirit. And He asked him, What is thy name? And he answered, saying, my name is Legion: for we are many. And he besought Him much that He would not send them away out of the country. Now there was there nigh unto the mountains a great herd of swine feeding. And all the devils besought Him, saying, Send us into the swine, that we may enter into them. And forthwith Jesus gave them leave. And the unclean spirits went out, and entered into the swine: and the herd ran violently down a steep place into the sea, (they were about two thousand;) and were choked in the sea. And they that fed the swine fled, and told it in the city, and in the country. And they went out to see what it was that was done. And they come to Jesus, and see him that was possessed with the devil, and had the legion, sitting, and clothed, and in his right mind: and they were afraid. And they that saw it told them how it befell to him that was possessed with the devil, and also concerning the swine. And they began to pray Him to depart out of their coasts. And when He was come into the ship, he that had been possessed with the devil prayed Him that he might be with Him. Howbeit Jesus suffered him not, but saith unto him, Go home to thy friends, and tell them how great things the Lord hath done for thee, and hath had compassion on thee. And he departed, and began to publish in Decapolis how great things Jesus had done for him: and all men did marvel."
—Mark 5:1-20.

A Wonderful Miracle
THE STORY OF the Gadarene Demoniac follows, as you will notice, immediately upon the story of the stilling of the storm. Now that was a startling wonder. That a raging tempest should in an instant,

at Christ's behest, become a great calm—there is nothing more marvelous in the story of Christ's life from first to last. It left the disciples filled with amazement that amounted to awe, and saying, one to another, "Who then is this, that even the wind and the sea obey Him?" (4:41, R.V.). And immediately after that amazing story comes the narrative of the healing of this demoniac. Does it strike you as a descent? As an anti-climax? Do you feel this story of the restoration of a man to his right mind is tame and commonplace, compared with the story of the stilling of the storm? I am prepared to maintain that, wonderful though the story of the stilling of the storm was, this story is more wonderful still. And amazing though the power was that subdued the wild storm and hushed it into a great calm, the power that swept this man's heart clean of the foul brood that haunted it, and reclothed a raging maniac in his rightful mind, is more amazing still. When we learn to estimate things truly, we shall always see that the moral miracle far transcends in grandeur the mere physical wonder. The greatest miracle of all is the restoration to moral soundness and health of a man, who has all his lifetime been "dead in trespasses and sins." People say sometimes that the age of miracles is at an end. The age of physical wonders may be, but not the age of miracles. Christ still works amongst us His most stupendous miracle of all, when He turns the sinner into a saint, when He restores and redeems the soul. And that is why I venture to regard the healing of the Gadarene Demoniac as a greater thing than the stilling of the storm. The one was a physical wonder; this is a great moral miracle.

And Its Critics

Now, as you know, there has been a great deal of controversy and discussion about this incident. Some years ago our magazines were full of it. Professor Huxley made a furious onslaught upon it, and with quite needless and offensive brutality spoke of it as, "The Gadarene pig affair." I mention that only to show how the great can be lost sight of in the little; how a man may get so absorbed in a detail as to lose sight of the central truth. These controversialists lost sight of the man while they wrangled over the fate of the pigs. But it was as an illustration of the redeeming power of Jesus Christ, over the most desperate of cases that the Evangelist presented this story. And for the present, I am going to confine myself rigidly and absolutely to this central theme.

The Demoniac

Let me first of all call your attention to what the Evangelist says about this man's abject and terrible plight. "There met Him out of the tombs a man with an unclean spirit, who had his dwelling in the tombs . . . And always, night and day, in the tombs and in the mountains, he was crying out, and cutting himself with stones" (vv. 2, 3, 5, R.V.). The other Evangelists add further touches to the ghastly picture. For Matthew says, that in his mad fury, the man was a terror to others; while Luke says that he wore no clothes. The picture we have is that of a mere wreck and hideous ruin of a man. And to what was the ruin and the wreck due? To sin. Trace back the suffering and misery of the world to its source—at the last you come to sin. Oftentimes we can see the connection between the two. We see the sin, and we see the hideous ruin it creates. The trembling hands and the shattered frame of the drunkard are the direct result of his sin. The premature old age and the death of the profligate are the direct results of his sin. In these cases we can trace the connection between sin and human misery and shame directly. In other cases you can only trace it indirectly. The suffering of the child may be the result of the sin of his father. Mental defect, moral twist in the offspring, may be the result of sin in the parent. Four-fifths of the physical wreckage with which our hospitals deal may, doctors tell us, be traced to moral evil, to sin, as the cause.

The Ruin Sin Makes

The probability is that this man's calamity was the result of sin. It may have been his own. The narrative, indeed, seems to suggest that it was, for he had not always been the unclean and raving maniac he was when Jesus met with him. At any rate, this naked, brutalized madman may aptly stand as an illustration of the ruin sin makes. It degrades, defiles a man. It pollutes the soul. It turns what was designed for a temple of God into a haunt of devils. We go into raptures of regret over the ruin wrought by the vandalism of past ages. We mourn the destruction wrought in ancient buildings. We grieve to think of the Acropolis, with its priceless treasures of architecture and art, battered into ruin by the cannon of the Venetians. We can never think of the ruined Persepolis without lamenting the mad act that laid it waste. But, more melancholy far than the destruction of the most famous statue, the most renowned temple, the most splendid city, is the destruction of a man, the ruin of the understanding, the perversion of the conscience, the wrecking of the soul. And that is the destruction that follows in sin's wake. You can see that destruction all around you. Sometimes it is to be observed in all its naked horror, in wrecked manhood and polluted womanhood, in the criminal and the profligate and the harlot. Sometimes it is less conspicuous, though not less real. For while outward respectability may be preserved, there may be a dulling of sensitiveness, a loss of the finer feelings, a blight upon the soul. "When truth is lost, and honor die," says Whittier, "the man is dead," and it is sin that does it. So I repeat that this demoniac, naked, maimed, a danger to himself and to others, a mere wreck and ruin of a man, may very well stand as a type of the awful ruin wrought by sin.

The Failure of Human Remedy

Now notice, in the second place, the failure of all human efforts to deal with this demoniac. Apparently they never attempted to cure him. They never tried to deal with the real mischief. They seemed to have realized that it was beyond their power. It was a more modest task they addressed themselves to. All they did was to try to keep the demoniac within bounds. All they tried to do was to restrain him; all they attempted was, to limit his power for mischief. So they had him bound with chains, and they made those chains strong; but it was all in vain. As often as they bound him, so often had this demoniac, with the convulsive strength of madness, plucked the chains asunder and broken the fetters in pieces. It seemed that no chain ever forged by blacksmith was strong enough for the task; and at the point at which our narrative takes up the story they seemed to have given up the effort to bind him as quite hopeless— "no man had strength to tame him"(v. 4, R.V.).

As Seen Today

And is not this a parable of the way in which human society seeks to deal with those wild passions that still rage in the hearts of men? All that society seeks to do with these fierce passions and lusts of the soul is to curb and restrain them, to keep them within bounds, to prevent them from becoming dangerous, to limit their powers of mischief. All our laws and prohibitions are to us what his chains were to this wild man of Gadarene. "Thou shalt not," says Law to us. It knows that the fierce fires of anger burn in the human heart, and it says, "Thou shalt not kill." It knows that unholy lusts surge in the soul, and it says, "Thou shalt not commit adultery." It knows that greed and covetousness are passions to which all men are prone, and it says, "Thou shalt not steal."

You will notice Law does not attempt to deal with the anger itself, or the lust itself, or the greed itself. All that Law seeks to do is to prevent the outbreak of these evil passions into the sinful act and deed. All it does, in a word, is to bind the man. It does not try to cure the mischief; it does not attempt to clear the soul of these evil things that lurk there. Law, backed up by prisons and reformatories, and policemen and punishments, has rarely attempted anything more than to restrain men; and even this modest ambition it has failed to realize. Law has been powerless to restrain men. Again and again men have broken through the chains by which Law has thought to restrain their fierce passions. Every case in our police courts is an illustration of the failure of the restraints of Law.

There has been a law against murder for hundreds of years, but murders still take place. In a score of ways Law has sought to penalize lustful passions; but in spite of everything, adultery and fornication are daily sins. There has been a law against theft ever since human society was constituted, but, in spite of the Law's restraints, thefts are of common occurrence. Nothing that man has been able to devise has been able to keep these wild passions of the human heart within bounds. No man has had strength to tame them; and what Law has failed to do, public opinion, fashion, custom, have failed to do also.

The Power of the Passions

I do not say that these are not powerful restraining forces. They are. But in spite of them all, the unruly human nature will break out. Under the fierce impulse of passion men break through them all. There is no need to quote instances. History teems with them. Common life teems with them. The daily newspaper teems with them. Men can tame and control the wild beasts of the desert, the lion and the tiger, but no restraints he has been able to invent have been able to tame the insurgent passions of his own heart. The restraints both of philosophic maxims and the terrors of the law, and the customs of society, have all failed. They have proved weak and useless. They are of no more avail than are the sand mounds a child builds on the seashore to check the assaults of the inrushing tide. They are as useless in face of passion and appetite as were the new ropes with which the Philistines tried to bind Samson, and which to him were no stronger than wisps of straw. Nothing that man has been able to invent in the way of restraint has been able to curb human passion. You can say of these evil and sinful hearts of ours what the Evangelist here says of this demoniac, "No man had strength to tame him."

The Power of Christ

Now in contrast with the impotence of human efforts to tame
this man, look at the mighty power of Christ. What all the
chains of Gadara could not effect, Jesus accomplished by a look, a
word. I need not go into the details of the cure. It may be, as some
commentators suggest, that the sight of the swine dashing down
the cliffs was necessary to deliver the man from the obsession that
a legion of devils had occupied his heart. But that, after all, is a
detail. The point to notice is, that Christ did what the Gadarenes
had failed to do. Yea, and much more. For all that the Gadarenes
attempted to do with their chains and fetters, was to restrain the
sufferer. Our Lord, by curing him, restored him once again to his
rightful mind. And here we come across the deep and radical difference between human methods of reform and the method of
Jesus Christ.

His Method of Reform

Men are always intent upon checking and restraining the
working of the evil passion they know to exist. Jesus, on the other
hand, removes the evil passions themselves. Men devote their
attention to the outward act. Jesus turns His towards the cure of
the evil heart. And our Lord's method is the only effectual
method. We are pinning our faith in these days to the method of
restraint. We are pinning our faith in the matter of the reform of the
drink evil, to legislative prohibitions against the traffic. In the matter of labor troubles we are pinning our faith to laws which shall
prohibit greed and oppression. I do not say that these things will
not help; but I do maintain they will never be an effective cure, for
we are never going to have a sober world so long as you have men
with the drink craving in their hearts. You are never going to have
perfect happiness between class and class, so long as greed continues to exist in the soul. You are never going to have the
millennium, so long as you have evil men. Christ's method is the
only effective method. He goes to the root of things. He looks on
the heart. He removes the lust, the passion, the appetite that is the
cause of the mischief, and so does away with the need for
restraints and prohibitions and chains. He creates a new man, so
making peace.

Change of Heart

That this is the right method, everyone can see. To change the
heart is the one sure way of restoration and reform. But can Jesus
change the heart? Yes, He can. This story of this demoniac whom

no man could tame, restored to sanity by a word from Jesus, is here to tell us He can change the heart, that He can accomplish this supreme miracle in the vilest and most desperate of cases. He did it in some desperate cases when He was here on earth. You could have discovered no more difficult cases than those of Zacchaeus, the woman who was a sinner, and the dying thief. And yet Jesus Christ gave them all a new heart. And He can do the same thing for men still.

John Watson tells the story of a barge man giving his experience at a Salvation Army meeting. In his unconverted days he had been addicted to profane swearing. But he heard Christ preached, and this was his subsequent testimony, "I just 'listed in His army, and look here, lads, I've never sworn since, and that was a year ago." Jesus had given him a clean heart and a clean tongue.

New hearts are what the world wants. And Jesus Christ can give them. He can give them to any one and every one. He can save to the uttermost. And when the new heart is given, everything else follows. "If any man is in Christ, he is a new creature; the old things are passed away; behold, they are become new" (2 Cor. 5:17, R.V.).

32

The Gadarenes and the Healed Man

"And they began to pray Him to depart out of their coasts. And when He was come into the ship, he that had been possessed with the devil prayed Him that he might be with Him. Howbeit Jesus suffered him not, but saith unto him, Go home to thy friends, and tell them how great things the Lord hath done for thee, and hath had compassion on thee. And he departed, and began to publish in Decapolis how great things Jesus had done for him: and all men did marvel."   —Mark 5:17-20.

LET US RETURN to the story of the Gerasene (as the R.V. reads) demoniac. So far I have confined myself to the actual healing, dwelling more especially on the man's pitiable plight; the failure of all human efforts to deal with him; and then the complete cure effected by the power of Christ. All this I have described as a parable of the inability of man to deal with the hurt and plague of sin, and of Jesus Christ's power to save to the uttermost. Now, there are all kinds of curious questions raised by the manner in which the man's cure was effected, all of which are learnedly and lengthily discussed by the commentators. I do not, however, intend to spend time upon those questions. Those who are interested in the problem of demonic possession, and wonder how devils can take possession of swine, had better refer to works discussing these things. My object is to get out of the narrative the lessons and truths that have some practical bearing upon our life today. And so I am going to pass by the method of the healing, in order to call your attention to what happened afterwards. There is food for study and thought; there are lessons of warning and inspiration to be derived from a consideration of the conduct, first, of the Gerasenes and secondly, of the healed demoniac.

The Conduct of the Gerasenes

First let us study for a moment the conduct of the Gerasenes as it is here described for us. When the swineherds had recovered from their first stupefaction at the sight of the herd rushing down the steep place into the sea, they fled, and began telling in the city and in the country what had come to pass. The result was that the people went surging and crowding out, to see things for themselves. The amazing sight that confronted them was the spectacle of him who had been possessed with devils sitting, clothed and in his right mind. The man, who had made the night hideous with his cries, who had made the road impassable by his fierceness, who had defied every effort made to tame and bind him—that man was now sitting there before their very eyes, obviously restored to moral soundness and bodily health.

What Might Have Been

Now what would you expect as the effect upon the observers of such a sight? Would you not have supposed that the vision of a human being saved, a human soul restored, would have stirred them to rapture and praise? If they had such a thing as a Doxology in those days, I should have expected that at the sight of this healed and restored man it would have broken spontaneously from their lips.

I should have expected next to read that these people at once proceeded to scour the city and the villages around for every possessed person, and every sick person, and every leprous person in their coasts and brought them to Jesus, in order that the saving power which had redeemed this demoniac might be exercised upon the others also.

That was what happened at Capernaum. Our Lord healed a lunatic man in the synagogue on the Sabbath day. The news of that gracious deed flew like wild fire through the town, and "at even, when the sun did set"—it was against their Sabbath law to do so earlier—"they brought unto Him all that were sick, and them that were possessed with devils. And all the city was gathered together at the door" (1:32, R.V.). And that is what I should have expected to read about Gerasa.

And Was Not

But what a different story it is that the Evangelist tells! Instead of begging Him to wait until they brought to Him other sufferers, upon whom to exercise His healing power, the people besought Him to depart out of their borders. They begged Jesus Christ to go! Is not this an amazing, is it not, indeed, almost an incredible, thing? And yet it was by no means an unusual thing. Gerasa was not the only place where they wanted to get rid of Christ. "He came unto

His own," says John, "and His own received Him not" (John 1:11). That was literally fulfilled in our Lord's experience. He went to Nazareth, eager to preach the Gospel to His townsmen, and to do amongst them the works He had done elsewhere; but the upshot of His visit was this, that His townsfolk took Him to the brow of the hill on which their city was built, in order that they might cast Him down headlong (Luke 4:29). He went once to a Samaritan village; they would not receive Him, because His face was as though He were journeying toward Jerusalem (Luke 9:53). He went to Jerusalem itself—they would have none of Him. So resolved were they to get rid of Him, that they nailed Him to the bitter tree. No; this was no unusual experience of Jesus. These Gerasenes were not alone in their folly. The Nazarenes, the Samaritans, the dwellers in Jerusalem, they all told Jesus to depart.

A Folly Also of Today

But I do not know that I need go back to New Testament times for any illustrations. This is not alone an ancient folly. It is a folly of today. There are men and women amongst us who prefer Christ's room to His company, and who beg Him to depart out of their borders.

Why Our Lord Was Rejected

They did that amazing and incredible thing in Gerasa long ago; and they continue to do that amazing and incredible thing still. Jesus comes with His offer of salvation. He comes offering to restore men to moral soundness and health. He is the only one who can do this great thing. And yet men beseech Him to depart, they turn Him out of their lives.

Now what was it that made the Gerasenes long to get rid of Christ? I think verse 16 supplies the key. "And they that saw it declared unto them how it befell him that was possessed with devils" (R.V.). Now I believe, if this story had ended at that point, these people would have hailed Christ as a public benefactor, and would have besought Him to stay. But the story did not end there. "They declared unto them how it befell him that was possessed with devils, and concerning the swine." That settled the matter. As soon as they heard the news concerning the swine, they began to beseech Him to depart from their borders. The restoration of the man was as nothing to them, compared to the loss of the swine, and so they begged Jesus to go, because He interfered with their business. It is quite probable that the keeping of swine was forbidden to these people. For to the Jew, the pig, you all remember, was an unclean animal. If these people were Jews, as quite likely they were, they had engaged in a forbidden trade for the sake of the profit of it. And they were not going to have that trade interfered with. They preferred their chance of gain to their chance of the Kingdom; they preferred their swine to Christ. Like Esau, they preferred their mess of pottage to the birthright.

A Cause Operative Today

These Gerasenes have had multitudes of followers. You remember how Demetrius and his fellowcraftsmen in Ephesus tried to kill the apostle Paul, and to prevent the preaching of the Gospel. It was interfering with their business. And they were having no Christ preached in Ephesus who interfered with their trade. And again there is no need to go back to New Testament times, for this same thing happens still. Preachers of Christ in the open air have again and again been obstructed on the ground that they interfered with trade.

Many a business man has bowed Jesus out of his establishment, because His presence interferes with his trade; many a merchant has bowed Him out of his office because He interferes with his profits; many a young fellow has bowed Him out of his life because He interferes with his pleasures. They have told Him to go. And if you inquire how it is men can be so foolish as to drive away One who has such blessings to bestow, you will find that the reason is always something sordid, unholy, unclean; it always concerns the swine. They think more of the world than of the soul, more of gain than of God.

The Appeal and Its Result

"They began to beseech Him to depart" (v. 17, R.V.), and Jesus went. He will not force His presence upon people against their will. If He is to enter anywhere, the door must be opened for Him. If He is to stay anywhere, He must be made welcome. He will take possession of no man's heart by storm. The puniest man behind the ramparts of his will can defy the Almighty Son of God. They besought Him to depart. They slammed the door in His face in Gerasa. So He went, and He never came back. Gerasa knew not the day of its visitation. It kept its swine, and lost its soul. O Gerasa, Gerasa, if thou hadst known, even thou, the things which belong unto peace; but now they are hid from thine eyes! Let us see to it that we ourselves recognize the day of our visitation. "Behold, now is the accepted time; behold, now is the day of salvation" (2 Cor. 6:2).

The Healed Man and His Plea

But if the Gerasenes wanted to get rid of Jesus, there was one man who wanted for evermore to keep by His side. "And as He was entering into the boat, he that had been possessed with devils besought Him that he might be with Him" (v. 18, R.V.). The Gerasenes felt they would never be happy and at ease until Jesus was gone; this man felt he could be happy nowhere else, save in the presence of his Lord. What are we to make of this request? Some commentators suggest that fear is partly accountable for it. The man feared, they say, that, once out of the presence of Jesus, the foul spirits from whose power he had been emancipated would come back again. He felt it was only the Person who delivered him who could also keep him. And if the healed man did think so, he was perfectly right in so thinking For all is not done when a man is "saved"; all is not finished by one act of deliverance; the saved man needs keeping, or else his last estate may be worse than the first. Just as a man is *saved*, so also he must be *kept* by the power of Christ. If this was the man's motive, the only mistake he made was in thinking that to be near Christ he had always to be in His physical presence. Left alone in Gerasa, Jesus would be with him still, and he would find himself kept by the power of God unto Salvation.

The Prompting of Love

But I think what prompted this request was not so much fear as love. You remember how in his gratitude to Peter and John the lame man whom they had healed clung to them. In the same way this man clung to Jesus. He felt he was no longer his own. He felt the manhood and strength which had been restored to him belonged now to the Savior who restored them. He wanted to dedicate his recovered faculties and sanity to the service of Jesus. "He besought Him that he might be with Him." Yes, I believe it was love, overflowing gratitude and love, that prompted this request. You can understand it, can you not? Have you never sung in a rapture of thankfulness, as you contemplated the Cross, "For ever here my rest shall be, close to Thy bleeding side?" Have you never sung, when you have thought of Christ's amazing love, "Take myself, and I will be, ever only, all for Thee!" It was exactly the same feeling that prompted this healed man to beseech Christ that he might be with Him. It was the request of a grateful and adoring love. Yet, though the request beyond doubt brought joy to the heart of Jesus, because it spoke of love, it was a request He did not grant. "He suffered him not, but saith unto him, Go to thy house unto thy friends, and tell them how great things the Lord hath done for thee, and how He had mercy on thee" (v. 19, R.V.).

The Lord's Command: Its Mercy

What shall we say about this command of our Lord? (1) Well, to begin with, what a revelation it is of His mercy! The Gerasenes had besought Him to depart. But He will not leave without leaving a witness behind. Usually He laid upon the objects of His healing power the command to tell no man. It is the opposite command He gives to this healed demoniac. "Tell," He said to him, "how great things the Lord hath done for thee." And I believe the variation in the command is due to His desire to give the Gerasenes another chance. They were driving Him away. He will leave this man behind, a monument of His redeeming mercy, and bid him tell the people the amazing story of his restoration. Perchance some would listen and repent. So the healed man became Christ's evangelist. He "began to publish in Decapolis how great things Jesus had done for him; and all men did marvel" (v. 20). And, as Bishop Chadwick says, when all men did marvel, we may hope that some were won.

Its Call to Action

(2) I see in this command a hint that the Christian life is not one of rapture and communion simply, but one of action and service also. This healed man asked for a privilege. Christ laid upon him a duty. He asked that he might be "with Him"; instead, He sent him forth to preach to his family and his friends and neighbors. The Christian life is not simply something to *enjoy*; it is also something to *do*. It is not rapture simply, it is service also. Peter, when he saw the Lord's glory on the holy mount, cried, "It is good for us to be here," and he was for building three tabernacles, that they might abide there for ever. But in a short hour or two Jesus was leading the way down from the mount to the plain, with its surging crowd and its human suffering, and its crying need for help. To sit at the Lord's feet and hear His word is a great and blessed privilege, but it does not sum up the whole of Christian duty. We have not only to receive, we have also to give. Christ will not suffer us to be always with Him; He will have us go and tell. Go and tell— that is the duty He lays upon the healed and saved soul. "Go and tell how great things the Lord hath done for thee and how He had mercy on thee." It is not fine sermons He expects of us; for that work He has His own called and chosen men. What He wants of us is testimony, the simple statement of what He has done for us, and how He has had mercy on us.

The Appeal to Ourselves

Have we given this testimony? If some doctor had healed you of a great and terrible disease, you would make it your business to trumpet that fact abroad. Have you published the fact that you know of One who can restore the soul? Have you gone and told? And where shall you begin your telling? Where this man began it? Go to your house unto your friends. That is the place to begin—at your own fireside, under your own rooftree. You need not wait for some great opening to occur, for some special opportunity to offer. The opening you need is to your hand. The opportunity you require is at your door. Begin at home. Not all the preaching in the world will have such effect upon the children as the simple recital by father or mother of the great things God has done for them, and how He has had mercy on them.

"They besought Him to depart out of their borders . . . He besought Him that he might be with Him." What contrasted feelings Christ does inspire! The Gerasenes and the healed demoniac stand between them for all mankind. For some hate Him, and some love Him. Some say, "We will not have this man to reign over us," and others say with adoring hearts, "Thou, O Christ, art all I want." Which do we?

33
The Woman with the Issue of Blood

"And when Jesus was passed over again by ship unto the other side, much people gathered unto Him: and He was nigh unto the sea. And, behold, there cometh one of the rulers of the synagogue, Jairus by name; and when he saw Him, he fell at His feet, And besought Him greatly, saying, My little daughter lieth at the point of death: I pray thee, come and lay Thy hands on her, that she may be healed; and she shall live. And Jesus went with him; and much people followed Him, and thronged Him. And a certain woman, which had an issue of blood twelve years, And had suffered many things of many physicians, and had spent all that she had, and was nothing bettered, but rather grew worse, When she had heard of Jesus, came in the press behind, and touched His garment. For she said, If I may touch but His clothes, I shall be whole. And straightway the fountain of her blood was dried up; and she felt in her body that she was healed of that plague. And Jesus, immediately knowing in Himself that virtue had gone out of Him, turned Him about in the press, and said, Who touched My clothes? And His disciples said unto Him, Thou seest the multitude thronging Thee, and sayest Thou, Who touched Me? And He looked round about to see her that had done this thing. But the woman fearing and trembling, knowing what was done in her, came and fell down before Him, and told Him all the truth. And He said unto her, Daughter, thy faith hath made thee whole; go in peace, and be whole of thy plague." —Mark 5:21-34.

The Reception at Capernaum

THERE IS A great difference between the reception Jesus met with in Gerasa and the reception He met with when He returned to Capernaum, on the other side of the lake. At Gerasa they had begged Him to depart, at Capernaum there was a great crowd waiting to welcome His return. They had been loth to let Him leave them the previous evening, and when, after His rebuff at Gerasa, His boat was sighted steering homeward, they thronged down to the landing-place to give Him greeting. Not that we are to suppose that these people of Capernaum had any real faith in Jesus. Later on, as we shall see, they deserted Him in shoals. But

for the moment they had been stirred to something like enthusiasm by the signs which Jesus did. Very likely that enthusiasm had
been intensified by the news of what had happened on the lake the
previous evening. For, as Mark reminds us, there were other boats
beside the one in which Jesus sailed, out in that wild storm, and
some of them, no doubt, had returned to Capernaum and told the
story of how Jesus at a word had stilled the tempest and rescued
them out of deadly peril. All this had added to the excitement in
Capernaum, and intensified the eagerness with which Christ's
return was anticipated.

Produced by Gratitude

But I think I should be doing an injustice to the crowd on the
shore that morning if I said that it was merely excitement that had
gathered them together. I think there were some there who had
been brought there by gratitude. There were some in Capernaum
who owed all their hope and happiness in life to Jesus. Mark tells
us the stories of some of them. There was the possessed man
whom Christ healed in the synagogue; and Simon's wife's mother; and the young man who had been cured of the palsy; and that
unnamed multitude who had been brought to Christ's door
after the sun had set on the Sabbath, on whom He had exercised
His healing mercy. I believe these folk, with their dear ones, were
in that crowd, eager to welcome their Deliverer.

And by Hope

There were others in the crowd drawn thither by a wistful hope.
It was not that they had already received blessing, but they wanted blessing. They had great sorrows in their souls, great burdens
on their hearts; and they were waiting there for Christ with some
kind of trembling hope that He might remove them. It is with two
of these folk, drawn to Christ by their need, that the rest of the
chapter deals.

The first of them was Jairus, the ruler of the synagogue,
whose trouble was that his little daughter was at the point of
death. The other was a woman who had suffered for twelve years
from a serious disease that had baffled all the efforts of the doctors
to cure, or even to alleviate it. Jairus was the first to make his sorrow known to Jesus; but the suffering woman was the first to
experience His healing power. For as He was walking along to
Jairus' house, this woman "touched Him in the press, and healing
virtue stole." Let us think first of this episode by the way, leaving
the story of Jairus' daughter for subsequent consideration.

Sorrow Revealing Itself to Sympathy

Before, however, I address myself to the incident itself, I want to call your attention to the way in which Jesus brought the sorrow of any place to the surface. People never knew how many sick folk, leprous folk, possessed folk, there were in any district until Jesus came. But the coming of the Healer brought all the hidden misery and heartache and suffering into full view. It is to the man of sympathetic soul and healing grace that misery reveals itself. You may walk through any town with careless heart, and see little or nothing of its pain. You may, indeed, report that there is no pain or sorrow there, that it is a town of gaiety and pleasure. But if people once begin to realize you have a sympathetic heart, if they once discover you have some of the Spirit of Jesus, you shall find there are sorrows and sufferings at your very doors.

Sorrow Urging Sufferers to Christ

Notice once again, not only how Christ draws the sorrow to the surface, but how sorrow drives people to Christ. Probably I am doing neither Jairus nor this woman an injustice when I say that I do not think anything but their desperate and apparently hopeless need would have driven them to Jesus. Jairus was a ruler of the synagogue. He was a man in high official and social station. He belonged moreover to the Pharisees—to that class which had already taken up an attitude of hostility to Jesus. It required a good deal to make Jairus beg a favor of the prophet of Nazareth; he had to pocket a great deal of pride. Indeed, the only thing that made him do it was this—his little daughter was at the point of death.

So, again, with this woman. Tradition says that her name was Veronica, and that she came from Caesarea Philippi. The tradition has in all probability a basis of truth. It is nearly certain that the woman was a Gentile. If she had been a Jewess, she would never, suffering as she did, have ventured into a crowd, and so infected with ceremonial uncleanness every one she touched. The probability is that the far-borne fame of Jesus had reached her in her Gentile home, and the resolve had risen in her heart that she would give this Jesus, the Healer, a trial. But it was as a last resort. If the doctors of Caesarea could have done anything for her, she would never have sought the help of Jesus. It was only because they had tried every nostrum they knew, and yet left her no better, but rather worse, that she made her way to Capernaum. Jesus was a last resource.

As Now

And still sorrow and trouble drive people to Jesus. With multitudes He is still a last resort. If sorrow never visited them, they would feel no need of Jesus. If they could find some other cure for their hurt, they would never seek His help. It is only when they find that nothing on earth can give the guilty conscience peace, or take away its stain; it is only when they find that no earthly help avails, in face of the tragic sorrows and losses of life, that they turn to Jesus, and cry, "Thou Son of David, have mercy on me!" The miracle of grace is this—Jesus never turns such applicants away. He knew Jairus would never have sought His help if he could have found help somewhere else; He knew this woman would never have come to Him, if she could have got a doctor to cure her; He knew He was the last resort. And yet He cherished no resentment. In both cases He answered prayer. And though still it is only the failure of every other supposed source of help and healing that drives men to Jesus, though they seek Him last, and come to Him late, He has no word of reproach; He drives no one away. Unwearied in forgiveness, still His heart can only love.

The Lord's Goodness by the Way

But now to come to this woman's story. Christ's goodness to this poor afflicted soul was an act of goodness by the way. He was going to Jairus' house, with a great crowd accompanying Him, when this woman edged her way past one and the other, until, stretching a trembling hand, she was able to touch the blue tassel of the garment of Jesus. And immediately she knew in her body that she was healed of her plague. It was the succor of Jairus' little daughter that Jesus had in His mind. The healing of this sick woman was—shall I say?—an incidental act of beneficence. It was goodness by the way.

Not a Solitary Act

Not a few of His acts of grace were so done. He was on the way to Jerusalem when those ten lepers (Luke 17:12) greeted Him with their piteous appeal for cleansing; and the urgency of His journey could not prevent Him from answering their prayer. Later on, in that solemn journey when His heart was full of what was going to happen to Him at Jerusalem, when He was absorbed in the thought of that great sacrifice He was to offer up for the sins of the world, He was greeted by the cries of the two blind beggars (Matt. 20:30), outside Jericho's gate; the crowd would have hushed their cries, from some vague feeling that Jesus was occupied with great things, and ought not to be disturbed by the cases of the two blind beggars. But He commanded them to be brought, and healed them by the way; He was so full of kindness and goodness that it overflowed, and lavished itself upon all who came within His reach.

Do We Seize Such Opportunities?

Do we practice this wayside goodness? I am not afraid of the neglect of great opportunities; but I wonder sometimes whether we take advantage of all the small opportunities that present themselves by the way. What struck me most in reading Sir Stevenson A. Blackwood's *Life* was the amount of good he did by the way. When traveling up and down the country on Post Office business, when representing England in great Congresses abroad, he was always on the look-out for opportunities of service by the way. His fellow-passengers in railway trains, and servants at the houses in which he stayed, all have reason to bless God for this wayside goodness. Are we on the look-out for it? Do we buy up these opportunities? If we will but look out for them, every day brings with it opportunities of saying a kindly word, and doing some gracious deed which may come with healing virtue to some sick and despairing soul.

The Cost of Mercy

It was on the way to Jairus' house that Jesus did this kindly deed, and He knew when the deed was done. He perceived, the Authorized Version puts it, "that virtue had gone out of Him." He perceived, says the Revised Version, a little more accurately, that the power proceeding from Him "had gone forth." There was always power going forth from Jesus; healing and saving influences were continually streaming from Him, and He perceived that this saving power had exercised itself at that particular moment. What have we here? What I will venture to call the cost of mercy. Doing good is no cheap and easy business. It costs something. There is no doing good without expense, without paying the price. We are apt to think that these miracles of healing which Jesus performed cost Him nothing—that it was merely a case of a word or a wave of the hand. But that is not how I read the Gospel story. Every miracle had its cost. "Himself took our infirmities, and bare our sicknesses" . . . says St Matthew (Matt. 7:17). He felt the dire ills that affected other men as if they were His own. And He was able to remove them only by what was virtually an impartation of His own life. The Cross, indeed, is in a sense a parable of every miracle, and every miracle is a type of the Cross. Just as Jesus could quicken those who were dead in trespasses and sins by the laying down of His own life, so He could only bring healing to the leprous and the diseased by the expenditure of vital force. Christ's goodness cost Him a price.

The Personal Effect in Goodness

The goodness that is healing and redemptive, always costs. There are a great many people who try to do good on the cheap. They give their money to this cause and that, and there is an end of it. But there is no redeeming quality in goodness of that kind. If you want to do real good, you must give more than money; you must give yourself. Virtue must go out from you. There is no redeeming quality in money; it is pity and sympathy and love that redeem.

Pressure and the Touch of Faith

It was the consciousness of this drain upon His powers that made Christ turn about and ask, "Who touched My garments?" To the disciples it seemed an absurd question, seeing that on every side the people were crowding on to Him. "Thou seest the multitude thronging Thee," they protested "and sayest thou, Who touched Me"? (v. 31). But Jesus knew that while many were in physical contact with Him, someone had touched Him with the touch of faith. There is all the difference in the world between thronging and crowding on Christ and thus, in faith, touching Him. Many rudely press upon Christ's body, says Augustine; few touch Him to their salvation. It is possible to come into closest contact with Christ and receive no blessing. Many do so come into contact with Him. The forces of custom, for instance, bring people to the service of the Church; they impel them to read their Bible; they perhaps lead them even to the table of the Lord. But Worship and the Word and the Sacrament profit them nothing, because they have no sense of need, and have come not expecting a blessing. But let a man touch Christ, let him reach out the trembling hand of even a timid faith, and seek Christ for the blessing He alone can give, and, though he be a publican or a dying thief, Christ's saving power will be exercised upon him.

The Woman's Blessing

"Who touched Me?" Jesus said (v. 31). "But the woman, fearing and trembling, knowing what had been done to her, came and fell down before Him, and told Him all the truth" (v. 33, R.V.). The woman thought to have stolen away unnoticed. But Jesus insisted on discovering her. It was, as Dr. David Smith says, natural modesty that made her court concealment. At first sight it seems harsh and almost cruel that He should have dragged her forward, and compelled her to divulge her secret in the presence of the crowd. Why did He do it? For Jesus could not really be cruel, and He certainly never did this thing for His own glorification. The author I have just referred to gives the answer. "Had she been suffered to steal away, she would have lost the chief blessing of her life. She would have gained the healing of her body, but she would have missed the healing of her soul. She would have proved the power of Jesus, but she would have remained a stranger to His love. For look what He said to her, as she lay there fearing and trembling at His feet: 'Daughter'—He had never addressed any woman by that gracious name before—'thy faith hath made thee whole; go in peace' (v. 34). If I know anything about human nature, I know this, that that woman would thank God all her days that she could not be hid. It was worth while to be put to shame in the eyes of the crowd, to hear that gracious word from the lips of Christ: 'Thy faith hath made thee whole.'"

Even Though Her Faith Was Imperfect

Yet this woman's faith was not great. The commentators are all able to point out its flaws. It was a timid faith, for it only enabled the woman to stretch a stealthy hand, and touch Christ in the throng. It was not equal to the task of sending her openly to Jesus. And it was a very superstitious faith, for she evidently thought there was some kind of magical efficacy in the mere touch of Jesus. But it was faith, nevertheless, and it was richly rewarded. Even our imperfect faith brings its blessing. The faith that can only cry, "Help mine unbelief!" does not fail of its reward. When Sir James Simpson lay dying, a friend said to him that soon, like John the beloved disciple at the Last Supper, "he might rest on the bosom of Jesus." "I don't know that I can quite do that," he replied, "but I think I have got hold of the hem of His garment." Perhaps some of us have no very firm grip. We have only stretched out a timid hand, but even that may draw from Our Savior the words of forgiveness and blessing.

34
The Raising of Jairus' Daughter

And when Jesus was passed over again by ship unto the other side, much people gathered unto Him and He was nigh unto the sea. And, behold, there cometh one of the rulers of the synagogue, Jairus by name; and when he saw Him, he fell at His feet. And besought Him greatly, saying, My little daughter lieth at the point of death: I pray thee, come and lay Thy hands on her, that she may be healed; and she shall live. And Jesus went with him; and much people followed Him, and thronged Him. . . . While He yet spake, there came from the ruler of the synagogue's house certain which said, Thy daughter is dead: why troublest thou the Master any further? As soon as Jesus heard the word that was spoken, He saith unto the ruler of the synagogue, Be not afraid, only believe. And He suffered no man to follow Him, save Peter, and James, and John the brother of James. And He cometh to the house of the ruler of the synagogue, and seeth the tumult, and them that wept and wailed greatly. And when He was come in, He saith unto them, Why make ye this ado, and weep? the damsel is not dead, but sleepeth. And they laughed Him to scorn. But when He had put them all out, He taketh the father and the mother of the damsel, and them that were with Him, and entereth in where the damsel was lying. And He took the damsel by the hand, and said unto her, Talitha cumi; which is, being interpreted, Damsel, I say unto thee, arise. And staightway the damsel arose, and walked; for she was of the age of twelve years. And they were astonished with a great astonishment. And He charged them straitly that no man should know it; and commanded that something should be given her to eat. — Mark 5:21-24, 35-43.

HAVING DEALT WITH the healing of the woman with the issue of blood, we can consider the story of Jairus' daughter as a whole, from the moment her father came to Jesus with his prayer for help, to that glad moment when the little one was restored sound and well to her parents' arms.

The Father

Of Jairus we know nothing beyond what the Evangelists tell us in connection with this incident. They all make a point of emphasizing his position. "He was a ruler," says Matthew. "He was a ruler of the synagogue," say Mark and Luke. Perhaps Jairus' social and ecclesiastical position is thus emphasized, because it was not many of his class and rank who sought the help of Jesus. It was amongst the poor and the outcast that Christ found the majority of His hearers and friends. "Not many mighty, not many noble, are called" (1 Cor. 1:26). If Scribes and Pharisees were to be found in Christ's congregations, they usually came, not as suppliants, but as critics. It was an unusual thing, it was an unprecedented thing, to see one so high in official and ecclesiastical position as Jairus, a ruler of the synagogue, falling down at the feet of Christ.

His Difficulties

I can quite believe that it cost Jairus a good deal to make this public appeal to Jesus. "How hardly," said our Lord—"with what difficulty"— "shall they that have riches enter into the Kingdom of God!" (Mark 10:23). It is always harder for the man who is rich in this world's goods, who is high in this world's place, to enter in by the strait gate, than it is for those who are poor and of lowly station. It was more difficult for Jairus to seek Christ's help than it was for the blind beggars and palsied persons upon whom He lavished His healing grace, or even for this Gentile woman, whose story is embedded in the heart of the Jairus narrative. Jairus had more to give up. He had more to face. He had to humble himself. Jairus was one of the chief men, if not the chief man, of the town, while Jesus was, in the public eye, only a carpenter from Nazareth; then, all Jairus' friends and colleagues, the Scribes and Pharisees of Capernaum, had already taken up an attitude of hostility towards Him, and therefore to seek His help meant to challenge their hatred and contempt. It is easy to realize how much it must have cost Jairus to fall at Jesus' feet and beg His aid. How hardly shall they that have riches or place or station enter the Kingdom of God.

Difficulties Overcome

Yes, it is hard, it is terribly hard, but, thank God, not impossible. It was hard for Jairus, but not impossible. His own ecclesiastical position, and his friendship with the Scribes and Pharisees of Capernaum, were tremendous obstacles in his way. Nevertheless, he went. "There cometh one of the rulers of the synagogue, Jairus by name; and seeing Him, he falleth at His feet" (v. 22, R.V.).

A Triumph of Grace

What a triumph of God's grace, what a revelation of God's power is this! We speak sometimes as if the final and capital revelations of God's power were to be found in the saving of the poor and the fallen and the degraded; but if I understand our Lord's teaching at all rightly, we are rather to see the final evidence of His power in the salvation of those who are rich, and increased with goods, and whose worldly station is high and splendid. It was a greater triumph of grace to save a Joseph of Arimathaea, or a Nicodemus than it was to save the woman who was a sinner; it was a greater victory to save this ruler of the synagogue than it was to rescue the dying thief. "How hardly!" yes, but even to that hard task the grace of God is equal. He can break down the barriers in every man's path. He gathers His saints out of every rank and station. He can save kings as well as beggars; princes as well as peasants. He can save to the very uttermost those—whatever their rank or means— who come to God through him.

Had Our Lord and Jairus Met Before?

The narrative contains a hint of a previous meeting. I turn to St Luke 7, and find that, at an earlier stage in our Lord's history, certain elders of the Jews came to Jesus, begging his help on behalf of a centurion who had built them a synagogue, and who had a very dear servant sick, and at the point of death. Jairus may have been, and in all probability was one of the deputation that pleaded the centurion's cause that day. At any rate, he must have been cognizant of that mission. And the memory of what happened then—our Lord's ready response to the appeal for His help, and the proof of His power in the healing of the centurion's servant— may all have come back to him now, in his own hour of need, and impelled him to beg Christ to come to the help of his little daughter, who was also at the very point of death.

Love Overcoming Pride

What enabled Jairus to act as he did? Love. Dr. Maclaren has a great sermon on Naaman's refusal to wash himself in Jordan—to do such a simple and paltry thing for his own healing— entitled, "Pride overcoming want." If I had to find a heading for this paragraph, which shows us this proud ruler of the synagogue falling down at Jesus' feet, I think I should suggest this one, "Love overcoming Pride." Pride and Love both tugged at the heart of Jairus that day: pride in his position, and love for his child. Pride whispered, "Don't demean yourself. Think what your friends will say." Love whispered, "Your little daughter is at the point of death." It was a battle royal between these two mightiest forces in the human soul—pride and love. But a look at his little daughter's face, with the pallor of approaching death spreading over it; the sight of her little frame shaken by her gaspings for breath; the thought of what his home would be if his little daughter, the light of his eyes, his only child, were taken away—that settled it. Love triumphed, and, throwing his pride to the winds, this man, this personage in Capernaum, made his way into the midst of the crowd of "common people," of publicans and sinners who surrounded Christ, and before the eyes of them all flung himself at the feet of Christ, sobbing out his prayer. In the Greek you can almost hear his sobs, and his broken phrases. "My little daughter is in extremity—that Thou come and lay Thy hands on her—that she may be saved, and live."

Jairus' Prayer

Now what shall we say about this prayer of Jairus? It is a good prayer, says Dr. Clover. It does not show, perhaps, the magnificent faith of the centurion whose cause Jairus had pleaded some weeks before. Still, it is a good prayer, a proper prayer.

The Prayer of Love

First of all, you can feel love throbbing and thrilling through it. "My little daughter," he sobs; and the term used is a fond diminutive, a term of endearment. What a world of pity and pathos there is in that appeal! It was love—the bleeding love of a parent's heart— that brought Jairus to Jesus!

The Power of Love

How often a similar cause has sent men to seek Christ's help! That was what brought the man about whom we read in the ninth chapter of this Gospel to Jesus. "Master," he cried, "I have brought unto thee my son, which hath a dumb spirit. . . . If thou canst do anything, have compassion on us, and help us" (Mark 9:17, 22). That was what brought the Canaanitish woman to Jesus, of whom we read in Matthew 15:22. "Have mercy on me, O Lord, Thou Son of David," she cried; "my daughter is grievously vexed with a devil." That is what has brought many a man and woman since their day! I have myself known many a father and many a mother driven to seek Christ's help by the power of love for their child. Perhaps they had not given a thought to Christ in their days of prosperity and ease, but when trouble threatened, when a little child lay sick, they went, like Jairus, to Jesus with the cry, "My little daughter is at the point of death." And the cry of love is one Jesus never disregards. God is love. And though perhaps He may not answer the prayer of love exactly as love asks,

He will surely come to the succor of every heart that calls for Him. "My little daughter," sobbed Jairus. "And Jesus went with him." That was our Lord's practical response.

The Prayer of Faith

Again, in this prayer I see faith. Jairus remembered what Jesus had done for the centurion's servant, and he argued that He could do as much for his little child. And so there is no suggestion of doubt or hesitancy in his prayer. He believed that Jesus had only to come down and lay His hands on her, and she should be saved from the grave, and live. "According to your faith be it unto you" (Matt. 9:29), said Jesus. He could do none of His mighty works in Nazareth because of their unbelief. He could not answer the prayer of the father of the demoniac lad for his child so long as there was an "if" in his petitions. But this prayer of Jairus He was able promptly and swiftly to answer. "I pray Thee," he said, "that Thou come and lay Thy hands on her, that she may be made whole, and live" (v. 23, R.V.). And faith won the answer. Straightway Jesus went with him.

The Delay of Jesus

I can imagine that a great hope sprang up in Jairus' heart when Jesus bent His steps towards his house, but "hope deferred," we say, "maketh the heart sick." And with Jairus it was a case of "hope deferred." When he left home his little daughter was in extremity. Unless help came soon, it would be too late. If ever there was an urgent errand, it was the errand on which Jairus came. If ever there was need for haste, there was need for the Healer to hasten, if He wanted to snatch the little girl from the jaws of death. But instead of haste there came stoppage and delay. For on His way to the house Jesus was arrested by the action of the woman with the issue of blood. I do not know how long the incident took, but to Jairus the minutes must have seemed ages. For his little daughter was at the point of death, and Jairus seems never to have thought that the power of Christ reached not only up to death, but beyond it. Time was to him of the essence of the case. Unless they hurried, they would be too late. Yet, instead of hurrying, Christ stopped—stopped until, as Jairus thought, He placed the recovery of his little child beyond hope. For, just as the Lord was giving His benediction to the woman, a messenger came from Jairus' house with the heart-breaking news that all was over, that his little daughter was dead, and that there was no need to trouble the Master any further.

The Discipline of His Delays

I wonder did hard thoughts about Jesus rise up in Jairus' heart? I wonder did he reproach Him for the delay? I should not be at all surprised if that were so. Christ's delays are puzzling and perplexing oftentimes. We raise an urgent cry to Him, and instead of hasting to our help, He tarries. "Master," was the message the sisters of Lazarus sent to Him, "he whom Thou lovest is sick" (John 11:3). And He abode still in the place where He was two days. What bitter thoughts may have filled the sisters' minds during those days of delay! "Lord," they said to Him when He came at length, two days too late, "if Thou hadst been here, our brother had not died." Similar thoughts may have risen up in the heart of Jairus. "If He had not stayed to discover and talk with the woman, He might have been in time to heal and save my child." But Jesus knew the temptation, and, turning to the broken-hearted father, said, "Fear not, only believe" (v. 36).

The Call for Faith

"Fear not, only believe!" So simple are the words! So hard and difficult is the lesson they inculcate! "Fear not," He said to Jairus, when all Jairus' worst fears had been confirmed. "Only believe," He said, when there seemed to be no longer any room for faith or hope. And He speaks the same word to us, in our dark and troubled days; in the days when sorrows threaten us, and all our hopes seem thwarted and broken; in the days when our prayers seem to go unanswered, and Heaven seems deaf to our appeal. "Fear not, only believe." For in spite of all apparent silence and neglect, God never forgets. In spite of seeming delay, no prayer goes unanswered. "Fear not, only believe." Stick to your faith in God. Even though He slay you, continue to trust in Him, and your righteousness shall come forth as brightness, and your salvation as a lamp that burneth. The discipline of delay is hard to bear. But the delay is not due to the fact that God grudges to bless; it is because He has other and better blessings in store for us than those for which we ask. "Only believe," He said to Jairus, when his last hope seemed shattered. And was not Jairus' faith justified? Was it not worth while to believe? Was not his child, raised and restored, the justification of this appeal? And so, if in our darkest days we still hold to our trust, we too shall one day be gloriously justified. "I waited patiently for the Lord"—it is not easy to wait patiently—"and He inclined unto me, and heard my cry. He brought me up also out of an horrible pit, out of the miry clay, and set my feet upon a rock, and established my goings. And He hath put a new song in my mouth, even praise unto our God" (Psa. 40:1-3).

Christ's View of Death

And so they pursued their way to Jairus' house—and who shall say what thoughts filled the father's desolate heart? Arrived there, Jesus hushed the hired wailers, who were already making the house resound with their shrill lamentations. "Why make ye a tumult, and weep? the child is not dead, but sleepeth" (v. 39, R.V.). The mourners, with their false and narrow literalism, thought that Jesus was doubting the reality of the child's death, and they laughed Him to scorn. But Jesus was not doubting the reality of the child's death. He was giving His view of death. What was death to Jesus? A sleep. "Our friend Lazarus sleepeth," He said; "but I go, that I may awake him out of sleep" (John 11:11). Jesus never talked of death. In His view "all live unto God." That was all that death meant to Him—a going to sleep, a closing of the eyes upon this world, to open them upon a better world and a fairer morning. "She is not dead, but sleepeth." Is there then no such thing as "death"? Yes, there is. "The wages of sin is death" (Rom. 6:23). "The sting of death is sin" (1 Cor. 4:56). Jesus knew what death was, for He Himself bore our sins. He submitted to all the shame and curse and horror of it. In a sense, Jesus is the only one Who knows fully what "death" means. *He tasted death for every man*. But, in a measure, every man, with sin on his soul and haunted by the fears sin always brings, knows what death means. But the Christian does not die, he falls on sleep. Stephen, "when he had said this, fell asleep" (Acts 7:60). The very place where the dust of the believer lies is no longer a graveyard, but a cemetery—a sleeping place.

Christ's Lordship over Death

A sleep implies a waking. "The damsel is not dead," Jesus said, "but sleepeth." And He proceeded to show that the little one was not beyond the reach of His voice. For, taking her by the hand, He said, "Little lamb, Arise." "And straightway the damsel rose up, and walked" (v. 42, R.V.). "Little lamb, Arise." How beautiful and tender: This is a revelation of the mother heart of Jesus, says one commentator. Yes, it is that. But it is much more. It is a revelation of the Lordship of Jesus. We want a mother-heart. But we want more. For what can the mother-heart do in the face of grim death?

The mother-heart is powerless; the mother-heart cannot save or redeem. The mother-heart breaks, as it sees death marching on its remorseless way. But there is more than mother-heart here. There is infinite Power. Here is One Who made even death unclutch his bony fingers. Is death the strong man who despoils our homes and goods? Here is One stronger than the strong. Here is One Who takes death and captivity captive. Here is One Who can redeem from the power of death and the grave. "The last enemy that shall be destroyed is death" (1 Cor. 4:26), says the Apostle. He has been destroyed.

What Jesus did for Jairus' daughter He will do for us all. "Death hath no more dominion over us." "O death, where is thy sting?" "O grave, where is thy victory?" (1 Cor. 4:55). "I am the Resurrection, and the Life: he that believeth in Me, though he were dead, yet shall he live. And whosoever liveth and believeth in Me shall never die " (John 11:25, 26).

35
Jesus at Nazareth

"And He went out from thence, and came into His own country; and His disciples follow Him. And when the Sabbath day was come, He began to teach in the synagogue: and many hearing Him were astonished, saying, From whence hath this man these things? and what wisdom is this which is given unto Him, that even such mighty works are wrought by His hands? Is not this the Carpenter, the Son of Mary, the Brother of James, and Joses, and of Juda, and Simon? and are not His sisters here with us? And they were offended at Him."   —Mark 6:1-3.

Our Lord and "His Own Country"

"HIS OWN COUNTRY" is quite obviously Nazareth. The excitement caused by the healing of the woman with the issue of blood, and the still more wonderful miracle of the raising of Jairus' daughter, was inconvenient and distasteful. And to escape from it our Lord left the crowded district round the lake, and withdrew into the much more quiet region of "His own country." Commentators find it most difficult to decide whether our Lord, after He began to preach, paid one visit to Nazareth or two. The account in these verses before us obviously refers to the same visit as is described for us in Matthew 13. The difficulty comes in trying to decide whether the visit which Matthew and Mark describe is the same as that recorded in Luke 4. There is, as you remember, a general similarity in the accounts all three Evangelists give of the reception Christ met with at the hands of the Nazarenes. All these tell us that Christ's townsfolk, blinded by prejudice, refused to acknowledge His greatness. "They were offended in Him" (v. 3, R.V.), and many scholars, impressed by this general similarity, have concluded that all three accounts refer to one and the self-same visit. On the other hand, there are certain points of difference that make equally competent scholars maintain that the accounts refer to two distinct and separate visits. Let me mention some of these points of difference. In Matthew's and Mark's accounts the Nazarenes content themselves with disparaging references to our Lord's family and occupation; but in Luke's account their fury against Him is so fierce that they make a determined attempt to kill Him. In Matthew's and Mark's accounts Jesus leaves Capernaum for Nazareth; in Luke's account, the hostility of His own people drives Him from Nazareth to Capernaum. But far more weighty than verbal differences of this kind is the fact that Luke places His visit right at the beginning of our Lord's ministry, while the visit recorded by Matthew and Mark took place *after* Jesus had been for months (eighteen months, Dr. Glover suggests) engaged in the work of teaching and preaching. On the whole, therefore, we are perhaps justified in concluding that Jesus paid two visits to His home town, and that it is the second of those visits that is referred to here.

His Prior Treatment at Nazareth

If this was a second visit, its import is the more striking. For He had, on a previous occasion, been badly treated in Nazareth. They had not only rejected His message; they had tried their utmost to kill Him. For at the end of the sermon "they rose up, and cast Him forth out of the city, and led Him unto the brow of the hill whereon their city was built, that they might throw Him down headlong" (Luke 4:29, R.V.). Jesus had scarcely a friend in Nazareth. His own brethren did not believe in Him. They thought Him mad, and with Mary, their mother, they came one day to lay hands upon Him. Indeed, so complete was the alienation between our Lord and the members of His own family, that in this incident which Mark records in chapter 3, He almost repudiates relationship—at any rate, He declares that the men and women in His congregation, listening with receptive and obedient minds, were more really His mother and sisters and brothers than were Mary and James and Joses and Judas and Simon and the sisters referred to in this paragraph. On the whole, considering the condition of things in His own home, remembering the reception He met with on His first visit, it would have been quite natural and intelligible if Jesus had never gone near Nazareth again.

Mercy for Insult

But our Lord is plenteous in mercy, "unwearied in forgiveness still, His heart could only love." The rude reception He met with, the contemptuous rejection of His claims, could not, and did not, quench or even chill His love. And so in process of time He went back again, to give Nazareth another chance. He made this second visit, says one of the baldest and driest of commentators, with the twofold purpose of renewing His relations with His mother and His brothers, and endeavoring again to commend Himself to His fellow-townsmen. That is exactly it. He went back, to give them all a second chance. You remember how the prophet, in the name of God, apostrophizes Israel. Israel has sorely grieved God, and rebelled against Him, and done despite to His law, yet He yearns over Israel, "How shall I give thee up, Ephraim?" He cries, "Mine heart is turned within me, my repentings are kindled together" (Hos. 11:8). And the heart of Jesus yearned over Nazareth, over His townsmen, over His old playmates, over His kinsfolk according to the flesh. This second visit to the town that had rejected Him was just the outcome of that yearning compassion and love.

The Second Chance

The love that believes in the second chance is characteristic of Jesus. "Let us go into Judea again," He said one day to His disciples. And the bare suggestion staggered them. "Rabbi," they protested, "the Jews of late sought to stone Thee, and goest Thou thither again?" (John 11:8). Again—back to the stones; to the men who had sought to kill Him? Yes, again, to give them another chance. What love this is! that after men have cast Him out, and sought to kill Him, will come back again! Yes, you and I need it all! My hope of acceptance and salvation lies here—that though I have stoned Christ and cast Him forth, He comes back again. By act and word we reject Christ, and repudiate Him, and rebel against Him, and bid Him depart! But, thank God, He does not leave us to our fate. He comes back again. He gives us another chance. The long-suffering of the Lord is our salvation.

And I am tempted to add this word before I pass on—this belief in the second chance that characterized Jesus, characterizes all who really possess His spirit. You remember the treatment Paul received at Lystra. This is what I read, they "stoned Paul, and drew him out of the city, supposing he had been dead" (Acts 14:19.) What a reception to meet with! Paul hereafter will surely eschew a city that treated him so cruelly! Yet what I read in the next verse but one is this, "And when they had preached the Gospel to that city, and had taught many, they returned again to Lystra!" (Acts 14:21). Back to the people who had stoned and well-nigh killed him, to give them another chance. And that is the spirit that will characterize all who have truly learned of Jesus. We shall always be eager to go again to those who have repelled and rebuffeted us.

The Perfect Humanity of Jesus

And now, let us look at what these Nazarenes said about Jesus, and the questions Jesus started in their minds. First of all, then, we have here their account of Jesus—of His family and upbringing and circumstances. "Is not this the carpenter," they said, "the son of Mary, and brother of James, and Joses, and Judas, and Simon? and are not His sisters here with us?" (v. 3, R.V.). This is a testimony from the Nazarenes to Jesus' true and normal humanity. He was made in all things "like unto His brethren" (Heb. 2:17), the writer of the Epistle to the Hebrews says, and here these Nazarenes place their seal to that great and comforting statement. Jesus was a true and genuine man. He had a normal and human development. As far as His humanity was concerned, the Nazarenes, it is clear, believed that Jesus was just like any one of themselves. They knew His mother Mary, His brothers and sisters; and, without entering upon the region of controversy, there is no adequate reason for supposing that these brothers and sisters referred to here were anything but real brothers and sisters, i.e. sons and daughters of Joseph and Mary. The were still amongst them—plain, ordinary everyday people. They remembered that Jesus Himself had just been a craftsman in their midst. "Is not this the Carpenter?" they said. They had in their possession barrows and ploughs and chairs and tables of Jesus' making. As far as outward circumstances were concerned, there was nothing to differentiate Jesus from any other Jew of humble birth.

But a Distinction Apparent

And yet there was a difference. That was the startling fact that forced itself upon the minds of these Nazarenes. There was a difference. There was all the difference in the world. Jesus had played with them, gone to school with them, worked with them and for them, and yet He was different from them. He had been brought up in the same home with James and Joses and Judas and Simon, and yet He was quite different from them. If these Nazarenes could have denied the difference they would. For all their local prejudices and jealousies and envies were up in arms. But the difference would not be denied. It would be as idle to deny that the sun shone as to deny the difference, the immeasurable difference, between Jesus and His own kind; yes, and every man they had either seen or heard of. And their problem came in trying to account for this difference.

"Whence," they said in their bewilderment, "hath this Man these things?" and "What is the wisdom that is given unto this Man?" and "What mean such mighty works wrought by His hands?" (v. 2, R.V.). If verse 3 is the Nazarenes' testimony to our Lord's real and normal humanity, verse 2 is their testimony to His absolutely unique greatness. The three questions that leaped to their lips emphasize three separate aspects of the greatness of Christ. "Whence hath this Man these things?" is the first question, i.e. these things that He is saying.

The Speech of Our Lord

Here is their testimony to the wonder of the speech of Christ. "Never man spake like this Man " (John 7:46) was the testimony of the officers who were sent to seize Christ, but who returned with their errand unfulfilled. That is to all intents and purposes the testimony of these Nazarenes. They "wondered," Luke says, in his account of His first visit, "at the gracious words which proceeded out of His mouth" (Luke 4:22). There was a charm and a winsomeness about Christ's speech that not even the most callous and insensible could fail to feel. Even the "publicans and sinners drew near for to hear Him." Even the "common people heard Him gladly." And not only was Christ's speech marked by grace and charm. It had the note of authority in it too. Perhaps this was the most astonishing thing about it. "He taught them as one having authority." He spoke as one who had the right to command. He preached as one who had power to supersede even Moses. There was a whole universe between Jesus and every other teacher the land contained.

The Wisdom of Our Lord

"What is the wisdom that is given unto this Man?"—this was the second question. He never "guessed at truth." He declared the truth as one who knew. There was no "perhaps, or "if" or "it may be," in His speech. The note of certitude rang through it all. And as Jesus declared His Gospel, men recognized its truth. Truth always has a self-evidencing power. And even these prejudiced Nazarenes could not fail to see that Jesus had a grip of truth, a knowledge of God, familiarity with the eternal, that no prophet or psalmist had ever possessed. And it left them speechless with amazement. "What is the wisdom that is given unto this man?" they said.

The Works by Our Lord

"What mean such mighty works wrought by His hands?"—that was their third question. The reference, no doubt, is to the miracles of healing wrought by Jesus, the news of which had reached His old home, and had set the whole place in a ferment. Acts of power were attributed to certain of the great prophets of the Old

Testament, but they were exceptional and rare. Power, on the other hand, streamed forth from Jesus. "As many as touched Him were made whole." No one in all their nation's history had performed such acts of power as Jesus did. He was victor over disease, over leprosy, over death itself. How came Jesus by this power, which neither Elijah nor Moses could equal? "What mean such mighty works wrought by His hands?" These were the qualities about Jesus for which the Nazarenes could not account.

People in these days try to account for a man by his ancestry and training. And these things undoubtedly have an almost incalculable influence upon a man's development. The Nazarenes did not talk as much as we do about heredity and environment. But obviously these things were in their mind, and they had some notion of their effect on life. But what they felt was that heredity and environment completely failed to account for Jesus. For there was nothing remarkable about Jesus' family. "Is not this the son of Mary," they said, "and brother of James and Joses and Judas and Simon?" It was not a case of inherited genius—which genius had come to its consummate flower in Jesus. Genius in any case is not sufficient to account for Christ's wisdom. But as a matter of fact there was no genius. His relations were just plain, average commonplace Jews. Nor was it a case of favorable environment; Jesus had had no early advantages. He had never been to college in Jerusalem. He had received the limited schooling a poor Jewish lad was wont to receive, and was then put to the carpenter's bench. They said, "Is not this the Carpenter?" And so Jesus remained a problem to these Nazarenes. Ignoring or rejecting any idea of Divinity in Jesus, they found Him an insoluble problem. They had no category in which they could place Him. And, rather than confess Him to be the Sent of God, they preferred to believe He was "inspired of the devil." "And they were offended in Him" (v. 3, R.V.).

The Humanitarian Theory

The Lord Jesus is still a problem to us. He confronts the world, and it is impossible to account for Him on merely humanitarian lines. I hold as tenaciously as anyone to His real humanity, but I have no patience with the attempts that many make to whittle away His uniqueness, to reduce Him to the proportions of a merely superior man. I know it is difficult to form an intellectual conception of how Jesus can be at one and the same time very God and true Man. But if that is difficult—to think of Him as mere man is impossible. "Whence hath this Man these things?" "What is the wisdom that is given unto this Man?" How is it this Galilean peasant surpasses the greatest human intellects in the grasp of truth? "What mean these mighty works wrought by His hands?" How is it Christ has been able to do wonders in the way of salvation no human agency has ever been able to accomplish? Not likeness but uniqueness is what I see. Shut out His Divinity, and Jesus becomes a stumbling-block. But let His wisdom and power produce their due impression, and you will see in Him Very God as well as Very Man, and will fall at His feet saying, "My Lord and my God."

36
The Nazarenes and Their Error

Is not this the Carpenter, the Son of Mary, the Brother of James, and Joses, and of Juda, and Simon? and are not His sisters here with us? And they were offended at Him. But Jesus said unto them, A prophet is not without honor, but in His own country, and among His own kin, and in His own house. And He could there do no mighty work, save that he laid His hands upon a few sick folk, and healed them. And He marvelled because of their unbelief. And He went round about the villages, teaching. —Mark 6:3-6.

The Life of Christ at Nazareth

WE HAVE NOW to consider the conduct of Christ's townsfolk, as the remainder of this paragraph reveals it to us. Now shall I very much startle any if I say that there was some slight excuse for the incredulity the Nazarenes displayed on the occasion of the first visit? There was no excuse, of course, for the murderous fury, but there was some slight excuse for their incredulity. For consider the circumstances, Jesus had lived in Nazareth as boy and man. We must dismiss from our minds all thought of the marvels with which the Apocryphal Gospels have embellished the story of those early years. Jesus lived an absolutely normal and healthy boy's life. The other boys who played with Him and went to school with Him were conscious of no difference between themselves and Him, except that there was an uprightness, a purity, a grace about Him they did not possess. They felt He was a better boy, but still a boy. And when He grew up, His experience was again the normal experience of a Jewish lad. He was apprenticed to a trade—His father's trade, and, as this paragraph plainly shows, carried that trade on until that memorable day when the Father's voice summoned Him to His mission. Then He left Nazareth for John's baptism, and His own inner conviction of a Divine call was confirmed by John's solemn announcement. He knew the hour had come, and to prepare for His great work He sought the solitude of the wilderness, calmly to face the Father's plan for Him, and to battle down all temptations to take any easier way to win the world. After the temptation, He entered on His work as a

165

Preacher of the Kingdom, and practically made straight for Nazareth, to declare His Gospel there.

The Sudden Claim

Now, try to realize the circumstances. Only some six or seven weeks had elapsed since Jesus had been, in the eyes of the people of Nazareth, one of themselves—a village carpenter. And now He was back again, making the most extraordinary claims for Himself! Transfer the circumstances to our own times and suppose that a working-man—known, it is true, for his piety, but still an everyday working-man—should one day appear in our midst declaring himself to be the founder of a new kingdom. Do you not think there would be some shakings of the head and some contemptuous epithets flying round? Well, that is exactly how it was with the Nazarenes on Christ's first visit. Familiarity does undoubtedly make it difficult for men to do homage to another's greatness. And I think there is some excuse for the incredulity the Nazarenes displayed on the occasion of our Lord's first visit.

The Second Appeal

But I confess I can find no excuse for their incredulity on this second visit. I am dumbfounded as I think of it. For, by this time, Jesus Christ's name and fame were spread throughout the land. These Nazarenes had heard and seen that very day for themselves evidences of our Lord's greatness and supremacy. They had heard His words; they had listened to His wisdom; they had seen apparently some of His mighty works. They could not help but acknowledge His uniqueness. Carpenter or no carpenter, this was no ordinary man. "Whence," they asked in wondering amazement, "hath this Man these things? and, What is the wisdom that is given unto this Man? and What mean such mighty works wrought by His hands?" (v. 2, R.V.). And having read these expressions of awe-struck wonder, I expect to read next that these Nazarenes, with their prejudices clean swept away by what they heard and saw, made confession like Nathanael, "Rabbi, Thou art the Son of God; Thou art the King of Israel" (John 1:49); or that they fell at His feet, like Thomas did, and cried, "My Lord and my God" (John 20:28).

Its Rejection

But what I read is something very different. "And they were offended in Him"—"they were caused to stumble," as the margin puts it, or, to translate the Greek verb quite literally, "They were scandalized in Him." This is a staggering thing—that people should recognize Jesus Christ's uniqueness and yet be scandalized in Him. What was the reason for it? It was in a word, prejudice. You remember how in his Holy War, John Bunyan stations one old Mr. Prejudice, with fifty deaf men under him at Ear-gate, to defend that particular gate into the citadel of Mansoul against the assaults of Prince Emmanuel. Well, it was Mr. Prejudice who stopped the ears and hardened the hearts of these Nazarenes against the appeals of Jesus that day. The second rejection was all Mr. Prejudice's work.

The Cause: Prejudice

"They were scandalized in Him"—and prejudice was at the bottom of it; prejudice born of nearness and familiarity. "A prophet," was the comment of Jesus Himself, "is not without honor, save in His own country and among His own kin, and in His own house" (v. 4, R.V.). We know the truth of this proverb in the common affairs of daily life. We are often blind to the worth of the familiar and the near. We find it difficult to admit the greatness of anyone whom circumstances seemed to mark as our equal, and who started side by side with us. Jeremy Bentham, Hazlitt says, was an illustration of this very proverb, for he was better known and more highly esteemed on the other side of the globe than he was in his own land.

I remember hearing a true incident about one of the great cotton lords of Manchester. He was supposed to be suffering from some particular complaint, and he traveled all the way to Vienna, to consult a doctor supposed to be a great specialist on this particular disease. "You are an Englishman?" the doctor said. "Yes," the patient replied. "May I ask from what part of England you come?" "Manchester," was the answer. "But why did you come from Manchester all the way to me? The greatest authority in the world lives in your own city"; and he named one of the medical professors of my old university. "The eyes of a fool," says the Wise Man, "are in the ends of the earth" (Prov. 17:24). It is a widespread folly. We see more worth and value in the things that are far off than in the things that are near. Distance with many of us magnifies importance. It is so in the case even of the "prophet" still. There are many people who seem to measure a preacher's worth by the mileage he travels. They find all sorts of virtues and qualities in the stranger they fail to see in the man who is in their own midst.

A Modern Error

It is so even in the case of Jesus Christ still. This sin of the Nazarenes is being—in a slightly different form—repeated by multitudes in our midst today. Do you not wonder how it is men are not won by the beauty of Christ, touched by the appeal of the Christian Gospel? Do you not wonder how it is that the story of the Cross leaves an English audience unmoved, while it melts the poor pagan Greenlander to tears? Do you not wonder how it is men are so indifferent to this old Book, while a Japanese reading it for the first time thrills with joy, and greets it as a veritable word of God? What is the reason for it all? Just this—familiarity has bred contempt. We are familiar with Jesus and with His words. We are so accustomed to His words, His wisdom, His mighty works, that we have ceased to wonder at them. Let us ask God to preserve us from the deadening effects of familiarity and routine. Let us ask Him to keep our hearts ever sensitive to the grace of Jesus and the wonder of the Gospel. When we lose our wonder we may commit again the sin of these Nazarenes, and count the blood of the covenant . . . an unholy thing (Heb. 10:29).

Its Results

The Nazarenes were offended in Jesus, and as a result Jesus could there do no mighty work. He Who away down in Capernaum had healed the woman by mere touch of His garment, Who had raised the young daughter of Jairus from the dead, Who in Gerasa had restored the man possessed of the legion to sanity and health, Who at a word had stilled the whistling wind and raging sea, in Nazareth could do no mighty work. "He could there do no mighty work" (v. 5). That is rather a startling sentence. "Cannot" is an ugly word to apply to Him into Whose hands the Father had committed all things. What are we to understand by it? Are we to understand that power for the moment had deserted Jesus? No, this "cannot" of which we read here was not the result of any physical arrest put upon Christ's powers. The "cannot," as Dr. Salmond says, is due to the fact that "the moral conditions were wanting." For I must remind you that every "mighty work" of which we read in the Gospels was the result of the fulfillment of two conditions.

The Power and the Conditions of Its Exercise

There was, first of all, the Divine power of Christ, and there was, in the second place, faith on the part of the receiver of the blessing. Take the two last miracles of which we have been reading. Hundreds of people touched Christ's garments, and received no benefit. How came it, then, that this woman, from her mere touch, received the healing of the plague with which she had been afflicted for twelve years? Jesus Himself supplies the answer, "Daughter, thy *faith* hath made thee whole" (v. 34). It was the humble faith and expectancy of the woman that liberated—shall I say?—the Divine power, and allowed it to do its beneficial work. Take the case of Jairus' daughter. At a certain stage in the journey certain of Jairus' friends or servants met them, and brought word that the little child was dead, and that therefore there was no need to trouble the Master any further. "Fear not," said Jesus, "only believe" (v. 36). And so they went on their way. To those people, who, as they would say, knew the facts, the continuance of this journey seemed absurd. But Jairus cherished a belief that it would not prove in vain. "Only believe," said Jesus. He could have worked no miracle without faith in the recipient. But because Jairus believed, it was possible for Him to summon the "little lamb" back again from the sleep of death.

This demand for a certain moral condition before exercising His healing power is still more vividly seen in the case of the healing of the demoniac lad at the foot of the Holy Mound. "If Thou canst do anything," cried the agonized father, "have compassion on us, and help us" (9:22). He talked as if it were solely and simply a question of Christ's power. But it was much more than that. "If Thou canst?" replied Jesus, as if to say, "It is not simply a case of My power; it is just as much a case of your faith. All things are possible to him that believeth." "Lord," sobbed the man, "I believe; help Thou mine unbelief"(9:24). This condition of faith must always be fulfilled before Christ's power can be exercised. For, if Christ performed His mighty works upon people irrespective of their moral condition, His miracles would cease to be moral acts at all. They would become mere acts of wonder. Divine blessing is always conditioned by the moral state of the recipient; the exercise of Christ's power depends upon the state of our own hearts. Whatsoever we ask believing we shall receive. But unbelief puts an effectual arrest on the output of Christ's power.

Is the Condition Met by Us?

"He could there do no mighty work" (v. 5). Is that the condition with us? We complain often of the dearth of conversions. We pray constantly for a revival. We cry out to our Lord and say, "It is high time for Thee to work." But let us lay this truth to heart—if there is an arrest of our Lord's power, it is not because His arm is shortened, that it cannot save. It is because the requisite moral conditions in us are lacking. When faith and expectancy are present, Christ never fails. When the Church fulfils the conditions on her side, Christ is never wanting. Every revival proves the truth of this statement. So I suggest a variation in our prayers. Instead of crying, "Awake, arm of the Lord, as in the ancient days," let us cry earnestly, unceasingly, "Lord, increase our faith."

The Saving Exception at Nazareth

"He could there do no mighty work, save that He laid His hands upon a few sick folk, and healed them" (v. 5). "Save that"—there is always the saving exception. The story of Christ's visit to Nazareth was not a story of complete and abject failure. Even in Nazareth there were few hidden ones, as Dr. Salmond says, with aclaim upon His compassion, and with the inward preparation for the healing gift; some open and guileless souls who amid the general prejudice and incredulity believed in Jesus, and so made it possible for Him to work.

Failures—and Failures

"He could there do no mighty work, save that"—that is typical of work for God. There is often much to depress; but it is never abject and complete failure. Elijah thought he had labored for nought and in vain; but there were 7000 in Israel who had not bowed the knee to Baal. Jesus died on the Cross of Shame—and the Cross was just the Symbol of the way in which the nation as a whole had rejected Him. He failed amongst His countrymen; but it was not total failure. "He could there do no mighty work"—save that He won some hundred and twenty souls, who loved Him, and lived for Him, and built their whole hopes for time and eternity upon Him. They laughed at Paul in Athens; his Athenian mission was to a large extent a failure—the most disappointing failure of any mission Paul undertook. And yet it was not a total failure. He could there do no mighty work —save that he won Dionysius the Areopagite and a woman named Damaris to the faith.

The converts at Sardis well nigh all turned apostate, and it seemed as if the preaching of the Gospel was to end in ghastly and tragic failure. And yet it was not total failure. There was no great and mighty work done in Sardis, save that there were a few who from the day of their conversion never afterwards defiled their garments. "Save that"— there is always this saving clause, to keep alive our faith in men, in the Gospel, in our Lord. We preach and preach, and we seem to accomplish nothing—save that, as we learn in unexpected ways sometimes, God used our poor and halting words to comfort some breaking heart, to strengthen some struggling soul. And sometimes we almost lose faith in the Gospel. We hear of it being preached far and wide, and it seems to accomplish so little. It does no mighty work, save that—yes, there is always a save that—we hear of souls being born again or of a whole nation revived.

The Wonder of Christ

"And He marvelled because of their unbelief" (v. 6). Commentators tell us that there were only two things Christ wondered at, and they were faith and unfaith. The faith of the Roman centurion was a wonder to Jesus: "He marvelled, and said, Verily, I say unto you, I have not found so great faith, no, not in Israel" (Matt. 8:10). It was a mighty faith, discovered in an unexpected quarter. And He marveled at the unbelief of Nazareth. It was unintelligible to Him. For it was unbelief in spite of knowledge. It was unbelief in spite of the recognition of His greatness. It was unbelief in spite of the evidence of His wonderful works. Unbelief is irrational. English people recognize His wisdom. They admit His supremacy. They see His mighty deeds. And yet multitudes do not believe. He wondered at their unbelief! Does He wonder at us? "The Son of Man, when He cometh, shall He find faith on the earth?" "Oh, foolish ones and slow of heart to believe!" "Lord, help mine unbelief."

37
The Sending of the Twelve

"And He called unto Him the twelve, and began to send them forth by two and two; and gave them power over unclean spirits; And commanded them that they should take nothing for their journey, save a staff only; no scrip, no bread, no money in their purse: But be shod with sandals; and not put on two coats. And He said unto them, in what place soever ye enter into an house, there abide till ye depart from that place. And whosoever shall not receive you, nor hear you, when ye depart thence, shake off the dust under your feet for a testimony against them. Verily I say unto you, It shall be more tolerable for Sodom and Gomorrha in the day of judgment, than for that city. And they went out, and preached that men should repent. And they cast out many devils, and anointed with oil many that were sick, and healed them."
—Mark 6:7-13.

Leaving Nazareth

WE RESUME THE thread of the Gospel narrative at the mission of the twelve Apostles. Jesus must have had a heavy heart when He took His leave of Nazareth. It seemed as if rejection was to be His invariable lot. For His rejection at the hands of the dwellers in Decapolis had been swiftly followed by this rejection at the hands of His own townsmen. At the one place they had begged Him to depart out of their borders; at the other they were scandalized in Him. And yet, as Bishop Chadwick says, we read of no statement of His labors. Men, after a hard and bitter experience, are apt to be discouraged and depressed. Elijah, seeing the apparent failure of his work in Israel, wished that he might die. But Jesus never gave way to these fits of despair. He never for one moment laid aside His work. "When they persecute you in this city," He said to His disciples, "flee ye into another" (Matt. 10:23).

A New Sphere: in the Villages

That was exactly the principle on which the Lord Himself acted. Rejected at Nazareth, Jesus did not abandon His work in high dudgeon. He simply changed the sphere of it. When the Nazarenes refused to listen to Him, "He went round about the villages teaching" (v. 6). "Round about the villages!" What an illustration this is of the condescension of Jesus! When you next read that verse (Matt. 11:29) in which He says, "I am meek and lowly in heart," put down in the margin this verse 6 as illustration and proof of the claim.

A Lesson in Lowliness

"He went round about the villages teaching." The villages! We townsfolk sometimes talk of the village with just a touch of scorn. And when it comes to being a village preacher, we think of him with a kind of superior pity. We talk of the village preacher as an "obscure" person, or say that a man of gifts is "buried" in a village. There is not a student leaving college who does not think himself too good for the village. Too good for the village? We may all of us well go to school to Christ, to learn the lesson of lowliness; to be taught to be willing to take the small opportunity, and to serve Him in a humble place.

With Christ as Our Teacher

I remember reading about a very prominent minister who one day announced from his pulpit that he would not give a sermon at his week-night service unless at least a hundred were present to hear him. It was not worth his while, he said, to preach to fewer than a hundred. And as I read, I could not help contrasting the conduct of his Master. Souls were of such priceless worth to Him that, if there was not a crowd, He was ready to preach to one. And I thought of Him speaking by night to Nicodemus, and then preaching that wonderful sermon to the Samaritan woman at the well! Christ never despised the small opportunity, and He never despised the humble place. He was "meek and lowly in heart." "He went round about the villages teaching." He cared not for the towns only, but for the villages also. He was a village preacher. And the brave, self-sacrificing men who, in quiet places, often amid great poverty and hardship, are preaching and teaching the Gospel may comfort themselves with this thought—that they are doing today the work the Lord Himself thought it worth His while to do nearly twenty centuries ago.

The Villager's Advantage

"He went round about the villages teaching." When I piece together the Gospel narratives, and supplement what I find here by the fuller account which Matthew gives, I gather that He met in the villages with a very different reception from that which He had experienced in Nazareth. The villager, as a rule, is less sophisticated than the townsman. He is of a simple and more open nature. He finds it easier to believe, and is therefore more susceptible to spiritual influences. And so it comes about that things which are hidden "from the wise and prudent" are often revealed to babes.

Their Ready Response

Take Christ's own preaching. It was in the country Christ won His triumphs; not in the towns. Look at His list of disciples; they are all countrymen, provincials! Not a Pharisee, not a ruler, is to be found amongst them. The people of the capital looked coldly on Jesus; it was in the country that He most readily found responsive souls; and even in countrified Galilee—and the more rural the district the readier the response. So, while Nazareth was scandalized in Him, the villages received Him with open arms. Christ found a glorious field in the villages. "The harvest," He explained to His disciples, as He noted how willing and eager these villagers were to listen—" the harvest truly is plenteous, but the laborers are few" (Matt. 9:37). A ready and responsive country-side Christ saw, waiting to hear the Gospel, and only Himself to preach it.

The Great Opportunity

"Pray ye therefore," He said further to them, "the Lord of the harvest, that He will send forth laborers into His harvest" (v. 38). Christ felt Himself unequal to cope with the great opportunity that offered. He was very much in the same position as our missionaries are today, with new fields opening, endless opportunities offering, and the forces actually available hopelessly inadequate to overtake the work. "Send," they make appeal in every letter, "more laborers." That is exactly how Jesus felt. Personally He could not overtake the work; He could not preach in every village that was willing to hear. He wanted "more laborers"; assistants, helpers, colleagues.

And the Great Need

And it was just this sense of the vastness of the work, and the inability of coping with it alone, that led our Lord to send forth the Twelve on their first mission tour. He multiplied Himself by sending them forth to preach, and so the good news of the Kingdom was carried into many a village and hamlet which otherwise might not have heard it.

"And He called unto Him the Twelve, and began to send them forth by two and two" (v. 7). This sentence sends me back to another in which the first calling of the Twelve is described. In chap. 3:14 I read this, "And He appointed Twelve, that they might be with Him, and that He might send them forth to preach." That was the object Christ had in view in the calling of the Twelve—that in course of time He might send them forth to preach. And now He proceeded to put His project into execution. "He began to send them forth." He had called these twelve men that they might be "with Him." He had invited them to come to school to Himself; and, that they might learn the lessons He had to teach them more thoroughly, He bestowed upon them the inestimable privilege of living in closest intimacy and friendship with Himself. He wanted them to witness His miraculous works, to hear His doctrine of the Kingdom, to behold His glory, to learn from Him how to pray and how to live.

A Mission of Help

But these great privileges were not bestowed upon them for their own sake merely. Christ saw the people as sheep not having a shepherd—all for lack of that Gospel which He had to proclaim. And He had those wandering and stricken people in His mind when He summoned Peter and James and John and the rest to come and live with Him as His friends. "He appointed Twelve that they might be with Him, and that He might send them forth." He bade them come and learn, that in due time they might be fitted to teach. He bade them come and receive, that in due time they might be fitted to impart. He made them His apprentices—shall I say?—that in course of time they might themselves become workmen needing not to be ashamed. He made them His disciples, that in course of time they might become apostles. And that time now seemed to have arrived. "And He called unto Him the Twelve, and began to send them forth by two and two." He began to send them forth to tell what they had heard, to teach what they had learned, to testify what they had seen. They had been listeners up to this point; now Christ sends them forth to make their first attempts as preachers.

The Master's Curriculum for Disciples

To pass, for a moment, from exposition, let me point out that we have here an illustration of the progress through which the Lord Jesus would have every one of His followers pass. First the school, then the field; first learn then teach: first disciples, then apostles. "Learn of Me, for I am meek and lowly in heart," that is the first call. Christ would have us be "with Him," that He may unfold His mind and will to us, that we may learn His purposes and imbibe His Spirit. We cannot teach others unless we have first learned of the Master ourselves; and the longer we have been learning the more competent we are to teach. Some young and eager spirits are eager to skip this "disciple" stage. "I do not want to waste my years in college," one young fellow wrote to me, not long ago. "I want to get out into the work." He forgot that Christ calls His workers to be "with Him," before He sends them forth to preach.

And Its Purpose

But while it is important to remember that we cannot teach unless we have first learned, yet the lesson which we perhaps need to have more clearly brought home to mind and conscience is this— we learn in order to teach; we are made disciples in order that we may become apostles; we are called to be with Him in order that in due course He may send us forth. "Oh, teach me, Lord," we sing in our familiar hymn. And what is the purpose of the prayer? "That I may teach the precious things Thou wouldest impart." That is it; our privileges are all for service; our personal blessings are all meant to serve the common good; what we know of Jesus is meant for the enlightenment of the world.

Questions for Ourselves

Have we ourselves reached this second stage? Many of us have been learners for years; have we become teachers yet? We have been disciples for a lifetime; have we started work as apostles? We have enjoyed the most delightful times with the Master; but have we as yet begun to go forth and preach? Of course, there is no suggestion in all this that we should all turn teachers or preachers in the technical sense; but, short of that, have we, as opportunity is given, begun to tell to others, and to share with others, what we know of Christ?

Witness-bearing and the Qualification for It

I am persuaded that here lies the main reason for the slow progress of the Christian faith—that some Christians have been too content to remain in school all their days, instead of going forth to teach; they have been receivers, not givers, listeners, not tellers. They need to hear our Lord's second command, "Go forth." And if someone tells me that they do not feel fitted for the work of preaching and witnessing, I answer, neither were these twelve. They had very much to learn—you know what blundering scholars they were. But there were certain things they already knew. They knew that the Kingdom of Heaven was at hand; they felt sure that Jesus was about to inaugurate that Kingdom; and they went and preached everywhere that, in view of the approach of the

Kingdom, men should repent. That is what Christ expects of us. We feel, no doubt, that we have a great deal to learn; indeed, while life lasts we shall never finish our learning. But in the meantime we know something. We know that Jesus brings God near. We know that He breaks the power of sin. We know that He imparts peace and harmony into this life. Will you tell of that? Speak of what you know; testify of what you have seen. The multitudes are still as sheep not having a shepherd, all for lack of that knowledge you possess. The world is waiting for it, longing for it, dying for it. The harvest is plenteous, the laborers are few. Pray the Lord of the harvest to send forth more laborers, and offer yourself as one. "Here am I, send me."

The Missionary Enterprise

This sending of the Twelve is the beginning of Christ's great missionary enterprise. You remember Ezekiel's vision of the river (Ezek. 47:1-5)? He saw the river, as he puts it, coming out from under the threshold of the house eastward. At its beginning it was but a tiny trickling stream. You could have turned its course with the hand. But a thousand cubits lower down the stream had grown, and the waters were up to the ankles; and a thousand cubits further on still, the water had grown still further, and reached up to the knees; and a thousand cubits further still, and they were up to the loins; and a thousand further still, and it was a river the prophet could not pass through. For the waters were risen; waters to swim in, a river that could not be passed through. And everything lived wheresoever this river went.

The Beginning of a Great Stream

"And He began to send them forth two by two"; this is the tiny and insignificant beginning of the stream. Six couples of preachers went through the towns and villages of Galilee, saying, "Repent, for the Kingdom of Heaven is at hand." There was nothing to create a stir or to attract notice. But every mission the centuries have known has sprung from this one. This is the tiny seed from which grew Paul's vast labors among the Gentiles of the ancient world; Columba's apostolic labors in Scotland; Francis' labors in Italy; Xavier's devoted toil in the Far East; John Eliot's and David Brainerd's self-sacrificing work amongst the American Indians; William Carey's service in India; John Williams' work in the South Seas; David Livingstone's in Central Africa; Hannington's labors in Uganda; James Chalmers' in New Guinea; the pioneering work of that splendid old man J. G. Paton in the New Hebrides, and the labors of many more of whom time would

fail to tell. The great missionary enterprise began with the sending
forth of these twelve men; but how vast is the multitude of the preachers! It began with the one small sphere of Galilee; but now the heralds
of the Cross have gone into every land. From north to south, from east
to west, preaching the good news of the Kingdom. The tiny trickling
stream of these verses has grown into a great river today; and wherever the river flows it gives life. Thank God, the stream is still flowing,
the waters are still rising, and rise they will until the knowledge of the
Lord shall cover the earth as the waters cover the sea.

A Ministry as Well for the Body as the Soul

We can see how in this first enterprise the ministry to the body
goes hand in hand with the ministry of the soul. One of the most
striking developments of the modern missionary enterprise is the
emphasis laid on medical missionary work. We feel the appeal of
physical suffering in these days more keenly than in any previous
age. And so, side by side with the evangelist, we send the healer.
It is worth while to send the doctor out for the physical good that
he can do. The work of healing sickness, alleviating pain, saving
life, is worth doing for its own sake. But, as a matter of fact and
experience, it is found that, by ministering to the body our medical men get rare opportunities of ministering to the soul as well.
And this development of medical missions is no innovation. We
are but following the best of all precedents. The Master Himself
was Evangelist and Healer all in one. And the first missionaries
were evangelists and healers too. For Jesus not only sent them
forth to preach; He also gave them authority over the unclean spirits, and, as is obvious from the last sentence of the paragraph,
power to cure sickness too.

Missionary Instructions: Companionship

He sent them forth "by two and two"; not singly, but in couples.
That is just an illustration, not simply of the considerateness, but
also of the wisdom of Jesus. "It is not good that the man should be
alone"; it is a principle that has many and various applications.
"Two are better than one." Yes, and two together are better than
two men separate from one another. Two men working individ-
ually are not so good, and cannot accomplish so much, as two men
working in partnership. And this is specially so in Christian work.
There are tasks impossible to the single worker that become fea-
sible when two are working side by side. And more than that. In
face of the discouragements and difficulties inseparable from missionary work, it is essential that there should be companionship,

that each may be strengthening the other's faith in God. And so two and two these men went forth: Peter and John, James and Andrew, Philip and Bartholomew, Matthew and Thomas, and so on. The same wise and excellent rule prevailed in later days; Barnabas and Paul, and later Barnabas and Mark, and Paul and Silas, taking the journeys together. Perhaps, as Dr. Chadwick says, our modern missionaries lose more in energy than is gained in area by neglecting so human a precedent, and forfeiting the special presence vouchsafed to the common worship of two or three.

Two Pregnant Messages

The Master has other instructions to give these first missionaries. At every autumnal gathering we have a valedictory missionary service, and some of our wisest and ablest ministers address a few words of counsel to those who are about to set out for heathen lands. This is our Lord's valedictory address. Think on every clause and line in it, for every clause and every line is pregnant with instruction for life and service today. But I will sum it all up in the two words which, as Dr. Bruce says, give us the soul and marrow of our Christ's farewell speech. These are the two, "Care not," "Fear not." I dare say the disciples felt timid and distrustful, as they set forth to their new toil. They had never parted from Jesus before. It was with these brave and high words Christ sent them forth, "Care not," "Fear not."

"Care Not"

"Care not." That is the essential meaning of these counsels about taking nothing for the journey, no bread, no wallet, no money in the purse. Some commentators tell us that this insistence upon the necessity of going unencumbered is an indication of the urgency of the errand. The Romans called an army's baggage impedimenta—hindrances. And all unnecessary personal luggage would have been so much hindrance in the way of these missionaries. No doubt there is truth in this suggestion. Others again, like Dr. Glover, see in all this a lesson of trust in man. The evangelists are to believe that there are good men in the world, who will provide them with shelter and food in return for the good news they bring. And this also I dare say is true. But primarily and principally the lesson is not of trust in man, but of trust in God. "Care not," says Jesus. For God cares. Take no money in your purse—your Father will provide. Go to your work without anxiety—God is with you, God shall supply all your need.

"Fear Not"

And "Fear not." Mark does not say much about this, but Matthew gives the message in more detail. They were going as sheep in the midst of wolves. They knew how Jesus Himself had been treated; very likely the same treatment would be measured out to them. "Fear not," said Jesus; God will protect, keep, and save you.

Messages Still Spoken and Heard

"Care not." "Fear not." They are still Christ's brave and cheerful words to His workers. "Care not"; your Father cares. "Fear not"; your Father watches. And men have gone forth in simple trust in those brave words of the Lord. When Carey set sail for India, the society that sent him had only £13 in hand—£13! But Carey went. He heard his Master saying, "Care not." Robert Morrison went alone to China. "Do you think you are going to convert those millions of Chinese?" "No," he replied, "but God can." "Fear not." "Care not." They are the Master's words to every Christian disciple. Life is full of anxieties and troubles. "Care not," He says; your Father knoweth. Yes; life is full of haunting terrors, and the worst terror of all waits for us at the last. "Fear not," says our Lord. No one can snatch you out of the Father's hand. Neither death, nor life, nor things present, nor things to come, shall be able to separate us from the love of God, which is in Christ Jesus our Lord (Rom. 8:38,39).

Oh for a simpler faith in the loving, keeping care of God! "Care not," "fear not," Jesus says! And as I hear Him speak I feel I can say back to Him, "I will both lay me down in peace, and sleep: for Thou, Lord, only makest me dwell in safety" (Psa. 4:8).

38
Herod and John the Baptist

"And king Herod heard of him; (for his name was spread abroad:) and he said, That John the Baptist was risen from the dead, and therefore mighty works do shew forth themselves in him. Others said, That it is Elias. And others said, That it is a prophet, or as one of the prophets. But when Herod heard thereof he said, It is John, whom I beheaded: he is risen from the dead. For Herod himself had sent forth and laid hold upon John, and bound him in prison for Herodias' sake, his brother Philip's wife: for he had married her. For John had said unto Herod, It is not lawful for thee to have thy brother's wife. Therefore Herodias had a quarrel against him, and would have killed him; but she could not: For Herod feared John, knowing that he was a just man and an holy, and observed him; and when he heard him, he did many things, and heard him gladly. And when a convenient day was come, that Herod on his birthday made a supper to his lords, high captains, and chief estates of Galilee; And when the daughter of the said Herodias came in, and danced, and pleased Herod and them that sat with him, the king said unto the damsel, Ask of me whatsoever thou wilt, and I will give it thee. And he sware unto her, Whatsoever thou shalt ask of me, I will give it thee, unto the half of my kingdom. And she went forth, and said unto her mother, What shall I ask! And she said, The head of John the Baptist. And she came in straightway with haste unto the king, and asked, saying, I will that thou give me by and by in a charger the head of John the Baptist. And the king was exceeding sorry; yet for his oath's sake, and for their sakes which sat with him, he would not reject her. And immediately the king sent an executioner, and commanded his head to be brought: and he went and beheaded him in the prison, And brought his head in a charger, and gave it to the damsel: and the damsel gave it to her mother. And when his disciples heard of it, they came and took up his corpse, and laid it in a tomb." —Mark 6:14-29.

Good News Spreads

THE MISSION OF the Twelve and the excitement caused by the works of power wrought through their hands (to which we find a reference in the closing sentence of the preceding paragraph) naturally spread abroad the name and fame of Jesus. For we may be sure that the Apostles made it clear to the people, as Peter and John did at a later day, that it was not by their own wisdom, or skill, or power, that they accomplished these wonderful cures, but in the name of "Jesus of Nazareth." And thus all Galilee rang with talk about this Jesus, so that at last it reached the palace and the ears of the King. "King Herod heard thereof."

Amongst the People

The report about Jesus was, I imagine, good news to the mass of the people of Galilee. If any were sick or had dear ones sick, the report about this Man who could cleanse the leper, cast out devils, give sight to the blind, hearing to the deaf, and life to the dead, must have opened a door of hope for them. And, quite apart from sickness, the advent of a One in whom such mighty works manifested themselves must have made the people at large realize that God had come near them. For when they heard of Jesus, they said, "This is Elijah," and others, "He is a prophet even as one of the prophets"—that is to say, as true a prophet as Isaiah or Jeremiah, or Amos or Hosea, or any one of the recognized order of prophets, of whom they boasted, and in whom they took such great pride. They did not, it is true, rise to the great faith that Jesus was Messiah Himself. But the report of His doings filled them with a solemn joy; they felt the Kingdom of God had come near to them.

And Reaches the King

"And King Herod heard thereof"; but it was no good tidings to him. The report about Jesus fell upon him like a clap of doom. It terrified him. It flung him into a perfect panic of fear. When he heard about Jesus and His wonderful works, his knees shook and his face blanched. He saw ghosts, and he gasped out, "John, whom I beheaded—he is risen from the dead!" Thereupon the Evangelist proceeds to tell us why it was that Jesus suggested John, and why it was that the thought of John filled this King Herod's heart with mortal terror.

Well-justified Alarm

It is a ghastly story. You know it well, and I scarcely need repeat it. Herod's shameful and incestuous union with Herodias, his brother Philip's wife; John the Baptist's plain and unvarnished rebuke of the monarch's sin; his consequent imprisonment in the castle of Machaerus; Herod's birthday feast; Salome's degrading and lascivious dance; the King's drunken vow to the girl who had so disgraced her sex; her demand for John the Baptist's head, and the murder of the prophet to glut a woman's hate—these are the steps in the lurid and awful story.

A Haunting Crime

It was a story Herod was for ever trying to forget. For he had been rushed into a crime he loathed by the stronger will of his wicked and cruel wife. He knew John for a just man and a holy. He reverenced him. He heard him gladly. The suggestion that he would ever soak his hands in the Baptist's blood would have shocked Herod. "Is thy servant a dog," he would have said, "that he should do this thing?" But he had done it. Driven by false shame and false pride, and the stronger will of the malignant Herodias, he had done the very thing he loathed. And ever since he had done it he had been trying to forget it. He had been trying to bury the ghastly crime out of sight. But it would not be buried. Here we see the wretched king confronted by his terrible sin. The report about Jesus did this for Herod—it conjured up the ghost of the murdered John. "John!" he cried, and you can almost hear the sentence come in jerky gasps from his ashen lips— "John, whom I beheaded —he is risen from the dead."

An Unwilling Criminal

When I read this sordid and awful story, I can find it in my heart to be sorry for Herod. For this very paragraph, which tells us of his wickedness and shame, is not without indications that under happier home conditions Herod might have been a very different man. His treatment of John the Baptist shows this much—that he was not insusceptible to the appeal of goodness and purity. Herodias hated, with a hate as cruel as the grave, the plain-spoken Baptist. From the first she set herself against him and desired to kill him. But, however pliable Herod might be in the hands of his wicked queen in other respects, he obstinately refused to yield to her wishes in this. "She could not," the Evangelist says, i.e. she could not kill him; "for Herod feared John, knowing that he was a righteous man and a holy, and kept him safe."

The Supremacy of Character

Now all this, as the commentators tell us, is an illustration of the supremacy of character. It is a testimony to the essential greatness of John. The king and his prisoner seemed to have changed places. It is not the prisoner who fears the king, it is the king who fears the prisoner. "Herod feared John, knowing that he was a righteous man and a holy." But if you look at that sentence for a moment, you will begin to see in it more than a tribute to the kingliness of John's character— as the commentators point out —you will begin to see that to a certain extent it is a testimony to Herod *himself*. Whatever Herod became in later days—and it was something terrible enough, seeing that he was able without a qualm to make a mock of Christ Himself—at this stage in his career his case was not hopeless. He was sensitive to goodness. He could feel the appeal of the beauty of holiness.

Herod as a Man

When we think of Herod we are apt to think of him as a man utterly and wholly wicked. The black in our mental picture of him is unrelieved by any single touch of white. But that is not at all the Bible picture of him. Even this paragraph is not all black. There are glimmerings and suggestions of white. There was something in him that responded to John's appeals. He had done much to smother the power of goodness in him and over him by his shameful union with Herodias. But he had not utterly stifled and extirpated it. I have read of a sufferer whose skin, through the effect of some serious malady, had lost all its sensitivity. Hands, limbs, body, all had been deprived of the sense of feeling. Only one tiny spot on the cheek responded to the touch. And by touching that spot friends could communicate with the imprisoned soul within. Herod had hardened his heart and seared his conscience by his sin with Herodias, but there was still a tender spot left, and John touched it. "He was much perplexed; and he heard him gladly." Goodness was making its final struggle in the soul of Herod during those days when he had listened to John. And when, later on, I see the king all eagerness to listen to his prisoner—it looks as if Herod might yet repent and turn to God. Indeed, that might have been the issue of the conflict going on in Herod's soul. But for Herodias' cruel craft, this Herod, who ended by making a mock of Christ, might have repented of his sin, and have taken a place at last amongst those saints, arrayed in the white robes, who stand before the throne of God and of the Lamb.

Herod's Failure

I can very easily believe that John himself had his hopes of the king. I can believe that he may have begun to comfort himself with the thought that his imprisonment was, after all, going to turn out a blessing in disguise; that he had been taken away from his work amongst the multitude in order to bring about the conversion of the king. But the story does not end with a converted king; it ends, as you know, with a murdered prophet. How came it about that the monarch who reverenced John so much, who, indeed, was almost a convert to his teaching, became John's murderer?

Its Causes

Looking at the narrative, I think that the real root reason is to be found in Herod's weak and vacillating will. In a sense Herod was not a deliberately wicked man, but he was a weak man, and, through his weakness, he allowed himself to be swept into this awful wickedness. He is in the New Testament what Ahab is in the Old Testament. Both of them were weak and sensual men. Neither, however, if left to himself, would have steeped his hands in blood. But they both had queens of masterful will. Driven by this stronger will of their queens, both these weak men committed great and awful wickedness.

The King's Irresolution and Timidity

Look at that expression, "He was much perplexed" (v. 20, R.V.). The whole secret of Herod's tragic failure is there. It gives us a picture of a weak and irresolute man. He could not make up his mind what to do. Between the Baptist and his own conscience on the one side, and his wicked queen upon the other, "he was much perplexed." He was torn by conflicting impulses. And so he temporized and procrastinated until that shameful day came when Herodias' cunning trapped him with the crime which in his sober moments he had steadfastly refused to commit. Yes, at the root of Herod's awful and tragic lapse lies his weakness and timidity and cowardice. Herod had not the strength of will to do the right thing in scorn of consequences. He could not rise above what the old Book calls "the fear of men." That was Herod's curse all his life through. He was weak-willed—was swept into crime he abhorred by wicked associates of stronger will than himself.

Herod as a Type

Herod is a type of multitudes still. Timidity, which takes the form of false pride, is accountable for the moral failure of thousands. Herod's story is being repeated every week in all our centers of population. We hear heart-breaking stories of moral lapses, amongst, for example, our young people. I will venture to say that in nine cases out of ten the cause of the failure is not so much wickedness as weakness. They come into the town from country homes. They find themselves amongst evil associates, who laugh at them and make fun of them and dare them. Then, through a false shame and a silly pride, they allow themselves to be swept into sins they loathe. "For the sake of them that sat at meat," in fear of his companions and associates, fear of their scornful comments, Herod became a murderer; and for the same reason men sacrifice their innocence and honor still.

The Will and the Way of Salvation

One condition of salvation is a resolute and steadfast will. I am not so sure that we do not talk too much and depend too much in our religious life about feeling, and too little about "willing." Because after all it is on willing, not feeling, that our salvation depends. That is to say, it costs effort and strong resolutions to enter the straight gate and to tread the narrow way. For men do not slip or glide or drift into it on the flood of some kindly and altogether admirable emotion. Listen: "Agonize to enter in by the strait gate." That is our Lord's warning. If it had depended on emotion, Herod would have been secure, for his feelings were all that could he desired. But he perished for lack of that strength of will which would have set Herodias and Salome and all the courtiers at defiance, and would simply and bravely have done the right. Do you remember John Bunyan's picture of the crowd outside the palace, the moral of which is that a man must be resolute and bold who would be a Christian? Let me remind you of it.

"Then the interpreter took Christian and led him up toward the door of the palace, and behold, at the door stood a great company of men, as desirous to go in, but durst not. There also sat a man at a little distance from the door at a table-side, with a book and his inkhorn before him, to take the name of him who should enter therein. He saw also that in the doorway stood many men in armour to keep it, being resolved to do the men that would enter what hurt and mischief they could. Now was Christian somewhat in a maze. At last, when every man started back for fear of the armed men, Christian saw a man of a very stout countenance come up to the man that sat there to write, saying, 'Set down my name, sir'; the which when he had done he saw the man draw his sword, and put an helmet upon his head, and rush toward the door upon the armed men, who laid upon him with deadly force; but the man, not at all discouraged, fell to cutting and hacking most fiercely. So after he had received and given many wounds to those that attempted to keep him out, he cuts his way through them all, and pressed forward into the palace; at which there was a pleasant voice heard from those that were within, even of those that walked upon the top of the palace, saying, 'Come in, come in; eternal glory thou shalt win.'"

The Strife of Him That Would Enter In

That is but a parable of the effort and courage it needs to force one's way into the Kingdom of God. Herod would fain have entered it, but between him and the gate stood his enemies in the shape of Herodias and his courtiers; and he had not the courage to force his way through them all, and say to the man with the inkhorn, "Set down my name, sir." He drew back into perdition. Between men and the gate of the palace there still stand many fierce foes — our own foolish appetites and sinful lusts, wicked companions and friends; and sometimes our worst foes are those of our own household. It needs courage to break from them all and through them all and say, "Set down my name, sir." "If any man hateth not his own father, and mother, and wife, and children, and brethren, and sisters, yea, and his own life also, he cannot be My disciple." There is some hacking and cutting to be done. But if we have the courage to do it the strength of will to do, to face the world for the right and the truth, we too shall hear the pleasant voice from the palace roof, "Come in, come in; eternal glory thou shalt win."

Herod's Fate

We cannot here pass without thought or comment on *Herod's Fate*. His promise and his failure are in this paragraph. His fate you may read for yourselves in Luke 23, when it is said, "And Herod with his soldiers set Him (i.e. Jesus) at nought, and mocked Him." Contrast these two facts, Herod feared John—Herod set Jesus at nought and mocked Him. In the contrast you see the calamitous issue of sin. This chapter is full of the most tremendous teaching about sin. The way in which it breeds— for all this tragedy sprang from Herod's unholy passion for Herodias. The way in which it haunts the conscience —illustrated in Herod's terror-stricken out-cry. The solemn fact of personal responsibility, "John, whom I beheaded." And the tragic doom of sin, "The wages of sin is death." It is no empty threat. It is no theological bogey. It is the inexorable law. See it working itself out. He feared John; but in a few months he had become so dead to purity and holiness that he could make a mock of Christ.

Sin's Penalty

You remember the sequence Paul traces in Romans 1—lusts of the heart, vile passions, a reprobate mind. It is illustrated in Herod's case. That was his doom, his fate, a reprobate mind. There is no whittling sin away, or minimizing its awful consequence. We make mistakes when we even postpone the punishment of sin to some future judgment. The punishment takes place here and now. The soul that sinneth, it shall die. The worst and most dreadful punishment of sin is the havoc it works in character—the loss of sensitiveness, the seared and hardened conscience. When faith is lost and honor dies, the man is dead. It came to that with Herod. He began by neglecting John; he ended by mocking Christ. He refused to have God in his knowledge, and this was the tragic result. God gave him up to a reprobate mind.

"Let Him Alone"

That is the final and dread issue of persistent neglect of conscience and repeated sin—a deadened conscience, a reprobate mind. The most terrible punishment of sin is that man ceases to feel it is sin. "Ephraim is turned to his idols," says God by the lips of one of His prophets. "Let him alone."

"Let him alone!" What a sentence of dread and doom and despair that is! There is no hope left when God despairs, when the Lord says, "Let him alone." It has not come to that with any one of us. But do not neglect the warning; a neglected conscience is a seared conscience, a life of sin may issue in the reprobate mind. Therefore, if you hear the call, do not put it off or procrastinate. But listen to it and obey it.

If Herod had only listened to John, what a different life-story his might have been! For though he had committed a terrible and awful sin, it was not an unpardonable sin. David, the man after God's own heart, had committed a sin every whit as black. But David, when Nathan rebuked him, and brought his sin to his remembrance, listened, and humbled himself, and repented in dust and ashes, and cried, "Be merciful to me, O God." And Herod might have been where David is; he might have sat at the same King's table as David does; he might have worn the white robe which David does; he might have joined in the song which David sings; he might have been called "a man after God's own heart," as David is—if only he had listened to John and humbled himself and repented. But though he listened and was much perplexed, he failed to repent, and so he makes his bed in hell. With Herod's fate before me, I proclaim the old message, "Now is the accepted time, now is the day of salvation." And I issue the old appeal, "Today, if ye will hear My voice, harden not your hearts."

39
The Return of the Twelve

"And the apostles gathered themselves together unto Jesus, and told Him all things, both what they had done, and what they had taught. And He said unto them, Come ye yourselves apart into a desert place, and rest a while: for there were many coming and going, and they had no leisure so much as to eat. And they departed into a desert place by ship privately. And the people saw them departing, and many knew Him, and ran afoot thither out of all cities, and outwent them, and came together unto Him." —Mark 6:30-33.

Apostles and Disciples

WE MAY ALMOST regard verses 14-29 as an interpolation in the sequence of the narrative. At any rate verse 30 links itself naturally to verse 13. The paragraph that extends from verse 7 to verse 13 tells the story of the sending of the Twelve. This paragraph tells the story of their return.

"And the Apostles gather themselves together unto Jesus" (v. 30). This is the only place in which Mark gives this official title of "Apostles" to the Twelve. But there is a special fitness and appropriateness in its use in this particular connection. For what does the word "Apostle" mean? It means literally, "one who is sent forth; a messenger." Now glance back at verse 7. What do we read? "And He called unto Him the twelve, and began to send them forth by two and two." The men who came back to Jesus were Apostles, because they were men who had been "sent forth" on the errands of the King. But for the rest Mark never applies the title to them, for the simple reason that this is the only instance of "sending forth" of which he tells us. All through the rest of the Gospel they are not Apostles— "men sent forth," messengers, preachers; they are disciples, students, learners. So apparently in Mark's Gospel the title "Apostle" is not used as a title of rank; it is the name of an office, and only when they actually discharged the functions of that office is the title applied to them. "And the Apostles gather themselves together (i.e. from the various towns and villages whither they had gone to preach) unto Jesus; and they told Him all things, whatsoever they had done, and whatsoever they had taught" (v. 30).

The Revision of the Master

The sending forth of the Twelve had been more or less of an experiment. They had by no means reached the end of the disciple stage.
They were far from fully understanding Christ's mind and entering
into His purposes. It was simply the pressure of an urgent need, the
vision of the plenteous harvest waiting for laborers, that induced Jesus
to thrust forth these twelve men, raw and immature as they were, to
try their prentice hands at the work of evangelism. Now the mission
tour is over, and the Twelve are all eagerness to tell their Master how
they got on in their first attempts at preaching; they relate to Him their
experiences; they tell Him "all things, whatsoever they had done, and
whatsoever they had taught."

For their mission had that twofold aspect—they were sent forth
to do something, and to proclaim something. Christ gave them
authority to heal the sick and cast out devils, and He bade them
proclaim whithersoever they went that the Kingdom of Heaven
was at hand. Dr. Host, in his book *Ecclesia*, says that this twofold
function is characteristic of the Apostle. Teaching and healing constituted his double duty. And so now these Apostles, on their
return from their first missionary tour, present their report to Jesus
under these two heads—"they told Him whatsoever they had
done, and whatsoever they had taught." They told Him of the
cures they had wrought, and the sermons they had preached, and
the reception their preaching had met with.

The Full Report

They told Him "all things." They kept nothing back from their
Master. Every little detail of their tour they submitted to Jesus for
His criticism and judgment. I am sure that the Master saw mistakes and blunders in the story of what they had done. Indeed, one
of the Evangelists suggests that He saw and had gently but firmly to rebuke a certain boastfulness they showed in their possession
of miraculous powers. But if they did make mistakes, they took the
very best means of correcting and avoiding them, for they told
Jesus "all things." And somehow, in the mere telling of their story
to Him, they became conscious of what was wrong and faulty in
their work. Whatever was amiss in their service revealed itself in
the presence of Jesus. I do not think that Jesus needed to point out
their mistakes to them, and say, "you blundered here and there."
When they came into touch with Him, when they looked at their
work in the light of His countenance, they instinctively recognized
what it was they had said or done amiss. "They told Him all
things." That was—shall I say?—the Apostolic safeguard. This was

how they discovered their faults and mistakes, and made themselves the great preachers they afterwards became—they told Him all things.

Of Things Done

With the example of these twelve Apostles before us, let me declare the duty and the inestimable advantage of telling Jesus all things. It would be for our eternal profit, if periodically, say, at the close of each day, we reported all our doings to the Lord Jesus Christ. I am persuaded that many people are making the most ghastly mistakes, that, indeed, they are going far towards making wreck and ruin of their lives, all because they do not cultivate this habit of telling Jesus "all things." For there are many things which at present we practice which we should feel constrained for ever to abandon, if we reported them to Jesus Christ. In His presence we should discover their essential unworthiness, not to say wickedness. For things that pass muster by the standards of human society, and seem all right when looked at in the crowd, seem all wrong when we speak about them to Jesus. And so, to save us from poor, base and ignoble living, to save us from those tragic mistakes that lay life waste, I urge you to tell Jesus all things.

The Practice of Recollection

In other words, we must practice what the Roman Catholics call the habit of recollection. "Recollection," according to Faber, "is a double attention which we pay first to God, and then to ourselves." It is the realization of the presence of God, and then the scrutiny in our own hearts and lives in that presence. It is the looking at all things whatsoever we have done in the light of God's countenance. I know all that can be said about morbid and unhealthy introspection. I know that there is danger in introspection, carried to an extreme. But I know also that without introspection, without this practice of looking at every thing in the presence of Jesus, the Christian life is not possible at all. I read of one of the ancient Stoics, that it was part of his spiritual and moral discipline each night quietly to review the events of the day, and to note where he had gone astray, and to make resolutions of amendment. That is the discipline I commend to you; only instead of talking over the day's doings just with ourselves, I invite you to talk them over with Jesus.

How It May Help Us

Do you not think that it would make a great difference to us if we did this? Supposing, for instance, the business man, when the day's work was finished, told Jesus all things whatsoever he had done, submitted his business books to His perusal. Do you not think that possibly he might see a necessity for amending some of his business methods? Supposing a serving man or maid, when the day's work was completed, told Jesus all things whatsoever he or she had done? Do you not think that each might possibly see things to be ashamed of? And supposing you and I, when the day was drawing to its close, reported all its doings to the Lord. Do you not think that we might see evil thoughts, foolish words, petty and malicious gossip, pride and envy and jealousy, of which we ought to repent in dust and ashes? I know that to be made to recognize our own faults and failures is an extremely painful discipline; but it is a very salutary one. To recognize our shortcomings is the first step towards amendment. Repentance is the condition of entrance into the Kingdom of Heaven. And so, in the interests of your own souls, make a habit of telling Jesus "all things" whatsoever you have done.

The Report of Things Said

"All things, whatsoever they had done, and whatsoever they had taught." They told Jesus not only about the cures they had wrought; they told Him also about the sermons they had preached. They submitted their sermons to Him, for criticism and judgment. I am filled with admiration for the wisdom of the Twelve in so doing. What an example to us preachers! I am sometimes tempted to think that we are in danger of submitting our preaching to the judgment of the wrong authorities. I do not think that many are guilty of the baseness of preaching to please their congregation. In spite of the often repeated charge made in our newspapers, and sometimes repeated by those who themselves ought to know better, I do not for one minute believe that we are guilty of the crime of believing one thing and preaching another; of reserving the truth we really accept, and only giving forth what we know congregations like to hear. But I do sometimes think that ministers and preachers go a great deal too much in fear of the Press, and the person who calls himself the "modern thinker." After all, the great concern of a preacher is not whether the reporter approves his words, or whether the man of modern mind says that at last he has found a religion that is rational. The great question is, whether Jesus Christ approves. And it would be our salvation as preachers if we carried our sermons, not into the limelight of public judgment, but into the pure light of the presence of our Lord. We shall never go far astray if we tell Him all things, whatsoever we teach.

Anticipating the Judgment Day

"And they told Him all things, whatsoever they had done, and whatsoever they had taught." Thus they anticipated the Judgment Day. For that is the judgment, when the soul reviews its doings and sayings in the presence of Jesus. The Lord, Paul says, "will both bring to light the hidden things of darkness, and make manifest the counsels of the hearts" (1 Cor. 4:5). "There is nothing hid," said Jesus Himself, "that shall not be manifested; neither was anything kept secret, but that it should come abroad" (Mark 4:22). That is to say, however painful the discipline may be, there is coming a time when we shall have to tell Jesus all things. But what a day it will be, if we have only a record of tragic mistakes and failure to tell! Happy they who deem every day a Judgment Day; who make a practice day by day of telling Jesus all things; who receive His gentle corrections, and find grace to amend their sinful lives! For such the other Judgment Day has no terrors—each man shall receive his praise from God.

The Need of Repose

"They told Him all things." In what conditions were these twelve men, now that they had returned from their tour? They were tired, and they were excited. They were in great need of quiet rest— not simply rest from physical exertion, but quietness for fellowship with their Master, which never failed to soothe and refresh their souls. And Jesus was quick to note their need. "Come ye yourselves apart," He said to these tired and excited men, "into a desert place, and rest a while. For there were many coming and going, and they had no leisure so much as to eat" (v. 31). Mr. David Smith, in his recent *Life of Christ*, finds the reason for this retreat across the lake in Jesus Himself. There was a plot afoot among the people, he suggests, to force Christ's hand, and make Him declare Himself King; and the disciples were privy to it. The ringleaders were intent on the business, and Jesus observed them going to and fro, so eagerly that they had not leisure so much as to eat. And it was to escape this zeal, which was not according to knowledge, that Jesus took Himself and His disciples away from the excitement of Capernaum to the quietness of the uninhabited lake. But, though it is quite likely there was some such excitement as Mr. Smith describes, his version does not tally with the Evangelist's story. It was not for His own sake, but for His disciples' sake that Jesus withdrew to a desert place apart. He was thinking, not of Himself, but of them, and so now I get another illustration of that quality so characteristic of Jesus—His tender consideration for others.

The Tender Consideration of Christ

"Christ pleased not Himself" (Rom. 15:3), the Apostle says. His concern was never for Himself, but for others. He forgot His own great grief and heavy burdens in His compassion for the griefs and burdens of others. "Weep not for Me," He said to the women of Jerusalem, as He toiled along up Calvary's slope with the cross upon His back, "but weep for yourselves, and for your children" (Luke 23:28). Indeed, Christ's life might be summed up from first to last in that little phrase, "for others." For Bethlehem was for others; and Nazareth was for others; the labors of Galilee were for others, and the cross of Calvary was for others. Now, at the right hand of the throne on high, He is still busy interceding for others. And that is what we see here: Jesus forgetting Himself in His tender care for others. He had just received news of the death of His kinsman and forerunner, John the Baptist. In itself that would have been a deep and piercing sorrow. Yet His own unfathomable grief did not make Him insensible to the lesser need of others. He saw these disciples of His tired and excited. He forgot His own sorrow in care for them. "Come ye yourselves apart, and rest a while." "Have this mind in you," says the Apostle, "which was also in Christ Jesus " (Phil. 2:5). It is the unselfish mind. We, too, should think about others and care for others. We are in the footsteps of Jesus when we cultivate

> "A heart at leisure from itself
> To soothe and sympathize."

The Costliness of Service

"Come ye yourselves apart, and rest a while." In that call of Christ I get a hint of the costliness of service. In a sense these twelve men were used to hard work. The majority of them were rough-hewn fishermen. They knew what it was to battle with the gale, to fight grim fights with wind and wave. They knew what it was to labor all through the long dark night. In some respects, I suppose, there is no task physically more wearying and toilsome than the fisherman's. But they had discovered that, toilsome and fatiguing though it was to catch fish, the work of catching men was more toilsome and fatiguing still. The one cost them physical energy and sweat, this latter made a drain upon soul and spirit. Their missionary tour left them spent and worn and exhausted. So spiritual service always costs. It exacts its toil from the man who renders it. There may be easy posts and places in life; I do not know—but there are no easy places in Christ's service. Fishing for souls is an exhausting business. For prayer is no mere form of words glibly repeated; prayer is a wrestle, an agony. Teaching is no easy performance; it is a pouring forth of the soul; it makes a drain upon the vital energies; it costs blood and tears. Think of Jesus Himself; how His teaching drained Him of strength, and left Him spent. Look at Him falling into a sleep in the stern of the boat—a sleep so deep that not even the roar of the storm could wake Him. That is only an illustration of the costliness of service. And these disciples were suffering in their measure from the same weariness and exhaustion. Their preaching tour had cost them nothing in money, but it had made vast demands upon their emotions and sympathies and spiritual energies.

The Provision for Refreshment

"Come ye," said Jesus to these tired men, "yourselves apart into a desert place, and rest a while." Here is our Lord's provision for the refreshing and renewal of these tired men. "Come apart into a desert place, and rest." The body needs periodic rest to recoup and refresh itself. God draws the curtain of night. He gives us the boon of sleep, and in the quiet restfulness of our sleeping hours, Nature repairs the physical losses caused by the labors of the day. And the soul too needs rest. Indeed, by so much as soul work is more costly and exhausting, by so much is the soul's need of rest and quietness the more urgent. And so Christ calls to us still to come aside and rest. The Christian life has a double aspect. It is a life of service, and of communion. Communion that does not end in service is unhealthy, but service without communion is sterile and barren, and in the long run impossible. It is the communion I am anxious about. I am not afraid of lack of activity, but do we give the soul its quiet times? Is our ineffectiveness due to the fact that our spiritual energies are exhausted? We must pay more regard to the soul's quiet times. As the prophet says, "Enter thou into thy chambers, and shut thy doors about thee" (Isa. 26:20). We shall emerge with new stores of power. "They that wait upon the Lord shall renew their strength" (Isa. 40:31).

40
The Feeding of the Five Thousand

"And Jesus, when He came out, saw much people, and was moved with compassion toward them, because they were as sheep not having a shepherd: and He began to teach them many things. And when the day was now far spent, His disciples came unto Him, and said, This is a desert place, and now the time is far passed: Send them away, that they may go into the country round about, and into the villages, and buy themselves bread: for they have nothing to eat. He answered and said unto them, Give ye them to eat. And they say unto Him, Shall we go and buy two hundred pennyworth of bread, and give them to eat? He saith unto them, How many loaves have ye? go and see. And when they knew, they say, Five, and two fishes. And He commanded them to make all sit down by companies upon the green grass. And they sat down in ranks, by hundreds, and by fifties. And when He had taken the five loaves and the two fishes, He looked up to heaven, and blessed, and brake the loaves, and gave them to His disciples to set before them; and the two fishes divided He among them all. And they did all eat, and were filled. And they took up twelve baskets full of the fragments, and of the fishes. And they that did eat of the loaves were about five thousand men."　　　—Mark 6:34-44.

The Search for Retirement

YOU WILL REMEMBER the events that led up to this great wilderness feast. The Apostles had just returned from their first missionary journey, tired and excited by their attempts at preaching. Jesus Himself had been pierced to the quick by the murder of John the Baptist in Machaerus. Both the Master and the disciples were in sore need of quietness and rest—quietness and rest which they could not possibly secure in Capernaum, where it was all bustle and excitement, and where there were so many coming and going that they had no leisure so much as to eat. Jesus accordingly proposed to the disciples that they should escape out of the tumult and excitement of Capernaum, by taking ship and crossing over to the quiet uplands on the other side of the lake. And so, with what privacy they could, they made their way down to the boat, and set sail for a desert place, apparently near the other Bethsaida, known as Bethsaida Julias.

A Baffled Quest

But Jesus was the hero of the hour. As the result of His wonderful works He was the object just now of an intense enthusiasm. The people never allowed Him out of their presence. And so it came to pass that He could not steal away to that quiet place to which He had invited His disciples unobserved. Some eyes were upon Him as He and His, perhaps in the gathering dusk, launched out upon the bosom of the lake. The news soon spread that He was gone, and in their eager enthusiasm the people began to crowd out of Capernaum, and hurried along the shores of the lake in the direction in which they had seen Him go. The number of people who did this is an index to the excitement earned by Christ's teaching and miracles—for all the evangelists agree that there were 5000 men, besides women and children. This vast number of people trudged it along the shore, "running all the way," says Dr. Bruce, with the result that when Jesus and His disciples reached the spot they were aiming for, instead of finding the quiet they desired, they found this excited and eager crowd there waiting for them. "And He came forth and saw a great multitude" (v. 34). And so our Lord's quest for privacy was baffled. The quiet He sought He could not get. In the desert uplands of Bethsaida Julias, just as much as in the crowded streets of Capernaum, the multitude was ever with Him.

The Trial of Interruptions

There is nothing so trying, as Dr. Chadwick says, "as the world's remorseless intrusion upon one's privacy." Supposing that you and I had been in Christ's place. Supposing that we had set out to gain quiet, and, instead of quietness, found a crowd, the very crowd we were trying to avoid. How should we feel? Supposing that you or I were the subject of this paragraph, how would it read: "And He came forth and saw a great multitude"? Yes; what would be the next sentence, if you and I had been the subject of it? Would it read like this: "And He was angry, and would not land. He was sore vexed, and returned back again"? For we get petulant and annoyed when our best-laid plans and cherished purposes are frustrated by the intrusion of other people. When I have promised myself half an hour or an hour's quiet reading—and the very rarity of the opportunity makes it the more welcome when it come—I know how easily and quickly I become impatient, when a ring at the telephone or a knock at the door tells me that I have to surrender my promised quiet to attend to other people's affairs. But how different it was with Jesus! He sorely needed quiet—quiet to talk to His disciples, quiet to talk with God, for His own heart was well-nigh breaking with sorrow. And yet, when He came forth and saw the multitude, and realized that there was after all to be no quiet for Him, there is no suggestion of petulance in His voice, as there was no shade of anger in His soul.

The Lord's Compassion

"And He came forth and saw a great multitude, and He had compassion on them" (v. 34). What an exquisite touch this is! And what a beautiful light it throws on the character of Jesus! It is just another illustration of that wonderful love that never sought its own, but always forgot its own needs and worries and sorrows in sympathy and care for the burdens and sorrows of other people. That was the feeling the sight of the crowd stirred in Jesus—not annoyance or vexation, but a deep compassion.

The Shepherdless Multitude

And this was what excited His compassion— "because they were as sheep not having a shepherd" (v. 34). Just think of the figure for a moment. You can scarcely conceive of a more pitiable object than an Eastern sheep without a shepherd to care for it. For, to begin with, pasture grounds were not easily found. It was part of the shepherd's duty to lead his flock into the green pastures and by the still waters. But a shepherdless sheep in a land of such partial and scanty pasturage might very easily perish for lack of sustenance. Then, in the second place, not only was pasturage scanty, but wild beasts were plentiful. A shepherdless sheep might easily fall victim to some prowling savage beast. And when Jesus looked out on that vast crowd, His heart was stirred within Him, for to Him they seemed just like poor shepherdless sheep. He saw before Him starving souls. You remember John Milton's line, "The hungry sheep look up, and are not fed." That is exactly how it was with these people. They had their pastors and teachers. But these never led them into the green pastures of God's Word or broke to them the bread of life. They talked to them about the traditions of the elders, and neglected mercy and truth. And so the people's souls were well-nigh perished with hunger. But He saw not only famishing souls—He saw also wandering souls, lost souls, souls in very imminent peril, because of those enemies that lie in wait to destroy. For scribes and elders were but blind leaders of the blind, and did nothing to guide their feet into ways of godliness and truth. He saw souls lost and out of the way, because there was no one to guide them and care for them. And as He looked at this great multitude of shepherdless sheep, famished and lost, the Lord had compassion on them and "began to teach them many things." "He began to teach them many things," i.e. He Himself shepherded these shepherdless souls. "He taught them many things." He led them into the green pastures of the Word. He spoke to them those words which were spirit and life. And how eagerly they listened! "The common people heard Him gladly." The hungry and famished sheep were being fed.

And the Good Shepherd

But He not only fed the hungry, He went after the wandering and the lost. He had always some word of hope and entreaty and appeal for the sinner. He followed them out into the wilderness of their sin. And He rescued many. Matthew the publican, the woman who was a sinner, Zacchaeus, the Samaritan woman— these are just specimens of lost sheep whom Jesus brought back into the safety of the fold. "And He taught them many things." Tired and weary though He was, He went on teaching the whole day. He spent Himself in the work. It was not a mistake; nor is it for us. It is worth any sacrifice to feed a fainting soul, to save a lost soul. It is worth our while to become all things to all men, if by all means we can save some.

The Marvelous Meal

But Jesus did more than teach them that day. He fed them too. He provided a meal out there in the wilderness for this vast crowd, and provided so bountifully that not only did all eat and were filled, but there were gathered up of broken fragments after the feast was done twelve baskets full. Now, avoiding more familiar ground, let me call your attention to a point that perhaps is not often thought about by us; I mean the motive of the miracle. For, as Dr. A. B. Bruce points out, this miracle appears to be a miracle without a sufficient reason. It cannot be said to have been urgently called for by the necessities of the multitude. There is that difference between the feeding of the four thousand and the feeding of the five thousand. The feeding of the four thousand was an act of, shall I say, necessity? The multitude had been with Jesus three days, and had nothing to eat, and if He had sent them away fasting, they would have fainted by the way, for some of them had come from far. But there was no such necessity in the case of the feeding of the five thousand. The people had only been with Him a few hours. There were villages near by, where, as the disciples suggested, the people could buy for themselves. Or, if worst came to worst, the disciples had sufficient money in the common purse to buy some £40 of bread; so that at any rate every one could have a little. There was clearly no necessity for the miracle. Why, then, did our Lord perform it? For, as Mr. David Smith puts it, it was never His wont to exert His miraculous power unless it was needed, and there was no other way.

A Foreshadowing of the Cross and Passion

It is not enough to answer that it did not need dire necessity to stir our Lord's compassion into exercise. As a matter of fact, except in this case He was a severe economist in the exercise of power. What, then, is the reason for this divergence? I think that Mr. David Smith and Dr. Bruce suggest to us the right answer. The real explanation of the miracle is to be found in the great discourse that in the Fourth Gospel succeeds it (John 6). That discourse on the bread of life, and on eating the flesh and drinking the blood of the Son of Man, has always been considered to throw light upon the sacrament of the Lord's Supper. But at its delivery it was a discourse on this miraculous feast. Its applicability also to the Last Supper is due to this fact—that this desert meal in a very deep and real fashion foreshadowed the Communion Feast of the Upper Room.

Let us call to mind again the mental and spiritual condition of our Lord on the day on which the miracle took place. He had just heard of the death of John the Baptist. And the news of the tragic end of His forerunner had made Him realize afresh that He too was marching straight to a cruel death. The cross rose stark and naked and cruel before His vision. And His soul was sore troubled within Him. It was because the thought of His own great sacrifice was filling His mind; it was because He was realizing with fresh vividness that He could only save the world by giving Himself for it, that He performed this miracle. It was an anticipation of that other feast, when He took the bread, and blessed and brake, and gave to the Twelve in the Upper Room, and it was meant to teach exactly the same lesson.

The succeeding discourse shows that all this was in Jesus' mind. And there is a little touch in John's account of the miracle itself that points the same way. John gives a note of time, "The passover was at hand" (John 6:4). Now that is not a note of time simply. It is meant as a clue to the meaning of the whole incident. This is how Dr. Bruce puts it: "It was Passover time, and Jesus was thinking of it, though He went not up to the feast that season." He thought of the paschal lamb, and how He, the true Paschal Lamb, would soon be slain for the life of the world; and He gave expression to these thoughts that were in His soul in the incident we are considering. Yes, this feast was prophetic of our Lord's cross and passion. By it He said to the multitudes, "I, the Son of God, am the Bread of life. What this bread which I break and give you is to your bodies that I am to your souls." "Except ye eat the flesh of the Son of Man and drink His blood, ye have not life in you" (John 6:53). If any man eat of this bread, he shall live for ever; and the bread that I will give is My flesh, which I will give for the life of the world" (John 6:51).

A Sifting Incident

By the very fact that the feast had this mystical and sacramental significance, it became a means of testing and sifting that vast crowd that participated in it. There were some casually minded people who saw in the feast nothing but bread and fish, and in Jesus no more than one who could minister to their material needs. The feast stirred their casual and worldly ambitions, and they were all for making Christ King instead of Herod. They saw no hint of its spiritual meaning. They discerned not the Lord's body. But there were some, just a few, who saw its deeper meaning, and who welcomed it as a sign and seal of the Savior's saving grace. The next day the sifting became visible. For when Jesus explained it all, and talked to them about eating His flesh and drinking His blood, many of them "went back, and walked no more with Him" (John 6:66). And the abandonment of this materialistic and casual crowd left Jesus with just the few who were in spiritual sympathy with Him. "Will ye also go away?" He said to His disciples. "Lord," asked Peter, "to whom shall we go? Thou hast the words of eternal life" (v. 68). That is the significance of this volunteered miracle. It is an anticipation of the Last Supper. It is a foreshadowing of the cross. The broken bread was just the sign and symbol of Christ's body broken and given for the life of the world.

And now, out of the many points in the narrative of the miracle itself that suggest themselves for our notice, I mean to confine myself to just one.

The Multiplication of Resources

"Give ye them to eat," said Jesus to His disciples, and pointed to the vast crowd before them. And the disciples were staggered by the command. It would take at least £40 worth of bread, they protest, to feed that host. "How many loaves have ye?" said Jesus. And they come back and say, "Five, and two fishes." And without sending to Bethsaida for the £40 worth of bread, He bids them feed the crowd with the scanty provision they had. Five loaves and two fishes, and a crowd of 5000 men to be fed! It looked absurd, did it not? But, after Christ had blessed them, those loaves and fishes multiplied in the giving, so that all had enough, and there were twelve baskets full of fragments left over; 5000 men fed on those loaves and fishes, and more was left at the end than there was at the beginning.

Duty Not Measured by Human Ability

Bushnell has a great sermon on that phrase, "Give ye them to eat," which he entitled, "Duty not measured by Ability." Christ is always bidding us do impossibilities. He commands us to do things which are quite obviously beyond our power. But the marvel is, they get done. "Give ye them to eat"; it sounded foolish, but it was done. No; "duty is not measured by ability." Christ can empower us to do the seemingly impossible things. But there is another word also to be added. Duty is not measured by ability, but ability is not measured by the sum-total of our resources. It was not with five loaves and two fishes that the disciples fed the crowd, but with five loaves and two fishes blessed and multiplied by Christ.

The Power Still with Us

The blessing and multiplying Christ is with us still, ready to make our scanty resources equal to any task to which He summons us. There are no impossibilities to men or churches, however weak, who have with them the blessing and multiplying Christ. We have giant tasks confronting us—unbelief and sin at home, the vast millions of paganism abroad; and we sometimes compare our resources with the tasks, and we grow faint-hearted and despairing sometimes. But why should we? We have the blessing and multiplying Christ.

When the modern missionary movement started with William Carey and £13, it did look absurd, did it not? No wonder sceptics laughed. But look at what has actually happened. The movement so begun bids fair to evangelize the world. Christ multiplied our poor loaves and fishes. Let us have faith in our Lord. Let us trust His power. There are no tasks impossible to us. "With three shillings Theresa can do nothing; but with Jesus and three shillings there is nothing Theresa cannot do." And let us bring our own poor resources for Him to bless and multiply— small gifts, scarcely the one talent. But in His hands what may they not accomplish! He may do much with you and me. For all through the ages we have been using weak instruments to do impossible things. "God hath chosen the foolish things of the world, to confound the wise; and God hath chosen the weak things of the world, to confound the things which are mighty" (1 Cor. 1:27).

41
The Storm

"And straightway He constrained His disciples to get into the ship, and to go to the other side before unto Bethsaida, while He sent away the people. And when He had sent them away, He departed into a mountain to pray. And when even was come, the ship was in the midst of the sea, and He alone on the land. And He saw them toiling in rowing; for the wind was contrary unto them; and about the fourth watch of the night He cometh unto them, walking upon the sea, and would have passed by them. But when they saw Him walking upon the sea, they supposed it had been a spirit, and cried out: For they all saw Him, and were troubled. And immediately He talked with them, and saith unto them, Be of good cheer; it is I; be not afraid. And He went up unto them into the ship; and the wind ceased: and they were sore amazed in themselves beyond measure, and wondered. For they considered not the miracle of the loaves: for their heart was hardened." —Mark 6:45-52.

The Change of Plan

AND "STRAIGHTWAY," THAT IS, as soon as ever the great feast was over, "He constrained His disciples to enter into the boat" (v. 45). Now why did our Lord do this? It seems a complete reversal of all His plans. He had Himself invited His disciples to cross over with Him to this spot, in order that they might have a little respite from toil, and opportunity to talk quietly together over their preaching experiences. Why, then, did He send them away? The natural and obvious thing would have been for Jesus to dismiss the multitude, and then for Him and the Twelve to enjoy the quietness they had come to seek. And it is quite clear the disciples did not want to go. Christ had to exercise pressure, to exert His authority. "Straightway He constrained His disciples to enter into the boat." What is the reason for this seemingly contradictory action of Jesus?

Its Cause

The reason may be found in a sentence in John's account. "Jesus therefore perceived that they would come and take Him by force, to make Him a King" (John 6:15). That explains everything. The miracle of the great feast had stirred the people to a wild and dangerous enthusiasm. Herod's castle was not very far off and they were for marching on to it, deposing that blood-stained monarch, and installing Christ as King in his stead. Even the disciples were infected with the same spirit. Their dreams still were of thrones and an earthly dominion. They were quite ready to join hands with these excited but worldly-minded enthusiasts from Capernaum, and inaugurate there and then a political revolution. They were very far from understanding that Christ's Kingdom was not of this world, and that He was marching not to a crown, but a cross. It was to get them out of this excited atmosphere, and to dissipate the carnal hopes that they had already begun to cherish, that Christ constrained, compelled, forced the disciples to go before Him unto the other side, to Bethsaida.

Its Reception

They went unwillingly. I should not be surprised to hear that they went resentfully. It must have seemed to them like throwing the chance of a life-time away. Here was the crowd ready to follow Him anywhere, and to risk everything for Him. Why did He not seize His opportunity, and win the promised throne? Perhaps the beginning of Judas' treachery dates back to this night. What was the use of following a Master who would not take the kingdom when it was within His grasp? It was all a mystery and a folly to these disciples. Christ's ways were not their ways, nor His thoughts their thoughts. They were a discontented, sullen company, as Christ constrained them to enter into the boat and to go before Him unto the other side.

The Master's Constraint

Does it not happen sometimes still that Christ constrains us to walk along paths which, left to ourselves, we should never dream of taking? Does He not sometimes constrain us to walk the way of suffering, to enter the wilderness of temptation, to face tempests of trial? I wonder sometimes whether St Paul wanted to take that last journey to Jerusalem. Friends tried to dissuade him. He himself knew that bonds and imprisonment awaited him. Still, on he went. And the reason for it was, he was under constraint, he was "bound in the spirit!" When Christ constrains us, let us implicitly obey. Even though we cannot understand His reason, let us obey. Even though we see it means trouble and distress, let us obey. After events will justify our obedience, for they will show our Lord knew best; Paul never regretted that, "bound in the spirit," he set his face to go to Jerusalem. All the troubles that befell him as the result of that journey turned out in the long run for the furtherance of the Gospel. Nor shall we ever regret our obedience. Christ's ways are love.

> "Though they transcend
> Our feeble range of sight,
> They wind through darkness to their end,
> In everlasting light."

The Praying Christ

"He constrained His disciples to enter into the boat, and to go before Him unto the other side" (v. 43), but He Himself, after He had taken leave of the multitude, "departed into the mountain to pray" (v. 46). You will have remarked how that Jesus met every crisis of His life by prayer. He was at a great crisis—perhaps the supreme crisis— of His life just now. At the moment He was the popular hero; on the morrow He was going to destroy His popularity and deliberately choose to become the despised and rejected of men. It does not need any great subtlety to see the crisis which confronted Jesus now.

In the Face of Temptation

We sometimes make the mistake of thinking that the temptations of Jesus were concentrated into those forty days He spent in the wilderness. But they were not. As if, indeed, to guard us against forming any such mistaken notion, the Evangelist tells us that the devil only departed from Him "for a season" (Luke 4:13). For a season! He returned again and again to the assault. He returned to the assault on the day of the feeding of the 5000. You remember that the second temptation wherewith he assailed the soul of Christ in the wilderness was that of the offer of the kingdoms of the world and the glory of them, if Jesus would only fall down and worship him. A short cut to the power that had been promised Him—a short cut that would avoid the garden and the cross; that was the bait Satan held out before the mind of Jesus.

It was with precisely the same temptation he assailed Him now. The people wanted to come and take Jesus by force and make Him King. Power was in His grasp. The kingdom, in the earthly sense, was being thrust upon Him, "all the Kingdoms of the earth, and the glory of them." The dazzling offer was being pressed upon Him afresh. We do no honor to our Master by saying this temptation could have had no sort of appeal to Him. It could. It did. Here was an opportunity of securing at once many things on which He had set His heart. His very passion for doing good lent force to the temptation. And, besides, it promised escape from so much. Yes, Jesus felt it. It was just because He felt it so much that He departed into the mountains to pray. And it was wrestling, agonizing prayer in which our Lord engaged that night. He faced the issues. A throne without trouble, or rejection, shame and death—the world's way, or God's way. He anticipated the agony of the garden on the hill top that night. But He won His fight.

The Victory Won

Once again the devil had to depart foiled and beaten. Christ rejected the glittering offer of the crown, and deliberately chose the Via Dolorosa of the cross. "The cup which the Father hath given Me, shall I not drink it"'(John 18:11)? And the very next day He let the crowd know that, if they were thinking of a throne, He Himself was thinking of a cross. He spoke to them of sacrifice and death. "The bread which I will give is My flesh, which I will give for the life of the world" (John 6:51). It shattered His popularity on the instant. "Upon this many of His disciples went back, and walked no more with Him" (John 6:66). He became from this time onward "the despised and rejected of men."

The Struggling Disciples

But while the Master was fighting out His great fight on the summit of the hill, the disciples were having a great struggle for life against the fury of wind and wave. The Lake of Galilee is notorious for the suddenness of its storms. What is a placid smiling lake one hour may be a seething, furious cauldron the next. One of these wild and sudden tempests overtook the disciples on this particular night. They had launched their boat about sunset; but they had not gone very far, not more than halfway across, when they found themselves in the clutches of the gale. With that gale they fought hour after hour. Not until the fourth watch did help come to them; that is to say, not until towards daybreak—between three and four o'clock in the morning. For all those weary hours the disciples only barely held their own against wind and wave. And as hour after hour passed, and hope began to give place to despair, it may be that they thought hard things of Jesus. Why had He constrained them to get into the boat? If He had only allowed them to remain with Him, as they wished, they would all have been safe and sound on the shore. Why, if He felt they ought to cross over, had not He Himself come with them? Some such thoughts, I have no doubt, passed through the minds of the disciples; possibly even some such remarks they may, in the bitterness of their souls, have made one to another. When troubles assail us it is hard not to throw the blame on God. We are all tempted to murmur and complain. We can understand Job's wife when, embittered by the trouble, she said, "Renounce God, and die" (Job 2:9, R.V.).

The Watchful Master

Yet the disciples were not the neglected and forgotten people they bitterly imagined themselves to be. Look at verse 47: "And when even was come, the boat was in the midst of the sea, and He alone on the land." The boat on the sea, Jesus on the hill; the disciples in the storm, Jesus in God's secret place. They are far apart. There seems to be no connection between them. But read on: "And seeing them distressed in rowing, . . . about the fourth watch of the night He cometh unto them" (v. 48). There was a very close and intimate connection after all. Jesus on the hill was watching His disciples on the sea. The disciples on the sea were safe, because Jesus was watching on the hill. Let me give you almost a companion picture. Down in the valley Israel and Amalek had met in the clash and shock of battle. Away yonder on the hill there was an old man, with his hands uplifted in prayer. They stand far apart. There seems to be no connection between them. But as a matter of fact the connection was most close and intimate. Moses on the hill was watching the course of battle in the plain. Israel down in the valley proved victorious because Moses held up his hands in prayer for them on the hill. And so now, Jesus was watching the disciples in their struggles, and seeing them distressed in rowing, "about the fourth watch of the night He cometh unto them, walking on the sea" (v. 48).

His Abiding Care for His Own

Here is a truth of quite infinite comfort; Jesus sees, and Jesus knows. We are often tempted, as these disciples were, when the storms of trouble buffet us and press heavily upon us, to think that our Savior does not see, and cannot care. If He saw and cared, He would surely hasten to our help. We forget that the very storm may have its work to do; we forget that whom the Lord loveth He chasteneth; we forget that in battling against storms we knit thews and sinews of strength in our souls. And so we cry that our way is hid from the Lord, and our judgment is passed over by our God. But that is a faithless cry. Our way is not hidden from Him. Our judgment is not passed over by Him. He sees, and He cares. And though because He sees it may be well for us He delays His coming, you may depend upon it that at the right hour He will come to our aid. Seeing them distressed, He came to them. Their extremity was His opportunity. He would not allow them to be tried more than they were able. Seeing them distressed, He came to them, and the wind ceased. And so He will come to us and bring us deliverance. "He shall bring forth thy righteousness as the light, and thy judgment as the noon-day" (Psalm 37:6).

> "Through waves and clouds and storms,
> He gently clears thy way;
> Wait thou His time, so shall this night
> Soon end in joyous day."

The Lesson to Faith

All the commentators agree that this miracle, like the last, was symbolic of spiritual truth. Mr. David Smith, for instance, thinks that, as the feeding of the 5000 with the broken bread was symbolic of Christ's death, the breaking of His body to give bread to the world, so this miracle, with its story of Christ's walking upon the water, was symbolic and prophetic of the Resurrection, when Christ would be possessed of a body raised above the laws which govern these earthly and material bodies of ours. The suggestion seems to me a little far-fetched. But I can see another truth, which I am quite sure this incident was meant to teach. It was meant to impress upon the disciples this fact—that they were in Christ's keeping, even when physically He was absent from them. I do not think they would have feared the tempest very much, if Jesus had been with them. For after the great experience of the previous storm recorded for us in chap. 4, they must have felt that "with Christ in the vessel," as our old hymn puts it, they could "smile at the storm." The trouble on this occasion was—as John's account explicitly states—"it was now dark, and Jesus was not come to them" (John 6:17). The lesson they needed to learn was, that they were just as much in His keeping when He was hidden from their eyes as they were when He was with them in the boat.

Whether Absent or Present

That was the great lesson this incident taught them. In a few months Jesus would be leaving them altogether. They would have Him no more for their daily companion. They would have to face their difficulties and temptations apparently alone. But Jesus assured them that though their eyes could not see Him He would yet be with them always unto the end of the world. With them always! And they believed the promise. They remembered how on this night of storm and peril the unseen Christ was watching over them and guarding them. And so they went to their work, and braved their manifold dangers with the joyful faith that their Lord was with them, and was keeping them, and that nothing could separate them from the love of God which was in Christ Jesus their Lord. Even so He is with us always. Our eyes have never seen Him: our hands have never touched Him; but He is with us always. We are safe in His keeping. No one can pluck us out of His hand.

The Misunderstood Christ

Let us notice, however, the reception the disciples gave to Jesus when He did appear to their rescue. When they saw Him walking on the sea, they supposed that it was an apparition, and they cried out, for they were troubled. In their terror they did not recognize Jesus, and so they were afraid of Him. It is always because men do not know Christ, because they do not recognize Him, that they fear Him and reject Him. It is always some unreal Christ, some caricature Christ, whom men repudiate and renounce. The real Christ is never unwelcome. When the Lord saw the disciples' panic He said, "Be of good cheer: it is I; be not afraid " (v. 50). And when they heard His voice, when they heard Him speak for Himself, they were glad enough to welcome Him into their boat. When Christ is allowed to speak for Himself men will gladly receive Him. Only let them hear Him who spake as never man spake, and they will gladly welcome Him.

The Slow Scholars

And when they received Jesus, the wind ceased, and they were sore amazed in themselves, "for," says the evangelist, commenting upon this amazement, "they understood not concerning the loaves, but their heart was hardened" (vv. 51, 52). Why should they have been amazed? Had not Christ demonstrated His power only the day before? The amazement of the disciples was evidence of the hardness of their hearts and their slowness to believe. They were poor scholars. The lesson of the previous day had been practically in vain. Are we, too, not slow scholars? Is it not a fact that we, too, fail to understand? Are not our hearts often hardened? Ought not the marvelous deliverance of past days teach us to expect great deliverances for all the days to come? Our panics of fear, our transports of surprise, are alike evidences of weak faith. Let the great things which our Lord has done for us have their due effect upon us, and teach us to ask great things of God, and to expect great things from God.

42
The Things That Defile

"And when they had passed over, they came into the land of Gennesaret, and drew to the shore. And when they were come out of the ship, straightway they knew Him, And ran through that whole region round about, and began to carry about in beds those that were sick, where they heard He was. And whithersoever He entered, into villages, or cities, or country, they laid the sick in the streets, and besought Him that they might touch if it were but the border of His garment: and as many as touched Him were made whole. Then came together unto Him the Pharisees, and certain of the scribes, which came from Jerusalem. And when they saw some of His disciples eat bread with defiled, that is to say, with unwashen, hands, they found fault. For the Pharisees, and all the Jews, except they wash their hands oft, eat not, holding the tradition of the elders. And when they come from the market, except they wash they eat not. And many other things there be, which they have received to hold, as the washing of cups, and pots, brasen vessels, and of tables. Then the Pharisees and scribes asked Him, Why walk not Thy disciples according to the tradition of the elders, but eat bread with unwashen hands? He answered and said unto them, Well hath Esaias prophesied of you hypocrites, as it is written, This people honoreth Me with their lips, but their heart is far from Me. Howbeit in vain do they worship Me, teaching for doctrines the commandments of men. For laying aside the commandment of God, ye hold the tradition of men, as the washing of pots and cups: and many other such like things ye do. And He said unto them, Full well ye reject the commandment of God, that ye may keep your own tradition. For Moses said, Honor thy father and thy mother; and, Whoso curseth father or mother, let him die the death: But ye say, If a man shall say to his father or mother, It is Corban, that is to say, a gift, by whatsoever thou might eat be profited by me; he shall be free. And ye suffer Him no more to do ought for his father or his mother; Making the word of God of none effect through your tradition, which ye have delivered: and many such like things do ye. And when He had called all the people unto Him, He said unto them, Hearken unto Me every one of you, and understand: There is nothing from without a man, that entering into him can defile him: but the things which come out of him, those are they that defile the man. If any man have ears to hear, let him hear. And when He was entered into the house from the people, His disciples asked Him concerning the parable. And He saith unto them, Are ye so without understanding also? Do ye not perceive, that whatsoever thing from without *entereth into the man, it cannot defile him; Because it entereth not into his heart, but into the belly, and goeth out into the draught, purging all meats? And He said, That which cometh out of the man, that defileth the man. For from within, out of the heart of men, proceed evil thoughts, adulteries, fornications, murders, thefts, covetousness, wickedness, deceit, lasciviousness, an evil eye, blasphemy, pride, foolishness: All these evil things come from within, and defile the man."* —Mark 6:53–7:23.

The Lapsed Multitude

THE BRIEF VERSES at the close of chapter 6 form a connecting link between the wonderful story of the walking upon the sea and that of our Lord's controversy with the Pharisees about the washing of hands. We know as a matter of fact that this incident did not follow immediately upon the miracle. For John tells us that on the day following the night of storm Jesus preached the wonderful sermon in which He announced Himself to be the Bread of life, and said that only by eating His flesh and drinking His blood could men gain eternal life. The result of that sermon was that Christ's popularity was shattered, and the multitudes who up to this point had been enthusiastic in His cause "went back, and walked no more with Him" (John 6:66). Indeed, Christ found Himself practically reduced to His twelve disciples as the only followers in whose devotion He could trust, and upon whose loyalty He could rely. After the crisis He appears to have left Capernaum, and visited Gennesaret.

And Their Eagerness for Material Benefits

But though the people had turned their backs on His teaching, they had by no means lost faith in His power. So His coming to Gennesaret converted the place into a kind of field hospital; for the people "ran round about that whole region, and began to carry about on their beds those that were sick, where they heard He was. And wheresoever He entered into villages, or into cities, or into the country, they laid the sick in the market-places, and besought Him that they might touch if it were but the border of His garment: and as many as touched Him were made whole" (Mark 6:55, 56). You notice that, if these people were not prepared to accept the spiritual truths Christ taught, they were only too eager to profit by the material blessings He bestowed. If they were not ready to take upon their necks His easy yoke, they were quite ready to fly to Him to get healing for their sicknesses and cure for their diseases. It is a curious phenomenon, this repudiation of Christ's authority, combined with willingness to make a convenience of Him. But it is by no means a rare phenomenon. There are plenty of people who refuse to obey Christ, and still fly to Him to help them in their troubles. There are plenty of people who turn their backs on Him when He speaks to them about eating His flesh and drinking His blood, who yet appeal to Him when they are in distress. This making a convenience of Christ—wanting His gifts, but not wanting Him—is a pitiful business.

The Breadth of Christ's Love

But the marvel is that Christ responds to the cry even of those who have refused to obey Him. "He is kind unto the unthankful and to the evil" (Luke 6:35). For see what happened in this case. These people were amongst those who "went back, and walked no more with Him." And yet, when they came seeking Christ's help, this is what I read, "As many as touched Him were made whole" (v. 56). He did not withhold His help because they had refused their obedience. "As many as touched Him were made whole." And He is the same compassionate and loving Christ still. We are often unthankful and disobedient. But when trouble drives us to Him, He does not cast our unthankfulness and disobedience in our teeth. He hurries to us with help. As the poet once wrote:

> "Unwearied in forgiveness still,
> His heart can only love."

Hostility at Work

Now it was about Passover time, as John tells us, that the miracle of the feeding of the 5000, and the incident of the storm, and the subsequent crisis amongst Christ's followers took place. Perhaps, as Mr. David Smith suggests, the rulers had expected that He would come up to Jerusalem for the feast, and that they would be able to compass His overthrow. Disappointed in this, they seem to have sent down from Jerusalem a deputation of Scribes and Pharisees, to co-operate with the local authorities of Capernaum in scrutinizing the actions of Christ—lying in wait for opportunities of bringing Him to book.

The Charge against Jesus

It was not very long before they found ground for complaint. As in their previous accusation against Him with reference to the Sabbath, it was apparently the conduct of the disciples, rather than that of Jesus Himself, that was at fault. But probably they argued—and they were perfectly right in so arguing—that the conduct of the disciples in a measure reflected the teaching of their Master, and that, if they neglected a certain ritual observance, it was because Jesus had made them feel that the observance in question was trivial and unimportant. Now the particular thing that scandalized these spying Pharisees and Scribes was the fact that the disciples ate bread with defiled—i.e. unwashen hands. And then Mark proceeds to explain to the Gentile readers how it was that a trumpery omission of this kind could be construed into a mortal offense. "For," he says, "the Pharisees, and all the Jews, except they wash their hands diligently, eat not, holding the tradition of the elders: and when they come from the market-place, except they wash themselves, they eat not: and many other things there be, which they have received to hold, washings of cups, and pots, and brasen vessels" (vv. 3, 4).

The Law and Tradition

Moses had, as Dr. Glover says, very freely commanded washing. Partly for sanitary reasons, and partly also to emphasize the separateness of the chosen race, the Law required ablution on certain occasions. But these occasions, the "tradition of the elders" had indefinitely multiplied. They not only washed in cases of actual defilement, as Moses commanded; but they washed, for fear of possible and unconscious defilement. And so, for instance, as Mark here mentions, when they came home from market they washed, lest in the market they should have contracted defilement by unconscious contact with a Gentile. And a multitude of similar puerile rules tradition formulated, until life became a veritable slavery. And any breach of these rules was counted a heinous sin, to be punished by excommunication. This was the charge these Scribes and Pharisees brought against the disciples. "Why walk not Thy disciples according to the tradition of the elders, but eat their bread with defiled hands?" (v. 5). They had committed the monstrous crime of breaking one of the multitudinous trumpery rules with which Rabbinism had burdened and encumbered human life.

The Charge Met

What had Jesus Christ to say in answer to this charge? If it would be right to use the epithet "scornful" of Jesus, I believe it would be right to use it of Him here. There is a kind of splendid scorn of the blind folly that could exalt the washing of the hands into an article of religion. His answer to the charge is to brand those who made it as hypocrites. "Well did Isaiah prophesy of you hypocrites." And what is a hypocrite? Well, literally, he is a man who plays a part on the stage. That was what these Scribes and Pharisees, with their insistence upon petty and trumpery rules, were—mere play-actors, men who wore a mask of religion. They paid outward deference to God, but their hearts were far from Him. What they had was not really a religion, but a ritual; and, as Isaiah reminded the Jews long before, you may have the ritual without the religion. "To what purpose is the multitude of your sacrifices unto Me? saith the Lord. . . . Your new moons and your appointed feasts My soul hateth; . . . I am weary to bear them" (Isa. 1:11, 14). It was a case of ritual without religion. It was the publican, and not the Pharisee who boasted of his punctiliousness in the observance of religious duties, who went down to his house justified. God had no pleasure in the Pharisee and his prayers. They meant ritual without religion.

Ritual without Religion
It was so in the case of these Scribes and Pharisees in our paragraph. They were scrupulous about ablutions, they held up their hands in pious horror at the bare thought of eating bread with unwashen hands, but they were careless about mercy and love and truth. Jesus calls them "hypocrites"—mummers, play-actors. Their punctiliousness was but ritual without religion. And I may go further, for not only may ritual exist without religion, but emphasized ritual is a dangerous enemy to religion. Laying undue importance upon the outward forms, you obscure the importance of the inner spirit. Once you exaggerate the importance of external rules, you minimize the importance of faith and love. Once ceremonialism comes in by the door, genuine religion has a way of flying out by the window.

An Example of Its Working
Palestine in our Lord's day is an illustration of the truth of this. Religion had been smothered beneath ritual. Washing the hands counted for more than the devotion of the heart. They were careful of petty rules, and careless of the great commands of God. Take the glaring and monstrous case which Jesus cast up against them. The fifth commandment in the Decalogue was this: "Honor thy father and thy mother." And by honoring them is meant not simply outward deference, but obedience in youth, and assistance, if required, in age. This filial duty is not only commanded by God, but it is ratified by the instinct of universal human nature. But Jewish casuistry had invent-

ed a way by which greedy and selfish men could evade that plain and obvious duty, and do so in the name of religion. Whatever was vowed to God was sacred to the uses of religion. It was *corban*— an offering— and must pass into the hands of the priests. It need not, and often was not paid at once; the money so dedicated was often employed by the owner during life, and only actually passed into the Temple treasury at his death. But the fact that it was *corban* placed it beyond the reach of ordinary claims; for they held it sacrilegious to apply to other uses what had once been dedicated to God. Now wicked and shameless men used this tradition about *corban* to evade some of their plain and primary responsibilities. Selfish sons, for instance, played this trick upon needy parents, and answered their piteous appeals for help by this very formula which our Lord here quotes, "That where with thou mightest have been profited by me is *corban*" (v. 11). The peculiar odiousness of it lay in the circumstance that it was done in the name of God. Religion was used to justify selfishness and greed; or rather, devotion to ritual was allowed to stifle and destroy religion; "making void," said Jesus, "the word of God by your tradition, which ye have delivered" (v. 13).

A Modern Peril

Now, has all this any message for us? Has it any pertinency to our time? I am persuaded that it has. These are days of developed ritualism. But let us never forget that ritual is not religion. The one can never take the place of the other. Religion is not a posture of the body; it is an attitude of the heart. God is a Spirit, and they that worship Him must worship Him in spirit and truth. In so far as ritual tends to emphasize the external rather than the internal, the form rather than the spirit, it is to be jealously guarded against, rather than fostered and encouraged. For you can not magnify the little external things of religion, without thereby minimizing the great and vital things.

Defilement—External and Vital

All this talk about externalism had arisen from the complaint made by the Scribes and Pharisees about the "unwashen" hands of the disciples. It was only outward defilement that they seemed to have any notion of. Christ proceeds now to show what the true sources of defilement are. It was a lesson that not only these spying enemies of His, but the whole body of people, needed to be taught. So He called to Him the multitude, and said to them, "Hear Me all of you, and understand: there is nothing from without the man, that going into him can defile him: but the things which pro-

ceed out of the man are those that defile the man" (v. 15). It was
one of those great sweeping truths that Christ delighted to utter. It
went right beyond ceremonial conditions to moral verities —
beyond the outward to the inward. By this one word He swept
away all those multitudes of regulations that tradition had accumulated, and indeed struck at the artificial distinction which the
Mosaic law made between things clean and unclean—a regulation
which had perhaps been useful in its day, but had served its time.

The Distinction and Difference

The disciples realized that it was a broad and sweeping statement, whose bearings they did not all at once take in. And so
when they were alone in the house they asked Him as to the parable. He, with some words implying rebuke, condescends patiently
to explain it to them. And the gist of His explanation comes to this
that, as Dr. Glover puts it, defilement arises not from food, but
from faults. The center of pollution is the evil heart. "Out of the
heart of men, evil thoughts proceed, fornications, thefts, murders,
adulteries, covetings, wickednesses, deceit, lasciviousness, an evil
eye, railing, pride, foolishness: all these evil things proceed from
within, and defile the man" (vv. 21, 23). "This He said," remarks
the Evangelist, "making all meats clean" (v. 19). Yes, He did that;
but He did much more. He revolutionized the whole notion of
defilement. In the deepest sense there is no defilement, save that
which is moral and spiritual. The only thing that really pollutes a
man is an unclean heart.

A Personal Application

Have we learned the lesson? I wonder whether even in
Christian countries there are not a great many people who are far
more troubled about dirty hands than they are about a dirty soul!
I wonder whether even to this day Society at large does not lay a
great deal more stress upon correct behavior than it does upon a
clean heart! But, at any rate, let us be under no delusion. Our Lord
"looketh upon the heart." He tests and measures everything by
what He sees there. A man is clean or defiled according as his
heart is clean or defiled; and what defiles the heart is the evil
thought. Go through this list, and examine yourself by it. Perhaps
we can honestly say that some of the things that are in this terrible
list are not in our hearts—fornication, thefts, murders, adulteries.
But what about covetings? And what about deceit? And what
about the evil and envious eye? And what about pride? Are none
of them there? And none of them enter the heart without leaving

a black and ugly smudge upon it. When I think of it all, I am tempted to cry out, like the leper, "Unclean! unclean!" For, like John Bunyan, I feel that sin and corruption do as naturally bubble out of my heart as water bubbles out of a fountain, until, like him, at the sight of my own vileness I fall deeply into despair. But there is One who can make my defiled heart clean again. No external cleansing can wash away the stains that evil thoughts make. "Though thou wash thee with lye, and take thee much soap, yet thine iniquity is marked before Me, saith the Lord God" (Jer. 2:22). "And the blood of Jesus Christ His Son cleanseth us from all sin" (1 John 1:7). And so I turn to Him with the prayer, "Create in me a clean heart, O God, and renew a right spirit within me."

43
He Who Could Not Be Hid

"And from thence He arose, and went into the borders of Tyre and Sidon, and entered into an house, and would have no man know it: but He could not be hid." —Mark 7:24.

The Limits of Christ's Ministry

JESUS FOR THE MOST part confined Himself to His own people. In Matthew's account of this incident the Lord says that He was not sent save to the lost sheep of the house of Israel (Matt. 15:24). This does not mean that His sympathies were limited to those of His own race. They ran out to those other sheep which were not of the Jewish fold; and never in all His life was He so moved as when He was notified of the desire of those Greeks who came to Philip, saying, "Sir, we would see Jesus." It was in the interests of His work that Christ confined Himself to Palestine. For the future of Christianity it was infinitely better that He should concentrate His energies upon a limited number, and impress them deeply, radically, vitally, than that He should dissipate Himself over larger numbers, and leave only a weak and ineffectual impression upon any. By concentrating His energies upon Palestine, and especially upon His twelve disciples, Jesus produced so deep and profound an impression that, even though He went, it was absolutely certain that the Christian faith would remain. But, all the same, I am glad He did not absolutely and entirely limit Himself to Israel.

The Visit to Phoenicia

Once at least Christ crossed the border and sojourned amongst the Gentiles. Here we reach the story of that visit to those who were strangers and aliens from the commonwealth of Israel. "And from thence He arose," says Mark, "and went away into the borders of Tyre and Sidon" (v. 24). What was it that impelled our Lord to take this long and tedious journey into pagan Phoenicia? What was it made Him break His rule of confining Himself to Palestine? I think it was His desire for solitude and quietness. You remember how, after the return of the Twelve from their first evangelizing tour, He had invited them to come apart into a desert place to rest awhile. He saw they needed rest after the excitements of their missionary labors, and He had Himself many things to say to them about the future which it was necessary they should hear and understand. But the rest sought on the other side of the sea they did not find. Instead of a solitude, they found a multitude. Instead of quietness, they had passed ever since from one excitement to another. First, the feeding of the 5000; then the storm at sea; then the crisis in Capernaum and the desertion of the crowds; and, finally, the controversy with the Jerusalem Scribes and Pharisees about ablutions.

In Search of Retirement

The opportunity for quiet talk with His disciples which Christ had so much wanted had never come. And yet every day that passed showed more and more clearly how urgently necessary such a time of quietness was. Even in the controversy about ablutions the slowness of the disciples had distressed Jesus. "Are ye so without understanding also?" He said. It became obvious to Jesus that if the disciples were to be ready for that time when He would be taken from them, He must somehow gain quietness and leisure to teach and train them. But the quietness He wanted it seemed hopeless to expect anywhere in Palestine. Experience had taught Him that, no matter where He went, the multitude was sure to follow. And so He turned His eyes to the land that lay to the northwest of Galilee.

The people of that country were the descendants of the ancient Canaanites, whom the Israelites had dispossessed on their entrance into the Land of Promise. They had once been the foremost maritime people in the world, though now fallen from their high estate. But to the Jew the land was an unclean and abhorred land, because of the loathsome and licentious idolatry practiced by its inhabitants. To this country Jesus now bends His steps. Its very loathsomeness to the Jew seemed to promise to Him the quietness and retirement He desired. He went away into the borders of Tyre and Sidon, hoping to be able to sojourn there unrecognized and undisturbed. But once again the rest had to be set aside.

"But He Could Not be Hid"

"He entered into a house, and would have no man know it," says Mark: "and He could not be hid"(v. 24). He could not be hid!" That is one of the penalties of greatness—privacy becomes impossible. Let our king travel abroad, and he cannot be hid. He may travel incognito, as we term it, but the ubiquitous newspaper man is ever on his heels, watching his every act, and his every movement is proclaimed to the world. And Jesus could not be hid. Not that the newspaper man existed, as we know him, in those far-off days. But His sayings and doings had set all Palestine in a ferment. He was the subject of conversation wherever men did congregate. Phoenician visitors who had heard of His wonderful works, and perhaps witnessed some of them, had carried His name and fame beyond the confines of His own land, and had astonished their own countrymen with the report of what they had seen and heard. Doubtless, in many a home in pagan Phoenicia, and especially in many a sick home, the name and power of Christ had been eagerly canvassed. Christ's fame had preceded Him into the borders of Tyre and Sidon.

The Power of His Personality

Quite apart from what report had done for Him, I believe there was something in the very aspect of Jesus that made people feel that here was no ordinary man. "Her very walk proclaimed her a goddess," says Virgil, about one of the characters in his *Aeneid*. And so there was something about the appearance, the manner, the speech of Jesus that proclaimed the secret He fain would hide. I was once discussing with my Bible Class the passage in which John tells how the officers of the Temple, who had been sent to seize Christ, returned with their errand unfulfilled, giving as their excuse, "Never man so spake." And I asked my class what they thought it was about Jesus that had so impressed and subdued these Temple officials. And one of them replied, "I think it must have been something in His very face." Technically, the answer was not the right one. But, all the same, I think it was profoundly true. I think there was something in the very face of Jesus, a nobility and a graciousness about Him, that stirred unwonted emotions in every heart.

No, Jesus "could not be hid." Face, speech, manner, all published abroad who and what He was. You may build, as some one has said, a high wall around your rose garden; yet you cannot hide the existence of the roses. Over the highest wall ever built the roses will waft their fragrance, and men as they pass will say, "There are roses near." And Jesus was the Rose of Sharon. Fragrant, gladdening, sweetening influences flowed forth from Him. Instinctively, men recognized that the Rose was in their midst. Jesus needed no trumpet to sound before Him, no herald to proclaim His coming. Men found Him out. He had not been an hour amongst these pagan strangers in Phoenicia before they knew that He was no ordinary man. "He could not be hid."

The Self-evident Christianity

Nor, suffer me to say in passing, can the true Christian either. If a man is able to hide his Christianity, it is probably because there is no Christianity to hide. When a man is a true Christian, all the world knows it. A genuine faith always proclaims itself by the influences it emits and the qualities it begets. "They took knowledge of them that they had been with Jesus." The men who have really been with Jesus "cannot be hid."

44
The Syro-Phoenician Woman

"For a certain woman, whose young daughter had an unclean spirit, heard of Him, and came and fell at His feet: The woman was a Greek, a Syrophoenician by nation; and she besought Him that He would cast forth the devil out of her daughter. But Jesus said unto her, Let the children first be filled: for it is not meet to take the children's bread, and to cast it unto the dogs. And she answered and said unto him, Yes, Lord: yet the dogs under the table eat of the children's crumbs. And He said unto her, For this saying go thy way; the devil is gone out of thy daughter. And when she was come to her house, she found the devil gone out, and her daughter laid upon the bed." —Mark 7:25-30.

The Unexpected

THE STORY THAT follows is a story full of difficulties, difficulties arising mainly from our Lord's conduct. Dr. Vaughan, of Kensington, had a sermon on the Cursing of the Barren Fig Tree, and this is how he always began it: "Curse a fig-tree! My Master curse a figtree! 'Tisn't like Him." And so, when I read of our Lord's treatment of this Canaanitish woman, I am tempted to say, "What! Turn a deaf ear to a cry for help? What! Mock at sorrow's appeal? What! My Master speak roughly to a woman? 'Tisn't like Him." No, it isn't like Him. And that is exactly the difficulty. For at first sight His treatment of this poor woman seems absolutely contrary to His custom. So much so, that some have found no incident in our Lord's earthly ministry more puzzling than this.

And Its Difficulties

The difficulty is twofold. There is, first of all, the difficulty of His reluctance to take any notice of the woman at all; and there is, secondly, the difficulty of His seeming harshness and cruelty.

The Difficulty of Christ's Reluctance

Let us deal with the matter of our Lord's reluctance first. It is the lesser of the two difficulties, and can, I think, easily be explained. Mark does not refer to it. It is in the fuller account of Matthew that we find it recorded. Let me give it you as Matthew narrates it.

"And behold, a Canaanitish woman came out from those borders and cried, saying, Have mercy on me, O Lord, Thou Son of David; my daughter is grievously vexed with a devil. But He answered her not a word. And His disciples came and besought Him saying, Send her away; for she crieth after us. But He answered and said, I was not sent but unto the lost sheep of the house of Israel" (15:22-24). Now that isn't like Him, is it?—to turn a deaf ear to a cry for help? It is a strange thing to find the disciples more forward than the Master. The Jesus we read about in the other pages of the Gospel never needed to be begged and urged and entreated to do a kindness. He was "swift to bless." Did the leper cry to Him, and say, "If Thou wilt, Thou canst make me clean"? His answer came swift as a flash. "I will; be thou clean." Indeed, in case after case, Our Lord never needed to be asked at all. He did not need to be asked to feed the 5000 in the wilderness. He had compassion on them, because they were as sheep not having a shepherd. He broke the bread for them of His own accord. He did not need to be asked to heal the impotent man at the pool of Bethesda. The sight of the man in his misery was enough for Jesus, and He Himself made the offer of healing, "Wilt thou be made whole?"' He did not need to be asked to raise the dead son of the widow of Nain to life again. He was so moved with pity for her sorrow that of His own accord He bade the bearers be still, and summoned the dead man back to life. That is the Jesus we most often read about in the Gospels—a Jesus who never needed to be asked twice, who turned away from nobody's call, who often anticipated men's prayers and appeals, who was "swift to bless."

He Did Not Deny Gentiles

It staggers one, therefore, to read that, when this Canaanitish woman came with her piteous plea, He answered her not a word; that even His disciples showed more compassion and pity than He. How was it? Most commentators explain it all on the ground that Christ's mission was first of all to the Jews, and that He was not called upon to confer His gifts upon the Gentiles. But the explanation is not satisfactory; for, as a matter of fact, Christ never hesitated to confer blessing upon Gentiles when they crossed His path, as, e.g., in the case of the Roman centurion. No, I think the explanation is a much simpler one. I believe that Jesus was genuinely reluctant to perform any wonder in these borders of Tyre and Sidon.

But He Sought Retirement

But it was not at all because the woman who entreated Him was a Gentile. It was because the performance of a great work of heal-

ing would defeat the very object for which He had journeyed
there. He had left Galilee and made His way to pagan Phoenicia
for quietness and rest —quietness to teach His disciples, and to
give them that training which they needed, in view of His coming
departure. To perform a miracle would make impossible the quietness He and they so sorely needed. So, to quote Mr. David Smith,
it was with a feeling of dismay that He observed the approach of
a suppliant. He foresaw the consequences of granting her petition.
The fame of the miracle would go abroad, and He would soon be
surrounded by a crowd—sufferers craving relief, and others
who came only to gaze and admire. And that is exactly the result
this miracle brought about. The report of it was spread abroad, and
Jesus had to seek elsewhere the seclusion denied to Him in the borders of Tyre and Sidon.

The Difficulty of Christ's Words

But the difficulty of our Lord's reluctance is not nearly so great
as the difficulty caused by our Lord's seemingly harsh and even
cruel speech. Let me remind you of the conversation that took
place between Him and this broken-hearted woman. No doubt the
woman overheard our Lord's answer to the disciples, that He was
not sent except to the lost sheep of the house of Israel. That in itself
was enough to quench the woman's hope. But love for her
daughter lent her importunity, and she followed the Master and
His disciples until they came into the house. When they took their
places at table she fell at Christ's feet with the pathetic prayer,
"Lord, help me." He took notice of her now, and answered
her—But what an answer! "It is not meet," He said, "to take the
children's bread, and cast it to the dogs" (v. 26). It was not only
refusal. It looked like refusal with insult. That is not like Him,
is it?

A Strange Contrast

When I turn over the pages of the Gospels, and read of His dealings with other grief-stricken souls, it is the Lord's tenderness and
gentleness that strike me. He comforted the woman who was a sinner with the gift of peace. He called the timid woman who had
won her blessing by stealth, "Daughter." Even for the woman who
was detected in sin and shame, He had only a solemn but
infinitely tender rebuke. "A bruised reed shall He not break, and
the smoking flax shall He not quench" (Isa. 42:3). All the more
staggering is it, therefore, to read of Him giving an answer like
this: "It is not meet to take the children's bread, and cast it to the

dogs" (v. 27). What explanation can we give of it? For it is impossible that our Lord could be really harsh or cruel.

Explained

The common, favorite explanation is to say that our Lord's roughness was all assumed. It was designed only to try the woman's faith, and possibly to show His disciples what even a heathen woman was capable of. And perhaps there is truth in all this, and we must judge the whole episode in the light of the boon bestowed and the blessing pronounced at the end. But, in addition to that broad and general explanation, a closer study of our Lord's words will mitigate somewhat their first impression of harshness. "Let the children first be filled," He said. It looks at first like a blank refusal. But a closer scrutiny reveals hope in what seems at first a flat denial. Look at that word "first." "Let the children first be filled." Surely there was a world of encouragement in it— encouragement which this quick-witted woman would not fail to grasp. First, it implied that her time would come, and that it was only a question of time. And that very word "dog" in the original is not nearly so harsh as it is in our English version. The form of the word which our Lord uses is the diminutive—and it may well be a diminutive of endearment. "Doggies," our Lord's word might be rendered. He does not use a word which would be suitable for those fierce and unclean beasts that prowl the streets and act as scavengers. He uses rather a term that would be applicable to little house-dogs, the household pets which played about the table at meal-time, and got occasional scraps from their masters. And so this very word which at first looks like mere and sheer insult, may itself have kindled hope in the woman's heart. There is no edge of cruelty; and, as Dr. Chadwick says, "It domesticated the Gentile world." It gave this woman a place, even though a humble and lowly place, in the household of God.

A Contest of Wits

Then Mr. David Smith suggests that both the answer of our Lord and the retort of the woman are proverbial—that it was something like a contest of of wits between them, and that in dealing thus with this Gentile woman Jesus only showed His incomparable insight into the human character. With a nimble and quick-witted Greek it was the very way to deal. "Truth, Lord. I am not better than a poor pet-dog; but then I am not asking much. I wish not more than scraps." Then I like to think that these words are to be always read, taking Christ's tone and look into account. A difference of tone will make all the difference between ugly insult and innocent raillery.

It depends upon the "look" whether an answer is to be taken as a refusal, or as a challenge to bolder confidence. This woman saw the looks and heard the tones of the Lord. And that took all the harshness and cruelty out of the words. There was a gentleness in His voice, and when she looked into His face she saw there such pity and grace, that this answer which we are so apt to regard as harsh, became to her just an encouragement to hope on, and so she returned her great answer, "Yea, Lord: even the dogs under the table eat of the children's crumbs" (v. 28).

Sorrow and the Savior

But now as to some of the main truths taught by this story. And first, of the way in which sorrow brings people to the Savior. "He could not be hid," says Mark. "But straightway a woman, whose little daughter had an unclean spirit, having heard of Him, came and fell at His feet" (vv. 24, 25). You notice who it was that discovered Christ—it was a woman in trouble. Do you ask me how it was she found Him out? I cannot tell. How does the bee discover the flower in which the honey is hidden? Instinct, you say. Well, I say it was the instinct of need that discovered where help could be found. The comfortable and prosperous people of Tyre would never have discovered Jesus. He might have spent His days in their borders undisturbed and unrecognized, as far as they were concerned. But misery has a keen scent and sure instinct for a helper. Probably this woman had heard reports of Christ's healing power. She had heard how He healed the sick, gave cleansing to the leper, and sight to the blind, and cast out devils. I can believe that again and again she had wished the Lord would come her way—for she had a little daughter plagued with an unclean spirit. And when she heard of this Jewish Stranger, accompanied by a band of disciples, who had come to sojourn at a neighbor's house; when she heard the description of Him her neighbors gave, with that wonderful intuition that women often possess—and especially women whose characters have been refined by trouble—she jumped to the conclusion that the great Healer of whom she had so often heard was at her very doors. And this was the result, "straightway . . . having heard of Him," she "came and fell down at His feet."

The Ministry of Trouble

I find here an illustration of the ministry of trouble; "By these things," i.e. by troubles and difficulties, says the prophet, "men live, and wholly therein is the life of my spirit" (Isa. 38:16). There is no truth that human experience more fully and richly verifies. Affliction and trouble have been the means of bringing to men some of their very choicest gifts.

The Sorely-tried Mother

See what they did for the woman of this story. When epilepsy or insanity—whichever it was— claimed the little child as its victim, this mother's heart well-nigh broke. I should gather from the tone of the narrative that this little daughter was the woman's only child. And, from the absence of all reference to a husband and father, I should conclude also that she was a widow. This little child was all she had in the world; so that her grief when the little one was stricken down was all the more bitter. You remember how Luke, to emphasize the sadness of that funeral which Christ met coming out of the gates of Nain, says of the young man who was being carried out to burial that he was "the only son of his mother, and she was a widow." This Syro-Phoenician woman's trouble was every whit as deep and bitter. For this little girl was also the only child of her mother, and she a widow. And though it was not a case of death, I am not at all sure it was not something worse than death. For reason had been dethroned, and her innocent little child had become possessed of an "unclean spirit." In face of all this you can understand that it was a heart-breaking sorrow, and that the poor woman's soul often rebelled and grew bitter whenever she gazed upon her daughter. And yet the greatest blessing of her life came to her through the ministry of this sorrow.

Tired and Refined

I will say nothing at this point about what the sorrow did in softening and refining her own character. Though I can well believe that through the sickness of her little daughter she gained a new tenderness and sympathy. There was an old Scottish saint who had for a crest a palm-tree with weights depending from its branches, and beneath the crest these words written: *Sub pondere cresco*—"I grow beneath a burden." There was a belief that the weighted palm grew straightest and fairest, and the old saint had discovered that character grows most fair when it too has loads to bear and griefs to carry. And I can readily believe that this woman's character developed and grew beneath the heavy burden of her daughter's sickness.

Wounded and Brought to the Healer

I pass that by with the bare mention, because one might fairly object that it is all a matter of conjecture and imagination. But there is one blessing this sorrow conferred upon her—and it is the greatest blessing of all, which is no matter of guess or conjecture, but is plain, historic fact—it brought her to Jesus Christ. Had she had no little daughter ill, Jesus might have come and gone, and she would never have sought His face. It was trouble that brought her to the Lord's feet. And in after days, when she found out Who and what Jesus was, when she found out that He met every need and craving of her soul, when she found out, as Paul did, that having Him she had all things and abounded, I think she would come to thank God for the great sorrow that crushed and embittered her life. For her sorrow brought her to her Savior, and gave her rest to her soul. This is almost a parable of life. When men are in trouble—at their wits' end, as the Psalmist puts it—then they cry unto the Lord. God has many angels who do His errands and summon men to Him, says Archer Butler; but the angel that has gathered most to the Savior's feet is the Angel of Sorrow. And that is literally true.

As Others Were

Think of the people who came to Jesus in the days of His flesh. What brought the lepers crowding to Jesus? Sorrow brought them. What brought the blind and the lame and the dumb wherever men said He was? Sorrow brought them. What brought the woman with the issue of blood to touch His garment, and the woman who was a sinner to wash His feet? Sorrow brought them. What brought the father of the demoniac lad to seek His help? What brought the proud Jairus as a suppliant to His feet? Sorrow brought them. I question very much whether any of these would have sought Christ out, had all been well with them, but the Angel of Sorrow gathered them all in. And it is so still.

As Others Are

In our days of health and happiness and prosperity we have no sense of want or need, and therefore we do not seek our Lord's help. But when health fails or the home is darkened, we want help and sympathy. When the strong waters come up against our souls, we need a mighty Arm to save us, and then we cry as this woman did, "Have mercy on me, Thou Son of David." It is perfectly true still that, "The hungry He hath filled with good things; and the rich He hath sent empty away" (Luke 1:53). And when the man impoverished by sorrow and trouble finds himself enriched with all the comfort and grace of Christ, he will learn to bless God, even for the sorrow that drove him into the Lord's arms. And so there are compensations for sorrow, and there are great enrichments in trouble.

"Is it raining, little flower?
Be glad of rain;
Too much sun would wither thee,
'Twill shine again;
The sky is very black, 'tis true,
But just behind it shines the blue.

Art thou weary, tender heart?
Be glad of pain;
In sorrow sweetest things will grow,
As flowers in rain.
God watches, and thou wilt have sun,
When clouds their perfect work have done."

Any trouble is worth bearing if it brings us into the arms of our blessed Lord, for He is all we need.

The Savior and the Alien

Again, this story is a story of Christ's compassion to a heathen and an alien. Mark is careful to emphasize this fact about the woman, she "was a Greek, a Syro-Phoenician by race," he says (v. 26). She was not only a Gentile, but she belonged to that race which was held in peculiar abhorrence by the Jews, not simply because they were the descendants of their ancient enemies, but also because of the loathsome character of their idolatries. It was upon a woman of this abhorrent and accursed race that Christ exercised His compassion. Is there no significance in that? Is not the universal mission of Christianity here, in symbol and figure? There is no race outside the love and compassion of that Christ Who stooped to heal and bless and save the most outcast and degraded races in the world.

A Great Precedent and a Glorious Promise

"The history of the Acts of the Apostles is here in spirit," is Bishop Chadwick's last word on this incident. So it is. Peter, when he went to preach the Gospel to Cornelius, the Latin centurion, thought he was doing an unheard-of thing, that he was introducing a serious innovation, and so he made an elaborate defense of his conduct. He might have spared himself the trouble. All the defense he needed to make was to point to his Master going to the borders of Tyre and Sidon and there extending His mercy to a Canaanitish woman. Peter's preaching to Cornelius, Philip's preaching to the eunuch, the preaching of those unknown missionaries to the Greeks at Antioch, Paul's superb and world-embracing missionary labors, they are all here in spirit. Christ broke down all distinction of class and race. His love embraces the world. His propitiation avails for the world. There are multitudes which no man can number around the throne clothed in white robes and with palms in their hands, of all people and tribes and kindreds and tongues, and of that vast multitude this alien woman is the sign and the pledge. She was the "firstfruit of the Gentiles." And Christ's compassion still runs out towards the circle of the earth. His face is still set towards the borders of the Tyre and Sidon of our own times—to the outcast, alien, degraded, sunken folk of the world. And amongst these alien, sunken, degraded folk there are many like this woman, who have sorrows and griefs to bear that only the Great Physician can heal. There are the multitudes of stricken souls longing for the Savior—here is the Savior longing to heal and bless them. Shall we not bring the sufferers and the Healer together?

The Triumph of Faith

But the central thing in the whole incident is the woman's strong, persistent and ultimately triumphant faith—faith in the sense of trust in the goodness of God and His willingness to bless. It was "faith" of some sort that brought this woman in the first instance to Jesus. The story tells us how her faith was tried. The seemingly harsh answers and refusal of our Lord put that faith of hers to the test. And it showed itself a strong faith—a faith that could persist and hold on, a faith that would not let the Lord go until He had blessed her. You and I— do we have faith? Probably most of us have, of a sort. But what sort of a faith is it? Is it a faith that will stand the test of trial? For often our Lord deals with us as He dealt with this woman. We come to Him with our troubles and appeals, and He seems to take no notice. "Lord," was the message the sisters of Bethany sent to Jesus, "he whom Thou lovest is sick." It was an appeal, a cry, an urgent entreaty. "Hurry to our help," it said, in effect. And Jesus seemed to take no notice of it. For, instead of hurrying off to Bethany, "He abode at that time two days in the place where He was" (John 11:6). I wonder what became of the sisters' faith in that interval? Judging by the way they greeted our Lord when at last He did come, I should say there was not much

faith left. And that is how the Lord often treats us. He delays His
coming; He answers us not a word.

Is the Trial Ours?

The faith of many is being tried in this way. Does the faith hold
out? Does it persist, in spite of trials like this woman's? Let me
remind you of a passage in St Peter about faith and its trials.
"Wherein," he says, referring to the hope of salvation, "ye greatly
rejoice, though now for a little while, if need be, ye have been put
to grief in manifold temptations, that the proof of your faith, being
more precious than gold that perisheth though it is proved by fire,
might be found unto praise and glory and honor at the revelation
of Jesus Christ: whom not having seen, ye love; on whom,
though now ye see Him not, yet believing, ye rejoice greatly with
joy unspeakable and full of glory: receiving the end of your faith,
even the salvation of your souls" (1 Pet. 1:6-9). That is a passage
about faith in the trial. And the Apostle says practically two things
about faith in the trial. He says that a faith that endures and persists through trial brings glory and honor to Christ. And he says,
further, that a faith that so endures shall win its great reward in the
blessing of salvation.

The Glory of Faith's Endurance

Consider those two points for a moment—a faith that persists
through trial and difficulty brings honor and praise to Christ. It
is— shall I say? —a compliment to the Lord. What a splendid tribute this woman paid to Jesus! She believed in His power. She
believed in His love. Nothing could shake her belief that Jesus both
could and would. And there was gratitude as well as admiration
in our Lord's comment, "O woman, great is thy faith." Nothing
exalts our Master like an unshaken trust in Him. What a compliment it was that David Livingstone paid to Jesus! He was in a
position of great difficulty, but he never lost heart, because he
knew he was in his Master's hands. And he had faith in his Master.
"My Master," he said, "is a perfect gentleman. He will never break
His word." Does our unshaken faith in times of difficulty and trial
bring glory and honor to our Master? Or do we by our complaints
and murmurs at the first onset of trial lead the world to believe
that we are disappointed in our Master, and that He is not to be
trusted? Nothing would sooner beget a belief in Christ than a persistent and cheerful faith on our part.

In the second place, not only does faith bring glory to Christ, but
in the long run it always brings blessing to ourselves. Faith is never

finally disappointed. It is always richly justified and rewarded. Look at this woman. Faith persisted, and what a blessing it brought her. "O woman," said our Lord (Matt. 15:28), "great is thy faith; be it done unto thee even as thou wilt." And she went away, and found her child laid upon the bed, and the devil gone out. "He that endureth to the end, the same shall be saved," said Jesus. And the faith that endures and persists shall win the blessing.

I am tempted to tell you a story of the mission field—it illustrates my point. The American Board established a mission among one of the many tribes of India. And for years and years the missionaries labored without result. Ten, twenty years passed, and no convert was made, and by and by this mission came to be known throughout the States as the Lone Star Mission. The Board at home took the case of the mission into consideration. Many thought it ought to be abandoned. They determined at last to write, and ask the missionaries in this trying field what they thought ought to be done. This was the reply that came back to the Board: "We are going on. With God nothing is impossible." Not long after their faith was abundantly justified. The blessing came. Thousands upon thousands accepted Christ; five thousand were baptized in one year, and the Lone Star Mission is quoted now, not as an example of missionary failure, but as a shining illustration of the triumph of faith. That is the kind of faith we want. Persistent faith is always in the long run triumphant faith.

A Sure Reward

In spite of all the delays and disappointments, the blessing will come. I do not say that the blessing will come in the exact form you ask; but it will always so come as to reveal to you the wealth of God's goodness and grace, for the end of your faith will be the salvation of your souls. And where shall you gain this faith? Where shall you gain this "Courage, your fainting heart to keep, and trust Him, though He slay"? I know of no place where faith can be gained save at the cross of our Lord. There we can believe that all things must work together for good; there we can believe that God who did not keep back His only Son, but freely gave Him up for us all, will also with Him freely give us all things. There we can believe that God is Love, and believing that, we can rest in the Lord, and wait patiently for Him, assured that He will fulfill our hearts' desires.

45

The Healing of the Deaf and Dumb

"And again, departing from the coasts of Tyre and Sidon, He came unto the sea of Galilee, through the midst of the coasts of Decapolis. And they bring unto Him one that was deaf, and had an impediment in his speech and they beseech Him to put His hands upon him. And He took him aside from the multitude, and put His fingers into his ears, and He spit, and touched His tongue."
—Mark 7:31-33.

A Ministry to Gentiles

THE HEALING OF the Syro-Phoenician's sick daughter had just that untoward effect that Jesus feared. It put an end to all His hopes of quietness and seclusion. It spread His name and fame abroad. But our Lord was so "full of grace," as John puts it, that no shade of resentment ever invaded His breast, even when His cherished plans were frustrated by the importunity of the people. When, instead of solitude, He found on the other side of the lake a multitude, His feeling was not one of annoyance; He was moved with compassion, because they were as sheep not having a shepherd. And so now in Phoenicia, when His identity became known, and the crowds began to gather, instead of being vexed and hurrying off to some other place for the quiet He had come to seek, apparently He stayed for a little time to preach to them and minister to their needs.

Just as He availed Himself of the opening made for Him at Sychar by His conversation with the woman at the well, and seeing the fields white already with the harvest, remained there two days, so now, seeing a "great and effectual" door opened to Him amongst these pagan people of Phoenicia, He tarried there some time, preaching the good news of the Kingdom of God. He visited Tyre, and then traveled northward along the shore of the Mediterranean to Sidon, and there, taking a circuit round, along the southern slopes of Lebanon and Hermon, He made His way along the east bank of the Jordan through the midst of the borders of Decapolis, until at length He came to Galilee again. It must have been a memorable journey, and it rejoices one to think that Jesus

233

Himself preached to Gentiles and to heathens. No record of the preaching has been preserved for us, and yet there are hints that it met with abundant success, for in after days Jesus quoted the reception given to Him in Tyre and Sidon as a melancholy and damning contrast to the unbelief of the cities of Galilee.

At Decapolis

It was apparently not in Galilee, but in the borders of Decapolis, that our Lord performed the miracle we now are to consider. It was not by any means the only miracle He performed on His way back. Matthew tells us that "there came unto Him great multitudes, having with them the lame, blind, dumb, maimed, and many others, and they cast them down at His feet; and He healed them: insomuch that the multitude wondered, when they saw the dumb speaking, the maimed whole, and the lame walking, and the blind seeing: and they glorified the God of Israel" (Matt. 15:30, 31). You notice that last phrase, "they glorified the God of Israel." It implies that many of those present were heathens. It is the confession forced from pagan lips and pagan hearts by the sight of the Lord's mighty works that the God of Israel was the King above all gods. And it exactly suits such a half heathen region as we know Decapolis to have been.

A Striking Change

Now the fact that such multitudes crowded upon Christ in Decapolis is very significant. It argues such a change of temper and feeling. For Christ had been into the borders of Decapolis before. In Mark 5 we have His visit to Gerasa, which He signalized by restoring to his right mind the man who had the legion. But the story of that visit ends with these words, "they began to beseech Him to depart from their borders" (v. 17). They were eager to get rid of Christ. They were impatient to see the last of Him. But it was a very different reception He met with on this second passing visit. There was immense excitement and enthusiasm. Wherever He went the crowds followed. And all that they saw constrained them to glorify God.

Its Cause

Now what accounts for this startling and radical change of manner? What is the reason for this so-different reception? I think I have discovered the reason for it. When Jesus was saying "goodbye" to Gerasa, the healed demoniac wanted, you remember, to go with Him. But Jesus would not permit him, but said to him, "Go to thy house unto thy friends, and tell them how great things the Lord hath done for thee, and how He had mercy on thee. And he went his way," I read, "and began to publish in Decapolis how great things Jesus had done for him; and all men did marvel" (vv. 19, 20). You notice, the healed man did not confine his witness to his own house and his own friends. He took a wider circuit. He published his wonderful news throughout the whole district of Decapolis. Into every one of the ten cities he went. And everywhere he told the same marvelous story. He told them how Jesus had found him a naked and untameable maniac, a terror to the whole country-side, and how by a word He had reinstated wisdom on her throne, and made a man out of a mere wreck. He spoke, that is, of the healing and saving power of Christ, and clinched and proved his speech by saying, "He healed and saved me." The result was, all Decapolis was on tip-toe of expectation. All Decapolis, especially the sick and maimed and the distressed of Decapolis, longed that Jesus would visit them. And so it came to pass that when Jesus took Decapolis on His way back to Galilee, the first intimation of His approach brought the crowd into His presence. The healed demoniac had been a most effective preacher. His witness to the healing and saving power of Christ made others eager to try Christ too.

The Need of Witnessing

In all of this there is an obvious lesson for us. We complain oftentimes of the indifference of our time. People nowadays do not seem to care for Christ. They show no eagerness to come to Him. They do not seem to think He can do anything for them. I wonder whether the indifference may not largely be our fault. Have we borne our witness to Christ's healing and saving power? Have we told them what great things the Lord hath done for us, and how He had mercy on us? Have we told them how He brought us pardon, peace, joy, and immortal hope? The witness of Christian people does infinitely more for the truth than any amount of preaching. Only the life must confirm the witness. That is to say, when you bear your witness that Christ has brought you pardon and peace and joy and hope, your lives must obviously be seen to be full of the pardon, peace, and joy of which you speak.

Are We Witnesses?

Do we bear that witness? Do we rejoice to tell people what Christ has done? And do our lives show that they are great things which He has done? Do you think, if men really knew that Jesus bestowed these great gifts they would remain indifferent and unconcerned? As a matter of fact, these are just the gifts men most deeply crave. For men are burdened by sin, they are harassed by fear, and they want forgiveness, peace, a settled hope. If only they saw that we obviously possessed these things, if they only saw that Christ really had bestowed them upon us, they too would turn to the Lord with eager hearts, saying, "Be merciful to me, and bless me also, Thou Son of God." The healed demoniac turned hundreds to the Lord. There is nothing still so potent to make men seek the Savior as the testimony of the saved man.

The Deaf and Dumb Man

Now, out of this multitude of acts of grace done upon the sick and the suffering of Decapolis Mark selects one for full and detailed description. It was the case of a deaf-stammerer. And I suppose that the reason why Mark picks out this particular miracle for detailed treatment is, as Archbishop Trench says, because it was signalized by some incidents which had not occurred on any previous occasion. It is really the conduct of Jesus Christ that the Evangelist wishes to emphasize. The miracle is not recorded—if I may so put it— because it was such a wonderful miracle. Christ did many a deed far more startling and amazing than that. The healing of this deaf and partially dumb man, from the point of mere wonderfulness, was not to be compared with the stilling of the storm or the feeding of the 5000, or the raising of Jairus' daughter from the dead. No; this miracle is recorded, not for the greatness of the act itself, so much as for the conduct of Jesus. That is what has stamped itself indelibly upon the memory of Peter. He can recall every detail of what happened. He can remember how Christ took the man aside privately; how He put His fingers in his deaf ears; how He spat and touched his tongue; how He looked up to heaven, and then groaned in spirit, and how finally He spoke that word of command, *Ephphatha,* "Be opened," and how as a result the man's "ears were opened, and the bond of his tongue was loosed, and he spake plain."

Different Cases, Different Treatment

Now, if it be true, as it probably is, that this incident has been preserved for us because of a certain peculiarity in Christ's treatment of this deaf and dumb man, then that very fact has a lesson of quite infinite importance to teach, viz., this: different men require different treatment. Christ Himself was never tied down to one stereotyped method. The friends of this deaf and dumb man take upon themselves to suggest a method to Jesus. They beseech Him that "He would lay His hand upon him." That—shall I say?—was the regulation and usual method of conveying visible power. Christ Himself occasionally employed it. "He laid His hands upon a few sick folk, and healed them" (6:5). But this time Jesus will not adopt that method. There was something about this man that required different treatment. I suppose, if, like Jesus Himself, we knew what was in man, we should see the reason why He employed varieties of methods in dealing with different persons—why, for instance, the woman with the issue of blood was healed in the crowd, and made to declare herself before the crowd, while this deaf and dumb man was taken aside privately to be healed; why the nobleman's servant was healed at a distance and by a word, while He laid His hand upon the leper and touched him; why He volunteered help in the case of the impotent man at the pool of Bethesda, and in the case of the Syro-Phoenician woman had to be appealed to again and again; why in the majority of cases He employed nothing but word or touch, while in the case of the man born blind He sent him to the pool of Siloam to wash, and in the case of this deaf and dumb man He touched his tongue with His own saliva.

With Good Reasons

If, I say, we knew everything about man, we should know why Jesus used a particular method in any particular case. For we may be quite sure of this—that the particular method was adopted not through whim or caprice, but because in some deep way it met the special need of the particular case. We may think we see the reason in this case and that; we may think we know why He volunteered help to the impotent man; we may think we know why He made the shrinking woman declare herself; we may think we know why He "touched" the leper. But whether we know or do not know the reason, we are sure there was one. We are quite sure, if we knew everything, we should see in the special method adopted in each particular case evidence of the wisdom of God.

The Lord's Diversities of Operation

But the main point for us to notice is that Christ has not one stereotyped method of bringing His gifts of healing and grace to men. He has diversities of operation. He adapts His method to the special case. He studies the individual soul. I wonder sometimes whether we do not forget this simple truth. In some quarters there is a tendency to limit and narrow the workings of Christ, to say that only in this way and that can He approach the soul. There are those who seem to think that Christ can only confer His blessing through one particular Christian communion; that He has only one "channel of grace"; and that only through that one channel can His healing and saving power be conveyed to the individual soul. So also there are those who seem to think that Christ has only one particular method of saving souls—that a man must have a kind of volcanic experience, a sudden upheaval of the whole nature, such as, let us say, Paul had on the way to Damascus, or the jailor had in Philippi, or Colonel Gardiner had in Paris, or the multitudes had who listened to John Wesley's and George Whitefield's preaching. They are inclined to doubt the reality of the salvation of the man who had never had any such revolutionizing experience, who, as Dr. G. Campbell Morgan once said, cannot remember having been born again.

But the Same Spirit

What we need to learn is, that Christ has more than one method of dealing with souls. There are twelve gates into the Kingdom—three on the north, three on the south, three on the east, three on the west, and by differing paths men may meet at last in the same beautiful city of God. To forget this, and to deny this, is to limit the Holy One of Israel. Christ, we may be sure, is just as much at home, and can confer His saving grace just as truly in the Salvation Army barracks, or the Quakers' meeting-house, as in a stately cathedral. Christ can save the soul just as surely by the gracious ministries of the home, as by the tumultuous or subduing experiences of a revival meeting. There are diversities of operations; but it will be well for us when we recognize that in and through them all works one of the same Spirit.

Example to Be Followed

If we are ourselves to deal wisely and successfully with men, we must, like our Lord, adapt our method to the special requirements of the case. We are fishers of men. And any man who wishes to become an expert fisherman must, according to Isaak Walton, "study his fish." We, too, must study men, if we are to catch men. All men are not to be won in the same way. What appeals to one does not appeal to another. Well-intentioned but tactless dealing may often repel instead of winning souls. That is what gave Henry Drummond his marvelous power over the students in Edinburgh. He knew student nature. He touched just those chords he knew would respond in every young student's heart, and so he turned hundreds to righteousness. That is the reason why in these days men are beginning to study boy and child nature in connection with our Sunday schools. They are beginning to realize that the man's way is not the child's way—that if the child's soul is to be won, they must find the right avenue, and tread it. We need to be wise to win souls, to be expert in the human heart. And if we say such wisdom is not ours, if we ask, God will give it liberally to us.

Christ's Treatment

And now note two points in Christ's special treatment of this case. "And He took him aside from the multitude privately, and put His fingers into his ears, and He spat, and touched his tongue" (v. 33). There are two points to notice—(1) The privacy, and (2) our Lord's symbolic actions.

The Symbolic Actions

Let us take that second point first, as it can be dismissed in a word or two. Why did our Lord put His fingers in this man's ears, and then touch his tongue with the moisture from His own mouth? To quicken and arouse faith. This was the only way Christ could communicate with the man. Deaf as the man was, our Lord could only speak to him by signs. And so He put His fingers into his ears, as if to bore through any obstacle there might be to hearing; and then touched his tongue, as if to convey to it the faculty of His own. And so He quickened expectation and faith, which was an indispensable condition of His every act of power.

The Privacy

And why did He withdraw him from the crowd? Not to avoid observation, as some suggest. Not that He Himself might be the more free to pray, as others say; but, as Archbishop Trench says, that the man himself might be more receptive of deep and lasting impressions. This leads me to say that Jesus takes us aside for the very same purpose still. In the din and clamor of the crowded street Christ cannot speak to us: the rush and pressure of life are prone to obliterate and efface the impressions of religion—indeed, often prevent any impression being made at all.

And Its Value

And so sometimes our Lord takes us aside into the sick-room, into which the tumult of the world cannot come; into the loneliness and solitude of bereavement, into the wilderness of sorrow, in order that He may speak His words of healing and life to us. We shrink from being taken aside like that; but it is worth while being laid aside from the rush and toil of life, if our ears become opened to heavenly harmonies, and we see the King in His beauty. Sorrow often leaves its blessing behind, in a healed and saved soul. In the meantime let us not wait for sickness or sorrow to draw us aside. Day by day let us draw aside of our own accord, that every day our souls may be refreshed, so that renewed we may go from strength to strength.

46
The Deaf and Dumb Man

"And looking up to heaven, He sighed, and saith unto him, Ephphatha, that is, Be opened. And straightway his ears were opened, and the string of his tongue was loosed, and he spake plain. And He charged them that they should tell no man: but the more He charged them, so much the more a great deal they published it; And were beyond measure astonished, saying, He hath done all things well: He maketh both the deaf to hear, and the dumb to speak."
—Mark 7:34-37.

THESE TWO POINTS already dealt with do not exhaust the details of our Lord's action in the case of this miracle. The Evangelist—deriving, no doubt, his information from Peter—says that before He performed the very act of healing our Lord looked up to heaven, and then He sighed, or rather groaned, and then He spoke the word of power, "Ephphatha," "Be opened." Dr. Maclaren has made these details of our Lord's action the basis of one of his most exquisite sermons, and it is almost impossible to say anything about them without following, however imperfectly, in his steps. But, at the risk of unfavorable comparison, let me say something about these details of our Lord's conduct, the light they throw upon His character, and the permanent lessons they have to teach us.

The Heavenward Look
The first thing Jesus did after He had taken the man aside, and by His symbolic action stirred hope within his breast, was this, "He looked up to heaven." It was not the only time that Jesus looked up to heaven before performing an act of power. I turn back to the account of the feeding of the five thousand, and read, "He took the five loaves and the two fishes, and looking up to heaven, He blessed, and brake the loaves" (Mark 6:41). Now why did Jesus look up to heaven? And what did He do when He looked up to heaven? I think the answer is plain and unmistakeable. He looked up to heaven because it was the source of His power, and what He did when He looked up was to pray.

The Secret of Power

What a lesson there is in all this for us! The heavenward look is still the secret of power. In other words, we can only do our work and win our triumphs in conscious dependence upon God. It is upon Him we must wait. It is to Him we must call. "As the eyes of servants look unto the hand of their master, . . . so our eyes look unto the Lord our God" (Psa. 123:2); for apart from Him we can do nothing. Prayer is the thermometer of the Church, people are very fond of saying. It is much more than that—it is the *power-gauge* of the Church. "This kind," the kind of ills the Church has to fight against and expel, "cometh forth by nothing save by prayer."

And Some Substitutes for It

Do we cultivate this heavenward look? In what is it that we put our trust? To what is it that we look for power and success? I wonder sometimes whether we do not put our trust overmuch, in these days, in mere mechanical and human devices. I think of some of the methods churches use to win the crowds—advertisements, music, popular lectures, socials, and the rest. They are, no doubt, all right in their way and place. But conquering power does not come that way. "My soul, wait thou only upon God, from Him cometh my salvation." Notice the sequence in our paragraph: Jesus looked up to heaven, and saith unto him, "Ephphatha" (v. 34). The heavenward look issued in the word of power. And still the Church that "looks up" shall be able to speak the word of power: it shall be able to free the prisoner, to cleanse the leper, to save the sinner, to quicken the dead, and nothing shall be impossible to it.

The Groan

"Looking up to heaven, He sighed." What is the meaning of this sigh, or rather groan, that escaped the lips of Jesus? It is surely a strange thing that, at the very moment our Lord was about to exercise His triumphant power, He should sigh. Some commentators explain it by saying that it was the deep voice of the prayer in which He was at that moment engaged. And others, again, say that what He sighed for was the unbelief of the multitude, upon whom every work of power seemed to be wasted, in that it failed to convince them. Others, again, hold that He sighed at the thought of those deeper ills of the soul which could not be healed by a word, as physical deafness could. And, yet again, Stier ingeniously suggests that Jesus sighed because He realized that the gifts of speech and hearing were so often abused, and might be abused by the very man on whom He was about to confer them—He sighed because He knew that "the gift of hearing is so doubtful a blessing, and the faculty of speech is so apt to be perverted."

And Its Meaning

But the simplest explanation is the truest and the best. The "groan" expressed, as Dr. Salmond puts it, "Christ's deep, pained sympathy." Our Lord was touched with the feeling of all our infirmities. He was full of the deepest and keenest sympathy. He was "moved with compassion" at every sight of sorrow. His eyes had been lifted up to heaven the moment before—the land where there is no sickness, no suffering, no pain. And now they are fixed upon an example of the woes and miseries of earth; and possibly the contrast between heaven, with its happiness and perfect health, and earth, with its suffering and pain, called forth this "groan." Our Lord "groaned" over this poor creature before Him, deaf and partially dumb, the mere wreck and ruin of a man. This was not man as God had made him. God looked on all that He had made, and behold it was "very good." This maimed and marred being was man as sin had damaged, defaced and disfigured him. And our Lord "groaned" at the thought of the ravages sin had made in God's fair world.

Not a Solitary Incident

There is another illustration of the same kind of thing in the story of the raising of Lazarus. When our Lord saw the sisters weeping, and the Jews who had come to comfort them also weeping, John tells us, "He groaned in the spirit and was troubled." And again when He came to the grave He groaned in Himself. In the Greek word there is a suggestion of anger and indignation. He groaned with indignant emotion. What was it that stirred this emotion within Him? He groaned with indignant emotion at the disorder of the world, at the pain and suffering and sorrow and death that sin had brought into the world. And so in this deaf and dumb man He saw an illustration of the work of the devil, of the ravage and havoc wrought by sin, and He "groaned"; He sighed—not so much with indignation this time (for the Greek word is not identical with that in John), but with pity and sympathy.

The Compassion of Christ

In this "sigh" you have our Lord's pity expressed for all needy, suffering, sin-burdened men. He did not walk through life with unheeding eyes and an unfeeling heart. He had eyes to see and a heart to feel. Sorrow always stirred His sympathies. He was "full of compassion." And we too need the pitiful heart, if we are to do Christ's work in the world. The world is full today of the sick and the poor and the suffering and the sinful. We ought not to be able to walk along life's ways with unmoved compassion. We want a "heart at leisure from itself, to soothe and sympathize." "A heart of compassion" is the first thing Paul mentions in that list of the shining garments of the new man. "Put on therefore, as God's elect, holy and beloved, a heart of compassion" (Col. 3:12). For we can do nothing towards the redemption of the world unless we have the compassionate heart.

The Groan and the Upward Look

It is worth noticing that the "sigh" or "groan"' of our Lord came immediately after the heavenward look. As Dr. Morison beautifully puts it, "The deepest sympathy for man springs from the loftiest communion with God." The fact is, we shall only learn to pity as we look up. It is only as we think of God that we learn something of His purpose with reference to man; it is only as we see man as he was meant to be, that we shall pity man as he is. I can conceive of one, who never lifts his eyes above earth and its things, having the springs of pity dried up within him. Here, for instance, is a man who writes, "This world is the best possible of worlds; man as he is, is as good as he can be; sin and misery are essentially human." We have only to hold a creed like that, and pity will die within us. But if we "look up," and see man as God meant him to be, we shall be filled with deep and unutterable pity for man as he is. Pity springing from communion with God is like a stream which, having its source high up in the eternal snows, flows cool and full, bringing refreshing verdure to the parched fields in the hottest days of summer.

The Look Away from Despair

Then again, as Dr. Maclaren suggests, the heavenward look is necessary to guard us from the pit of despair. If we look simply and only at this world and its miseries, we may easily fall into despair. There is a profound pity in the heart of some of our great Pessimists. Thomas Hardy, for instance, has a deep concern for the sorrows and sadnesses of this world, which with such terrible realism he describes for us in his Wessex novels. It is such a hopeless pity; he sees no remedy or cure. But the heavenward look flashes the gleam of hope into the very eye of pity. "Jesus groaned." He sighed over the plight of this deaf and dumb man; but it was not a hopeless sigh, for He knew at the very moment that God would enable Him to repair the ravages which sin had made. And so exactly will it be with us; the sight of the world's sin and pain ought always to stir us to deepest and tenderest pity; but if we look up to God it will never stir us to despair, for we shall know then that God can save to the uttermost, that He can undo and repair the ravages of sin, that He can set the most broken and marred perfect before His throne.

Christ's Word

Then, following the heavenward look and the sigh, came the word of power. "Looking up to heaven, He sighed, and saith unto him, Ephphatha, that is, Be opened" (v. 34). You notice that in this case, as in that of the daughter of Jairus, the very Aramaic word that Jesus spoke has stamped itself upon Peter's memory and is reproduced here. There is a close connection between the word of power and the sigh and the heavenward look that preceded it. It was the pity of His heart that prompted the desire to help. It was His union with God that gave Him the power to help. Looking up to heaven, "He sighed, and saith, Ephphatha, that is, Be opened. And his ears were opened, and the bond of his tongue was loosed, and he spake plain."

Pitifulness, Prayerfulness and Power

The lesson of all this for us is obvious. Pitifulness and prayerfulness are the conditions of power. For without pitifulness we shall not have the wish to save the burdened and sin-stained all about us; and without prayer we shall not have the power. But supposing we have the pitifulness, and supposing we have the prayerfulness, supposing we have the sensitive heart and the expectant faith, then we too shall be able to speak the word of power, and we too shall see God's saving and restoring grace exercised through and by us. Do you not long to see the Church of Jesus Christ speaking the word of power? Do you not long to see it declaring its Gospel with such authoritativeness that men would be convinced and converted by it? Do you not long to see blind eyes opened, deaf ears unstopped, dead hearts quickened? Here are the conditions— a great pity and a great faith. A Church that has great pity for men, and great faith in God, shall have great and irresistible power. And when once the Church of Christ shows that it possesses that power, men will cease to scoff at it and think lightly of it.

And Results

Notice what happened as a result of the deed of mercy Christ performed on this deaf and dumb man. "And they were beyond measure astonished, saying, He hath done all things well: He maketh even the deaf to hear, and the dumb to speak" (v. 37). The sight of our Lord's redeeming power extorted praise from the people, and quickened faith amongst them. "He hath done all things well," they said. And Matthew adds, "And they glorified the God of Israel." Praise and faith on the part of the people will always be the result, when the effects of Christ's redeeming power are seen. It is only an impotent Church that men scoff at. It is only because the Church has to some extent lost its power of working moral miracles that men treat God with indifference, and speak as if there was nothing in the Christian faith.

47
The Leaven of the Pharisees

"In those days the multitude being very great, and having nothing to eat, Jesus called His disciples unto Him, and saith unto them, I have compassion on the multitude, because they have now been with me three days, and have nothing to eat: And if I send them away fasting to their own houses, they will faint by the way: for divers of them came from far. And His disciples answered Him, From whence can a man satisfy these men with bread here in the wilderness? And He asked them, How many loaves have ye? And they said, Seven. And He commanded the people to sit down on the ground: and He took the seven loaves, and gave thanks, and brake, and gave to His disciples to set before them and they did set them before the people. And they had a few small fishes: and He blessed, and commanded to set them also before them. So they did eat, and were filled: and they took up of the broken meat that was left seven baskets. And they that had eaten were about four thousand: and He sent them away. And straightway He entered into a ship with His disciples, and came into the parts of Dalmanutha. And the Pharisees came forth, and began to question with Him, seeking of Him a sign from heaven, tempting Him. And He sighed deeply in His spirit, and saith, Why doth this generation seek after a sign? verily I say unto you, There shall no sign be given unto this generation. And He left them, and entering into the ship again departed to the other side. Now the disciples had forgotten to take bread, neither had they in the ship with them more than one loaf. And He charged them, saying, Take heed, beware of the leaven of the Pharisees, and of the leaven of Herod. And they reasoned among themselves, saying, It is because we have no bread. And when Jesus knew it, He saith unto them, Why reason ye, because ye have no bread? perceive ye not yet, neither understand? have ye your heart yet hardened? Having eyes, see ye not? and having ears, hear ye not? and do ye not remember? When I brake the five loaves among five thousand, how many baskets full of fragments took ye up? They say unto Him, Twelve. And when the seven among four thousand, how many baskets full of fragments took ye up? And they said Seven. And He said unto them, How is it that ye do not understand?" —Mark 8:1-21.

The Feeding of the Four Thousand

I AM GOING to omit any extended treatment of the paragraph which describes the feeding of the 4000. The outstanding lessons are mainly identical with those suggested by the feeding of the 5000 (see pp.

247

196-202). The only noticeable point of difference is this—that, while the feeding of the 5000 was not a work of necessity, but was deliberately performed by our Lord to symbolize His dying and the giving of His flesh to be the food of the world, this later wilderness feast was provided in order to meet an urgent necessity. It found its motive, not in any truth Jesus wished to teach, but in His sympathy and compassion. The crowd had been with Him three days, and had had nothing to eat, and He would not send them away fasting to their homes lest they should faint by the way, for many of them had come from far. The presence of 4000 people with Him in the wilderness would seem to show that the popularity lost by the sermon on the Bread of life had to a large extent been recovered.

Retirement Sought

But Christ was more in love with quietness than popularity. What He wanted most was opportunity for quiet talk with His disciples. And so, when the great feast was over, He entered into the boat with His disciples, and came into the parts of Dalmanutha. Where Dalmanutha was, it is impossible to say, for this is the only place where the name is mentioned. "He came," Matthew says, "into the borders of Magadan" (Matt. 4:39). But that does not help us, as Magadan is as impossible to locate as Dalmanutha, Matthew's account being the only place where the name occurs. Travelers and geographers have suggested identifications with various sites, one or other of which may possibly have been the Dalmanutha mentioned here, though it is by no means certain. The fact seems to be that Dalmanutha and Magadan—whether they are two names for one place, or two places adjacent to each other—were very obscure places. And it was their obscurity that constituted their attractiveness to our Lord. He made His way to these hidden, out-of-the-way spots, whose very location has passed out of the recollection of men, because they seemed to promise Him an undisturbed retreat, where at length He could enjoy that opportunity for quiet speech with His disciples about Himself and the shameful end He knew was in store for Him — an opportunity which hitherto He had sought in vain.

He was, however, again disappointed in His hope. When He passed northwards into the borders of Phoenicia, He could not be hid—need, misery discovered Him. Now, when He proceeded eastward to these obscure villages, He could not be hid—hate discovered Him.

Enemies Afoot

"And the Pharisees came forth," says Mark—Matthew tells us that some Sadducees were also with them—a fact we should have gathered from Christ's subsequent conversation with His disciples, even if Matthew had not told us so explicitly. Pharisees and Sadducees were, as a rule, at daggers drawn. They were separated from one another by deep religious and political differences. The Pharisee stood for the strictest orthodoxy; the Sadducee was more or less of a rationalist. The Pharisee was politically an enthusiastic, not to say fanatical, nationalist; the Sadducee was willing to accept foreign rule, and, indeed, to identify the Messianic anticipations of Israel with the Herodian dynasty. But for the time Pharisees and Sadducees had forgotten their mutual antagonism in a common hate of Jesus. They had thwarted and opposed Him before, as we have already seen. Perhaps, when they saw the crowds desert Him after His sermon on the Bread of life, and discovered that He had gone northwards into Phoenicia, they may have flattered themselves that they had finally got rid of Him. But His return, and the crowding out of so many thousands into the wilderness to hear Him, stirred them to renewed activity. He had scarcely reached His retreat before they were on the scene. They had probably come forth from Capernaum, and their object was to ply Christ with captious questions, and, if possible, to "catch Him in His words."

A Sign Demanded

They began their policy of entangling questions, by reiterating their demand for a "sign." This was a strange demand, was it not? For our Lord's career as a Teacher had been marked by an abundance of "signs." That is what all of our Lord's miracles were—they were "signs." That is John's comment, after the first of them, "This beginning of His signs did Jesus in Cana of Galilee, and manifested His glory" (John 2:11). And ever since that first sign, signs the most wonderful and subduing had continued to mark our Lord's course. Wherever He went He left behind Him some monument of His power and grace.

Monuments of Mercy Seen

When Eleanor, the wife of King Edward I., died at Harby, they brought her body to Westminster for burial, and in every town at which her body rested for a night they built a cross; you can trace the route of that funeral procession by the crosses that still remain. So you could trace Christ's progress through Palestine by the healed men and women to be found in every place, monuments to His compassion and love. He went to Jerusalem, and He left His monument there in the person of the impotent man whom He restored to health and strength. He went to Cana, and He left His monument there in the person of the nobleman's son rescued from the very jaws of death. He went to Decapolis, and He left His monument there in him who had had the legion but was clothed and in his right mind. He went into the borders of Phoenicia, and left His monument there in the person of the daughter of the Canaanitish woman, whom He delivered from the tyranny of an unclean spirit. He went to Jericho, and He left His monument there in the person of blind Bartimaeus restored to sight. He went to Bethany, and He left His monument there in the person of dead Lazarus called back again to life. And as for Capernaum, from which place these carping Pharisees had come, He had done so many signs in Capernaum that, if He had done the like in Tyre and Sidon, they would have repented long ago in sackcloth and ashes.

And Yet Ignored

And yet, in spite of all this, these Pharisees and Sadducees came to Him asking for a sign. Other people were awed and subdued, and convinced by what they saw. Nicodemus declared that no one could do such mighty works except God were with him; the multitudes, when they saw the palsied man restored, glorified God, saying, "We never saw it on this fashion"; even the half pagan people of Decapolis, when they saw the deaf and dumb man able to hear and able to speak, declared, "He hath done all things well," and glorified the God of Israel. But these Pharisees and Sadducees affected to be still in doubt;—they insinuated that there was room in all these signs for illusion and delusion, and so they come to Him clamoring for a sign about which there should be no controversy or dispute— they seek of Him a sign from heaven.

A Sign from Heaven Sought

From heaven, because heaven was supposed to be a place where Satan had no power. In their bitterness and malice they had not hesitated to suggest that some of our Lord's miracles were done by Satan's help and power. But a sign from heaven would prove past dispute the Divineness of Christ's mission. They do not specify what precise sign they want; "that He should stop the sun or rein in the moon, or hurl down thunder or the like," says Chrysostom. Probably they had in mind the manna sent down from heaven in answer to the prayer of Moses, or the fire called down by Elijah or the thunder and rain called down by Samuel at any rate, some sign from heaven, that they might see and believe.

The Sorrow of Jesus

And when He heard this request our Lord "sighed deeply in His spirit," or rather, groaned deeply. What evoked this deep groan from the spirit of Jesus? We saw before that His sigh over the deaf and dumb man was a sigh wrung from Him by the thought of the havoc sin had made in a world which God made "very good." This deep and vehement groan is a groan over sin itself. If it had been weak faith crying out for succor and confirmation our Lord, you may depend upon it, would have done or said something to meet its need. But the demand for a sign was not the cry of weak faith. It was the final evidence of callousness and obduracy of heart. Christ had already given signs more than sufficient to men of open and honest heart. But these were men who did not want to believe. Their request for a sign from heaven was made, not in the interests of belief, but as an excuse of unbelief. And that was why Christ groaned deeply. Here were men hardening their hearts against the evidences of God's grace, doing despite to the Holy Spirit of God, deliberately sinning against the light. It was over this that Christ sighed. I find that scarcely anything stirred Christ to deeper emotion than the thought of the people's unbelief. It was one of the things over which He is said to have "marvelled." And when He burst into that passion of tears and grief over Jerusalem, the cause lay in the obduracy and unbelief of the people.

A Personal Question

All of this suggests the question whether Christ has any occasion to sigh over us. For confessedly He accomplishes in our midst the most wonderful "mighty works." He restores the morally blind, He heals the morally leprous, He quickens the morally dead. His Divine Commission would seem to be sufficiently attested; yet multitudes refuse to believe on Him. And their obduracy causes infinite pain and sorrow to His heart. He sighs deeply in His spirit. Does He sigh over us?

The Refusal of the Sign

The reply of Jesus to the demand was, "Why doth this generation seek a sign? verily I say unto you, There shall no sign be given unto this generation" (v. 12). Now, why did Jesus refuse these people a sign? Various reasons have been suggested, and there is probably something in every one of them. (1) To begin with, the motive that prompted the request was wholly wrong. As I said, it was not confirmation of a struggling faith that these people wanted, but rather an excuse for unbelief. (2) Then again, as some commentators suggest, even a sign from heaven would have been wasted upon these people. You remember what our Lord said in the parable of Dives and Lazarus, "If they hear not Moses and the prophets, neither will they be persuaded, if one rise from the dead!" (Luke 16:31). An extraordinary preacher, says Jesus, would produce no effect upon men who could remain unmoved under the preaching of Moses and the prophets. And the same principle held good with reference to these Pharisees and Sadducees. Men who could remain untouched and unpersuaded—who could convince themselves there was nothing Divine in the healing of the palsied, the feeding of the 5000, the raising of Jairus' daughter—would not be persuaded though Christ should give them a sign from heaven. They would try to explain even that away. They did try to explain it away. For when the voice from heaven came saying, "I have both glorified it, and will glorify it again," those who stood by said it was only thunder.

The Reason for Refusal

But I think there were other and deeper reasons why Christ refused this "sign from heaven." First of all, as far as I can make out from a study of the Gospels, Christ never performed any miracle from motives of mere display. They were never done for spectacular effect. He never performed a miracle, as far as I can discover, to prove His Deity, or to constrain people to believe on Him. The result of His miracles often was that people did believe on Him, because through them they beheld His glory. But that was never the motive. The motive was always our Lord's pity and kindness and desire to do good. He never performed a useless miracle. He never displayed His power for display's sake. His works were always a revelation of His grace. But such a "sign" as these Pharisees asked for would have been contrary to our Lord's whole method. Every element of mercy, humanity, and instruction would have been banished from it. It would have reduced Christ to the level of the magician, the mere wonder-worker, and He refused to do it. (3) And there is this further fact. Christ, as Mr. Latham points out in his *Pastor Pastorum*, never overwhelmed the human mind and will by His miracles. Their evidence was never irresistible. That is to say, if men wished to find a loophole for doubt, they could generally find one. It had of necessity to be so; otherwise religion would, as Mr. Latham says, be not a faith, but a science; trust in Christ would cease to be a moral act.

There is no moral quality about our belief that two and two make four; we are so made that we must believe it. You can see that if the "signs" which Christ did proved His Divinity in the same mathematical and irresistible way, faith in Him as the Divine Savior would be as void of moral quality as our belief today that two and two make four. It seems a paradox, but in reality it is sober truth to say, that before a genuine faith can be exercised, there must be room for question and doubt. For there is always an element of the venturesome in faith. People crave for certitude. They have a hankering after mathematical proof in the realm of religion. They are hankering after the impossible. The law of religion is, "we walk by faith, not by sight." If Christ had given an absolutely irresistible "sign from heaven"—such a sign as left men powerless to disbelieve—He would not have created faith, He would have destroyed it. He would have overwhelmed the mind, He would not have convinced it. So He declined this final and irresistible sign. He left room for the exercise of "faith." He has given us "signs" enough to persuade the honest and sincere heart. If men refuse to be persuaded, it is because they have an evil heart of unbelief. And so a man's faith or unfaith becomes an index to his moral nature.

The Leaven of the Pharisees

"There shall no sign be given unto this generation," Christ said. And having said that He left them, and again entering into the boat, departed to the other side. But though He left them, He could not forget them. While His disciples were busy attending to the boat, Christ brooded over the obduracy and blindness and malignant hate of these people He had just left. And then, as Dr. A. B. Bruce says, "Abruptly, and as one waking out of a reverie, He uttered this solemn warning to His disciples, 'Take heed, beware of the leaven of the Pharisees and the leaven of Herod'" (v. 15). I need not refer to the stupid literalism of the disciples, who actually thought at first Christ was warning them against purchasing bread that came from the hands of the Pharisees and Herodians. Their colossal misunderstanding only shows how urgent was their need of that special training Christ was eager to give, how far as yet they were from appreciating the spiritual character of the Kingdom. But I pass all that by. They understood at length, as Matthew puts it, that He "bade them not beware of the leaven of

bread, but of the teaching of the Pharisees and Sadducees"
(Matt. 16:12). Now what was there in the teaching of the
Pharisees and Sadducees that made Christ warn His disciples
thus solemnly against it?

Hypocrisy

The Pharisees are again and again denounced by Christ as "hypocrites." They made a great show of religion; but it was a case of
much cry and little wool. The form was there, without the
power. They paid tithes of mint and anise and cummin, and
neglected mercy and righteousness and truth.

Formalism

Formality was the besetting sin of the Pharisees. That was the
"leaven" against which Christ warned the disciples. For "formalism"is ever the foe of true religion. The man who magnifies the
outward and mechanical is always in danger of minimizing and
neglecting the inward and the spiritual. Formalism in Palestine
nineteen centuries ago was so much the foe of religion that it
nailed the Lord of life to the tree.

Materialism

And if formalism was the leaven of the Pharisees, materialism
was the leaven of Herod. For the Herodians—who were mainly
Sadducees—were people who abandoned their national hopes and
ideals, attached themselves to the usurping and half-pagan
Herodian dynasty, for the sake of present material advantage. And
materialism again is the deadly foe of religion. It is the antithesis,
denial of religion. "Love of the world is enmity against God."
"Beware," said Jesus, "of these two things." They had stifled out
the religion in the hearts of these Pharisees and Herodians. They
would stifle out the religion in their hearts, if allowed to enter.

Has the warning any pertinency for our day? Surely, my
brethren, it has. These are the two most menacing perils of our
own day—formalism and materialism, the leaven of the Pharisees
and the leaven of Herod.

Take Heed!

These are not ancient perils. They are perils of today. There is no
warning more needed by us than this—"Take heed, beware of the
leaven of the Pharisees and the leaven of Herod." Beware of formalism, the leaven of the Pharisees. God is a Spirit, and they that
worship Him must worship Him in spirit and in truth. Beware of

materialism— the leaven of Herod. "Love not the world, neither the things that are in the world. If any man love the world, the love of the Father is not in him. For all that is in the world, the lust of the flesh, and the lust of the eyes, and the vainglory of life, is not of the Father, but is of the world. And the world passeth away, and the lust thereof: but he that doeth the will of God abideth for ever" (1 John 2:15-17).

48
The Healing of the Blind Man at Bethsaida

"And He cometh to Bethsaida; and they bring a blind man unto Him, and besought Him to touch him. And He took the blind man by the hand, and led him out of the town; and when He had spit on his eyes, and put His hands upon him, He asked him if he saw ought. And he looked up, and said, I see men as trees, walking. After that He put His hand again upon his eyes, and made him look up: and he was restored, and saw every man clearly. And He sent him away to his house, saying, Neither go into the town, nor tell it to any in the town." —Mark 8:22-26.

Christ and the Twelve

THE CLUE TO our Lord's movements at this stage of His career is that desire for quietness, and the opportunity for speech and converse with His disciples which quietness would afford, to which I have already referred more than once. How urgent was the need for instructing and teaching the Twelve the conversation about leaven that took place as they crossed the sea only too plainly revealed. There is a sense of disappointment in Christ's word to them, "Why reason ye, because ye have no bread? do ye not yet perceive, neither understand? . . . Having eyes, see ye not? and having ears, hear ye not? and do ye not remember?" (vv. 17, 18). It was saddening to Jesus that, in spite of all their associations with Him, when He talked of the leaven of the Pharisees and of the leaven of Herod, they should think that He was talking of bread. It was disheartening that, in spite of the miracle of the 5000, and the subsequent miracle of the 4000, these disciples should get into something like a panic, because they had only with them one loaf. And these were the men upon whom would rest the whole burden of the work when He was gone, and upon whose zeal and understanding (humanly speaking) the future of the Kingdom would depend. In view of all this, you can understand our Lord's anxiety for quietness, wherein to devote Himself to the instruction and the discipline of these disciples. Indeed, it is not too much to say that from this time forth this was the work upon which Christ concentrated His energies. In the first part of His career He gave Himself up to the work of public preaching; in the second part of His career He gave Himself specially to the work of "training the Twelve." In His desire for quiet, in order to be able to undertake this "training" work, He had gone from place to place. But always something intervened. He had gone to the borders of Phoenicia, and the woman with a sick daughter had found Him out; and after that there was no privacy for Him. He had come down into the coasts of Decapolis; but His fame had preceded Him, until soon there was a crowd of 4000 men hanging on His lips for days at a time in the wilderness. He escaped to Dalmanutha; but even in that obscure and out-of-the-way place hate discovered Him, and the Pharisees and Herodians dogged His steps. So once again Jesus moved on.

At Bethsaida

Leaving Dalmanutha He took ship, sailed to the other side, and came to Bethsaida. This is not the Bethsaida, the city of Andrew and Peter, situated near Capernaum, and so frequently referred to in the Gospel story. This is Bethsaida Julias, once a mere village, but now raised by one of the Herods to the rank of a city, situated on the north-eastern corner of the Sea of Galilee, near the river Jordan. Jesus was really on His way to the coasts of Caesarea Philippi, in the north, for it seemed hopeless to expect privacy anywhere in Galilee. He visited Bethsaida Julias only because it was on His route. But, passing visit though it was, someone recognized Him, and soon He was confronted by a little company of people who brought to Him a man who was blind, and besought Him to touch him. And the five verses that follow tell us of the miracle Christ wrought upon this particular sufferer. I have said that Christ wherever He went left His monument behind Him, in the shape of a household blessed, or a man or woman or child healed. He was only passing through this city of Bethsaida Julias, and yet He left His monument there too, in the person of this blind man restored to sight. It was a case of goodness by the way.

Now this miracle, like that of the healing of the deaf and dumb man which we have already studied together, is peculiar to St Mark. And in several of their details the two are very much alike, and suggest very much the same reflections and lessons. Upon these similarities I shall only very lightly touch, in order that I may have time to emphasize the one or two lessons that are special and peculiar to this narrative.

The Blind Man

"And they bring to Him a blind man" (v. 22). There is no deprivation more pitiable than that of blindness, and in the East, especially in Egypt and Syria, there is none more common. The conditions of climate and life, the glare of the sun, the dust, account for this. One-tenth of the population of Joppa suffer from ophthalmia. In Cairo, out of a quarter of a million of people, there are 4000 blind. Sightless, blear-eyed, fly-infected, miserable men and women confront travelers in every Syrian town and village today, and make one of the most distressing spectacles of Eastern life. I suppose it was the prevalence of this terrible affliction that made the prophet anticipate, as one of the blessings that Messiah would bring with Him, that, "the eyes of the blind shall be opened." So, when John the Baptist sent from prison to ask Jesus if He really were the long-expected Messiah, Jesus bade the messengers go back, and tell John what they had seen and heard, and amongst other things this, that "the blind receive their sight."

Led to Jesus

It was one of this sorry, afflicted class who was brought to Jesus as He passed through Bethsaida. Some preachers have made a great deal of the word "bring"—"they bring to Him a blind man." They have pressed the word, to suggest that the desire and faith were all in the friends of the sufferer, and not in the sufferer himself; some going so far as to make out that the patient was a passive and even unwilling subject. And on this exegesis they have built homilies about the duty of our bringing our friends to Jesus for help and healing. The lesson they teach is admirable enough; the highest service one friend can render to another is to introduce him to Jesus, but the exegesis upon which in this particular instance it is based is quite unwarranted. The word "bring" in this case carries with it no implication of unwillingness; it has reference solely and simply to the man's blindness. Just because he was blind, he had to be brought, led to Jesus. And then Jesus does two things to this blind man, similar to two things He had done in the case of the deaf and dumb man.

Privacy Sought

First of all, the miracle is performed in privacy. "He took hold of the blind man by the hand, and brought him out of the village" (v. 23). He Himself led him out, upon which Bengel makes the remark, "wondrous humility!" Yea, so it is, but not rare or uncommon in the case of Jesus. That is what He was always doing.

Jesus was not like an Eastern monarch, haughty, inaccessible, dispensing favors from a throne. He stooped to become a friend of the poorest. Indeed, this is what He did for the whole race when He took flesh. He took hold upon the seed of Abraham. He took our fallen, guilty, sin-stained race by the hand. He took this blind man by the hand, and I do not think it is fanciful to suppose that there would be something in the warm pressure of our Lord's hand that would assure the sufferer that he was in the company of a friend. Had he been able to look into the Master's face, he would have seen love and kindness shining there; the hand clasp was meant to assure him of the love he could not see. "He took hold of the blind man by the hand, and brought him out of the village" (v. 23) He took him aside from the staring and gaping crowd. Partly, no doubt, for the man's own sake, for Christ's best lessons are taught when He can get a man alone. But partly also, as the narrative makes abundantly clear, for His own sake. Jesus was in search of privacy. A great wonder wrought before the eyes of a great crowd would entirely have defeated His object. It would have brought the multitudes about Him. It would have created a dangerous enthusiasm. So He did His act of beneficence by stealth. He took the blind man out of the village, and when He had accomplished His act of healing, He sent him away to his home, saying, "Do not even enter into the village" (v. 26).

Symbolic Action Used

And secondly, in this case, as in the case of the deaf and dumb man, He used symbolic action "When He had spit on his eyes, . . . He laid His hands upon him" (v. 23). Now saliva was supposed to have some healing medicinal quality. And the object Christ had in anointing the blind man's eyes with His saliva was—as in the case of boring the deaf man's ears—to quicken a spirit of expectancy and faith within him. All of which, says Dr. Alexander Maclaren, is the way in which Christ stoops to the use of material helps, in order to minister to sense-bound natures. The ordinances of worship, the Sacraments, they are great means of grace; but from one point of view they are accommodations to our human weakness. The pure spirits in heaven need no such aids for their worship. "I saw no temple therein." But, composed as we are of flesh and spirit, an absolute and naked spirituality of worship is impossible to us; we need the sacred day and the sacred place, and the sacred symbols of bread and wine. Only let us always remember this—that, just as the healing power was not in this saliva with which Jesus anointed the blind man's eyes, but in the Lord

Himself, in His will and commanding word, so the grace is not in the ordinance, in the place, or in the symbols, but in the present living Christ. The holy place is visited in vain, and the worship is shared in in vain, and the bread and wine are partaken of in vain, unless we come into direct and immediate contact with the saving and redeeming Christ.

But now I pass on from these points of similarity, to points which are special and peculiar to this particular miracle.

The Gradual Illumination

And the first point I want you to notice is that of the gradualness of the cure. Usually in the record of our Lord's miracles, the sick man, whatever his disease might be, was cured at once by a word. But in this case the man was healed not at once, but at twice. After spitting on his eyes and laying His hands on them, Jesus asked the blind man if he could see anything. "And he looked up, and said, I see men; for I behold them as trees, walking" (v. 24). That is to say, he could discern large objects in motion and though they looked like trees, he concluded that they were men, for the simple reason that they were walking about. So again Jesus "laid His hands upon his eyes; and he looked steadfastly, and was restored, and saw all things clearly" (v. 25).

The Lord's Way with Souls

The commentators make a great deal of the fact that all this is in closest accord with later scientific discovery. But I confess it is not its truth to scientific discovery, but the broad fact of the gradual nature of the cure, that interests me. For it seems to me that we have in this miracle a symbol, parable of the way in which Christ works in the matter of the illumination of the soul. Take it on the broadest platform, to begin with. What is the Bible? It is the story of the progressive revelation of God to the human race. But there is a vast difference between the first beginnings of revelation, as we have them in Genesis let us say, and the full and perfect revelation given to us in Jesus Christ. God, we are assured, spoke "unto the fathers in the prophets by divers portions and in divers manners" (Heb. 1:1). He revealed Himself, the verse seems to suggest in fragments. These patriarchs of our race saw God, they were vividly and intensely conscious of Him; but you cannot read the Old Testament books without seeing that they did not see God clearly. There is much of error and mistake in their ideas about God. But their knowledge grew from more and more, until at length it was granted unto men to see the full light of the glory of God in the face of Jesus Christ.

Progressive Spiritual Vision

Take it on the narrower platform of the individual life, and there again it is true that our spiritual vision is progressive. We do not see everything clearly at the first touch of Christ. The whole teaching of the New Testament insists upon progression in our apprehension of Christian truth. When Christ first opens our eyes to eternal things, all does not at once become clear. We see things dimly, darkly, indistinctly. The heights and depths of Christian truth are not revealed to us. The lengths and breadths of God's love are not comprehended by us. The meaning and power of the cross of Christ, for instance— that is not something that breaks upon us in a flash; it grows upon us more and more. I suppose my own experience is but a sample of that of thousands of others. It was but a poor and imperfect vision of the cross of Christ I had when I started my Christian life. But it has become clearer and clearer to me as the years have rolled by. My study of God's Word, my experience of life, my better acquaintance with the sins and wants of my own heart, all these things have helped me to fuller understanding of the great mystery of Christ's death and passion. I do not say that "I see clearly" even yet; but I see heights and depths, glories and mercies in the cross of Christ today that were hidden from me twenty years ago. And this is only an example. The same truth could be illustrated in the matter of prayer and providence, and the person of Christ. We do not see all or know all at once. The knowledge is progressive. And vision grows in clearness as we receive "grace for grace," unceasingly renewed, and enter into the secret of the Lord which is with them that fear Him.

But Contact with Christ

But notice that a man may have been really touched by Christ, even though his vision may be vague and dim. "I see men," said this sufferer, "for I behold them as trees walking." And yet he had really experienced the touch of Christ. And so there are men and women whose notions of truth may be very crude and ignorant, who yet have come into that direct and immediate contact with Christ which really constitutes the salvation of the soul.

The Perfect Vision

But while the story teaches the truth that spiritual illumination is gradual, it also brings us the assurance that Christ will not leave His work till He has given us perfect vision. He was not content to leave this man in that condition of imperfect and uncertain sight when men appeared to him as trees walking. Our Lord touched his eyes again, and he was restored, and saw all things clearly. And this is just a parable of what Christ will do for the soul. Before He has finished with us, we too shall see all things clearly. "The path of the righteous is as the shining light, that shineth more and more unto the perfect day" (Prov. 4:18). Light, the "shining light." And you have perhaps watched the light of dawn.

You have seen it first touch in the hills, while the valley lay shrouded in darkness and night; and then gradually creep down the hillside, sweeping the night before it, until at length it has invaded every nook and cranny, and filled them with sunshine and brightness. The path of the just shall be like that; it shall lead him into fuller and fuller light, until at length it is "perfect day" with him—perfect day. I know how hard it is to bear the dim twilight of the dawn. I know how fiercely some of us long to see and to know. How we chafe at the limitations of our vision!

I had a letter only a few days ago from a father who had just lost a daughter of fifteen. How that father wants to know! He wrote to me pathetically, asking me questions that are as much hidden from me as from him. But Christ will not leave us for ever in the twilight, with only a groping and uncertain knowledge. He will bring us into the "perfect day."

I do not know that the "perfect day" will ever be ours in this life. The skies will grow brighter for us, and the vision clearer year by year, if we really follow on to know the Lord; yet to the end there will be many things that are not plain. But as to the life beyond, "there shall be no night there," no shred of darkness left, sacred high eternal noon, the "perfect day." And then at length we shall "see clearly."

To Be Attained at the Last

There were two stages in this man's experience. He saw men as trees, the stage of imperfect vision. He saw all things clearly, the stage of perfect sight. There are two similar stages in our experience. This is how Paul states them: "Now we see in a mirror darkly; but then face to face: now I know in part; but then shall I know even as also I have been known" (1 Cor. 13:12). Let us live in hope. Christ will in His own good time complete the work He has begun. He who is the Author is also the Finisher of our faith. He will not leave as in the night; He will bring us at length into the perfect day, when we shall see all things clearly.

49
Questions and Answers

"And Jesus went out, and His disciples, into the towns of Caesarea Philippi: and by the way He asked His disciples, saying unto them, Whom do men say that I am? And they answered, John the Baptist: but some say, Elias; and others, One of the prophets. And He saith unto them, But whom say ye that I am? And Peter answereth and saith unto Him, Thou art the Christ. And He charged them that they should tell no man of Him." —Mark 8:27-30.

To Caesarea Philippi

WE COME NOW to what is in many respects the most critical episode in the life of our Lord. I have emphasized the fact that at this particular stage in His career Christ tried to escape the crowds, in order to find opportunity for quiet speech with His disciples. In view of the cross, which He could plainly see looming up on His horizon, He urgently desired to speak with His chosen Twelve about Himself, and about His passion. For this reason He sets His face northwards, to a remote and retired part of the country which He had not yet visited in the course of His ministry. "Jesus went forth, and His disciples, into the villages of Caesarea Philippi" (v. 27).

A Pagan City

This Caesarea Philippi lay some twenty-five miles to the north of the Sea of Galilee. It was named Caesarea in honor of the Roman Emperor Augustus, and it was called Caesarea Philippi, "Philip's Caesarea," after the Herod who had rebuilt it, and made it splendid, and to distinguish it from that other Caesarea on the sea coast, where Paul was afterwards imprisoned. This Caesarea was situated in the grandest and most romantic part of Palestine. Planted on a terrace about 1100 feet above sea-level, at the foot of Lebanon, surrounded by groves of oaks and poplars, with fertile plains stretching westwards, and the snowy mass of Hermon to the north-east, it had a beauty beyond any other town in the land. It was a pagan city. Indeed, its ancient name was Paneas, and it was so called from the Pancivir, a sanctuary of the god Pan, in a deep cavern in the neighborhood.

As showing the hold this pagan cult had of the district, it is interesting to note that the old name gradually asserted itself, and survives to this day in the name Panias. It was to this pagan and to a large extent foreign city that Jesus now traveled with His disciples. Though apparently even here Jesus did not venture into the city itself. In Caesarea some one would have been sure to recognize Him. He kept Himself outside, in the country districts. "He went forth, and His disciples, into the villages of Caesarea Philippi." And there at length He seems to have gained the quietness He needed, and opportunity to speak with the Twelve about the things that lay so near His heart.

A Critical Discourse

It is one of the conversations that took place between Our Lord and His disciples that we are to consider now. I gather myself from a study of the various narratives, that our Lord regarded this conversation as a critical and vital one. For from Luke's account we learn that before He asked the question with which the conversation started He spent some time in solitary prayer. That was our Lord's habit, when any specially difficult or delicate task lay before Him. Before, for instance, He went on His first preaching journey through Galilee, He rose up a great while before day, and departed into a desert place, and there prayed. Before He engaged in the delicate and all-important task of choosing His twelve Apostles, He continued all night in prayer to God. And apparently the conversation which He was now about to hold was of such solemn moment and of such vital consequence that our Lord felt constrained to prepare for it by earnest and continued prayer. And what was the subject of this conversation to which our Lord attached such extraordinary importance? In a word, it was a conversation about His own Person.

The Place of Christ in Christianity

And here I pause just for a moment, to say that evidently Christ attached immense importance to what men thought about Himself. Men are very apt in these days to say it does not matter very much what views we hold about Jesus, so long as we accept His teaching, and obey it. And they dismiss all attempts at defining the Person of Christ, as metaphysical and theological subtleties, which are of no importance for daily life. All I have to say is, that that is not what Jesus Himself thought. He attached the most tremendous importance to the account people gave of Him; the whole future of the Gospel depended in some vital way upon what men thought of Him.

Yes, let us be under no delusion. Our Lord regarded the future of Christianity as bound up with a right understanding of His person. Those who tell us it does not matter much what views we hold, and who make that the excuse for holding inadequate and unworthy views, misread the entire Gospel. They reduce the Gospel to a new teaching, a new philosophy, a mere code of morals. But if there is one thing the New Testament makes abundantly clear, it is this—that the Christian Gospel is not a teaching merely, or a philosophy merely, or a morality merely; it is, as Dr. Van Dyke says, the Gospel of a Person. It centers not simply in what Jesus says, but in what He was and did. Indeed, that is what differentiates Jesus from every other teacher and prophet the world has ever seen. He insists upon Himself. It sounds very plausible to say, "Let theologians quarrel about the Person of Christ; let us be content to obey His teaching"; but, as a matter of fact, in the light of an incident like this, and the whole trend of the Gospel narrative, there is only one thing to be said about this Christianity without Christ—it is another Gospel, which is not another.

The Popular Verdict

Now, passing from that broad and primary lesson of the significance of Christ's Person, I want you to notice the first question Jesus put to His disciples, and their answer. It was this, "Whom do men say that I am?" (v. 27). Or, perhaps, in order to bring out the exact shade of meaning, the question might be rendered thus, "Who do the people say that I am?" Jesus did not ask what the rulers and the Pharisees thought of Him. They had only too plainly shown what they thought. They had called Him a glutton, a drunkard, a friend of publicans and sinners, an agent of Beelzebub. What Christ wanted to know was the opinion of the people at large. For He knew that in every market and at every fireside they had discussed Him, and He wanted to know what the effect of His teaching and wonderful works had upon them, and who they said He was.

A Favorable One

The disciples answer quite frankly, and say, "John the Baptist; and others, Elijah; but others, One of the prophets" (v. 28). Now you will notice from this answer that, as Dr. A. B. Bruce says, "the opinions prevalent among the masses concerning Jesus were in the main favorable." They did not make the calamitous mistake prejudiced Scribes and Pharisees did, of writing Jesus down as an emissary of Satan. There is nothing like prejudice for distorting the vision and perverting the judgment. The mass of the people, with simple and guileless hearts, recognized that, to say the least, Jesus was a specially inspired man. They felt that no one could speak as He spoke, and no one could do the work that He did, except God were with Him. They did not recognize His essential glory. They did not identify Him as their promised Messiah. And perhaps there is some excuse for them, inasmuch as Jesus was so unlike the Messiah they had been taught to expect. But they did recognize that Christ was inspired of God in an altogether unique way, and so they classed Him with the great prophets who were the glory and pride of their race. They said that He was John the Baptist, or Elijah, or One of the prophets.

Christ and the Prophets

Will you notice further, as that same great scholar and thinker points out, that the very variety of opinion about Jesus—the fact that one saw John the Baptist in Him, another Elijah, and another Jeremiah, and another this prophet or that—is in itself proof that Jesus was greater than any of the prophets to whom they compared Him? I daresay the people themselves did not feel the force of this, but quite obviously it is so. Each of the prophets was identified in the popular mind with some one striking and predominant quality. John was remembered for his stern and strenuous call to repentance; Jeremiah was remembered for his melting tenderness and compassion. Ezekiel and Daniel for their parabolic discourses. But here was some One far greater than John, greater than Jeremiah, greater than Ezekiel, greater than Daniel; for He united John and Jeremiah, Ezekiel and Daniel, all in Himself. I think I could construct an argument for the Divinity of Christ out of the opinions of the multitude, confessedly imperfect though they are. The very diversity of them, when you think of it, is proof that Jesus was more than man.

But possibly, as some commentators suggest, the first question was only asked in order to open the conversation. The second was the all-important one.

The Disciples' Faith

"But whom say ye that I am?" Jesus asked (v. 29). It is not the opinion of the crowd He is asking about now, but the faith of these twelve men whom He had called to be with Him, whom He had admitted to His closest intimacy, who had seen Him at close quarters. "Ye, my chosen ones, who say ye that I am?" I need not point out to any of my readers how absolutely critical this question was. For on the answer to it depended the success or failure of His work. To a large extent He had failed with the populace. Not one of them had recognized the glory. If He had failed also with the Twelve, if He were no more than a prophet to them, then He had failed utterly. Humanly speaking, if these disciples had not recognized His Messiahship, there would never have been a Christian faith or a Christendom.

Peter's Answer

But Simon's answer soon dispelled all fears. In the name of the Twelve, without hesitation or doubt, Simon replied, "Thou art the Christ." These disciples were very slow scholars, as we have had occasion to note over and over again. They had their mistakes and their misunderstandings. But let us do them fair play and bare justice, and let this be set down to their infinite credit that, while Pharisees and Scribes denounced Jesus as having a devil, and the populace in their most exalted guesses never thought of Him as more than a great man, these humble Galileans "beheld His glory," and beneath His lowly state recognized the majesty of the only begotten Son of God. "Thou art the Christ," says Peter. God hid the glorious truth from the wise and prudent, and revealed it unto babes.

The Force of This Profession

I do not say that this is a confession of the Divinity of Christ, in the sense in which the Nicene Creed is. But again, as Dr. A. B. Bruce puts it, it is a clear recognition that Jesus was more than man. "Thou art the Messiah, God's anointed One"; that is what Peter said. That is to say, he recognized in his Master that Great One who was the hope of the Jewish nation, of whom the prophets had spoken and psalmists had sung. He applied to Jesus all the splendid predictions of the Old Testament. Jesus was a prophet like unto Moses; the promised Deliverer who would set at liberty them that are bruised, and preach the acceptable year of the Lord. He was Wonderful, Counsellor, the Mighty God, the Prince of Peace. He was the King whose kingdom was to be an everlasting kingdom, and whose name was to endure throughout all generations. All these magnificent and glowing prophecies pointed to Jesus, and found their fulfillment in Him. "Thou art the Christ," said Peter. It was a noble confession. Christ had not failed. His words, His miracles, His life had not been wasted upon these disciples. This answer is the proof of it. They beheld His glory, glory as of the only begotten of the Father, full of grace and truth.

And Its Reception

And Jesus was satisfied with their confession. With characteristic modesty, Peter omits from his account the great eulogy which our Lord, in the overflowing gratitude of His soul, pronounced upon him. But the other Evangelists have preserved it for us. "Blessed art thou, Simon Bar Jonah: for flesh and blood hath not revealed it unto thee, but My Father which is in heaven. And I also say unto thee, that thou art Peter, and upon this rock I will build my Church; and the gates of Hades shall not prevail against it" (Matt. 16:17, 18). Here let us note—(l) that with any confession falling short of this great confession of Peter, our Lord is not satisfied. The popular verdict classed Jesus with the prophets, with the very greatest of them.

The Significance of the Episode

It put Him on a level with the most inspired and gifted of men. It ranked Him with Elijah, Jeremiah, John the Baptist. But Jesus declined to be so classed. He claimed a higher place. He was not Elijah's or John's or Jeremiah's equal. He was their Lord. This has its special pertinency for our own day. The Person of Christ has once again become the subject of debate. And I do not think I am doing the "new theology" movement any injustice when I say that it is the view of the populace it gives as to the person of Christ, and not the belief of Peter. It is numbering Jesus Christ once more among the "prophets." It is whittling away the difference between Jesus and the rest of humanity, and assuring us that we are all "potential Christs." All I have to say about it is, that Christ repudiates the classification. He is not satisfied to be greeted as Teacher, Prophet, not even as the greatest of Teachers, and the greatest of Prophets. He is in a class by Himself. He is unapproached, unapproachable. Jesus is not the fine flower of the race. He is the gift of God. And no view of His Person satisfies Him until, like Peter, we are ready to say, not "One of the prophets," but, "Thou art the Christ, the Son of the Living God."

A Personal Question

But (2), after all, the important question is the personal one. I do not make light of the views and opinions the people at large hold about Christ. They are most of them hopelessly inadequate. Just at present the favorite view seems to be that Christ was principally a Social Reformer. But the important and vital question for you and me is, not what the people think, but our own answer to the Lord's question. There must be no hesitation about our reply. There are some beliefs held and cherished by our fathers which we can, perhaps, surrender without loss. But belief in the Divinity of Christ is of the very essence of our faith. Degrade Him to a "prophet," and you destroy the Gospel. Count Him simply as one amongst others, and upon a faith, or rather want of faith, like that Christ cannot build His Church. And so I am glad that we are confronted with this question, "Whom say ye that I am?"

For my own part, I am ready with my answer. Are you ready with yours? And will it be such an answer as will fill Him with confidence about the future of His Church? My prayer is that our studies in the life of Christ may help to establish our faith, so that, amid all the present upheaval and distress, we may answer with quiet and settled confidence, "Thou art the Christ, the Son of the Living God."

50
Pointing to the Cross

"And He began to teach them, that the Son of man must suffer many things, and he rejected of the elders, and of the chief priests, and scribes, and be killed, and after three days rise again. And He spake that saying openly. And Peter took Him, and began to rebuke Him. But when He had turned about and looked on His disciples, He rebuked Peter, saying, Get thee behind me, Satan: for thou savorest not the things that be of God, but the things that be of men."
—Mark 8:31-33.

A Turning-Point

PETER'S CONFESSION LED on to an announcement by our Lord that filled His disciples' hearts with desolation and sorrow. "And He began to teach them that the Son of man must suffer many things, and be rejected of the elders, and of the chief priests, and the scribes, and be killed, and after three days rise again" (v. 31). "And He began to teach them"—this marks the occasion, as Dr. Salmond says, as being an important turning-point in Christ's work. Hitherto our Lord had never spoken in plain and unmistakable terms about His death. Not that He was unaware that the cross lay at the end of His earthly life. I differ in toto from those scholars and critics who tell us that it was the failure of our Lord's work, as far as the leaders of the nation were concerned, that first made Him realize that a violent death would be the end of it all. I believe Holman Hunt's picture is far nearer the truth.

I believe that the "Shadow of the Cross" lay over our Lord's life from the first. He knew all along that He must be delivered up into the hands of men. But up to this point all His allusions to His death were more or less veiled. As J. A. Alexander says: "Having now drawn from them a profession of their faith in his Messiahship, he enters on the delicate and painful task of teaching them that although he was the Messiah and by necessary consequence a king, the manifestation of his royalty must be preceded not only by prophetic but priestly functions, or in other words that he must suffer before he reigned (see Luke 24:26)."

270

From Veiled Speech

So far, all of His references to His death were of the nature of riddles. As Dr. Bruce says, their meaning became clear after the event, but at the time, although they may have chilled the heart with a momentary fear, no one clearly understood them. He had spoken, for instance, of a temple which was to be destroyed, and rebuilt in three days; He had said that, as the serpent was lifted up in the wilderness, so must the Son of man be lifted up; He had forewarned His disciples of a time when the Bridegroom would be taken away from them, and when therefore they might well weep and fast; He had spoken in strange and mystic language about giving His flesh for the life of the world. After our Lord's Passion the disciples understood these things, but at the time they were uttered, though they may have created a passing vague alarm, their meaning escaped them.

To Plain Intimation of the Passage

But after Peter's confession our Lord dropped hints and suggestions and parables, and began to speak of His approaching death in a perfectly direct, matter-of-fact, unmistakable way. "He spake the saying openly," He left them in no manner of doubt. This was the end towards which He was marching—rejection and death. Now the Evangelist clearly wishes us to understand that there is a connection between Peter's confession and this first announcement of the cross. It was because Peter, speaking in the name of the Twelve, confessed Him as the Messiah, that Christ "began to teach them, that He must suffer many things . . . and be killed."

The Time Was Come

Can we see what the connection was? Can we understand why it was Jesus took this occasion to speak the saying openly? I think we can. (1) To begin with, no doubt, as Dr. Bruce suggests, the circumstances were such as to make it advisable to tell the disciples what the end would be. For the signs were growing ominous. Storm- clouds were gathering in our Lord's sky. In the hate of the Pharisees there could be recognized the first mutterings of that tempest that broke in all its fury upon our Lord's head in the judgment hall and on Calvary's hill. If Christ had allowed His death to come upon Him without a word of warning to His disciples, it would have shattered their faith completely. Even as it was, it went far towards doing it. But He told them all about it before it came to pass, so that when it did come to pass they might believe.

The Hearers Ready

(2) It was not only natural, but Peter's confession also told Him that now it was safe. That is why it was at this precise point that Jesus began to teach them that He must suffer many things. Christ always reveals His truth to men as they are able to bear it. It would not have been safe to tell the disciples right away at the beginning that the cross was going to be the end. They had been bred to believe that the Messiah's career was to end in a throne, so that if Jesus had spoken of a cross at the very start, they would obstinately have refused to believe He was the Messiah at all. First, Jesus taught the disciples to believe in Himself—then He spoke to them about His end. First, He revealed to them the glory of His Person; then He began to speak about His sacrifice. Now that their faith in Him as God's Christ was established; now that they were persuaded He was the Son of the living God, our Lord knew that they were prepared to bear the announcement of the cross, that their faith would stand the strain of it. And so He began to teach them that the Son of man must suffer many things, and be rejected, and be killed.

The Fact of Importance

(3) And I think there was yet another reason why Jesus took this particular occasion to announce His coming death and passion, and that was because His Messiahship was intimately and inseparably associated with the cross. He could not have been God's Messiah to the world without the cross. The idea most closely identified with Messiahship was that of redemption and deliverance. But the Jews interpreted these ideas wrongly. The redemption they looked for was redemption from political servitude; the deliverance they expected was national deliverance. And so they looked for a Messiah who would wield a sword, and march to a throne. But the redemption God's Messiah came to accomplish was the redemption of the soul; and the deliverance He came to achieve was deliverance from sin. This redemption could only be achieved by dying and this deliverance could only be effected through the cross. And so when Peter said, "Thou art the Christ," when he proclaimed Jesus as Messiah, our Lord began to teach them that the Son of man must suffer many things. As if to say, "You are right, Peter; I am the Messiah of God; and to accomplish My Messianic deliverance I must suffer many things, be rejected, and die." It was the Messiahship that necessitated the cross. Christ might have evaded the cross, perhaps; but if He had done so He could not have been the Messiah.

The two things—Messiahship and the suffering of death—were inseparable. It behoved the Christ to suffer. And that was why the confession of His Messiahship was followed immediately by the announcement of His passion.

The Surprising Sequence

"Peter answereth and saith unto Him, Thou art the Christ. . . . And He began to teach them, that the Son of man must suffer many things" (vv. 29, 31). What a strange, and at first sight disappointing and confusing, sequence that is! It is not at all what we should have expected. This is the kind of reply they would have expected: "Flesh and blood have not revealed this unto thee, Simon, but My Father Who is in heaven; and because I am the Son of God, all My enemies shall be confounded, priests and elders shall be put to shame, and My cause shall prosper." But how tragically different the sequence is! "Thou art the Christ," said Peter. "And Jesus began to teach them, that He must suffer, and be killed." As if He should say, "Yes, I am the Son of God, and because I am the Son of God I shall be slain." The sequence, I repeat, is staggering. To the disciples it was absolutely bewildering. And yet, when you look at it a little more closely, how pathetic, how beautiful, how subduing it is! And what a light it casts upon what is after all the essential glory of God! The attribute which was most closely identified with the idea of God in the minds of these disciples was that of power. That Jesus was the Son of God meant to them that He would trample all His foes beneath His feet.

And the Divine Revelation

But there are things infinitely more beautiful and Divine than power, and they are, pity and sympathy and love. And it is the pity and sympathy and love of God that shine forth in this sequence. For the "must" in this sequence was just the "must" of our Lord's pity and sympathy and sacrificial love. He had power enough to avoid the cross, had He wished. Did He not say to His captors that at a word He could summon to His aid ten thousand legions of angels? Did He not tell Pilate that He could have no power against Him, except it was given from above? But I love Christ the more that He left His power unused, and for love and pity's sake meekly consented to die. "If Thou art the Son of God," said mocking and taunting Jews, "come down from the cross" (Matt. 27:40). But He showed Himself Son of God in far more effective fashion by refusing to come down to save Himself, and enduring it, that He might save others. "And He began to teach them that He must suffer." It was a disappointing, almost a heart-breaking sequence to the disciples at the time. But it has brought

infinite comfort to a sinning world. For it has taught us to associate
with our conception of God the ideas of mercy and love and
self-sacrifice. It would have been human, if Jesus had used His
power to escape death. By this we know He was the Son of
God indeed—that having the power to live, He yet for love's
sake chose to die.

Peter Rebuked

But to Peter and the rest the announcement was a bitter disappointment. Because Christ was the Messiah, they had pictured a
glowing future both for Himself and them. They looked forward
to a day of splendid triumph, when Christ should sit on His
throne, and they too should sit on twelve thrones, judging the
twelve tribes of Israel. They never dreamed of associating ideas of
suffering and death with Messiah. And so when Jesus talked about
suffering and rejection, and death, the thing seemed absolutely
monstrous to them. And Peter, warm-hearted and impulsive Peter,
took His Master aside, and began to rebuke Him for cherishing
any such notion, and said, "God forbid; this shall not be unto
Thee."

No doubt the remonstrance sprang from the Apostle's warm-
hearted affection for his Lord; but it was presumptuous
nevertheless. It was disrespectful and irreverent. He tried to over-
bear and contradict and even bully his Master into putting away
from His mind these gloomy forebodings of coming ill. And it was
punished by the sternest and most scathing rebuke that ever fell
from our Lord's lips. "Get thee behind me, Satan: for thou mind-
est not the things of God, but the things of men" (v. 33). What a
swift and sudden change we have here! The most unstinted of
eulogies is followed by the sharpest of rebukes. The same man
who a few moments before was acclaimed by Jesus as speaking by
inspiration of God, is now denounced as the mouthpiece of Satan.
The same man who was declared by Jesus to be the rock on which
He would build His Church, is now stigmatized as a stone of
stumbling and a rock of offense. "Verily," said John Bunyan, "there
is a way to hell from the very gate of heaven"; and this man Peter,
lifted to heaven by our Lord's eulogy, is brought down to hell by
our Lord's censure and rebuke.

For Doing Satan's Work

"Get thee behind Me, Satan," said Jesus. And He said it with
vehemence, and almost with passion. It seems mercilessly severe.
But the rebuke was deserved, and even that hard word Satan,

which, as Dr. Bruce says, is the sting of the speech, is in its proper place. For that is exactly what Peter was doing. He was doing Satan's work for him. Luke says that when the devil left Jesus in the wilderness, it was only for a season. He came back again, Luke implies, and renewed the temptation. And one of the times he came back and renewed the temptation was this time, when Peter rebuked the Lord at the bare mention of the cross, and said, "God forbid; this shall not be unto Thee."

For this was the wilderness over again. Peter here tried to do for his Lord what the devil tried to do then. For, strip the struggle in the wilderness of everything that is merely incidental, and what did the temptation amount to? It was a temptation to take an easier way to the throne than the way of the cross. "Why tread that bitter way, when you can have the world on easier terms?" said Satan. Why sacrifice yourself and die? And Peter, the first and prince of the Twelve, tempted his Lord now in exactly the same way. And Jesus recognized His old adversary. He thrust the temptation from Him with horror, "Get thee behind Me, Satan."

An Unholy Office

And so one of Christ's fiercest temptations came from one of His nearest friends. "Satan fashioneth himself," Paul says, "into an angel of light" (2 Cor. 11:14). But he is most dangerous of all when he appears in the guise of a friend. Peter was a stumbling-block in his Master's way. He made it hard for Jesus to do the will of God. And still many a friend does the same unholy office for another. When we bid our friends think more of comfort than of duty; when we bid them consider their own interests rather than God's call, we are committing Peter's folly and sin over again. Robert Morrison's friends, for instance, tried every device they knew to shake him out of his resolve to go to China as a missionary. Do you remember what Mr. Worldly Wiseman said to Christian, when he met him with the mud of the Slough of Despond upon him? "Hear me," he said, "for I am older than thou; thou art like to meet with in the way which thou goest, wearisomeness, painfulness, hunger, perils, nakedness, sword, lions, dragons, darkness, and, in a word, death, and what not!" These things are certainly true. And why should a man so carelessly cast himself away? Peter was Christ's Mr. Worldly Wiseman. Why, said he, so carelessly cast thyself away? And we, when we dissuade our friends from the way of sacrifice and the cross, are playing Mr. Worldly Wiseman's wicked part. And you remember Worldly Wiseman's doom. "It were well for him if a millstone were hanged about his neck, and he were thrown into the sea, rather than that he should cause one of these little ones to stumble." Let us ask for grace each to be not a Worldly Wiseman, but a Great-heart.

51

Discipleship and the Cross

"And when He had called the people unto Him with His disciples also, He said unto them, Whosoever will come after Me, let him deny himself and take up his cross, and follow Me. For whosoever will save his life shall lose it but whosoever shall lose his life for My sake and the gospel's, the same shall save it. For what shall it profit a man, if he shall gain the whole world, and lose his own soul? Or what shall a man give in exchange for his soul? Whosoever therefore shall be ashamed of Me and of My words in this adulterous and sinful generation; of him also shall the Son of man be ashamed, when He cometh in the glory of His Father with the holy angels. And He said unto them, Verily I say unto you, That there be some of them that stand here, which shall not taste of death, till they have seen the kingdom of God come with power."   —Mark 8:34–9:1.

Cross-bearing: A Duty for All

THERE IS THE closest and most vital connection between these verses and those just preceding them. It was Peter's protest against the intimation of the Passion that drew from our Lord this solemn declaration that cross-bearing is the universal and indispensable condition of discipleship. "God forbid!" Peter had said, in his own hot and impulsive way, "this—a violent death at the hands of elders and priests and scribes —shall never be unto Thee." "Say you so?" Jesus replies in effect (I quote Dr. A. B. Bruce's paraphrase), "I tell you that not only shall I, your Master, be crucified, but ye too, faithfully following Me, shall certainly have your crosses to bear. If any man would come after Me, let him deny himself, and take up his cross, and follow Me." To lend emphasis to the announcement, to make it quite clear that this was a universal law, Jesus did not say this to the Twelve alone. "He called unto Him the multitude with His disciples." This was not a law for the Apostles merely, it was equally binding upon the humblest believer; not for teachers and leaders only, but for the least and most insignificant of followers as well; not a law for the first Christians only, but for Christians of every age.

277

King Arthur insisted upon conditions before a man could become a Knight of his Round Table. Everyone had to swear to speak no slander, no, nor listen to it; to live sweet lives in purest chastity; to ride abroad redressing human wrongs; to honor his own word as if his God's; to break the heathen, and to uphold the Christ. But here is a law insisted upon by a greater Captain than King Arthur—the condition of entrance into a still nobler order of chivalry—"If any man would come after Me, let him deny himself, and take up his cross, and follow Me" (8:34).

Master and Disciple

The first truth all this suggests to me is that of the correspondency that exists between the Master and the disciple. Christ is not a solitary cross-bearer; every true Christian is a cross-bearer too. Our Lord warned us that His lot and ours was bound to be the same. "A disciple," He said, "is not above his master, nor a servant above his lord. It is enough for the disciple that he be as his master, and the servant as his lord" (Matt. 10:24, 25). There will be a correspondency, He said, between your fate and Mine. And so it was. As John puts it in his Epistle, "As He is, even so are we in this world" (4:17). "So are we"; the lot of the Master was the lot of the disciple also: in this respect among others, that the disciple, like the Master, had to bear a cross.

The Solitary Cross

But when I talk about the Lord bearing a cross, and the disciple also bearing a cross, I do not want to be misunderstood. I do not say that the Master's cross and the disciples' cross are one and the same. There is a sense in which our Lord's cross is solitary and unshared. In its redemptive aspect Christ's cross stands alone. People talk about a "continuous atonement." I do not know what they mean by it. If they mean that Christ's work on the cross needs to be completed and perfected by some suffering or work of ours, I answer, first, that nothing we can do can possibly add to the atoning work of Jesus. We are sinful men and women; we cannot atone, we need atoning for. And, in the second place, I answer that Christ's sacrifice does not need completing. It is complete. The sacrifice of the cross is a full, perfect, and sufficient sacrifice, oblation, and satisfaction. "It is finished." Nothing remains to be done. Christ did it all when He submitted Himself to death and shame. As a redeeming sacrifice the cross of Christ remains for ever unshared.

And the Fellowship of Suffering

But while the cross from one point of view is a redeeming sacrifice, from another point of view it represents the sacrifice of self, and the pains and penalties Christ endured because of His absolute and complete devotion to the righteous will of God. And in this respect we too must bear the cross as well as Christ. In this respect there is a strict correspondency between Master and disciple. We must enter into the fellowship of His sufferings. "As He is, even so are we in this world." For that is what the Christian life is on its practical side; it is a life of conscious devotion to the holy will of God. And obedience to the will of God inevitably means the cross; for it means the hostility of the world, and the sacrifice of self. It means outward trouble and inward conflict. See what it meant for some of these disciples. If tradition speaks truly, following Christ meant for some of them not persecution only, but death. It meant a scaffold in Jerusalem for James, a cross in Rome for Peter. They drank of their Lord's cup, and were baptized with their Lord's baptism. They had literally to take up their cross and follow Him. And though these killing times are past, it remains true to this day that they who will live godly must suffer persecution.

The Hostility of the World

The man who makes the will of God his law must make up his mind for the scorn and contempt of men. We can escape it only by cowardice and compromise. Many people refuse to rank themselves among Christ's avowed followers because they are not prepared for this cross. "Nevertheless," says John, "even of the rulers many believed on Him; but because of the Pharisees they did not confess it, lest they should be put out of the synagogue" (John 12:42). That is it, they shrank from the cross. But there can be no compromising between the world and Christ. We must face the world, and defy the world, and break with the world. We must let the world do its worst. If we want to go after Christ, we must take up this cross, and follow Him.

The Surrender of Self

And in addition to the hostility of the world, there is the sacrifice of self, the surrender of whatever there is in us which is contrary to the will of God, the extermination of those unholy desires and passions of the soul, so dear to the natural man, so alien to the law of God. And what a cross that is! No man can tell what another man's cross is. But we have all a cross of some kind. You have yours. I have mine. They differ from one another; but there is not one of us who does not know that there are things in us to be fought, and repudiated, and torn up by the roots, if we would follow Christ. Do not confine what I am saying to what we speak of as the grosser sins. We can see that the drunkard and the profligate have to say good-bye to their evil habits before they can follow Christ, and we know what agony that means in many cases. But it is not to them alone this demand applies. It applies also to us. For there is not one of us who does not know perfectly well that in our own hearts there are things to be repudiated and put away, if we want to follow Christ.

A Real Crucifixion

The putting away of these things, the denial of self and sense, what a conflict it is, and what agony it entails! There was no punishment so torturing as crucifixion. But what crucifixion was in the physical realm, that the denial and repudiation of self is in the spiritual. Indeed, crucifixion is the very word Paul uses for the process. "I have been crucified with Christ," he cries (Gal. 2:20). "Our old man," he says in another place, "was crucified with Him" (Rom. 6:6). "The world," he says in yet a third place, "hath been crucified unto me, and I unto the world" (Gal. 6:14). While in another place he states his own experience as a general law, and in the very spirit of this text says, "They that are of Christ Jesus have crucified the flesh with the passions and the lusts thereof" (Gal. 5:24). "The flesh," their own flesh. It is upon themselves they have executed this judgment. It is upon themselves they have inflicted this agony. They have driven the nails through their own quivering affections and lusts. In this respect of the denial of self in obedience to the holy will of God, Christ is but the first cross-bearer of a great host. That was the sign that a Knight had entered for the Crusades, in olden days—the cross upon the shoulder. This is the sign that we have entered the service of Jesus— the cross in the life, the marks, the stigmata, the nail-prints of Jesus, in the heart. "If any man would come after Me, let him deny himself, and take up his cross, and follow Me" (v. 34).

Three Reasons for Cross-bearing

Now I can imagine that, when the disciples heard this law first laid down, many of them may have said in their hearts, "This is a hard saying, who can bear it?" And perhaps some of them may even have contemplated leaving Jesus, and following no more after Him. He was making the price of discipleship so costly. I believe Jesus Himself realized that thoughts like these were arising in their minds, that many listening to Him were asking the question, "Is it worth while?" And so He proceeds to deal with that unexpressed doubt. "It is a heavy price to pay," He says to these doubting and hesitating folk, in effect, "but it is worth while. Discipleship means the cross but it is worth the cost." And He proceeds to enunciate three reasons, each one of them introduced by a "for," to show that it is worth while to follow Him, even though it means the cross and the daily self-denial. Let us glance briefly at each of the reasons Christ adduces.

(1) The Paradox of Losing and Saving

(1) This is the first—"Whosoever would save his life shall lose it; and whosoever shall lose his life for My sake and the Gospel's shall save it" (8:35). To understand this paradox—a paradox embodying so much of essential and vital truth that our Lord repeated it on more than one occasion—we must bear in mind that the word "life" is used here in a double sense. In the one connection it stands for mere life; in the other it stands for the "good of life," life worthy of the name. It is life on the lower and the higher plane. As Paul would put it, it is life "after the flesh," and life "after the Spirit." So that this saying might be paraphrased thus, "Whosoever will make it his first business to save or preserve his natural life and worldly well-being, shall lose the higher life, the life indeed; and whosoever is willing to lose his natural life for My sake, shall find the true eternal life." And we know by experience that this is true.

And the Price of Ease

If we concentrate our thought upon the lower self, upon comfort, and wealth, and sensual indulgence, the higher life suffers. You remember that grim verse in the Psalms, "They lusted exceedingly in the wilderness, and tempted God in the desert" (Psa. 106:14, 15), lusted for mere material good, for the flesh-pots of Egypt, "and He gave them their request"—they got what they wanted. But at what a price! for "He gave them their request; but sent leanness into their soul." That is a sequence we see illustrated too sadly often before our very eyes. We see men getting their desires, getting comfort, ease and wealth; we see them pampering their lower self, and we see them paying for it in leanness of soul. On the other hand, when a man dies to self, when he crucifies his flesh, with the affections and lusts thereof, he rises with Christ into a new life, a rich life, an eternal life. Sacrifice of some kind must be made. The only question we have to settle is, which we will sacrifice, the lower or the higher, what the world calls life, or what He calls life. Here there is the first reason for obeying Christ's call, and bearing the cross. By sacrificing self, by crucifying the flesh, by losing the lower life, we gain the life which is life indeed.

(2) The Profit and Loss Sum

(2) And here is the second reason—it follows closely upon the first, and is indeed explanatory of it—"For what doth it profit a man to gain the whole world, and forfeit his life? For what should a man give in exchange for his life?" (8:36, 37). Here is our Lord's profit and loss sum. He puts the lower life and the higher life in the scales, and weighs them against each other. For the lower life is just the "worldly" life, the life given up to things of time and sense; the life that seeks to satisfy itself with creature comforts and sensual joys. Supposing that a man gains the world, enjoys everything the world can give, is rich and increased with goods, and in need of nothing; like Dives, is clothed in purple and fine linen, and fares sumptuously every day; supposing that he gains the whole world at the cost of the life of his soul, he is a loser by the bargain. On the other hand, the whole world is too small, an utterly inadequate price to pay for the ransom of a soul once lost.

An Ever-present Alternative

Christ's question remains still unanswered. We are all of us confronted by this alternative, the world or the soul. And many of us are tempted to sacrifice the soul to the world. That is especially our peril in these materialistic days. But whoever sacrifices his soul to the world makes a bad bargain. For he is sacrificing the inward and essential to the outward and accidental, the enduring to the transient, the eternal to the temporal. Supposing a man gains the world, he cannot keep it. "The world passeth away." "The rich man died," that is his end. And the man who has made the world his choice loses everything. He is ushered into the next world, poor and miserable and blind and naked. For a man's genuine and permanent wealth does not consist in cash, but in character, not in what he possesses, but in what he is. I know the world measures what a man is worth by the amount of money he has; but the real worth of man is measured by the amount of soul he has, by the amount of faith and hope and love and purity there is in him. And in face of this I want to know what shall it profit a man to gain the world, and lose his real life—his soul life? Profit! there is no profit in it, only sheer and utter loss. Indeed, that is the only person Christ describes as "lost," the man who has lost his soul. And supposing a man has "lost" his soul, what can he give to buy it back?

What shall a man give in exchange, or rather as an exchange, for his soul? Many a man, coming to the end of his life, would give anything and everything to get his lost soul back. He has got his wealth, perhaps; but face to face with eternity he sees his wealth is mere dust and dross compared to the soul, and he would give all he has to buy it back. But "it cannot be gotten for gold, neither shall silver be weighed for the price thereof" (Job 28:15). It is in view of all this that Christ urged men to crucify the world to themselves, and themselves unto the world, to deny themselves, and follow Him. It may mean poverty, as far as this world is concerned, but they shall be rich unto eternal life.

(3) The Time of Reckoning

(3) And the third argument for cross-bearing is drawn from the Second Advent. I am not going just now to enter upon any discussion as to what we are to understand by the specific references to the Second Coming in the Gospel, and even in this particular passage. There is no doubt the disciples expected that coming to take place speedily. Indeed, the words that follow this verse, words which naturally belong to it (9:1), seem to promise that it shall take place within the lifetime of some who were then standing by our Lord and listening to His words. It may be that our Lord spoke of two comings, one near at hand, and another at the end of the world, and that these two got more or less confused in the recollections of the disciples. But be that as it may, one fact is quite clear: our Lord spoke of a day of triumph, when He should appear invested with the manifest glory of Messiah, and attended with a mighty host of ministering spirits— *His* reward for bearing His cross of ignominy and shame. And in that day of the Lord's triumph those who have borne the cross and followed Him shall triumph too. Those who have suffered with Him shall also be glorified together. Those who have fought His battles shall wear the crown. "For whosoever shall be ashamed of Me and of My words in this adulterous and sinful generation, the Son of Man also shall be ashamed of him, when He cometh in the glory of His Father with the holy angels" (8:38). In the great and awful day of judgment and searching and sifting, the one thing worth having will be the life-giving recognition and smile of the Lord; but if we have never enlisted in His army, if we do not bear the "marks" of the cross, what can He say but this, "I never knew you; depart from Me, ye that work iniquity"?

A Searching Call

"If any man would come after Me, let him deny himself, and take up his cross, and follow Me"; it is a stern and searching call. And yet it is a reasonable call. For, just as Jesus endured the cross and despised the shame for the joy that was set before Him, so too, if we remember the "joy "set before us, we shall have strength to bear our cross. And let us remember this, farther. When we bear our cross we are in the blessed fellowship of Jesus. He marches at the head with His great and heavy cross. We follow after. And our crosses are light compared with His. "Shall Jesus thus suffer, and shall we refuse?" "Who shall dream of shrinking, by our Captain led?" "We will not shrink!" "Master, I will follow Thee whithersoever Thou goest" (Matt. 8:19).

52

The Transfiguration: The Transfigured

"And after six days Jesus taketh with Him Peter, and James, and John, and leadeth them up into a high mountain apart by themselves: and He was transfigured before them. And His raiment became shining, exceeding white as snow; so as no fuller on earth can white them. And there appeared unto them Elias with Moses: and they were talking with Jesus. And Peter answered and said to Jesus, Master, it is good for us to be here: and let us make three tabernacles, one for Thee, and one for Moses, and one for Elias. For he wist not what to say; for they were sore afraid. And there was a cloud that overshadowed them: and a voice came out of the cloud, saying, This is My beloved Son: hear Him. And suddenly, when they had looked round about, they saw no man any more, save Jesus only with themselves."

—Mark 9:2-8.

A Miracle Unique

THE GREAT EVENT that took place on one of the slopes of Mount Hermon is, of course, to be regarded as a miraculous, supernatural occurrence. But it differs from every other miracle the Gospels record for us. And the difference is this—in every other miracle Christ is the Giver of grace; in this He is the Receiver of glory. The reason for every other miracle is obvious and plain. Our Lord Himself announced that He was come to preach good tidings to the poor, to proclaim release to the captives, and recovery of sight to the blind, to set at liberty them that were bruised, and when He went about doing good, healing the sick, cleansing the leper, giving liberty to the devil-possessed, He was doing the very work for which He was sent.

Its Purpose

But what good end was the Transfiguration meant to serve? In whose interests and for whose benefit did it take place? These are questions that inevitably suggest themselves, as we read how, on this high and solitary and unnamed mountain the Lord was transfigured, "and His garments became glistering, exceeding white; so as no fuller on earth can whiten them" (9:3).

The Subject and the Witnesses

Now, in answering these questions we must notice that there were two sets of participants in this great and never-to-be-forgotten scene. There was our Lord; and there were the three disciples, Peter and James and John. I leave out of account the heavenly visitors, for quite clearly the Transfiguration did not take place for their sakes; they appeared in it for the sake of the others. We need to consider our Lord and the three disciples. When I am asked for the sake of which of these two sets did the Transfiguration take place, I answer, for both. I believe that, primarily, the Transfiguration took place for Jesus' sake. But not for Jesus' sake only. You remember how John tells of the voice from heaven which said, "I have both glorified it, and will glorify it again" (John 12:28). Jesus remarked, "This voice hath not come for My sake; but for your sakes" (v. 30). So exactly the glory of the holy mount was not exclusively for Jesus' sake; it was also partly for the sake of these three disciples, who, though heavy with sleep, beheld the glory, and never afterwards forgot it. But here we will confine ourselves to a consideration of the Transfiguration in relation to Jesus. What end was it meant to serve, as far as Jesus was concerned? What was it meant to do for Him?

The Transfiguration and the Cross

The very first words of the narrative will help us to our answer to that question. All the Evangelists who give us an account of this wonderful incident make a special point of the date. They are all particular to mention that it took place about a week after another event; and the obvious inference is that in the minds of the Evangelists these two events were closely connected together. As Dr. A. B. Bruce puts it, this note of time is like a finger-post pointing back to the previous paragraphs, and saying, "If you want to understand what follows, remember what went before." What is it that comes before? It was Christ's first announcement of the cross; His first plain, direct, unmistakable declaration that His career on earth was not going to end in a throne, as the disciples had fondly imagined, but in a cruel and shameful death. Now that announcement produced something like dismay and consternation in the apostolic band. Peter's indignant but mistaken protest is just an index of their recoil from the thought of a cross for their Master. And it is no dishonor to our Lord Himself to say, that the thought of the cross was accompanied by a sense of repugnance in His own soul. Remember the prayer at Gethsemane and the agony (Matt. 26:39, 42; Luke 22:42, 44). It was this that lent such deadly force to the temptation which Peter's mistaken affection put in His way. That was the mood of Jesus and of His disciples during the intervening week; and we must realize all this—the despair of the disciples, the grief and shrinking of our Lord—if we want to realize the meaning and purpose of this wonderful event that took place upon Hermon. For the primary end the Transfiguration was meant to serve was that of encouragement; the encouragement of the disciples, whose faith had been well-nigh shattered by Christ's announcement of His death, and the encouragement of our blessed Lord Himself. What happened on Hermon strengthened Him to bear the cross, and by the grace of God to taste death for every man.

The Prayer

Luke alone of the three Evangelists recording the Transfiguration says that Jesus went up into the mountain "to pray." He took His three closest and dearest disciples with Him, as He did subsequently in the garden, both for their advantage, and because, true Man as He was, He craved human sympathy, and appreciated to the full the help and encouragement which human sympathy gives. "He went up into the mountain to pray." Very likely to plead for His disciples, that when the dreaded blow actually fell, their faith might not utterly fail. But also He went up this mountain that by communion with God He might be strengthened to face and bear it. Read the story of our Lord's prayer in Gethsemane: "Father, if Thou be willing, remove this cup from Me: nevertheless not My will, but Thine, be done" (Luke 22:42). It was the same agonized prayer our Lord offered upon the holy mount. He prayed for strength and courage to drink the bitter cup to its dregs.

And the Response

And, just as in answer to His prayer in the garden, an angel appeared from heaven strengthening Him, so He was heard for His strong crying and tears on the holy mount. For, as Luke puts it, "As He was praying, the fashion of His countenance was altered, and His raiment became white and dazzling" (Luke 9:29). "As He was praying"; the miracle happened while our Lord was in the very act of prayer. Before He called, His Father answered; and while He was yet speaking His Father heard. The glory, the company of Moses and Elijah, the heavenly voice, were all in answer to prayer. "They that wait upon the Lord shall renew their strength; . . . they shall run, and not be weary; they shall walk, and not faint," says the prophet (Isa. 40:31). Our Lord waited upon God; He too received His strength, and walked without fainting straight to the bitter cross.

Prayer and Transfiguration

What an encouragement all this is to prayer! What blessings descend upon the praying soul, and especially this—the transfiguration and transformation of character. "As He was praying, the fashion of His countenance was altered"; the miracle happens still. There is nothing for transfiguring face and character like communion. Moses went up to the mount, and stayed there forty days, and when he came down again there was such a radiance in his face that the children of Israel dared not look upon him (Exod. 34:30; 2 Cor. 3:7). And that is no solitary experience. "They looked unto Him," said the Psalmist, "and were lightened" (Psa. 130:5). They were lit up. Their faces shone like the sun for joy. David begins one Psalm, "Out of the depths have I cried unto Thee, O Lord" (Psa. 130:1), but communion with God dispels the cloud, and soothes the sorrow and trouble, and before the end the fashion of his countenance is altered, and he is saying, "O Israel, hope in the Lord; for with the Lord there is mercy, and with Him is plenteous redemption" (v. 7). And the same transformation takes place still.

Prayer leaves its mark on the character, on the very face. The look of care, as Dr. Glover says, relaxes into peace; lines of anguish change into those of joy. Dr. J. G. Paton mentions the rapt look on his old father's face when he came out of the tiny room where he held communion with God. It was almost the very first thing that impressed him with the reality of religion. And the transformation goes deeper than the face. It reaches down to the very heart. I know of nothing that so effectually removes all hateful things from the soul, and begets love and hope and faith in it, as prayer. As we behold Christ, and meditate upon Him, we are changed into His image, from glory to glory.

Prayer and Sustaining Power

But I must pass on. Our Lord received a rich and full answer to His prayer. "Cast thy burden upon the Lord," says the Psalmist, "and He shall sustain thee" (Psa. 55:22). It is not exactly the sequence we should expect. We should have expected something like this, "Cast thy burden on the Lord, and He will take it away."

But that is not God's method. It may be necessary to bear the burden, as it was for Paul's good to have his thorn in the flesh. What God does for those who cast their burden upon Him, is what He did for the great Apostle of the Gentiles. He gives grace sufficient for the burden. That was what He did for His beloved Son on the holy mount. He did not take the bitter cup away from His lips. He did not take the cruel and shameful cross away; but He so strengthened Christ's soul that, after this great experience on Hermon, He steadfastly set His face to go to Jerusalem.

The Glory at the Transfiguration

Three things happened on the mount to cheer our Lord's heart, and thus to strengthen Him in His great redeeming purpose: The glory, the visit of Moses and Elijah, and the heavenly voice. First of all, there was the glory. "He was transfigured before them," Mark says, "and His garments became glistering, exceeding white; so as no fuller on earth can whiten them" (vv. 2, 3). Questions have been asked whether this glory was a glory conferred upon Christ from without, or whether it was His inner and essential glory shining through. I do not know that the question can ever be satisfactorily answered. The essential point is, that for a brief space Christ was "in glory."

Some fanciful commentators have suggested that Christ could then and there have stepped into glory without passing through the pain and humiliation of the cross; that when Jesus left the holy mount with its heavenly visitors, and came down again to the plain, He humbled Himself a second time, as He had done before, when He condescended to be born in Bethlehem. But with all respect I venture to say that is an entire misinterpretation of the narrative, and a misunderstanding of the character of our Lord. Christ's glory, according to the uniform testimony of Scripture, springs out of His shame. It is because He humbled Himself unto death that He has received the name which is above every name. The glory He enjoyed on the mount was a foretaste of the glory that would be His after the cross had been borne. John Bunyan, before he brings Christian and Hopeful to the cold waters of Jordan, takes them for a brief space to the land of Beulah, whose air was very sweet and pleasant, and where the sun shone night and day, and where they had rapturous visions of the golden city whither they were journeying, with the result that the pilgrims were eager to cross the Jordan, and be there. And in much the same way Jesus enjoyed the glory of the holy mount and the converse of the shining ones before He tasted of the shame of the judgment and the cross. "For the joy that was set before Him," says the Apostle, "He endured the cross, despising the shame" (Heb. 12:2). And of that joy He had a foretaste in the glory of the Transfiguration Mount.

The Heavenly Visitors

The second encouragement was the visit and the converse of Moses and Elijah. "There appeared unto them Elijah with Moses: and they were talking with Jesus" (v. 4). Commentators have speculated as to why these two Old Testament saints in particular were sent to hold converse with Jesus. The general opinion seems to be that these two were the great representatives of the Law and the Prophets, and as such had been the great Forerunners of the Lord in preparing the way for His Kingdom. Others suggest that these two men were chosen because each of them had borne a heavy cross, and each had achieved a great deliverance. And yet others find the reason for the choice of Moses and Elijah in the singularity of their end. The one never had a shroud, the other never had a grave.

Their Converse

But I am not half so concerned as to why these two particular saints were chosen, as I am about the theme of the converse they held with our Lord. "They were talking with Jesus," Mark says. And what did they talk about? It is Luke who supplies the answer to that question, "they spake of the decease which He was about to accomplish at Jerusalem " (Luke 9:31). His dying was the subject of their converse. But it is quite a peculiar word they use to describe His dying. Our English version renders it "decease," but the Greek word is "exodus." They talked of the exodus which He was to accomplish at Jerusalem. Notice, the cross is not presented as a death which Christ endured, but as an exodus which He accomplished. It was not something which He suffered; it was something which He achieved.

What does the very word exodus suggest? It suggests emancipation, redemption, deliverance. And that was what the cross meant: emancipation, redemption, deliverance for a world. Christ's disciples did not understand this. The bare mention of death flung them into a panic of despair. But the saints in glory knew what the cross meant. It meant not defeat, but deliverance. By dying Christ was to accomplish an exodus. And they came and talked with Jesus about it. Peter and the rest would fain keep Jesus from the cross. To them it meant the overthrow of all their hopes. Moses and Elijah knew better. They came down to strengthen Christ's hands in God. They talked about the exodus—the great deliverance He was to accomplish at Jerusalem.

The Heavenly Voice

Thirdly, there was the Heavenly Voice. At every moment of His life and at every stage of His career Christ had the Father's favor resting upon Him. "I do always the things which please Him." But on certain occasions He received for His encouragement certain special and extraordinary proofs of God's good pleasure. More than once in His career a voice came from heaven. And the significant thing is these voices came when Christ in some special way accepted the shame and pain of our sin. The voice came at the Baptism, when Jesus by that act made our sin His own. It came again on this Transfiguration Mount, when the cross rose stark and cruel before Him, and He accepted it as the price of man's redemption. It came later, when with troubled soul at the thought of death Jesus was yet able to say, "Father, glorify Thy name." And if the Son's obedience gave the Father pleasure, the Father's pleasure gave the Son strength. "The cup which the Father hath given Me, shall I not drink it?" (John 18:11). What did it matter though His foremost disciple should protest and condemn, so long as God said of Him, with His cross upon His back, "Thou art My Beloved Son"? And so the Transfiguration was the answer to our Lord's urgent and believing prayer. There is for every burden the necessary strength. There is for every cross the needful grace. There was even for His. The glory, the heavenly visitors, the Father's good pleasure, so nerved and confirmed our Lord's soul, that, "foreknowing, choosing, feeling all," He did not shrink

> "Until the perfect work was done,
> And drunk the bitter cup of gall."

53
The Transfiguration: The Witnesses

"And after six days Jesus taketh with him Peter, and James, and John, and leadeth them up into an high mountain apart by themselves: and He was transfigured before them. And His raiment became shining, exceeding white as snow; so as no fuller on earth can white them. And there appeared unto them Elias with Moses: and they were talking with Jesus. And Peter answered and said to Jesus, Master, it is good for us to be here: and let us make three tabernacles; one for Thee, and one for Moses, and one for Elias. For he wist not what to say; for they were sore afraid. And there was a cloud that overshadowed them; and a voice came out of the cloud, saying, This is My beloved Son: hear Him. And suddenly, when they had looked round about, they saw no man any more, save Jesus only with themselves." —Mark 9:2-8.

The Chosen Three

NOW AS TO the part the three disciples played at the Transfiguration, and its effect upon them.

"And after six days," Mark says, "Jesus taketh with Him Peter, and James, and John, and bringeth them up into a high mountain apart by themselves: and He was transfigured before them" (v. 2). Only three out of the twelve disciples went up with Jesus to the holy mount. Why were Peter and James and John especially chosen? No doubt because they were in some way nearer to Christ than the rest. I do not mean to suggest that Christ had His favorites, though John is called "the disciple whom Jesus loved." But there were degrees of faith and understanding and affection among the Twelve. And these three were chosen because on the whole we may well believe that they understood Christ best, and sympathized with Him most.

In ordinary and secular matters the order is—first see, then believe. But the opposite is the order in the spiritual realm—first faith, then vision. Seeing does not lead to believing, but believing leads to seeing. "He that loveth . . . knoweth." That is why our Lord's choice fell upon Peter and James and John, as it did once again, in the hour of His mortal agony and conflict in Gethsemane—because out of the circle of the Twelve these three clung to Him most closely, and were nearest to their Master in spirit.

The Rewards of Faith

Those who cling closely to Jesus see some wonderful sights, and enjoy some unspeakable privileges. I do not deny that they have also to bear some heavy crosses and to share in the fellowship of the Lord's suffering; to accompany their Lord into Gethsemanes and up Calvaries. But now and again they are taken up like these three were, to the holy mount, when their enraptured eyes are privileged to behold the very glory of the Lord. "If I find Him, if I follow," we ask, in the once familiar and favorite hymn, "what His guerdon here"? And we answer our own question, "Many a conflict, many a labor, many a tear." And that is true so far as it goes. But it does not tell the whole story. "What His guerdon here?" Gethsemane; yes, but the holy mount also. Christ's reward is not simply "many a conflict, many a labor, many a tear." Along with the conflicts and labors and tears there will certainly come many an hour of glorious vision and high and holy fellowship. And the vision of the holy mount always compensates for Gethsemane. "I reckon," says St Paul, "that the sufferings of this present time are not worthy to be compared with the glory" (Rom. 8:18).

Peter's Proposal

Luke gives us to understand that Peter, James and John did on the mount exactly what they afterwards did in the garden. While the Lord prayed they slept. And apparently it was only when Moses and Elijah were preparing to return to the heaven which they had for a brief space left that the glory broke upon their gaze. That is to say, they might have enjoyed more of the glory than they did, had they only watched, instead of sleeping. But when at last the disciples were fully awake, and they beheld the glorious vision, their souls were clean ravished within them, and they desired above all things that the glory might last. Peter was, as usual, the first to speak; but by his words the thoughts of the hearts of all three of them stand revealed. "Rabbi," he said, "it is good for us to be here, and let us make three tabernacles; one for Thee, and one for Moses, and one for Elijah" (v. 5). Afterwards he realized that was a foolish request to have made. And in the next verse you have his apology for his rashness and foolishness (for, though the Gospel is written by St Mark, I see no reason whatever for doubting the old tradition that Mark got his material from St

Peter). Here is his apology, "For he wist not what to answer; for they became sore afraid" (v. 6).

The Voice of Self

Now, let us ask ourselves what Peter's proposal amounted to. This, says Dr. A. B. Bruce: he wanted to enjoy the felicities of heaven without any preliminary process of cross-bearing. Peter was exactly in the same humor as when he took Jesus aside, and presumed to rebuke Him because He spoke of rejection and suffering and death. "Why need we go down to face captious Pharisees and plotting priests, why run the risk of rejection and suffering and death at all; why not remain in this blessed company and on this holy hill? This is heaven begun—why go back to earth, with its sorrows and its sins?" The glory without the shame, the crown without the cross—that was what Peter wanted. He knew afterwards it was a foolish request. He came to realize that even for Jesus humiliation was the way of exaltation; that, if Christ had shirked the cross, there would have been no redemption for the world; that it behoved the Christ to suffer. But all that was in the future. At present he feared and hated and loathed the very idea of a cross. And once again in this speech of his on the holy mount he invited his Lord to shirk and decline it. "He wist not what to say"—that is all the excuse that can be made for it. It was the foolish appeal of an ignorant, worldly heart. Moses and Elijah, who knew what the cross meant, did not seek to dissuade our Lord from it. They spoke with Him of the exodus, the glorious emancipation and redemption, He was to accomplish at Jerusalem. And so the glory of the holy mount could not detain Him. He steadfastly set His face towards Jerusalem.

And the Call of Duty

That is the primary meaning of Peter's proposal. But most preachers widen the import, and say that he desired to prolong the time of rapture and communion, at the expense of the time of labor and conflict. And for practical purposes it may be legitimate to give this wider interpretation to it. One can understand Peter's wish for a prolongation of the scene. What a blessed privilege it was to be in such celestial company! What a rapturous joy it was to hear their high and holy converse! I can quite understand that this blessed communion on the mount was more to Peter's taste than the wrangle with the Pharisees, and the sights and sounds of disease that were sure to meet them again, as soon as ever they reached the foot. And yet he learned afterwards that this wish too was a foolish wish. Times of rapture are exceedingly grateful and refreshing when they come; but they are not meant to last, they are sent to refresh and strengthen us. We visit the mountain, not to escape the toil and conflict of the plain, but to be the better able to play our part in it. The Christian life is not communion only, it is conflict as well. It is not rapture only, it is service and labor also. That is a notable sequence in Isaiah's prophecies. "They that wait upon the Lord shall renew their strength; they shall mount up with wings as eagles; they shall run, and not be weary; they shall walk, and not faint" (Isa. 40:31).

The Supremacy of Christ

But as to Peter's first words. "Rabbi," said he, "it is good for us to be here." What made him say it? I daresay many things combined. But perhaps the thing that weighed most with Peter was the presence of Moses and Elijah. He thought more, that is to say, of the ministering servants than he did of the Lord. But it was the presence of the Lord that made the mountain a holy place. I think that even in these days we are inclined to make Peter's mistake—to think more of Moses and Elijah than we do of the Lord, to attach undue importance to secondary and subsidiary things, and to forget that the one thing that really matters is the presence of the Master.

But just because it was the presence of Jesus that mattered, there was no need to remain on the mountain-top. It was just as good to be with Jesus in the valley fighting with disease, in the Temple preaching the word of life, beyond Jordan in exile, in Gethsemane, in the judgment hall, upon the very cross. Wherever Jesus is, it is good for us to be there. And before today men have found it good to be afflicted; they have found it good to have burdens to bear; they have found it good to be passed through a very furnace of trial, because there was with them in it One like unto the Son of man. And I think that was the lesson that was taught Peter and his fellow-disciples on the mount. They were taught there the all-importance of Christ. But they learned not only the all-importance, the supremacy of Jesus, but also His all-sufficiency.

The All-sufficiency of Christ

"Suddenly looking round about, they saw no one any more, save Jesus only with themselves" (v. 8). Was there some shade of disappointment and regret when they found Jesus only with themselves? Perhaps it was God's way of teaching them that Jesus only was enough. Jesus only, as Dr. Glover says, was complete Law. Jesus only was complete Prophecy. He did not need the help of

Elijah to declare the will of God. He did not need the help of Moses and his sacrifices, to make an open way for sinful men to the Presence of God. He Himself was the Truth. He Himself offered the one full and perfect oblation and sacrifice. They had all they needed in Jesus. As St Paul puts it, they were "complete in Him." Jesus only! That is where we are still. But Jesus is enough.

The Effect on the Disciples

I have said that the Transfiguration was meant for the encouragement of our Lord's soul in view of the cross. It was also meant for the confirmation of the disciples' faith in view of that same cross. The cross was bound to be a trial to them. Bred up to believe that Messiah's destiny was to be a throne, the sight of their Lord, "mocked, insulted, beaten, bound," was certain to make them doubt whether He was the Messiah at all. So this great experience was given to them, to strengthen their faith, that it might not fail in that day of bitter trial. For when they saw Jesus hanging on the accursed tree, and heard all Jerusalem railing at Him, they remembered they had seen His glory; they remembered also the voice which said, "This is My beloved Son." And so, though Jerusalem crucified Him as an impostor and a malefactor, they held fast the faith. During the dark days until Jesus was declared to be the Son of God with power by the Resurrection from the dead, the memory of the holy mount, with its glory, and its celestial visions and its heavenly voice, was their sheet-anchor and their stay. Nothing could destroy their conviction, then formed, that Jesus was the Son of God.

Great Experiences and Their Value

That is one great and happy end our great experiences are meant to serve. They keep faith alive in days of stress and trial. Dark days come to us all. Days when faith almost falters. What shall we do then? Recall our great experiences. "Call to mind," says John Bunyan, "the former days, and years of ancient times; remember also your songs in the night, and commune with your own hearts. Have you never an hill Mizar to remember? Have you forgot the close, the milk-house, the stable, the barn, and the like where God did visit your souls?" Remember, that is the Dreamer's advice, your hill of Transfiguration. Recall the fact that you too have seen the Lord's glory, that you too have heard His voice, that you too have felt His power. Through all your days of doubt and difficulty and eclipse, hold fast to your experiences. Remember the holy mount. And it shall happen to you, as to these disciples, that the gloom and despair of Passion Week will end in the joy and triumph of the Resurrection morning, doubt shall give place to joyous certainty.

> "Wait thou His time,
> So shall thy night
> Soon end in glorious day."

54
The Descent from the Hill

"And as they came down from the mountain, He charged them that they should tell no man what things they had seen, till the Son of man were risen from the dead. And they kept that saying with themselves, questioning one with another what the rising from the dead should mean. And they asked Him, saying, Why say the scribes that Elias must first come? And He answered and told them, Elias verily cometh first, and restoreth all things; and how it is written of the Son of man, that He must suffer many things, and be set at nought. But I say unto you, That Elias is indeed come, and they have done unto him whatsoever they listed, as it is written of him."
—Mark 9:9-13.

The Wealth of Holy Scripture
AT FIRST SIGHT these five verses do not seem to suggest much of practical profit. But Scripture is always surprising us by its unsuspected wealth. You remember the words of Job: "The stones thereof are the place of sapphires, and it hath dust of gold" (28:6). That verse always seems to me to be an admirable description of the Bible. Its very stony places turn out to be full of precious gems; its very dust is dust of gold. We come across what looks at first sight like a barren and desert tract, but as we gaze at it and study it all kinds of hidden beauties reveal themselves, until what we thought desert blossoms as the rose, and the wilderness becomes a veritable garden of the Lord. And so it may be with this paragraph.

The True Order in Service
"And as they were coming down from the mountain." So Peter's prayer that they might make tents, and abide on the top of the mountain, was not answered. They took their way down from the holy hill to the toil and conflict of the plain. And it was the same Lord, Who now led them down, Who had a few hours before taken them up. Here in a figure you get the two aspects of Christian life. Christ bids us at one time go up the mountain with Him, for communion. And then He bids us go down the mountain

with Him to service. It is of no use going down into the valley to try to minister to the needs and wants of men, unless we have first of all gone up. And that is the peril of our own day. We believe in going down in these days. That is to say, we believe in service. There was never so much done in the way of philanthropy. People were never in all their history so busy as they are today. And yet have you never been struck by the curious ineffectiveness of much of our philanthropy?

Is It Neglected?

We were never busier in our ministry, and yet we seem to do so little. Vice, temptation, sin— all appear to grow no less. We seem quite impotent to cast the evil spirit out. I wonder why it is? Is it that we have forgotten the path to the hill? Is it that we have gone down to the field of service without first going up to the hill of prayer? "Apart from Me," said Jesus to His disciples, "ye can do nothing." Apart from the Divine aid we can cast out no devils, we can change no hearts, we can bring about no radical reformations. Mere human philanthropies are sterile and impotent. But when men go up first, and then go down, what mighty power they wield! That is the first call we need to hear still—the call to come up. If we will follow our blessed Lord, He will take us, as He did these three disciples, up to some mountain apart to pray. But He will not let us remain up. He takes us up in order that later on He may lead us down again. He carries us up into the blessed fellowship of the holy mount that subsequently He may lead us down to the common levels of everyday life, that there we may fight against sin and vice and evil, and minister to the needs and wants of our fellow-men. Labor apart from prayer is ineffective: prayer that does not issue in toil is a pretense and a sham. The genuine Christian follows his Lord up and down, shares in the glory of the mount, and the conflict of the plain.

The Profit of Communion

"And as they were coming down from the mountain"—they came down unwillingly, with a certain disappointment in their souls. And yet they did not come down exactly as they went up. They were not quite the same men after this great experience as they were before. They never forgot the glory. It established their faith. It made them braver, stronger, truer men. The mountain made a difference. It always does so. No man ever comes down the hill exactly as he went up. Moses went up an ordinary man. He came down a transfigured saint. And although no halo surrounds our heads as the result and issue of our communion, the mountain never fails to leave its mark upon us. "Strength and beauty," says the Psalmist, "are in His sanctuary" (Psa. 96:6). Of the man who makes the Most High his refuge, the Psalmist also says, "Thou shalt not be afraid for the terror by night, nor for the arrow that flieth by day" (Psa. 91:5). "The mountains shall bring peace to the people" (Psa. 72:3), says yet a third Psalm. Strength for life's difficulties, calm fearlessness, a quiet spirit, beauty of character, these are the marks of the mountain. No man can hold real fellowship without having his faith quickened, his strength renewed, his love confirmed.

The Lord's Charge

With what sort of feeling did the three disciples come down from the mountain? With feelings of regret and disappointment that they were not permitted to remain and enjoy the glory longer, no doubt; but also with hearts and minds excited and full of anticipations of triumph. Possibly the vision of our Lord's glory revived again the hopes which Christ's announcement of the cross had well-nigh dashed to pieces. They began again to dream of crowns and thrones. Our Lord's perception of the kind of thoughts surging up in His disciples' minds induced Him to lay the injunction upon them that He did. They were bristling with eagerness to tell their fellow-disciples what they had seen on the mount; but Jesus charged them that they should tell no man what things they had seen. This was not at all an infrequent injunction on the lips of Jesus. "Tell no man," He said to the healed leper. "Tell no man," He said to the deaf and dumb man. "Tell no man," He said to Jairus and his wife. He lays here the same charge upon the three disciples. As Dr. Salmond puts it, "The injunction to silence which had been laid on others who would have proclaimed His miracles is now laid upon the chosen three with regard to the mighty work done on Himself."

Its Reason

Why did our Lord lay this embargo upon His disciples? First of all, because He did not wish to stir up an undesirable excitement. The populations of Galilee were in a very inflammable condition. Already, more than once, roused to enthusiasm by our Lord's acts of power, they had tried to take Him by force and make Him a King. If this story of His glory on the mount had reached them, and had won their credence, their enthusiasm and excitement might have become uncontrollable, and the purely spiritual nature of the Lord's Kingdom might have been compromised. Jesus would have no story told the populace that would for a moment stir to dangerous activity their desire for a worldly Messianic Kingdom. But, further, I think that, as Bishop Chadwick suggests, our Lord did not wish this experience of theirs to be exposed to ridicule and cross-examination. For if they had told the story immediately on their coming down from the hill, there were plenty of people, like Thomas, of a sceptical turn of mind, and others, like the scribes, bitterly hostile to their Master, who would not hesitate to say that they did not believe it. They would laugh at the story, and say they had been dreaming. And indeed it was a strange and wondrous story to ask the people to accept. They would look at Jesus in His seamless cloak—one of themselves in garb and manner and speech—and the assertion of the three disciples that a few hours before He had shone with heavenly glory, and had Moses and Elijah to visit Him and converse with Him, would seem wildly and hopelessly incredible. And so Jesus bids them keep silence about it, in order that "the impression of this great experience might be forced back upon the depths of their own spirits, and spread its roots beneath the surface there"; to tell no man, until another event had taken place, which would make the story of what happened on the holy mount a natural and congruous story, which it would be no longer difficult to believe, but which it would be blameworthy to disbelieve. They were to tell no man what things they had seen, save when the Son of man should have risen from the dead. They could venture to tell it then. The Resurrection would make the Transfiguration believable. Men would find no difficulty in believing that He who was declared to be the Son of God with power by the Resurrection from the dead, for one brief hour shared on the mount in the glory which He had with His Father before the world was.

The Central Place of the Resurrection

And this leads me to call attention to the central and critical place which our Lord evidently assigns to His Resurrection. It is to throw light upon many a mystery. It is to explain many a difficulty. It is to make many a hard thing credible. In the old days, sixty or a hundred years ago, the miracles of our Lord were quoted as evidences of His deity. But in the meantime there has grown up such a sense of the invariable order of the universe, that the miracles themselves, instead of becoming an aid to faith, have become one of our present-day stumbling-blocks and difficulties.

Its Relation to Other Miracles

But the miracles cease to be difficulties, and become believable events, in the light of the Resurrection. It is with the Resurrection we must start. In a sense it is the one and only thing that matters. It is the keystone of the whole arch. It is, as Dr. Chadwick says, "the center of all the miraculous narratives, the sun which keeps them all in their orbit." There are certain wonderful events narrated in the Gospels which would stagger belief if they stood there isolated and detached. But no wonderful deeds are impossible to Him who rose again the third day. Supernatural works are, shall I say it, "natural" to such a supernatural person. The Resurrection really carries every other miracle with it. And the Resurrection is one of the best-attested facts of human history. It has not only the witness of the apostles and other disciples, it has the still more striking and commanding witness of the Church, and the whole history of the past nineteen centuries, a history which if the Resurrection is denied becomes absolutely irrational and incoherent. The Resurrection is one of the great certitudes of the faith, and every act and deed of our Lord's life is to be considered in the light that streams from His open grave.

Elijah's Coming

"Risen again from the dead," said Jesus, and I imagine that word would strike a chill to the three disciples' hearts. They had just seen their Lord's glory, and the vision of the glory had almost banished from their minds the sad and solemn words their Master had spoken a week before, about rejection, and suffering, and death. In the light of their experiences on the hill, they had begun to dream once again about thrones. But here is their Lord talking about "death" once again. He will allow them to cherish no false or misleading hopes. The cross was as visible as ever to His undazzled eyes. He warns them once again that it was to "death" He was marching. But it was all an enigma to the disciples. They obstinately refused to believe that in the bare and literal way Christ could die. So on their way down, while Jesus marched on in front, "They questioned among themselves what the rising again from the dead should mean" (v. 10). They did not like to ask Jesus Himself; they had the timidity of men who fear unpalatable truth, and so they forbore to inquire. But there was one question they asked their Lord. It was about Elijah. They had just seen Elijah on the holy hill. The scribes, basing themselves on a prophecy of Malachi, had taught the people that before Messiah came Elijah would reappear, to prepare the Lord's way. Was that transient, fleeting appearance of Elijah on the mount all that the prophet meant? And the Master, in answer to their question, said, "Elijah indeed cometh first, and restoreth all things: and how is it written of the Son of man, that He should suffer many things and be set at nought?" (v. 12). At first sight these two sentences appear to have not the slightest connection with one another, and a German commentator speaks of the latter sentence as one that has "vehemently harassed interpreters." But really there is no difficulty. Our Lord wishes the disciples to connect with the prophecy about Elijah another prophecy about Himself. The disciples—following the example of their teachers—had been eclectics in their reading of the Scriptures. They had picked and chosen. They had made much of those passages that spoke of Messiah's glory and reign. They had ignored all those other passages that spoke of His suffering and death.

"But I say unto you," Christ added, "that Elijah is come, and they have also done unto him whatsoever they listed, even as it is written of him" (v. 13). Elijah had come—and at that a veil dropped from their eyes, and they recognized that Jesus spoke of that lonely ascetic of the wilderness whose cry had rung throughout the land, "Repent, for the Kingdom of God is at hand," and who in that way had prepared the way of the Lord.

A Past Event

John had come in the power and spirit of Elijah; but they did with him as they had done with his prototype in the ancient days. They did with him and to him whatsoever they listed. They rejected him, and repudiated his message, and allowed him, without protest, to be put to death by a weak king at the bidding of an adulterous queen. They knew not the day of their visitation. They did not recognize Elijah when he came.

Foreshadowing Another

"They have also done unto him"—that little word "also" is full of significance. It implies that there was another whom they were treating in the same way as John. And that other was John's Lord. "The Son of man must suffer many things, and be rejected by the elders, and the chief priests, and the scribes, and be killed" (8:31). John's baptism was rejected: John's Lord was crucified. They neither recognized the forerunner nor the Messiah Himself. They did unto both whatsoever they listed. The Lord still visits us, and proffers Himself to us. Do you recognize the day of your visitation? Or do you do with Him whatsoever you list? "Kiss the Son, lest He be angry, and ye perish in the way, for His wrath will soon be kindled. Blessed are all they that put their trust in Him" (Psa. 2:12).

55

The Disciples' Failure

"And when He came to His disciples, He saw a great multitude about them, and the scribes questioning with them. And straightway all the people, when they beheld Him, were greatly amazed, and running to Him saluted Him. And He asked the scribes, What question ye with them? And one of the multitude answered and said, Master, I have brought unto Thee my son, which hath a dumb spirit; And wheresoever he taketh him he teareth him: and he foameth, and gnasheth with his teeth and pineth away: and I spake to Thy disciples that they should cast him out; and they could not. He answereth him, and saith, O faithless generation, how long shall I be with you? how long shall I suffer you? bring him unto Me. And they brought him unto Him: and when He saw him, straightway the spirit tare him; and he fell on the ground, and wallowed foaming. And He asked his father, How long is it ago since this came unto him? and he said, Of a child. And ofttimes it hath cast him into the fire, and into the waters, to destroy him: but if Thou canst do anything, have compassion on us, and help us. Jesus said unto him, if thou canst believe, all things are possible to him that believeth. And straightway the father of the child cried out, and said with tears, Lord, I believe; help Thou mine unbelief. When Jesus saw that the people came running together He rebuked the foul spirit, saying unto him, Thou dumb and deaf spirit, I charge thee, come out of him, and enter no more into him. And the spirit cried, and rent him sore, and came out of him: and he was as one dead; insomuch that many said He is dead. But Jesus took him by the hand, and lifted him up; and he arose. And when He was come into the house, His disciples asked Him privately, Why could not we cast him out? And He said unto them, This kind can come forth by nothing, but by prayer and fasting. And they departed thence, and passed through Galilee; and He would not that any man should know it." —Mark 9:14-30.

The Need and the Call

"LORD, IT IS good for us to be here," Peter had said, when enjoying the glory of the holy mount. But as soon as he reached the foot of the hill, he must have felt that it would not have been "good" if the Lord had remained longer on the mountain. For here at the mountain's foot were people in sore and urgent need of Him. Here was a poor lad dehumanized almost by an evil spirit; here was a father agonized with concern and grief on his account; here were His disciples disappointed and defeated, and at their wits' end; and here was a multitude bewildered by the disciples' failure, and in danger, as a result, of losing what little faith they had in Christ Himself. There was imperative need for the presence of Jesus.

The Appeal That Failed

At the foot of the hill there was a crowd about the nine disciples, and scribes questioning with them. Our Lord asked what all the excitement was about. An answer was quickly forthcoming, not from the disciples, nor yet from the scribes, but from an individual in the crowd. "Master," he cried, "I brought unto Thee my son, which hath a dumb spirit; and wheresoever it taketh him, it dasheth him down: and he foameth, and grindeth his teeth, and pineth away: and I spake to Thy disciples that they should cast it out; and they were not able" (vv. 17-19).

The Causes of Failure

Now how was it the disciples had failed? Was it from first to last a case of presumption? In undertaking to cast the evil spirit out of this boy, had they undertaken a task for which no authority or power had been conferred upon them? No; that was not so. Jesus had conferred on them certain authorities and powers, and amongst others this, "He gave them authority over the unclean spirits" (6:7). And this power was not conferred upon them in vain, for one of the things over which the Twelve, and even the Seventy, rejoiced most was this, "Even the devils," they said, "are subject to us in Thy name." This, then, was no case of undertaking a task for which they had no authority.

Lowered Spiritual Vitality

Why, then, had they failed here? Probably several reasons cooperated. Possibly they were out of heart. Their Master was away. Their three strongest companions were away. And above everything else, the announcement of Christ's approaching rejection and suffering and death had stunned them, and well-nigh shattered their faith. Only a week or so had elapsed since that first announcement of the cross. Of that week we have absolutely no record. Apparently nothing was said, nothing was done. They spent it, as Godet says, in a kind of stupor of bewilderment and grief. That was very much their spiritual condition when this distracted father brought to them his demented son, and besought them to heal him. And their spiritual condition to a large extent explains their failure. What a person can give out depends upon what he has within. The power he exerts depends upon the power he possesses. Before a man can breathe hope into another, he must have stores of hope in himself. Before he can create faith in another, he must have strong faith of his own. That is the principle underlying our Lord's word, "According to your faith it shall be unto you." Now, this father brought his lad to the disciples when their spiritual vitality was at its lowest ebb. They could work no miracle, because they themselves possessed no spiritual energy. They could do no mighty work, because they themselves had no faith. "O faithless generation," cried Jesus, "how long shall I be with you? how long shall I bear with you?" (v. 19).

Lack of Prayer

If you ask why the disciples had no faith, you find the reason in the reply Jesus gave to their query, "Why could not we cast it out?" "This kind," answered Jesus, "can come out by nothing, save by prayer" (v. 29). That was the ultimate cause of failure. Lack of prayer. Faith and prayer stand almost in the relation of cause and effect. You cannot neglect one, and retain the other. You cannot omit prayer, and keep faith. For what is prayer? It is the meeting of spirit with spirit. It is man communing with God. It is the mortal laying hold upon the eternal. It is man talking with God; yes, and God talking with man. Now if anyone neglects prayer, if he does not speak to God, and hear God speak to him, God becomes vague, distant, unreal to him. He loses his sense of God, his assurance of the presence of God, the resistless force and power the assurance of God's presence always brings. And losing his hold of God, he becomes impotent and paralyzed.

Failure and Reproach

The failure of the disciples exposed them and their faith and their Lord to the scorn and mockery of an unbelieving crowd. When Jesus reached His disciples He found the multitude surging around them, and scribes questioning with them, "disputing with them," the word might be translated. The failure of the disciples caused exultation to the scribes. They taunted the disciples with their failure. Starting from this obvious and complete failure, they threw doubt upon their possession of any authority to cast out evil spirits. They suggested that all their so-called successes were impostures and make-believes. They managed even to make the disciples' failure bring the Master Himself into discredit. Our impotence and failure always tend to bring the whole of religion into discredit, and to bring reproach on our Master Himself. And is not that why in these very days of ours men calmly suggest that Christianity is played out, and the Lord Jesus has had His day? They would not say it if Christ's people were manifestly exerting redeeming, regenerating power. It is our feebleness and weakness which cause the enemy to blaspheme.

The Vindicating Lord

But, while the dispute was at its height, Jesus arrived. "And straightway," Mark says, "all the multitude, when they saw Him, were greatly amazed, and running to Him saluted Him" (v. 15). Commentators have puzzled themselves over the reasons for the amazement which Mark here records. Some of them say that Jesus, when He came down from the hill, retained in His face, like Moses, traces of the shining glory. I prefer to think with Dr. Salmond that the cause was the suddenness and opportuneness of the Lord's coming. The scribes were just saying that Jesus Himself was an impostor, and He appears to vindicate His claim. The disciples were at their very wits' end. Their Lord comes to their aid, to rescue them from their trouble, and to establish and confirm their faith. And the Lord is always appearing like this, "in the nick of time," for the confusion of His foes and the reinforcement of His friends. In the eighteenth century Bishop Butler says that people were so convinced that Christianity was false and played out that they did not even trouble to discuss it. Then the Lord vindicated His cause, and strengthened the hearts of His people by working the stupendous miracle of the Evangelical Revival. It is always so. When we are at our wits' end, our blessed Lord comes and turns our defeat into victory. So let us be of good cheer. Christ will always vindicate His own cause. His arm is not shortened that it cannot save. And in our days of despondency and despair He will always confound His foes, and surprise His friends by showing that He can save to the uttermost those who come to God through Him.

The Father of the Sufferer

So much for the disciples. But what of the anxious father? There are in effect in this paragraph the stories of two miracles. The first and the most obvious is our Lord's triumph over the evil spirit. The second is not so obvious, but is in many ways more wonderful still. Jesus not only drove the evil spirit out of the boy, but He won a triumph for faith in the soul of his father. When He came down from the hill it was to find His disciples in the midst of a seething, excited crowd, and the scribes engaged in a vehement

dispute with them. "What question ye with them?" He asked
(v. 16). A certain man of the multitude answered Him. "Master," he
said, "I brought unto Thee my son, which hath a dumb spirit; and
wheresoever it taketh him, it dasheth him down, and he foameth
and grindeth his teeth, and pineth away; and I spake to Thy disciples that they should cast it out; and they were not able"
(vv. 17, 18).

Love Impels

Ah, the impetuous eagerness of love! It may have been to His
disciples, or to the questioning scribes or to the excited multitude,
that our Lord addressed His question; but it was the father who
replied. He could not wait while the scribes or the disciples
explained matters to the Master. He himself without a moment's
delay rushes in, so to speak, and pours his sad story into the ears
of the Lord. It was, indeed, to Jesus the man really meant to have
brought his son. "I brought unto Thee my son," he says. But Jesus
was away on the hill, so in his distress the father turned to the nine
disciples, and besought them that they would cast the evil spirit
out. And they tried, and failed. That was the pitiful story this
father had to tell.

The Fruits of Failure

The recital was significant. For, as the failure sprang from lack
of faith, so its effect was to weaken and destroy faith. The faith of
this father had suffered. Look at the title by which the man
addresses Christ. There is no sense of devotion in it. There is no
suggestion of personal trust. It is not "Lord." It is not "Master." It
is not "Son of David." It is the cold title, "Teacher," which he
employs. He had started from home with some measure of faith in
his heart. But the failure of the disciples had practically shattered
it. He sees in Christ at this point nothing but a "teacher." What
wonder that Christ broke out into the cry, "O faithless generation,
how long shall I be with you? how long shall I bear with you?"
(v. 19).

The Restorer of Faith

But a bruised reed our Lord never broke, and smoking flax He
never quenched. And so, instead of treating with scorn and contempt this broken and shattered faith, He set about rebuilding it,
revivifying it, restoring it. "Bring him unto Me," He said. "And
they brought him unto Him." But "when he saw Him, straightway
the spirit tare him grievously; and he fell on the ground, and wal-

lowed foaming" (v. 20). Now our Lord was tender of heart, and "swift to bless." Now what one might have expected in such a case as this was an instantaneous cure. But while this poor lad lay wallowing and screaming at His feet, the Lord turned to the father, and said, "How long time is it since this hath come unto him?" (v. 21). Very likely the poor impatient father thought Jesus might have cured his lad first, and asked His questions afterwards. But that was never our Lord's way. He never hurried.

The question was designed to reveal to the man himself the moral state of his own heart. It brought all the belief and unbelief of the man to the surface. "And he said, From a child,"—it was a stubborn and longstanding mischief. "And ofttimes it hath cast him both into the fire and into the waters, to destroy him: but if Thou canst do anything, have compassion on us, and help us" (vv. 21, 22).

A Type
"If Thou canst!" To a large extent this man, with more doubt than faith in him, to a large extent he represents the age in which we live. There are some ages in the world's history which deserve the title, "The Ages of Faith," because for some reason or other the verities of the unseen and external world were so near and real and vivid, that men found it easy to believe. But our age is not an age of faith. It is, as Dr. Van Dyck entitles it, "An Age of Doubt." It has not utterly discarded Christ. But it wonders whether He can really do anything to meet its sore and bitter need. It is conscious of its misery and woe and sin, as it never has been in all its history. And it looks wistfully at Jesus. But it is not at all sure that He can help. It is not confident that He can heal. All it is capable of in the way of faith is a timid, trembling, hesitating, "If Thou canst do anything, have compassion on us, and help us." John Bunyan, in his immortal dream, pictures some men of sturdy and almost aggressive faith— men like Great-Heart and Standfast, and Valiant-for-Truth, and Hopeful and Faithful, and the rest. But he also gives us the picture of men whose faith is timid and trembling, who scarcely believe, in the persona of Mr. Little-Faith, Mr. Fearing, and Mr. Feeble-Mind, and Mr. Ready-to-Halt. And in this age of ours there are a great many more Little-Faiths and Fearings and Feeble-Minds than there are Great-Hearts and Standfasts and Valiants-for-Truth. We find the very temper of our time in this Mr. Fearing's word to Jesus, "If Thou canst do anything, have compassion on us, and help us."

How Treated by Our Lord

But see how our Lord deals with this doubtful and distracted soul. To get the exact account, you must follow the Revised rather than the Authorized Version. Jesus did not answer, as the A.V. represents, "If thou canst believe, all things are possible to him that believeth." He takes up the man's own phrase, "If thou canst!" He says—and He utters it, as Dr. Salmond notes, with a touch of compassionate rebuke—"If Thou canst," thou sayest; but it is not a question of My power, it is a question of thy faith —for "all things are possible to him that believeth." Christ rolls the responsibility back upon the man himself. He thought it all depended on Jesus; Jesus tells him it depended upon himself. An overwhelming consciousness of power breathes through this answer. Christ will have no "if" applied to Him. But He shows that the secret of success and failure is in ourselves. We do not forget that the excellency of the power is always of God, and not of ourselves. But according to our faith it is done unto us. And so, whenever we fail, instead of casting the blame upon God, we had better search our own hearts—for we may depend upon it that it is in ourselves the fault lies. We are never straitened in God, we are only straitened in ourselves. If we are ever tempted to think that "Christ does nothing for us," if we are honest with ourselves, we shall always find it is not really that Christ has failed; it is because our grip of Him has loosened, it is because our vision of Him has become dim.

The Father's Prayer

The answer our Lord gave this poor agonized father revealed to him that the first help he needed was help for himself, help for the faith which was almost overborne and quenched by unfaith; and so the appeal for bodily relief for his son changes now into a "contrite prayer for grace for himself." "Lord, I believe," he cried; "help Thou mine unbelief." Here, faced as we are by a stricken world in sad and sore need of healing, is the best prayer we can offer. Before we can be used of God to save the world, God must be allowed to have His own way with us. This contrite prayer for "grace for ourselves"; that is the first thing we need. To win our own battles over our besetting sins, to be effective in Christian service, we ourselves want a strong grip of God, a firm and confident trust in the Lord Jesus. So let us take our doubting, distrustful hearts to Him, and say, like this distressed and troubled father, "Lord, I believe; help Thou mine unbelief." And what mighty power there is in feeble faith! "If ye have faith as a grain of mustard-seed," said our Lord, "ye shall say unto this mountain, Remove hence unto yonder place; and it shall remove; and nothing shall be impossible unto you" (Matt. 17:20).

Faith and Response

As a grain of mustard-seed, weak, tiny, infinitesimal. That is all this father had. But look at the result. A mighty exercise of power and a restored son. Even a small faith exercises wondrous power. The Lord is wonderfully compassionate. He hears and answers and blesses a feeble cry like this. He gives even to Little Faith, and Mr. Fearing, and Mr. Ready-to-Halt, the victory and the abundant entrance. O tender and compassionate Jesus, O pitiful, loving Jesus! Our faith is feeble, overborne almost by misgivings and fears. We can do little more than cry sometimes, "Help mine unbelief." Yet He will not disregard even that faltering prayer. When Sir James Simpson, the greatest Scottish physician of his time, lay dying, a friend said to him that, like John the beloved disciple, he would soon be resting on the bosom of Jesus. "I don't know that I can quite do that," he said, "but I think I have got hold of the hem of His garment." And that is all that some of us have been able to do. We have stretched out timid hands, and have just touched the hem of His garment, and even that has brought its unspeakable blessing. "As many as touched Him were made whole."

56

The Training of the Twelve

"And they departed thence, and passed through Galilee; and He would not that any man should know it. For He taught His disciples, and said unto them, The Son of man is delivered into the hands of men, and they shall kill Him; and after that He is killed, He shall rise the third day. But they understood not that saying, and were afraid to ask Him. And He came to Capernaum: and being in the house He asked them, What was it that ye disputed among yourselves by the way? But they held their peace: for by the way they had disputed among themselves, who should be the greatest. And He sat down, and called the Twelve, and saith unto them, If any man desire to be first, the same shall be last of all, and servant of all. And He took a child, and set him in the midst of them: and when He had taken him in His arms, He said unto them, Whosoever shall receive one of such children in My name, receiveth Me: and whosoever shall receive Me, receiveth not Me, but Him that sent Me."   —Mark 9:30-37.

A Need of Ministry

THE TWELVE DISCIPLES, chosen by our Lord for the purpose of continuing His work and extending His Kingdom, were as yet wholly unfitted for their appointed task. Left to themselves in their present condition, the disciples would have been helpless. For, as any can see who reads even this paragraph, the disciples had so far neither the temper nor the spiritual understanding necessary to enable them to carry on Christ's work. They still hugged their carnal conception of an earthly empire, and either could not or would not understand Christ's purpose of winning an empire of souls by way of suffering and death. To the training of the Twelve the Lord now principally devoted Himself. In the paragraph before us we see how Jesus sought to train them in the understanding of Christian truth, and in the exercise of Christian temper.

Instruction in the Divine Plan

And the first lesson of which our paragraph gives record, is a lesson in the understanding of Christian truth. "And they went forth from thence," says Mark, i.e. from the foot of Mount Hermon, which was the scene of the healing of the demoniac boy, "and passed through Galilee" (v. 30). It was for the last time, and apparently they avoided the highways, and followed quiet and secluded paths. "He would not," says the Evangelist, "that any man should know it." As a rule, Jesus frequented the town and the busy street and the crowded synagogue, for He had good tidings to proclaim, which were to all people. But on this particular journey it was privacy and quietness He wanted most, for, says Mark, supplying the reason for this secrecy and seclusion, "He taught His disciples," or rather, to translate the Greek quite literally, "He was teaching His disciples." And this was the subject of His teaching: "The Son of man is delivered up into the hands of men, and they shall kill Him; and when He is killed, after three days He shall rise again" (v. 31).

The Redeemer's path led not through triumph to a throne, but through rejection to a cross—that was the subject of Christ's lesson. The disciples had been brought up on Psalm 72; Jesus reminded them of Isaiah 53. Their idea was that of a Jewish kingdom founded on force; Christ's was that of a spiritual and universal kingdom founded on sacrificial love. So He set Himself to make them realize that only by His dying could redemption be achieved, and that only by uttermost sacrifice could His Kingdom be established. "The Son of man is delivered up into the hands of men, and they shall kill Him" (v. 31). It was not the first time our Lord had set Himself to teach the disciples this lesson. After Peter's Great Confession, I find that "He began to teach them, that the Son of man must suffer many things, and be rejected by the elders, and the chief priests, and the scribes, and be killed, and after three days rise again" (8:31). That lesson had been given only some eight or nine days before. Why does Jesus repeat it again so soon? Because the disciples failed to take it in. Indeed, they utterly refused to believe that such a fate as death could be in store for their Lord. That first lesson of the cross had made no real impression. If the announcement had made the disciples uneasy and apprehensive for a little time, its effects soon passed.

The Patience of the Master

And so Jesus repeats the lesson, "The Son of man is delivered up into the hands of men," He said, "and they shall kill Him." Notice the patience of Jesus. Like the prophet, He condescends to teach men line upon line, precept upon precept, here a little, and there a little. And He does not cast off any because they are slow to learn. He will patiently repeat the lesson again and yet again. And how much need these disciples had of the Lord's patience! They were dull scholars. They were slow of heart to believe. They either could not or would not see their Lord's meaning. "But they understood not the saying, and were afraid to ask Him." "They understood not the saying." Their minds were so warped by prejudice that they refused to take the words in their plain and obvious meaning. What marvelous patience our Lord had! Many a teacher would have dismissed these men as hopelessly obtuse and dull. But Jesus does not dismiss them. The failure of the first lesson and the failure of the second lesson only make Him repeat the lesson once again.

And with Us, Too

Jesus will be patient with us, though we too are so slow to learn His lesson and catch His spirit. We have been to school to Christ, some of us, for years; but we are poor scholars. We have scarcely mastered the A B C of the Christian faith as yet. We have not learned the lesson of self-denial, we have not learned the lesson of forgiveness, we have not learned the lesson of love. Yet our patient Lord bears with us, He repeats the old lessons again and again. Verily, as Peter says, the long-suffering of the Lord is our salvation. And as the patience of Jesus with these disciples makes me able to believe He will be patient with us, so what He made of these dull and slow disciples makes me able to believe He can do something with the dullest and slowest of us. Peter and John and the rest of them—they would have broken an ordinary teacher's heart—but Jesus bore with them. And His patience met with its reward. Peter learned the lesson at last. And John penetrated deep into his Lord's meaning and purpose at the last. And Thomas and Philip learned to glory in the cross at the last. Even so I can believe He will do equally great things for us, and that that daring word of the Apostle will become true of us, "We shall know even as also we are known."

The Fear of the Truth

"But they understood not that saying, and were afraid to ask Him." "And were afraid to ask Him." Why? "They had seen how Jesus could rebuke even Peter, when he spoke rash words on a former occasion," remarks Dr. Salmond. But I do not think that was what prevented their asking Jesus. The alternative explanation given by the same commentator comes far nearer the truth. "The awe of His words made them shrink from a closer acquaintance with their purport." That is it exactly. They did not understand what Jesus meant, but they felt He meant something sad, something sorrowful, something tragic. And they feared to ask Him to explain, because they felt they did not want to know the stern and grim reality. They were afraid to ask Him, not because Jesus might have rebuked them, but because they themselves did not want to know. "It is a natural impulse," says Bishop Chadwick, "not to want to know the worst." Insolvent tradesmen leave their books unbalanced. They do not examine into their accounts, lest they should have to face the bitter fact that they are bankrupt. And so the disciples refused to ask what Jesus really meant, for fear the truth should dash to fragments every hope they had ever cherished. They preferred not to know, that they might continue to live in their world of make-believe. It was a kind of moral cowardice by no means unknown in these days of ours. There are many things which we cover up and hide. We fear, if we began to investigate and ask questions, what we might discover would fill us with shame. For instance, how few of us honestly ask ourselves how we stand in face of death and the judgment? When Falstaff in his last sickness began to talk of God, "I bade him," says Dame Quickly, "not talk of that." That exactly catches the temper of our day. We choke off all discussion on these solemn themes. We will not let our souls dwell on the thoughts of God and eternity.

A Futile Policy

It is a futile and suicidal policy. If a tradesman is losing ground, the sooner he faces the fact the better, or else total business ruin may be his fate. And if we are growing spiritually impoverished, the sooner we know it the better. There is a chance for the man who knows he is wrong and wants to mend. There is none for the man who though he is wrong persists in believing he is all right. "Remember," is the Lord's advice to a bankrupt Church, a Church that had become spiritually impoverished, and had lost its first love, "whence thou art fallen, and repent, and do the first works." Compare your past with your present, He says, remember what you used to be, and what you used to do. And retrace your steps. Resume your old habits. Begin again your old practices. Do the first works. And that is the counsel He would give to you and me. "Remember whence you have fallen." Make inquisition of your own heart and life. See where you have fallen and failed. Face the facts. The recognition of the tragic fact of failure and loss is the very first step towards moral and spiritual recovery.

A Lesson on the Christian Temper

And now let me pass on from our Lord's lesson in Christian truth to the lesson He gave His disciples upon the Christian temper and spirit. On the way Jesus noticed that a discussion which developed into a vehement dispute had taken place amongst the disciples. And when they reached Capernaum He asked them what it was all about. "What," said He, "were ye reasoning in the way?" "But they held their peace," says Mark; "for they had disputed one with another in the way, who was the greatest" (vv. 33, 34). What an amazing and startling contrast we have here! The Lord is in front, absorbed in thoughts of His cross and passion, thinking of the death He was to taste for every man; His disciples, following a little behind, quarrel and wrangle about precedence and position. This was a favorite bone of contention amongst the disciples. Perhaps it was the fact that Peter, James, and John had been chosen to accompany the Lord up the mount, coupled with the fact of the humiliation of the other nine by their failure to cast out the evil spirit, that gave rise to the dispute at this particular juncture. But whatever the cause there was the fact, while Christ was marching to His cross, these disciples were quarrelling about places. "What were ye reasoning in the way?" asked Jesus. "But they held their peace." There was no answer from any one of them—not even from Peter. Why? They were ashamed. They had advanced their own claims and asserted their rights loudly enough amongst themselves; but all this eagerness for rank and place seemed paltry and unworthy in the presence of Jesus. "They held their peace." Things change their aspect when we view them in worldly society, and in the presence of Jesus. We too fret and fume, if we feel our proper place is not given to us. We grow hot and jealous about rank and position and the rest of it. But how mean and petty it all looks when we bring it into the presence of Jesus! It would do us good to bring our ambitions and desires and plans constantly into the presence of the lowly Jesus, and test them there.

Exaltation by Service

But they held their peace. But Jesus divined what the dispute was all about, and calling them to Him, He sat down, as the Jewish Rabbis were wont to do when about to teach— because He was about to deal with the matter as a teacher— solemnly. And to the conscience-stricken and humiliated Twelve He laid down the law of greatness in His Kingdom. "If any man would be first, he shall be last of all, and minister of all" (v. 35). The condition of greatness in Christ's Kingdom is humility, humility that glories in service, the service not of a class, but of all. The Kingdom of Christ is not a kingdom of self-seeking, but of self-sacrifice. And he is greatest in it who loves best and serves most. "I serve," that is the motto of England's Prince of Wales. That is the way to becoming a Prince in God's Kingdom, by service. Christ stooped to death. He became the minister of all. And all who would attain to greatness in His Kingdom must follow in His train.

Is This Ministry Ours?

Are we on the way to this Divine and eternal greatness? Do we live, not to be ministered unto, but to minister? Are we ready to stoop to humble services? Do we go about doing good? We may be among the weak things, and the despised things, and the things that are not, of the earth. But for the humblest of us a higher rank is open than earthly potentates can ever bestow. We can become great in the Kingdom. If we wear the motto and live the motto "I serve," we shall become kings and priests unto God. For here is the one eternal law of greatness and true nobility —"If any man would be first, he shall be last of all, and minister of all."

57
A Lesson in Charity

"And John answered Him, saying, Master, we saw one casting out devils in Thy name, and he followeth not us: and we forbade him, because he followeth not us. But Jesus said, Forbid him not: for there is no man which shall do a miracle in My name, that can lightly speak evil of Me. For he that is not against us is on our part." —Mark 9:38-40.

The Occasion

IN THESE THREE verses our Lord is still engaged with the training of the Twelve. He had just taught them a lesson in humility; now He teaches them a lesson in tolerance. We must remember, in discussing these various lessons which our Lord taught His disciples, that they are not, as Dr. A. B. Bruce remarks, continuous and set discourses on announced themes. For the most part they are of the nature of Socratic dialogues, and are often suggested by a remark made or a question asked by one of the disciples. The immediate occasion of this lesson in charity was John's account of a meeting which he and his brother, or possibly all the twelve, had with a man who was casting out devils in the name of Christ, but was not a follower of the Master.

What was it that caused John to tell the story at this particular juncture? Possibly it was an attempt to change the subject, and to divert the conversation into another channel. John smarted under the rebuke just administered to himself and the other Apostles for their strife about places. Perhaps the consciousness that he and his brother aspired to the highest thrones in the kingdom made him feel that the rebuke was almost especially aimed at him. So he thought he would let the Lord know that if he had certain ambitions for himself, he was also active in his Master's service, and jealous for His honor. But I prefer to think that John recalled the incident because, in the light of what Jesus had just said, it suddenly dawned upon him that he had committed a great mistake in seeking to stop the man at all. For it was in Christ's name this exorcist had been doing his work. And, instead of "receiving" him, as the Lord's words seemed to suggest he ought to have done, he had denounced him, sought to hinder him, repudiated him. Had he acted rightly in so doing? Up to that moment probably John had been rather proud of his action. But, in view of what Jesus said, he became doubtful and uneasy. So, with a frankness and a candor that are altogether to his credit, he told his Master the whole story, that He might pass judgment upon it.

The Motives

Now what were the motives that lay behind the interdict which the Apostles sought to lay upon this unrecognized worker? There may have been in it a touch of jealousy for the Master's honor. They may have felt that a man who did not openly confess Christ by joining the circle of His avowed disciples, had no right to use His name. And so they may have honestly thought they were defending and asserting the honor of Christ by forbidding him any more to use Christ's name. It is a good thing to be "very jealous of the Lord," but we have need to be careful that we are jealous after a godly sort. Some of the most monstrous crimes this world has seen perpetrated have been committed from a mistaken sense of jealousy for the honor of God. But, from the way in which the narrative is worded, one would gather that jealousy for the honor of God was not half so powerful a motive as personal pique. A sense of wounded dignity breathes through the very words. "We forbade him, because he followed not us." They looked upon themselves as the only accredited and authorized agents of the Lord Jesus, and they were indignant that an outsider should take to himself what they considered their prerogatives.

The Act

But, whatever the motives that animated them, the practical result was an act of exclusiveness, and narrowness and intolerance. They ruled this man, whom they ought to have received as a brother, out of their communion; they tried to stop his work; they denied his right to work at all, and all because he did not belong to their little circle. They never stayed to inquire what kind of a man he was; they paid no heed to the fact that he must have had some kind of faith in Christ, or he would never have used Christ's name; they disregarded the fact that the man's ministry was obviously owned and blessed of God. They denied the right of anyone outside their circle to work in the name of Christ at all; they set themselves up as the exclusive channels of Christ's grace, and the sole dispensers of His power. "We forbade him," says John, not "because he followed not Thee"—but "because he followed not us."

The Spirit of Intolerance

Is there any lesson for us in all this? Has it any pertinency for our own day? Our Lord, as we shall see in a moment, utterly and wholly repudiated this exclusive and intolerant spirit. Did His rebuke eradicate it for ever from the hearts of His disciples? Is this the first and last instance of narrowness and intolerance we read of in the Christian Church? Alas, no! In spite of this rebuke and repudiation of our Lord, the hearts of many of His disciples in every age have been filled with this narrow and intolerant spirit. It has resulted in crimes that bring the blush of shame to the cheek. It developed into the faggot and the fire. It substituted, as Hugh Black says, the doctrine of the stake for the doctrine of the cross. It set up the Inquisition in Spain. It kindled the fires in Smithfield. It drove the Pilgrim Fathers across the seas; it silenced Richard Baxter; it flung John Bunyan for twelve years into Bedford Gaol; it drove John Wesley from the pulpit to the fields.

And what about today? Alas, the same spirit prevails. You can trace much of the strife and consequent weakness and shame of Christ's Church back to it. We are all of us far too prone to think our way is the only way. We are far too ready to forbid other men, because they follow not us. And we rend and paralyze and shame the Church of Christ in consequence.

Christ's Lesson in Tolerance

Now let us turn to our Lord's comment on John's story. It was not for nothing John's conscience had been uneasy. The answer Christ made confirmed him in his fears that their action had been unwarrantable and wrong. For the recital of the story calls forth from our Lord's lips a short and sharp rebuke. "Forbid him not," He said. They had no right to place this man under an interdict, or to try and stop him in his gracious work. Christ will have none of their exclusiveness and intolerance. And He proceeds to give His reasons, and in these reasons the voices of wisdom and charity unite. The first reason is personal to the particular man in question. "There is no man which shall do a mighty work in My name, and be able quickly to speak evil of Me" (v. 39). They had treated this man as if he were an enemy. They could not have acted more harshly by him, had he been an open and determined foe. But, said Jesus, he clearly was not an enemy. Nor was he likely easily to become one. His use of the name of Christ to a certain degree committed him to the cause of Christ. They ought to have treated him, though outside their circle, as an ally and a friend. "For there is no man which shall do a mighty work in My name, and be able quickly to speak evil of Me." The second reason He casts into the form of a general truth. "For he that is not against us is for us."

Contrasted Sayings

This maxim recalls another like it, and yet unlike. In Matthew 12:30 we find Jesus saying, "He that is not with Me is against Me." Now the commentators all tell me that these two sayings, though apparently contradictory, are really not contradictory, but supplementary. And in all kinds of ingenious ways they proceed to reconcile the two. "The principle in both sayings is the same," says Dr. Salmond. "It is the simple principle that we cannot be for and against, friend and foe at the same time." "The two sayings," is Dr. Bruce's comment, "are harmonized by a truth underlying both—that the cardinal matter in spiritual character is the bias of the heart. If the heart of a man be with me, then though by ignorance and error, isolation from those who are avowedly my friends, he may seem to be against me, he is really for me. On the other hand, if a man be not in heart with me (e.g. the Pharisees), then though by his orthodoxy and zeal he may seem to be on God's side, and therefore on mine, he is really against me." The impossibility of neutrality in the spiritual sphere—this, according to the commentators, is the great truth that both sayings are meant to emphasize. But, ingenious though these explanations are, I do not think they really meet the difficulty; for in the one passage, as Dr. Chadwick puts it, "seeming neutrality is reckoned as friendship, while in the other it is denounced as enmity."

Reconciled

Doubtless the true explanation is to be found in a closer examination of the two sayings. The saying in Matthew refers exclusively to a man's relations to Christ. "He that is not with Me is against Me"; and that is inevitably so. There can be no such thing as a neutral attitude towards Christ. The man who says that he simply is indifferent to Christ, is unwittingly, perhaps, increasing the mass of opposition that has to be overcome by Him. But in the saying we have just now under consideration it is His disciples rather than Himself that Christ has in mind. In Luke's account, indeed, that is how the saying is given, "He that is not against you is for you." It is a warning to the disciples not to suppose that loyalty to their organization, although Christ was with them, was the same thing as loyalty to Him. It was quite possible for people to be outside their circle—not "with them" or "of them," in that narrow and mechanical sense—and yet to be in Christ and loyal to Him.

And if a man was "in Christ" and loyal to Him, even though he did not belong to their circle, he was really "for them"; he was helping on their work and furthering their cause. It was so with this unknown worker. He was not "of them," in the sense that he did not belong to their circle, but inasmuch as he was doing good and spreading Christ's name he was really on their side.

A Warning to Ourselves

And it is so still. The various denominations into which Christ's Church is divided are not antagonists—if they only knew it, they are allies. Over our furious controversies, and our ugly intolerances, Christ whispers this word, "He that is not against us is for us." When we consider the great work which all churches exist to further, people of other communions are seen to be not against us, but for us. It is when we think only of our particular organizations that those not belonging to us seem against us. When we think not of our Church, but of Christ, and Christ's Kingdom, we see those who belong to other communions, and who worship and work in different ways from ours are not against us, but for us. There is nothing we need more than the increase of the spirit of brotherhood, a frank and unreserved recognition of our deep and real unity in Christ our Lord.

58
Offenses

"For whosoever shall give you a cup of water to drink in My name, because ye belong to Christ, verily I say unto you, he shall not lose his reward. And whosoever shall offend one of these little ones that believe in Me, it is better for him that a millstone were hanged about his neck, and he were cast into the sea. And if thy hand offend thee, cut it off: it is better for thee to enter into life maimed, than having two hands to go into hell, into the fire that never shall be quenched: Where their worm dieth not, and the fire is not quenched: And if thy foot offend thee, cut it off: it is better for thee to enter halt into life, than having two feet to be cast into hell, into the fire that never shall be quenched: Where their worm dieth not, and the fire is not quenched. And if thine eye offend thee, pluck it out: it is better for thee to enter into the kingdom of God with one eye, than having two eyes to be cast into hell fire: Where their worm dieth not, and the fire is not quenched." —Mark 9:41-48.

The Reward of Helpful Service

IT IS WITH the sure and rich reward of all helpful service that our Lord is concerned in the first verse of our paragraph. "Whosoever shall give you a cup of water to drink, because ye are Christ's, verily I say unto you, he shall in no wise lose his reward" (v. 41). Let me, if I can, make clear what I conceive to be the sequence of thought. Jesus has finished His comments on John's story with the sentence, "He that is not against us is for us." As if to say, "That man who was casting out devils in My name was not a foe, he was a friend. He was not to be denounced and hindered; he was to be encouraged. He was really helping us." And then He goes on to say that whoever helps His disciples, even though it be only to the extent of a cup of cold water, he shall by no means lose his reward.

The sequence is perfectly natural and intelligible. You may say, indeed, that this is the Lord's blessing upon that interrupted and excommunicated stranger. John and his companions had denounced him, and tried to hinder him. The Master blessed him. The disciples thought he was their enemy, and so they forbade him: the Master saw he was their friend and ally and helper, and so He said that that unknown stranger should in no wise lose his reward. But though I think that our Lord had the interdicted man especially in mind when He uttered this saying, He cast it into the form of a general statement. "Whosoever shall give you a cup of water to drink, because ye are Christ's, verily I say unto you, he shall in no wise lose his reward." Broadly speaking, you may say that is an assertion of the sure reward of every helpful Christian service. Looking a little more closely, we shall find the saying suggestive of two or three other truths beside that main and central one.

Act and Motive

First of all, what a suggestion we get here as to the constitution of genuine Christian giving! Christian giving is giving for Christ's sake. Christian service is service in Christ's name. The giving of a cup of cold water was a service common enough in a hot country like Palestine. What transfigured that common act into a Christian act, was when the cup of water was given to a disciple because he was Christ's. In a word, it is the motive that decides whether an act or a gift is Christian or not. There is a great deal of giving in our world that is not Christian. A great many give because it is the fashion and custom to give. A subscription list is started for the relief of distress, and we feel we must for respectability's sake have our names upon it. I do not know that giving prompted by such motives counts for anything in Christ's sight. Then there is a great deal of giving that springs from humanitarian motives. Men are touched by the thought of human misery, and give. That is philanthropy. I do not say that is not admirable. It is. But there is a higher plane to be reached by us. Our giving becomes Christian when we give for Christ's sake.

The Quality of Service

Then see how our Lord omits from His notice not even the slightest and humblest service. Nothing could be cheaper, in a sense, no service could be simpler, than the gift of a cup of cold water; and yet the Lord notices that small service, and of it He says it shall by no means lose its reward. We sometimes deplore that the gifts we can offer and the services we can render are so small. This saying is for our special encouragement. Cups of cold water—it is only humble and trivial services of that kind we seem capable of. But it is not the quantity so much as the quality of the work that decides its value in God's sight. Go on giving your cups of cold water, rendering your little kindnesses, speaking your simple words, in the name and for the sake of Christ—go on doing these things. Christ notices them. Verily I say unto you, you shall in no wise lose your reward.

The Certainty of Reward

And now as to this certainty of reward. Is it true? Yes. The man who does a kindness to another because he is Christ's, receives his reward in an enlarged capacity for kindness, in spiritual enrichment. Life somehow becomes richer and deeper for him; every little act of Christian service seems to lift his own life on to higher levels. Of course, in spite of all this, a man may allow his baser instincts to get the mastery over him, and so the reward may have been bestowed upon him in vain. But there is no doubt about the reward. "The deepening of spiritual capacity," as Bishop Chadwick says, "is one exceeding great reward of every act of loyalty to Christ." And that reward never fails.

Offenses against Little Ones

And this truth about the sure reward of every act of Christian service suggests to our Lord the converse and opposite truth of the inevitable punishment of every offense. "Whosoever shall cause one of these little ones that believe on Me to stumble," He said, "it were better for him if a great millstone were hanged about his neck, and he were cast into the sea" (v. 42). The commentators all say that Jesus had the little child referred to in verse 36 still in the midst, and that it was the little child He had in mind when He spoke of "one of these little ones." That may be so. But I am not at all sure that it was not that interdicted and excommunicated exorcist He was still thinking about. What had been the effect of the harsh action of the disciples upon him? Perhaps they had shattered the faith he had in Christ. What if the harshness of the disciples had driven him back? What if they had quenched the flickering wick of his faith? They had done it thoughtlessly. But what irreparable harm they might have caused—the loss and shipwreck of faith, the ruin of a soul! And so our Lord issues this solemn warning, and says it is better that a man should lose his life, be sunk in the depth of the sea, rather than that by his conduct he should cause one of these little ones who believe on Him to stumble.

Stumbling-blocks and Their Makers

This is a solemn saying. The truth that supplies its justification is the truth of the infinite and supreme worth of the soul, the soul of even the humblest and the weakest in the sight of God. Far better, says our Lord, lose life than to destroy a soul. "It must needs be that offences come," said our Lord, on another occasion, "but woe to that man through whom the offence cometh." Our Lord becomes stern, severe, menacing, when He thinks of those who put stumbling-blocks in a brother's way. And yet there are amongst us those who do it, who constantly and deliberately do it. I think of those writers, men and women, who produce prurient and suggestive books; who flood our land with base literature which defiles and pollutes the minds of our youth. I think of the evil companions who at every corner lie await to destroy, who tempt young men and women to their ruin and shame. What a fate is theirs! There are lost and ruined and blighted souls set down to their account. They have robbed God of some of His children. Good were it for such men if they had never been born.

Consideration for the Little Ones

No one, I suppose, who reads this would deliberately set a stumbling-block in a brother's way. We would shrink with horror from the thought of luring, goading, tempting a soul into sin. But it is possible even for us to be guilty of causing a brother to stumble. I am constantly being told by men and women that their greatest stumbling-block is found in the inconsistencies of Christian people. Remember there are "little ones," weak ones, Little Faiths, Fearings, Ready-to-Halts all about us. And some lapse, some selfishness, some uncharitableness, as in the case of these disciples, may easily cause them to stumble. Look, therefore, carefully how you walk—not as unwise, but as wise. For here is this solemn word set for our warning. "Whosoever shall cause one of these little ones that believe on Me to stumble, it were better for him if a great millstone were hanged about his neck, and he were cast into the sea."

Offenses Against One's Own Soul

Then the Lord again, by a perfectly natural transition, passes from the thought of offenses against a "little one" to offenses against one's own self. In a sense the two classes of offenses merge into one. For a man's sin against another is always also a sin against his own soul. Still, it is possible in thought to distinguish between the two classes; and in the remaining verses of our paragraph our Lord is dealing with offenses against a man's own soul. "And if thy hand cause thee to stumble," He says, "cut it off: it is good for thee to enter into life maimed, rather than having thy two hands to go into hell, into the unquenchable fire" (v. 43). And He repeats the same formula about the foot and the eye. Here we must beware of a bald literalism. The truth He is emphasizing is this—we must shrink from no spiritual surgery to save the life of the soul. It is not a physical mutilation our Lord is advocating here. That would be to countenance the Manichean heresy, that matter is essentially evil. And our Lord knew that the ultimate source of sin was not the members of the body, but the corrupt and sinful will. Our Lord uses hand and foot and eye here in a metaphorical and symbolic sense. Spiritual hurt, as Dr. Salmond says, may come from some part of a man's nature which he has suffered to become unsound. It is his wisdom, therefore, to cut off the occasion, at whatever cost, and wherever it may lie, whether in hand or foot or eye.

Lines of Offenses

But while it is spiritual surgery our Lord has in His mind, and while hand and foot and eye are not to be taken literally, they are most suggestive of various kinds of sin which enslave and destroy the soul. The hand, this wonderful instrument, may, as Dr. Chadwick suggests, stand for some harmless accomplishments that somehow or other have become fraught with evil suggestiveness; it may stand for a business, a livelihood that is entangled with dishonest ways. And the foot that carries us into our various fellowships and companionships—it may well stand for some association or friendship which corrodes and degrades the soul. "Some walk in the counsel of the ungodly." And the eye may stand for unholy desire and passion. Through Eye-gate what temptations assault men. That was how the first sin came into the world, according to the old story. "The woman saw that the tree was good for food, and that it was a delight to the eyes" (Gen. 3:6).

The Way of Duty

Now what our Lord says about all these things is this, that they must ruthlessly be excised, if they injure the soul. If some accomplishment becomes a snare, it must be surrendered. If business cannot be carried on with a good conscience, it must be given up. "If thy hand cause thee to stumble, cut it off." And if any otherwise pleasant companionship insensibly deadens the soul, takes the edge off our sensitiveness, it must be abandoned. "If thy foot cause thee to stumble, cut it off." And if certain books you read, certain sights you behold, bring evil desires into your heart, shut the books, and shun the sights. "If thine eye cause thee to stumble, cast it out." It is no new doctrine. It is the doctrine of self-denial and self-sacrifice that is taught on every page of the Christian gospel. The Christian life is not an easy one. There is much lopping and cutting and maiming to be done. There is agony to be endured, and blood to be shed.

Self-Preservation

But two things are to be noticed. (1) The sacrifice is not for sacrifice sake. The end of sacrifice, as the philosophers say, is self realization. The purpose of the surgery and the mutilation is to preserve life. Some people tell us that every instinct and desire of human nature is to be gratified. That is the so-called gospel of Naturalism. It would be more truly and properly called the cult of Animalism. But, as a matter of fact, you cannot give the rein to the passions and instincts of the lower nature without imperilling the higher. You cannot live only to gratify the flesh, without polluting and destroying the soul. And it is to preserve that life of the soul that Jesus bids us use the knife to those desires and lusts that threaten it. "It is good for thee to enter into life maimed, rather than having thy two hands to go into hell." The surgery is all in the interests of life.

And the Sacrifice Worth Making

(2) And secondly, the life is worth the sacrifice. Do you remember that wonderful conversation about life and death in *Lavengro*, between Jasper the gipsy and Lavengro himself? "Life is sweet, brother," said Jasper. "Do you think so?" replied Lavengro. "Think so; there's night and day, brother, both sweet things; sun, moon, and stars, brother, all sweet things; there's likewise the wind on the heath. Life is very sweet, brother; who would wish to die?" "I would wish to die," replied Lavengro. "You talk like a fool," retorted Jasper; "a gipsy would wish to live for ever." "In sickness, Jasper?" "There's the sun and stars, brother." "In blindness, Jasper?" "There's the wind on the heath, brother; if I could only feel that, I would gladly live for ever." Life is the supreme thing; and the gipsy was ready to endure and suffer anything for life. But there is a better and nobler thing than the life of which he spoke. It is the life of which Christ speaks here. For this is soul life, divine life, eternal life. And that is worth anything, everything. Life is very sweet, and it is worth while to sacrifice hand, or foot, or eye to secure life. It is worth while to live a maimed, mutilated, darkened life down here, that our souls may win the life eternal. It is worth while to beat the body black and blue, to "crucify the flesh with the passions and lusts thereof," if only the soul may live for ever.

59
Salted with Fire

"For every one shall be salted with fire, and every sacrifice shall be salted with salt. Salt is good: but if the salt have lost his saltness, wherewith will ye season it? Have salt in yourselves, and have peace one with another."
—Mark 9:49, 50.

Some Difficulties

THESE TWO VERSES are obscure. In verse 49 there is scarcely a word that does not offer difficulty. "For every one" seems to imply some causal connection with what has gone before. What is that connection? To whom does the "every one" refer— to unbelievers or to disciples? "Every one shall be salted." Which of the two radically different meanings of "salt"' are we to accept as correct? And what does "salting with fire" mean? No wonder that expositors lament over this passage. "It is exceedingly difficult," says Grain. "It is exceedingly vexed," says Wolf. "It is exceedingly vexing," remarks another. "It has put to the rack the ingenuity of many learned men," says Grotius. While an English commentator remarks, "There is perhaps no passage in the New Testament which has so defied all efforts to assign to it any certain interpretation." In face of all that, it seems perhaps almost presumptuous to attempt to expound it at all. But, accepting the view Dr. Morison suggests, I believe a sound and perfectly intelligible account can be given of this most difficult passage.

The Text

Let us begin by accepting the text as it stands in the R.V., where the latter half of the verse is omitted. The uncertainty about the correct reading is no doubt due to the fact that, from the very beginning, the passage was felt to be difficult; and so in various MSS. the text was slightly altered, and in some cases an additional sentence was inserted, in the hope of making the meaning a little more clear. That may account for the insertion of the phrase, "and every sacrifice shall be salted with salt," which you find in the A.V. The scribe probably thought that the old Levitical custom of salting the sacrifice might throw light upon the passage. But we may accept the R.V. view, that Mark only wrote, "For every one shall be salted with fire."

The Persons Indicated

But what exactly does that mean? To whom, to begin with, does the phrase "every one" refer? Some commentators confine the reference to the unbelieving. But it is not to unbelieving men that Christ has been speaking; it is to His own disciples. It is not of unbelieving men He has been speaking; it is of His own. He has been warning them that they may find stumbling-blocks in their own natures, and telling them that they must practice unsparing spiritual energy; that they must cut off the hand and the foot and cast out the eye rather than incur the doom of those who yield to their fleshly lusts. "For," He says, "every one shall be salted with fire." The "every one" clearly refers to the people who have been the subject of the preceding verses. In other words, this assertion refers to believing men, to Christ's own disciples.

The Salt

What, then, does our Lord mean when He says that every one of His disciples shall be salted with fire? "Salt" and "fire" must be used here, not literally, but metaphorically; otherwise, in the conjunction of salt and fire, we should get a conjunction of two incongruous ideas—preservation and destruction. Metaphorically considered, however, they are perfectly congruous. The two ideas that are most prominently associated with salt are those of seasoning and preservation from corruption. Here the whole idea is that of preservation—preservation from the worm which dieth not, and the fire which is not quenched. It is, as Dr. Morison says, "the antiseptic property of salt" that the Savior has in His mind. So that, substituting for the actual word the idea for which it stands, we might read the sentence thus: "Every one of My disciples shall be preserved from corruption by fire."

The Fire

Let us now pass on to the second term, "fire." It is suggested, no doubt, by the reference to "fire" in the preceding verse. But there is a difference. The fire of Gehenna was destructive, penal. It utterly consumed all the corruption and filth and abominations that were cast into it. But this fire is not destructive, it is cleansing; it is not penal, it is purifying. "Every one shall be preserved from corruption by fire." For fire, as we know, has this cleansing power. It purifies, for instance, the metal cast into it. It cleanses it of the dross mingled with it, so that it issues forth refined silver, pure gold, as the case may be. But while the action of fire in this instance is meant to be regarded as purifying rather than as penal, the idea of pain is still associated with it. You cauterize a wound; it is a cleansing and healing, but it is also a painful process. And so our Lord says that every disciple of His will be preserved from corruption by something which purifies, but which in the process hurts and blisters and burns. What is that something? The Holy Spirit, some commentators say. "Fire" is one of the symbols of the Spirit. When He enters the heart, He flames against all unrighteousness and sin; He burns out all that is unholy and base and foul. He is a Spirit of burning. And that means that the Spirit's work in the heart is often painful work. It is agonizing work, and we shrink from it in fear. "Who among us," cried the prophet, "shall dwell with the devouring fire? who among us shall dwell with everlasting burnings?" (Isa. 33:14). We may say, then, that the essential meaning of the passage is this, "Every one of Christ's disciples is preserved from corruption by the fire of an unsparing self-sacrifice, kindled by the energies of the Spirit of God."

The Pain of Sacrifice

Two practical truths are suggested by this explanation. (1) The Christian life involves pain and sacrifice. Here is a truth stamped on every page of the New Testament. It is suggested by every figure used to describe the Christian life. It is emphasized in every appeal to live the Christian life. Christ calls His disciples, not to a velvet path, but to a narrow way. He summons them, not to ease and comfort, but to sacrifice. He promises them, not a smooth and pleasant time, but suffering and a cross. There is much of agonizing, cutting, maiming, burning to be done in the Christian life. Everything great and good costs effort and sacrifice. The greatest achievement of all is the attainment of a Christian character. And as it is the greatest, so is it also the costliest. There is no such thing as being a Christian on the cheap. Discipleship costs its price. "Every one shall be salted with fire."

And Its Profit

(2) But the pain the Christian disciple undergoes all tends to profit. "Burning"—it does not suggest a pleasant process. It suggests agony, torture. But the end of it all is, cleansing and health. I cannot help thinking that there is between verse 48 and 49 a deliberate and purposed antithesis. The two verses present

to us alternative fires. As our old commentator puts it, "He sets one fire over against another, the present one against the future." There is the fire of Gehenna, of which the ceaseless burnings of the Valley of Hinnom were the type and symbol, and there is the cleansing fire of the Spirit of God. And it looks as if Christ meant us to understand that into one of these fires every man must go. If he refuses to part with what is corrupt and sinful, then there waits for him the penal fire, into which everything corrupt and sinful is cast. But if he submits himself to the cleansing fire of the Spirit, that fire cleanses and purifies him of all that is foul and base, and leaves nothing in him on which the penal fire of Gehenna could feed.

The Saltless Salt

"Salt is good," our Lord goes on to say, "but if the salt have lost its saltness, wherewith will ye season it?" (v. 50). The connection between this sentence and the preceding one is verbal rather than logical. I mean, that it was the mention of the word "salt" that suggested this further remark to Jesus. "Salt" is still in His mind the great preservative. And as He uses the term here, He evidently means by it "the spirit of Holiness, the Christian character"; that which, when men have it, makes them in turn "the salt of the earth." But what if the salt has lost its saltness? What is the use, He asks, of a profession out of which all the reality has gone, of a nominal Christianity out of which the genuine Christian spirit has evaporated? Is there such a thing as "saltless salt" in the spiritual world? Alas, yes, there is. I read, for instance, of a Church which the Lord of the Church thus described, "Thou hast a name that thou livest, and thou art dead" (Rev. 3:1). There was a Church that was not fulfilling its function—"Saltless salt." I read of another Church of which the Lord said, "I have this against thee, that thou didst leave thy first love" (Rev. 2:4). The process was not complete, but the degeneration had commenced. The salt was losing its saltness. I read of some men in St Paul's second letter to Timothy, "holding a form of godliness, but having denied the power thereof" (3:5). There was the profession without the substance; the appearance of salt, with none of its pungency and preserving power.

Still to Be Found

Saltless salt—there is a great deal of it in the world still; profession without practice, name without deed, fire without life. I do not know but that if we began to examine our own consciences and hearts we might have to confess that this degenerating process has to some extent taken place in us. The salt has begun to lose its saltness. We exercise little preserving and purifying power on the life of the world around us. "Salt is good," says our Lord. The genuine, vital, and uncompromising Christian is a center of healthful and healing and purifying influence. By his mere presence he arrests and stays corruption. Dr. Stalker tells about a young lad so transparently and unmistakably Christian that, by his mere presence, within a month he banished the foul speech for which his office had been notorious. There is nothing the world wants more than men and women of the same sincere and unashamed Christian character. But why is it that we Christians produce so little effect on the world; that in spite of our presence, evil and base and corrupt practices flourish on every hand? Is it because the salt in us has lost its saltness? Is it because our Christianity is so feeble and compromising and formal? What hope is there for the world, if Christianity fails it? "If the salt have lost its saltness, wherewith will ye season it?" (v. 50).

Holiness and Peace

And so our Lord passes on to His practical conclusion. "Have salt in yourselves," He says, "and be at peace one with another." Our Lord here has a side reference to their interference with the man who had been casting out devils. It was not their business to interfere with another man, because he worked in what they considered to be unorthodox fashion; it was their business to see to it that they did their own duty in the world, that their own Christian faith was real, that their own lives were such that they would exercise a cleansing and purifying influence upon the world. And this they could only do as they had the spirit of holiness and consecration within them. "And be at peace one with another." For the disciples had been quarreling about places. They had been disputing which of them was greatest. And their disputes had threatened to break up the unity of the apostolate, and to militate against the success of their work. "Be at peace one with another," the Lord says. For real peace would inevitably result, if they had "salt in themselves."

Things to Be Desired

The wisdom which is from above is first pure, then peaceable. Holiness and peace. Those are the things Christ desires for His disciples. Those are the things that Christ's disciples need most still. What a change would come over our world if Christian people were only at peace one with another, and gave to the world an example of holy living! A conquered world would be the result. Let us pray for these two things—greater holiness and mutual concord. The world will be ours when we have salt in ourselves, and are at peace one with another.

60
Divorce

"And He arose from thence, and cometh into the coasts of Judea by the farther side of Jordan: and the people resort unto Him again; and, as He was wont, He taught them again. And the Pharisees came to Him, and asked Him, Is it lawful for a man to put away his wife? tempting Him. And He answered and said unto them, What did Moses command you? And they said, Moses suffered to write a bill of divorcement, and to put her away. And Jesus answered and said unto them, For the hardness of your heart he wrote you this precept. But from the beginning of the creation God made them male and female. For this cause shall a man leave his father and mother, and cleave to his wife; And they twain shall be one flesh: so then they are no more twain, but one flesh. What therefore God hath joined together, let not man put asunder. And in the house His disciples asked Him again of the same matter. And He saith unto them, Whosoever shall put away his wife, and marry another, committeth adultery against her. And if a woman shall put away her husband, and be married to another, she committeth adultery."

—Mark 10:1-12.

Bridging a Gap

SOME INTERVAL OF time elapsed between the conversation recorded in the last chapter and the conversation we are now to consider. During that interval many things had happened. If we want to "fill in" this gap which Mark leaves in his story, we must turn to Luke and John. From a comparison of these other Gospels we find that in the meantime Jesus had sent out the seventy disciples; He had gone up to Jerusalem to the feast of Pentecost; He had retired from Jerusalem to Perea; He had again gone up to Jerusalem to the feast of Dedication; and once again, to avoid the murderous plots of the Jews, had gone away beyond Jordan, to the place where John was at the first baptizing. It is probably just at this point that the question as to divorce is to be placed.

The Causes of the Question

From John's account it is clear that the preaching of Jesus beyond Jordan was attended by more than ordinary success. It was probably, as Mr. David Smith suggests, the results of our Lord's

335

preaching that stirred His enemies once again to activity. Perhaps they had flattered themselves that, when they had driven Him out of Jerusalem, they were finally rid of Him. But when they heard that the crowds were resorting to Him beyond Jordan, and that people in numbers were believing on Him, they were greatly perturbed, and it was not long before certain emissaries of the Pharisees appeared on the scene, with the deliberate object of thwarting Him in His work. The method they adopted was that of bringing to Christ a captious question, a question which would put Him on the horns of a dilemma, and, however He might answer it, might impair and imperil His authority. The question chosen dealt with divorce. "Is it lawful for a man," they asked, "to put away his wife?" i.e. at his pleasure, or, as it is expressed in so many words in Matthew's account, "for any cause"? And this they said "tempting" Him; not because they really wanted guidance or instruction, but because they wanted to ensnare and trap Him in His speech.

The Conditions as to Divorce

Now, to understand the special difficulties connected with a question like this, we must know something about the position of marriage and divorce in our Lord's time. The Mosaic Law had allowed divorce in case a husband found any "unseemly thing" in his wife. The phrase "unseemly thing" was ambiguous, and the Rabbis quarreled violently amongst themselves as to its true interpretation. One school took the stricter and nobler view, that what the Law meant was that a wife could only be put away for unfaithfulness. Another held the meaning of the phrase to be that, if for any reason the wife had become distasteful to the husband, he could put her away, "for any cause." And so, as Mr. David Smith says in his Life of Christ, Rabbis had arisen who taught the people that if a husband for any reason conceived a dislike to his wife, or if he saw any other woman who seemed fairer in his eyes, or even if her cooking did not quite please him, for these and other reasons, equally trumpery, he was at liberty to send his wife away. Now, a lax doctrine of morals is always agreeable to the natural man, and the second was the interpretation currently received. Jewish society was accordingly disgraced by an appalling laxity in this matter of divorce. Family life was imperilled by it, and an intolerable wrong was done to womankind. It made woman the slave of man, putting the wife at the husband's mercy. For while she could not for any cause divorce him, he might for no cause at all divorce her, and cast her upon the world.

The Question Put

This, then, was the question the Pharisees brought to Jesus. "Is it lawful for a man to put away his wife?" i.e. for any custom allowed. They made quite sure that whether Jesus said "Yes" or "No," He would lay Himself open to attack. For if He said "Yes," they could at once represent Him to the people as sanctioning a low morality, and holding baser views about marriage than some of their own teachers; and that would have been the end of our Lord's moral authority. On the other hand, if He said "No," they could represent Him as repudiating the authority of their own sacred Law, by which divorce was expressly allowed, and as thus in violent opposition to the popular sentiment. For the Jews cherished this facility of divorce as a signal privilege, accounting it a singular grace vouchsafed to Israel, and withheld from the Gentiles. Perhaps, too, they also hoped that, if He said "No," it would stir Herod to enmity. For Herod had put away his own wife, and married Herodias, his brother's wife, while that brother was still alive. They remembered that Christ's Forerunner had come to the dungeon and the block because of his plain and faithful speech on this very question. And they doubtless hoped that a plain answer from Christ might arouse Herodias again to fury, and so bring Christ to share in the Baptist's doom. All these calculations and hopes were in the minds of these Pharisees. They asked their question "tempting Him."

The Reply Given

Our Lord in His answer first refers these plotting Pharisees to the authority they themselves recognized. "What did Moses command you?" He asks. They reply, "Moses suffered to write a bill of divorcement, and to put her away." They take care to say nothing about the causes and reasons for which divorce was permitted. "For your hardness of heart," returns our Lord, "he wrote you this commandment." That is to say, Moses could go no further than he did in the way of regulating and restraining divorce, because the moral condition of the people would not allow it. All that Moses did was by way of putting a check upon divorce. He made summary dismissal impossible; he secured delay, by making a formal bill of divorcement necessary, and so gained time for reflection. It was a vast improvement over the laxity common before his day. But it was not a perfect law. It did not accomplish all Moses himself desired; but it was the best possible under the circumstances. Solon, the great Athenian law-giver, once said that his laws were not the best that could have been devised, but they were the best the Athenians could receive. And so Moses was compelled to adapt his marriage legislation to the moral condition of the Israelites.

The True Ideal of Marriage

And then Christ proceeds to set forth the true ideal of marriage—the Divine intention of the marriage relation. No consideration of popularity or of personal safety weighs with Him. Boldly, frankly, plainly, He declares what the relations between man and woman were meant to be. "From the beginning of the creation," He said (quoting the very words of Scripture), "male and female made He them." That is to say, God made man and woman complementary to each other, so that only in union with its opposite does either find its true perfection. There may be special reasons calling certain men and certain women to celibacy. But celibacy is not, as the Roman Church seems to hold, a higher state than marriage. Our Lord's plain teaching here is that God's plan and ideal was that man should find his perfection in a holy union with woman, and woman similarly in a holy union with man. "From the beginning of the creation, male and female made He them." "For this cause," Jesus says, "shall a man leave his father and mother, and shall cleave to his wife; and the twain shall become one flesh: so that they are no more twain, but one flesh" (vv. 6-8). The union of man and woman in marriage is so profound and vital, that husband and wife cease, as it were, to be two separate and distinct individuals, and become so merged together that they constitute one unit of being. Each becomes part of the very existence of the other, "so that they are no longer twain, but one flesh," "the two-celled heart beating with one full stroke." This union, down to the very foundations of being, and instituted by God, is not to be at the mercy of man's whims and caprices. Ideally and essentially, marriage is a permanent and indissoluble relation. "What therefore God hath joined together, let not man put asunder" (v. 9).

Reaffirmed

To those who heard it, this was a staggering reply. What, no relief from the marriage bond, even in case of insupportable incompatibilities? The disciples themselves were bewildered, and, when they got into the house, pressed Jesus further upon the point. They said (as Matthew tells us) that if the bond of marriage was an indissoluble one, then it were better not to marry at all. But their questions and protests only evoke from our Lord another affirmation of the essential permanence and indissolubleness of the marriage relation. "Whosoever shall put away his wife, and marry another, committeth adultery against her; and if she herself shall put away her husband, and marry another, she committeth adultery" (vv. 11, 12). The wanton breach of this holy bond, the putting away of wife or husband for this and that reason, was, our Lord said, a violation of the seventh commandment. No "incompatibilities" suffice to dissolve this union. There ought to be no "incompatibilities." For marriage is not to be engaged in rashly, thoughtlessly or lightly, but advisedly, reverently, and in the fear of God. There is only one thing, according to our Lord's teaching, that can break the marriage bond, and that is the awful sin that poisons married life at its source. Short of that, marriage is indissoluble. "What God hath joined together, let not man put asunder."

Christ as Defender of the Weak

Now, apart from the main issue, let us remark how our Lord appears here as the defender of the weak. In the ancient world, no one suffered crueller wrong and indignity than woman. And here our Lord appears as the defender of woman and the lifter up of her head. Woman, according to our Lord's teaching, is not man's slave or toy, to be dismissed and cast off at the merest whim and caprice; she is man's complement and counterpart; and matrimony is a holy estate, in which woman has equal rights with man. The emancipation of womankind began with a declaration like that which is contained in these verses. The honor, respect, and chivalrous deference paid to woman today she owes chiefly if not entirely to the influence of Jesus.

And of the Family

Our Lord appears here also as the defender of the family. In the long run the life of the nation, yes, and the prosperity of the kingdom, depend upon the life of the family. And the life of the family, again, depends upon the sacredness and sanctity of marriage. It needs no pointing out from me that laxity of marriage law inflicts irreparable injury upon family life. I think sometimes of what happens to the children when fathers and mothers divorce one another, as they do in some civilized countries today, for all sorts of flimsy and ridiculous reasons. What becomes of the children? And with what kind of a conception of morality are they likely to grow up? In speaking as He did, our Lord was safeguarding the interests of the children, defending the family, preserving the home, and so securing the very foundations on which the fabric of society rests.

A Present-day Need

No subject needs to be more plainly and emphatically spoken about in our day than that of marriage. There is a growing tendency towards laxity in views about it. Divorces become ever more and more numerous. Legislatures are inclined to multiply the reasons for which relief from the marriage-bond can be obtained. Writers are busy making attacks upon the whole system of marriage. Novelists—and women novelists amongst the most prominent—advocate temporary alliances, or sing the praises of a promiscuous love which is nothing but gross and naked animalism. A certain school of social reformers repudiate marriage altogether. These are serious and menacing signs. You threaten the very life of the state when you relax the ties of marriage and weaken the family bond.

There is nothing we want more than a new grasp of our Lord's teaching—that there is but one moral law, and that law is the same for man and woman. The sacredness of marriage ought to be a subject upon which we have no doubts. On this point it is well not to have an open, but a closed and settled, mind. Let no specious and plausible talk about "unhappy marriages" unsettle that conviction. The remedy for "unhappy marriage" is not greater facility of divorce, but increased thought and seriousness in the contraction of marriage. Laxity in this will mean rottenness sweeping in like a flood. It is ours to maintain and assert the more austere and exacting view of Christ. Marriage is an ordinance of God. It is meant for the perfecting of character. It is essentially and ideally permanent and indissoluble. "What . . . God hath joined together, let not man put asunder."

61
Christ and the Children

"And they brought young children to Him, that He should touch them: and His disciples rebuked those that brought them. But when Jesus saw it, He was much displeased, and said unto them, suffer the little children to come unto Me, and forbid them not: for of such is the kingdom of God. Verily I say unto you, Whosoever shall not receive the kingdom of God as a little child, he shall not enter therein. And He took them up in His arms, put His hands upon them, and blessed them." —Mark 10:13-16.

The Defense of the Child

THERE IS NO hint in the narrative as to the exact time or place where this blessing of the children occurred. We are not to conclude that, because it follows upon the account of our Lord's conversation with the Pharisees about divorce, it must have happened on the same day or about the same time. All that we can say about it is, that it happened during our Lord's last journey southwards, and probably while He was still in Perea. But while I do not think that the contiguity of this passage about the children to the passage about divorce is meant to imply that both events happened the same day, or even the same week, I think the Evangelist set them down here side by side with a purpose. The connection between them is not chronological, it is one of idea and point of view. They are put down here the one after the other, because they both illustrate a certain aspect of our Lord's character.

A Defense of the Weak

I have said that in defending the cause of woman in the matter of divorce our Lord showed Himself the defender of the weak and the oppressed, guardian of the family and family life. This story of the reception and blessing of the children sheds further light upon that gracious aspect of our Lord's character. Here too He appears as the defender of the weak. For what is so weak and helpless as the little child, the babe? And in that cruel, ancient world, who was so oppressed and abused and ill-treated as the child? You see a reflection of the ancient world's estimate of the child in the conduct

341

of the disciples. The disciples "rebuked those that brought them." Babes, they thought, were beneath the notice of Christ. He could not be troubled with them. But He who never broke the bruised reed, who was always the defender of the weak and the oppressed, said, "Suffer the little children to come unto Me," and took them up in His arms, and blessed them (v. 14).

And a Defense of the Family

And here too He appears as the defender of the family. In the last paragraph He maintains the rights of the wife. In this paragraph He maintains the right of the child. Now there are three parties to the family—husband, wife, child. The place of the husband was sufficiently safeguarded by the customs and laws of ancient society. But the wife was subjected to cruel wrong, and the child was often the subject of shameful neglect. By His teaching on divorce our Lord gave the wife her proper place in the family. By His love for the children He redeemed childhood from neglect, and made the little ones the object of loving regard and care. And so our Lord defended and safeguarded family life. The emphasis our Lord laid upon the family deserves to be called "extraordinary," says a noted American professor. Not only did He always express sympathy with domestic life in all its phases; not only did He display great reverence for women and tenderness for children; not only did He adopt the terminology of the family to express the relations between Himself and His followers, and even the relations between man and God, but the family was the only institution upon which Jesus laid down any specific legislation.

The Family the Social Unit

All this emphasis upon the importance of the family arose from our Lord's sense of the vast part the family plays in the development of human character. To Him, the family was the social unit, and it was through the regenerated family that the regeneration of the world was to be effected. We need to learn of our Lord in all this. The home is the strategic point. Decay of family life spells ruin to the nation, and a block to the progress of the Kingdom of God. Therefore we must do all we can to defend and safeguard it, to defend it against the menace to its integrity by the slackening of the marriage-tie, to defend it against the menace to its happiness and usefulness, from the neglect of the little child. The sanctified family is a pledge and promise of the redeemed world.

The Whole Duty of Parents

And now, turning to the story itself, let us notice the part the parents played in this incident. "And they brought unto Him little children, that He should touch them" (v. 13). There can be no doubt who the "they" refers to, viz., the parents of the children. I say "parents" deliberately, because fathers as well as mothers were evidently concerned in this. The fathers of these children have hardly had fair play at our hands. I have seen many pictures of this incident, but I cannot remember one which depicts a father as taking any part in it. But the narrative makes it plain that there were fathers as well as mothers present, for the participle in the Greek is in the masculine. Here, then, we have fathers and mothers bringing their children to Jesus, children young enough to be taken up in His arms. And the word which is translated simply "brought" in our version really means "offered." It is the word used of the "offering" of gold and frankincense and myrrh by the wise men to the infant Jesus. These fathers and mothers "offered" their little children to Christ. It was a solemn act of dedication and consecration. They "offered" little children to Him.

Duty Where Unexpected

And it was the parents of Perea who did this. Now Perea, the geographers tell us, was part pagan, as well as part Jewish. I have no doubt its people were despised and scorned by the proud Jews of Jerusalem. But some at least of the parents of Perea had sufficient insight to recognize that to be blessed of Christ would be the choicest gift that could fall to the lot of their children. It is worth noticing how the finest tribute to Christ, the finest illustrations of faith and love, occur amongst pagan and half-pagan people. It was the faith of the centurion that made Jesus marvel at its strength; it was in a Syro-Phoenician woman He found a persistent love that would not be denied; it was in Samaria He met with the swiftest and most general response to His preaching; and now amongst those half-pagan people of Perea parents pay Him the finest tribute all through His career—they "offered" their children to Him, that He might touch them. Here in parable we have the whole duty of parents—to offer their children to the Lord; to consecrate them in their very infancy to Christ, to do as Hannah did with young Samuel, to grant them to the Lord all the days of their life.

A Duty Often Neglected

It is just here, in this critical and all-important duty, that many fond and loving parents fail. They take every care of their chil-

dren's health and education and manners. They do their level best
to further their worldly success. But many of them take little
account of their children's souls. And yet that is really the
supreme duty. You remember Angel Charity's cross-examination
of Christian. It all gathered round this one point. Here are some of
her questions. "Why did you not bring your children along
with you? Did you pray to God that He would bless your counsel
to them? Did you tell them of your own sorrow and fear of
destruction? Did you not by your vain life damp all that you by
words used by way of persuasion to bring them away with you?"
Charity never asked Christian what he had done to promote his
children's worldly prosperity. The crucial thing was, what he had
done for their souls. We, to whom the charge of children has been
given, may well take this to heart. If we were half as anxious to
offer our children to the Lord as we are to educate them well, to
place them well, to marry them well, there would be a different
story to tell about some of our homes than there is at present; and
the world would be a far sweeter and better place than it is. First
things first; and the first duty of a parent to his child is this—to
offer him to the Lord.

The Hindering Disciples

"They brought unto Him little children, that He should touch
them: and the disciples rebuked them." And this in spite of the
stern and solemn warning about putting a stumbling-block in the
way of a little one. Why did they rebuke the parents? Why did
they try to hinder them from coming to Christ? Out of concern,
says Dr. Salmond, for the Master's dignity and ease. Because, says
Professor Warfield, the children did not need healing, and could
not receive instruction. The disciples thought of Jesus as a
Teacher sent from God, and a Healer.

Their Mistake

As these little children had no sickness or disease, and were too
young to profit by the Lord's teaching, they thought it was putting
Him to needless toil and trouble on their behalf for His notice. So
they rebuked those that brought them, and rather roughly tried to
thrust them away.

And Ours

You may wonder that any men, and especially these men, could
so misinterpret and misunderstand the Christ. But let us not be too
hard upon them. Do we not sometimes commit the same tragic

mistake? Are not some tempted to deny that the child can receive the Spirit of God; to think that children, while children, cannot come to Christ? If I am asked how soon children may become susceptible to the operation of God's grace, I must answer that I do not know at what time they are not. Beware, then, of slighting the spirituality of the child. Who are we, to say that this or that child is too young to come to Christ, seeing that this Holy Book tells us of a Jeremiah who was sanctified, and a John the Baptist who was filled with the Holy Ghost even from his mother's womb?

The Welcoming Lord

The disciples rebuked those who brought them, and were for driving them and their children away; but when Jesus saw it He was moved with indignation—He took it ill, as our old English commentator expresses it, that the Twelve should so entirely misunderstand and ignore His teaching, should act so entirely contrary to every principle He had laid down—and "said unto them, Suffer, permit, the little children to come unto Me; forbid them not; for of such is the Kingdom of heaven." "Suffer, permit, the little children to come." All sorts of people had in their time made their way into Christ's presence. As Dr. Glover says, Pharisees had come in their bitterness and hate to catch Him in His words: strings of sufferers—the blind, the deaf, the halt, the leprous—had come to Him to be healed; greedy people flocked out to Him because they ate of the loaves, and were filled; pious people pressed upon Him to hear His words of spirit and life; sinful people forced their way into His presence, and fell at His feet, praying that they might be forgiven. But no people ever came into our Lord's presence who were so welcome to Him as these little children. Suffer them to come, He said. And He took them up in His arms, laid His hands upon them, and blessed them.

The Children's Friend

Here is our Lord as the children's Friend. The little ones were dear to His heart. "Feed My lambs" was the charge He laid upon the chief of His Apostles. And when He took the little ones up in His arms He took captive every parent's heart. "Remember this, my boy," said Hood Wilson's mother to him, on the day of his ordination, "every time you lay your hand on a child's head, you are laying it on a mother's heart." There is no aspect of the Lord Jesus that appeals with more constraining force to a parent's heart today than the sight of Him with the children in His arms.

The Children's Charter

"For of such is the Kingdom of heaven." What a word was this! I have heard the charter of the Society for the Prevention of Cruelty to Children spoken of sometimes as "the Children's Charter." But this is the real Children's Charter. It is this great word of Christ that has given the child his royal place. Here is the child's spiritual rank and heritage. "Of such is the Kingdom of heaven." "Heaven lies about us in our infancy," says Wordsworth; but that is not half so emphatic a statement as this of our Lord—"Of such is the Kingdom of heaven." And this very dictum, which asserted the child's spiritual prerogative, has given him his earthly place of regard and affection and love. When Jesus said, "Of such is the Kingdom of God," He rescued the child from the neglect and contempt with which he was regarded in the ancient world.

The Child and Paganism

Evidence abounds in the ancient writers to prove how children were neglected and abused. Heathenism had no place in its thought or care for child life. Exposure was a common practice; infanticide was counted no crime. Listen to just two or three extracts from Latin writers. Stobacus says, "The poor man raises his sons, but the daughters, even if one is poor, we expose." Quintillian says that "to kill a man is often held to be a crime, but to kill one's own children is sometimes considered a beautiful action among the Romans." And Seneca writes thus: "Monstrous offspring we destroy; children, too, if weak and improperly formed, we drown. It is not anger, but reason, thus to separate the useless from the sound." In these sentences you get the temper and spirit of the ancient world.

The Child in Christianity

But Jesus rescued the child, and set him upon high; made him the object of loving regard and care, so that the very tenderest feelings of our present day gather and cluster around our little ones. And this He did by revealing the child's spiritual prerogative. Just as He redeemed the humblest of men from contempt, and broke the shackles of the slave, by revealing the infinite worth of the individual soul in the sight of God; just as He redeemed women from degradation, by revealing her as being, in God's sight, the complement and counterpart of man, so He redeemed the child by saying of him, "Of such is the Kingdom of God." The history of the past eighteen centuries has been a history of enlarging liberty and social amelioration. And all these liberating and ameliorative movements spring from spiritual sanctions. It is the new conception Christ gave of the place of the woman and the child, and even the slave, in the regard of God, that has gradually wrought out their emancipation and redemption. The child can never be neglected again. Here is his charter, "Of such is the Kingdom of heaven."

The Man as Child

Then our Lord, having vindicated the child's dignity, went on to lay down this law, that only the childlike could enter the Kingdom at all. "Whosoever shall not receive the Kingdom of God as a little child, he shall in no wise enter therein" (v. 15). It is not a case, as we think sometimes, of the child waiting till he becomes a man, it is a case of the man having to become a child again. The reference may be to the child's innocence; or to the child's simplicity; or to the child's humility. Probably, however, the main thought is the child's helplessness and utter dependence. We must "receive" the Kingdom of God as a little child. We are as helpless in the matter as a child in its mother's arms. The children of the Kingdom enter it infants for whom all must be done, humbly receiving, and doing nothing. "By grace have ye been saved through faith; and that not of yourselves: it is the gift of God" (Eph. 2:8). "The free gift of God is eternal life in Christ Jesus our Lord" (Rom. 6:23).

The Restart

"As a little child"; what regrets the very phrase stirs within us! What would we not give to shake off the defilements, the evil knowledge, the sinful entanglements the years have brought? Is it possible again to become as "a little child"? Yes, it is. "Ye must be born again," said Jesus, and He never gave a command which was not also half a promise. I read in the Old Book of a leprous man who at the command of the prophet of the Lord dipped seven times in Jordan, and his flesh came again, like unto the flesh of a little child. But there is a better fountain than Jordan, in which you and I can wash away the defilements of the years, and become again in soul and spirit like "a little child." "The blood of Jesus Christ His Son cleanseth us from all sin" (1 John 1:7).

62
The Rich Young Ruler

"And when He was gone forth into the way, there came one running, and kneeled to Him, and asked Him, Good Master, what shall I do that I may inherit eternal life? And Jesus said unto him, Why callest thou Me good? there is none good but one, that is, God. Thou knowest the commandments, Do not commit adultery, Do not kill, Do not steal, Do not bear false witness, Defraud not, Honor thy father and mother. And he answered and said unto Him, Master, all these have I observed from my youth. Then Jesus beholding him loved him, and said unto him, One thing thou lackest: go thy way, sell whatsoever thou hast, and give to the poor, and thou shalt have treasure in heaven: and come, take up the cross, and follow Me. And he was sad at that saying, and went away grieved: for he had great possessions."
—Mark 10:17-22.

The Questioner
THIS RICH YOUNG ruler had come into contact with Jesus before; he must at any rate have heard Him preach, and have been profoundly impressed by Him. Mr. David Smith suggests that he may have been in the synagogue in Jericho, some three months before, when a certain scribe stood up, and, tempting Jesus, asked this very same question, "What shall I do to inherit eternal life?" He had heard our Lord's controversy with that scribe; he had listened to that exquisite parable of the Good Samaritan, and the arrow of conviction had entered his soul. For three months he had been, as the old Puritans would say, "under concern." For three months he had been unhappy in his mind. He could bear the suspense and unhappiness no longer, so when Jesus was resuming His southward journey he ran forth and kneeled to Him, and asked Him, "Good Master, what shall I do that I may inherit eternal life?" (v. 17).

His Spirit
It was the very same question that the scribe had asked in Jericho; yet in what a different spirit it was asked. The scribe did not ask the question because he really wanted to know; he asked simply because he thought that this question might put Jesus in a

corner. This young ruler asked it because it was the one thing above everything else he wanted to know, and felt he must know. You know that difference of temper and spirit. It is not unfamiliar in our own days.

His Circumstances

All this comes out in the minute little touches of Mark's narrative. To begin with, it needed a great deal of courage and resolution to make this young ruler come at all. He was a man of some wealth—all the Evangelists make a point of that; he was also, according to St Luke's account, a "ruler," i.e. probably a ruler of the synagogue. He was a young man, therefore, not simply of wealth, but of official and acknowledged standing. Now, I repeat, it was not easy for a young man of such a position to come to Jesus at all. For the wealth and officialism of Palestine had taken up an attitude of hostility towards Jesus. "Publicans and sinners" came together to hear Him; it was comparatively easy for them. But this young ruler had to set his own class at defiance; he had to brave the anger and scorn of the official world to which he belonged.

His Eagerness and Courage

There was intense eagerness in the manner of his coming. He "ran" to Him, He felt the business on which he came brooked no delay. It was pressing, urgent, vital business. "As He was going forth into the way, there ran one to Him" (v. 17). And when he reached the Lord, regardless of all the proprieties, and careless of the scowls and frowns of his friends, he flung himself upon his knees in the dust before Him. "There ran one to Him, and kneeled to Him." Other rich men who felt the influence of Jesus, appear in frank and open courage to come far behind this young man. I cannot imagine Joseph of Arimathea bending the knee to Jesus in a public place. Joseph thought of his "honorable counsellorship," and kept his discipleship secret, for fear of the Jews. I cannot imagine Nicodemus doing this. Nicodemus believed that Jesus was a teacher sent from God. But he never said so openly. He too thought of his position and his reputation. I cannot imagine Nicodemus falling on his knees before Jesus in the public street, and calling Him "Good Master" in the ears of men. Nicodemus preferred to do his homage to Christ "secretly by night." But this young ruler cast all considerations of precedence to the wind. He risked his reputation. He risked the goodwill of his friends. It was vital that he should know the secret of eternal life, so down in the dust he went at the Lord's feet, braving all the shrugs and the jeers of the onlookers, crying out, "Good Master, what shall I do that I may inherit eternal life?"

His Sense of Need

With all his courage and reverence for the Lord, the young ruler had a passionate desire to have his question answered, and to know the way of life. He was conscious of his need. He was keenly alive to the fact that he lacked something. He had kept the commandments, as he subsequently told Jesus, He had lived a blameless life. There was not a smirch or stain upon his character. Touching the righteousness which was in the law, he was blameless. And yet he was unsatisfied; his soul had no rest. He was like Paul in his Pharisee days, laboriously and punctiliously performing every legal duty, and yet finding out there was no righteousness by the works of the law, ready, although he had kept all the commandments from his youth, to cry, "Wretched man that I am, who shall deliver me from the body of this death?" All this sense of need, his dissatisfaction, his unrest, the trouble of his soul, find expression in his urgent and passionate cry, "Good Master, what shall I do that I may inherit eternal life?" If only men and women in these days were half as concerned about eternal life as this young ruler was, and had half his courage in seeking out and confessing Christ!

Christ's Faithful Dealing

Now, if I have rightly understood the character of this young ruler, and accurately portrayed it, he will seem just the kind of person to touch our Lord's sympathy, and to win from Him a ready and gracious response. "A bruised reed," the Evangelist says of Him, "shall He not break, and smoking flax shall He not quench" (Matt. 12:20). But when I turn to the narrative I find Christ dealing coldly, harshly, almost sternly with this young ruler. Why was it? There is only one answer. Christ had a way of encouraging the weak and timid, and of checking the forward and impulsive, by confronting them with the stern facts, with the realism of the Christian life. As in the case of the scribe who wanted to follow Christ, to whom Christ said sharply almost, "Foxes have holes, and birds of the air have nests, but the Son of man hath not where to lay His head." And perhaps there was something superficial and facile about this young ruler; at any rate, Christ Jesus meets his impassioned inquiry with a preliminary objection. He said, "Why callest Thou Me good? none is good save one, even God" (v. 18).

The Young Man Questioned

Controversy has raged about this sentence. The Socinian inter-prets it to mean that Christ disclaims the epithet "good," and argues from it that He totally disclaims any idea of being put on an equality with God. But that quite clearly cannot be the meaning of the sentence. For, according to that interpretation, it would amount to a denial not simply of Christ's divinity, but of His good-ness as well. And, as we know from the whole tenor of the Gospels, Christ knew Himself holy, harmless, undefiled. This is certainly no confession of imperfection. Nor is it simply a rebuke to the young ruler for using a word without meaning it. Apparently the purpose of the question was to drive this young ruler back upon his foundations, to make him investigate his own half formed beliefs, face the issues of his own confession. "You have called me good,'" He says. "Consider what your language means. 'Good' is a title which belongs to God. You have given it to Me. Do you really mean it?" Far from being a repudiation of sin-lessness, and a disclaimer of Divinity, rightly interpreted this question becomes a challenge and a claim.

The Young Man Answered

And then our Lord proceeds to answer the young ruler's ques-tion. He refers him to the law of Moses. "Thou knowest the commandments, Do not kill, Do not commit adultery, Do not steal, Do not bear false witness, Do not defraud, Honor thy father and mother" (v. 19). The answer was a grievous disappointment to the inquirer. For all these commandments he had punctiliously and painfully obeyed, thinking thereby to attain to peace. Sadly and wearily, therefore, he replied, "All these things have I observed from my youth. What lack I yet?" (Matt 19:20). He knew there was something lacking. In spite of all his scrupulosity and punctil-iousness, his heart was a stranger to peace and joy. The eternal life, the Divine life, the life he felt Jesus had, was not his. "What," he cried, "lack I yet?"

The Inexorable Demand

And as the Lord looked at him, so earnest and appealing, His heart was touched. "He loved him," Mark says. Or it may possibly mean that He "kissed him." This young man, with the clean record and the hungry heart, appealed to our Lord's sympathy and affec-tion. "Jesus looking upon him, loved him." And then He set before the young man the inexorable demand of the kingdom, the stringent condition of eternal life. "One thing thou lackest; go, sell whatsoever thou hast, and give to the poor, and thou shalt have treasure in heaven: and come, follow Me" (v. 21). Now we must be careful in our interpretation of this demand of our Lord. It does not mean that every one who wants to lay hold on the eternal life must sell all his goods and give to the poor; it is not a general condition, but a demand made to meet the young ruler's case. Our Lord, like a skilful physician, diagnosed the disease before prescribing the remedy. He saw that this young ruler was suffering from a "divided heart." It wavered between love of God and love of gold. And there is never any peace for a divided heart; only war and strife and misery. "Sell whatsoever thou hast," Christ said to this young ruler, "and give to the poor, and thou shalt have treasure in heaven." In other words, He asked him to surrender to God an undivided heart.

Made of Us Also

That is what God asks of us—not the punctilious observance of external rites and ceremonies, but a surrendered heart. Thus alone are life and peace to be gained; not by the works of the law, but by the surrendered heart. Have we learned the lesson? I look around, and see much labored "keeping of the commandments": a careful and exact obedience given to the moral law: a punctilious observance of the externals of religion. Yet people are not at rest. No; and they never will be along those lines alone. The experience of this young ruler, the experience of Paul himself, only illustrates the truth of the Apostle's saying, "By the works of the law shall no flesh be justified" (Gal. 2:16). Peace only comes by way of a consecrated and surrendered heart.

The Great Refusal

"Sell that thou hast, and give to the poor," said our Lord. But the demand was too much for the young ruler. He who, in his enthusiasm and eagerness, came "running" to Christ, went away with a face like a "lowering" sky, which forebodes "foul weather"; for he had "great possessions," and for those "great possessions" he sacrificed his Lord. Granted, it was a stringent demand. And yet the demand carried its compensations along with it. "Sell whatsoever thou hast, and give to the poor," said Jesus, "and thou shalt have treasure in heaven: and come, follow Me." The compensation outbalanced the sacrifice, for there was the blessed company of Jesus all the way; the inheritance incorruptible and undefiled at the last. But he clung to his gold, and sacrificed the company of Jesus, and the internal inheritance. "He went away sorrowful."

Some people find it hard to believe that so promising a young man, whom Jesus "loved," could really make a final refusal. They point out that he went away "sorrowful"; and they choose to think that, some time later, he chose the "better part" which here he refused. That may be so, though his present refusal made it harder for him later to choose aright. But, as a matter of fact, Scripture says nothing about a later acceptance. As far as Scripture is concerned, that is the last view we get of him. And many like him have thus "gone away." They would have been glad to have been Christians on easier terms, but this inexorable demand for sacrifice was more than they could bear, and they "went away." What about ourselves? Christ asks still for a completely surrendered heart. He demands still the expulsion of everything that disputes the dominion with Him. What will you do? Will you also go away? God give us grace to say with Peter, "Lord, to whom shall we go? Thou hast the words of eternal life" (John 6:68).

63
Christ's Teaching about Wealth

"And Jesus looked round about, and saith unto His disciples, How hardly shall they that have riches enter into the Kingdom of God! And the disciples were astonished at His words. But Jesus answereth again, and saith unto them, Children, how hard is it for them that trust in riches to enter into the Kingdom of God! It is easier for a camel to go through the eye of a needle, than for a rich man to enter into the Kingdom of God. And they were astonished out of measure, saying among themselves, Who then can be saved? And Jesus looking upon them saith, With men it is impossible, but not with God: for with God all things are possible." —Mark 10:23-27.

Why the Lesson Was Given

The conversation here given followed immediately upon the incident of the rich young ruler, and was indeed suggested by it. The departure of the young ruler was the text, and these verses were the sermon Christ preached upon it. Or, if you like to put it in a slightly different way, in the preceding paragraph you have the story; in this paragraph Christ points the moral. The departure of the young ruler showed how fierce and strong are the foes that come between a man and eternal life. There is, as John Bunyan puts it, a crowd barring the way to the palace gate. And a man needs to be not only of a stout countenance, but also of a very brave heart, if he is to bid defiance to that armed throng, and say to the man with the inkhorn, "Set down my name, sir." We have all to "agonize," if we would enter in by the strait gate. And that is why, when the young ruler went away, "Jesus looked round about, and saith unto His disciples, how hardly"—i e. with what difficulty—"shall they that have riches"—or rather, "shall they that have the riches, the possessions of the world"—"enter into the Kingdom of God!"

The Lord's Look and Words

"He looked round about"; withdrawing His gaze from the retreating figure of the young ruler, he turned it upon the Twelve. He knew that the love of money, which had caused the young

354

ruler to make the "great refusal," was already doing its deadly work in Judas' soul. And perhaps it was on Judas' face the eyes of the Lord rested, as it was to Judas' heart and conscience that He spoke, when He said, How hardly—with what difficulty— shall they who have the good things of life enter into the Kingdom of God?

The Disciples' Amazement

"And the disciples," we read, "were amazed at His words" (v. 24). They destroyed every notion about wealth the disciples had ever cherished. They had been brought up on the Old Testament; and there wealth is repeatedly spoken of as a sign of God's favor. So the Wise Man says of wisdom, "Length of days is in her right hand, and in her left hand are riches and honor" (Prov. 3:16). Thus Christ's dictum overturned all their inherited ideas. They themselves were looking forward to material rewards—to princedoms and dominions and thrones. And here Christ declares that that very thing which they had been taught to desire, and to regard as a proof of the Divine favor, was not a blessing, but something like a curse; not a help, but a hindrance, an almost insurmountable obstacle to the possession of the Kingdom. And here I prefer the reading noted in the Revised Version margin, which omits the words "those that trust in riches." According to the oldest MSS., what Jesus said when He saw the bewilderment His first remark had caused, was this, "Children, how hard it is to enter the Kingdom of God!" He enlarges His field of vision. He makes His first statement, "Children"—you notice the tenderness of His address—"I said a moment ago, it is hard for the rich man to enter the Kingdom of God. It is hard for every one. There are barriers in every one's way. It is a strait gate and a narrow way for all. But it is specially hard for the rich. It is easier for a camel to go through a needle's eye than for a rich man to enter into the Kingdom of God."

The Camel and the Needle's Eye

Attempts have been made to soften this figure of the camel and the needle's eye. Some have suggested that the word "camel" in the Greek is a mistake for "cable." And others, accepting "camel" as correct, have suggested that the "needle's eye" is to be understood as a small side-gate near the great gate in Jerusalem. But the phrase must be accepted just as it stands. It is exactly the kind of striking, hyperbolical figure in which an Eastern speaker would delight. Southey caught its spirit when he wrote:

"I would ride the camel,
Yea, leap him flying, through the needle's eye,
As easily as such a pampered soul
Could pass the narrow gate."

It is a proverbial expression, meant to represent vividly and
memorably the extraordinary difficulty of discharging the responsibilities and overcoming the temptations of riches, So the Lord's
answer to the disciples' wonder was simply to emphasize His former statement.

The Difference God Makes

The Lord's repetition of His statement only intensified the disciples' amazement. "They were astonished exceedingly," saying
unto Him, "Then who can be saved?" They began to be dimly conscious of difficulties of which they had never before dreamed.
Their minds had traveled beyond the cares of the rich. A new conception of the Kingdom began to dawn upon them. They began to
tremble about anyone's salvation. "Who then can be saved?" they
asked. And Jesus replied, "With men it is impossible, but not with
God" (v. 27). If it depended upon men themselves, their own
unaided efforts, their own righteousness, they would never gain
the Kingdom. But with God all things are possible. With God to
help, the impossible may become actual, and man, yes, even the
rich man, may enter the Kingdom of God.

And now as to the light this passage throws upon our Lord's
teaching about wealth. Upon the general subject I will say but one
or two words. There is a school amongst us that asserts that Jesus
condemned wealth altogether, and that a rich Christian is therefore
a contradiction in terms. I think, from my study of the Gospels,
that this school is quite wrong. Of course ill-gotten wealth is absolutely debarred to the Christian. Money made in dishonest ways,
or gained by oppression, by sweated labor, for instance, is
unchristian money. But I do not see how anyone can read the
Gospels without finding that Jesus admits the legitimacy of
wealth. It is implied in the parables of the Talents and the
Pounds. It is implied here in this story of the young ruler. Jesus
does not deny the man's right to his wealth. He only urges the surrender of it as the way to perfection. That is to say, the surrender
of wealth is not an economic principle, it is simply in this case a
matter of moral choice. Jesus does not enjoin the monkish vow of
poverty upon His followers. Anthony, who, on reading the story
of the young ruler, forthwith distributed to the villagers his large
fertile estates, inherited from his father, sent his sister to be edu-

cated with a society of pious virgins, and then settled down to a rigidly ascetic life, was imitating the letter, and not the spirit of Scripture. And when Itenan says that the monk is in a sense the only true Christian, he is repeating Anthony's mistake. Jesus nowhere holds that every Christian must sacrifice his wealth, and take the vow of poverty.

And Its True Use

Not only so, but our Lord obviously teaches that wealth may be made beneficent; that it can minister not simply to the good of others, but also to the good of a man's own soul. That is surely the whole teaching of the parable of the Unrighteous Steward. Men can make friends even of the unrighteous mammon. They can turn a thing so pregnant with peril as wealth into a great means of blessing. Surely we have seen illustrations of all this in the cases of men—of whom our own days supply many striking and familiar examples—whose wealth has been employed in a gracious, helpful and Christian ministry.

The Perils of Wealth

But, while Jesus admits the legitimacy of wealth, and allows that money may be transfigured into a minister of grace, no one can read the New Testament with any attention without seeing that the main point He emphasizes is, not its legitimacy, nor its possibilities of gracious ministry, but its perils—its menacing and deadly perils. Again and again He bids men be on the watch against the fascinations of wealth. He obviously regards mammon as the chief rival and antagonist of God in the affections of men. Again and again He bids men beware of covetousness. And perhaps His insistence upon the perils of wealth reaches its climax in the words, "It is easier for a camel to go through a needle's eye, than for a rich man to enter the Kingdom of God" (v. 25).

Men Absorbed in Wealth

Now can we discover what, according to our Lord, are the perils of wealth that make Him so insistent in His warnings against it? I think we can. (1) First of all, our Lord saw that wealth had a strange but fatal power of absorbing the affections of the soul, and so becoming the rival and antagonist of God. That is what had happened in the case of this young ruler. God claims the first place in every soul. He will not take the second place; He will be loved best, or not at all. I dare say the young ruler thought he loved God best. But when the choice had to be made, it was his gold he loved best. He did not possess his riches, his riches possessed him. They had monopolized God's place. Living as we do in a materialistic age, we do not need any one to tell us that there are multitudes of mammon-worshippers all about us still, men who give to wealth the place in their hearts that properly belongs to God.

Men Trusting in Wealth

(2) A second peril which Christ saw attached to wealth was this—those who had great possessions were always tempted to trust in them. Money has not only the power of absorbing the heart, it has also the power of satisfying it. Take the parable of the Rich Fool as an illustration. His barns and storehouses were full; he seemed quite immune against trouble and distress. "Soul, thou hast much goods," he said, "laid up for many years, eat, drink, be merry." The fact that he had such abundant wealth blinded him to his lack of spiritual things. He thought himself rich and increased with goods, and in need of nothing, and when he was ushered into eternity that night, he went into it as a blind and miserable and naked soul. This is no imaginary peril. The possession of earthly wealth may blind a man to his need of lasting riches. The man who has much treasure on earth is in danger of not feeling the need of treasure in heaven. And so the possession of "uncertain riches" often spells the ruin of the soul; and "great possessions" often mean the sacrifice of the inheritance incorruptible and undefiled. For the condition of receiving the "eternal life " is a sense of need. "He hath filled the hungry with good things." But those who have this world's goods often feel no sense of need, and so the rich go empty away. What profit is it for a man to have all his treasures on earth, when he himself is made for eternity? "Do you know," said a man—I think to John Bright—"he died worth a million." "Yes," replied Bright, "and that was all he was worth." What unutterable tragedy such a sentence hides! "All he was worth." And it had all to be left.

Men the Prey of Covetousness

(3) Further, the possession of wealth is apt to beget a spirit of covetousness, and covetousness is itself a sin, and the fruitful mother of sins. "Take heed," said our Lord, "and keep yourselves from covetousness." Covetousness, He knew, was one of the most deadly enemies of the soul. It warps and shrivels and deadens the soul. It makes it insensible to the higher and holier appeals. Men grow in fortune, and get further and further away from God. Their bank balances increase, and their stock of sympathy and pity and

love diminishes. There is nothing like covetousness for stifling the religious life. It chokes the Word, so that there is more hope for the drunkard and the sensualist than for the man whom avarice holds in its grip. And not only is covetousness itself a sin, but it begets sin. "The love of money is a root of all kinds of evil," says the Apostle (1 Tim. 6:10). It was so in the Lord's own day. Witness the Pharisees devouring widows' houses, and the priests turning the very Temple into a den of thieves. It is so now. Think what greed is doing in this land of ours. Most of the wrongs from which we suffer spring from this one bitter root. There would be scarcely any social problem left, if only men's hearts were delivered from this blighting and sinful love.

The Christian's Duty

What, then, is to be the Christian attitude towards wealth? Wealth, remember, is a relative term. I have known the small patrimony of the poor as perilous to the soul as the mighty fortunes of the rich. Covetousness is not necessarily a matter of thousands or millions. Silas Marner with his small store of gold coins was as much a victim of it as any financier who is adding his thousand to thousand. What, then, is the Christian's duty towards his wealth, whether it be great or small? Must he deny himself of it? Not necessarily. But he must keep himself master of it. He must not let it master him. I have a friend who said to me that when he was about twenty-five years of age, when money began to come to him, he found he had to face the question whether he would be master of his wealth, or would let his wealth master him. He said that by God's grace he would be master of his wealth. It was no vain resolve; he holds his money with a loose grip; it is to him an agent for usefulness. He gives, as he puts it, pound for pound of his income to the Lord. He has made to himself friends of the mammon of unrighteousness. That is the way to treat wealth, whether large or small—be its master. And with none of us must wealth be the aim of life. "Little children, guard yourselves from idols "(1 John 5:21). It is the last word of Scripture. And mammon is the idol most of our people worship. But the new earth would be here, if we seriously heeded these words of Christ, "Be not therefore anxious, saying, What shall we eat? or, What shall we drink? or, Wherewithal shall we be clothed? . . . But seek ye first His Kingdom and His righteousness" (Matt. 6:31, 33).

64
The Hundredfold

"Then Peter began to say unto Him, Lo, we have left all, and have followed Thee. And Jesus answered and said, Verily I say unto you, There is no man that hath left house, or brethren, or sisters, or father, or mother, or wife, or children, or lands, for My sake, and the gospel's, but he shall receive an hundredfold now in this time, houses, and brethren, and sisters, and mothers, and children, and lands, with persecutions; and in the world to come eternal life. But many that are first shall be last; and the last first."

—Mark 10:28-31.

The Impulsive Peter

ALL THE EVANGELISTS notice that it was Peter who said this. It was just the kind of remark you would expect Peter to make. There were things Peter said which, on calmer reflection, he would have wished unsaid. But this habit nevertheless constitutes part of the charm of his character. His hot-headedness and impulsiveness make him the most open and transparent and human of the Twelve.

His Inquiry

His question here arose directly out of the incident of the rich young ruler. He had heard our Lord demand of that young man that he should sell his possessions, and follow Him. He had seen the young ruler go away sorrowful. He had heard the Lord's startling comment that it was easier for a camel to go through a needle's eye than for a rich man to enter the Kingdom of God. And though for a moment, like the rest of the disciples, staggered by that austere saying, he quickly recovered his spirits, and with a great deal of self-satisfaction let his mind dwell on the difference between the conduct of the rich young ruler and that of himself and his fellow disciples. "We," he thought to himself, "have done the very thing which the Master asked the rich young ruler to do. We have done that hard thing; we have left all, and followed Jesus. Surely sacrifice so great and so difficult will win a rich reward?" The thought had no sooner formed itself in Peter's mind than, with

360

characteristic impulsiveness, he was giving it expression. "Lo," he said to Jesus, "we (with an emphasis on the we: we, in contrast to the rich young ruler who refused to make the sacrifice), we have left all, and have followed Thee" (v. 28). And Peter did not stop there, according to Matthew's account, for he went on to ask, "What then shall we have?" (Matt. 19:27).

Peter's Sacrifice

It is very easy to criticize this question of Peter. For, when Peter asked, "What then shall we have?" he spoke in the very tone and temper of the hired servant. There is a touch of the sordid and the mercenary about it. "No longer do I call you servants," said Jesus on one occasion; "but I have called you friends'" (John 15:15). But Peter here does not speak as a "friend"; he speaks as one who only works for wages, a "hired servant," and as one eminently pleased with himself. But when critics go on to object that Peter's all did not amount to much, that in his case there was no such sacrifice as was demanded in the case of the young ruler, they take a very different view of the case from that which Christ took. I do not find Christ ridiculing or disparaging the sacrifice the disciples had made, as scarcely worth mention. Christ never measured anything by mere bulk; He measures by the love and sacrifice involved. And so He joyfully acknowledged that these men had sacrificed their all, and, with a "verily" that was full of tender assurance, He promised them a reward that outran their wildest dreams.

The Master's Response

To the Twelve themselves, according to Matthew's account, He promised that they should sit on twelve thrones judging the twelve tribes of Israel. Peter, for the sacrifice of his boat and his nets, Matthew, for the surrender of his tollbooth, were each to receive a throne. And it was no delusive promise. The throne Christ gave was not perhaps the kind of throne the disciples expected. They wore none of the trappings of royalty, but no king that ever sat upon a throne wielded such sovereign authority as do these twelve humble men, who first heard Christ's call and followed Him. But Mark passes the special reward of the apostles' sacrifice by without notice, in order to lay stress on the reward Christ promises to everyone who makes sacrifices for His sake. "Verily I say unto you," said our Lord, "there is no man that hath left house, or brethren, or sisters, or mother, or father, or children, or lands, for My sake, and for the gospel's sake, but he shall receive a hundredfold now in this time, houses, and brethren, and sisters, and mothers, and children, and lands, with persecutions; and in the world to come eternal life" (vv. 29, 30).

The Divine Generosity

In this overwhelming promise you will notice the Divine generosity of the reward. That is the way in which the Lord blesses—a hundredfold. This is the way in which He compensates for sacrifice— a hundredfold. The very magnificence of the reward has, as Dr. Bruce says, a sobering effect upon the mind. It tends to humble. For nobody, no matter what sacrifices he has made, or what devotion he has shown, can pretend that he has earned the "hundredfold." All talk of merit is out of the question here. When we have done our best—if we are honest with ourselves—we have to confess we have been unprofitable servants. The reward is so obviously out of proportion, as to make us realize it is not of debt, but of the Lord's mercy and grace. We do not earn these blessings; the free gift of God is eternal life.

The Doctrine of Rewards

There are those in these days who say that in the Christian life we ought not to think of reward at all. Christianity, we are told, ought to be disinterested, and the man who is always thinking of the reward at the end is really turning his religion into a kind of glorified selfishness. Now there is an element of truth in this objection. If people were Christian simply for the sake of the reward, and not for love, they would not in any true sense be Christians at all. I sometimes wonder whether Peter was a real Christian, when he asked, " What then shall we get?" I am quite sure he was a real Christian when he said, "Lord, Thou knowest all things, Thou knowest that I love Thee." Our Lord Himself repudiated what I may call mercenary discipleship, when He charged the crowds with following Him only because they ate of the loaves, and were filled. A Christian is a man who follows Christ and obeys Christ and gives Himself to Christ for love's sake. But Christ never calls a man to an unreasonable service. The life Christ calls a man to, is the best life and the highest life, the rich life. And that is what the Christian doctrine of rewards amounts to; it is the assertion of the supreme reasonableness of the Christian life.

The Reality of the Reward

But now as to the reality of this reward. It is an overwhelming promise—is it a true one? This promise of a hundredfold now and eternal life hereafter, is it a mocking mirage, or is it a reality? Let us examine the promise for a moment. It falls into two parts. It promises reward now, and in the world to come. Now as to the promise of eternal life in the world to come, we have to take that on trust. We believe, we gladly believe, that for Christ's friends death does not bring life to an end. But life enters upon a new stage. It becomes larger, deeper, richer, fuller. It becomes life in the very presence of God, a life of perfect bliss. But that, as I say, we take on trust. As far as that portion of the promise is concerned, we walk by faith, not by sight.

But in so far as the Lord's promise deals with this present world and this present life, we can bring it to the test of facts and experience. What then of the hundredfold which they who make sacrifices for Christ are to receive in this time? Does that get fulfilled? In answering this question we must beware of a bald literalism. A bald and naked literalism will make nonsense of this gracious word. Of course, Christ does not mean that for every house we give up we shall get a hundred houses given back to us. The promise essentially means this—that discipleship means the immense and untold enrichment of life even now. Is that true? Absolutely and utterly true.

It is true even of material things. Religion tends to prosperity. Godliness has the promise of the life which now is. But it is not on that low and rather sordid plane that I would argue the truth of this promise. The hundredfold comes to the disciple in other and better ways. "A hundredfold in this time." Is it true? Yes, says Dr. Bruce, if you take the long view; and he bids us notice how, through the sacrifices of Christian people, the little one has become a thousand, and the small one a strong nation, and the prophetic picture of an ever-widening Christian dominion has been to a large extent realized.

But essentially the promise is true, not simply of the centuries and the generations; it is true of the individual. The Christian life means untold enlargement and enrichment. "All things are yours," cries Paul; "whether Paul, or Apollos, or Cephas, or the world, or life, or death, or things present, or things to come; all are yours, and ye are Christ's" (1 Cor. 3:22, 23). "I have all things, and abound," wrote the same great-hearted Apostle (Phil. 4:18). He had stripped himself bare for Christ; he had stripped himself of home and friends and reputation and prospects; but Paul did not walk through life like a beggar, he walked through it with the proud step and light heart of one who had inexhaustible and unsearchable riches. "I have all things, and abound."

With Persecution

"With persecutions," the Lord adds. And we are not to read this phrase as if it were the bitter put in to counterbalance the sweet. The Lord means us to reckon persecutions as another item added to the inventory of the disciple's blessings. The hundredfold is realized, not in spite of persecutions, but to a larger extent because of them. The phrase carries us back to that other striking and memorable word, "Blessed are ye when men shall reproach you, and persecute you, and say all manner of evil against you falsely, for My sake. Rejoice, and be exceeding glad; for great is your reward in heaven" (Matt. 5:11, 12). "But," He added, "many that are first shall be last, and the last first."

A man's place in the Divine order of precedence is not settled by length of service or conspicuous service. These twelve were the first in time, and the most conspicuous in position. It did not follow that they were to be the first in heaven. Judas by transgression fell, and went to his own place—the first became last. The persecuting and blaspheming Saul, though born out of due time, came not a whit behind the very chiefest of the Apostles—the last became first. In the external world every man finds his proper niche; every man is appraised at his true value. For God judges not by the outward appearance; He judges by the heart. Not by our conspicuous station, or by our Church standing, but by the amount of genuine love and sacrifice there is in our discipleship. "Many that are first shall be last"; it is a word of solemn warning. It is well we should examine our hearts, and ask ourselves where, judged by that test, shall we stand— amongst the first or amongst the last?

65
On the Way to Jerusalem

"And they were in the way going up to Jerusalem; and Jesus went before them: and they were amazed; and as they followed, they were afraid. And He took again the twelve and began to tell them what things should happen unto Him saying, Behold, we go up to Jerusalem; and the Son of Man shall be delivered unto the chief priests, and unto the scribes and they shall condemn Him to death, and shall deliver Him to the Gentiles: and they shall mock Him, and shall scourge Him, and shall spit upon Him, and shall kill Him: and the third day He shall rise again." —Mark 10:32-34.

The Sequence of Events

A WORD AS to the exact chronological position of this journey to Jerusalem. Mark's is, as everyone knows, the briefest of the Gospels, and we are not to conclude that incidents that follow one another in the narrative necessarily came immediately the one after the other. For the sequence of events, we must compare Gospel with Gospel. Now, as far as I can judge from a comparison with the other Gospels and especially with St John, several notable events had happened since the incident of the rich young ruler and the subsequent conversation, and, amongst them, the raising of Lazarus from the dead. That astounding and overwhelming miracle had caused immense excitement, with the result that the Sanhedrin met together and deliberately resolved that they would put Christ to death. Jesus got to know of their resolution, and, inasmuch as His hour was not yet come, He departed into a city called Ephraim, about twenty miles to the north of Jerusalem. There apparently He remained for some time, until, indeed, His Passion drew nigh. Then of His own free will He journeyed back, to face His foes and meet His death. That is the exact point in our Lord's career to which this paragraph brings us. He is setting out on His last journey to Jerusalem. His hour has struck. It is no longer the hour for flight and concealment. It is the hour to go forth and drink the cup and bear the cross and die.

The Manner of the Going

What a journey that was! Never in all human history was ever so wonderful and subduing a march undertaken as this! The wonder of it, the awe of it, smote those who witnessed it with amazement and fear. Look at Mark's vivid account, "And they were in the way, going up to Jerusalem; and Jesus was going before them." Usually, our Lord walked along in the very midst of His disciples, but on this last march He strode in front of them. He "was going before them." "And they were amazed," not simply because the action was unusual; there was about the attitude and appearance of Jesus that which filled the Twelve with wonder; "and they that followed," i.e. the larger crowd that always hung about the steps of Christ—the multitude that pressed upon Him and thronged Him—"they that followed were afraid."

The Obedient Christ

I am not surprised that the disciples were "amazed," and the multitudes were "afraid"; for surely the sight of Jesus marching on to Jerusalem is an awe-inspiring sight. What a glimpse we have here of the obedient Christ! Obedience, from one point of view is the key to the life of Jesus. It was the explanation He Himself gave of His conduct and actions. "Wist ye not," He said to His earthly parents, "that I must be about My Father's business? "(Luke 2:49). "I am come down from heaven," He said to the multitude, "not to do Mine own will, but the will of Him that sent Me" (John 6:38). "We must work the works of Him that sent Me," He said on another occasion, "while it is day; the night cometh, when no man can work" (John 9:4). All through His life Christ submitted Himself absolutely and without reserve to the Father's will. He spoke the words the Father gave Him to speak. He did the works His Father gave Him to do. And there was no limit to His obedience. He shrank from no sacrifice or pain. He became obedient unto death even the death of the cross.

The Heroic Christ

What a glimpse, too, we have here of the heroic Christ! He knew to what He was going. Not one item in the bitter tragedy of the garden and the judgment hall and the cross escaped Him. And yet deliberately and willingly He faced it all. The courage of the soldier on the battlefield—wonderful as it often is—pales beside the courage, the majestic and overwhelming courage, of the Son of God marching to the cross. The soldier faces wounds and death, but can always hope to escape them. There was no escape for

Jesus. It was to death He marched, to a cruel death, to a shameful and bitter death, and yet He never hesitated or blenched. He stead-fastly set His face, says St Luke, "to go to Jerusalem."

The Eager Christ

What a glimpse we have here of the eager Christ! "He was going before them." "I have a baptism to be baptized with," He said one day; "and how am I straitened till it be accomplished!" (Luke 12:60). "How am I straitened!" There was a sense of urgency and pressure about our Lord's whole life; that urgency and pressure you see in His march to the cross. It was not the haste of fear. It was not the haste of a man anxious to get as quickly as possible over an ordeal from which he shrinks. Light is thrown upon this eagerness of our Lord, in Hebrews, where the writer says that Jesus "for the joy that was set before Him endured the cross, despising shame" (Heb. 12:2). It was not a timid and shrinking and nervous haste; it was a glad and triumphant haste. He did not march in front as one who was broken or dismayed, else His disciples would have drawn near to comfort Him. He walked majestic.

That is the Christ we see in this incident—the obedient Christ, the courageous Christ, the eager Christ, and the loving and sacrificial Christ. Why did He hasten to the cross? "All," as our old hymn puts it, "All to ransom guilty captives." All for love! "He loved me, and gave Himself for me." Well may we go on to say, "Flow, my praise, for ever flow."

The Amazed Twelve

But I pass now from talking of the Christ revealed in this incident, to say just a word about the picture of the disciples we get here. The Twelve were "amazed," we read. Christ was continually giving them things to "wonder" at. When He gave utterance to that hard saying about the rich man and the kingdom of God, the disciples, we learn, were amazed (it is the very same word). Their surprise then was at the Lord's speech; their surprise now is at the Lord Himself. It was at the staggering nature of His sayings, they wondered in verse 24; it is at the majesty of His Person they wonder here. And what perennial sources of wonder those two are! The Lord's words constantly fill us with surprise. They are so fresh, so deep, so inexhaustible. Like those who first heard them, we are always "astonished" at His teaching. And the wonder of His Person surpasses even the wonder of His words. Christ is greater than His speech. As we study His life, some new revelation of His love, or wisdom, or majesty, or power is constantly filling us with the kind of "amazement" of which the narrative speaks.

The Anxious Multitude

But it is not so much the description of the Twelve that invites notice, as the description the Evangelist gives of the more indiscriminate multitude. "And they that followed were afraid." It is the conjunction of these two almost contradictory statements that has struck me; they were "afraid," but still they "followed." "Forebodings of evil smote them, and filled them with vague terrors," says Dr. Salmond; but yet they followed. They looked at Jesus striding on in front, and were filled with trembling fear; and yet they followed. There is a phrase in the Old Testament that seems exactly to describe the moral and spiritual condition of these people. Here it is:

"Faint, yet Pursuing"

"Faint, yet pursuing" (Judges 8:4). You remember where it occurs. After Gideon and his three hundred had surprised the host of Midian by their night attack, the work of pursuit began. They allowed their foes no chance to reform and give battle again. In hot haste they pressed them. They did not stay even to take food. Right up to Jordan, Gideon and his band kept up the work. Yes, and beyond Jordan they were still at it— "faint, yet pursuing."

Not Men of the Stoutest Hearts

And that was very much the condition of these unnamed friends and disciples of Jesus. These men were not cast in the heroic mould. They were not men like Paul, who, when his friends tried to dissuade him from making the journey to Jerusalem because bonds and imprisonment awaited him there, replied that he was ready not to be bound only, but also to die for the name of the Lord Jesus (Acts 21:13). They were not men of the dauntless spirit of Martin Luther, who, when his friends warned him of danger if he persisted in going to Worms, replied that though there were as many devils in Worms as there were tiles upon the housetops, yet would he go. Mr. Glover compares these men to John Bunyan, who, though he had just married a second time, and had a little blind daughter dependent upon him, and though he knew that a warrant was issued for his arrest if he should persist in preaching the Gospel, went to keep his engagement at the little village of Samsell. His wife, his blind daughter, his own liberty—John Bunyan risked them all in his loyalty to Christ.

But Like Mr. Fearing

But my own feeling is that these people find their real representative, not in John Bunyan himself, but in that Mr. Fearing whom John Bunyan pictures for us with such inimitable felicity. You remember all about Mr. Fearing—a man made up of doubts and timidities. For about a month, the Dreamer tells us, he lay roaring at the Slough of Despond, not venturing to cross it, yet equally determined that he would not go back. And when he came to the wicket gate, there he stood shaking and shrinking, letting many another pass in before him, before he dared raise the hammer and give a timid knock. So it was also at Interpreter's door. He lay about in the cold a good while before he would adventure to call; yet he would not go back, "though the nights were long and cold then." He was surrounded by timidities and fears, yet he would not go back. He was faint; yet he continued to pursue. He was afraid; but he followed. And Mr. Fearing at last won his way into the gates of the Celestial City. This was a crowd of Mr. Fearings— as they followed they were afraid.

They were afraid, but they followed. I find comfort in the thought that these men who followed Christ on His last journey were not strangers to fear. It brings them all very near to us. For most of us are much more like Mr. Fearing and Mr. Ready-to-Halt than we are like Mr. Greatheart and Mr. Valiant-for-Truth. "Fightings without and fears within," that is our condition. We, too, are full of timidities and hesitations. And yet, fears and all, let us follow. Faint though we are, let us pursue. Like Mr. Fearing and Mr. Ready-to-Halt, we shall win home at the last.

Made Bold by Jesus Christ

"As they followed, they were afraid." And what was it kept them following, in spite of their fears? It was the influence of Jesus upon them. As they looked at Him, they were constrained to follow, though they were afraid. Here is the courage of Jesus, says one of the commentators, overcoming fear in the disciples. "Consider Him," says the writer of the Epistle to the Hebrews, "that endured such gainsaying of sinners against Himself, that ye wax not weary, fainting in your souls" (12:3). Consider Him; there is inspiration in the example of Christ. The vision of the heroic Jesus banished the cowardice out of their souls. It has done so for thousands. They went cheerfully to the stake and the block and the gibbet. "Who shall dream of shrinking," they said, "by our Captain led?" But I am not at all sure that it was a case of the Lord's courage shaming them out of their cowardice. I am inclined to think it was a case rather of love overcoming fear. These people felt it was worth while to be with Jesus, whithersoever He might lead them. They knew somehow that Jesus was their life. And so, though they felt vaguely that trouble was impending, they still clung to Him. They were afraid; but they followed. They were faint; but they pursued. And that is what will overcome fear for us—love! Perfect love casteth out fear. Yes, even an imperfect love will overcome it. To feel that Jesus is our life, to feel that He has loved us, and given Himself for us, that will make us cling to Him, despite all the sufferings and trials His service may entail. Even though our hearts be as overwhelmed with fear, as John Bunyan's was in the days before he became a preacher of the Gospel, even though we feel that verse after verse of Scripture rises up to condemn us, we shall, like him, cling to Christ. "My case being desperate," he writes, "I thought with myself, I can but die; and if it must be so, it shall once be said that such an one died at the foot of Christ in prayer." That is it—full of fear; but love keeps us following to the very end. This is the secret of the perseverance of the saints. "The love of Christ constraineth us."

The Journey's End—and Beyond It

At a certain stage in the journey the Lord fell back, and took the Twelve aside, and told them what it was He was marching to. It was the third time He had announced to them His Passion. He did it this time with greater circumstantiality and detail than ever. "Behold, we go up to Jerusalem, and the Son of Man shall be delivered unto the chief priests and the scribes; and they shall condemn Him to death, and shall deliver Him unto the Gentiles; and they shall mock Him, and shall spit upon Him, and shall scourge Him, and shall kill Him; and after three days He shall rise again" (vv. 33, 34). It was not to a throne He was marching; still His ultimate triumph was sure. For while He spoke of death He also spoke of "rising again." But what lay immediately in front of Him was rejection, insult, and a shameful death. The prospect did not appall them. Not one of them drew back, save the son of perdition. They continued with Christ in His temptations. And it is a similar prospect Christ holds out before His followers still. His ultimate triumph is certain. Away yonder there is waiting a palm-branch and a throne. But immediately and now discipleship means tribulation, suffering, sacrifice, and the cross. Shall we draw back? No, though we be afraid, we will follow. Though we be faint, we will pursue. "We are not of them that shrink back unto perdition, but of them that have faith unto the saving of the soul" (Heb. 10:39).

66

The Sons of Zebedee

"And James and John, the sons of Zebedee, come unto him, saying, Master, we would that thou shouldest do for us whatsoever we shall desire. And He said unto them, What would ye that I should do for you? They said unto Him, Grant unto us that we may sit, one on Thy right hand, and the other on Thy left hand, in Thy glory. But Jesus said unto them, Ye know not what ye ask: can ye drink of the cup that I drink of? and be baptized with the baptism that I am baptized with? And they said unto Him, We can. And Jesus said unto them, Ye shall indeed drink of the cup that I drink of; and with the baptism that I am baptized withal shall ye be baptized: but to sit on My right hand and on My left hand is not Mine to give; but it shall be given to them for whom it is prepared." —Mark 10:35-40.

A Strange Plea

I SUPPOSE THAT no one ever reads this paragraph without considering how it came about that the sons of Zebedee could come to Jesus with so ambitious and selfish a prayer at this particular juncture. Jesus had just told them in plain and unmistakable language that He was going to be rejected, mocked, spat upon, scourged, killed; and these two disciples chose that particular moment to plead with Him for thrones. One would have thought that Christ's emphatic announcement would have banished from His disciples' minds this foolish dreaming.

And Its Explanation

To find the explanation you must turn to Luke's Gospel. This is the comment Luke makes, after narrating our Lord's solemn announcement of His passion:" And they understood none of these things; and this saying was hid from them, and they perceived not the things that were said" (Luke 18:34). "And they understood none of these things." You wonder why. The announcement was plain and straightforward enough. But in this matter of the cross the disciples were so wholly possessed by their own preconceived notions that they could not and would not take in the warning.

371

Mr. Prejudice at Work

You remember how John Bunyan, in his Holy War, puts Ear-gate into the charge of Mr. Prejudice, who had sixty completely deaf men under him as his company, men eminently advantageous for that service, inasmuch as it mattered not one atom to them what was spoken in their ear either by God or man. That is only John Bunyan's picturesque way of saying that prejudice can make men dull and deaf to all warnings and appeals. Mr. Prejudice and his sixty deaf men were, let us say, in charge of the disciples' ears in this matter of the cross. They were so steeped in materialistic notions of Messiah's empire, they were so completely possessed by their belief that Messiah's path ended in an earthly throne, that they closed their ears against every mention of the cross. Christ's words mystified them, no doubt. But they put them down as parables. They obstinately refused to take them in their plain and literal meaning. "They understood none of these things." We must remember all this, otherwise it is inexplicable how James and John should still be dreaming of thrones when Christ was contemplating the cross.

A Contributory Cause

Probably we should bear in mind this fact also, that only a short time before Christ had worked that most stupendous and overwhelming of His miracles. He had raised Lazarus from the dead, after he had been in the grave four days. It was a sign that filled all who had witnessed it with wonder, and all who heard of it with excited anticipation. Jerusalem and Judea were stirred from end to end. People began to ask whether any one but the Messiah could work such mighty signs as these. In a word, the people at large were ready to welcome and acclaim Jesus as Messiah, as indeed they did on the occasion of His triumphal entry into Jerusalem. The disciples knew all this. They were conscious of the kind of thrill there was in the air. They felt the throb of the popular expectancy. They made sure, therefore, that on the occasion of this visit to Jerusalem there would be some great apocalypse of our Lord's Messianic dignity and power, and that the Kingdom of God would immediately appear. And so, full of anticipations of this kind, at a certain stage in the journey, James and John, accompanied by their mother Salome—Salome, indeed, being the spokeswoman—came to Jesus with their request for the two chief thrones.

The Plea of the Two

"Master," they said, "we would that Thou shouldest do for us whatsoever we ask" (v. 35). They wish Jesus to give them a kind of blank check. Eastern kings were occasionally wont, in their large and ostentatious way, to promise persons who had won their regard anything they might ask—just as Herod promised Herodias' daughter anything, up to the half of his kingdom. Salome's two sons hoped to be dealt with thus.

And the Faith Behind It

It was no doubt, as Dr. Salmond says, "a large, bold, and inconsiderate demand." But let us do this credit to Salome and her sons—the very boldness of the request shows that they believed that Christ had unlimited power. He wore nothing but the seamless cloak, but to this woman and her sons the seamless cloak could not hide His royal dignity. To them He was even now King of Kings and Lord of Lords, and all things were His to give. It was an inconsiderate, it was a foolish request, but there was faith behind it, a mistaken faith, perhaps, but, nevertheless, a great and magnificent faith.

At Large Request

But Christ was no Eastern despot, bestowing His favors, so to speak, blindfold; and so He replies to the disciples' request with a question, "What would ye that I should do for you? " (v. 36). He will have them state in definite and specific terms what it is they have in their mind. Perhaps James and John did not quite care to put into words what really was in their hearts. Possibly they felt a trifle ashamed of their own ambitiousness. But Christ, as Dr. Morison says, will have these two disciples spread out, under the light of His observation and of their own reflection, what was lying in their hearts.

With an Aim

And so they tell Him—or perhaps Salome tells Him for them—what it was they really wanted. "Grant unto us," they said, "that we may sit, one on Thy right hand, and one on Thy left hand, in Thy glory" (v. 37). The murder was out. What these two men wanted was the highest station in the kingdom. They wanted specially, says Dr. A. B. Bruce, "to steal a march on Peter." The primacy seemed to rest between themselves and Peter, for Jesus had obviously chosen out Peter and themselves as leaders among the Twelve. But the words spoken by our Lord to Peter at Caesarea had rankled in their minds, and had made them fear that amongst the three Peter would be first. So here they try to steal a march on Peter, and beguile their Lord into promising the chief places in the kingdom to themselves. "Grant unto us that we may sit, one on Thy right hand, and one on Thy left hand, in Thy glory."

Its Faults

Now it is a very easy matter to criticize this request of these two disciples and their mother. Dr. A. B. Bruce, in his *Training of the Twelve*, gives a long catalogue of the faults contained in it. It was a presumptuous request, he says, because it virtually asked Jesus their Lord to become the tool of their ambition and vanity. And it was as ignorant as it was presumptuous, showing that they were poles asunder from their Lord in their thoughts of the kingdom. And it was as selfish as it was ignorant. Their own self-aggrandizement was the burden of it. Yes, this request of the sons of Zebedee was all that. Almost every fault that could attach to a prayer stares us in the face in this brief plea.

The Lord's Reply

And yet, our Lord's reply is singularly mild and gentle. There is no indignant denunciation. If there is a tone of rebuke, it is of the kindest and tenderest. Can it be that Jesus saw something beside presumption and ignorance and selfishness in this prayer? Can it be that He saw something which was grateful to His soul? I think He did. And when I look again at this prayer, I can almost guess what it was. "Grant unto us," they said, "that we may sit one on Thy right hand, and one on Thy left hand, in Thy glory." It was a mistaken prayer, it was a foolish prayer.

Taking Count of Faith

But there was, as I have already said, a superb faith in it. Whatever others might think of Jesus, these two men believed that He deserved the kingdom, and would yet receive it. Do you not think that this would be grateful to the heart of Christ, in view of the "rejection " at the hands of chief priests and scribes which He knew was soon to be His fate?

And of Courage

And there was courage in it. Probably they did not understand what Jesus had just told them about the cross. They refused to take it literally. But I daresay they felt there was some sort of a crisis and conflict coming, and so it became a time when the feeble and craven-hearted abandoned Christ. But these men never dreamed of leaving Him. They take that moment of solemn warning to declare that, whatever might be in store, they attached themselves definitely and finally to the cause of Christ.

And of Love

And surely there was more than faith and courage in the prayer; there was also love in it. Here was the thing these two craved above everything else, to be near their Lord. It was not altogether that they wanted to be above Peter and the rest. They wanted to be near Christ. John, we are told, was the disciple whom Jesus loved. Between himself and Jesus there was a bond of closest and deepest affection. And it was the height of John's ambition, and of James' too, that in the glory the old close and tender relationship should still continue. There was deep and consecrated love in this prayer. That was heaven to these two men, to be close to Jesus. "Grant to us that we may sit, one on Thy right hand, and one on Thy left, in Thy glory." And so our Lord's answer was, as Dr. Bruce says, "singularly mild." The selfishness and presumptuousness of it were distressing Him, but the faith of it, and the courage of it, and the love of it, were grateful to His soul.

Ignorance in Prayer

Now let us turn to look at our Lord's answer. "Ye know not what ye ask," He said (v. 38). A throne is never a comfortable seat. "Uneasy lies the head that wears a crown." But never was such a throne as Christ's. For His throne was the bitter cross. They did not know what suffering and agony they were asking for, in asking for a throne by the side of Christ. It was an ignorant prayer. And of how many of our prayers could not our Lord say, "Ye know not what ye ask"? Especially is that so when we ask for great things for ourselves. We little realize what risks we run, and what a price has to be paid. In our ignorance it is, as Matthew Henry quaintly puts it, folly to prescribe and wisdom to subscribe to God.

The Cup and the Baptism

Then our Lord puts the question to them, "Are ye able to drink the cup that I drink? or to be baptized with the baptism that I am baptized with?" "The cup that I drink," "the baptism that I am baptized with," they are highly significant terms. They may refer, as some commentators think, the "cup" to inward agony; the "baptism" to outward and visible suffering. In which case it would be true to say, with Dr. Glover, that the "cup" was fullest in Gethsemane; and the "baptism" was most overwhelming on Calvary, when all God's waves and billows went over the Redeemer's head. Or it may be, as Dr. Chadwick suggests, that the "cup" may refer to sufferings voluntarily accepted, and the "baptism" to sufferings into which we are plunged. But the former is the better explanation. The baptism, the public shame and ignominy; the cup, the secret pain and sorrow. Anybody could see how awful a baptism Christ endured in the judgment hall and on the cross. Yet our Lord's bitterest pangs were not those caused by physical suffering, but those caused by agony of soul. "My God, My God, why hast Thou forsaken Me?"—who can fathom the desolation involved in that cry? That was part of the Lord's bitter cup. But take them together, and the "cup" and the "baptism" stand for the totality of our Lord's suffering. They stand also for the price of His throne. Christ did not inherit His throne. He won it. With His agony and bloody sweat, with His cross and passion, with His death and burial, He paid for it. And there is no throne in the spiritual realm except by paying a like price. That is the meaning of the question that Jesus puts to His disciples. "Thrones," He says, "are not to be had for the asking, Thrones are to be won and paid for. And this is the price—sharing My cup and baptism."

The Price of Glory

Suffering with Christ is the condition of being glorified together. We must be ready to be baptized with His baptism; we must be ready to suffer for righteousness' sake; we must be ready to bear scorn and insult rude; we must be ready to face the world's hostility and contempt, in our allegiance to the will of God. And we must drink the Lord's cup. We must share in His agony for human sin. We must feel the pressure of it upon our hearts, as He did upon His. This is the condition of sharing the throne with Christ—entering into the fellowship of His sufferings. In a character sketch of a certain prominent statesman, accounting for his ineffectiveness, in spite of his manifold gifts, the writer quoted a remark made by his tutor upon him while still a youth. "He wants the palm without the dust." Perhaps that is what these disciples wanted. Perhaps that is what we want, the palm without the dust, the crown without the cross, the Throne without the agony and sweat. And what Jesus is saying here to these two disciples, and to His disciples for all time, is, that thrones in the spiritual realm cost their price. They can only be purchased at the price of the cup and the baptism.

The Answer to the Lord's Question

"Are ye able to drink the cup that I drink? or to be baptized with the baptism that I am baptized with?" asked Jesus. "And they said unto Him, 'We are able'" (v. 39). And this answer, the commentators all unite to tell me, is almost as foolish and ignorant as their original request. "They knew not what they asked," says Dr. Glover, "and now they know not what they say." And I suppose the commentators are right. It was a light-hearted and thoughtless answer. They would have spoken far otherwise, says Dr. David Smith, "had they known whereto they were pledging themselves, had it been revealed to them that a week later their Lord would be lifted up, not on a throne, but on a cross, with a cross on His right, and a cross on His left. Their love for their Master would surely have kept them faithful; but they would have spoken with faltering lips, and their answer would have been a trembling prayer for strength to drink that bitter cup and endure that bloody baptism." Yes, I believe all that. And yet there was more than ignorance and thoughtlessness in this reply. There was honest purpose in it; there was heroic love in it; there was uttermost consecration in it. These two men felt ready to go anywhere and endure anything, to drink any cup, to be baptized with any baptism, for the Lord's sake. "We are able," they said. And Christ knew that, although they were ignorant of how bitter the cup was, and how bloody the baptism, they would not falter or quail. "The cup that I drink," He said to them, "ye shall drink; and with the baptism that I am baptized withal shall ye be baptized" (v. 39, R.V.).

The Ambition Realized

It all came true. I turn to the book of the Acts of the Apostles, and I read this, "Now about that time Herod the king put forth his hands to afflict certain of the Church. And he killed James the brother of John with the sword" (Acts 12:1, 2). That is where James' loyalty and zeal brought him— to a premature and cruel death. First of all the apostolic band he was called to tread the martyr way. And he never faltered or quailed. If the old tradition be true, he went to his death like a conqueror to a triumph, like a king to his crowning; he drank his Lord's cup, and was baptized with his Lord's baptism. I turn to the Revelation 1 and I read of John, the second of these brothers, an exile in Patmos, "for the word of God, and the testimony of Jesus." That is where John's love and loyalty brought him—into loneliness and exile and imprisonment. And he never faltered or quailed. He drank of the Lord's cup, and was baptized with the Lord's baptism. And so I leave it to others to criticize their reply. I am subdued by the loyalty and courage, and utter devotion which they showed, and, as I think of them, the one going to exile, the other to the block, the prayer comes to my lips,

> "To me, O God, may grace be given,
> To follow in their train."

The Lord's Way with Us

These men asked for thrones, and instead of thrones they received the promise of a cup and a baptism. It is often so. We get from our Lord what we never asked for, what, in fact, we did not desire. We never ask for the bitter cup and the bloody baptism, but oftentimes God chooses them for us. And, like these two brothers, we sometimes come to thank God for giving us the things for which we did not ask, for we see that even these things work together for our good. But what of the thrones? What of the right hand and the left hand?

Place in the Heavenly Realm

"It is for them for whom it has been prepared." Place in the heavenly realm is determined, not by favor but by fitness. Christ can promise to every disciple a cup and baptism. But He cannot promise to any disciple the first or second place in heaven. Every man there gets the place he deserves. "His own place." It is for them for whom it hath been prepared. But this may be added—though our Lord does not say it in so many words—to drink the Lord's cup, and to be baptized with the Lord's baptism is the sure way to the throne. Our present light affliction worketh for us a far more exceeding and eternal weight of glory. Faithfulness unto death is the condition of receiving the crown of life. And that was in John's mind when he wrote that word in his Apocalypse, "He that overcometh, I will give to him to sit down with Me in My throne, as I also overcame, and sat down with My Father in His throne" (Rev. 3:21).

67
Greatness in the Kingdom

"And when the ten heard it, they began to be much displeased with James and John. But Jesus called them to Him, and saith unto them, Ye know that they which are accounted to rule over the Gentiles exercise lordship over them; and their great ones exercise authority upon them. But so shall it not be among you: but whosoever will be great among you, shall be your minister: and whosoever of you will be the chiefest, shall be servant of all. For even the Son of man came not to be ministered unto, but to minister, and to give his life a ransom for many. And they came to Jericho: and as he went out of Jericho with his disciples and a great number of people, blind Bartimaeus, the son of Timaeus, sat by the highway-side begging. And when he heard that it was Jesus of Nazareth, he began to cry out, and say, Jesus, Thou son of David, have mercy on me. And many charged him that he should hold his peace: but he cried the more a great deal, Thou son of David, have mercy on me."
—Mark 10:41-48.

The Attitude of the Jews

"AND WHEN THE ten heard it," i.e. heard the request James and John had made for the two chief places in the Kingdom, "they began to be moved with indignation concerning James and John" (v. 41) How they heard it we are not told. Perhaps they overheard it, though that is scarcely likely. James and John were not eager to put their wish into precise and definite terms, even to their Master Himself. They had to be pressed to do it. I do not think they could have been brought to do it at all, if the other ten disciples had been standing by listening to them. The probability is they guessed that the two brothers were asking something for themselves. For when the two with their mother came into the presence of Jesus they took up the attitude of suppliants. They came, says Matthew, "worshipping Him." And when the other disciples saw James and John on their knees before the Master, they inferred that they were begging for something, and perhaps begging for something to the detriment of others. So when the whole incident was over they began to cross-examine the two brothers as to the subject of this private interview of theirs, and it was not long before they had wormed the ugly secret out of them. Then the ten "began to be

379

moved with indignation against James and John." And no wonder.
From their own point of view, it was a mean and rather despicable
action of which James and John had been guilty.

Their Own Ambition

What a light this sentence throws upon the temper of the disciples! Why were they so angry over the action of these two
disciples? Possibly because there was not a man of them who did
not want the chief place himself. Christina Rossetti has a beautiful
little poem, which she entitles "The Lowest Place":

> "Give me the lowest place; not that I dare
> Ask for that lowest place, but Thou hast died
> That I might live and share the glory by Thy side.
> Give me the lowest place; or if for me
> That lowest place too high, make one more low,
> Where I may sit and see, my God, and love Thee so."

But these disciples were in no mood for the lowest place. They
wanted the highest. Ambitiousness was not the fault of James and
John alone, it was the fault of the entire twelve; they were
always quarrelling amongst themselves as to who should be greatest. It is a curious thing that the faults we most keenly resent in
other people are just the faults to which we are specially prone ourselves. We have always, as the authors of *Guesses at Truth* say, "a
sharp eye for a rival." It takes a conceited man to spot conceit in
another; it takes a passionate man to detect bad temper in another; it takes a jealous man to discover jealousy in another. And so
these ambitious disciples were quick to discover the ambitiousness
of James and John, and were correspondingly irritated by it.

And the Anger It Bred

"They began to be moved with indignation concerning James
and John," and so one fault begat another. That is one of the most
terrible characteristics of sin—it breeds. Sin never stands isolated
and alone. A man cannot commit an act of sin and have done with
it, so to speak. It brings with it a whole train of attendant sins. It
often involves others in its lamentable and disastrous consequences. It is the latter result we see illustrated here. The selfish
request of the brothers stirred up anger and bitterness in the hearts
of the ten. It disturbed the kindly relationship hitherto existing. It
bred the ugly feelings of jealousy and hate. It undid the work of
the Lord.

The Lord's Intervention

But Jesus did not allow the mischief to go far. "The ten began to be moved with indignation concerning James and John." But He did not allow them to get beyond the beginning. He did not wait till the indignation had developed into a heated altercation. Words might have been spoken and deeds done that would have created a breach beyond the possibility of healing, if Jesus had allowed the quarrel to develop. He nipped it in the very bud. At the first signs of indignation and anger upon the faces of the ten He called them to Him, and began to instruct them once again in the laws of greatness in His Kingdom.

He Deals with Them All

He called them all to Him; not James and John alone, nor the ten alone, but the two brothers and the ten. For they were all in the same condemnation. They were all of them still in the gall of bitterness and the bond of iniquity. They were all guilty of the same selfish ambitiousness. They all cherished the same material notions of greatness. So He calls them all to Him, and propounds to them once again the law of greatness in the Kingdom of God. I say "once again" advisedly. For, if you will turn back to chapter 9 v. 34, you will see He had already given the same lesson once before. The disciples were amazingly slow scholars. It had to be "line upon line and precept upon precept" with them. But, happily, the Master was as patient as the scholars were slow. With amazing condescension He would repeat and repeat the lessons He had to teach. I can understand, as I read the Gospels, why Peter should say that "the long-suffering of our Lord is salvation" (2 Peter 3:15). So He repeated the old lesson on the law of greatness. In His Kingdom greatness comes to him who stoops to serve. "Ye know," He says, "that they which are accounted to rule over the Gentiles lord it over them; and their great ones exercise authority over them. But it is not so among you; but whosoever would become great among you, shall be your minister; and whosoever would be first among you, shall be servant of all" (vv. 43, 44). The King is the type of greatness in the world; the slave is the type of greatness in the Kingdom.

The World and the Kingdom

It was the former kind of greatness James and John had asked for. It was the former kind of greatness the ten were keen about. Their idea of greatness was to occupy a high place, and to have multitudes beneath them, serving them. It was a Herod's pomp or a Pilate's state they coveted. But the ideals of the Lord's Kingdom are totally different. It is not the man who has most people serving him, but the man who himself serves the most people, who is greatest there. These disciples by their very self-seeking were really destroying their chances of high place. For not to the man who exalted himself above his fellows, but to the man who stooped to serve them would the chief place go.

Greatness by Service

Have we learned the lesson? Greatness out in the world is often a matter of the accident of birth. High place is for some hereditary, going to those who have never occupied a servile position, but have always been served. I do not know that Jesus means here to criticize this arrangement. There are advantages in hereditary rank, and it seems almost inevitable that it should be marked by a certain amount of parade and state. All that Jesus is doing here is to say that greatness in His Kingdom is of an entirely different kind, and is won by different methods. Greatness in the eternal Kingdom is not a matter of rank or birth or favor; it is a matter of service. It cannot be inherited; it must be deserved. It cannot be bestowed as a favor; it must be won. And the mark of the great man in the Kingdom is not that he has multitudes of people waiting upon his beck and nod, but that he himself is everybody's minister and servant. We recognize this in the case of others; but the vital question is, Do we act upon that truth ourselves? Do we seek the real kind of greatness? It is strange how keen some are about earthly rank and station. But what do these things matter, after all? The only thing that matters is position in the eternal Kingdom. And that goes not to rank or station; it is not reached by favor or scheming. You must win it and deserve it—by service.

Do We Seek It Thus?

"Come, ye blessed of My Father, inherit the kingdom," I hear the Lord say. That is the invitation I want one day to receive. Who are the happy people who get it? The people who have spent themselves in service. "I was an hungred, and ye gave Me meat; I was thirsty, and ye gave Me drink; I was a stranger, and ye took Me in; naked, and ye clothed Me; I was sick, and ye visited Me; I was in prison, and ye came unto Me" (Matt. 25:35, 36). Are we busy in this holy service? Do we visit the sick, and feed the hungry, and befriend the stranger? Earthly rank is beyond the reach of most of us. But we may all of us, if we will, become great in the eternal Kingdom. The motto of the Prince of Wales is *Ich dien*—I serve. That motto indicates the way to princely rank in the Kingdom of God. "Whosoever would be first shall be servant of all."

The Example of Christ

Our Lord enforces His teaching by an appeal to His own example. "For verily the Son of Man came not to be ministered unto, but to minister, and to give His life a ransom for many" (v. 45). Let us look at the first statement. "The Son of Man came not to be ministered unto, but to minister." There are two ideas here. (1) There is, first of all, the appeal to example. Jesus Himself had none of the marks of external rank and power. He was not born in the purple; He was born in a stable. He had not a multitude of servants to wait on Him; He was Himself a working carpenter. Jesus was not a Master; He was in the midst of men as One that served. He did not lord it over them; He ministered unto them. He was at everybody's beck and call. Take a sentence like this, "He had not leisure so much as to eat," and let its meaning sink into your minds. For what does it imply? It means that Jesus was so absolutely at the service of the needy and the sick that He had no time to think of Himself. Martha and Mary could send for Him; the Roman centurion could claim Him; Jairus could command Him; the Caananitish woman could lay hands on Him; and a multitude of others, halt and blind and dumb and leprous, could make their appeal to Him, and none in vain. Jesus was everybody's servant. He lived not to be ministered unto, but to minister. And in the very reminder there is an appeal. The disciples must be content to be what He was, "If I then, the Lord and the Master, have washed your feet, ye also ought to wash one another's feet" (John 13:14).

The Way to His Kingdom

(2) There is, secondly, the suggestion that it was through ministry that Christ Himself was seeking His Kingdom. For let us never forget Christ was a King; and the establishment of a Kingdom was, from one point of view, the object of His coming. Yet it was not by "lording" it over men that He proposed to establish His Kingdom, but rather by serving them. It was, indeed, in His power to use the other method. He might have established an earthly kingdom, had He so wished. He might have rivalled the Roman procurator, or Herod, or even great Caesar, in the matter of pomp and state, had He so willed. But He chose the path of service. And by that path He has entered upon a Kingdom such as no Herod or Caesar ever knew. For that is what has given Christ His

empire. He rules in innumerable hearts, because He loved men and served men to the uttermost. The cross was the last service love could render. To serve the race He loved Christ did not shrink from that last and uttermost sacrifice. And the cross has given Him His Kingdom. You remember how Paul couples the two things together. He became "obedient unto death, yea, the death of the cross. Wherefore also God highly exalted Him, and gave unto Him the name which is above every name" (Phil. 2:8,9). That is it. He became "servant of all," and He is now the first of all. And that is the way to greatness for the disciple as well as the Master. There is no other path for us to the throne and the Kingdom, save the path He trod. No cross, no crown. But if we suffer with Him and serve with Him, we shall also be glorified together.

The Ransom

And now I pass on to dwell for a moment on the last clause in this great verse. "The Son of Man came not to be ministered unto, but to minister, and to give His life a ransom for many" (v. 45). "A ransom for many." "This great saying," remarks Dr. David Smith, "has a priceless value." "It is only a metaphor," he says further, "but it expresses a truth which is the very heart of the Gospel, and without which there is no Gospel at all." Let us examine the saying, to discover if we can what is the truth which constitutes the Gospel which it expresses. All hangs on the meaning we attach to that word "ransom." What idea would the word "ransom" suggest to the disciples who heard Christ use it? Dr. A. B. Bruce suggests that it would at once bring to their minds the half-shekel which every adult Jew paid into the Temple Treasury at Passion time, "a ransom for his soul unto the Lord." But Dr. David Smith contends, and Dr. Morison agrees with him, that it would inevitably suggest to the minds of the disciples another idea as well, viz. the price of deliverance paid for the redemption of captives. But, whichever explanation we prefer, the essential point remains the same. Our Lord represents His life as laid down in order to win redemption for many. It is a life given "instead of" many. And that life so given is the redemption price that sets the many free. Christ thinks of men as bondslaves under sin; exposed to the doom and penalty of sin. And by His own death somehow or other He delivers men from this doom; He opens the way for a new relation to God, so that men are no longer criminals, but sons of God and heirs of eternal life.

The Doctrine and the Gospels

It is said that there is no suggestion of a doctrine of the Atonement in the Gospels; that the doctrine of the Atonement as we know it is the result of apostolic and especially Pauline philosophizing about the death of Jesus. It is true that in the Gospels you get no elaborated and articulated doctrine of the cross. That is not surprising. Christ had to die before the meaning of His death could be understood and explained. But, unless you wipe out sayings like these, it is simply untrue to say that Atonement is an invention of the Apostles.

All that Paul says, and all that Peter says, and all that John says, is implied in a saying like this. For if the passage means anything at all, it means vicarious suffering. When John said, "Unto Him that loveth us, and loosed us from our sins by His blood" (Rev. 1:5), he is only repeating what Jesus Himself says here. When Peter said, "redeemed, not with corruptible things, as silver or gold . . . but with precious blood, as of a lamb without blemish, and without spot" (1 Peter 1:18, 19), he is only repeating what Jesus Himself says here. And when Paul says, "Christ redeemed us from the curse of the law, having become a curse for us" (Gal. 3:13), he is only repeating what Jesus Himself says here. He bought our freedom and our life by the sacrifice of His own. That was the object of His coming.

People speculate as to whether Christ would have come into our world, had there been no sin. I do not know. All that I do know is, that it was to deliver us from sin that He actually came. "The Son of Man came to give His life a ransom for many." And He paid the ransom. He offered the one full and perfect oblation and sacrifice. He set men free from the law of sin and death. And that is the Gospel. There is no Gospel for a sinning world without it. But what a Gospel this is,

> "Bearing shame and scoffing rude,
> In my place condemned He stood,
> Sealed my pardon with His blood,
> Hallelujah."

"The Son of Man came . . . to give His life a ransom for many."

68
Blind Bartimaeus

"And they came to Jericho: and as He went out of Jericho with His disciples and a great number of people, blind Bartimaeus, the son of Timaeus, sat by the highway side begging. And when he heard that it was Jesus of Nazareth, he began to cry out, and say, Jesus, Thou son of David, have mercy on me. And many charged him that he should hold his peace; but he cried the more a great deal, Thou son of David, have mercy on me. And Jesus stood still, and commanded him to be called. And they call the blind man, saying unto him, Be of good comfort, rise; He calleth thee. And he, casting away his garment, rose, and came to Jesus. And Jesus answered and said unto him, What wilt thou that I should do unto thee! The blind man said unto him, Lord, that I might receive my sight. And Jesus said unto him, go thy way; thy faith hath made thee whole. And immediately he received his sight, and followed Jesus in the way." —Mark 10:46-52.

The Accounts of the Miracle

I SHALL NOT discuss the differences between the various accounts the three Evangelists give of this particular incident. No two of them tell the story in exactly the same way. Matthew and Mark, for instance, both agree that the miracle took place as Christ was leaving Jericho. Luke says it took place as our Lord was entering the town. But even Matthew and Mark do not agree among themselves, for Mark only mentions one blind man, while Matthew says there were two.

How Reconciled

Various ingenious attempts have been made to reconcile these differences. The fact that Mark mentions only one blind man, while Matthew mentions two, may perhaps be explained on the ground that Bartimaeus was far the more prominent and active of the two, and so overshadowed his companion that, in the memory of those who witnessed it, the miracle came to be especially identified with Bartimaeus. But the discrepancy between Matthew and Mark on the one side, and Luke on the other, does not admit of such easy explanation. Bengel suggests that what really happened was this—

that Bartimaeus made his first appeal to Christ as he entered the city, but that Christ did not answer his appeal then; so Bartimaeus taking a blind friend along with him, waylaid Jesus as he went out of the city the next morning; that this time his appeal was answered, and both he and his friend were cured. Others, again, convinced that the two accounts cannot be reconciled, say that what really happened was this, that there were two different miracles performed by Jesus at Jericho, one as He went into the city, and the other as He left it. This, however, is a suggestion of despair and lands us in more and greater difficulties than it removes. There was only one miracle performed at Jericho.

The Value of Divergencies

But if we cannot reconcile in every detail the accounts the Evangelists give us of it that need not trouble us. The fact that there are slight divergencies in the various narratives does not discredit them; it does the very opposite, it adds to the weight of their witness. For quite obviously it shows that we have here three independent testimonies. If they slavishly copied one another in every detail, we should suspect that we had in them only three versions of one and the selfsame story. But the very divergencies and contradictions show that what we actually possess is three separate and independent accounts. And in the mouth of two or three witnesses every word shall be established.

The Lord, the Needy One, and the Crowd

Let us now turn to the story, as Mark, in his own vivid and characteristic way, tells it. There are three actors or sets of actors in it—the Lord, the crowd, and Bartimaeus. We may gather many a profitable lesson from a study of the conduct of our Lord in this incident. For every miracle that our Lord ever did is, as John says, a sign. It is an index to His character and spirit. It is a window into His soul. And His dealings with Bartimeaus throw light upon His purposes of grace. "Thy gentleness hath made me great," says one of the Psalmists (18:35). Bartimaeus might well have taken that for his motto for the rest of his days. It is an illustration of how the gentleness of the Lord stooped to a poor blind beggar, and made life rich and glad for him. We might gather salutary lessons of warning from the conduct of the harsh and unfeeling crowd, that would fain have hushed Bartimaeus' cries, and so prevented him from finding his Deliverer. Surely, if ever a crowd came near falling under that stern condemnation the Lord pronounced upon those who put stumbling-blocks in their brothers' way, this crowd did, when, as Bartimaeus lifted up his voice and cried for help and healing, it bade him hold his peace. But it is upon Bartimaeus I want to concentrate attention.

The Blind Man and His Hope

It is interesting to notice that Mark is the only one who has pre-served the name of Bartimaeus for us. The probability is, as Archbishop Trench suggests that by the Lord's gracious dealings with him Bartimaeus was drawn into the circle of the disciples and was sufficiently well known in the Church of later days to make it a matter of interest to many that he, and no other, was the object of Christ's healing power. At the time at which we are introduced to him in this narrative, however, Bartimaeus was only a blind beg-gar. He took his stand on the side of the road leading to Jerusalem. He chose that particular spot because of the number of pilgrims passing along on their way to Passover at Jerusalem. And Bartimaeus knew, like the lame man at the Beautiful Gate of the Temple, that there was a close and intimate connection between religion and philanthropy; that no persons were so likely to have pity on him in his blindness as those who had the love of God in their hearts.

The Passing Throng

Pilgrims who usually travelled on that Jerusalem road went in companies, for it was a road of evil reputation. On this particular morning Bartimaeus, with that quick and subtle instinct the blind possess, knew it was not an ordinary band of pilgrims that was passing. It may be, as some suggest, that instead of the singing and laughing groups that went by, this one moved on hushed and silent, still held in wondering awe by the appearance of the Christ. I am inclined myself, however, to favor a simpler and more obvi-ous explanation, and say that it was the size of the crowd that communicated itself to Bartimaeus. With that sharpened sense of hearing which often comes to the blind as a partial compensation for the loss of sight, Bartimaeus knew it was no ordinary band, that it was a throng, a multitude. He seems to have made inquiries of some passerby as to what all the excitement was about, and he received for answer the information that Jesus of Nazareth was passing by. "And when he heard that it was Jesus of Nazareth," Mark says, "he began to cry out, and say, 'Jesus, Thou Son of David, have mercy on me'" (v. 47).

And "Jesus of Nazareth"

Now, something must be assumed, in order to understand this cry. Bartimaeus must have heard of Jesus. And he must have heard also of His mighty works. Remember once again that, only a short time before, Christ had performed the mightiest of all His miracles, in raising Lazarus from the dead after he had been in the grave four days. That miracle had put all Judea into a ferment of excitement. News of it had no doubt reached Jericho, and had come amongst others to the ears of Bartimaeus. It had stirred hope within him. It had made him long that the same Jesus would come his way; for the Jesus who could raise a dead man to life could, he argued, restore sight again to his blind eyes. And now that very Jesus was actually passing, the Jesus who had raised Lazarus, the Jesus into whose presence he had longed to come.

The Blind Man and His Opportunity

Jesus of Nazareth was passing by. It was the opportunity he had longed for, but scarcely hoped ever to obtain. Quick as a flash the prayer leaped to his lips, "Jesus, Thou Son of David, have mercy on me." And that is the first thing I want you to notice about Bartimaeus, that he was a man who recognized his opportunity and seized it. Bartimaeus was, as Dr. Glover says, like those wise virgins whom our Lord speaks of in His parable. As soon as ever the cry is made that the bridegroom cometh, he trims his lamp of prayer and faith, and goes out to meet Him. He is like those servants who, when their Lord cometh, are found watching. He had often thought of Jesus; often prayed in his heart that Jesus might pass his way; and so, though the Lord came suddenly and unexpectedly Bartimaeus was not unprepared. Supposing that Bartimaeus had not seized his opportunity? He would never have had another, for Jesus never returned that way again. Bartimaeus, if he had missed this opportunity, would have missed healing, sight, eternal life. All this is a commonplace about opportunity. The neglect of opportunity is often punished by the loss of it.

> "There is a tide in the affairs of men,
> Which taken at the flood, leads on to fortune.
> Omitted, all the voyage of their life
> Is bound in shallows and in miseries."

The Unready and Their Loss

There were two Saxon kings named Ethelred, and of the reign of the second of them Freeman says it was "the worst and most shameful in our annals. This country of ours was raided and harried in every direction. And the secret of the national disgrace and shame is to be found in the nickname they gave the king; they called him Ethelred the Unready." The unready man is always doomed to loss and shame. It is so in spiritual, as well as merely material things. That is why the Bible lays such stress upon today. That is why it insists that now is the day of salvation. That is why it makes a reiterated appeal to us to be ready. Opportunities of grace come swiftly and suddenly to us, and, if not seized, they pass. Jesus, for instance, came one day to a Samaritan village, and the inhabitants would not receive Him. John and James were so angry they wanted to call down fire from heaven. No, Jesus would have no fire from heaven. And yet those Samaritans were punished, sorely, terribly punished. For this is what I read, "They went to another village." Jesus left them. They missed their chance. And men may miss Christ today, unless they are ready to call to Him when He passes by them, and to welcome Him when He knocks at the door of their hearts. There comes to us gracious seasons of spiritual emotion. Noble impulses are stirred within us. Our hearts melt and become tender in response to some moving appeal. The Lord Jesus is calling us. But if we refuse to act. What happens? The light fails and the glow cools, the gracious impulse departs, perhaps never to return.

Divine Patience and Its Limits

We glory in the patience of our Lord. The long-suffering of the Lord is salvation. But it is not a limitless patience. I read a solemn sentence like this, "My Spirit shall not strive with man forever." And again, "Ephraim is turned to his idols, let him alone." I read of some folk whom the Apostle describes as being "past feeling," people whose opportunity is gone. Let us take warning by these statements. "Jesus of Nazareth is passing by." Let us cry to Him. Let us make our appeal to Him. Lest it should ever have to be said to us, "Jesus of Nazareth has passed by," and we should be classed amongst the "unready," who missed the tide, and lost their chance.

The Blind Man and His Faith

Next let us see in Bartimaeus a man of strong and vigorous faith. It comes out in the very words of the appeal he addressed to Jesus. The answer the passersby gave to his question was that Jesus of Nazareth was passing by. "Jesus of Nazareth"; so they spoke of Him. There is no suggestion that they saw in Jesus any glint of the heavenly and the Divine. But it is not Jesus of Nazareth Bartimaeus calls him. "Jesus, Thou Son of David," he cries, "have mercy on me." "Thou Son of David!" this blind beggar gives Jesus the Messianic title. Physically blind though he was, he saw further into spiritual things than the multitude. He had heard about Jesus, about His wonderful words, and still more wonderful deeds. He had meditated upon it all in his heart. And while other people were quarrelling and debating who Christ was, this blind man had made up his mind that this Jesus Who was giving sight to the blind, and cleansing to the leper, and life to the dead, was none other than the promised Christ. Scribes and Pharisees spoke of Christ as an emissary of Beelzebub. Bartimaeus was persuaded he was the long-looked-for Messiah. And the faith of his soul expresses itself in his cry, "Jesus, Thou Son of David, have mercy on me!"

A Faith Not Daunted by Discouragement

There are all shades of faith and unfaith recorded for us in the New Testament, from the blank unbelief of the Nazarenes and the hesitating and halting faith of the father of the demoniac boy, up to the centurion's superb and splendid faith, which compelled the wonder and admiration of our blessed Lord Himself. Bartimaeus' faith was akin to that of the centurion. It was faith of the heroic and intrepid sort. And the strength and courage of Bartimaeus' faith come out in this—that it was not daunted by discouragement. When he began to cry out many rebuked him, Mark tells us, "that he should hold his peace." Some commentators say they rebuked him because they were offended by his application to Jesus of the Messianic title; but my own belief is that when they tried to hush Bartimaeus, they thought they were being kind to Christ. Perhaps Christ had still that rapt and exalted expression on His face which, as we read in verse 32, filled those who followed Him with wonder and awe. They felt that Christ had great concerns and cares of His own. And so, when Bartimaeus cried out, they tried to silence him; they felt it was something like sacrilege to intrude upon Christ just then; they felt that it was an impertinence on the blind beggar's part to claim attention from One Who was obviously occupied with great thoughts and cares.

Mistaken Kindness

They were cruel to Bartimaeus, in their efforts to be kind to Christ. It only showed, of course, how completely they misunderstood the Lord. We may write down this as axiomatic. We are never really kind to Christ if we are harsh or stern to the least of His people. Christ came to seek and save the lost, and we are defeating the very purpose for which Christ came, when we keep the least and the lost away from Him. Bartimaeus, however, refused to be silenced. His faith was not to be daunted by discouragement.

The Faith That Wins the Blessing

The effect of the rebukes of the crowd was this, according to Mark's account, "He cried out the more a great deal, Thou Son of David, have mercy on me" (v. 48). Bartimaeus' faith was a faith that bore up and pressed on, and persevered. And that is the kind of faith that wins the blessing. There are plenty of voices to bid us hold our peace when we cry to Christ. Worldly friends laugh at us. Common sense says that it is useless. A guilty conscience urges that it is impossible that Christ should notice us. We need the faith that can bear up against all these things. We shall reap in due season, if we faint not! You remember how John Bunyan stuck to his praying, in spite of sore temptation. This is how he describes his own experience, "Then the Tempter laid at me very sore, suggesting that neither the mercy of God, nor yet the blood of Christ, did at all concern me, therefore it was but in vain to pray. 'Yet,' thought I, 'I will pray.' 'But,' said the Tempter, 'your sin is unpardonable.' 'Well,' said I, 'I will pray.' 'It is to no boot,' said he. 'Yet,' said I, 'I will pray.' And so went to prayer to God. And as I was thus before the Lord, that Scripture fastened on my heart. 'O man, great is thy faith,' even as if one had clapped me on the back, as I was on my knees before God." That is it exactly. It is the faith that will not be discouraged that gets the blessing It is persevering and believing prayer that finds the answer. We fail because we are so easily daunted. Here is a prayer for us all: "Lord, increase our faith."

Faith Triumphant

The crowd was for passing Bartimaeus by, but as soon as his cry reached the ears of the Lord, He stood still, and said, "Call ye him." Our Lord never turns a deaf ear to the cry of need. And the very people who had before rebuked Bartimaeus, now that Christ takes notice of him, change their tone, and say, "Courage, rise. He calleth thee." Bartimaeus did not need a second invitation. With impetuous eagerness he cast away the outer garment that rather impeded his movements, and came to Jesus. And Jesus answered him and said, "What wilt thou that I should do unto thee? And the blind man said unto Him, Rabboni, that I may receive my sight (v. 51). And Jesus said unto him, Go thy way; thy faith hath made thee whole. And straightway he received his sight" (v. 52). Nearly every sentence in this colloquy suggests thought. But I pass everything by, just to say that here we see faith triumphant. Here we see prayer answered. Is any true, deep, earnest prayer ever unanswered? "Thou satisfiest the desire of every living thing," says the Psalmist (145:16). "Every one that asketh receiveth," says our Lord (Matt. 7:8), "and he that seeketh, findeth." So let us, as Dr. Glover says, sow the seeds of prayer on the heart of God. There is no hard ground, or rocky soil, or thorny ground there. His heart is the good soil of tender and gracious love. Let us scatter the seed of prayer, and we shall get a harvest of blessing. According to our faith it shall be unto us.

The Man of Loyal Obedience

A final word about the end of Bartimaeus' history—And he "followed Him in the way" (v. 52). One of the greatest sorrows of our Lord's life was that so many took His benefits without giving Him their hearts. "Were there not ten cleansed?" He asked one day. "Where are the nine ?" They had accepted His gift, they neglected the Giver. He healed numbers of sick folk and leprous folk, and blind folk and lame folk, and palsied folk, during the years of His brief ministry. Where were they all, when Jerusalem rang with the cry, "Crucify Him"? Apparently there was not one grateful enough to lift up his voice on His behalf. But, however disappointed Christ may have been in others, He was not disappointed in Bartimaeus; for this was the use Bartimaeus made of his new found sight, "he followed Him in the way." He did not go home to his friends, he clung to Him Who had healed and saved him, "he followed Him in the way." His experience of Christ's mercy was followed by a life of obedience.

Is That Obedience Ours?

We too have experienced the saving mercy of Christ; are we following in the way? How many there are who receive Christ's benefits yet neglect Him still! Are we amongst them? "Happy," says Bishop Chadwick, "is the man whose eyes are open to discern and his heart prompt to follow the print of those holy feet." And so Jericho was kind to Christ. Jericho gave two new disciples to Christ. At the time when others were turning their backs upon Him, two men—Zacchaeus, the chief publican, and Bartimaeus gave their hearts to Him as He trod the way that led to the cross. Are we also with them and following Him in the way?

69

The Triumphal Entry

"And when they came nigh to Jerusalem, unto Bethphage and Bethany, at the mount of Olives, He sendeth forth two of His disciples, and saith unto them, Go your way into the village over against you: and as soon as ye be entered into it, ye shall find a colt tied, whereon never man sat; loose him, and bring him. And if any man say unto you, Why do ye this? say ye that the Lord hath need of him; and straightway he will send him hither. And they went their way, and found the colt tied by the door without in a place where two ways met; and they loose him. And certain of them that stood there said unto them, What do ye, loosing the colt? And they said unto them even as Jesus had commanded: and they let them go. And they brought the colt to Jesus, and cast their garments on him; and He sat upon him. And many spread their garments in the way: and others cut down branches off the trees, and strawed them in the way. And they that went before, and they that followed, cried, saying, Hosanna; Blessed is he that cometh in the name of the Lord: Blessed be the kingdom of our father David, that cometh in the name of the Lord: Hosanna in the highest." —Mark 11:1-10.

Our Lord in Galilee

In his account of the life of our Lord Dr. David Smith calls attention to one significant and striking difference between Christ's methods in Galilee and His methods whenever He visited Jerusalem. In Galilee He kept His Messiahship veiled. He forbade the noising abroad of His wonderful works. He commanded His disciples to keep silent about the glory of the holy mount. Again and again, when excitement and enthusiasm were growing high, He would escape from the crowds, and hide Himself in some solitude beyond their reach.

The reason for this reserve on the part of Jesus in Galilee is not hard to discover. Galilee was in an inflammable condition. The people were on the tip-toe of expectancy. Every Messianic pretender was sure of finding a following in Galilee. If Jesus had plainly announced Himself as Messiah, the smouldering excitement would have blazed up into a flame of open revolt. Swords would have leaped out of their scabbards, and insurrection would have been the order of the day. As it was, they tried on more than one occasion to take Jesus Christ by force and make Him King.

And in Jerusalem

But He followed a policy the precise opposite of this whenever He visited Jerusalem. He paid only a few brief visits to the capital in the course of His ministry, but the significant thing is this—He never visited Jerusalem without in one way or another asserting His Messiahship. He did so the first time, by sweeping out of the sacred precincts those who bought and sold, and by speaking of the Temple as His Father's house. He did so the second time by healing the impotent man at the pool of Bethesda on the Sabbath day, and by claiming, in response to the challenge of the Jews, that He shared in the privileges and prerogatives of God. He did so the third time by proclaiming Himself the "Light of the World," by healing the man who had been born blind, and by declaring plainly, in response to the blind man's query, that He Himself was the long-promised Messiah of God.

A Last Appeal and a Final Warning

Again, the reason for this change of policy is not far to seek. Jerusalem was the capital. In Jerusalem lived the priests and rulers of the nation. Upon Jerusalem's attitude Christ's fate, humanly speaking, hung. And so He took every opportunity of presenting His claims to the rulers and citizens of Jerusalem with all possible emphasis and clearness. If, after all, they rejected Him, they should not be able to plead ignorance. They should do so in face of the plainest and most unequivocal declaration on His own part. They should be without excuse. And so in Jerusalem our Lord made no secret of His claims. Without reserve He announced Himself as the Messiah of God. But no declaration of His Messiahship was so unmistakable, so impressive, so deliberate, as that which He made on the first day of the week of His Passion, when He rode in lowly state into Jerusalem sitting on an ass's colt. Everybody knew what it meant. The pilgrims knew what it meant, and they rent the air with the cry, "Hosanna to the Son of David." And the rulers and Pharisees knew what it meant, for they were indignant that the people should apply the Messianic name to Jesus, and when He refused to rebuke them, they went away, and took counsel how they might kill Him. This triumphal entry put an end to all reserves and concealments. By riding like a king to His capital, Jesus declared to every one plainly who He was. You may say, it was at one and the same time a last appeal and final warning. It was a last appeal. An appeal to Jerusalem to repent and believe while its opportunity lasted. And a warning that their hate and rage were directed against One Who was none other than God's Anointed. There is nothing to be said in excuse for the crime of the Friday after the triumphal entry of the Monday. Priests and elders sinned with their eyes wide open.

The Order of Events

To get the true chronology of this incident we must compare Gospel with Gospel. From a comparison with St John's Gospel, it would appear that Mark has got his account of the Bethany feast slightly out of the true order. Mark postpones his account of that feast and Mary's unforgettable deed, the implication being that it happened after the triumphal entry. But the probability is that John's order is the true one, and that it was after Martha's feast that the entry took place. We must assume then that on the Sabbath Jesus and His disciples rested at Bethany, that He spent His last Sabbath on earth in the home that was dearest to Him, and amongst the friends He loved the best. And on the first day of the week—that is, on our Palm Sunday—He made this triumphal march into the capital.

A Settled Plan

We know how on previous occasions the crowd was eager to force royal honors upon Jesus; in this case He arrogates them to Himself. The whole is of our Lord's initiation and devising. In the morning of the day He sends off two of His disciples to an unknown friend who had an ass's colt whereon no man ever yet sat. The procedure, no doubt, had been arranged between this man and our Lord. For Jesus had more disciples in the world than others thought. Not one of the twelve, it would seem, knew this man, but Jesus knew him. In one way or another Jesus had come into contact with him, just as He had with the good man of the house about whom we shall read later on. He had arranged with the owner that some day He would requisition this young colt. They had settled a sort of pass-word, "The Lord hath need of him." And when the two disciples appeared, and in answer to the questions put to them gave the pass-word, "The Lord hath need of him," the owner made no further demur. And when they had brought the colt to Jesus, they cast on it their garments, and so improvised a saddle, and set Jesus thereon. Seated on that ass's colt Jesus set out on His "state-entry" into Jerusalem.

A Fulfilled Prediction

Now when our Lord chose to enter Jerusalem in that fashion, He deliberately proclaimed Himself the fulfillment of ancient prophecy. There was a prophecy which, Dr. David Smith says, was much discussed by the Rabbis, and which at the sight of Jesus making a public entry into Jerusalem in such guise, was bound to leap into men's minds. It was a prophecy of Zechariah about the advent of the Messiah king. "Rejoice greatly, O daughter of Zion, shout, O daughter of Jerusalem; behold, thy king cometh unto thee; He is just, and having salvation; lowly, and riding upon an ass, even upon a colt the foal of an ass" (Zech. 9:9). Now Jesus meant by His action to remind the people around Him of that ancient prophecy. He meant them to find in Him its fulfillment. And the people did not fail to catch Christ's meaning. They at once leaped to the significance of the action. There was a considerable company of people who had traveled up from Jericho with Jesus. There was a still larger contingent of pilgrims, who, stirred by the story of Lazarus' raising from the dead, and hearing that it was the intention of Christ to enter the city that morning, had come out to see this wonderful Prophet for themselves. As soon as these pilgrims saw Jesus riding down the Mount of Olives, sitting on this ass's colt, the meaning of it all flashed upon them. Here was the long-promised and long-expected Messiah Himself. So in their enthusiasm some took their garments, and spread them in the way, and some took branches of trees, which they cut and brought from the adjacent fields, and all the way from Bethany to Jerusalem those that went before and those that followed after cried as they marched, "Blessed is He that cometh in the name of the Lord. Blessed is the kingdom that cometh; the kingdom of our father David: Hosanna in the highest" (v. 10).

The Kingship of Christ

Such, then, is the story. Its central significance is this—that here is the proclamation of Christ's kingship. At last, as Bishop Chadwick says, "Jesus openly and practically assumes rank as a monarch, and allows men to proclaim the advent of His kingdom." This day of His triumphant entry was our Lord's proclamation day; not His crowning day, for proclamation and crowning are not one and the same. I remember very well that on a certain day in January, 1901, the Bournemouth corporation in their robes of office gathered in the square, and the Mayor for the time being read a State paper which declared Edward VII to be King of these realms. That was proclamation day. But coronation day did not come around for eighteen months after that.

His Proclamation and His Coronation

Now our Lord too had His proclamation day and He had also His crowning day. His crowning day came when they nailed Him between two thieves. It was then they actually placed Him upon the royal seat, and set the crown of empire upon His brow. But He was proclaimed, publicly and solemnly proclaimed as King, when He rode in triumph into Jerusalem, and the multitude sang as He moved along, "Hosanna, Blessed is He that cometh in the name of Jehovah." In the forecasts of seer and prophet the kingly aspect of Messiah's office looms large. In the Jewish mind it almost obscured and hid every other aspect, with the result that they did not recognize "the King" in the meek and lowly Jesus. But, meek and lowly though He was, Jesus knew Himself to be a king, and by this state-entry He declared and proclaimed it. Just as a few days later, in answer to Pilate's question, "Art thou a King then?" He answered, "Thou sayest that I am a king," so now, by riding in lowly state into Jerusalem, and accepting the plaudits of the people as His due, He announced Himself to the world as the promised King whom God would yet set upon His holy hill of Zion.

The Lord as Savior, Friend and Brother

Do we often think of Christ in that way? Do we think of Him as King? Do we often dwell upon His majesty and right to rule? I wonder if I am wrong in thinking that the kingship of Jesus is to a large extent a forgotten and neglected truth? We prefer to lay the emphasis upon the other aspects of Our Lord's office and character. We like to speak of Him as the Savior, Who in His pity and love stooped to the cross to save us from sin and death. We like to speak of Him as our Friend, bone of our bone, flesh of our flesh, touched with the feeling of our infirmities. We like to speak of Him as Brother, willing to enter our homes and to share with us the burdens and sorrows and trials of our mortal life. It is the gentler and more condescending aspects of our Lord's character upon which we lay the most stress. It is part and parcel of that tendency, marked enough in the religious life of our day, to ignore every attribute of God save His love, and so to magnify His pitifulness and compassion as to obscure His holiness and majesty.

But King Also

Now I rejoice in the fact that Christ is my Savior, my Friend, my Brother. I rejoice that in the strength of love He stoops to take my hand, to make my heart His home, and my life His care. But I would not forget that this same Jesus, who is Savior, Friend, and

Brother, is also King; that this Jesus, Who is full of grace and truth, is also Lord of glory, before Whom cherubim and seraphim veil their faces, Whose steps legions of angels attend, Who has all authority given to Him in heaven and on earth. Perhaps, in these days, we need nothing more than the recovery of the bracing sense of the authority, majesty and kingship of Jesus. Dr. Dale has left it on record how in a time of weakness and prostration it was this thought of Christ as King, that steadied him, and gave him courage and strength. History also bears witness to the fact that the strongest and most fearless Christians the world has ever known are those who realized most vividly Christ's kingship, Whose watchword was the crown rights of the Redeemer. A realization of the same truth will tone and brace up our religious life. It will be well, then, for us to stand again and again with these applauding crowds, and sing, "Hosanna, Blessed is He that cometh in the name of Jehovah," and to speak of Him not simply as Savior, Brother, Friend, but to say of Him, in words familiar to us all, "Thou art the King of Glory, O Christ, Thou art the Everlasting Son of the Father."

The Nature of Christ's Kingship

But we may not simply learn from this story the truth that Christ is King; we may gather from it also suggestions as to the kind of kingship Christ's is. The Jews were right in expecting Messiah to be a king. Where they went wrong was in expecting that He would be a king like Herod or like Caesar. They dreamed of a material empire, and of a monarch who used carnal weapons to win it. How different is the idea of kingship we get from this story! "My Kingdom is not of this world," said Jesus to Pilate. And the story of His triumphal entry is the best commentary upon that statement. Whenever an earthly monarch makes a state entry into any place it is marked by pageantry, and the display of military force. What a contrast is Our Lord's triumphal procession! There is nothing of the pomp and pageantry of royalty about His appearance; He rides, not on the warlike horse, but on an ass's colt. There is no suggestion of armed force. The Roman soldiers looked out from the fort on the throng, as the procession approached the city, and they felt no anxiety or concern; for all the escort Christ had was a crowd of singing pilgrims.

The Kingdom of Peace

Verily, the Kingdom was not of this world. It was a Kingdom of peace! Christ came not to make war upon men, but to preach peace to them that were far off, and peace to them that were nigh; to make peace between a man and his own self, between man and his neighbor, between man and God.

How Established

This Kingdom was not to be established by carnal weapons. "He is meek," says one of the prophets, "and having salvation." He is meek. And how this incident proclaimed it! There is here no war horse, no weapon. His attendants carry palms, not spears. Those who accompany Him, as Dr. Glover says, spread their garments in the way, but don no armor. It is obvious this King does not mean to win His Kingdom by force of arms. Nor does He. "Conquering by gentleness," that is the Lord's plan. All human government must, in the last resort, depend upon force; but not the rule and government of Christ. He trusts for His Kingdom absolutely to spiritual forces. His empire is one of moral influences: He trusts to the truth; He trusts to His love. He needs no worldly support, no patronage of states or governments to promote His empire. He will leave truth and love to do their own work upon human hearts. He is meek. But what did He Himself say about the meek? "Blessed are the meek, for they shall inherit the earth." And the meek Jesus, Who trusted entirely to the power of truth and the force of love, He too has inherited the earth. His Kingdom already stretches from sea to sea, and from the river to the ends of the earth. He has founded an empire the like of which for endurance and extent the world has never seen. "Alexander, Ceasar, Charlemagne and I," the great Napoleon is reported to have said, "have founded great empires. But upon what did these creations of our genius depend? Upon force. Jesus alone founded an Empire upon love, and to this day millions would die for Him." Christ trusted to His love. He did not coerce; He appealed. He did not threaten; He wooed. And the meek have inherited the earth.

The Applauding People

Now look away from Jesus, the central figure, in the applauding people. Nothing could exceed their enthusiasm. No royal honors were too great to be paid to Jesus that day. People spread their garments and branches of trees in the way, and as He rode on, those who went before and those who followed after cried, "Hosanna, Blessed is He that cometh in the name of Jehovah." But pass on to the Friday when Jerusalem echoed with a far different cry; when this Jesus, now saluted as King, was hounded as a criminal; when the shout of "Hosanna" gave place to the hoarse and savage cry, "Crucify Him!" Where were those applauding multitudes on the Friday? Not one of them then lifted up a voice on behalf of Christ. It may well be that these same people who sang "Hosanna" on the Sunday helped to swell the shout of "Crucify Him" on the Friday. For there are strange fluctuations of feeling, and this enthusiasm on the Sunday may have been nothing more than a brief and transient emotion. But, in any case, they must have let the plaudits of Sunday take the place of steady and daily obedience. It is easier far to applaud Christ than it is to obey Him; to cheer Him, than to do His will. But it is obedience He asks for.

Is Christ Our King?

If He is King, and we acknowledge Him as such, He wants our loyal and unhesitating allegiance, our faithful service. These people did not give it Him. Are we giving it? Is Christ our King? Do we live by His laws? Are we consciously and deliberately doing Him service? These people confessed Him, and crucified Him within a week. Is it an ancient crime? Do we never act in similar fashion? Do we not pay our homage to Him on the Sunday, and then crucify Him during the week? We sing in church, "Thou art the King of Glory, O Christ"; but do we not by our actions outside often say, "We will not have this man to reign over us"? And yet it is obedience Christ wants. "Why call ye Me Lord, Lord, and do not the things which I say? He that hath My commandments and keepeth them, he it is that loveth Me." Are we, then, loyal subjects? The Lord is before us, and I say, "Behold your King! Your King; the only Being Who has authority to rule and a right to your obedience." And I ask you, what will you do with your King? Will you say, "Away with Him!" Or will you say with me, and mean when you say it,

> "My gracious Lord, I own Thy right
> To every service I can pay,
> And call it my supreme delight
> To hear Thy dictates, and obey."

70

The Barren Fig-Tree: Difficulties

"And Jesus entered into Jerusalem, and into the temple: and when He had looked round about upon all things, and now the eventide was come, He went out unto Bethany with the twelve. And on the morrow, when they were come from Bethany, He was hungry: And seeing a fig-tree afar off having leaves, He came, if haply He might find any thing thereon: and when He came to it, He found nothing but leaves; for the time of figs was not yet. And Jesus answered and said unto it, No man eat fruit of thee hereafter forever. And His disciples heard it." —Mark 11:11-14.

The Visit to the Temple

BEFORE DISCUSSING THE difficult passage which tells the story of the barren fig-tree, let us look at verse 11, in which Mark tells us what happened after our Lord's triumphal entry into Jerusalem. "And He entered into Jerusalem," says the Evangelist, "into the Temple." "Into the Temple," surely the terminus of the procession is significant. It is significant as to the nature of Christ's Kingdom, and the character of His Kingship. Had it been an earthly kingdom our Lord was set upon establishing, had it been Herod's or Caesar's throne He wished to occupy, He would have marched, not to the Temple, but to the castle or the procurator's palace. But Jesus had no designs against Caesar's soldiers; no wish to sit in Pilate's or Herod's room; and so He bent His steps, not to the palace, but to the Temple.

Its Import

The Temple was the shrine and center of the Jewish religion. By marching on the day on which He was acclaimed as King straight to the Temple, our Lord declared to the world that it was a spiritual kingdom He came to establish, and it was in men's hearts He desired to reign. When He reached the Temple, He "looked round about upon all things." He cast a searching, scrutinizing glance upon all the was taking place in the Temple precincts. He saw much that grieved and pained Him, and on the morrow, as we shall see, He took sharp and drastic action. But on the day of His entry He contented Himself with this all-embracing gaze. He "looks round about upon all things."

The Searching Look

How full of solemn suggestion a little phrase like this is! The Lord still visits His temple! He comes to visit His Father's house. And when He comes nothing escapes His notice. I wonder what it is He sees. He sees no one buying or selling. There are no seats of the money changers to overthrow. And yet He may see things equally incongruous with the purpose of a house of God. His house is a house of prayer. But is it the prayerful and believing spirit Christ always sees? Do we never bring the proud and unforgiving spirit with us? Do not foolish and sometimes foul thoughts go racing through our minds even in a sacred place like this? Are we not often busy with worldly plans and cares, while to outward appearance engaged in worship? And by bringing these things with us into the house of God we desecrate it just as badly as did these Jews who bartered and haggled in the Temple courts. And whatever we bring with us our Lord sees. The foolish thought, the evil temper, the wandering imagination, the unholy desire, nothing escapes His notice. Every time we gather in church, the Lord is present too, and He "looks round about upon all things." I never think of that solemn, searching, scrutinizing gaze without feeling constrained to take the Psalmist's prayer on my lips and to say, "Let the words of my mouth and the meditation of my heart be acceptable in Thy sight, O Lord, my Rock and my Redeemer" (19:14). With that solemn and searching glance our Lord contented Himself on the day of His entry; for apparently, as His lowly procession had made its way down Olivet and into Jerusalem, the day had waned; and as it was now eventide, He went out into Bethany—out of the reach of His bitter foes, to the restfulness and quiet of Martha and Mary's house.

Returning to Jerusalem

But Jerusalem was to be the scene of His labors during these last few days. He had a witness to bear, and at all risks and costs it must be borne. So, when the next morning comes, He takes the journey to Jerusalem once more. And on the way He realized He was faint and hungry. It is possible He had risen a great while before day, to seek the Father's face in prayer; and absorbed in communion with God He had clean forgotten His physical necessities. That was often the case with Jesus. Again and again it happened that He had no leisure so much as to eat. But the needs of the body cannot for long be neglected. And so Jesus, lifted in the exaltation of His spirit above any sense of need, suddenly realized that He was going to face a long and trying day in Jerusalem, and He was faint and spent almost before it began.

"He Hungered"

"When they were come out from Bethany He hungered" (v. 12). Does that seem a trivial thing? Does it almost seem derogatory to the dignity of Christ to mention a fact like that? Personally, I am grateful for it. It makes one realize how truly Jesus was man, and how completely He was touched with the feeling of our infirmities. "He hungered."

The Barren Fig-Tree

And ahead of Him on the road He saw a fig-tree, which promised the sustenance He needed; for although it was not the regular season of figs, this particular tree was in full leaf, and in the fig-tree, we are told, fruitage precedes leafage. But when Jesus reached it He found that the tree bore nothing but leaves. All that show of foliage was a cheat and a delusion. There was not a fig on the whole tree. And so our Lord "answered" (note the word; it is as if the tree had refused to give fruit), and said unto it, "No man eat fruit from thee henceforward forever" (v. 14). The disciples heard the sentence; and next morning, as they were making their way again into the city they saw that the barren fig-tree had withered away.

Difficulties: Our Lord's Knowledge

(1) Now certain obvious difficulties are raised by this story. (1) The first and most obvious is concerned with Christ's knowledge. Did our Lord really expect to find fruit on the tree? Was He really ignorant that it was a barren tree? This was the difficulty that gave most trouble to ancient commentators. To admit ignorance seemed to them equivalent to denying our Lord's perfection. "If He really sought fruit," says Augustine, "He erred." And so they resort to various shifts to reconcile our Lord's pretended ignorance with His honesty. Their explanations amount practically to this—that He only feigned to seek the fruit. The whole action, we are told, was symbolic; it was a "wrought" parable. The entire episode was simply meant to teach the lesson that large professions without practice, as illustrated in the case of the Jewish

nation, inevitably come under the judgment and condemnation of God. Many prefer, however, the simple explanation of our Lord's conduct in connection with this fig-tree, namely, that He did not know it was barren. It was not the regular season for figs, Mark says. But our Lord inferred from its luxuriant leafage that there were sure to be figs upon it. It is urged that this interpretation in no way detracts from His Divinity (for that rests in the last resort upon His sinless life and His power to impart life to others); but that it does help to make His humanity a more real and genuine thing.

Difficulties: The Tree Not a Moral Agent

(2) A further difficulty is felt by some who hold that a tree, not being a moral agent, not being capable either of good or of evil, ought not to have been punished. But we answer the objection by the language we use of trees. We talk of "good" trees and "bad" trees. We say such and such a tree "ought" to bear well, while another perhaps cannot be "expected" to do much. That is to say, we attribute moral qualities to trees, and ourselves pass judgment upon them. All of which, again, implies that there is a certain analogy between trees and men. Indeed, our Lord more than once employs the analogy. In one familiar parable, for instance, He compares Israel to a barren fig-tree, which is only spared through the importunity of the gardener who begged for another year of grace. So now it was Israel—so rich in professions, so poor in practice—that He saw symbolized in that barren tree, and when He pronounced judgment upon it, it was Israel that He had in mind. It was a solemn warning to His countrymen of the doom that would surely fall upon them, if they satisfied themselves with empty professions, and brought forth no fruits meet for repentance. The physical injury was intended to teach a great spiritual lesson.

Difficulties: The Severity of Our Lord

(3) But behind all this, there lies a feeling that judgment of this kind is alien from the spirit of Christ. The tendency of our own day is to ignore every suggestion of sternness and austerity in the character of our Lord. We emphasize the kindly, gracious aspects of our Lord's character. "Gentle Jesus," we call Him. "A bruised reed He will not break," we say of Him, "and smoking flax He will not quench." We delight to remember that He came to seek and to save the lost, and that He was the friend of publicans and sinners. And all this is of course, quite true. But there is another aspect of our

Lord's character. He is not merely gentle and kind; He is also majestic and austere. He is not only Savior; He is also Judge. I will admit, if you like, that judgment is strange work, distasteful work to Him. "Curse a fig-tree?" so Dr. Halley used to begin a great sermon of his on this incident. "Curse a fig-tree? `Tisn't like Him." I grant it is not like Him. It is not work in which He takes delight. He came to save men's lives, not to destroy them.

But He Is Judge as Well as Savior

But we are blind to whole tracts of the New Testament teaching if we ignore the fact that Christ is Judge as well as Savior. He does not bear the sword in vain. We are not exalting Christ, we are doing a grave wrong to men, if we induce them to believe that Jesus is mere indulgent good-nature, and that He can view sin and wrong with easy indifference. And I am not sure that our over-emphasis on the gentleness and kindness of Jesus has not already inflicted that grave wrong upon men. "No one is afraid of God now," said Dr. Dale to Dr. Berry one day.

To a large extent Dr. Dale's remark remains true. The sense of God's holiness and purity has been lost and submerged in the sense of, I will not say His love, but His good-nature. And the result is that the edge has gone from our sense of sin, and our hatred of it. But the fear of the Lord remains to this day the beginning of wisdom. And an incident like this teaches us that neglected truth of the fear of God. Men may banish the "wrath of the Lamb" from thought and speech. But, in spite of our silence, that "wrath " remains a reality. In parable it is here in the cursing of this barren fig-tree.

God's Goodness and Severity

"Behold, then," says St Paul, "the goodness and severity of God" (Rom. 11:22). The goodness and the severity! We talk much, as a rule, about the goodness, and say nothing about the severity. But, as a matter of fact, there can be no goodness apart from severity. The indulgent father, the father who is never severe, the father who never steels his heart to punish, is not a good father. He is a weak father and a foolish father, and from the child's standpoint, a bad father. In the same way exactly a God who winked at and never punished sin would not be a good God. He would not be good in Himself; for good-nature is not the same as goodness. And He certainly would not be good towards men. I can conceive of nothing more fatal to human souls than that God should allow them to sin on without penalty or rebuke. By ignoring the austere and severe aspects of our Lord's character, we really sacrifice His holiness and perfection. Moreover, paradoxical as it may sound at first, it is a fact that we sacrifice the very kindness and love of Christ, if we ignore His severity. "Thy chastisements are love," says our familiar hymn. So they are. They are the final and consummate proof of love.

A Last Appeal

Love is seen even in the very severity of this action. He had already compared Israel to a persistently barren tree. They made loud professions of religion; they had all the outward parade of it; they offered sacrifices and made long prayers, but the genuine effects of religion—obedience, mercy, love and truth—were conspicuous by their absence. They were like this fig-tree, with a profusion of leafage, but no fruit. And by this act of blighting the barren fig-tree our Lord made a kind of last appeal, and gave a kind of final warning to Israel. He inflicted this act of penal justice upon this tree, that thereby barren Israel might be warned to escape the wrath to come. He destroyed a fig-tree that He might save men's souls.

The Pity of the Lord

The yearning pity of the Lord shines out of an act like this. There was an intention of saving grace at the very heart of it. This is the one miracle of judgment our Lord ever performed. And when He felt constrained to assert the holiness and righteousness of God, He did not do it, Archbishop Trench remarks, like Moses and Elijah, at the expense of the lives of many men; but only at the cost of a single, unfeeling tree. His miracles of help and healing were numberless, and on men; His miracle of judgment was but one, and on a tree. Behold the "goodness and severity" of the Lord!

And His Solemn Warning

And yet, though we may assuredly see love and kindness shining through it, the story is a solemn story. Let us not ignore its austere and searching teaching. Christ is Judge as well as Savior. He is full of patient and seeking love for the sinner, but He burns with a flame of holy wrath against sin. And sooner or later the judgment upon sin will fall. There are limits to the patience even of the patient Christ. The blow fell upon Israel, rebellious and barren Israel, in shattering fashion, some thirty years later, when the Lord they had rejected, by the hand of the Roman power, broke the nation in pieces like a potter's vessel. And the sin that provokes

judgment need not be some great and positive offense. It is barrenness that incurs the doom mentioned in the story. "Inasmuch as
ye did it not," that was the charge. "Depart from Me," that was the
doom. Let us "kiss the son, lest He be angry, and ye perish in the
way. Blessed are all they that put their trust in Him " (Psa. 2:12).

71
The Barren Fig-Tree: Messages

"And on the morrow, when they were come from Bethany, He was hungry: And seeing a fig-tree afar off having leaves, He came, if haply He might find any thing thereon: and when He came to it, He found nothing but leaves; for the time of figs was not yet. And Jesus answered and said unto it, No man eat fruit of thee hereafter for ever. And His disciples heard it. And in the morning, as they passed by, they saw the fig-tree dried up from the roots. And Peter calling to remembrance said unto Him, Master, behold, the fig-tree which Thou cursedst is withered away. And Jesus answering saith unto them, Have faith in God. For verily I say unto you, That whosoever shall say unto this mountain, Be thou removed, and be thou cast into the sea; and shall not doubt in his heart, but shall believe that those things which he saith shall come to pass; he shall have whatsoever he saith. Therefore I say unto you, What things soever ye desire, when ye pray, believe that ye receive them, and ye shall have them. And when ye stand praying, forgive, If ye have ought against any: that your Father also which is in heaven may forgive you your trespasses." —Mark 11:12-14, 20-25.

Christ as Judge

SO MUCH FOR the difficulties associated with this story of the barren fig-tree. Now let us deal with the solemn teaching of the story itself. I have said that this incident revealed Jesus in His capacity as Judge. Judgment is Christ's prerogative. "The Father hath given all judgment unto the Son," says John (John 5:22). "We must all be made manifest before the judgment-seat of Christ," says St Paul, "that each one may receive the things done in the body, according to what we hath done, whether it be good or bad " (2 Cor. 5:10). While Jesus Himself asserts that before Him as Judge all the nations shall be gathered; and it is His judgment that sets the sheep on His right hand, and the goats on His left. Thus the uniform witness of Holy Writ is that Christ is Judge as well as Savior. Whoever ignores this aspect of our Lord's office shuts his eyes to whole tracts of New Testament teaching.

Principles of His Judgment

But this incident does more than proclaim the fact that Jesus Christ is Judge. It also sets forth the principles of His judgment, showing us the things that fall under our Lord's condemnation, and suggesting the penalties He inflicts. I have said that it was the Jewish people our Lord saw symbolized in this barren fig-tree; and it is their judgment which in parable is set forth in this incident. But our Lord's judgments are never arbitrary or casual; they are based on great principles; they are governed by eternal law. So that from any individual case we are justified in deducting a general rule; and we may be sure that though this is primarily a judgment upon the Jews, the principles embodied in it are valid for all time.

Barrenness—a Sin

Observe first that barrenness is a sin. That was the fault of this tree. It was not that it was spoiling the landscape by its ugly appearance, or blighting all vegetation near by its poisonous exhalations. As a matter of fact, it was doing no harm, and it was fair to look upon. It was barren; that was all. It was doing nothing. It was failing to fulfill the true end of its existence. And for that it was condemned. It seems to me we need to broaden our conceptions of what sin is. We are apt to cherish a narrow, mechanical, external idea of sin. "Sinner," as we commonly understand the word, means someone who has committed a glaring, gross, and open offense. To be a sinner in the eyes of most people, a man must have done something positively shameful and wicked. But if we turn to a story like this, its first and most obvious lesson is that barrenness is a sin. A man need not do anything openly wicked in order to come under the condemnation of Christ. He comes under that condemnation if he does nothing, if he is simply barren and useless.

The Repeated Warning

When I read the instances of judgment given to us in the Gospels, I find that in nearly every case the men so condemned were condemned not because of any positive harm they had done, but because, like this fig-tree, they had done nothing. Take the judgment picture as given to us by our Lord in Matt. 25. Upon some was pronounced this terrible judgment, "Depart from Me, ye cursed, into the eternal fire." What awful wickedness had they perpetrated to merit a doom like that? Nothing. It was not what they had done; it was what they had not done. There were at their doors hungry people to be fed, naked people to be clothed, thirsty people to be refreshed, sick people to be visited and comforted—

and they had done nothing. "Inasmuch as ye did it not . . . depart from Me, ye cursed." Take the parable of the talents. Upon one of his servants the householder pronounces this sentence, "Cast ye out the unprofitable servant into the outer darkness: there shall be the weeping and gnashing of teeth" (Matt. 25:30). What enormity had this servant committed? Had he defrauded his lord, and robbed him of his money? No; for when his lord came back he returned to him the talent he had originally received. Again it was not a case of what he had done; it was a case of what he had not done. His lord had given him a talent to trade with, but instead of using it, he hid the talent in the earth and did nothing. Take the story of Dives. "In Hades he lifted up his eyes being in torments" (Luke 17:23). What awful and monstrous sin had Dives committed, to find himself at the last in that flame? It is not charged against him that he had committed obvious sin. Possibly he had lived what would be considered an eminently respectable life. I should not be surprised if he had had a large funeral, and if the local Rabbi pronounced a eulogy over his coffin, extolling the virtues of the dead man. What, then, had he done, to be thus "in torments"? Again, it was not a case of what he had done; it was a case of what he had not done. Lazarus had lain at his gate in his poverty and sores day after day, and this rich man, clothed in purple and fine linen, and faring sumptuously every day, had done nothing for him.

A Warning Still Needed

We miss, then, the entire point of our Lord's repeated teaching, unless we see that barrenness is a damning sin. Of many we need not fear that they will ever stand convicted of open and flagrant crime. Their danger is of another kind; it is the sin of barrenness. We are sent here to this world for a purpose. The Westminster Catechism expresses it this way, "The chief end of man is to glorify God." And we glorify God as our Master did, by lives of usefulness and service. Here, then, is the matter that will decide our destiny. Are we fulfilling the purpose God had in mind? Are we going about doing good? Failure in this brings the condemnation upon us, "The God in Whose hand thy breath is, and Whose are all thy ways, hast thou not glorified" (Dan. 6:23). So ran the reason given to a Babylonian king for the doom that was about to fall upon him.

Where Is Our Fruit?

How do we stand such a test? Do we bear the fruits of righteousness? Or are we barren trees? "The fruit of the Spirit," says the Apostle, "is love, joy, peace, long-suffering, kindness, goodness, faithfulness, meekness, temperance" (Gal. 5:22, 23). Are such fruits seen in us? Are we living lives of active and positive beneficence? It is not for me or any other man to judge, but one cannot help feeling that there are a large number of "barren trees" about. By worldly standards, these people live lives respectable enough; but they are colorless, ineffective, useless. It is not that they do much positive harm, but rather that in a world full of need and misery and sin, they do nothing. Upon all such fruitless, useless, barren lives the Divine judgment will fall.

Profession and Practice

The next truth I find suggested in this story is this—that barrenness may exist where there is much promise of fruit. That was the characteristic of this particular fig-tree; there was much promise, but no performance. There was any amount of leafage, but not a single fig. The tree was not only barren, it was deceptive and false into the bargain. And this tree which promised so fair, but was so barren, reminded our Lord, as I have said, of the people of Israel. There was much of the show and parade of religion in Judea. The Temple smoked with sacrifices. Priests were ever busy at the altars. The people ceaselessly trod its courts. One type of Jew, condemned by our Lord, was wont, if I may so put it, to advertise his religion. He tithed his mint and anise and cummin. He stood at the corner of the streets and made long prayers. He made broad his phylacteries. By his actions and observances he called the world's attention to himself, and said, "I am a religious man." He was like this fig-tree, there was any amount of profession and promise, but the real thing was conspicuous by its absence. Mercy and truth were sadly to seek. These very men, so scrupulous about the washing of pots and pans and brazen vessels, carried within them foul and unclean hearts. These very men who stood at the corners of the streets and made long prayers were not above devouring widows' houses. All through their lives this contradiction ran. They served God with their lips, but their hearts were far from Him. They sacrificed, but did not obey. They were like this tree, nothing but leaves.

A Modern Evil

And still we find this same humbling phenomenon, barrenness where there is profusion of promise. Fruitless lives are to be found even amongst those who profess to be followers of Jesus. One of the sights that Interpreter pointed out in his garden to Christiana and her children was that of a "tree whose inside was all rotten and gone, yet it grew and had leaves." Then said Mercy, "What is this? " "This Tree," said Interpreter, "whose outside is fair, and whose inside is rotten, it is to which many may be compared that are in the garden of God, who with their mouths speak high in behalf of God, but in deed will do nothing for Him; whose leaves are fair, but their hearts good for nothing, but to be tinder for the devil's tinderbox." And that is just the old Dreamer's way of stating the moral of this tree, that had abundance of leaves but nothing else. There are men and women, alas, many of them, who are all leaf, and no fruit. Church membership, attendance at public worship, participation in the Holy Communion, these are the leaves. But where is the fruit? There is nothing in their lives to demonstrate the reality of their faith. Their profession often leaves their life untouched. It all ends with the profession and the promise. It is a case of "nothing but leaves." Now, a life all barren is bad enough; but a life that makes promise, and yet remains barren, is worse still; for it adds the sin of falsity to the sin of barrenness. Or, to put it in a slightly different form, a fruitless life is bad enough; but a fruitless life on the part of a professing Christian is the worst of all. Better make no profession than make a profession without practice.

The biggest obstacle to religion today is not the man who is frankly not a Christian, but the man who says he is a Christian and does not live like one. Profession without practice brings the whole of religion into contempt. It causes the name of God to be blasphemed.

How Is It with Us?

We do well, therefore, frankly to ask ourselves, Have we the power of godliness as well as the form? Do we love Christ as well as profess Him? Or does it all end with the profession?

"Either put on courage, or put off the name of Alexander," said that great monarch to a soldier who was showing signs of cowardice in one of his battles. So I say, "Either put on Christ, or put off the name of Christian." To profess Christ and to live for self, is not simply to be fruitless, but to be hypocrites into the bargain. Profession without practice, leaves without fruit, avail nothing with God. "Not every one that saith unto Me, Lord, Lord, shall enter into the Kingdom of heaven; but he that doeth the will of My Father which is in heaven" (Matt. 7:21).

The Doom of Barrenness

Now mark the doom of barrenness, as exemplified in this incident. "No man eat fruit from thee henceforward forever" (v. 14), said our Lord. And in the morning the disciples noticed that the "fig-tree was withered away from the roots." The punishment of barrenness, as Dr. Glover says, was judicial barrenness. Or, to put it in less technical language, the punishment of this fig-tree that refused to bear fruit was permanent inability to bear fruit. All this is neither arbitrary nor capricious, but in strictest accord with the principles of judgment, as we see them at work all about us.

The Law of Atrophy

There are two laws with whose working we are quite familiar, which are illustrated in our Lord's judgment on the fig-tree. They are closely connected with each other, indeed, may be regarded as complementary to each other. The first—shall I call it the law of atrophy?—is one of the observed laws of science, that powers and faculties unused, decay and perish. Muscles, e.g. unexercised, grow limp and flabby. The condition of retaining a faculty is its use. Now that is true in higher regions than the physical. The condition of retaining the *spirit* of generosity is the *exercise* of generosity. The condition of retaining the spirit of unselfishness is the *practice* of unselfishness. The man who never does a generous deed soon loses the capacity for generosity. The man who never does an unselfish deed loses the very power to be unselfish. Neglect is punished by loss. That is the principle illustrated in the doom of this tree. It refused to bear fruit; it lost the power of bearing fruit. "Henceforth no man eat fruit from thee for ever."

The Law of Permanence

The second law I see illustrated is the law of permanence. It is the positive side of the law of atrophy. We lose what we fail to use. But what we choose and practice, that we tend permanently to become. This fruitless tree, what was its punishment? Permanent fruitlessness. It is a stern and awful law. But it is one whose working we see on every hand. It is the law set forth in that sequence which says that actions repeated become habits, habits long continued become character, and character settles destiny. The man who does mean and miserly actions tends to become permanently miserly; the man who acts selfishly becomes selfish in the very grain of his nature; the man who allows himself to brood over foul and filthy things becomes filthy to his very core. Character is always tending to permanence. I can conceive no doom more awful than that a man should be permanently what he has made himself. And that is the principle of the Divine judgment. "He that is unrighteous, let him do unrighteousness still; and he that is filthy, let him be made filthy still; and he that is righteous, let him do righteousness still" (Rev. 22:11). In a sense Christ's judgment is simply the ratification of our own choice. We become permanently what we ourselves choose to be.

The Responsibility of Hearing

"And the disciples heard it," says St Mark, "heard," that is, the sentence pronounced upon the barren tree; taking in not merely the words, but, then or later, the solemn import of them.

Now, we ourselves have heard with our ears once again this story of the barren fig-tree. Have we heard it with the ears of the soul? Have we listened to and received its solemn warning? "If ye know these things," said our Lord, "happy are ye if ye do them." "Herein is My Father glorified, that ye bear much fruit; and so shall ye be My disciples" (John 15:8). If we have "heard" this solemn story aright, we shall ask God for His enriching and life-giving Spirit, we shall pray that that Spirit may come upon us, and that our barrenness may rejoice to own His fertilizing power. For the fruit of the spirit is love, joy, peace, goodness, kindness, meekness, temperance; and against such there is no law, no judgment, no doom; no, but then comes the "Well done, good and faithful servant, enter thou into the joy of thy Lord."

72
The Cleansing of the Temple

"And they come to Jerusalem: and Jesus went into the temple, and began to cast out them that sold and bought in the temple, and overthrew the tables of the money-changers, and the seats of them that sold doves; and would not suffer that any man should carry any vessel through the temple. And He taught, saying unto them, Is it not written, My house shall be called of all nations the house of prayer? but ye have made it a den of thieves. And the scribes and chief priests heard it, and sought how they might destroy him: for they feared him, because all the people was astonished at his doctrine."
—Mark 11:15-18.

The Scrutiny of the Temple

ON THE DAY that our Lord made His entry in lowly state into Jerusalem, He went straight to the Temple; for it was not Caesar's or Herod's throne that He sought. The empire He came to establish was not material, but spiritual. His mission was not political; it was religious. Our Lord, however, took no action of any sort on His visit to the Temple, on the day of His triumphal entry. He contented Himself with a sweeping and searching scrutiny of the things that were being done within its precincts. "He looked round about upon all things." The look was, no doubt, with a view to action. But it was eventide, and the action itself was postponed until the next day. "When He had looked round about upon all things, it being now eventide, He went out unto Bethany with the Twelve" (v. 11).

The Things Seen

Now, what was it our Lord saw when He looked round about upon all things? To put it in a word, He saw the Temple desecrated. There were men bartering and haggling, cheating and overreaching one another in the very house of God.

The Reason for the Traffic

We remember, of course, that it was not a case of general trafficking; all the buying and selling that went on was with a view to the requirements of the Temple worship. Jews came up to worship at the Temple from all parts of Palestine, from all parts of the world. You can see how inconvenient, even how impossible, it would be for them to bring their sacrifices with them. Take the Passover sacrifice. Pilgrims came flocking in their thousands and tens of thousands for that great feast. It would have been the extremity of inconvenience if they had had to bring the sacrificial lamb along with them. So, to meet their convenience, arrangements were made whereby the pilgrims could purchase the lambs they needed, in Jerusalem, or indeed in the Temple itself. It was the same with the money-changing. Jews coming from foreign countries would naturally be provided with the money of those countries. But the Temple tax had to be paid in Jewish coin. So again, to meet their convenience money-changers attended in the Temple precincts, to exchange the diverse sorts of money the pilgrims brought for the Jewish half-shekel.

Its Scene

Further, we are not to think of this traffic as taking place in the shrine itself. Around the Temple there were a series of courts, and the largest and the outermost of these was the Court of the Gentiles. It was in this great Court of the Gentiles that the buying and selling took place. The Jew scarcely, perhaps, reckoned this court as a holy place. It was almost a profane place, for the uncircumcised Gentile could enter into it. The probability is that the Jew would have revolted in horror from the idea of permitting trafficking in the court where he himself worshipped; but he did not think that it mattered very much what happened in the Court of the Gentiles.

The Real Offense

All this is not by way of excuse for the conduct of the Jews, but in order that we may see just wherein their offense lay. I do not think it was the mere buying and selling and money-changing that desecrated the Temple. If the motive of these actions had been a genuine desire to meet the convenience of the pilgrims, and to minister to their necessities, if kindliness and a spirit of helpfulness lay behind the buying and selling, I do not think that our Lord would have blazed up in holy anger against it, nor would He have accused those who engaged in it of turning His Father's house into a den of robbers.

The Sacred and the Secular: How Distinguished

In our Lord's sight actions were sacred or profane according to the spirit that prompted them. We have ourselves a rough and mechanical division of things into things secular and sacred. A hymn, for instance, is a sacred thing; a speech is a secular thing. But in Christ's sight the hymn may be a secular thing, and the speech the sacred thing. An irreligious spirit makes the most sacred hymn a profane thing; a worshipful spirit makes a speech even on a secular theme a religious exercise. Now there is nothing more secular from our narrow point of view than buying and selling. But even buying and selling can be translated into Divine service. We all of us believe that, or else there is but a poor prospect for those engaged in commerce. Supposing, then, that these people buying and selling in the Temple courts had been animated solely by the desire to help the pilgrims from all parts of the world, do you think that He Who said that God wanted mercy, and not sacrifice, Who in the very next chapter endorses the scribes' declaration that to love God and to love one's neighbor as oneself is much more than all whole burnt offerings and sacrifices, do you think that He would have denounced them as "robbers," and driven them in holy wrath out of the Temple precincts? I tell you nay. I do not think He would have rebuked them at all. Such buying and selling would have been converted into Divine service, and would not have been incongruous, even in a place set apart for prayer.

The Temple-Market Perverted

It was not, then, the buying and the selling that in itself was wrong; it was the spirit in which it was carried on. Originally instituted to meet the convenience of the pilgrims, it was carried on from motives of cupidity and greed. The priests who permitted the traffic no longer thought of the pilgrims and their needs; they thought only of their own gains. The sale of animals for sacrifice became a source of profit. The exchange of money became an opportunity for extorting an oppressive discount. This market in the Temple, instead of being a help, became a burden to the worshipper. The sordid, mercenary spirit of the priests turned everything, as Dr. Salmond says, to "desecration, profanity, greed and fraud." It was this ugly and greedy spirit that stirred our Lord to indignation. They turned the very service of the Lord into an oppression. They turned the worship of the Temple into a way of gain. They brought the spirit of the world in its basest and foulest form right into the Holy Place. This it was that defiled the

Temple. They were guilty of cheating and defrauding and oppression in the name of religion. Literally, they turned the house of prayer into "a den of robbers."

Houses of God Misused

All this has its most solemn teaching for us today. We should never dream of setting up a cattle-market or even a shop within sacred precincts, though in these days men are often puzzled as to what is permissible and what is not permissible in buildings set apart for the worship of God. My own strong feeling is that it is conducive to the spirit of worship to preserve these buildings entirely for worship, though I cannot assert that those who put them to other uses are wrong. But, even if we keep them rigidly and absolutely for worship, we may yet desecrate and pollute them. For, as I have tried to point out, the real character of an action is decided by the spirit in which we do it. You may have profane hymn-singing and secular preaching. God asks to be worshipped "in spirit and in truth," but when we come together, and assume the form of worship while our hearts are all the while far away from God and holy things; when we sit in pews, and allow our minds to busy themselves with worldly affairs; when we bring pride, and jealousy, and uncharitableness with us; when we allow coarse and base and foul thoughts to go coursing through our minds, we are as really and truly polluting God's house as were these traffickers who desecrated the Temple precincts. In the ultimate resort it is the sinful heart that is the real cause of the pollution. And there is one prayer we may well offer whenever we come up to God's house, and that is, "O God! make clean our hearts within us," for holiness becometh God's house for ever.

The Jew, the Gentile—and Jesus Christ

Our Lord's action, then, was first of all a condemnation of the evil spirit of greed that turned religion into a source of profit. In the second place, it was a protest against the differentiation made between the sacredness of the court in which the Jews themselves worshipped, and that in which the Gentiles worshipped. By turning the Court of the Gentiles into a cattle-market they as good as labelled it as a profane place. They said, in effect, that it did not much matter what was transacted there. It was an illustration in action of the traditional Jewish contempt for the Gentile. But Jesus knew no distinction between Jew and Gentile. Each was equally dear to the heart of God. The Temple, as He said, was a "house of prayer for all the nations." In God's great house Gentile and Jew

were equally welcome, and the place where the Gentiles worshipped was every whit as sacred as the inner court where the
Jews performed their devotions. And so He swept the dealers out
of the Court of the Gentiles, and overthrew the tables of the
money-changers, and the seats of them that sold the doves, and
thereby declared their acceptance with God and their equal
rights with the Jews. There was as little room in the house of God
for the spirit of religious pride as for the spirit of avarice and greed.
The presence of either was a desecration of the Holy Place. Both
came under the judgment of our Lord when He swept this mob of
traders out of the Court of the Gentiles, saying, "Is it not written,
My house shall be called a house of prayer for all the nations? but
ye have made it a den of robbers" (v. 17).

Having thus pointed out the sins which came under the lash of
our Lord's condemnation, let us note some lessons which the incident as a whole is calculated to teach.

The Sovereignty of Christ

First of all, observe the royal bearing of Jesus throughout this
incident. The day previous the crowds had acclaimed Him as King,
and He had gone to the Temple in triumph, as if to His royal seat.
In this incident He proceeds to exercise His royal authority: He acts
as King. He proclaims Himself Master and Lord in the Temple.
"The Lord," it had been said by one of the prophets "shall suddenly
come to His Temple." By driving these traffickers helter-skelter out
of the sacred courts Jesus proclaimed Himself the long-awaited
King of Jewish expectation. All who witnessed the incident knew
exactly what it meant. It was the Lord laying claim to His
Messiahship. He had kept it hidden and secret in Galilee. But in
Jerusalem, and especially during this last week, He publicly and
repeatedly declared it. Notice, too, how He speaks of the Temple.
When He purged it of its desecrations at the commencement of His
career, He spoke of it as His "Father's house." But see how He
speaks of it now. "My house shall be called a house of prayer." My
house! "By what authority doest Thou these things?" the chief
priests asked of Him. It was a proper question to ask. For no mere
man had a right to act as if he were Lord of the Temple, and no
mere man had a right to speak of the Temple as "My house."

The Moral Authority of Christ

Notice again what an illustration we have here of the moral
authority of the Lord Jesus Christ! He was only one man. There
were scores, possibly more, of these traffickers and money-chang-

ers. And yet before this one man unarmed this mob of men fled in
something like abject panic. Jesus was vested with no external
authority. He wore no badge of office. To outward appearance He
was only a Galilean peasant—that and nothing more. How came
these men to flee from before Him? There was a double reason. This
is the first, sin is always weakness. Men who know they are in the
wrong often show themselves timid in the face of righteousness.
"Conscience doth make cowards of us all." These men knew they
were doing a wrong, an indefensible thing. And so, when Jesus
challenged them, not a man dare stand his ground. But this is more
than an illustration of the weakness of evil—it is also an illustration
of the moral authority of Jesus. There was a purity and holiness in
His very appearance before which evil could not stand. "Who may
abide the day of His coming? and who shall stand when He
appeareth? " (Mal. 3:2), the prophet asks. Not these traffickers and
money-changers, caught in the very act of desecrating God's house.
They fled before Him, conscience-stricken and ashamed.

Moral Authority in Daily Life

We know something of this moral authority in every-day life.
There was a shameful scene in our House of Commons some years
ago, when, in the heat of party passion, members came to blows.
The Chairman of Committees was in charge of the House when
the storm broke. But he was powerless to quell it. So some one sent
in a hurry for Speaker Peel. When he appeared, and looked in his
own grave and dignified way upon the ugly scene, the men who
had forgotten themselves, subdued by not so much the official as
the moral authority of the Speaker, shrank like whipped school-
boys to their places. There is immense moral authority in
character. Men instinctively yield to it. But no one had it in such
preeminent degree as Jesus. The crowd who brought before
Him that wretched woman whom they had discovered in sin, stole
away one by one, unable to bear the scrutiny of those clear eyes.
The soldiers who came to seize Him went backward, and fell to the
ground. These traffickers fled pell-mell before Him. The ungodly
shall not stand in the judgment, "but are like chaff which the wind
driveth away" (Psa. 1:4).

The Holy Indignation of Christ

Observe, again, the holy indignation of Jesus Christ, as illustrated in this incident. He was filled with just anger against these
men who brought their avarice and greed into the Holy Place and
turned God's house into a den of robbers. In our conceptions of

Jesus we must make room for indignation and anger. He was not gentle or tolerant towards persistent and continued sin; more especially towards the sin of those who inflicted wrong upon their fellows. It is the penitent sinner toward whom Christ is all tenderness and pity.

Cleansing Temple and Church

Christ, then, has just proclaimed His Kingship, and the first act of His reign, so to speak, is to cleanse the Temple. Surely the action is suggestive of the cleansing of His Church. For the Church is the instrument through which Christ will establish His Kingdom; but a corrupt and tainted Church is useless for such a work. When there is a corrupt Church and a corrupt ministry, you get a corrupt people. The wickedness of the sons of Eli made men abhor the offering of the Lord. And it is so still. Weakness, corruption, worldliness in the Church itself set religion at a discount amongst the people; and so judgment must begin at the House of God. Has not all this its meaning for our own time? Things are slack amongst us. Somehow or other religion seems to be losing its hold. The progress of the Kingdom is arrested. Can it be that the fault lies with the Church? Have things crept into the Church which have destroyed its effectiveness and weakened its power? We are constantly praying for a revival. Perhaps it is we ourselves who need to be cleansed and purified. Is it not a fact that doubts and timidities have crept into our speech? Is it not a fact that our prayers are often lifeless, and our enthusiasm cold? Is it not a fact that we have condescended to some perilously worldly methods in our efforts to win what we call success? And is it not a fact that by our mutual jealousies and strife we oftentimes make religion a laughing-stock to the world around us?

Our Need Today

What we need today is that our Lord should come and cleanse His Church of these things that defile her in the eyes of men, and make vain all her efforts. A doubtful Church, a divided Church, a worldly Church is a powerless Church. A cleansing and purification of the Church is our sorest need. Let us all unite in the prayer that God will inspire continually the universal Church with the spirit of truth, unity, and concord; let us beg of Him that all they that do confess His holy name may agree in the truth of His Holy Word and live in unity and godly love. For a cleansed, redeemed and sanctified Church means a converted and rejuvenated world.

73
Prayer and Its Power

"And Jesus answering saith unto them, Have faith in God. For verily I say unto you, That whosoever shall say unto this mountain, Be thou removed, and be thou cast into the sea; and shall not doubt in his heart, but shall believe that those things which he saith shall come to pass; he shall have whatsoever he saith." —Mark 11:22, 23.

An Unexpected Reply

ON THE TUESDAY morning of that eventful week, when again our Lord and His followers made their way to Jerusalem, Peter noticed that the once leafy and luxuriant fig-tree was limp and wilted and dying. He remembered the episode of the previous morning, and said to Jesus, "Rabbi, behold the fig-tree which Thou cursedst is withered away. And Jesus answering saith unto them, Have faith in God" (vv. 21, 22). Now, that is not at all the kind of reply we should have expected Jesus to make to Peter's remark. At the first sight, it scarcely seems to the point. The kind of answer that would have seemed to us natural would have been some reference about the sure fulfillment of all His words. Instead of that, "Jesus answering saith unto them, Have faith in God." That was, according to Jesus, the central and all-important truth to be learned from the withering of the fig-tree, a lesson of faith and its limitless power.

Christ accomplished His mighty works through the power of God resting upon Him, and the power was His because of His perfect and absolute union with the Father. Christ was never ineffective or impotent (like the disciples at the foot of the transfiguration hill), for the simple reason that He was never out of touch with God. He Himself worked the works of Him that sent Him (John 9:4); and His disciples, by faith might enter into enjoyment of the same power. "He that believeth on Me, the works that I do shall he do also." Nay more—"greater works than these shall he do, because I go unto the Father" (John 14:12). Our Lord, therefore, went on to declare, in startling terms, the power faith confers. "Whosoever shall say unto this mountain, Be thou taken up and cast into the sea; and shall not doubt in his heart, but shall believe that what he saith cometh to pass; he shall have it" (v. 23). This figure about "removing mountains" was, the commentators tell us, a favorite figure of speech for things passing ordinary capacity. And a vivid and striking figure it is. For what is so solid and unmovable as the mountains "fixed in their everlasting seats"? And yet "to faith," Jesus says, the task of removing mountains is no impossibility. No task, then, is too mighty for "faith" to accomplish. No difficulty is too stupendous for "faith" to overcome. For faith links a man up to God. It reinforces man with the omnipotent energies of God. "This is the victory that hath overcome the world, even our faith" (1 John 5:4).

A Task for Faith

There are some who hold that when Jesus said, "This mountain" He pointed across the valley to the hill on which the Temple stood, all flashing and gleaming with its marble and gold; that what He meant to suggest was that these twelve disciples of His with a great faith in their hearts could remove "that mountain"; could break down and overthrow the fabric of Judaism; could cast the knowledge of God and the worship of God— supposed hitherto to be confined to that mountain—into the midst of the sea, i.e. could diffuse it amongst all nations. I am doubtful whether the saying is to be interpreted in that specialized way; and yet the diffusion of Christianity, in spite of all efforts to crush and destroy it, is a most striking illustration of its truth. It is one example of the "removing of the mountain." For if any enterprise ever seemed hopeless, it was the enterprise on which the Apostles at the bidding of Christ set out. There was Judaism, on the one hand—stable, as it seemed, as one of the eternal hills. And here were twelve illiterate and humble provincials on the other. Twelve men against a nation, a nation reinforced by adherents in every part of the world. To expect these twelve men to break up the fabric of Judaism seems as absurd as to expect twelve men with pick-axe and shovel to shift Mont Blanc. But, when the time came, they had a mighty faith in their hearts, and the seemingly impossible did not daunt them. Within fifty years there was no Temple on Mount Zion, and Judaism as a sacrificing system was no more. The mountain was cast into the midst of the sea.

Mountains Removed

This triumph of faith assuredly does not stand alone. After Jerusalem, the early disciples found themselves confronted by

Rome, in some respects the mightiest and most colossal fabric of empire the world has ever seen. A handful of Jews on the one side, and mighty Rome on the other.

In the Early Days of the Church

But with faith in their hearts they addressed themselves to the task their Master had assigned them. "I am ready to preach the Gospel to you also that are in Rome" (Rom. 1:15), declares Paul. He was all eagerness to give himself to the task. "Remove!" he cried. And "Remove!" cried his followers and successors. And the mountain began to totter. Rome, that once persecuted and harried and slew the Christians, in time showed signs of yielding, until at last with Julian's baffled and defeated cry, "Thou hast conquered, O Galilean!" you behold the mountain cast into the midst of the sea.

In India

Many another mountain has been removed since those far-off days. When William Carey went out to India to preach Christianity a great many people felt that he might as well try to shift the Himalayas as try to replace Hinduism with Christianity. Sydney Smith (himself a clergyman), in the pages of the *Edinburgh Review*, made fine sport of the foolish enterprise of the "consecrated cobbler," as he dubbed him. William Carey knew the difficulty. He was aware that to make an impression on India was like trying to remove mountains. But he had faith, superb and magnificent faith, and so, weak and lonely as he was, he went out to India, and, confronting the mountain of Hinduism, began to cry, "Be thou removed." Others followed in Carey's wake, and took up the same cry. A little army of missionaries is today saying, "Be thou removed." It is true Hinduism is not yet cast into the sea. But will anyone look at India and say the mountain has not moved? All India has been shaken out of its old allegiance. Its faith in its million gods is dying. The mountain is yielding, crumbling, falling; our successors should see it cast into the midst of the sea.

In the South Seas

When John Williams went out to the South Seas, a lustful and cannibal paganism had those fair islands in its grip. John Williams went from island to island, and faced that paganism—solid and unshakeable as the mountains, so it seemed, because so inextricably intertwined with the entire social life of the people. He faced that paganism in island after island, crying before it, "Be thou removed! Be thou removed!" It seemed a hopeless and impossible enterprise; but look at the result. Islands have been cleansed, civilized, Christianized. The Christian Church has taken the place of the cannibal feast. The mountain has been cast into the midst of the sea.

The day of miracles is not over. "The works that I do shall ye do also," said Jesus, "and greater works than these shall ye do." The power that worked in and through Christ is willing to work in and through us. This is the one condition—have faith in God.

Faithless Prayer

From speaking of faith our Lord proceeds to speak of prayer. The transition is quite a natural one. It is prayer that expresses faith. It is because we believe in God that we pray to Him at all. It is in prayer we open our souls to God's indwelling. But prayer which is not the expression of faith is mere waste of breath. The only effectual prayer is believing prayer—prayer animated and informed by a living faith. "Therefore I say unto you, All things whatsoever ye pray and ask for, believe that ye have received them, and ye shall have them" (v. 24). Believe that ye have received them. Why, we offer many prayers without expecting answers to them—just exactly as members of the Church at Jerusalem offered prayers for the release of Peter, and were frightened almost out of their wits when Rhoda came and told them Peter was actually knocking at the door. We pray for revivals, but we scarcely expect them. We pray for conversions, but we should be surprised if people really did cry, "Men, brethren, what must we do is be saved?" We do not believe that we have the things we ask for. Faith does not animate our prayers, and as a result they fail.

And Its Result

I wonder whether this may in part account for the ineffectiveness of the Church. We still have a good deal of prayer (of a sort), but it is not this expectant, believing prayer. And perhaps it is our lack of faith that accounts for our weakness. Unbelief interferes with our supply of power. You perhaps remember that incident about a Colorado village which Mr. Gordon narrates in his *Quiet Talks on Power*. The rainfall is slight out there, and so some public-spirited citizen made a reservoir away up in the hills, and by means of pipes brought an abundant supply of fresh, sweet water into every house in the town. But one morning, when the housewives turned the taps, there was only a little damp splutter; no water came. The men set out to investigate. They thought something must be the matter with the reservoir. But there was nothing amiss up there; it was full of clear, cold, sparkling water. They examined the pipes as far as they could, but they could find no break. And so it went on for a day or two, until the little village was threatened with a water famine. Then one of the officials got a note which said, "If you will first pull the plug out of the pipe about eight inches from the top you'll get all the water you want." So up the men went again, and dug open the pipe, and found a plug which some mischief-maker had inserted. That plug was keeping the water away from the town. The full reservoir was of no use to the town because of that plug.

Pull Out the Plug

May it not be so with us and the Divine power? There is no failure in God. The reservoir of grace and power is as full as ever it was. And yet somehow or other we are short of power, we lack force, we have no strength. What is the matter? There is a plug in the pipe. There is something that stops the outflow of the Divine energy of grace. And what is that something? Unbelief. We have not a living, utter trust in God. We do not believe that we have the things for which we ask. And before the power will come we must take out the plug. We must do away with unbelief. We are not straitened in God, we are only straitened in ourselves. It is faith, daring and triumphant faith, we want—a living and whole-hearted trust in God. According to our faith it shall be unto us. "Lord, increase our faith."

74
The Authority of Jesus

"And they come again to Jerusalem: and as He was walking in the temple, there come to Him the chief priests, and the scribes, and the elders, and say unto Him, By what authority doest Thou these things? and who gave Thee this authority to do these things? And Jesus answered and said unto them, I will also ask of you one question, and answer Me, and I will tell you by what authority I do these things. The baptism of John, was it from heaven, or of men? answer Me. And they reasoned with themselves, saying, If we shall say, From heaven; He will say, Why then did ye not believe him? But if we shall say, Of men; they feared the people: for all men counted John, that he was a prophet indeed. And they answered and said unto Jesus, We cannot tell. And Jesus answering saith unto them, Neither do I tell you by what authority I do these things." —Mark 11:27-33.

The Lord and the Temple

THE ACTIONS OF Christ during Passion Week had greatly exercised and disturbed the religious authorities; more especially His action in sweeping out of the Temple those who bought and sold within it. They had looked on, almost speechless with anger, while Christ on the Sunday rode in lowly triumph into Jerusalem, attended by applauding crowds. The triumphal entry, however, did not seem to them the best occasion for attacking Jesus, for the events of that day might, with a show of reason, have been set down to the uncontrollable enthusiasm of the people. But for the cleansing of the Temple the entire responsibility lay at Christ's door. He Himself took the initiative. From first to last, the action was His own. And no action our Lord took was more significant. He acted as if He were the Lord of the Temple; as if the Holy Place were His; and as if the right to lay down regulations for its use belonged, not to the priests, its official custodians, but to Himself. To the Jerusalem leaders this assertion of authority must have been peculiarly galling. For it involved the repudiation of their own. It was, in effect, a public declaration that what authority they possessed they had flagrantly and wickedly abused, and here was the Lord of the Temple come to take away from them an authority with which they could not be trusted. High priests and rulers seem to have been too surprised and stupefied to make any protest at the moment. The moral majesty of Christ overawed them, their own consciences made cowards of them. But our Lord's action rankled in their minds. They smarted under a sense of exposure and condemnation. And when our Lord withdrew Himself for the night to Bethany, they met, I imagine, in secret conclave to discuss what they were to do with Him. For quite clearly to allow His action in cleansing the Temple to pass unchallenged was equivalent to abdicating their own position.

The Question of Its Custodians

Here we get the result of their deliberations. You will notice they do not challenge the rightness of the action itself. They knew quite well that for their conduct in allowing the Temple courts to be used for purposes of greed and unholy gain they were absolutely without defense. On that point they allow judgment to go against them by default. What they challenge is not the rightness of the action, but Christ's right to take it. So when our Lord appeared in Jerusalem on the Tuesday morning, as He was walking in the Temple, there came to Him the chief priests and the scribes and the elders; and they said unto Him. "By what authority doest Thou these things? or who gave Thee this authority to do these things?" (v. 28).

A Factious Question

We may take it for granted that the chief priests and scribes did not ask this question because they were in difficulty, and really wanted to know. If that had been their motive, you may depend upon it Christ would have given them a plain and gracious answer. Christ was not the person to tantalize a man honestly perplexed, and to send him away mystified and confounded. The way in which Christ treated these men makes me quite sure that they asked this question out of spite, and rage, and hate, and not because they wanted to know. What they wanted was, to revenge themselves, if they could, for their humiliation of the day before. They asked the question, tempting Him. They hoped it might put Him in a difficulty. Perhaps, as Dr. David Smith says, they hoped to elicit from Him, not merely an assertion of His Messiahship, but some declaration of His oneness with God, like that which on a previous occasion had made the Jews take up stones to stone Him. That was their hope—that Jesus would say something which would inflame the mob, and so enable them to wreak upon Him that vengeance which was denied them so long as the multitude was on His side.

But a Plausible Question

And yet while behind the question there lay a hate which was as cruel as the grave, the question itself was eminently plausible. It was the kind of question which the man in the street would feel the chief priests and elders had a perfect right to ask. For these people were the religious rulers of Judaism. It would therefore appear a perfectly natural thing for them to ask Jesus what His authority was for teaching and preaching. For He held no office, and by men He had never been appointed to His work. It would therefore appear a very natural and reasonable thing for the regularly constituted and recognized authorities to come to Jesus with the question, "By what authority doest Thou these things? or who gave Thee this authority?"

Recognition of Christ's Authority

First of all, notice that even Christ's bitterest foes make confession of His authority. They could not help it. Authority was one of the most striking characteristics of our Lord's manner. That was what struck everybody who either heard or saw Him. Turn to the Sermon on the Mount for one illustration. The dominant impression left upon the minds of the hearers was that of the authoritativeness of the Preacher. There was the note of certitude in all He said. And, more than the note of certitude, there was that regal tone which distinguishes one who knows Himself to be the final court of appeal. This comes out most noticeably in the attitude He takes up toward Moses. You remember how, in the course of that sermon, He passes in review certain precepts and counsels of the Mosaic law. These He undertakes to revise and alter and abrogate on His own *ipse dixit*. "Ye have heard that it hath been said by them of old time," He begins, and then enunciates the Mosaic rule. "But I say unto you," He proceeds, and undertakes on His own authority to set up a new law and standard. He places Himself above Moses. He constitutes Himself the final court of appeal. When He had spoken, the last word has been said. It is not surprising that the people, trained up to regard every letter of the Mosaic law as sacred, were surprised. "The multitude were astonished at His teaching; for He taught them as one having authority, and not as their scribes" (Matt. 7:28, 29).

Authority in Action

The authority which was so marked in His speech was equally noticeable in His actions. He claimed, for instance, the authority to forgive sins; and if an outward miracle is any proof of an inward grace, He not only claimed it but exercised it. He claimed and exercised authority over unclean spirits, so that when He commanded them to come out, they immediately obeyed Him. He claimed and exercised authority over disease and death. And on the preceding day He had claimed and exercised authority over the Temple. The authority was not only claimed, it was exercised, it was acknowledged, it was obeyed. It was no use trying to deny the reality of that authority before which the traders had fled, panic-stricken and demoralized, the day before. These chief priests and elders do not attempt to deny it. They only profess a wish to know what kind of an authority it was, and whence Christ derived it.

Authority Recognized

But what an amazing admission even this confession is! God is continually making the wrath of men to praise Him. From the lips of Christ's critics and foes some of the most wonderful testimonies to His greatness have issued. The officers who were sent to seize Him had to admit that never man spake like He spake. The Herodians who came to tempt Him had to confess that He did not regard the person of men, but taught the way of God in truth. These chief priests and elders are constrained to bear unwilling witness to His unique authority. "Out of the mouths of babes and sucklings Thou hast perfected praise" (Matt. 21:16), said Jesus, as He listened to the shouts of the children who acclaimed Him, as He rode in triumph into Jerusalem. That praise should come out of the mouths of babes and sucklings is wonderful enough. But here is something more wonderful still. "Out of the mouths of enemies and foes hast Thou perfected praise." Enemies and foes are constrained to bear witness to Him. Chief priests and elders bear testimony to His unique and unparalleled authority. This is the kind of witness that stills the enemy and the avenger, and puts to silence the ignorance of foolish men.

The Counter-Inquiry

The suggestion that lay behind the question of the chief priests and scribes was that Christ, being neither priest nor scribe, was an unauthorized and irregular teacher, and had therefore no right to teach. Our Lord meets their question with the suggestion that lay behind it, by asking them another question. "The baptism of John,

was it from heaven, or from men?" (v. 30). Now, first of all, I want
to make it quite clear that this was not an attempt to snatch a
dialectical victory. This was not an attempt to escape from a difficult question by posing His questioners with another. It was, no
doubt, as Dr. David Smith says, "a masterpiece of dialectic." But it
was also, as he adds, very much more. At first you might be tempted to ask, "What has the question of the origin of John's baptism
to do with the question of Christ's authority? " Christ's counter-
question at first sight seems to be hopelessly irrelevant.

Not Irrelevant

It does not appear to have the remotest bearing upon the question originally asked. As a matter of fact, however, it went down
to the very roots of things. It had the most close and vital bearing
upon the question of Christ's own authority. The answer to
Christ's question about John's baptism would supply them with
the answer to their own question about Christ's authority.

John an Unofficial Preacher

For, to begin with, John, like Jesus, was an unauthorized
preacher. That is to say, though the son of a priest, John was himself
never in the priest's office. He owed absolutely nothing to
Jerusalem. Priests and elders had never authorized him to preach.
He had had no sort of "orders" conferred upon him. John
belonged not to the priests, but the prophets. The priest is created
by human appointment; the prophet is made by the direct inspiration of God. Priesthood was a matter of family and succession
and "order"; prophecy was the gift of the Spirit. John preached and
taught, not because of any authority conferred upon him by man,
but because, like Amos, like Jeremiah, like Elijah, like Isaiah, the
word was as a fire in his bones, and he knew himself called of God.
Now all Judea believed that John was a prophet. The people felt
that through him God spoke to their souls. Even priests and scribes
and elders had been moved and impressed by John. They had felt
the Divine power working through him. "Ye were willing to rejoice
for a season in his light" (John 5:35), Jesus had said of them, on an
earlier occasion. They knew that John was a teacher sent from God;
they knew that his baptism was from heaven. But then to admit
that about John, was to give away their case against Jesus; for John,
like Jesus, was an unauthorized teacher; and to admit that John was
sent of God, was to admit also in the case of Jesus that, though
Jerusalem was ignorant of Him, and the priests acknowledged Him
not, His authority too might be derived from heaven.

John's Witness to Christ

In the second place, John himself had witnessed to Christ's Messiahship. He had borne repeated and emphatic witness to it. It was he who said, "Behold, the Lamb of God, who taketh away the sin of the world!" It was he who said, "This is He of whom I said, After me cometh a man which is become before me. . . . And I have seen, and have borne witness that this is the Son of God" (John 1:29, 34). If they admitted that John's baptism was from heaven—as they knew it was, though through their pride and hardness of heart they had rejected John's call, and refused to submit themselves to the baptism of repentance—then Christ would naturally retort upon them, "Why, then, did ye not believe him, and especially in regard to John's witness to Myself?" Believing John, they ought to have passed as naturally into the ranks of Christ's disciples, as did Andrew and John.

The Dilemma

This, then, was the question Jesus propounded to the so-called leaders of religion in Palestine, "The baptism of John, was it from heaven, or from men?" It put our Lord's questioners on the horns of a dilemma. If they should give the true answer, and say, "From heaven," it was giving their whole case against Christ away; it was more, it was laying themselves open to the charge of perverse and obstinate unbelief. On the other hand, if they took refuge in the obviously false answer, "From men," they feared the people. It was a risky thing to deny John's divine commission, "for all verily held John to be a prophet" (v. 32). For a minute or two they hesitated, embarrassed, and not knowing what to say. "Answer Me," insisted Jesus. And then they blurted out the helpless and feeble confession, "We know not." They confessed themselves, that is to say, incapable of telling whether John was a charlatan or not; they confessed themselves incapable of distinguishing between a genuine and a sham religious movement. They confessed that in these high spiritual matters they could not judge. And by that miserable confession they put themselves clean out of court. They had come to Jesus proposing to adjudicate about His claims. But who were they, to be able to decide upon the claims of Jesus, when they confessed themselves incapable of deciding upon the work of John? These things are spiritually discerned, and they had pronounced themselves spiritual incapables, blind leaders of the blind. "Neither tell I you," was our Lord's rejoinder, "by what authority I do these things" (v. 33).

The Nature and Source of Christ's Authority

Now let us turn our attention to the subject of Christ's authority, and consider the nature and the origin of it. "By what authority doest Thou these things? Or who gave Thee this authority to do these things?" There is a twofold inquiry in this question. There is an inquiry as to the kind of the authority, and as to its source.

It Was Moral and Spiritual

First, then—as to the kind of authority—it was moral and spiritual, not official. Christ filled no office. He was neither priest nor Levite, nor elder nor scribe. And yet He spoke with an authority they could never hope to equal. The scribes had all the advantages of official status, but they wielded no power. Jesus came, a peasant from Nazareth, without any badge of office, and He exercised resistless power. It was moral authority. It was spiritual power. It was the authority of a holy character. Christ not only preached the truth, He was it. He was incarnate holiness. And men instinctively bowed to the authority of a perfectly pure and holy life. It was the authority of knowledge. Men instinctively recognize whether a man is or is not speaking of things he knows; whether it is an authentic word or a second-hand message they are listening to. The scribes dealt in traditions. All their speech was second-hand. Jesus spoke with the sure accents of one in direct touch with eternal realities. He spoke that which He knew, and testified that which He had seen. And the result was, He was invested with an authority which all men recognized, and before which all men of honest and good heart instinctively bowed.

Its Source Was the Father

In the second place—as to the source of the authority—Jesus derived His right to speak and act as He did from God. It was His Father Who had commissioned Him. It was the Father's works He did. It was from His Father He had received His commandments. Priests and elders thought that they were the source of preaching and teaching authority. They claimed that no one had the right to teach or speak unless he had received his "orders" from them. Jesus had asked for no authorization from them. He had never been humanly "ordained" to this work. From the priestly point of view, He was not in "orders." He was a mere layman. But Christ had no need of commission from priests and elders. He derived His authority from a higher source. He was commissioned by the Most High. His right to preach and teach was, that the Father had sent Him.

Moral Authority Dependent on Character

Two permanent lessons this story has to teach— lessons of vital importance to us still. This is the first. There is no moral authority without character. "As the man is, so is his strength." Office in itself will never confer moral authority. The sons of Eli had office. But they had not character. What was their influence? Nothing; worse than nothing. Because of them men abhorred the offering of the Lord. If we want to wield power for God, we must first of all be ourselves men of God. To do good we must *be* good. Without character, though we have all official guarantees, we are no better than sounding-brass or a tinkling cymbal.

God the Authority for the Ministerial Office

The second lesson is this—the ultimate source of authority to teach and preach is God. No man is ordained unless he is ordained of God. Nobody is really "in orders" unless he is placed in them by God. All that men can do is to ratify God's ordaining. No man, called of God, needs human authority to speak for Him. I have no word to say by way of disparagement of human ordination; I have been ordained myself. I have myself been set aside by the laying on of the hands of the presbytery. I believe that ordination tends to orderliness in the Church. And yet I would never forget that the real authority to preach comes from a higher source—it comes from God. And He can and does give it to men on whom no human hands have ever been laid. The Spirit bloweth still where He listeth, and the man dowered with the Spirit is the man ordained of God.

75
The Wicked Husbandmen

"And He began to speak unto them by parables. A certain man planted a vineyard, and set an hedge about it, and digged a place for the winefat, and built a tower, and let it out to husbandmen, and went into a far country. And at the season he sent to the husbandmen a servant, that he might receive from the husbandmen of the fruit of the vineyard. And they caught him, and beat him, and sent him away empty. And again he sent unto them another servant; and at him they cast stones, and wounded him in the head, and sent him away shamefully handled. And again he sent another; and him they killed, and many others; beating some, and killing some. Having yet therefore one son, his well beloved, he sent him also last unto them, saying, They will reverence my son. But those husbandmen said among themselves, This is the heir; come, let us kill him, and the inheritance shall be ours. And they took him, and killed him, and cast him out of the vineyard. What shall therefore the lord of the vineyard do? he will come and destroy the husbandmen, and will give the vineyard unto others. And have ye not read this scripture: The stone which the builders rejected is become the head of the corner; This was the Lord's doing, and it is marvellous in our eyes? And they sought to lay hold on Him, but feared the people: for they knew that He had spoken the parable against them: and they left Him, and went their way."

—Mark 12:1-12.

THIS PARABLE, THE parable of the wicked husbandmen, as we call it, is, on the whole, perhaps the saddest and sternest that ever fell from the lips of Christ. Dr. A. B. Bruce classifies it as a parable of judgment. And such undoubtedly it is. And the judgment appears the more severe and stern because judgment is Christ's strange work; and the doom pronounced appears the more awful, because it falls from the lips of Him Who said of Himself that He had not come into the world to judge the world, but that the world through Him should be saved. Before I begin to discuss this poignant and heart-breaking parable, let me put it in its right context.

The Two Sons
After their humiliating experience in the discussion about authority, the priests and the elders would very gladly have with-

drawn quietly away. But Jesus did not permit them to do that. He carried the war into the enemy's camp. They had come to challenge Christ's authority. He was not content to expose their spiritual incompetence. By means of the parable of the Two Sons, He roundly charged them with the sin of insincerity. They were like the elder son in that parable, who, when his father bade him go and work in the vineyard, replied, "I go, sir," and went not. Theirs was all profession, without practice. They made a great parade of their reverence for God, and did not obey Him. And so it would come to pass, Jesus said, that the publicans and harlots would go into the Kingdom of God before them. For while by their wild and reckless life the publicans and harlots had seemed to refuse obedience to God, like the younger son, who, when his father bade him go and work, said, "I go not"; yet at the call of John these people had repented of their sin, and returned to God, like the younger son, who afterwards repented and went. This parable Jesus seems to have spoken directly to the priests and elders, and it bit deep; for they themselves must have known how true it was that while they worshipped God with their lips, their hearts were far from Him.

The Wicked Husbandmen

But even after uttering the parable of the Two Sons, Christ had not done with these unhappy priests and scribes. Turning away from them, He addressed Himself to the crowd that was standing round, and spoke to them this parable of the Wicked Husbandmen. After having spoken to them, He proceeded to speak about them to the crowd. In the parable of the Two Sons He had charged the priests and elders directly with the sin of insincerity. In this parable He speaks to the multitude of the doom that is sure to fall upon these men who professed religion, and did not practice it; upon these religious leaders who were not religious themselves; upon these so-called religious guides who had rejected and persecuted and slain every servant God had sent to them. Their high place was to be forfeited; all their privileges were to be taken away. They were to fall under the holy wrath of God. "He will come and destroy the husbandmen, and will give the vineyard unto others" (v. 9). And the priests and elders recognized the point of the story. They needed no labored explanations. It carried its terrible meaning on its face. It was of their faithlessness, and their wickedness, and their rejection and doom Christ had spoken. And if the parable of the Two Sons bit deep, this pierced them to the very heart. In their rage and hate, they would have murdered

Christ on the spot, had they dared. "And they sought to lay hold on Him; and they feared the multitude; for they perceived that He spake the parable against them" (v. 12).

The Judgment of Faithlessness

Now let me turn to the parable itself. It is, primarily, as I have already said, a parable of judgment; and it is from that point of view I want in the first place to look at it. The broad drift of the meaning of the parable is sufficiently evident. It was still more evident to those who first listened to it. For in a sense this was not a new parable to the Jews; it was an old and familiar parable. Long before, Isaiah (Isa. 5) had pictured Israel as a vineyard, and had sung a song of what God had done for it—how He made a trench about it, and gathered out the stones thereof and planted it with the choicest vine, and built a tower in the midst of it, and also hewed out a winepress therein. But Israel disappointed God, for when He looked that it should bring forth grapes, behold, it brought forth wild grapes. That allegory of Isaiah was familiar enough to every Jewish mind; and what Jesus does here, is to take that old and familiar allegory, and adapt it to His own special purpose. As soon as the first sentence about the man planting a vineyard fell from His lips, His listeners knew it was of Israel, i.e. of themselves, Christ was speaking.

The Story and Its Application

Now in interpreting the parables we must not try to find a specific spiritual equivalent for every little detail in the picture. If we begin to puzzle over what the hedge means, and what the wine press means, and indeed, what exactly the vineyard means, we shall become hopelessly mystified and confused. The analogy between the earthly story and the spiritual truth it is meant to teach, is an analogy in broad outline, and does not extend to minute particulars. Let me in such broad outline set forth the truth this tragic story is meant to teach. The owner of the vineyard in this case is God. The husbandmen to whom He let it out are the Jews, and especially the Jewish leaders—the elders and chief priests and scribes about whom we read in the preceding paragraph. The vineyard itself is not quite so easy satisfactorily to interpret. Some say that it stands for the Church; others that it stands for the Kingdom of God. Let us be content to think that the "vineyard" stands for those unique religious privileges and opportunities God bestowed upon Israel. God did for Israel what He did not for any other nation. He made them the recipients of a unique revelation. He made them the depositaries of the true faith. And He did everything that could be done to secure that Israel should keep the deposit, and preserve and diffuse the revelation. But Israel was false to its trust. Again and again the people turned apostate. Instead of keeping and spreading the true faith, Israel again and again forsook the Lord, and turned after strange gods. Israel was indeed a vineyard from which God did not receive the expected fruit.

The Servants and the Husbandmen

Again and again He sent His servants to this perverse and rebellious people. Prophet after prophet summoned them back to the service of God. But there was scarcely a prophet whom they did not repudiate and persecute. The description in this parable is literally true. Some they beat, and some they wounded in the head, and handled shamefully, and so with many others, beating some, and killing some. Elijah, Micaiah, Isaiah, Jeremiah, John the Baptist—they had all suffered. They pleaded and reasoned with Israel in vain. Rejection had been their invariable lot. And the climax of Israel's rebellion and persistent faithlessness came in their treatment of Jesus.

The Mission of the Son

When His servants all failed, God sent His only Son. "They will reverence my Son," He said. But when these wicked husbandmen saw the Son they said, "This is the heir; come, let us kill Him" (v. 7). That is to say, Jesus prophesies that as they had treated the prophets, so they would treat the Son. And it all came true. Before the week was out the Jews, incited by their leaders, had nailed the Son Himself to the bitter tree!

Neglected Opportunities and Divine Sentence

That was the history of Israel—a history of opportunities neglected, privileges abused, a great trust betrayed. God got no fruit from this vineyard He had so carefully planted and so jealously guarded. All the labors of prophets and Psalmists had been in vain. Far from spreading the faith, Israel had not even kept it. Far from extending the Kingdom, Israel itself had been rebellious. "What therefore will the lord of the vineyard do?" asked Jesus (v. 9). And the people gave back the answer, "Miserable men! He will come and destroy these husbandmen, and will give the vineyard unto others" (Luke 10:15, 16). And although, according to Luke's account, the priests and rulers broke in with a passionate "God forbid!" Jesus accepts the people's verdict. That is exactly the fate that shall overtake faithless Israel. The vineyard shall be taken away from them. They shall lose their high place. They shall cease to be God's chosen instruments. He will entrust the cause of the Kingdom to other hands.

The Sentence Executed

It all came true. Faithless Israel was destroyed. Forty years after this parable was spoken the nation was shattered, crushed, and broken. Religiously, Israel ceased to count. God put the care of His Kingdom into other hands. Like His Apostles, He turned to the Gentiles. He let out the vineyard to others, who were aliens from the commonwealth of Israel, and strangers to the covenants of promise. And from them has God's fruit been found.

Privileges and Responsibility

That is the story, a story of tragic import to the Jews who heard it, and full of the most solemn warning to us as well. I can scarcely do more than point out some of its most obvious lessons. Notice, first of all, how the parable insists upon it that privilege carries with it responsibility. If God lets out a vineyard, He expects fruit. That is to say, gifts and privileges are all for service and use. God expects a return for them. As Dr. Glover says, "We have a rent to pay for every privilege." It does not matter what the privilege may be. One man's gift may be wealth, and another's may be learning, and another's may be leisure. It matters not; God expects wealth, learning and leisure to be used for His glory, for the good of men. And especially is this the case in respect of religious privileges. They are given for use. God expects rent for them. And the rent He expects is their employment for the benefit of others. "Necessity is laid upon me, and woe is me if I preach not the Gospel," that is the rent. We have been signally favored in regard to religious privileges. Is God getting the rent He expects? Are we diffusing the light? Are we spreading the kingdom? Is God's cause profiting by us? Does the Lord get His fruit?

The Progression of Sin

Then notice, secondly, what an illustration we get here of the progression of sin. These husbandmen begin by beating a servant, they end by killing the Son. They began by being merely perverse and willful, they ended by being wicked and devilish. That is one of the terrible characteristics of sin. Evil grows. "Is thy servant a dog?" (2 Kings 8:13), said Hazael, when the prophet foretold some awful enormity that would be perpetrated by him. He was indignant at the bare suggestion. And yet he did all the atrocious things predicted. Sin dulls the sensibilities, and sears the conscience, and so gradually the sinner becomes capable of crimes from which in his more innocent days he would have shrunk in horror. Thus it came about that Jerusalem, which began by rejecting the messages of the prophets, ended by crucifying Christ between two thieves.

The End of Faithfulness—Deprivation

But, of course, the central lesson of all is this, that faithlessness is punished by deprivation. It is so all through life. Any possession, any power, any gift that is not put to use, is taken away. Atrophy is one of Nature's tragic truths. The condition of the retention of any faculty is its employment. And it is so especially with religious place and privilege. If we lose our first love, and cease to do our first works, the result will be that our candlestick will be removed out of its place. Many candlesticks have been removed. Many transferences of privilege have taken place. The Jew was rejected, and the Gentile put in his place. Early in the story of Christianity, the Eastern Church lost its pride of place, and the Western Church led in its stead. In the sixteenth century the Roman Church failed to shake itself free of its superstitious falsities, and so the leadership fell to the Churches of the Reformation. God has raised us, as a people, high amongst the nations. He has conferred upon us signal honor and privilege. But let us remember that a Britain that ceases to be faithful may be thrust from her high place, and her glory may be given to another. We hold our place only on condition that we bring forth fruit. A faithless Britain may be a cast-away Britain. God may give the vineyard to others. We may become as Nineveh and Tyre. There is need to pray, "Lord God of Hosts, be with us yet, lest we forget, lest we forget!"

The Divine Patience

But this parable is not simply a parable of judgment upon human faithlessness. It is also a parable of the Divine patience, and of the unique and unshared glory of Christ. It is a parable of the Divine patience. Dr. A. B. Bruce says that no landlord would ever have acted as this landlord did. The whole story has an air of improbability, not to say impossibility. An ordinary landlord would very speedily have evicted these troublesome and rebellious tenants. Quite so. Jesus had to tell an improbable, almost an impossible, story if He was to convey any notion of the patience and long-suffering of God. For God's patience does pass all the limits possible to us men. As Faber puts it, "His fondness goes far out beyond our dreams." Indeed, in its primary application, this parable is not a parable at all, it is simple, matter-of-fact history. This is how God treated Israel. He sent to them servant after servant, prophet after prophet. And though Israel turned a deaf ear to the appeals of God's prophets, from Amos to John the Baptist, even then God's patience was not exhausted. He had yet one, a beloved Son; He sent Him last unto them, saying, "They will reverence My Son!" What marvellous and subduing patience this is!

A Patience That Still Lasts

And all this is true of the patience of God still. That is the chief characteristic of the love of God—it lasts! It outlasts. "How often shall my brother sin against me, and I forgive him?" asked Peter one day; "until seven times?" And I have no doubt that in suggesting seven times he thought he was making a most generous offer. "I say not unto thee, Until seven times," said Jesus, "but, Until seventy times seven" (Matt. 18:21, 22). Seventy times seven, that is the way in which the Divine love forgives. That is the way in which the Divine love pleads and entreats. It does not depart at the first rebuff. It returns until seventy times seven. "Behold, I stand at the door and knock," says the Lord. Or, as the Greek verb might be translated, "I have been standing a long time, and am standing still" (Rev. 3:20). It is not once He knocks. He continues to stand, and continues to knock, until seventy times seven. If there had been no second chance, if the Lord had left us at the first rebuff, it would have gone hard with some of us. But the long-suffering of the Lord, as Peter says, is salvation. We may have rejected His offers again and again and again, but our rejection will not be cast up against us.

> "If I ask Him to receive me,
> Will He say me nay?
> Not till earth, and not till heaven,
> Pass away."

The Unshared Glory of Christ

Again, this is a parable not only of the judgment of faithlessness and the Divine patience, but also a parable of the unshared glory of Christ. Here He tells the people what was the ground of His authority to cleanse the Temple, to forgive sins, to abrogate the law of Moses. It comes out in verse 6. "He had yet one, a beloved Son;

He sent Him last unto them, saying, They will reverence My Son."
Now in that verse Christ is speaking of Himself. He is the Son
whom the Lord of the vineyard sent as His last hope. "The verse
is of immense significance," Dr. Bruce says, "for the self-consciousness of Jesus." And its significance consists in this. Jesus is
here drawing a distinction between Himself and the prophets,
between Himself and Isaiah and Jeremiah and Elijah and Moses.
What were they? Servants. What was He? A Son.

The Glory of the Son

He places Himself in a category quite apart from the greatest
and noblest of men. Even Moses was but a slave in God's house.
Jesus was a Son over it. That was Christ's answer to the question,
"By what authority doest Thou these things? or who gave Thee
this authority to do these things?" His right to do these things was
that He was God's only and beloved Son. His authority roots itself
in His personality.

His Claim to Obedience

That is where Christ's authority roots itself still. Christ is the
Master-light of all our seeing. He is the Lord of our consciences.
His veriest word is law. That is too vast and august an authority to
entrust to the best and noblest of men. The only justification for it
is that Christ is more than man, that He is God's beloved Son, that
He is God Himself incarnate in the flesh, and by word and deed
declaring His holy will concerning us. That is just what He was. A
greater than the greatest of the prophets—God's beloved Son. To
God's Son we cannot render homage too complete, or obedience
too explicit. He has a right to His unquestioned authority. It was
God Himself Who, speaking of Jesus, said to the three disciples on
the holy mount, and through them to all men and women for all
time, "This is My beloved Son; hear Him." Do we hear Him? And
obey Him? and bow to His authority? "Blessed are all they that put
their trust in Him."

76

The Tribute Money

"And they send unto Him certain of the Pharisees and of the Herodians, to catch Him in His words. And when they were come, they say unto Him, Master, we know that Thou art true, and carest for no man: for Thou regardest not the person of men, but teachest the way of God in truth: Is it lawful to give tribute to Caesar, or not? Shall we give, or shall we not give? But He, knowing their hypocrisy, said unto them, Why tempt ye Me? bring Me a penny, that I may see it. And they brought it. And He saith unto them, Whose is this image and superscription? And they said unto Him, Caesar's. And Jesus answering said unto them, Render to Caesar the things that are Caesar's, and to God the things that are God's. And they marvelled at Him."
—Mark 12:13-17.

The Enquirers

"AND THEY," i.e. the chief priests and elders, "send unto Him certain of the Pharisees and of the Herodians" (v. 15). The young men who actually submitted the question about tribute to Jesus were not the originators and instigators of this plot. They were only the instruments and tools. Behind the actual questioners, in the background I see the sinister figures of Caiaphas and Annas, the high priests. Their own humiliating defeat in their debate with Christ about authority had only intensified their malice and rage, and hardened their resolve to catch Christ, if possible, in His talk. So this chapter tells us of a series of difficult questions which were submitted to Christ, and the plotters who concocted them all were the chief priests and the elders. To ask this question about tribute they choose certain young disciples of the Pharisees, and along with them certain young men of the Herodian party.

Why Chosen

Their choice of young men was cunningly made. Their very youth, they argued, would give to the deputation an air of guilelessness and sincerity, and so would help to throw Jesus off His guard, and induce Him to speak with dangerous freedom. And the combination too of Pharisees and Herodians was a clever move. For as a rule Pharisees and Herodians were at daggers drawn. They stood for different ideals. The Pharisees were the patriotic party, who held that the Jews were God's chosen people, meant not simply for independence, but for supremacy; who accordingly felt the Roman yoke to be a constant and almost unbearable irritation. The Herodians, on the other hand, were the courtly party, attached primarily to the Herodian dynasty, but through them to the Roman empire, to whose favor the Herods owed their thrones. The Pharisees were the irreconcilable opponents of Rome. The Herodians, as Dr. Salmond says, accepted Roman rule, and profited by it. They sent these young Pharisees and these Herodians to Jesus. They thought it would look as if these eager young rabbis had been debating the question with the Herodians, and that in their failure to agree they had decided to submit the matter to Christ, and to appeal to Him as arbitrator.

The Manner of Their Enquiry

That is exactly the attitude the deputation assume in their approach. There is all the difference in the world between the manner of this deputation and the manner of the chief priests and elders when they came to Christ with their question about authorities. The chief priests and elders talked down to Christ; they put Him in the dock, so to speak; ordered Him to defend Himself, and undertook themselves to adjudicate on His claims. These young Pharisees and Herodians talk up to Christ, they treat Him as the Master, and salute Him as the Authority Whose word on the subject of debate will settle the quarrel.

Allied Powers of Evil

"Master," they say, "we know that Thou art true, and carest not for anyone; for Thou regardest not the person of men, but of a truth teachest the way of God. Is it lawful to give tribute unto Caesar, or not? Shall we give, or shall we not give?" (vv. 14, 15). First of all let us notice what an unholy alliance there is here. As I have already said, as a rule Pharisees and Herodians were at daggers drawn. They stood for different national ideals. They were as far apart, shall I say? as the Clerical and the Free-thinker in France. But they hated Jesus more than they hated each other. And in their deeper hate of Him they forgot for the moment their mutual animosities, and became allies and friends. All the varied interest of hypocrisy and sin combine and unite to persecute Jesus. That is a suggestive little sentence in the Gospels—"And Herod and Pilate became friends with each other that very day" (Luke 22:12). What day was that? The day when between them they allowed Jesus to be done to death. And many a Pilate and a Herod, at enmity amongst themselves, become friends when it is a case of opposing and persecuting Jesus. Mr. Malice, and Mr. No Good, and Mr. Love Lust and Mr. Heady, these brave citizens of Vanity Fair, had no doubt their own private quarrels; but they acted as one man when it came to dealing with Christian and Faithful, who had dared to despise and denounce their fair. A common hate unites all evil principalities and powers against the Lord.

And Their Defeat

Yet these evil alliances are all in vain. As easily as our Lord overthrew these Pharisees and Herodians, with their cunningly concocted question, so easily does He overthrow and break down all evil combinations against Him, to this day. "The Kings of the earth set themselves, and the rulers take counsel together, against the Lord, and against His Anointed. . . . He that sitteth in the heavens shall laugh: the Lord shall have them in derision" (Psalm 2:2, 4). All unholy alliances against Christ, however formidable they may appear, are doomed to defeat. "He that falleth upon this stone shall be broken to pieces; but on whomsoever it shall fall, it will scatter him as dust" (Matt. 22:44).

Their Testimony to Jesus

But what a magnificent testimony these Pharisees and Herodians bear to Jesus! Look at it. "Master," they say, "we know that Thou art true." True, that is, as Dr. Morison says, ingenuous, honest, transparent; or, as the Twentieth Century New Testament translates it, "we know that Thou art an honest man"; "and carest not for anyone," that is, absolutely frank and fearless; Jesus was one who would not trim or whittle away the truth out of fear of the great and mighty; "for Thou regardest not the person of man," or, as the Greek might literally be translated, "Thou lookest not into the face of man"; in which phrase, says Dr. Morison again, there is a hint of the law-courts. Justice is always represented as blindfold. Who the parties to a suit are, makes no difference to Justice. She never looks upon the faces of the suitors at her bar. But the venal judges of the East were often in the habit of looking into the faces of their suitors; partiality often took the place of justice, and the stronger suitor was favored at the expense of the weaker. But Jesus never, in this sense, looked into any man's face, He was inexorably and perfectly just, completely and entirely impartial.

"Thou payest no regard to a man's position, but teachest the Way of God in truth." It was the "way of God," and not any mere human philosophy that Jesus taught. His word carried upon it the impress of its own Divineness.

Not Flattery but Truth

Now look at all that these Pharisees and Herodians attribute to Christ: honesty, fearlessness, perfect impartiality, a unique knowledge of the way of God. Of course it may be held that all this was said by way of flattery. Granted readily. But even flattery, if it is not to defeat itself, must proceed on a basis of truth. Flattery consists in the exaggeration of good qualities already existing. If a man attributes to another qualities he does not possess, the man is not flattered, he is insulted. He feels that the other is making a fool of him. Granted, then, that these men were intent on flattering Jesus, and that their reverence was feigned, it nevertheless remains true that they were only able to attribute these various qualities to Jesus because He verily possessed them. The eulogium was well founded, though the motive that prompted them to make it was as false as could be. This then is the involuntary tribute His bitter foes were constrained to pay to Christ. God makes the very wrath of men to praise Him, the Old Book says (Psalm 76:10), and from the lips of His adversaries and foes some of the noblest testimonies to Christ have come.

The Many Hostile Witnesses

It seems to me that if I had nothing but the witness of Christ's enemies to go upon, I should be constrained to believe He was more than man. "Never man spake like this man" (John 7:46), said the officers who had been sent to seize Him. "I find no fault in Him" (John 19:6), said Pilate. "He saved others, Himself He cannot save" (Matt. 27:42), said mocking priests at the foot of the cross. "Certainly this was the Son of God" (Luke 23:47), said the centurion who had charge of the execution. Unwilling testimony to His unique and unshared greatness is wrung from the lips of men who would gladly have discovered some fleck or flaw in Him. And it is so still, the very men who criticize Christ are constrained to glorify Him. Sceptical men like John Stuart Mill can think of no better rule for life than so to live that Christ would approve the life. Strauss says, "It will never be possible to rise above Him, or to imagine anyone who should even be equal to Him." Renan declares that between Him and God there is no distinction. Now who was this man, about whom His very critics and foes bear testimony that He was unlike every other man the world has ever seen—that He was greater, wiser, holier than any man the world has ever seen? People talk sometimes about the difficulty of believing that Jesus was the Son of God. My difficulty is in believing anything else. "I say, the acknowledgment of God in Christ," wrote Browning, "accepted by the reason, solves for thee all questions in the earth, and out of it."

The Attempted Dilemma

Now let me continue the story. It was not because of any genuine difficulty about the matter that these Pharisees and Herodians brought this question about tribute-money to Jesus. Their question was designed as a trick, a plot, a snare. They thought that it would put the Lord on the horns of a dilemma, and that, whichever way He replied, He was bound to deliver Himself into their hands. For if He answered in the Herodian sense, and said, "Yes, it is lawful to pay tribute," the Pharisees would have at once denounced Him as a traitor to His race, and His popularity would have been destroyed on the instant. On the other hand, if He had taken the side of the Pharisees, and said, "No, it is not lawful to pay tribute," the Herodians would have at once denounced Him to Pilate as being guilty of the crime of high treason. Whichever way the Lord answered the question, He seemed bound to come into collision either with the people or with Pilate.

The Dilemma Met

But it is an ill business trying to lay plots for the Lord. He was not deceived by the plausibility of their question, nor by the flattery of their address. He saw into the wicked and murderous intent behind it all. He read the hearts of these men like an open book. "Why tempt ye me!" He said. And then He cried, "Bring me a denarius, that I may see it." Tribute was paid, not in the Jewish money used for Temple purposes, but in the Roman silver coinage. When a denarius had been handed to Jesus He asked, "Whose is this image and superscription?" He held up to their view the coin, bearing on one of its sides a medallion of the emperor, and on the other the name of the emperor and his title of Pontifex Maximus. They said unto Him, "Caesar's." And by their answer they had replied to their own question. For it was an accepted principle that when any king's coinage was current, that king's sovereignty was recognized. Their own Rabbis had laid down that law for them. "Render unto Caesar," said Jesus, "the things that are Caesar's."

The Snare Avoided

But that scarcely brings out the exact force of the Greek. The question the Pharisees and Herodians had asked was, "Shall we give?" Jesus' reply is, "Give back, pay unto Caesar the things that are Caesar's." By accepting the advantages of Caesar's rule, they had also consented to its obligations. They had traded as Roman subjects; they must pay the Roman tribute. The payment of tribute had become a matter of obligation and debt. "Pay back," He said, and perhaps there was a touch of scorn in His voice as He said it, "to Caesar the things that are Caesar's," and He added, "and to God the things that are God's." He had answered their question; and yet He had avoided their snare. Yes, and He had done more. He had laid down a profound and permanent principle. "And they marvelled greatly at Him," says Mark (v. 17). The word is an exceptionally strong one—"they were utterly amazed at Him"— not simply at the ease with which He foiled their plot, but with the wisdom of His answer. And who knows but that some of these men may have been constrained to ask in wonder, "Who is this?" and, though they went to ensnare and catch Him, may have stayed to worship and adore Him?

Duties to the State

Now, as I said just a moment ago, this answer of our Lord's is far more than a happy way of escape out of what looked like an inextricable difficulty, it is a satisfying answer; it lays down great principles which avail for guidance in every similar difficulty. Primarily, the topic in debate was the duty men owe to civil government. The Pharisees thought that they were by their loyalty to God forbidden to pay tribute to Caesar. In other words, they felt that religion interfered with their civil obedience. The principle Christ lays down here is that those who accept the privileges of the State must discharge the just demands of the State. Christ was no Anarchist. He recognized the necessity and utility of rulers and governments. There was a certain sphere of human life within which they had a right to the exercise of authority. The Apostle was only interpreting Christ's mind when He said, "The powers that be are ordained of God " (Rom. 13:1).

Our Obedience to the State

Everyone who accepts the advantages of the rule of the State is bound to discharge his just obligations to the State; that is the principle here laid down. Take our own case. Our citizenship confers upon us great privileges. The State, for instance, cares for our safety. By means of its armies and its fleet it has warded off from us the dangers of foreign attack. By means of its system of law it safeguards our persons and property. And, in order to be able to do all this, the State makes certain demands upon us in the way of taxes. Now what our Lord here says is that no man has a right to receive the advantages of membership in this State unless he is willing to discharge his duties to the State. It is the same when you come to the narrower sphere of municipal life. Every well-ordered municipality does a multitude of things for our comfort and well-being. It makes and keeps our roads; it lights our streets; it looks after the health of our town; it maintains a staff of police for our protection. Now if we accept the benefit of all this, we must pay for it. If we enjoy the benefits of the municipality, we must discharge our duties to the municipality. In other words, the demand-notes of the Income Tax commissioner and of the rate-collector have a certain Divine authority behind them. People are all too apt to think that if they can cheat the State or the municipality, there is not much harm in it. As a matter of fact, what Jesus teaches here is, that the payment of our rates and taxes is a religious duty. "Render unto Caesar the things that are Caesar's."

With Its Limitation

And yet the obedience which Jesus here commands us to render is not unlimited. The State has its own province, and within that province it has a right to obedience. But there is a province in which the king's writ and the corporation's demand note do not run. "Render unto Caesar the things that are Caesar's, and unto God the things that are God's." The Pharisees were right in thinking that when the State made demands which clashed with their sense of what was due to God, it might be their duty to disobey the State. But that point had not been reached by this demand for tribute. There the State was well within its rights. But there was this limitation upon State right and the obedience of subject; it was all subject to consideration for the rights of God. "We must obey God rather than men," said Peter to the Sanhedrin (Acts 5:29). In seeking to interfere with their convictions and stifle their witness, the authorities had travelled beyond their province. Scores and hundreds of Christians refused to sacrifice incense to the emperor in the early days; they disobeyed the command of the State, preferring to be loyal to God, even though it cost them their lives. Scores of people in England refused to turn back to Rome at the bidding of Queen Mary; they disobeyed the command of the State, preferring to be loyal to God, even though it meant dying in the flames of Smithfield. The duty of obedience to the State is not unlimited. It is subject always to our obedience to God. "My authority ends," said Napoleon in a wise and weighty sentence, "where the authority of conscience begins." That is why, when the State travels beyond its province, it may be resisted and disobeyed.

Our Debt to God

But after all the emphasis of our Lord's saying is not on the negative limitation, but upon the positive duty. These Pharisees, in their excitement about this tribute money, were forgetting the weightier matter of the Law. They would no doubt have defended their objection to Rome, on the ground of their allegiance to God. "And to God the things that are God's," said Jesus to them. All this fret and fume about the Roman tax was not what God really wanted. Their debt to God was far other than they conceived. "What did God want?" "Son," that is the Divine answer, "give Me thine heart." All this fuss about the independence of Israel did not compensate God for the refusal of the heart. "Give back pay to God the things that are God's." For this also is but the discharge of a debt. God has put His image and superscription upon the heart of man, and we are defrauding God of His due if we do not give Him a consecrated and devoted heart.

A Question for Ourselves

Have we given God His due? Have we given to God the things that are God's? Have we given our hearts to Him? We shall give every one else his due, if first of all we give God His. But the mischief of it is, so many of us fail just here. We give God's things to Caesar. We give our hearts to money and pleasure and social position, and so God never gets His own from us. "Seek ye first the Kingdom of God and His righteousness," then everything else will be added unto us; everything else will fall into its proper place; everything else will receive its legitimate due. We shall know exactly what to give Caesar when we have honestly given to God the things that are God's. Life will be balanced, proportionate, orderly and fair, when we are ready to say to God—

> "Take my heart, my lord, I pour
> At Thy feet its treasure store.
> Take myself, and I will be,
> Ever, only, all for Thee."

77
The Life of the World to Come

"Then come unto Him the Sadducees, which say there is no resurrection; and they asked Him, saying, Master, Moses wrote unto us, If a man's brother die, and leave his wife behind him, and leave no children, that his brother should take his wife, and raise up seed unto his brother. Now there were seven brethren: and the first took a wife, and dying left no seed. And the second took her, and died, neither left he any seed: and the third likewise. And the seven had her, and left no seed: last of all the woman died also. In the resurrection therefore, when they shall rise, whose wife shall she be of them? for the seven had her to wife. And Jesus answering said unto them, Do ye not therefore err, because ye know not the scriptures, neither the power of God? For when they shall rise from the dead, they neither marry, nor are given in marriage; but are as the angels which are in heaven. And as touching the dead, that they rise: have ye not read in the book of Moses, how in the bush God spake unto him, saying, I am the God of Abraham, and the God of Isaac, and the God of Jacob? He is not the God of the dead, but the God of the living: ye therefore do greatly err." —Mark 12:18-27."

More Questions

WHENEVER I READ this paragraph I am left wondering at the audacity and conceit of the Sadducees. I should have thought that the way in which Jesus answered first of all the priests and the elders, and then the Pharisees and Herodians, and not only answered them, but covered them with confusion, would have warned off every other plotting questioner. I should have thought that the way, the effortless way, in which Jesus escaped the snares priests and elders and Pharisees and Herodians so cunningly laid for Him, would have been sufficient to teach anyone the lesson that it was a poor and hopeless business to catch Jesus in His words. But apparently it took two more questions and two more answers from the lips of Christ to persuade these people that the man was not born who could entrap Him in His speech.

The Sadducees and Their Problem

There were people who thought that where priests and elders, Pharisees and Herodians have failed, they might succeed. Possibly the failure of the Pharisees spurred them on to make their attempt. They may have relished the discomfiture of the Pharisees; they may have chuckled over the way in which Jesus made them and their question both ridiculous. At any rate, they thought they saw an opportunity of catching Christ, and scoring off their rivals at the same time. They came with an air of insolent confidence. Christ's triumph over His other questioners had not even taught them humility. They pay Him no compliment. There is no deference in their attitude, such as the Pharisees and Herodians had shown. They come in the manner of "superior persons." They submit their precious problem, which was meant to demonstrate the absurdity of the resurrection-belief to Jesus, and the tone they adopt is as if they would say, "There! Answer that, if you can."

The Sadducees and Their Tenets

Let us look at the questioners, and then at their question. These men were Sadducees. They belonged to the party who were the Rationalists of their day. Numerically they were not a large party; they were, indeed, a small minority of the nation. But they were the aristocratic party and the official party, and these things of course gave them influence and importance. In matters of faith they had, if I may so put it, a different Bible from the Pharisees. The Pharisees laid great store by the "traditions of the elders"; the Sadducees repudiated them. It is said that they rejected the Prophets and the Psalms, and accepted only the Books of Moses. At any rate, if they did not wholly reject them, they gave them an entirely inferior and subordinate place. The Pentateuch—the Books of the Law—was their rule of faith and practice, and to all intents and purposes constituted their Bible. Now the hope of immortality does not shine very brightly in the Books they received. What glimmerings we get of this great truth are found mostly in the prophets and the Psalms. In the Books of the Law, immortality and the resurrection are scarcely referred to. And, taking the Book of the Law as their Bible, the Sadducees denied the resurrection, personal immortality and retribution in a future life. Wealthy and comfortable themselves, they felt no need, as one writer puts it, for a future life to compensate for the inequalities of the present.

Their Problem

The problem which they submitted to Jesus was meant to show the absurdity of a belief in a resurrection. It was based on a familiar feature in Jewish life. To be childless was almost the greatest calamity a Jew could conceive of. So long as a Jew had descendants, some sort of immortality seemed to be his. To meet this craving for the perpetuation of the name, Moses had laid down the law that in the case of brothers living together, in case the elder should marry, and die without children, instead of allowing a "stranger" to marry the widow, and so letting the elder brother's name perish, the second brother should marry the widow, and any issue of this second marriage should be considered in law to be the son of the dead brother, and should perpetuate his name. This custom is known as the Levirate Law. Starting from this law, the Sadducees state a case which they thought reduced the doctrine of a resurrection to an absurdity. There were seven brothers, they said. The first married, and died childless. The second took the widow to wife, and likewise died childless. She passed in succession to all seven, and all seven died childless. Then the woman died last of all. Now, they ask triumphantly, in the resurrection life, of which you speak, whose wife shall she be?

A Possible Answer

Now Jesus might fairly have declined to answer this question. It was asked in levity, and He might have answered it with scorn. This was an imaginary case the Sadducees had submitted to Him. The contingency they pictured could hardly have taken place. Moreover, according to the very Law they quote, the woman was not "married" to the second brother. To quote the exact words of the old ordinance, he would "perform the duty of an husband's brother unto her" (Deut. 25:5). That would probably have been the answer a Pharisee would have given. But Jesus does not repay levity with scorn; He does not brush aside the whole miserable question with contempt. For the sake, not simply of His questioners, but of them that stood by, His own disciples perhaps, who had often been puzzled and perplexed by difficulties like these, He gave it an answer which made faith in the resurrection and the life beyond easier for all who heard it.

The Lord's Reply

Let us turn to the answer of Christ. Remember the question in dispute is not the marriage law, but the resurrection life. "Ye do err," He said to His questioners, "not knowing the Scriptures, nor the power of God" (Matt. 22:29). The Sadducees had come up to Jesus quite confident that they were going to expose both Jesus and the Pharisees, as being grotesquely and absurdly mistaken in their belief about a resurrection. Jesus fastens the charge of error upon them. Their whole difficulty about the resurrection arose from mistaken views of what the resurrection meant. Their objection proceeded on the assumption that the resurrection life was simply a continuation of life down here. They took it for granted that all the relationships of earth would be resumed in heaven. They thought of the life beyond in terms of life in the flesh. As Dr. Chadwick puts it, "They had no conception that the body can be raised otherwise than as it perished; and consequently they imagined all sorts of unhappy complications as likely to follow such a resurrection."

The Sadducees' Error Based on Ignorance

It was from this initial blunder that all their difficulties arose. Clever men though they thought themselves to be, they were wrong in the very premises from which they started, and their mistake, Jesus goes on to say, was due to two reasons: (1) They were ignorant of the Scriptures, (2) they made no allowance for the power of God. It is with the second mistake that our Lord deals first. The difficulties of the Sadducees about the resurrection life were due to this first of all—that they made no allowance for the power of God.

Ignorance of the Power of God

They assumed that the new life was simply a reproduction of the life here. They assumed that the body that is, is the body that shall be. They made absolutely no allowance for any exercise of the power of God. Clever people though they were, they were the kind of person Paul addresses when he says, "Thou foolish one, . . . that which thou sowest, thou sowest not the body that shall be, but a bare grain, it may chance of wheat, or of some other kind; but God giveth it a body even as it pleased Him" (1 Cor. 15:30, 37). It was God the Sadducees had left out of their calculation in all their thoughts about a future life. Had they known the power of God, they would have known that what is, is no measure of what may be. And that is our answer still to all difficulties about the future life. We remember the great power of God. There are difficulties, and we all feel them. There are many questions we cannot answer. But we may rest our hearts in the remembrance of the "power of God." With God all things are possible.

In Relation to the Resurrection Life

And then our Lord proceeds to hint to these Sadducees one of those mighty changes which shall be brought about in the resurrection life by the power of God. The entire conditions of life shall be altered. "For when they shall rise from the dead," He said, "they neither marry, nor are given in marriage; but are as angels in heaven" (v. 25). These words of our Lord have struck a chill into loving and united hearts before today. But really there is no threat of the dissolution of any affectionate and enriching relationship, when we rightly understand them. Let us try to see exactly what they mean. We are apt to forget that human life as it is, is not human life as God meant it to be. Death is in the world. Now marriage is the counterpoise of death.

And to Marriage

Marriage is God's ordinance for the replenishing of the life of this world, which otherwise would be destroyed by the ravages of death. But in the world to come death is swallowed up of life. One feature of the New Jerusalem which John delights to dwell upon is this—"there shall be no more death"; and because there is no more death, there is no more need of marriage. Marriage becomes an anachronism. So far as marriage has a physical basis—and it is on the physical basis of marriage the question of the Sadducees proceeded—it is an earthly thing. It has no place in the heavenly kingdom. But love is not dependent on marriage. And the love is the all-important and essential thing. Husband and wife shall be as dear to one another in the world to come as they are down here. Only the relationship between them shall be sublimed of every suggestion of the earthly; it shall not be "marriage" any more, it shall be something more glorious and beautiful than marriage. It will be love, without a touch of earth about it—love, holy, sacred, perfect. "They shall not marry," no, but we shall know each other and love each other, and contribute to each other's gladness there as here.

The Life of the World to Come

The life beyond has a natural fascination for us. So many of our friends are already in it; we ourselves are hastening towards it. So we are eager to know what it is like. We try to peer through the veil that hides it from us. But it is only "broken glimpses" of the life beyond that the Bible gives us. The Koran gives the Mohammedan a detailed and sensuous account of the joys of his Paradise; the Bible contents itself with hints and suggestions and gleams of the glory. It does not draw back the veil. "Eye saw not, and ear heard not. . . . Whatsoever things God hath prepared for them that love Him" (1 Cor. 1:9). About heaven, we have to walk by faith, not by sight. But even the scattered hints and suggestions we get in the Bible are sufficient to fill us with joy unspeakable and full of glory. The life of heaven is not loss, but immeasurable gain.

Its Fulness

I am not going to attempt to describe for you a life which the Bible has purposely left obscure and veiled. I content myself with simply saying this, we shall miss nothing in heaven that is really worth having. Heaven will rob us of no real joy, of no genuine delight, of no enriching love. Heaven means joy at its full: happiness in its perfection. Now the holy gift of love is the very gladness of our life. The love of wife for husband, and of husband for wife; the love of parent for child, and child for parent—it is love that makes life sunny for us; it is love that constitutes its joy. Without love, life itself would be meaningless. And heaven is not going to rob us of such love. "Love is of God," says John, "and everyone that loveth is born of God, and knoweth God" (1 John 4:7). Love is a bit of heaven on earth; it is a bit of the eternal in time. "Love is of God," and therefore love is eternal. For can anything that is "of God" die? That love is the symbol of eternity is not merely beautiful poetry; it is good theology as well. And so this love of ours will abide, only cleansed and purified and glorified. It does not end at the grave. It is not buried in the coffin. You remember the inscription on the gravestone that marks the place where Charles Kingsley and his wife both lie buried: *Amavimus, Amamus, Amabimus,* "We have loved, we love, we shall love." We shall continue to love, all through the age of eternity. And so I say to any who have loved ones within the veil, *Sursum Corda!* Lift up your hearts! Love shall abide, only it shall lose its dross.

"As Angels"

"They neither marry, nor are given in marriage, but are as angels in heaven." "As angels." We shall not *become* angels. The difference between angels and men will still exist. They are unfallen beings; we are sinners redeemed. But in the new life we shall be as angels, in the sense that we shall be spiritual, not fleshly beings. That word in itself was sufficient to demolish the Sadducean difficulty. They were arguing as if up yonder, just as down here, we should still be fleshly and perishing beings. No, says Jesus; up yonder we shall be "as angels," spiritual and immortal. "As angels," what a prospect! For the angel is a pure and holy being, of a whiteness as unsullied as that of a dove's wing. And you and I shall, in the life of the world to come, be "as angels." And the angel is for ever engaged in the holy service of God. And you and I, whose service is now so broken and fitful, shall then be constant and devoted, for we shall be "as angels." The angels gaze ever upon the glory of God. And you and I, who here catch only fleeting glimpses, and see through a glass darkly, shall then be "as angels." So let us be of good cheer. We do not know everything about the world to come. But we know this: we lose nothing that is worth keeping. Life will be enriched, deepened, glorified for us. We shall be "as angels." Let us leave it there. Let us remember the "great power of God." Let us content ourselves with this, "In Thy presence is fulness of joy; in Thy right hand there are pleasures for evermore" (Psa. 16:11).

78
The Resurrection

"And as touching the dead, that they rise: have ye not read in the book of Moses, how in the bush God spake unto him, saying, I am the God of Abraham, and the God of Isaac, and the God of Jacob?" —Mark 12:26.

Simple Hearts and Simple Faith

OUR LORD'S REPLY to the Sadducees asserts that this time, at any rate, the people at large were right, and they, the Sadducees, the clever people, the superior people, the cultured people, were wrong. As a matter of fact, culture is apt to be more than a little critical of religion. The superior person sometimes looks down with a touch of superciliousness and scorn upon the simple faith of the humble and trusting soul. But when it comes to religious truth, I would far rather trust the simple heart than the merely cultivated mind, the instinct of the Christian commonalty than the judgment of the "superior person." For when it comes to religion, to God and the soul and the eternal life, the intellect is not the sole, or even the chief organ of knowledge. *Pectus facit theologium*, says the old proverb. "It is the heart that makes the theologian." The man of loving and open heart knows more, and sees further into spiritual truth than the man only of keen and cultivated mind. How does the Beatitude run, "Blessed are the cultivated in mind"? No. "Blessed are the trained in intellect"? No. But "Blessed are the pure in heart, for they shall see God." The Jewish people at large believed eagerly, passionately in a resurrection and a life beyond the grave. These Sadducees, the clever, cultured people, scoffed at the belief. But it was the Sadducees, and not the people, who were wrong. It was only another illustration of things being hidden from the wise and prudent, and revealed unto babes.

"Not Knowing the Scriptures"

We have already dealt with one cause of their mistake. There was another; and it was this— "Is it not for this cause that ye err," Jesus said to them, "that ye know not the Scriptures?" (v. 24). That was a startling charge to bring against these Sadducees, for no

459

doubt they were well versed in those portions of the Old Testament which they reckoned as Scripture. But it is possible to read the Scriptures without knowing them, it is possible to be letter-perfect in them without understanding them. There is, in literary history, a curious example of reading without understanding. John Milton was one of the best, and most gifted men God ever gave to England. But there is no great man without his foibles, and John Milton had his. Though he had views on education that were far in advance of his time, he did not believe in the education of women. So he would not allow his daughters to learn languages; one tongue, he used to say with a gibe, was enough for a woman. But, when his eyesight failed, it was essential that his daughters should be able to read to him in various languages. So he went to the trouble of teaching them how to pronounce the words, but not what the words meant. Thus they had to read to their father in Latin, Italian and Greek without understanding a single word.

A Widespread Error

But is not there a great deal of Bible-reading of that sort? Men read the words without grasping the truth. "Understandest thou what thou readest?" asked Philip of the Ethiopian eunuch. "How can I," replied that humble soul, "except some one shall guide me?" (Acts 8:31, 32). He was reading without understanding. And many beside the Ethiopian were doing the same thing only they had not the humility to confess it. Take that fifty-third chapter of Isaiah which the eunuch was reading. Had not the whole Jewish nation read it without understanding it? They were familiar with its words; but as far as realizing the truth taught by it, the great passage might as well never have been in the Book of the Prophet at all.

How to Understand

And we do that same thing still. We often read the Scriptures without understanding them, just exactly as we may say our prayers without praying. We have our Scripture-reading schedules; we pledge ourselves to read some portion of this Holy Book every day. So far, so good! But remember, it is possible to have a superficial knowledge of Scripture, and to miss its vital points. You may know its sentences by heart, but miss its spirit. The letter killeth; it is the Spirit that giveth life. To know your Bible, you want more than ability to read. You want an illumined mind, a mind illumined by the Spirit of God. It is the Spirit who breathes upon the

Word, and brings the truth to light. You want also the obedient will. To understand the Word, you must be a doer of it, as well as a reader. "He that doeth the will," said Jesus, "shall know of the teaching." To know the Scriptures, you need, then, more equipment than the schools can supply—you need prayer, obedience and the Spirit's light.

The Unobserved Truth

"Ye know not the Scriptures," said Jesus of these Sadducees. He illustrates and substantiates His charge by quoting them a passage out of the Pentateuch. He does not quote either Psalmist or Prophet. The Sadducees would not have acknowledged their authority. He goes to the Books they themselves acknowledged as authoritative Scripture. And out of their authoritative Scripture He quotes perhaps the most familiar passage of all—a passage as familiar to them as, let us say, "Our Father" is to us. The doctrine of immortality—which these Sadducees denied—was in their Scriptures all the time, if they had eyes to see it, and in the most familiar passages too. "But as touching the dead, that they are raised," said Jesus; "have ye not read in the book of Moses, in the place concerning the Bush, how God spake unto him, saying, I am the God of Abraham, and the God of Isaac, and the God of Jacob?" (v. 26). Why, yes, they had read the passage scores, hundreds, thousands of times. But immortality and the resurrection are involved and implied in the passage; for "God," said Jesus, "is not the God of the dead, but of the living." They had read without understanding. "Ye do greatly err," said Jesus.

Christ's Argument for Immortality

Now let us look for a moment at Christ's argument for immortality as He states it here. The Sadducees made quite sure that there was no immortality in the Pentateuch. The doctrine was a later accretion, they said, and had no place in the revelation made to their great Lawgiver. Now it would have been passing strange if the Jews—God's chosen and peculiar people—had been left without witness of the world beyond. For the instinct for immortality is everywhere. Tennyson's lines,

> "Thou madest man he knows not why,
> He thinks he was not made to die,"

represent the universal belief. I say, it would have been passing strange, it would have been inexplicable, if the Jews had not shared in the expectation. But, as a matter of fact, Jesus finds the hope, almost the assertion, of immortality embedded in these Scriptures of the Law to which the Sadducees so confidently appealed. He recalls to their minds that familiar passage in which the story of the appearance of God to Moses in the Bush is told, and in the name God gives to Himself there our Lord finds the fact of immortality taken for granted.

Founded on the Character of God

What is the argument which Christ here propounds? It is the argument for immortality which is based upon the character of God. There is an argument for immortality which is based upon the nature of man. The very fact that man is a moral being, that he cherishes ambitions and hopes which in this life never get realized; the fact that there is so much incompleteness and waste in life; and that there are such serious inequalities that need to be rectified— all these things argue a life beyond the grave, unless you are to write down this world as a chaos, and life as a torture and a mockery. But there is a stronger argument for immortality than that which is based upon the nature of man, and that is the argument which grounds itself upon the character of God. It is that mightiest and most irrefutable of arguments that Christ advances here.

The Announcement of Moses

Let us see what this argument amounts to. This was how God announced Himself to Moses at the Bush: "I am the God of Abraham, and the God of Isaac, and the God of Jacob." Now in that title which God then applied to Himself the doctrine of immortality is involved. For the God who revealed Himself to Moses in the Bush was a God able to enter into covenant relations with men; who admitted men into His friendship and fellowship. He became Abraham's God, Isaac's God, Jacob's God. There was a covenant between these men and Him. They pledged and plighted themselves one to another. It was not a case simply of Abraham, Isaac and Jacob giving themselves to God; God entered into relations with them.

Not One of Merely Passing Relationship

But could such relations be merely temporary? Could death rob God of His friends? Did God pledge Himself to Abraham, saying, "I am thy God, and thine exceeding great reward," if the grave were to be the end of it all? You perhaps remember how Omar Khayyam describes the relationship between men and God:

> "We are no other than a moving row
> Of magic Shadow-shapes that come and go
> Round with the Sun-illumined lantern held
> In midnight by the Master of the Show;
> But helpless pieces of the game He plays
> Upon this chequer-board of Nights and Days;
> Hither and thither moves, and checks and slays,
> And one by one back in the closet lays."

Of course, if men are no more to God than the pieces on the chess-board are to the player, if they are mere puppets with which He amuses Himself, then we are robbed of our argument for immortality, and we shall conclude, with the old Persian poet, that this life is all, and we had better make the best of it. But that is not the picture of God suggested by our Lord's reference. That is not the God we know by our own personal experience. Men are not with Him mere pieces in the game. They are His friends. And the fact that God makes a friend of man, enters into personal relationships with him, is a pledge of immortality. It is impossible that death should rob God of His friend. The character of God is at stake. For to say otherwise, is to say that death, and not God, is Lord of the world.

A Sure Instinct of Soul

This truth you find expressed by Christ Himself. "Father," He said, as He hung a dying, "into Thy hands I commend My spirit." You find it on the lips of the Apostles. "I am persuaded," wrote St Paul, "that neither death, nor life, nor angels, nor principalities, nor things present, nor things to come, nor powers, nor height, nor depth, nor any other creature, shall be able to separate us from the love of God which is in Christ Jesus our Lord" (Rom. 8:38, 39). You find it on the lips of seers and poets.

> "For though from out the bourne of time and space
> My bark should wander far,
> I hope to see my Pilot face to face,
> When I have crossed the bar."

So wrote Tennyson. "God is love," said Browning. "I build on that," and so he "greets the unseen with a cheer." All this is a sure instinct of the soul. If we can enter into loving fellowship with God, into personal relations with Him—and there are thousands and tens of thousands to testify that we can—then it is impossible that death should be the end. The resurrection of Jesus Christ is the ratification of that instinct. His coming back has told us that that instinct was true. Yonder, as here, we are in our Father's hands. Nothing can separate us from Him. There are many things we do not know about the beyond, but we can say, with Whittier,

> "I know not where His islands lift
> Their fronded palms in air;
> I simply know I cannot drift
> Beyond His love and care."

And that is enough. Yonder, as here, we shall be with Him. It is impossible that God's friends should die.

79
The Great Commandment

"And one of the scribes came, and having heard them reasoning together, and perceiving that He had answered them well, asked him, Which is the first commandment of all? And Jesus answered him, The first of all the commandments is, Hear, O Israel; The Lord our God is one Lord: And thou shalt love the Lord thy God with all thy heart, and with all thy soul and with all thy mind, and with all thy strength: this is the first commandment. And the second is like, namely this, Thou shalt love thy neighbor as thyself. There is none other commandment greater than these. And the scribe said unto Him, Well, Master, Thou hast said the truth: for there is one God; and there is none other but He: and to love Him with all the heart, and with all the understanding, and with all the soul, and with all the strength, and to love his neighbor as himself, is more than all whole burnt-offerings and sacrifices. And when Jesus saw that he answered discreetly, He said unto him, Thou art not far from the kingdom of God. And no man after that durst ask Him any question." —Mark 12:28-34.

The Scribe

MATTHEW IN HIS account of this incident says that this question, like the questions about authority and tribute and the resurrection, was asked with an evil motive. He says that the lawyer asked him a question, tempting him. Mark gives a kindlier interpretation of his action. It is obvious that the Scribe had been in the group of listeners who had heard Christ's answers first to the priests, and then to the Pharisees and Herodians, and finally to the Sadducees. I believe that at the first he had desired the discomfiture of Christ. For like all his class he was prejudiced against Him, and bitterly hostile to His claims. But as he listened to Christ's wonderful replies, as he recognized not simply their dexterity and ease, but also their reach and depth, his prejudice changed to a great wonder, and his hate became converted into an almost worshipful admiration.

An Honest Enquirer

This Scribe, in spite of all his prejudices, was a man of candid mind and honest heart. He did not try to explain away Christ's answers, as the Pharisees tried to explain away His works by attributing them to Beelzebub. He recognized Divine wisdom and truth in Christ's answer. He recognized that here was a Teacher of rare and wonderful insight who trod firmly when the best of human teachers only faltered. And recognizing that, "knowing," as Mark puts it, "that he had answered them well," he thought he would ask him a question of his own. I think he asked it because he honestly wished to know and because he believed that Jesus could tell him. If you will look at the question you will see it differs entirely from all the others that had been submitted to Christ. The others were every one of them tricky and obviously meant to ensnare Him. This question is plain, direct, straightforward. There is no "catch" about it. The other questions were obviously made up and dealt with paltry and imaginary difficulties, this question equally obviously goes down to root and deals with a vital issue.

His Perplexity

It is a great question asked in all seriousness and earnestness. For the Scribe was seriously perplexed about this matter. This question about the first commandment was, indeed, one of the vexed questions of the schools. The Rabbis held that the Law contained 613 precepts, distinguished as "heavy" and "light." Very keen was the disputation between the strict school of Shammai and the more liberal school of Hillel as to the distinction between these precepts. It was commonly agreed that there were "heavy" precepts to which the penalty of death was attached: and these were in the main, laws regarding circumcision, the eating of unleavened bread, Sabbath observance, sacrifice and purification. Now, I believe that this Scribe had had his doubts for long enough as to whether these ceremonial precepts were really the weighty and serious things of the law; that for a long time he had an uneasy consciousness that these things could not be the principal things in religion. He saw, now, an opportunity of resolving his doubts, of getting guidance upon what was to him an urgent and vital matter. Recognizing the Divine Wisdom that spoke through the words of Christ, he braved the astonishment and scorn that revealed themselves in the faces of his companions, and as an "anxious enquirer" brought his difficulty to Christ.

His Question

"Of what kind," he asked, "is the first commandment of all?" Our English rendering scarcely reproduces the exact force of the

Greek. It was not numerical order he had in mind. "First in this context means principal," or, as John Wesley put it, "the most necessary to be observed." The Rabbis' distinction between the "heavy" and the "light" was in his mind. Were the ceremonial precepts, upon which the Rabbis laid such immense stress, after all, the principal things in the Law? Did the Law lay the emphasis upon the ceremonial or the moral obligation? Was ritual in very truth the principal thing in religion? That was the information which his question asked for.

The Lord's Answer

Jesus answered, "The first is, Hear, O Israel: the Lord our God the Lord is One: and thou shalt love the Lord thy God with all thy heart, and with all thy soul, and with all thy mind, and with all thy strength. The second is this, Thou shalt love thy neighbor as thyself. There is none other commandment greater than these." When our Lord gave that reply, He answered all that was involved and implied in the Scribe's question. He read this man's heart like an open book. I believe that He saw there the incipient revolt against the deadly formalism and externalism of current Judaism. He saw before Him a soul genuinely anxious to know what was the essential thing in religion. And He gave him his answer. In effect He said, "The principal commandment, the essential thing in religion is love—love to God, and love to man. Among the 613 precepts of your law there is none greater than this."

The Answer Desired

In giving that answer Jesus told the Scribe all he wanted to know. The Rabbis laid emphasis upon circumcision, upon sacrifice, upon Sabbath observance. These were to them the "weighty matters" of the Law. But of these external, mechanical, and merely ceremonial obligations the Lord said not a word. He declared to this Scribe and through him to the wide world and to all time that religion is not ceremonial but moral, that the thing that really matters is not outward rite but the love and consecration of the heart. As compared with the Judaism then practiced and taught by the Rabbis this was an altogether new view of religion. The Jews had exalted the ceremonial at the expense of the moral. They had tithed mint and anise and cummin and neglected justice, mercy and truth. Jesus restored the moral obligation to its supreme place and left ceremonialism entirely out of account.

The Scribe's Response

The Scribe's heart leaped up in joyful response to our Lord's declaration. It met and satisfied the deep instincts of his soul. He set himself by the Lord's side. He adopted the Lord's view. To this extent at any rate he proclaimed himself in sympathy with Jesus. "Teacher," he exclaimed, "Thou hast said truly that He is One and there is none other but He; to love Him with all the heart, and with all the understanding, and with all the strength, and to love his neighbor as himself is much more than all whole burnt-offerings and sacrifices." And upon this discerning answer of the Scribe's our Lord put the stamp of His approval when He turned and said to him, "Thou art not far from the Kingdom of God."

The Moral and the Ceremonial in Religion

On the whole, then, this colloquy between Jesus and the Scribe resolves itself into a statement as to the relative place of the moral and the ceremonial in religion. And the teaching of the incident is that the moral demand is everything and that the ceremonial does not count. A certain amount of ceremonial appears to be inseparable from religion. We seem as if we cannot engage in worship without some amount of form. We have an order of service; we stand to sing; we kneel and close our eyes to pray; though these customs are not universal. A certain amount of ceremonialism seems, then, to be inseparable from religion. And at the beginning no doubt every ceremony was adopted as being helpful to worship. Much of such ceremony was, in its inception, symbolic. But the danger of all ceremonialism is that the thing signified should be lost sight of in the symbol itself. That is what happened in Judaism. The Jews thought everything of the visible and external act and nothing of the inward feeling the act was supposed to represent; everything of the offering and nothing of the surrendered will; everything of the lamb and nothing of the penitent heart. And so among the Jews religion was choked and smothered out of existence by ritual, and the prophet could say that amongst them wickedness and worship went hand in hand. It was so in Christ's own day. But it was no new development of Christ's time. It was the besetting peril of Israel all through its history. The people were always confusing ritual with religion. Against that confusion the prophets made ceaseless protest. It was the burden of the prophet's witness that religion was not external but spiritual, not mechanical but moral.

Our Lord's Testimony

In this respect, Jesus Christ took up the protest of the prophets. He called men back to the true idea of religion. "The essential things," said the Rabbis, "are circumcision and Sabbath keeping and sacrifice." "No," said Jesus, "the essential thing is to have the heart right with God. Religion is not outward but inward; its demands are not ceremonial but moral: it is not a posture of the body but an attitude of the heart." "Thou shalt love the Lord Thy God with all thy heart, and with all thy soul, and with all thy mind, and with all thy strength, and thy neighbor as thyself." No man, in fine, is religious, however scrupulous as to ritual he may be, until he love God and his neighbor thus. And the man who loves God and his neighbor thus is religious though he observe no ceremonial at all.

Its Application Today

We have not got beyond the need of this teaching of our Lord's even in these days of ours. I have already said that I believe a certain amount of ceremonialism to be inseparable from religion, especially upon its public side; and further, that to certain natures ceremonialism may be helpful. At the same time we do well to look with a jealous eye upon any tendency to emphasize ceremonial. We know how quickly men lose sight of the spiritual in the mechanical, how easily ritual may come to take the place of religion.

Rites and Rifts

At the bottom, it is this emphasis upon rite and ceremony that, more than anything else, sunders the Church and keeps Christ's people apart today. Our schisms and divisions spring not so much from differences on questions of faith, as from differences about questions of order, rite and ceremony. These divisions, which are our weakness and shame, could never have arisen if we had really taken to heart Christ's teaching in this place that the essential thing in religion is love—love to God and love to one's neighbor. And as this emphasis on ceremony so largely occasions the divisions of Christendom, so is it also a peril to individual souls. Lay the emphasis on ceremony and is it not fatally easy for people to think that when they have performed the ceremony they have done everything? Here, to a large extent, may be the reason why religion today is so formal and barren and cold. The idea many people have of religion is that it means attending at public worship, possibly, also, paying a pew rent, subscribing more or less generously to religious objects, and participating in the Lord's Supper. Unhappily it is possible to do all that and to have no scrap of true religion in the soul. The essence of religion is love to God issuing in love to man. Our church-going, our religious services, our holy sacraments are only means to an end; they are meant to teach and help us to love. When they are exalted into ends in themselves they become the death of religion. God is not satisfied with our outward religious observances. Do we love Him? That is the critical question. Religion is not a ceremonial demand, it is a moral and spiritual demand, and we are not religious until God is enthroned within and we love Him with all our heart, and with all our soul, and with all our mind, and with all our strength.

"Not Far from the Kingdom"
That the Scribe should recognize all this; that he should publicly declare that love was better than all burnt-offerings and sacrifices showed that he had an honest heart; and more, it showed that he was an earnest seeker after truth. This man was no dilettante in religion. He wanted the real thing. And the Lord, when He noted his candor, his earnestness, and his spiritual sympathy, said to him: "Thou art not far from the Kingdom of God." "Not far from the Kingdom": there is scarcely a phrase in the Gospels so pregnant with hope and fear as this little phrase. "Not far"—did he actually enter in? "Not far"—or was he after all shut out? Both possibilities seem wrapped up in the phrase. I would give a great deal to know the after history of this Scribe; but Scripture leaves him here—"not far from the Kingdom."

Modern Parallels
"Not far from the Kingdom," how aptly it describes the condition of many in our own midst. They have a wistful desire for the truth, they have an admiration for Christ, they have a keen interest in religion, they come regularly to worship and yet they never take the final step and openly avow their faith in Christ. "Not far from the Kingdom"—and yet not in it. For, as Dr. Chadwick says, we may know and admire and confess the greatness and goodness of Jesus without forsaking all to follow Him.

A Tragic Position
There is something especially tragic about the case of those who are "so near and yet so far." The case of the young man who went away because he had great possessions has an additional note of tragedy in it because he came so near and yet fell away. "A miss,"

we say, "is as good as a mile." We may be church-goers, and church members, we may take an interest in religious matters and yet come short of the Kingdom. To be in the Kingdom we must not only know what religion is, as this Scribe did; we must practice it. We must not only admire Christ and praise Him; we must obey Him and love Him. There is not one of us "far from the Kingdom." But are we in it? Do we love God with all our heart and soul and mind and strength? Do we really obey and follow Christ? Is there any one of us who after having come so near will yet fall away? Happy are we if we can say that "we are not of them that shrink back unto perdition; but of them that have faith unto the saving of the soul" (Heb. 10:39).

80
Great David's Greater Son

"And Jesus answered and said, while He taught in the temple, How say the scribes that Christ is the son of David? For David himself said by the Holy Ghost, The Lord said to my Lord, Sit Thou on My right hand, till I make Thine enemies Thy footstool. David therefore himself calleth Him Lord; and whence is He then his son? And the common people heard him gladly."
—Mark 12:35-37.

The End of Captious Questions

"AND NO MAN," WE read at the close of our Lord's conversation with the discerning Scribe, "after that durst ask Him any question," that is, as Dr. Morison remarks, "in a captious or argumentative way." It is necessary to make that differentiation. For it would be giving a totally false impression of our Lord to interpret this sentence as meaning that men who had honest questions to ask no longer felt they dared approach Him. It was to Jesus the man with honest doubts and genuine difficulties naturally appealed. He invited questions and questioners of that type and gave them gracious and satisfying answers. The illuminating character of His answer to the Scribe, and the kindly tone of it, far from frightening the man with real difficulties away, must have made him feel that Jesus was the one Person to whom he could take them with the assurance of getting a helpful answer. But as far as those men were concerned who made it their business to concoct cunning questions and propound dilemmas in order to catch Christ in His words, the series of colloquies of which this chapter tells had taken all the fight out of them. "No man after that durst ask Him any question." We might have looked for some such sentence at the close of chapter eleven. The priests and elders might have recognized their defeat in the debate about authority. But love is not the only thing that makes people blind.

The Blindness of Hate

Hate makes people blinder still. Hate made Christ's enemies blind to every suggestion of Divine wisdom contained in His speech. To them He was simply the uncultivated teacher from Nazareth. It was absurd to think that they—the clever, cultivated people of the capital—could not gain a dialectical victory over Him. And so they returned again and again to the attack. Pharisees and Herodians followed the priests and the elders; the Sadducees followed the Pharisees and the Herodians. Priests, Pharisees, Herodians, Sadducees had all to be overwhelmed with shame and confusion before they could be persuaded that it was a hopeless enterprise to try to ensnare the Lord.

A Reluctant Conviction

But the utter hopelessness of it dawned upon them at last. It was not that Jesus avoided the dilemmas they set for Him, but there was such a reach and a depth in the answer He gave. They were full of Divinest wisdom; He laid down great principles which all who heard them recognized as containing the eternal truth. Every question submitted to Him became simply an opportunity for the revelation of some new aspect of His understanding and truth. Here was a Man Whose wisdom was equal to every difficulty! Here was a Master of the mind Who had never to confess Himself puzzled or beaten! At last, I say, Priests, Pharisees, Herodians, Sadducees, recognized that they had entered upon a hopeless contest. "No man after that durst ask Him any question."

Who Is This?

All this naturally and inevitably suggests a question: Who and what was this man, Who spake as never yet man spake? Read through these colloquies again, note the ease and mastery which Jesus displays, notice above everything else His matchless insight, His grasp of spiritual truth. Whence hath this man this wisdom? Here are the clever and educated men on the one side, and there is Jesus of Nazareth on the other—and it is Jesus who shines forth as the Lord of Truth and the Light of men. How do you account for it? I account for it by saying that God was in Christ and therefore that in Him all the treasures of wisdom and knowledge are hidden.

Our Lord's Question

After our Lord's conversation with the Scribe He seems to have resumed His teaching in the Temple. A great multitude was listening to Him, and, as is quite evident from Matthew's account, His foes, though they durst not ask Him any more questions, were still there on the watch for anything that they might be able to pick up and use against Him later on. Jesus saw them there, and in the course of His teaching He turned to them with a question of His own. They had been asking Him questions all the morning; He will now ask them one. They had been testing His wisdom, He will now test theirs. He carries the war, so to speak, into the enemies' camp. For the full account of what happened, we must turn to Matthew's version (Matt. 22:41-45). Mark's account is abbreviated and compressed. The Pharisees were the people to whom Jesus specially addressed the question, and the question itself was this: "What think ye of the Christ? Whose Son is He?" "What do you think about the Messiah"; that is, "whose son is He?" And to these men learned in the law, brought up in the tradition of the elders the question seemed absurdly simple, and they replied glibly, like children repeating their catechism, "David's." "Then," retorted Jesus, "how is it that David, by inspiration, calls Him Lord?" and with that He quoted some familiar verses from Psalm 110: "The Lord said unto my Lord, Sit Thou on My right hand, till I make Thine enemies the footstool of Thy feet." If, then, David calls Him Lord, how is He his son?

The Psalm and Its Authorship

Now it is necessary to say a word about certain difficulties which have been created by the verdict modern scholarship pronounces upon the Psalm Jesus here quotes. For it holds that David was not its author, and that our Lord's argument therefore falls to the ground. But everybody of course knows that Psalms by various writers are included in the Psalter. The titles prefixed to the Psalm are by no means to be taken as sure guides to the authorship of them. Yet, even according to the titles, we have, in the Psalter, Psalms by Moses, and Asaph and Solomon, and the sons of Korah and Elhan. The Psalter as a whole, however, was generally spoken of as by "David." The Jews had a dislike of anonymity, and were wont, Dr. David Smith says, to bring everything under the shadow of a great name, so they came to ascribe to David the great majority of the songs that gradually got gathered together into their Psalter. Psalm 110 is a case in point.

Our Lord's Use of the Psalm

Even so, how could our Lord use this argument? Let us see. Jesus is here disputing with the Pharisees. He meets them on their own ground; He fights them with their own weapons. This Psalm according to Pharisaic belief was of Davidic authorship. It was also of Messianic purport. There were two fixed points in the thought of the Pharisees about this Psalm: David was the writer of it, and the great King Whose invincible prowess is the subject of it was "great David's greater son." Now our Lord is not here discussing the rights or wrongs of that belief. He is dealing with men on their own ground. And in arguing with them of course had to start from some position which they admitted. "You hold," Jesus says in effect to them, "that the Messiah is the Son of David. Now there is a Psalm that you assert David wrote. In this Psalm David calls Messiah 'Lord.' How do you reconcile the two things?" The argument so far as those Pharisees are concerned to whom it was originally addressed depends not upon the fact that David was the author, but upon the fact that they believed he was; and the truth Christ seeks to inculcate by the quotation loses none of its validity even though scholarship should prove beyond cavil or dispute that David could not have written it. That truth is that a merely human conception of Messiah, the conception of Him, for instance, as a Conquering Prince, does not cover the Bible representation of Him. He is more than human, He is Divine. He is more than David's Son, He is David's Lord.

The Pharisees and the Scriptures

Now turning to the question itself notice that by means of it Christ does two things, He convicts the Pharisees of a partial and imperfect knowledge of their own Scriptures and He makes an immense claim for Himself. First of all, Jesus convicted the Pharisees of an imperfect acquaintance with their own Scriptures. He turns the tables upon His foes. They had tried to catch Him in His words. They had tried to humiliate Him in the eyes of the people. Now, by means of this brief colloquy, He, in the presence of the people, convicts them of ignorance of these very Scriptures in which they professed themselves to be expert. "What think ye of Christ?" He asked. "Whose Son is He?" And they answered him, like so many parrots, "David's." That is how they had been brought up to think of Messiah. He was to be David's Son. He was to be one of David's royal line. And He was to revive the ancient glories of David. He was to be a great King and to found a great Empire, and to give the Jews the place of supremacy amongst the nations of the earth. That was their notion of Messiah—it was materialistic, gross, earthly. The Messiah was to be David's Son. "But," said Jesus to them, "does not David say this of Him: 'The Lord said unto my Lord, Sit Thou on My right hand, till I make Thine enemies the footstool of Thy feet'?" David himself calleth Him Lord. Whence is He his son? "Your Bible," says Jesus to them, "speaks of a Messiah Who is much more than David's son—a prince of his royal line; it speaks of a Messiah Who is in some wonderful way David's Lord."

Where the Pharisees Erred

Jesus convicts them of a partial reading of the Scriptures. They had come to their Bibles with this preconceived notion in their minds. They were sure that the Messiah was to be a conquering Prince, and every passage that suggested anything different they ignored or passed by: The Jews could never have cherished their materialistic conceptions of Messiah and His work if they had honestly searched the Scriptures. What of this Psalm 110, where He is spoken of as David's Lord? What of Isaiah 53, where He is spoken of as God's suffering servant? Passages like these did not enter into the Jewish calculations. And so it resulted that when Jesus came they refused to acknowledge Him; they even crucified the Lord of Glory.

Ourselves and the Scriptures

It is at our peril we become eclectics in the matter of Bible reading. And yet how prone we are to partial and imperfect reading of the Scriptures. There are multitudes today who emphasize every line that speaks of Christ's humanity; but who strike out the passages that speak of Christ's Divinity. They want to see Christ as David's Son; they do not want to see Him as David's Lord. And if we are not guilty of that particular partiality, yet there are many of us who pick and choose in other ways. We pick out the passages, for instance, that speak of God's compassion and neglect the passages that speak of God's holiness and righteousness; we delight in the passages that speak of the infinite love of Christ, but we turn a blind eye to solemn verses like that which speaks of the "wrath of the Lamb." The temper is general. And yet a one-sided and partial reading of the Scriptures may have as disastrous effects in our case as it had in the case of these Pharisees. Indeed, is not the present limp and anaemic condition of our religious life, and especially our loss of the sense of sin, due to a partial reading of the Scriptures? It is the nemesis of our emphasis upon divine love to the exclusion of holiness. Every Scripture is profitable; and, in the interests not simply of truth, but of the religious life, neither ministers nor people must pick and choose, but declare and receive "the whole counsel of God."

David's Son and David's Lord

Then notice, in the second place, the great claim which Christ here makes for Himself. They were looking for David's Son. Christ was David's Son according to the flesh, though, because He wore none of the trappings of royalty, the Pharisees had failed to recognize Him. But He was something infinitely greater than David's Son. He was David's Lord. The fault with the Pharisees was not that they had thought too highly of Messiah. They had not thought highly enough. The Messiah in their thought of Him was never anything but human. Jesus here declares Him to be Divine—so Divine that the great David hails Him as Lord. And in making this stupendous and staggering claim for Messiah, Jesus was making it for Himself. He had already done it this very week by riding in lowly triumph into Jerusalem, and by claiming authority over the Temple. The Pharisees therefore knew all that was implied in this word about David's Lord.

The Great Claim

Now upon all this, I content myself with making a couple of comments. And, first of all, this—in spite of every attempt to whittle away the Gospel narrative, the Jesus Whom the Gospels portray is a One Who makes the most amazing claims for Himself. You may leave the fourth Gospel entirely out of account but you cannot reduce Jesus to the dimensions of a simple unsophisticated Galilean teacher. He makes the most astounding claims. He walks through the pages of the Gospels—great, majestic, exalted—as One Who knew Himself the Son of God. You cannot eliminate these claims, for He and His claims are one. So that the old dilemma confronts us and we cannot escape it; either Jesus was what He claimed to be or He was both a deceiver and deceived. That is to say, you cannot sacrifice Christ's Divinity without sacrificing His goodness at the same time.

And Its Justification

The second is this—the character of Jesus justifies His regal claim. This Man Who spake as never man spake: this Man Who wrought such mighty works: this Man Whom death could not hold: this Man Who lived the sinless life: this Person Who occupies this unique and solitary place, Who exercises this unique and solitary power—I cannot find room for Him in the ordinary human categories. He is more than David's Son, He is David's Lord. He is more than my brother, He is my God. And because He is the Lord, He will win His triumph. Jesus was on His way to the Cross. The hour of darkness and seemingly utter defeat was close upon Him. But He looked beyond and saw the certain victory. He strengthened His own heart with this great word, "The Lord said unto my

Lord, Sit Thou on My right hand [the place of authority and power] until I make Thine enemies the footstool of Thy feet." His enemies were to win no final triumph. Every enemy was to be put beneath His feet. And we may hearten ourselves with the same word. If Jesus were a mere Man—an everyday fallible human being—His cause might meet with defeat and He Himself might be superseded. But amid discouragements and disappointments and seeming defeats, I remember He is David's Lord. He is the mighty God, the Everlasting Father, the Prince of Peace. And when I remember that I feel I can trust and not be afraid. "The Lord is my strength and song, and He is become my salvation" (Ps. 118:14).

81
The Great Indictment

"And He said unto them in His doctrine, beware of the scribes, which love to go in long clothing, and love salutations in the market-places, and the chief seats in the synagogues, and the uppermost rooms at feasts: which devour widows' houses, and for a pretence make long prayers: these shall receive greater damnation." —Mark 12:38-40.

The Scribes and the Lord

ALL THROUGHOUT OUR Lord's career His Scribes and Pharisees had taken up an attitude of hostility against Him. From the very first they had criticized His actions, disputed His claims, and in every way tried to discredit Him in the eyes of the people. Neither the wisdom of Christ's words, nor the beneficence of His works stirred any feeling of wonder or appreciation in their breasts. Mr. Prejudice, with his sixty deaf men, was in possession of every gate that led to the citadel of their souls. How inveterate was the prejudice, and how bitter the hate may be judged by the account they gave of His mighty works. "He hath Beelzebub," they said, "and by the prince of the devils casteth He out devils." It was the Galilean Scribes who in their blind and obstinate prejudice had said that wicked thing against the Lord. But the Jerusalem Scribes were of the same bigoted and bitter temper. They saw no beauty in Christ that they would desire Him. In public, they continually tried to thwart Him in His work and to humiliate Him in the eyes of the people; in secret they constantly plotted His death. This day of questioning and debate had sufficiently displayed the spirit they were of. For Jesus knew, and probably the people knew also, that the questions which had been submitted to Him were prompted not by a genuine desire to know, but were the offspring of a malice and an envy and a hate that were as cruel as the grave.

The Lord and the Scribes

And now, when the questionings were all over, Jesus turns to the crowd and speaks to them about the character of His questioners. In one of the most terrible and awesome passages, not only in Scripture but in the whole of literature our Lord tears away the garb of sanctimoniousness and piety these rabbis wore, and revealed them for the hypocrites, the mummers, the playactors they really were. I have wondered sometimes how these Scribes must have felt as Jesus went on with His searching and remorseless exposure of their hypocrisy. In Revelation 6:15-17 we read of certain men who cry to the mountains and to the rocks, "Fall on us, and hide us from the face of Him that sitteth on the throne, and from the wrath of the Lamb." And I have imagined that these Scribes and Pharisees must have wished they could hide anywhere out of sight of those clear eyes that read their souls like an open book, and out of hearing of those terrible words that fell upon their ears like the stroke of doom. It is the merest résumé of the Great Indictment that we get here. For the complete and detailed account of our Lord's denunciation of the Scribes you must turn to Matthew 23. From the account Matthew gives we know that our Lord piled up one solemn and terrible "woe" upon another—until the indictment became absolutely crushing and overwhelming. It is only the gist of that terrific speech that Mark gives us here, and we must read and interpret what Mark says in the light of Matthew's fuller narrative.

The Wrath of the Lamb

But before we examine Christ's accusations against the Scribes, let us note that the chief interest and importance of this paragraph consists, not in the exposure it makes of the hypocrisy of the Scribes, but in the light it throws on the character of Jesus Himself. We see our Lord here in a strange aspect! This Man Who cries, "Woe unto you Scribes and Pharisees, hypocrites," is not like the "gentle Jesus" we sing about. There is something fierce, hot, scorching about the whole of this passage. What we get here is not the gentleness of Christ, but the anger of Christ. No! I withdraw that word anger. It carries with it just a suggestion of personal passion and pique. And there was no trace of personal temper in the whole of this tremendous indictment. The word for the burning, holy indignation of this passage is not anger but wrath. The wrath of Christ! We do not often speak of it. Perhaps in our conceptions of Christ we leave no room for it. And yet, my reading of the Gospels convinces me that Christ's wrath is as real as His love.

The Tenderness of Jesus Christ

It is, indeed, impossible to exaggerate the tenderness of Jesus. Nothing could be more gentle and gracious than His treatment, for instance, of Jairus' little daughter; or of that poor timid soul who touched the hem of His garment in the press, and stole healing virtue from Him; nothing could be more exquisitely tender than His treatment of Zacchaeus, and indeed the whole publican class; nothing could be more beautifully kind than His treatment of the weak but penitent Peter. But with all His kindness, and gentleness, and tenderness Christ was not soft. There is another and very different aspect to Christ's character. If you want to get the complete view of Christ's character you must read not only the story of how He welcomed publicans and sinners to Him—you must read also that other story of how He swept the Temple Courts clean of the mob of traffickers who bought and sold in its courts.

And His Sternness

If you want the complete view of Christ's character you must not only read the story of how He said to the outcast publican, "Thou also art a son of Abraham"—you must read also the story of how He cried out against the religious leaders of the day, saying, "Woe unto you Scribes and Pharisees, hypocrites." The wrath of Christ is as real as His love, and room must be made for it in any conception of the Christ that aspires to be complete.

Its Necessary Place in His Character

I will go a step further and say that Christ's wrath is an element in the perfection of His character. We conspire to ignore it in these days under the mistaken idea that somehow or other it takes from the glory and perfection of Christ to suppose that He could be wrathful. On the contrary, it is the people who ignore the wrath who sacrifice the perfection of Christ. I will for ever refuse the epithet "good" to the man who is incapable of a holy flame of indignation in the presence of wrong and sin. The man who is never angry is morally anaemic. He is not good; he is weak. The father who can never be wrathful with his child, who weakly smiles at his child's wrong-doing, is not a "good" father, he is about as bad a father as a child could have. It is high time we revised our ideas of what goodness is and ceased to identify it with a weak and soft amiability. Christ's holy wrath is, then, an element in His perfection. He was no soft and weak sentimentalist as a great deal of current religious thought and speech make Him out to have been. He was holy as well as tender, He was entirely good. In His passion for purity He flamed like a refiner's fire, and wicked men could not abide the day of His coming. That is the aspect of Christ we get here.

A Modern Need

There is scarcely anything we need more in these days than a quickened sense of the holiness of our Lord and His sacred wrath against sin. We have lost the saving and purifying sense of fear. "Nobody," as Dr. Dale said to Dr. Berry, "is afraid of God now." And as a result, the seriousness and the solemnity and the awe have passed out of our religious life. Religion has degenerated into an amiability—into a cheap optimism. There is nothing wrong— or if there is, everything and everybody will come all right and (as in the popular novel of the day) we are all going to be happy ever after. It would do us good to read a terrible passage like this upon our knees, that we may learn that the "wrath" of Christ is no figure of speech, and may acquire that godly fear which is the very beginning of wisdom.

Christ as Savior; but Judge Also

And while this passage reminds us that we must make room for holy wrath as well as for love in our conception of Christ, so it reminds us that He is not simply Savior—He is Judge as well. Am I wrong in saying that this again is an oft neglected aspect of the office and work of Christ? We are constantly talking about Jesus as Savior. And we cannot talk too much. For the announcement of His Saviorhood is the very core of the good news we have to proclaim to the world. That is how Christ was first announced in the ears of men. "There is born unto you this day in the city of David a Savior which is Christ the Lord." But that is not all. No one can read the New Testament without seeing that Christ is more than Savior, He is also Judge. The Father "hath committed all judgment unto the Son" (John 5:22). Before Him all nations are to be gathered. By their attitude to Him men's destinies are to be settled. Let us never forget that He Who wants to be our Savior is certain to be our Judge.

Love on Fire

I should be giving a wrong impression of this passage if I made out it was all wrath and indignation. There is love in it as well, for the word "woe" which fell time after time from Christ's lips, is an exclamation no less of pity than of condemnation. We speak of a thing as a "woeful pity." And so one of the old Greek Fathers entitles this terrible passage, "Christ's Commiseration of the Scribes and Pharisees." Even while pronouncing sentence upon them, He yearned over them with a great compassion. There is love in the very wrath of the Lord.

There is a wistful pleading even in His indignation. His wrath, as someone has said, is but His love on fire.

Can Man Speak as Christ Spoke?

This paragraph raises another very interesting and important question, and that is this—how far is this terrible indictment of our Lord's to be imitated by modern ministers in their preaching? I will content myself with just two words on this point. First of all, before we speak with the severity and directness of this great sermon, we ought to be able to read the human heart as Jesus did. He had a right to speak like this, for He knew what was in man; He read the hearts of these Scribes like an open book. But for the rest of us, who do not thus know the heart, perhaps we had better recall the word of the Lord where He says, "Judge not, that ye be not judged." And yet, in the second place, we must remember that the Christian preacher is not set in his place to prophesy smooth things. He is set in his place to declare the truth—even when the truth is bitter, unpalatable and painful. His duty is not merely to denounce sin in general terms. He must also, when occasion demands, rebuke the sinner; he must dare to say to him, with the plain, remorseless severity of the old Book, "Thou art the man."

The Sins Denounced

And now let us look at the accusation itself. The Scribes, remember, were the religious teachers of the Jews—they were, as we should say, the ministers of that day. Look at the charges Jesus brings against these men who paraded as the ministers of God.

Ostentation and Pride

He accuses them of ostentation and pride. They walked about, as Dr. Salmond says, in stately, flowing robes, like those of king and priests. They were all eagerness to have salutations in the market-places, i.e. to have sounding titles like Rabbi addressed to them in public. They liked also to have the chief seats in the synagogue—the seats or benches Dr. Salmond explains, reserved for the elders in front of the ark and facing the people. They were sticklers for order of precedence. They insisted upon their dignity.

Avarice

But pride and ostentation were not the chief sins of the Scribes. They were also guilty of avarice. "They devoured widows' houses," says our Lord. For they were lawyers as well as religious teachers. Necessarily they would be used for the making of wills and other legal business. And they used the opportunity their legal position gave them to enrich themselves at the expense of the poor and the defenseless. Dr. David Smith reminds us that in pre-reformation times, it was a custom in our own land, when a peasant died, for the priest to visit the stricken dwelling not to comfort the widow and the orphans but to claim the "cors-present"—the best cow and the coverlet of the bed or the deceased's outer garment. And the Scribes were guilty of a similar rapacity so that one great Rabbi could say about the impoverishment of a certain widow, "The stroke of the Pharisees has touched you." And our Lord's indignation waxed hot against these false shepherds who, instead of caring for the defenseless sheep of their charge, harried and rent them.

Hypocrisy

But even avarice was not their blackest and deepest crime. Their wickedness culminated in this, "for a pretence they make long prayers." In other words, although they were the religious teachers of Judea, their religion was all a sham. Their piety was all a parade and a pretense. They were—to use the word, which, according to Matthew's account, Jesus again and again applied to them—hypocrites, mummers, make-believes, play-actors. And they adopted this cloak of piety in order that under the shadow of it, they might the more easily practice the wickedness to which they were in their hearts addicted. So we may take this terrible indictment as Christ's condemnation of the religious sham.

Our Own Danger

There are no Scribes or Pharisees in these days of ours, but the sin which called down upon Scribes and Pharisees this stern indictment exists still. The religious pretender, the counterfeit Christian is alive still. Indeed it will profit us all in face of this great indictment to fall on our knees and ask, Is it I? Is it the substance of religion we have or only the shadow of it? Are we good coin or base metal? Do we do the will or do we simply say, "Lord, Lord"? And this is our Lord's condemnation of those who are religious simply to please men. I ought to withdraw that word religious and say those who make a show of religion in order to please men. That is what the Scribes and Pharisees did; they gave their alms and offered their sacrifices and said their prayers to be seen of men. And there is a parade of religion which men and women still adopt in order to be respectable. Society around them may demand a certain amount (not too much) and a certain type of religion. And so they go to church—because it is the correct thing—to be seen of men, not to hold fellowship with God. And this terrible sermon is our Lord's condemnation and repudiation of that miserable conventional religion. It is also His stern condemnation of those who make religion a cloak for wrongdoing. "The man who lives for avarice and ambition has his condemnation. But the man who does this under the cover of a loud religious profession has greater condemnation still." These scribes made their long prayers a means of devouring widow's houses the more easily. They turned religion into an instrument of wickedness.

"The Greater Condemnation"
"These shall receive greater condemnation"—greater than that of the open, avowed, and notorious sinner. Greater than that of the publicans and harlots and sinners whom these Scribes cast out. It is a singular thing that Christ's sternest words were reserved not for the open and notorious sinners but for the hypocrites, the sinners who wore the mask of goodness. Sham religion, false goodness was, in our Lord's eyes, worse than open badness, and it would receive "greater condemnation." None of us is likely to be reckoned amongst the publicans and sinners! But it is possible some of us may fall under the condemnation of these Scribes.

Tests
Is our religion real, genuine, true? There are two or three tests which it will profit us to apply to our religion. Here is one— "Let everyone that nameth the name of the Lord depart from unrighteousness" (2 Tim. 2:19). Here is another—"By this shall all men know that ye are My disciples, if ye have love one to another" (John 13:35). Here is yet a third—" Every one that hath this hope set on him purifieth himself even as He is pure" (1 John 3:3). Here is yet a fourth—"Pure religion and undefiled before our God and the Father is this, to visit the fatherless and widows in their affliction, and to keep himself unspotted from the world" (James 1:27). Do we satisfy the tests?

82
The Widow's Mites

"And Jesus sat over against the treasury, and beheld how the people cast money into the treasury: and many that were rich cast in much. And there came a certain poor widow, and she threw in two mites, which make a farthing. And He called unto Him His disciples, and saith unto them, Verily I say unto you, That this poor widow hath cast more in, than all they which have cast into the treasury: for all they did cast in of their abundance; but she of her want did cast in all that she had, even all her living." —Mark 12:41-44.

A Moving Contrast

THE CHANGE FROM the terrific sermon in which our Lord denounced "woe" upon Scribes and Pharisees, to this exquisite story of the widow and her offering, is like the change from the fury of a day of storm to the quiet beauty of a summer evening. When I read through the "Great Indictment" I seem to hear the roar of the thunder and to see the flash of the lightnings of Sinai; when I read Christ's eulogy upon the widow and her humble gift, I seem to be led into the green pastures and by the still waters. It is a welcome change from the judgments to the commendations of the Lord; and to none, perhaps, so welcome as to Christ Himself. I think it was Moody who used to say that no one should preach about hell and the judgment without tears. The man who can talk about the judgment without deep and overpowering emotion has not yet learned of Christ. May we not detect the breaking pain of the Lord's heart in these tremendous woes? It must have cost Him something to utter them. And at the very end of the sermon love broke out in one last despairing cry against judgment. "O Jerusalem, Jerusalem," He cried, "how often would I have gathered thy children together as a hen gathereth her chickens under her wings, and ye would not!" For judgment was Christ's "strange work." "I came," He says, "not to judge the world, but to save the world" (John 12:47).

The Loving-Kindness of Our Lord

But if judgment was Christ's "strange" work, He delighted in kind words and loving speech. You remember the antithesis in our

familiar hymn, "Slow to chide . . . swift to bless"—that is it exactly. Christ was slow to blame, but quick to praise. Slow to expose
and denounce men's sin but quick to see and to praise any good
that was in them. I remember that in the obituary notices of the late
Mr. M'Connell, the presiding magistrate of the London Session,
this was said about him, and I thought it was about as fine a thing
as could be said about any man holding a position like his. You
know that after a prisoner has been convicted, the police bring up
all his past history, and if he has been in the hands of the law
before, every previous conviction is mentioned to the judge. But
Mr. M'Connell was never satisfied with hearing merely the evil
about a man. When the police had made their report, he used to
turn to the prisoner and say, "Now, tell us something good about
yourself." And that was the very spirit of Jesus. He had no pleasure in exposing and denouncing men's evil deeds, but He had the
keenest delight in discovering something good about them. It was
a bit of genuine, unaffected goodness he saw in the poor widow
and her gift. And how He delighted in it! For our Lord's was that
loving heart that rejoiceth not in iniquity but rejoiceth with the
truth.

Christ at the Treasury

Let us now turn to the story itself as Mark tells it. It was in the
Court of the Gentiles that Jesus had run the gauntlet of all those
cunningly concocted questions and had ended up by pronouncing
that tremendous condemnation against the Scribes and Pharisees.
After that terrific sermon there could of course be no possible reconciliation between Him and them. And so Jesus, leaving the
crowd to wrangle about His words and His Person, proceeded to
quit the temple for ever. Their house was verily left unto them desolate. But before passing finally out, He made His way into the
Court of the Women, and just as in His weariness He had sat down
by Jacob's well to rest, so now spent and worn by all the excitement and emotion of the preceding hours, He sat down to rest for
a brief space on the steps that led up to the women's court. Now
in the Colonnades that surrounded this court there were thirteen
boxes called shopheroth or "trumpets" because they were shaped
like trumpets, swelling out beneath and tapering upward into a
narrow mouth or opening. They were set there to receive the offerings of worshippers for the support of the temple services. And as
Jesus sat on the steps leading to the Court He had these offering
boxes in full view.

The Givers

Very soon his attention was drawn to the conduct of the crowd of worshippers as they passed these boxes. "He beheld," or more exactly, "he was beholding," He was deliberately observing, how the crowd of people cast money into the treasury. A man's attitude towards the collecting box is a very fair index of character. Goethe tells a story of Lavater that one day, when it was his business to hold the bag for worshippers to drop in their coins as they left the Church, he resolved that without looking into the faces of the givers he would watch their hands. He thought that the very manner in which people dropped their gifts into the bag would tell him something about the characters of the people, and many were the interesting conclusions he had to communicate to Goethe when it was all over.

And Their Offerings

Our Lord anticipated Lavater. He sat watching how the people cast their gifts into the treasury, watching with interest their manner as they drew near the "trumpets" and made their offerings. He saw that many of the rich kept casting in much. With a certain ostentation they put a handful of coins into the trumpets. But somehow or other these large gifts did not call forth Christ's admiration. Perhaps He saw that they gave their many coins, as they said their long prayers, for to be seen of men.

The Poor Widow

But by and by as He watched, His attention was riveted, as Edersheim puts it, by one solitary figure. Mark's description of her is at once vivid and pathetic. And there came "one pauper widow"; she came, as Edersheim says, "alone," as if ashamed to mingle with the crowd of rich givers, ashamed to have her offering seen, perhaps ashamed to bring it; a "widow," in the garb of a desolate mourner, her condition, appearance, bearing, that of a "pauper." Our Lord's attention was drawn to her, and He watched her. She held in her hands "two perutahs"—two "mites" as our version puts it—the smallest of Jewish coins—a "perutah" being about an eightieth part of a denarius or shilling. Ten mites would be needed, Dr. Salmond says, to make an English penny. She had these coins in her hand. Shyly and timidly she dropped them into one of the "trumpets" and then hurried away as if ashamed of the meagreness of it all.

The World's Judgment Reversed

But our Lord knew what those two mites meant to that solitary pauper widow, and calling His disciples to Him He said, "Verily I say unto you, this poor widow cast in more than all they which are casting into the treasury, for they all did cast in of their superfluity: but she of her want did cast in all that she had, even all her living." The widow's two mites, said Jesus, formed the greatest gift put into the treasury that day. They outweighed the silver and the gold the rich cast in. It was a complete and total reversal of the world's judgment. "There are last which shall be first," said Jesus, "and there are first which shall be last," and this eulogy upon the widow woman and her gift is an illuminating commentary upon that text.

Christ and the Lowly in Heart

Now, turning to the lessons the story has to teach, notice first of all, Christ's unerring eye for modest, unobtrusive and humble goodness. His denunciations of the Scribes showed that loud profession could not deceive Him: His commendation of this pauper widow shows that shy and retiring goodness cannot escape Him. And it is this latter quality that endears Christ to us. There is something terrifying in the thought of those clear eyes which pierce through all pretenses and excuses. But there is something cheering and comforting in the thought of those eyes that never miss an act of genuine kindness and piety however humble. The Bible makes a great deal of the minuteness of God's care and attention. Not a sparrow falls to the ground without Him. He counts the very hairs of our head. And the minuteness of God's attention and care comes out specially in this, that He has eyes not simply for men of great and outstanding powers and services, but also for those quiet, humble, lowly folk whom the world never notices, and who never get their names into the newspapers. "This poor man cried," says one of the Psalmists, "and the Lord heard him" (Psalm 34:6). "I am poor and needy," cries another, "yet the Lord thinketh upon me" (Psalm 40:17). That is it! Not one is overlooked and forgotten. Cornelius was an officer amongst the troops in Caesarea—a man of no great station or influence. But in his own quiet and humble way he tried to serve God. And God had not overlooked him. "Thy prayers and thine alms," said the angel to him, "are gone up for a memorial before God" (Acts 10:14). Nathaniel was a humble Galilean provincial who waited for the consolation of Israel. Jerusalem knew nothing of him; the chief priest had never heard his name; but God knew all about his piety and his prayer.

"When thou wast under the fig tree, I saw thee " (John 1:48). And
in exactly the same way our Lord was quick to notice the piety and
devotion of this poor widow's act. No one else in the Temple recognized it. The attendant priest, and even our Lord's disciples had
eyes only for the rich men and their large gifts, but our Lord had
respect unto the lowly.

Heaven's Standard of Values

Another lesson I gather from the story—a lesson as to heaven's
standard of values. The widow's two mites, from one point of
view, was the smallest offering cast into the treasury that day.
Indeed this was the very least offering which was allowed by the
Rabbinical rules. On the other hand some of the rich men cast in
much—as we should say, they put silver and gold upon the plate.
And yet from our Lord's point of view the widow's mite constituted the biggest gift put into the treasury that day. He
picked up the widow's farthing and the rich man's sovereign and
He said the farthing was the bigger gift. "She hath given," He
said, "more than they all." The disciples for a moment looked
bewildered, and then our Lord proceeded to show how a farthing
could be better than a sovereign—in other words He proceeded
to state heaven's measure of values. "Every one else," He said,
"put in something from what he had to spare, while she, in her
need, put in all she had—everything she had to live on." Which
being translated into a general principle amounts to this—
Heaven measures our gifts and our services by the amount of
self-sacrifice involved in them.

The Difference

The rich men cast in their gold; but they never missed what they
gave. They had not to deny themselves a single luxury. They had
not to give up anything. They had not to dress in cheaper clothes
or keep a plainer table. They had not, as a result, to do without
anything. But it was otherwise with the poor widow. Her two
mites made little difference to the amount of the collection. But it
made a vast difference to her. It meant giving up her bite of bread,
or drop of milk, or morsel of honey for that day. It was all she had
to live upon until she worked for more. And so heading the list of
subscriptions for that day there comes not the name of any of the
eminent Rabbis, or proud Sadducees, or rich merchants of
Jerusalem, but the name of this poor widow who gave a farthing.
The amount of sacrifice involved in it decides the value of a gift in
heaven's sight.

A Warning Note

Now I find a double lesson in all this. I find a suggestion of warning in it. I begin to wonder how much our gifts and services are worth in heaven's sight, measured by this standard. How much genuine sacrifice is there in them? Like the disciples, we take a very mechanical and materialistic view of things. We measure gifts by their amount. It is almost inevitably so. And I frankly confess that the gold, and the banknote and the check are exceedingly welcome. But this incident teaches us that Christ not only counts our offering, He weighs it. He weighs it to see what amount of sacrifice is in it. In a way there is no more curious perversion and misuse of a text, than the misuse people make of this Scripture about the widow's mite. People are asked for a gift to some branch of Christian work and they say, "Well, I'll give you my mite." And by that they mean they will give a little. But this widow's mite was not a little. It was everything she had, it was all her living. If only people gave after the pattern of this poor widow our religious treasuries would be full to overflowing. With this story before me, I suggest that we should go honestly over our subscription lists and ask ourselves what our Lord thinks about them? I dare say from the human standpoint they look sufficient, perhaps even generous. But how do they look from heaven's standpoint? Is there real sacrifice in them?

A Note of Encouragement

The other lesson is one of encouragement. Our Lord knows exactly the value of even a small gift. It is accepted, Paul says, according as a man hath and not according as he hath not. So long as there is genuine sacrifice in the gift, we need not worry about the amount. And there is often, as in this case, much more sacrifice in the smaller than the larger offerings. We have generous gifts to our Missionary Society for instance. But there is one servant girl who out of hard-earned wages brings me a half-crown for the work of Christ in foreign lands. I have often wondered whether in our Lord's sight hers is not the largest subscription of all. At any rate let us lay this comfort to our heart, that if only we do our best, if there is genuine sacrifice in our gifts, even though the world thinks them meagre and beneath notice, Jesus marks, understands, and estimates aright.

The Gift and the Love Behind It

Another lesson the story suggests to me is this, that the acceptability of a gift depends upon the love that is in it. The poor widow was the only one who made sacrifices that day. Measured by sacrifice it was the largest of all the gifts offered to the treasury. But what prompted the sacrifice? Love. And while the sacrifice made the gift large, love made it acceptable. People cast in their offerings from various motives. Some of the rich men put their gold in to gain credit and glory with men. Others put their offerings in as a matter of usage and convention. But this poor widow gave her two mites "for love." For there was no law compelling her to give. And the Temple treasury was not like so many religious treasuries of today—in dire and urgent need. This "poor widow" might very well have passed the "trumpets" by. But, as a matter of fact, her heart was overflowing with love to God. Hers was a hard lot and yet she felt God had been inexpressibly good to her. And the best she had to offer was but a poor return for all His goodness to her. So out of sheer gratitude and devotion she gave her all—all she had to live upon. And that was what made the gift acceptable and dear to God. "Her heart went with her two mites." And this lesson is one which again we need to lay to heart. It is love God wants and our gifts are only acceptable as love prompts them. We do a lot of giving in various ways. But am I wrong in thinking that sometimes it is more than a trifle grudging? We part with our subscription with a grumble, and sometimes the poor collector has a rather hard time of it. I wonder how much the gift is worth in God's sight? The Lord loveth a cheerful giver. "The gift without the giver is bare."

No Praise—but Remembrance

You will notice that not a word passed between our Lord and this pauper widow. She did not know that Christ's eyes were upon her. She did not know that He had noticed her gift. She never knew of this eulogy that Christ pronounced upon her to His disciples. You may think if you like that there was a great joy in her heart, that there was sunshine in her soul as she left the Temple that day. But of earthly recognition there was none. Even our Lord refused to mar the pure devotion and sacrifice of her gift by a word of praise. "His silence was a tryst for heaven," says Edersheim. But the fragrance of this deed of hers, like the fragrance of Mary's alabaster box, has remained in the Church all down the centuries. And when she reached the Father's house she received her rich reward. These two mites had transmuted themselves into the unfading riches.

The Sure Reward

The ultimate reward of all loving and sacrificial service is still sure. Though the world may take no notice, the record of all faithful loving service is kept in heaven. Every offering of love is down in the Lamb's Book of Life. Acts as simple and lowly as this widow's gift, acts which had passed clean out of mind and memory, will be recalled to us then, and Christ will say, "Inasmuch as ye did it to the least of one of these, ye did it unto Me."

83
The Last Things

"And as He went out of the Temple, one of His disciples saith unto Him, Master, see what manner of stones and what buildings are here! And Jesus answering said unto him, Seest thou these great buildings? There shall not be left one stone upon another, that shall not be thrown down. And as He sat upon the Mount of Olives over against the Temple, Peter and James and John and Andrew asked Him privately, Tell us, when shall these things be? and what shall be the sign when all these things shall be fulfilled? And Jesus answering them began to say, Take heed lest any man deceive you: for many shall come in My name, saying, I am Christ; and shall deceive many. And when ye shall hear of wars and rumors of wars, be ye not troubled: for such things must needs be; but the end shall not be yet. For nation shall rise against nation, and kingdom against kingdom: and there shall be earthquakes in divers places, and there shall be famines and troubles: these are the beginnings of sorrows. But take heed to yourselves: for they shall deliver you up to councils; and in the synagogues ye shall be beaten: and ye shall be brought before rulers and kings for My sake, for a testimony against them. And the gospel must first be published among all nations. But when they shall lead you, and deliver you up, take no thought beforehand what ye shall speak, neither do ye premeditate: but whatsoever shall be given you in that hour, that speak ye: for it is not ye that speak, but the Holy Ghost. Now the brother shall betray the brother to death, and the father the son; and children shall rise up against their parents, and shall cause them to be put to death. And ye shall be hated of all men for My name's sake: but he that shall endure unto the end, the same shall be saved. But when ye shall see the abomination of desolation, spoken of by Daniel the prophet, standing where it ought not (let him that readeth understand), then let them that be in Judea flee to the mountains: and let him that is on the house-top not go down into the house, neither enter therein, to take anything out of his house: and let him that is in the field not turn back again for to take up his garment. But woe to them that are with child, and to them that give suck in those days! And pray ye that your flight be not in the winter. For in those days shall be affliction, such as was not from the beginning of the creation which God created unto this time, neither shall be. And except that the Lord had shortened those days, no flesh should be saved: but for the elect's sake, whom He hath chosen, He hath shortened the days. And then if any man shall say to you, lo, here is Christ; or, lo, He is there; believe him not: for false Christs and false prophets shall rise, and shall shew signs and wonders, to seduce, if it were possible, even the *elect. But take ye heed: behold, I have foretold you all things. But in those days, after that tribulation, the sun shall be darkened, and the moon shall not give her light. And the stars of heaven shall fall, and the powers that are in heaven shall be shaken. And then shall they see the Son of Man coming in the clouds with great power and glory. And then shall He send His angels, and shall gather together His elect from the four winds, from the uttermost part of the earth to the uttermost part of heaven. Now learn a parable of the fig tree; When her branch is yet tender, and putteth forth leaves, ye know that summer is near: so ye in like manner, when ye shall see these things come to pass, know that it is nigh, even at the doors. Verily I say unto you, That this generation shall not pass, till all these things be done. Heaven and earth shall pass away: but My words shall not pass away. But of that day and that hour knoweth no man, no, not the angels which are in heaven, neither the Son, but the Father. Take ye heed, watch and pray: for ye know not when the time is. For the Son of Man is as a man taking a far journey, who left his house, and gave authority to his servants, and to every man his work, and commanded the porter to watch. Watch ye therefore: for ye know not when the master of the house cometh, at even, or at midnight, or at the cock-crowing, or in the morning: lest coming suddenly he find you sleeping. And what I say unto you I say unto all, Watch."* —Mark 13:1-37.

The Doom of the Temple

IT WAS AS JESUS and His disciples were passing out of the Temple that the colloquy took place with which this chapter opens. "Teacher," said one of His disciples, "look what fine stones and buildings these are!" And Jesus replied, "Do you see these great buildings? Not a single stone will be left here upon another which shall not be thrown down." That solemn word must have sounded like the stroke of doom in the ears of the disciples. For they were Jews, and to them as to every Jew the Temple was the holiest place on earth. I can quite imagine that all conversation was silenced by that tragic word. It was in an awed quietness they crossed the Kidron, and set their faces towards that steep path across the Mount of Olives which was to lead them to their evening's rest in Bethany.

At the top of the ascent Jesus paused and sat down to rest, with the Temple whose destruction He had just predicted full in His view. What His thoughts were as He gazed at it in its glory who shall tell? But taking advantage of the few moments of rest, four of His disciples came to Him to ask questions about the solemn prediction He had uttered a few minutes before. Peter and James and John and Andrew approach Him. Doubtless they acted on this particular occasion as representatives of the Twelve. There may have been something so rapt and exalted and awe-inspiring about the very appearance of Jesus that no individual disciple dared ask Him any question.

The Question of the Four

Four of them therefore approached our Lord together, and those four the four chiefest and most influential of the Twelve Apostles. They came to Him privately (i.e. apart from the rest of the Twelve) and asked Him, "Tell us, when shall these things be, and what shall be the sign when these things are all about to be accomplished?" It was the prophesied destruction of the Temple they had in mind, and they wanted to know two things—when that destruction would take place, and what warning would be given them when that destruction was near.

And the Questions They Might Have Put

There were other and better questions they might have asked, says Dr. Glover. They might, for instance, have asked, "Why? Why must all these things be?" They might have asked their Lord to unfold to them the sin which necessitated so stern a judgment. They might have asked Him humbly what it was in the conduct of their nation that had provoked so awful a doom. Or they might have put yet another question—"How can this doom be averted?" and that perhaps would have been the best question of all. I should have thought better of the disciples if in face of this stern and solemn word they had felt sufficient concern for their nation to make them ask their Lord if there were no way of arresting and averting judgment. Abraham entreated the Lord for corrupt and pagan Sodom; could not these disciples have entreated Him for their own countrymen and for Jerusalem their Holy City? But curiosity, or personal concern, was apparently the dominant feeling in their minds, and the only question they asked was about the date and the sign. It was in answer to that question that, according to Mark's account, our Lord uttered the great eschatological discourse which occupies the rest of the chapter.

The Double Catastrophe

I designedly refrain from discussing the critical questions raised by this chapter. Our aim is mainly devotional and personal; the critical difficulties in no way impair the solemn message of these words to ourselves. Looking broadly at this discourse of our Lord we can see that there are two horizons in it—the one near, the other far. There are two "ends" in it—the end of Jerusalem and the end of the world. The first "end" dated for that generation; the other "not yet." And though the disciples interpreted all these sayings as if they referred to one "end" only, they yet reported them so faithfully that we with our clearer insight can distinguish between them. Judgments may vary about single verses, but roughly speaking vv. 3-8, 14-23, 28-31 seem to refer to the fall of Jerusalem; the rest of the chapter refers to the end of the world. But in speaking about the counsel Jesus gives to His disciples, in view of the coming judgment, whether I gather my lessons from the verses that refer to the nearer or the remoter coming makes no difference as far as their spiritual validity is concerned.

Preparation for Judgment

"When shall these things be? and what shall be the sign when these things are all about to be accomplished?" asked the disciples. And Jesus in answering them, instead of fixing the date, said, "Take heed that no man lead you stray." At first it sounds irrelevant. As a matter of fact there is a profound lesson in it. It is as if Christ said, "Date-fixing is not your concern. That is in God's hands. Your business is to take heed to yourselves, to do your own duty faithfully and well." The best way, then, of preparing for the Lord's coming is to work day by day with two hands earnestly as unto the Lord and not unto men. We have not got over our curiosity about dates even yet. Some people pore over the pages of the prophet Daniel and puzzle their brains about the number of the beasts in Revelation—thinking that from these passages they may discover the date when the Lord will come back. It is a futile task. The day and the hour God has kept within His own authority.

By "Carrying On"

But, if you really want to prepare for the Lord's coming, I can tell you how to do it. "Take heed to yourselves." Attend faithfully to your own duty and task. You remember the old and familiar story about the American legislature. They were in the midst of a debate when a deep and appalling darkness spread over the sky, until one member could not see another's face. In that darkness as of night strong men were seized with panic. They cried that the day of judgment was come. They wanted to adjourn the sitting and to betake themselves to prayer. Then one man got up and said, "Whether it be the day of judgment I know not: but one thing I do know, that it is the will of God that we should save our country. Mr. Speaker, I move that candles be brought in, and that we proceed with the business." Surely he was right. "How would a man rather be found than just doing the work which his Lord had committed to him?" Was it not John Wesley, who, when asked how he would spend the day if he knew it was his last, replied that he would just go through with the program of preaching and visiting and traveling arranged for him and then quietly lay himself down to rest at night? That is the best way to prepare for the judgment. Leave your star-gazing and your date-fixing. Take heed to yourselves. Do your appointed task faithfully.

By Steadfastness

And that we may be found in that "happy posture," bravely and faithfully doing our appointed task, there are two qualities we shall need. One is Steadfastness. "He that endureth to the end, the same shall be saved." The endurance here spoken of is not, as the commentators tell us, the passive virtue of patience, in our sense of bearing things without murmur or resistance; but the manlier and more positive grace of perseverance or steadfastness. Josephus, Dr. Salmond says, uses this word to describe the indomitable constancy of the heroes of the Maccabean struggle. It is a positive and energetic grace. It is courage that cannot be broken.

A Needed Grace

And we shall want that grace if we are to be prepared for the coming of Christ. For the Christian life is not an easy one. Look at the troubles that were in front of these disciples. They were to be delivered up to councils, and beaten in synagogues and set before kings. Their nearest and dearest would rise up against them and plot their death. They would have to face the hatred and contempt of a world. To be faithful to Christ these first disciples needed an unflinching and steadfast courage. And though the forms in which the hatred of the world expresses itself have changed—the Christian life remains a hard life, a difficult life, an arduous life. Whoso would live it needs the high gift of courage. For it is not enough to have loved Christ once and served Him once! It is not enough to have made a beginning! It is not what we were years ago, but what we are at the moment of Christ's coming that matters. Men who started well like Judas and Demas ended their career amongst the cast-aways. If we are to be ready for the "Coming" we want steadfast courage. Courage, not only to begin, but that finer courage that in spite of all difficulties bears up and presses on; for it is he who endureth to the end who shall be saved.

By Watchfulness

Secondly, we need the grace of watchfulness. "Watch, therefore," says Christ, for "ye know not when the Lord of the house cometh." And He ends the discourse by repeating the warning, "What I say unto you, I say unto all, Watch." "The price of liberty," said Burke in a notable and familiar sentence, "is eternal vigilance." It is the price of salvation as well. We must be eternally alert, watchful, vigilant. For we may fail in our Christian life not simply through cowardice but also through presumption. We may flatter ourselves that all is well with us and so let down our guard that at the very time when we were saying peace and safety sudden destruction may come upon us. That was the trouble with the disciples in the garden—not cowardice but presumption. Instead of watching they slept, and so their enemies got them unawares. You remember where John Bunyan leaves Presumption—in a bottom chained by the heels. Overconfidence may result in the Lord when He comes finding us sleeping. So that if on the one hand we need to pray to be delivered from weakness and fear, on the other hand we need to pray this further prayer, "Keep back thy servant also from presumptuous sins. Let them not have dominion over me" (Psalm 52:13). Overconfidence may be as fatal as cowardice. "What I say unto you, I say unto all, Watch."

This is a chapter about the Lord's Return. The disciples were most anxious about the date of it. Jesus was most anxious that they should be ready to welcome Him whenever He did come. And that is what really matters—that whenever the Lord comes we should be ready to receive Him.

Are We Ready?

I believe in what is technically known as the Second Coming of Christ. I believe that He will come back again to take His power and to reign. But I never trouble myself to ask when that coming will take place. There is another coming that may be nearer far. For Christ comes to the individual soul in death. And when that day and hour may be we cannot tell. But I do not know that this matters. The question is, are we ready to meet Him whenever He comes? Are we watching for Him? Are we steadfast, unmovable, always abounding in the work of the Lord? Are we bravely, faithfully doing our task? If so, all's well. We shall be amongst those who love His appearing. Suppose the message reached us, "Behold, I come quickly," what would our answer be? Happy the man who can say back, "Even so, come, Lord Jesus."

84
Mary and Her Alabaster Box

"After two days was the feast of the passover, and of unleavened bread: and the chief priests and the scribes sought how they might take Him by craft, and put Him to death. But they said, Not on the feast day, lest there be an uproar of the people. And being in Bethany in the house of Simon the leper, as He sat at meat, there came a woman having an alabaster box of ointment of spikenard very precious; and she brake the box, and poured it on His head. And there were some that had indignation within themselves, and said, Why was this waste of the ointment made? For it might have been sold for more than three hundred pence, and have been given to the poor. And they murmured against her. And Jesus said, Let her alone; why trouble ye her? she hath wrought a good work on Me. For ye have the poor with you always, and whensoever ye will ye may do them good: but Me ye have not always. She hath done what she could: she is come aforehand to anoint My body to the burying. Verily I say unto you, Wheresoever this gospel shall be preached throughout the whole world, this also that she hath done shall be spoken of for a memorial of her." —Mark 14:1-9.

Our Lord at Simon's House

WHENEVER JOHN'S ACCOUNT of the sequence of events differs from the account given by the Synoptics, my own inclination is always to accept John's account as the more accurate. For John wrote his Gospel last, when the three other Gospels were already widely known throughout the Church; and I cannot conceive of John giving a different account from that with which the Church was already familiar unless it was with the deliberate intention of correcting the accounts already current. Accordingly I accept John's date for the feast in Simon's house. From its position in Mark's narrative we might gather that it took place just two days before our Lord's Passion. But John in his record of the same feast, in chapter 12 of his Gospel, states definitely that it took place six days before the Passover: that is to say, according to John's chronology, it took place before the Triumphal Entry. If that be so, Mark does not give the story quite in its proper setting.

A Striking Contrast

But what an eye for artistic effect that Evangelist had when he placed side by side these two scenes—the chief priests plotting in the palace and Mary breaking her alabaster box in Simon's house! I do not mean to suggest that Mark's choice and arrangement of subjects were dictated simply by considerations of artistry. Nevertheless, if he had been a literary artist, intent mainly upon effect, he could not have grouped his incidents more admirably than he has done here. These two brief paragraphs give us a couple of contrasted pictures, and the effect of each is heightened by its contiguity to the other. The bitter hate of the chief priests appears all the more malignant by contrast with Mary's devoted and enthusiastic love; and Mary's devoted and enthusiastic love shines out the more splendidly against the black and bitter hate of the priests.

Christ as a Divider

It is the contrast between the two scenes that suggests the first thought to which I wish to call your attention. With what varied feelings different people regarded Christ! Simeon, when he took the young child in his arms in the Temple, in words that must have struck a chill to the heart of the proud young mother, prophesied that He would become a divider and a sunderer. He was set, he said, for the "falling and rising up of many in Israel" (Luke 2:34). All would not love Him. All would not be drawn to Him. Some would oppose and antagonize Him. He was to be a "sign which is spoken against." And our Lord when He entered upon His ministry, took up Simeon's parable and reaffirmed his prophecy about Himself only in plainer and more emphatic language still. "Think not," He said, "that I came to send peace on the earth; I came not to send peace, but a sword. For I came to set a man at variance against his father, and the daughter against her mother, and the daughter-in-law against her mother-in-law" (Matt. 10:34, 35). He was to become a principle of division and because of controversies and disputes and differences about Him, the closest and dearest of humanities would be snapped and severed.

A Prediction Fulfilled

That prophecy was fulfilled to the letter. The whole of Palestine was divided about Jesus. He drew some: He repelled others. He moved some to deepest devotion: He stirred others to well-nigh ungovernable rage. And that division of feeling with which men regarded Christ is all flashed upon us within the limits of these

nine verses. Here you have, side by side, bitter hate and passionate love; blind fury and utter devotion; the high priests plotting
and Mary anointing.

The Plot against Jesus

Look at the first picture. "And the chief priests and the scribes
sought how they might take Him with subtilty and kill Him." The
chief priests and scribes—they were the religious leaders of the
nation! Here is a strange occupation for ministers of religion—they
were busy plotting murder. And it was near Passover time!
Passover was the feast which reminded the Jews of the great deliverance which God had wrought out for them. And the chief priests
and scribes gathered together on the eve of that glad and blessed
season. For what? For prayer? For thanksgiving? No. "They
sought how they might take Him with subtilty and kill Him." You
may measure the intensity of their hate by the fact that they were
planning murder even in Passover time. For times of gladness and
rejoicing naturally dispose men's hearts to clemency and kindness.
So in Palestine even the stern and impartial Roman law relaxed a
little at the Passover season. To be in harmony with the prevailing
spirit of rejoicing it was the custom of the Roman governor to
release one prisoner at the feast. But the near approach of
Passover did not move the hearts of these people to pity or kindness toward Christ. They hated Him with a hate as cruel as the
grave. "The chief priests and scribes sought how they might take
Him with subtilty and kill Him."

Causes of the Plot

What stirred this cruel and deadly hate? Probably several reasons combined. I am willing to believe that some of the plotters
honestly thought Christ a deceiver. They had been brought up to
expect a certain type of Messiah, and their prejudices prevented
them from seeing the "Desire of Nations" in Jesus. They thought
that Christ was an impostor, leading the people astray; and so, like
Saul at a later date, they thought they ought—that they were under
obligation—"to do many things contrary to the name of Jesus of
Nazareth" (Acts 26:9). But this does not apply to the great majority of those who now gathered together to plot the death of Christ.
If you ask me why these people wanted to get rid of Christ, I
answer that the reason is to be discovered in the history that Mark
has narrated for us in the preceding chapters. Recall it. First of all,
Christ swept the mob of traffickers out of the Temple court. By so
doing He placarded the priests who permitted it as desecrators of

the Temple, and at the same time interfered with their ill-gotten gains. Further, on the great day of questioning, again and again by His answers He humbled them in the sight of all the people. Then followed that tremendous indictment, in which Christ denounced these people as hypocrites, men whose religion was a deceit and a sham. Looking back over these chapters, I am not surprised they hated Him. It was the hate of men whose wickedness had been publicly exposed. It was the hate of bad men for a good Man.

Some of the Plotters

In spite of the fact that these men were the religious leaders of their day, many of them were bad men. Dr. Geikie, in his *Life of Christ*, describes some of the persons who were probably present at this murder council. Caiaphas would preside; and Caiaphas was known amongst the people as "the Oppressor." Annas, his father-in-law, and those five sons of his who all occupied the high-priestly office in succession one to another, were present. To Annas and his family for their cruel craftiness the people had given the nickname of "the vipers." And other priests were there equally infamous. Is it any wonder that men of this type wanted to put Christ out of the way? The mere presence of a good man is an offense to a bad man.

The Foes of the Just

When Aristides was ostracized from Athens, one man who voted for his exile gave as his reason that he was tired of hearing him always spoken of as "Aristides the Just." Perhaps a better illustration still is to be found in the trial of Faithful in Vanity Fair as John Bunyan tells it for us. You remember the list of the Jurymen—Mr. Blind-man, Mr. No-Good, Mr. Malice, Mr. Love-lust, Mr. Live-loose, Mr. Heady, Mr. High-mind, Mr. Enmity, Mr. Lyar, Mr. Cruelty, Mr. Hate-light, and Mr. Implacable. Is it any wonder that such a Jury condemned Faithful to death? Why, his very existence was an offense and an irritation to them. "I hate the very looks of him," said Mr. Malice. "Away with such a fellow from the earth," said Mr. No-good. "I never could endure him," said Mr. Love-lust. "Nor I," said Mr. Live-loose, "for he would always be condemning my way." And in Christ we have Faithful's Captain and Lord; and in these chief priests and scribes we have the High-mind and Heady, and Love-lust and Live-loose and Malice and No-good of that day. What wonder that they hated Him? What wonder that they "sought to take Him with subtilty and kill Him"? They never could endure Him—for He was always condemning their way.

Self-Condemned

But notice this, that in hating Christ and seeking to kill Him these people pronounced their own condemnation. "This is the judgment, that the light is come into the world, and men loved the darkness rather than the light, for their works were evil" (John 3:19). In Jesus light had come into the world, purity had come, truth had come, love had come, absolute goodness had come. When these men plotted to kill Jesus it was proof that they had in their souls no love of truth and holiness and goodness. There could be no severer judgment. Thereby they declared to the world that their works and their hearts were evil. And that is why Scripture insists upon it that a man's destiny is settled by his attitude to Christ. There is nothing arbitrary or irrational about it. It is an infallible criterion of judgment. For, as Simeon said, Christ came "that thoughts out of many hearts may be revealed." The bias of the soul declares itself. Christ is the great touchstone of character. All who love goodness and purity will love Him. If men hate Him, it is because in their hearts they have said, "Evil, be thou my good."

The Master's Friends

Now turn to the other and contrasted picture. If Christ repelled some, He attracted others. If He filled some with cruel and malignant hate, He inspired others with uttermost and enthusiastic love. If in Jerusalem chief priests and scribes were plotting to kill Him, there were in Bethany lowly hearts who counted no honor too high to pay Him. There were some to whom Christ was the altogether lovely. There were some who kept the warmest place in their hearts for Him. There were some who reckoned their homes most blest when He was the honored guest. And first and chiefest of these who loved Christ and honored Him and were ready to give their best to Him was the little household at Bethany. Brother and sisters—they were Christ's dear friends. "Now Jesus loved Martha and her sister and Lazarus." And so while chief priests and scribes plot Christ's death in Jerusalem, kindly loving hearts make a great feast for Him in Bethany.

Simon and His Feast

I ought, however, to say that behind this feast and Mary's sacrificial deed there was more than ordinary love—there was love intensified by gratitude for supreme mercies given. The feast was spread in the house of Simon the leper. Now various ingenious guesses have been made as to the relationship between Simon and Lazarus and his sisters. Some commentators suggest that he may have been Martha's husband. But all such guesses are futile, as Scripture gives us no indication of what the relationship was or indeed that any relationship at all existed. We had better be satisfied with what is told us. Simon had been a leper. "Had been," I say, for of course a feast at his house would have been impossible had he been a leper still. He had once suffered from that most loathsome of all diseases, and had been cured of it. We are not told so in so many words, but I will hazard the guess, which with me is not a guess but a conviction, that Simon was one of the many lepers whom Jesus healed. And this feast of his was a feast inspired by gratitude to the Healer.

Behind Mary's sacrificial offering, again, there lay the memory of a great and unspeakable mercy. If you want to understand this lavish and splendid deed you must read again that eleventh chapter of St John's Gospel which tells how Lazarus sickened and died; and how at the call of the sisters Jesus came back out of Peraea, whither He had gone to seek shelter, and not only sympathized with the sisters but restored Lazarus to them alive and well, after he had been in the grave four days. Ever since that never-to-be-forgotten day, this was the question the one sister had put to the other, "What shall we render unto the Lord for all His benefits toward us?" Nothing was too great or good for this mighty Friend Who had done such great things for them. And this paragraph tells us their passionate gratitude sought to express itself.

Mary's Offering

The busy, energetic Martha served at this great feast. But Mary did a far more startling and amazing thing. While the feast was in progress, she stole up to the couch upon which the Master lay, with an alabaster cruse of ointment of spikenard, very costly, in her hand, and broke it over the Lord's head and "feet," says John. Now in describing an act like this one would wish to eschew prosaic details. But a word or two must be said to make clear the sacrificial character of this deed. Anointing the head with oil was a common practice in the dry and hot East. It was a little attention which, like water for the feet, hosts were in the habit of paying to their guests. But this was no ordinary anointing oil. The cost of the ordinary anointing oil would not have been more than the widow's mite. This was spikenard ointment—the most costly of all the fragrant oils of the world. Except in drops, it was only used by kings and the richest classes, says Dr. Sloon, and was costly enough to be made a royal present. Mary had bought an alabaster cruse of this ointment; she must have paid for it, said

Judas, at least three hundred denarii—or shillings—let us say, taking money at its present value—several hundred dollars. And it was not a drop or two only of the costly oil which she used. She broke the cruse; she emptied its whole contents. Nothing of it was reserved for commoner use. And it was not upon the Lord's head alone she poured this precious ointment—she anointed His sacred feet with it as well—an unusual act, says Dr. Salmond, a token of deepest humility and veneration, reserved for the greatest, and said not to have been known even among the Roman emperors till Nero's time. All this must be borne in mind if we would appreciate the full significance of Mary's act, the worship implied in it, the sacrifice involved in it.

The Master's Tribute

The deed stirred some of those sitting at the feast to indignant remonstrance. "To what purpose hath this waste of the ointment been made?" they said. But it stirred Jesus to thanksgiving and praise. "Let her alone," He said to her critics; "she hath wrought a good work," or rather, "a beautiful deed, on me." A beautiful deed! "Verily I say unto you," He added, "Wheresoever the gospel shall be preached throughout the whole world, that also which this woman hath done shall be spoken of for a memorial of her." What a eulogy! With the widow of the two mites, Mary of Bethany received the noblest praise ever bestowed by Christ on man or woman. It is as if He held her out to the notice of the wide world, and said, "This is what I want."

The Love behind the Offering

What was it in Mary's act that drew this eulogy? Not the fact that the ointment was costly but the lavish, enthusiastic, sacrificial love of which that costly ointment spoke. "What a wanton waste," said Judas. Yes, but then real love is always lavish, and, if you like, wasteful. Real love knows nothing of the "nicely calculated less or more." Real love never enters into a profit and loss account. Prudence may enter into minute reckonings as to how much will suffice, but love always wants to give to the utmost. If Mary had just used the few drops necessary to fulfil the obligations of hospitality, this story would not have been in the New Testament. Her gift would then have meant nothing beyond the fulfillment of the demands of etiquette. But this lavish offering bore witness that behind it there was a loving and consecrated heart. And that made it a "beautiful deed" in Christ's eyes. For it is love Christ wants. "Simon, son of Jonas," was His three-fold question to the penitent Peter, "lovest thou Me?" (John 21:15, 16, 17). "Son, daughter," He says to you and to me, "give Me thine heart."

Is It "Waste"?

"What waste!" That is what they said of Henry Martyn when, prominent minister though he was, he went out to India as a missionary. "What waste!" That is what they said about a brilliant young teacher in the United States, who, after the conclusion of the Civil War, felt it to be her duty to go and teach the emancipated slaves; who, after a few months of toil, sickened and died far away from home. "What waste!" But it is lavish, prodigal, wasteful love like that, that Christ wants! "I will most gladly spend and be spent out!" says the Apostle Paul (2 Cor. 12:15, R.V. Margin). This willingness to be spent out is the proof of a genuine love. Does such a love dwell in us? Are we so enthusiastic in the cause of Christ, so prodigal of strength, and labor, and money, that the world criticizes us and says, "What waste!"? Is not this the mischief with us today, that our love is so cold; that we are so prudent and calculating in all our religious service? There is no suggestion of abandonment in our love. This is the prayer for us—"Warm our coldness we implore." For it is when we begin to "spend" ourselves "out" that Jesus says, "They have wrought a good work."

Where Are We?

The high priests plotting murder: Mary lavishing love. These are representations of the two classes into which Jesus divides mankind. Some hate Him; some love Him. Some reject Him; and some worship Him. There is no third class. When Christ is presented to us we inevitably take our place in one or other of these two classes—His deniers or His lovers. In which class do we stand? "Blessed is he," said our Lord, "whosoever shall not be offended in Me."

85
Judas' Criticism

"And there were some that had indignation within themselves, and said,
Why was this waste of the ointment made?" —Mark 14:4.

The Contagion of Evil

"A MAN IS tried by his praise" (Prov. 27:21). His character is
revealed by his admirations. It would be equally true to say, "A
man is known by his blames"; by the things he dislikes and cen-
sures. These too reveal his character; and Judas' character stands
revealed to us—sharp-cut and clear—in the criticisms he passed
upon Mary. It is from John's account (John 12:4, 5) that we know
Judas to have been the chief critic of Mary's act. Indeed, from
John's account we might gather that the grumbling was confined
to Judas. But there is really no contradiction between John and
Mark. What happened, I imagine, was this. The grumbling began
with Judas: his was the evil heart that Mary's deed filled with malice and rage. Then his plausible excuse of care for the poor stirred
other disciples with some sort of indignation against the lavishness
and extravagance of the deed. If this be so, the "indignation" of the
others was all the result of Judas' evil influence upon them. And
here I find an illustration of a solemn truth. There is contagion in
evil. A little leaven leaveneth the whole lump. It is in the power of
one bad man to corrupt the company in which he is placed. Put
one suspicious, evil-minded, censorious person in the midst of a
knot of average men and women, he can infect all of them with his
own censorious and suspicious spirit. The presence of one fault-
finder is often enough to disturb the harmony of a Church. There
is a natural tendency in us all to be suspicious and fault-finding.
This is one convincing evidence of original sin that our bias is to
put the worst construction on things. We are always ready to think
and believe the worst. And one evil man acting on that natural tendency of ours may work endless mischief.

Flee the Censorious Spirit

One word of homely counsel: avoid the grumbling spirit. Do not be a fault-finder. Ask for the love that hopes all things and believes all things. Do not harbor suspicions, and, as you love your soul, do not insinuate your suspicions into the minds of others. Here is a word that ought for ever to silence every ugly insinuation, every evil suspicion, every sinister interpretation before it finds expression by our lips. "It must needs be that offences come, but woe to that man by whom the offence cometh" (Matt. 18:7).

The Motive of Judas

In the case of Judas, not only was the criticism essentially false but it sprang from a bad motive. "This ointment," he said, "might have been sold for three hundred shillings and given to the poor." Now that sounds, at first hearing, a kindly and thoughtful thing to say. It is not known that Judas had himself been conspicuous in his concern for the poor up to this point. Possibly, when a beggar made an appeal to him, he tightened his purse-strings. But all of a sudden, when he saw the ointment poured over Christ's head and feet, he was seized with a tremendous sympathy for the poor. "Think of all the poor people the money that ointment cost would have helped!" he said, fuming with indignation. And the other disciples—good, kindly men—were deceived by it, and began to grumble against Mary's devoted act.

Selfishness

The concern of Judas for the poor was a deceit and a sham. That was not the real reason why Judas was angry with Mary. The real reason was too ugly to be mentioned. But John tells us the naked truth. "Now this he said," remarks John, with a sort of burning contempt in his speech, "not because he cared for the poor, but because he was a thief, and" (I quote the Twentieth Century New Testament translation) "being in charge of the purse, used to take what was put in it." There you get the ugly root from which Judas' indignation sprang. It was not the poor he was thinking about, but himself. If only those three hundred shillings had been put into the common purse of which he had charge, some of them would have stuck to his own fingers. It is not the concern of the philanthropist you have here, but the rage of a disappointed thief, parading itself as the concern of a philanthropist. In truth, there are actions men do, the real motives of which they dare not confess to the world; they scarcely dare confess them to themselves. So they try to dress vice up in the cloak of virtue so as to lead astray, if possible, even the elect. They seek to cover the real meanness and baseness of their acts by making a parade of generous motives. Demetrius raised a riot against the Apostle Paul in Ephesus. His real reason was that the Christian preaching had interfered with business: his profits were decreasing: his craft was in danger. But in the public square Demetrius says not a word about his trade. You would never have thought that such a mercenary consideration had ever crossed his mind. In public, Demetrius is only moved by a great concern for the honor of religion—and so he and his fellow-craftsmen for three hours together cried, "Great is Diana of the Ephesians." The cry of "religion in danger" was far more respectable than the cry of "diminishing profits."

Examine Your Motives

It will do us good to analyze frankly and honestly the motives that lie behind our actions. Let us get right down to the naked facts. However plausible may be the excuses we may advance to the world, if the real reasons for any proposed action are base and mean, leave it alone! For it is not what the world thinks of any action, but what God thinks, that really matters. And the Lord knows our hearts! In the last resort the character of an act will be appraised not by its assigned, but by its real motive. "How kind," some of the bystanders, I have no doubt, said about Judas. But all this indignation of his went down in the great accounts books as the malice and spite of an evil and sinful heart.

Christ and the Poor

Again, doubt any criticism that sets Christ and the poor, religion and philanthropy, in antagonism one with another. The whole point of Judas' criticism is this—that if Mary had done less for Christ she might have been able to do more for the poor. The criticism was as false as fake could be. I wonder which of these two did most for the poor, Judas the critic or Mary the criticized. No man ever did less for the poor because he did more for Christ. No man ever neglected philanthropy because he was too much taken up with religion. As a matter of fact, Christ will not allow any friend or disciple of His to forget the poor. He Himself "came to preach good tidings to the poor." He was the friend of publicans and sinners. He went about healing the sick and doing good. Philanthropy is a necessary result of religion. If a man really loves Christ he must also serve and help the poor.

An Assumed Antagonism

And yet Judas' criticism is repeated in these days of ours. In some respects it represents the temper of the day. For instance, people object to the missionary cause, they object to spend money on extending the kingdom of Christ, on the ground there is so much poverty and need at home. "What waste!" they say about our missionary subscription lists. "Think what that money would do at home!" "Less for Christ; more for the poor"—that is their cry. But it does not appear that those who speak of missionary work as "waste" are the leaders in philanthropic effort at home. My own experience is that those who give of their substance to spread Christ's kingdom abroad are just the people who minister most generously to the poor and needy at home. Or take another illustration, social reform is in these days being set in some sort of opposition to religion. We give, it is said, too much of our time and money to puny religious purposes and too little to the amelioration of human conditions. But does any one imagine that if we spent less upon religion the cause of social betterment would be advanced? Take the churches of this town with which I am most familiar—they represent the money we have spent on the cause of Jesus Christ. Has it been "waste," as far as the social well-being of Bournemouth is concerned? Would it have been better that all the money had been given to the poor and no churches had been built at all? Would the poor of Bournemouth be better off if all that had been expended on church and chapel building had been set aside for them, and Bournemouth were today a churchless town? The question answers itself.

Religion the Mother of Philanthropy

There is nothing so shallow and so utterly and wholly false as the opinion so popular today, that if only we spent less on religion we should spend more on philanthropy. Again I ask, are the people who spend nothing on religion the people who spend most on philanthropy? Is it secularism that built hospitals and orphanages and homes? Is it atheism that is foremost in caring for the little child? Look around over those great charitable institutions that are the glory of our land. The answer is there. Let us, as Carlyle used to say, clear our minds of cant and face the facts frankly. The universal testimony of history and experience is that religion is the mother of philanthropy, that from the philanthropic point of view no money is ever wasted that is spent on Christ. The Church has been all down the centuries the best friend of the poor—you only damage the cause of the poor themselves when you exalt philanthropy at the expense of religion. "He that hath pity upon the poor lendeth unto the Lord," says the wise man (Prov. 19:17). And that is beautifully true. The Lord reckons every act of kindness done to the poor as done to Himself. But I could alter that proverb and make it read like this, "He that lendeth to the Lord hath pity on the poor," and it would be every whit as true. All that we do for Christ comes back in blessing upon men. The more we do for our Lord, the more we are moved to do for our brother also. No! what we spend on Christ is not waste. In the interests of the poor themselves, it is the best of all investments. Mary is always a better friend to the poor than Judas. The man who loves God is always the man who loves and serves his brother.

The Son of Waste

Judas, when laying the charge of "waste" against Mary, was accusing her of a fault of which he himself was guilty. "What waste!" Judas said, when Mary lavished her love upon the Lord. But it was not waste; it was wisdom. Mary's love was laying up for her treasure in heaven and making her rich to all eternity. The "waste," the real "waste" was on the part of Judas himself. "Not one of them perished," said Jesus, speaking of His disciples, "but the son of perdition" (John 17:12). Or as it might be translated, "Not one of them is lost save the son of loss." The "Son of Loss" or the "Son of Waste"—no other name fitted this man who seemed the very incarnation of worldly wisdom. The "Son of Loss!" What had he lost? What had he wasted? Opportunity, light, grace, character. He had lived for three years in closest fellowship with Jesus, the Incarnate goodness and truth. Yet all the splendid opportunities of those years were thrown away upon Judas. His opportunities of knowing the truth, of growing in grace, of winning heaven—he wasted them all. This man Judas—like Peter and James and John—might have had his name graven on the foundation of the new Jerusalem. Instead of that, this was his end—"He went away and hanged himself" (Matt. 27:5). He was a "Son of Loss."

Loss and Gain

Men make the same mistake still. Men allow their hearts to become absorbed with the love of the things of this life as Judas did. They regard devotion and worship and Christian zeal as "waste." They are practical men, and they sweat and strain after the more tangible rewards which this world offers! Men talk of them as rich. But are they really rich? There is nothing we need more than to revise our notion of loss and gain. A young lady of brilliant intellectual achievements went out to China as a missionary and died within the twelve months. "What waste!" Was it waste? "He that saveth his life shall lose it." On the other hand I read of men who were rich and increased with goods and in need of nothing. What wisely ordered lives! Were they? I read of a rich man who said to his soul, "Soul, thou hast much goods . . . eat, drink, be merry." He had made the best of life. But the Lord said, "Thou foolish one" (Luke 12:19, 20). He was not rich at all. He was "a son of loss." How can we sum up our lives? In terms of loss or gain? Are we laying hold of the good part, which shall never be taken away from us, or are we "sons of waste"? The only abiding wealth is the wealth of the soul. "Thou foolish one," said Christ of the rich man who thought of every thing but his soul. And He added, "So is he that . . . is not rich toward God" (Luke 12:21).

86
Mary's Praise

"She hath done what she could: she is come aforehand to anoint My body to the burying. Verily I say unto you, Wheresoever this gospel shall be preached throughout the whole world, this also that she hath done shall be spoken of for a memorial of her." —Mark 14:8, 9.

IN THE PREVIOUS chapter we considered the criticisms of the disciples, and especially of Judas, upon Mary's devoted act. In this we will look at the eulogy Christ pronounced upon the same loving deed.

Contrasted Judgments

How amazingly people will differ in their judgments upon one and the self-same deed. Look at the marked contrast in this narrative. Mary came in and broke her alabaster box and the disciples said, "What waste!" while their Master said, "She hath done a beautiful deed." They saw precisely the same thing—but they formed absolutely contrasted judgments. The fact is, we see the things we have the faculty of seeing. Or, to put it in another way, it is not the eye but the heart which is the true organ of vision, at any rate in the region of the spirit. The scientist sweeps the heavens with his telescope, examines the rocks with his hammer, analyses a flower beneath his microscope, and may find a soulless universe. The pure in heart will go out into the same world, and in the skies and the rocks and the meanest flower that blows he will see God. The man of selfish, cynical soul is always passing harsh judgments; the man who is in himself bad cannot believe that anybody else is good. But a man of honest, kindly, loving heart always hopes the best and believes the best.

The Heart of Jesus Christ

Now Jesus had a heart as pure as the driven snow, a heart untouched by evil, a heart overflowing with tenderness and grace; and the consequence was none judged so kindly, so tenderly, so gently as He did. A bruised reed He never broke and smoking flax

514

He never quenched. He saw good where no one else saw anything but evil. He had an unerring eye for every sign or promise of holiness. That was why He became the friend of publicans and sinners. That was why He named the unstable Simon—Peter, the Rock. That was why He spoke of Zacchaeus as a son of Abraham. And that really accounts for the difference in judgment upon Mary's deed. The disciples with their materialistic temper only thought of the money it cost, and they said, "What waste!" Jesus—with that clear vision which is born of a pure soul—saw the love for which it stood, and said, "What a beautiful deed!"

The Beauty of Sacrifice

"A beautiful deed," and of course it was the love expressed in it that made it beautiful in our Lord's eyes. Not the cost of it; not the rarity of the ointment; but the love it implied. We are inclined to be impressed by mere cost in these days. We give our admiration to offerings that strike us by their size. We applaud the $1000 offering; we let the five dollar gift pass by unnoticed. But mere size, mere cost is nothing to Jesus. It is the love that counts with Him. Here is His praise of a gift that cost in our money about £60—three hundred shillings. But lest we should imagine that it was the costliness of the gift that delighted our Lord, the Evangelist has already told us the story of another woman and another gift, which brought equal pleasure to our Lord's heart. It was not £60 the poor widow gave, but two mites, which make a farthing. Yet the gift gladdened our Lord's soul. Mary and the poor widow stand very much in the same category. They won from our Lord's lips very much the same kind of eulogy. The one gift, I am almost tempted to say, was as splendid as the other. When it comes to the love and sacrifice involved, I do not know which of the two gifts was the greater. For what did this three hundred shillings represent to Mary? All her savings, I believe. "She hath done what she could," Jesus said. And what did the two mites, which make a farthing, represent to the poor widow? All she had, even all her living. It was the sacrifice involved in Mary's gift that made it so meaningful to Christ.

Found in Its Motive

Yes; but not the sacrifice only; there was the love behind the sacrifice. For our Lord takes no pleasure in sacrifice for sacrifice's sake; but only in sacrifice which stands for love. There is no virtue in the mere act of forsaking father and mother. But when we give up father and mother for His sake and the Gospel's, with such a sacrifice Christ is well pleased. It is the love that counts with Christ. Love has the power of making the simplest act rich and glorious. Three of his soldiers heard David one day utter a wish for some of the water from the well by Bethlehem's gate. That night they determined they would risk their lives to give David his desire. So they crept down to Bethlehem, guarded as it was by watchful foes, and brought back a cup of the water of the old well and presented it to their chief. But what a sacred and beautiful thing that cup of water was to David! "Is not this the blood of the men that went in jeopardy of their lives?" he said. It was too precious for David to drink; he poured it out before the Lord. Love that risked all and dared all transfigured even the cup of water into a thing beautiful and divine. And that was what made Mary's act "a beautiful deed"— her deep, passionate, whole-hearted love.

"What She Could"

"She hath done what she could," said Jesus about Mary and her beautiful deed. It was not every kind of service that Mary was equal to. She could not, for instance, have taken her sister Martha's place, or have done her work; but what she could, she gladly and willingly did. "What she could." I find in this little phrase a hint as to the kind of service Christ expects of us. I find it from one point of view a word of encouragement.

Encouragement

Christ does not expect from every one the same amount or the same kind of service. He is no unreasonable Master; He does not expect as much from the man of one talent as He does from the man who has five. The service He expects from us is service "according to our several ability." Here is the word of cheer for the man who knows he only possesses humble and commonplace gifts. All Christ expects is that such an one should do what he can. And nobody who has done what he could—however insignificant—shall miss the reward.

And Challenge

But I find also in this commendation a word of rebuke and searching challenge. "What she could." Mary did all that lay in her power. She gave up to the very hilt of her ability. She spent herself to the uttermost. "What she could": and I confess that I feel a stab at my conscience as I read the little phrase. How many of us can say that? How many of us are fit to stand with Mary? How many of us will our Lord set in the same class with her, because like her we did all we could? This is a question we may well put to our conscience: Are we doing all we can? Are we making the best of our powers? Do we buy up every opportunity of service? Do we give to the point of feeling? Think of China and India in their urgent need today; have we done and given all we can? Or think of the need at home, the bitter cry of the city slum, the call there is in every department of Christian service for workers, the urgent demand there is—in view of the appalling indifferentism and irreligion—for bold and unashamed Christian witnessing—have we done all we can? Have we honestly done all in our power to further Christ's cause? Is it not a fact that we all lie in the same condemnation? We are all constrained to confess, "We have left undone . . . things that we ought to have done." And that is why Christ's kingdom tarries. The blessed day of our Lord's coming would not delay if only all Christ's people had Mary's love and devotion.

Mary's Sympathy

"She hath done what she could," said our Lord. "She hath anointed My body beforehand for the burying." And what are we to make out of this strange sentence? Is this a case of our Lord's putting upon Mary's act a meaning which she did not herself intend, interpreting her deed in the light of what He knew was so soon to happen? Or are we to take it that Mary herself had some foreshadowing of the doom that was so quickly to fall upon the Lord? I am myself inclined to adopt the latter view. Christ had often spoken solemn words about His dying, but as far as His disciples were concerned, they had fallen upon deaf ears. Mary, however, heard—and understood. Her love gave her sympathy and insight. She felt the silent sorrow of her Lord. She was conscious of the deepening shadows gathering around His path. She knew about the hate of the priests, and, with the prophetic instinct of love, she felt that death was coming. Remember, it is always those who love most who see furthest. And so while the Twelve were still dreaming about their thrones, she came with her alabaster box of ointment of spikenard, very precious, and anointed Him beforehand for His burying. She might not save Him from the death that was awaiting Him; she might not stand by His side when Jerusalem raged against Him; but she could show her love for Him. It was in no unhonored grave He should lie—the fragrant ointment of kings should be His—so beforehand she broke her alabaster box over His head and feet.

Looking Forward

"She hath anointed My body aforehand for the burying." "Aforehand." Mary showed her love for her Lord, while as yet He was alive to be comforted and strengthened by it. What a lot of human appreciation comes too late! We delay our appreciations until our friends are dead; then we say all sorts of kindly things about them and heap the coffin lid with flowers. Perhaps it would have been a rare help and encouragement to some of them if we had only given expression to the appreciation we felt while they were still alive to hear it. But Mary did not wait till Jesus was dead to declare her adoring gratitude and love for Him. She anointed His body "aforehand." Nicodemus and Joseph brought a hundred pounds' weight of spices to anoint Jesus' body when He was dead. It would have helped the Lord if only they had declared their faith and devotion sooner. But Mary appreciated in time. She expressed her devotion while Christ was alive to be refreshed by it.

Mary's Memorial

That was the great service Mary rendered the Lord by her devoted deed at Simon's feast. By the outpouring of her love she refreshed and strengthened Christ's soul. For I must remind you that in face of the Cross, our Lord's soul was exceeding sorrowful nigh unto death. It was a hard and bitter way to tread, and heart and flesh cried out against it. And by her act in Simon's house Mary cheered her Lord as He trod that toilsome way and strengthened Him in His great resolve that He would taste death for every man. Verily, it was "a beautiful deed." Therefore, said Jesus, in the gratitude of His soul, "Wheresoever the Gospel shall be preached throughout the whole world, that also which this woman hath done shall be spoken of for a memorial of her." And so it has come to pass. Mary has won her immortality. Wherever the Gospel is preached Mary's name is known. The whole world has been filled with the fragrance of that ointment which first filled the room in Simon's house, and Mary and her alabaster box are forever coupled together.

And the Lord's Remembrance

For all who display Mary's spirit and do what they can for the succor and help of their Lord, a similar remembrance is ensured! For still, Christ waits to be refreshed and strengthened by our love! Still He waits to be cheered by our devotion. Still we can come to the help of the Lord against the mighty. We can do "our bit" in

Christian service. We can minister to Christ's little ones. And every such act He reckons as done to Himself and He never forgets. Men often have a short memory for benefits. "Yet," I read in the Old Book, "did not the chief butler remember Joseph, but forgat him." But there is no danger of Christ forgetting. "The righteous shall be held in everlasting remembrance." Not the smallest act of love will be overlooked or forgotten. "Whosoever shall give to drink unto one of these little ones a cup of cold water only, in the name of a disciple, verily, I say unto you, he shall in no wise lose his reward."

The Legend of Mary's Translation

Mary, according to legend, in the days that followed the Resurrection, was with Martha and Lazarus driven by persecution out of Palestine, and with them sailed the sea until together they reached Massilia in Gaul. For thirty years, the story goes, she lived her beautiful and saintly life amongst the people of that land, and then one day she disappeared. She did not die, they said she was carried to heaven by the angels. So, it may be truly said of those who, like Mary, do their very best for the Lord, and offer Him not a broken alabaster box, but their broken, consecrated and devoted hearts. They never see death. The angel of God escorts them through the valley and across the river, and all the trumpets sound for them on the other side.

87
Judas' Crime

"And Judas Iscariot, one of the twelve, went unto the chief priests, to betray Him unto them. And when they heard it, they were glad, and promised to give him money. And he sought how he might conveniently betray Him."
—Mark 14:10, 11.

Remembrance of the Just and the Unjust

We pass now from Mary and her devoted act to Judas and his treachery. In the last clause of the previous paragraph, Jesus, speaking of Mary, had declared that her name and her deed should never be forgotten: "Wheresoever the Gospel shall be preached throughout the whole world, that also which this woman hath done shall be spoken of for a memorial of her." But there are two kinds of remembrance: there is a remembrance of honor and glory; there is also a remembrance of infamy and shame. It was the former remembrance Christ promised to Mary, and she is enjoying it today. But the remembrance of her arch-critic Judas is just as sure. Only while it is an immortality of honor that Mary enjoys, an immortality of infamy and shame is the portion of Judas. Wherever the Gospel goes, the name of Judas goes too, to be remembered with loathing and contempt. He and his traitor's deed are for ever coupled together. Just as we never think of Mary without thinking also of her broken alabaster box, so we never think of Judas apart from his crime. He is always Judas Iscariot, "which also betrayed Him."

The Start and the Finish

Judas and Mary are as the poles apart. The one illustrates the heights to which love can rise: the other the depths to which hate can stoop. Dr. Bruce says somewhere in his *Training of the Twelve* that he would be compelled to believe in heaven and hell if only to find a place for Mary and Judas respectively. And he is right. Mary and Judas are types of heaven and hell; for heaven is love, and hell is hate; and Mary is the incarnation of love, while Judas is the incarnation of hate. Nevertheless, though in these verses Mary and

520

Judas are as far as the poles asunder, as far apart as heaven and hell, they may have been much alike at the start.

Both were blessed with similar advantages in their upbringing: and both at the start had their feet set in the same direction. For did Mary love to sit at the Lord's feet and hear His word? Judas too was sufficiently earnest in his devotion to Jesus to be chosen as one of the Twelve who should be with Him, the Twelve whom He would send forth to preach His Gospel. And yet there was all the difference between heaven and hell separating them at the finish. Mary for love brought her alabaster box and broke it; Judas in his hate went away unto the chief priests, that he might deliver his Master unto them.

Together—Apart

This is no isolated instance. Every age and every walk of life will furnish illustrations of men who started from the same mark but who finished far asunder. There were two famous brothers in the last century—John Henry Newman and Francis W. Newman— whose intellectual development worked out in precisely opposite directions. They began together; but one became the advocate of authority and the other of freedom, until they ended up with all the difference between Romanism and agnosticism between them. In the highest realm of all—in the region of morals and the spiritual life—the same amazing differences are to be found. Out of the very same household there will issue a Jacob and an Esau: a Reuben and a Joseph.

The Divide

As you ride by rail between Dolgelley and Bala you come to a point in the hills which forms the watershed. And just at that point two streams take their rise. They have, it is practically true to say, the very same birthplace—but one tiny stream turns to the right and the other turns to the left and so the Dee and the Mawddach, born together, are the entire breadth of Wales apart at the finish. One falls into the sea facing the cold, gray north; the other ends its course facing the golden west. And that is how it is with men. They start together and the divergence sets in and they finish far apart.

> "So from the heights of will,
> Life's parting stream descends
> And as a moment turns its slender rill,
> Each widening torrent bends.
> From the same cradle side,

From the same mother's knee,
One to long darkness and the frozen tide,
One to the peaceful sea."

The Decisive Factor

I dwell upon this to emphasize once again the old point—
human destiny is not at the mercy of conditions. Environment is
not the decisive factor, else men starting alike should finish
alike, sharing the same advantages they should meet with a like
success. Man himself is the decisive factor. You remember that
verse in Omar Khayyam:

"I sent my soul through the Invisible,
Some letter of the after-life to spell;
And by and by my soul return'd to me
And answer'd 'I myself am Heav'n and Hell.'"

Yes, that is true. "I myself am Heav'n or Hell." It is from the
height of will life's parting stream descends. Life is a sort of raw
material. The stuff of devilry and the stuff of sainthood are both
in it. And it depends on ourselves—on the set of our wills—
whether we end with Mary or with Judas—in heaven or in hell:
amongst those who win eternal glory and renown, or amongst
those who have a portion of shame and everlasting contempt.

The Way of the Fall

"And Judas Iscariot, he that was one of the Twelve, went away
unto the chief priests." He flung himself out of Simon's house with
a fierce and bitter anger in his heart. Christ's commendation of
Mary and His implied rebuke of himself were the last straw. There
and then Judas made up his mind to renounce his allegiance and
to go over to the camp of Christ's enemies and foes. It was "the last
straw"; for the perversion and apostasy of Judas were not sudden
and unexpected. A whole train of circumstances led up to the
betrayal. There is a history of moral deterioration behind Judas'
appalling crime. The fact is, that a man becomes neither a saint nor
a devil all at once. "Heaven is not reached at a single bound," says
J. S. Holland.

"But we build the ladder by which we rise
From the lowly earth to the vaulted skies,
And we climb to its summit round by round."

And the story of every saint illustrates the truth of those lines. Sainthood is no sudden attainment. It is by little and little we get the victory over our sins. It is by little and little we grow in grace and in the knowledge of our Lord and Savior Jesus Christ. And if men do not leap into sainthood at one bound, neither do they fall into devilry by one appalling and awful lapse. Behind every shameful apostasy and fall there is a history of deterioration and degeneration.

The Way of Judas

There is such a history behind Judas' fall. The presence of Judas among the Twelve at all is a mystery. It presents problems difficult if not impossible to solve. I reject absolutely the suggestion that Christ chose Judas to be one of the Twelve just because He foreknew that he would eventually become a traitor—that is to introduce an element of artificiality that is altogether alien to the character of Jesus. I reject absolutely also the suggestion that Judas deliberately became a follower of Jesus with treacherous intent. In spite of the difficulties with regard to our Lord's knowledge of man which the view I hold involves, I believe that Judas, when he became a disciple, was as much in earnest as either Peter or John. I believe more; I believe that Jesus saw in him the material out of which an Apostle might have been made—the clay out of which a vessel unto honor might have been shaped. "Of Judas even in his darkest hour," says Professor Tasker in a most illuminating article, "the words of Lavater are true: 'he acted like a Satan, but like a Satan who had it in him to be an Apostle.'"

The Motives of Judas

But how was it that the man who had in him the makings of an Apostle became a Satan? How was it that this Judas who had in him the makings of a saint sank so low that the gentle Jesus said of him, "he hath a devil"? I dismiss entirely as unworthy of serious notice the suggestion that Judas was inspired by good motives in his dealings with the priests; that his real purpose was, not to betray Jesus Christ to death, but to hasten on His Messianic triumph by constraining Him to declare Himself. That theory owes its popularity to De Quincey, and it has been reproduced in our own day in the writings of perhaps the most widely-read lady novelist. But while the theory may do for a work of fiction, it is absolutely impossible to one who takes the Gospel seriously. To hold the belief that Judas was an honest but misguided man you must brush aside the Gospel story, and the stern and solemn words of our Lord Himself. Assuming then, as beyond dispute, that the betrayal was a deed of deliberate wickedness, I want to ask what were the motives that prompted Judas to do it. How was it that the man who might have been a saint became a devil? I agree with Professor Tasker that the answer is not to be given in a single word. This appalling deed had more than one evil root. The Gospels perhaps lay the most emphasis upon Judas' covetousness. But that was not the only evil passion at work in Judas' heart. In and by itself it scarcely accounts for the heinousness of Judas' deed. In addition to covetousness, ambition and jealousy ran riot in Judas' soul, and it was as the result of the joint action of covetousness and ambition and jealousy that Judas was hurried into the crime of history.

His Covetousness

First of all, the Gospels assert that Judas was a covetous man. In his early days, he had perhaps been known as a hard business man remarkably keen at a bargain. Under the spell of Christ's speech, a "new affection" sprang up in Judas' soul, and for the time it expelled his selfish greed and made Judas willing like the rest of the disciples to leave all and follow Christ. But though for the moment subjugated and overcome, Judas' love of money was not wholly eradicated. His heart was like the thorny ground Christ spoke of in the parable—good ground enough, but not clean. The thorn root of covetousness was hidden there. And by and by as Luke says, as he went on his way his heart was "choked" with the cares and riches of this life. The Apostles made him Treasurer of their little band, and Judas' temptation came to him along the line of his duty. The handling of money stirred up the latent passion for money. There began a system of petty pilfering. He used to take what was put there. He became a thief. The thought of the opportunities of aggrandizement that would have been his if Mary had only put her 300 shillings into the purse of which he had the custody—angered him and maddened him. He went immediately off to the high priests to make money out of his Master. First a covetous heart; then the pilfering from the bag; then the selling of his Master for thirty pieces of silver—a slave's ransom—that is the story of Judas' crime.

As a matter of fact, Mammon is a mighty power, and for money, men still deny and betray their Lord, and crucify Him afresh and put Him to an open shame.

His Ambition

But covetousness was not the only passion at work in Judas' heart. If money had been his one and only aim, he would have demanded a bigger price for his Lord's life. These high priests cherished so deadly a hatred of Jesus that they would have been ready to pay any price he had asked. But all he asked apparently was thirty pieces of silver —about £4— a slave's ransom. There was something almost contemptuous in the price asked. At any rate it makes it impossible for us to think that money was the only motive. And so alongside covetousness I see, first of all, ambition. To say that Judas was ambitious is to say about him no more than could be truly said of all the other disciples. Their motives in following Christ were not unmixed and pure. Mingled with a genuine love for Christ, there was a certain hope of reward. They were continually talking about thrones. They believed that when Jesus established His Messianic kingdom, they would all be princes in it. "What shall we have?" was a question often on their lips. In all these ambitious hopes Judas shared. The difference between the eleven and Judas was this, that while in the case of the eleven their love for Christ became stronger than their ambition—in Judas ambition got the better of love. When Jesus began to talk not of triumph but of death, not of a throne but of a Cross, Judas in heart became a deserter. When Mary anointed His head and feet, Jesus had said that it was against His burying she had done it. The word laid in ruins all Judas' ambitions of place and power. Death and a grave—were they to be the end? Then every hope he had cherished had proved to be delusive and vain. It was defeat and extinction that was in store for Jesus. Why stick any longer to a Person Who had cheated him? And so enraged at the disappointment of his ambitions, Judas went away to the high priests and covenanted to deliver Him unto them.

His Jealousy

With ambition I will set down jealousy as one of the motives that hurried Judas into this wicked deed. The wording of this passage is peculiar and scant. The R.V. translates it, "he that was one of the Twelve," but the Greek of the R.V. literally translated reads like this: Judas Iscariot "the one of the Twelve." The one! And this, according to a distinguished Biblical scholar, can only mean "the first of the Twelve." Perhaps that translation is scarcely justified; yet as Professor Tasker says, the phrase may preserve a genuine reminiscence of a time in the earlier ministry of Jesus when Judas, the treasurer of the Apostolic company, had a kind of priority. Judas, the leader of the Twelve—the foremost man in the little company—that is how he started. But precedence in the kingdom is settled by character, and gradually Judas saw Peter and James and John admitted into an intimacy with Jesus from which he was excluded. He saw the last become first, and himself—once first—become last! And Judas became furious with malice and envy. Now jealousy is, we say, as cruel as the grave. In Judas it combined with his covetousness and his ambition to drive him into the murder of the Son of God. It is a tragic story. There are almost fathomless mysteries in it. Explain it wholly perhaps we never can. But this we can say with Dr. Bruce, "He was bad enough to do the deed of infamy, and good enough to be unable to bear the burden of its guilt. Woe to such a man! Better for him, indeed, that he had never been born."

Lessons for Ourselves

As for the lessons we may take to our own hearts from the story of Judas' tragic career, they are many. I confine myself to two. (1) Judas is a solemn warning of the dangers of an incomplete conversion. That was the mischief with Judas. He was only half converted. He did not give his Lord an undivided heart. He did not count all things but loss. He did not slay utterly. He left roots of covetousness and ambition in his soul. And this tragedy was the result. (2) And Judas is a solemn illustration of privileges abused. Look at the phrasing of the text: "He that was one of the Twelve." That constitutes the peculiar enormity of the crime. He was one of the Twelve. Christ was wounded in the house of His friends. It would not have been surprising if one of the priests or scribes or elders had set his mind on betraying Christ. But it was one of the Twelve! Judas had lived in the fellowship of Christ, in the company of Christ; he had enjoyed the unspeakable privileges of hearing Christ's speech and seeing His wonderful deeds, and yet this was the man who went out and betrayed Him. Opportunities were wasted upon him. Privileges were abused by him. And there he stands a flagrant and terrible example of the failure of the favored. We are highly favored even as he. We have the Bible, we have the place of prayer, we have the preaching of the Gospel, we have the knowledge of Christ! If it were in the power of privilege to save, we ought all of us to see salvation. And yet all these privileges may go for nothing: in many cases they *do* go for nothing. Men sin against the light! They misuse the favor and goodness of God. What about our use of these privileges? Are they the aroma of life unto life or of death unto death? If the salt has lost its savor wherewith shall it be seasoned? It is fit neither for the land nor for the dunghill. Men cast it out.

88

The Goodman of the House

"And the first day of unleavened bread, when they killed the passover, His disciples said unto Him, Where wilt Thou that we go and prepare that Thou mayest eat the passover? And He sendeth forth two of His disciples, and saith unto them, Go ye into the city, and there shall meet you a man bearing a pitcher of water: follow him. And wheresoever he shall go in, say ye to the goodman of the house, The Master saith, Where is the guest-chamber, where I shall eat the passover with My disciples? And he will shew you a large upper room furnished and prepared: there make ready for us. And His disciples went forth, and came into the city, and found as He had said unto them: and they made ready the passover."   —Mark 14:12-16.

The Date of the Last Supper

I AM NOT going to discuss at length the difficult question of the exact date of the Last Supper and the Resurrection. I think—in spite of all the efforts of commentators to harmonize the accounts—that John gives a different date from that of the Synoptists. If we were left to the Synoptists, we should conclude that the feast to which Jesus and the Twelve sat down together in the Upper Room was the actual Passover Feast, and that Jesus was crucified on the following day. But John is quite clear and emphatic that the feast Christ ate with His disciples anticipated the real Passover Feast by twenty-four hours, and that the Crucifixion took place on the day on which the lamb was sacrificed. As John wrote last, and with the three other Gospels before him, I am driven to believe that all his corrections are intentional and deliberate; and as there is something beautifully congruous in the thought of Christ dying on the day the Paschal lamb was sacrificed, I incline to accept John's account as being the one which is chronologically correct. But I do not know that we need to trouble to try and settle that vexed controversy. It is sufficient for us to know that Jerusalem was all astir with preparations for the Passover; and it was ordained that at that feast, when men offered a lamb in sacrifice in memory of their deliverance from bondage and death in Egypt, the Lamb of God should offer Himself up in sacrifice for the sins of the world.

527

The Lord and the Means of Grace

I say, Jerusalem was all astir with preparations for the Passover. It was natural therefore that the disciples should come to Jesus and say, "Where wilt Thou that we go and make ready that Thou mayest eat the Passover?" You notice the form of the question: "Where wilt Thou that we make ready?" They do not ask Him if He means to observe it. They take that for granted. All they ask is as to the room He has arranged for its observance. All of which throws an interesting side-light upon the character and habits of Jesus. The fact that the disciples took it for granted that Jesus would observe the Passover shows that He had been in the habit of observing it. Jesus paid scrupulous respect to the forms and rites of the Jewish faith. He kept the Sabbath. He attended the synagogue. He observed the Passover. Ht did not brush them aside as mere empty forms. He "fulfilled all righteousness." He showed respect for the outward means of grace. He recognized that they were of grace, and that they ministered to the life of the soul.

An Example for His People

In all this we may learn a lesson from our Lord. I know it is easy to make too much of forms. But it is possible also to make too little of them. Perhaps this latter is our particular peril. We say that the spirit is the essential thing, that God is a spirit and that they who worship Him must worship Him in spirit and in truth. That is all true enough but, if we make the spirituality of religion an excuse for neglecting the forms and offices of religion, we seriously hurt and impoverish ourselves. For while it is true that you may have the form without that spirit—as in the case of the Pharisees of old—it is important to remember the complementary and balancing truth, that there can be no religious life without some measure of form. So let us follow our Lord in His respect for the means of grace. Let us cultivate the assembling of ourselves together, let us frequent the assemblies of the Church for prayer; above all things when the Table of the Lord is spread let us remember His dying love until He come. The preaching of the Word, united worship, the sacraments—they are all designed for the nourishment of our spiritual life and that life inevitably suffers by their neglect.

The Chosen Place

"Where wilt Thou that we go and make ready that Thou mayest eat the Passover?" asked His disciples. Instead of giving a direct answer and naming the house at which He had arranged to celebrate the feast, Jesus sent two of them (probably Peter and John) off into the city with these mysterious instructions—they were to go to a certain public fountain and there they would find a man bearing a pitcher of water. There would be no chance of failing to identify him— for water-carrying was, as a rule, a woman's business, and a man bearing a pitcher was always a more or less conspicuous object. This man they were to follow to the house to which he returned. Arrived there, they were to ask the goodman of the house for the guest-chamber he had promised to Christ. In the Upper Room which he would show them they were to make all the needful preparations for the observance of the feast.

Pre-arranged

Now it is obvious from all this that there had been an arrangement made between Jesus and this unknown friend of His. They had come to an understanding even as to this little plan by which the disciples were to be led to the chosen rendezvous. The goodman of the house had promised to send one of his servants to this particular fountain, and Jesus on His part arranged to send two of His disciples to follow him from that spot home. There was nothing haphazard or accidental about the meeting at the fountain. There was certainly nothing accidental about the choice of house. All had been planned and arranged beforehand between Jesus and His unknown host.

The Reason

But the question at once arises—why was all this mystery made about the rendezvous? Why could not Christ have named the street and the house at which He had arranged to eat the feast? Why all this secrecy? Dr. David Smith suggests the true answer. There was a traitor amongst the Twelve. Judas was on the look out for an opportunity to deliver Christ to His foes. Had Judas known exactly where Christ had determined to eat the feast, he might have arranged with the priests to seize Him in the very midst of the supper. But Jesus purposed to observe this feast with His disciples undisturbed. So with the goodman of the house He settled His plan. Judas got no clue from Christ's orders to Peter and John and he dared not track the messengers. That was the reason for the secrecy. Jesus was so beset with foes, that He could only secure these brief hours for quiet converse with His disciples, as it were by stealth!

The House and the Host

The two disciples went and they found it even as the Master had said. There at the fountain was the slave with his pitcher of water, obviously watching and waiting for some one. As soon as he caught sight of Peter and John (for no doubt he would know them) he took up his pitcher and made straight for his master's house and there the disciples found "the large Upper Room furnished" which in some private conversation with Jesus the goodman of the house had already offered. Many are the guesses that commentators have made as to the identity of this goodman of the house. Some guess Nicodemus, some Joseph of Arimathea, and others, with greater probability, John Mark. But who he really was we shall never surely know till that great day when all secrets are revealed. One thing however is quite obvious from the narrative—and that is, that he was one of the Lord's friends and disciples. Look at the wording of verse 14. "The Master saith—where is *My* guest chamber?" "The Master" saith! Such language could only be addressed to one who acknowledged Christ's authority and rule. "Where is My guest chamber?" Such language could only be addressed to one who looked upon all that he possessed as belonging to Jesus Christ. So, whoever he was, it is as plain as daylight that he was a friend and a disciple.

Christ's Unknown Friends

The goodman, then, was one of Christ's unknown friends. There are two classes of Christ's friends, as Dr. John Watson suggests. There are those who may be called His public friends and there are those who may be called His private friends. The public friends of Christ were the twelve disciples. They were always at Christ's side. Wherever He went, they went too. In the public eye they were inseparably identified with Christ's cause. But in addition to these public friends, Jesus had private friends of whom the Sanhedrin and even His disciples knew nothing. And amongst those private friends were Nicodemus, who came to Jesus by night, and the goodman of the house, who gladly placed his best room at the disposal of the Lord and His disciples. I daresay when the disciples asked the question, "Where wilt Thou that we go and make ready that Thou mayest eat the Passover?" they wondered whether in all Jerusalem a house could be found to open its doors to Jesus, for by this time He was indeed the despised and rejected of men. At this point, the priests and elders were bent upon His death! And they doubted whether in all Jerusalem there was one who would care to run the risk of being known as their Master's friend.

But Jesus has always more friends in the world than we are inclined to think. Elijah thought he was the only faithful soul left in the whole of Israel. But God knew better. In many a quiet country home there were humble but brave and loyal folk who had never turned their backs upon their father's God. "I have yet seven thousand in Israel," He said to His discouraged and despairing servant, "who have not bowed the knee to Baal." Paul thought Corinth was barren soil. He was out of heart because he could count, as he thought, the Christians in Corinth upon his fingers. But his Lord knew better. He appeared to His desponding servant in a vision by night with the message, "Be not afraid . . . for I have much people in this city." And so in Jerusalem—full of deadly hate as it was—when even His disciples doubted whether a single house would receive Him, Jesus had this goodman for His friend who counted it a joy and an honor to welcome Him to his Upper Room.

His Undistinguished Friends

It is like that still! Christ has more friends in the world than we think. For we do not exhaust the list of Christ's friends when we mention our religious leaders and those who are prominent in Church life. Thank God for these people who take their stand in the high places of the field; but let us not forget that Christ has other friends than these. There are modest, retiring, silent people in the world—people who have never taken part in a meeting in their lives, who have never offered a prayer in public in their lives, who have never held office in a Christian Church in their lives. Their very names are unknown to the leaders of our Churches; and yet among these humble, retiring, shrinking folk Christ has His friends, His staunch, loyal and trusty friends; and the first of all such was the goodman of the house, who, most probably had not the gifts of an Apostle or a preacher, but showed His love for Christ by offering Him a room.

The Goodman: A Brave and Trusty Friend

How this friendship between Christ and the goodman of the house began the Scriptures do not tell us—but this brief story makes it clear that he was not only a friend, he was one of the bravest and staunchest of friends. Dr. Watson in his beautiful little book, *The Upper Room*, remarks that the times when Christ's public friends withdraw and disappear, are often the seasons when His private friends show themselves. It was so in this last and awful week. Judas, one of the Twelve, betrayed Him; but Nicodemus prepared spices for His burying. Peter cursed and swore he did not know Him; but Joseph owned Him before the Sanhedrin, went boldly to Pilate and asked for His body and buried Him in his own new grave. And in much the same way, in our Lord's hour of peril, this goodman of the house showed himself His friend. "A friend in need," we say in our old proverb, "is a friend indeed." Well, this man was a "friend indeed" to Jesus, for he was a friend "in need." In the days of our Lord's popularity men like Simon the Pharisee were quite ready to open their doors to Christ. But in these closing days, not a Pharisee amongst them wanted Jesus for his guest. Then came forward this goodman of the house and said, "Be a guest in my house. The best I have to offer is Thine." The stars, they tell me, shine even during the day, but at high noon, in the full blaze of the sunshine, they are hidden, obscured, dazzled out of sight. But when the sun disappears, and darkness creeps over the sky, then the mild but beautiful stars steal out. There were quiet unobtrusive friends of Christ, who were hidden away in the background, and buried in obscurity when our Lord was in the full blaze of His popularity, but when the dark days came when the crowd turned their backs upon Him then these friends stole out of their modest hiding-places and stood loyally by His side. And the goodman of the house was one of them, for, when every other door in Jerusalem was closed against the Lord, he flung his wide open; and when it had become perilous to confess oneself a disciple he stood boldly by the Lord's side, delighting to avow himself His friend.

A Generous Friend

The goodman showed himself not only a brave and trusty friend, but he fulfilled the office and function of friendship. For is this not the mark of a true friendship—that it keeps nothing back, that it does its best for the loved one? This goodman of the house showed himself a generous friend for he did his very best for Christ. Unless the Greek of this passage entirely misleads me, he did for Christ more than He asked. When Christ sent Peter and John to this unknown friend of His, it was with this message, "Where is My guest chamber where I may eat the Passover with My disciples?" Now the word translated guest-chamber, means primarily an inn, and is so translated in the narrative of Christ's birth. But the word "inn" suggests to us more than the original implies. It would denote no more than the place where the beasts of burden were unloaded, shoes and staff or dusty garment put down, if an apartment at all, only one opening out on to the courtyard and certainly not the best. That was all Christ asked for. But it was not to this shelter that the unknown friend showed the disciples, but the Upper Room, the most retired and honorable room in the house, the best and chiefest apartment and that heavily and richly furnished with tables and couches and cushions. He was not content to give Christ merely what He asked: a place in the caravanserai; he gave the very best he had to give—not the hall, but the Upper Room.

The Offering of True Friendship

This is ever the mark of a true and genuine friendship. It gives its best. Its question is not how little need it do, but how much can it do? And this suggests to me the question, Have we fulfilled the office and function of friendship? We profess to be Christ's friends; have we given Him the chief place, the Upper Room? Yes, I know we have most of us, if not all of us, given some sort of hospitality to Christ. But with many of us, it is the mere lodging we have given, not the "Upper Room." We like to have some connection with Christ, but we do not let Him in very far. We keep Him on the outside, near the door, down in the hall. It is a poor external apartment we have set aside for His occupation. But He wants to live not in the hall but in the Upper Room. Not on the outside but in our heart of hearts. "Son, daughter, give Me thine heart," and it is a plea for the Upper Room. Have we given it to Him?

The Reward of Friendship

This goodman of the house showed himself a friend of Christ. What a rich reward he has reaped! "Verily, verily, I say unto you," our Lord remarked one day, "whosoever shall give to drink unto one of these little ones a cup of cold water only in the name of a disciple, he shall in no wise lose his reward." Not the smallest kindness ever done to Christ fails of recompense. Think of the reward this goodman reaped. First of all, he is known throughout the world as the friend of Jesus. Where ever the Gospel is preached this also that he did is spoken of as a memorial of him. It is said of the famous Lord Holland, that he wished to be remembered as "the friend of Charles James Fox." This man has a far nobler memorial. He is known as the man who in a time of mortal peril befriended Jesus Christ. Think what a train of events the granting of this Upper Room led to. I have been in some great houses and have been shown bedrooms, magnificently decorated and furnished, which are regarded with pride by the owners of the houses because some great person or other once slept in them. I remember for instance being shown in "Burleigh House," the room in which our Maiden Queen once slept. It was never used. It was kept like a sacred place and shown to visitors as Queen Elizabeth's room. In one sense it would have been honor enough that the goodman should have been able to say of his Upper Room that this was the room in which Jesus ate the Supper with His disciples, and spoke those wonderful words which John has preserved for us.

A Sacred Room

But a whole train of consequences followed the use of the Upper Room for this feast. It was to that Upper Room the disciples instinctively made their way after the crucifixion; it was in that Upper Room that the risen and victorious Christ appeared again to the disciples saying, "Peace be unto you." It was in that Upper Room He showed Himself to Thomas saying, "Reach within thy finger and see My hands; and reach within thy hand and put it into My side." And it was in that same Upper Room that the miracle of Pentecost happened, when the disciples were baptized with the Holy Ghost and with fire. "Christ pays richly for His entertainment," says quaint old Matthew Henry. "Men gain—not lose—by giving Christ their best," says Dr. Glover.

The Great Reward

But the best reward of all came, as Dr. Watson suggests, when the "goodman of the house" found an Upper Room prepared for him by Christ's own hands in the Father's house of many mansions. The reward for this man's welcome to Christ in the day of His trouble and distress was a welcome from Christ in the day of His exaltation and glory. Thousands and tens of thousands have found an entrance into the Celestial City, but none received gladder welcome than this man who first gave Christ His heart and then provided Him with a home. The hospitality of the heart is always repaid by the hospitality of heaven. If we ask Christ to sup with us today, the day will surely come when we shall sup with Him. The welcome we shall receive depends on the welcome we give. Have you asked the Lord to come into your Upper Room? Then surely you shall at the last take your place with the goodman of the house, and all the saints who have been the friends of Christ, and have done their best for Him, at the Marriage Supper of the Lamb.

89

The Announcement
of the Betrayal

"And in the evening He cometh with the twelve. And as they sat and did eat, Jesus said, Verily I say unto you, One of you which eateth with Me shall betray Me. And they began to be sorrowful, and to say unto Him, one by one, Is it I? and another said, Is it I? And He answered and said unto them, It is one of the twelve, that dippeth with me in the dish. The Son of man indeed goeth, as it is written of Him: but woe to that man by whom the Son of man is betrayed! good were it for that man if he had never been born."

—Mark 14:17-21.

WE COME NOW to that paragraph, that poignant little paragraph, which tells how, when Christ and the Twelve had taken their places for the festal meal, He made the announcement that it was one of the chosen band who should betray Him.

The Context

But before I begin the study of the paragraph itself, let me say again that Mark's account is not a complete account of what happened in the Upper Room. Mark's is the briefest of all the Gospels. He picks out what seem to him the salient parts of the story, and these he narrates for us in an incomparably vivid way. But if you want the complete story, an accurate scheme of the sequence of events, you must compare Mark's Gospel with the other three and insert here and there with his abbreviated narrative various scenes and incidents passed over by him but preserved for us in the records of the other evangelists. At this point, e.g. the announcement of the betrayal follows immediately upon the verse in which Mark describes their assembly in the Upper Room. Had we been left to Mark we should have concluded that this was the very first thing that happened when they had gathered together in that quiet chamber. But, when we compare the accounts of the other evangelists, we find Mark has passed over without notice a good many things, such, e.g. as the strife among the disciples as to which of them was greatest, and that most moving and pathetic incident of the washing of the disciples' feet. You must insert all that between verses 17 and 18 if you would have the full and complete sequence of events before you.

The Things Unrecorded

It must also be remembered, as Dr. Glover points out, that a good many things had happened which are mentioned by none of the evangelists. They had gathered in that Upper Room for the Paschal meal, and the Paschal meal was observed with a certain amount of fixed and definite ritual. Jesus, no doubt, had taken His place at the head of the table as the Master of the Feast. Following the usual practice He had explained the significance of the Passover, and spoken of the mighty deliverance of which it was the memorial—with what thoughts of that grander and more glorious Exodus which He was to accomplish for all mankind on the morrow who shall tell? And then they had sung some of the appointed Psalms—Psalms breathing of gratitude and rest and hope. Very likely they had already passed round that cup which was so essential a part of the Passover celebration. All these things had happened in the Upper Room before there fell from the lips of Christ this tragic announcement which changed their festal gladness into grief and fear.

The Prediction of the Betrayal

Why did Christ make the announcement at all? Some commentators suggest that He had a design in making it. He was just about to institute the feast of the Supper. "He had gathered the Twelve in the Upper Room," says Dr. David Smith, "not merely that He might eat the Passover with them, but that He might institute a sacred rite which should perpetuate the remembrance of His immortal love. Now the Supper is the family feast, at which only those who really and sincerely love the Lord have any right to sit. That is the reason why the Apostle says, "Let a man prove himself, and so let him eat of the bread and drink of the cup" (1 Cor. 11:28). It is no feast in which a traitor has any right to participate. Our Lord could not celebrate that first Passover with Judas present, and so He makes this fateful announcement in order to be freed from Judas' oppressive presence, and to be at liberty to celebrate His love-feast with those who were really and sincerely His own. There is a good deal of plausibility about the suggestion, but personally I do not feel inclined to accept it. For you have to assume that Judas left before the Supper, which is itself a very doubtful point. And it seems to me to artificialize the whole narrative.

Not a Disclosure But a Cry

If you ask how I think this tragic announcement came to be made, I reply, Christ could not bear the awful burden a moment longer. I do not think there was any *design* in it. I do not think it was meant to cure the pride of the disciples. I do not even think it was meant to give Judas a glimpse of the perdition before him and thus awake repentance. I think Dr. Chadwick comes nearest the truth when he says this was not so much a *disclosure* as a *cry*! A cry from the Lord's bruised and wounded spirit! He could not help Himself! After all, our Lord was not only "very God" but also "very Man," a man with an exquisitely sensitive soul! And just as when He came in sight of Jerusalem, the pity of His heart showed itself in tears which He could not suppress, so now the sorrow of His soul broke out in this agonizing cry. Dr. David Smith suggests that at the very moment He may have had the bitter herbs of the Passover Feast in His hand. And the bitter herbs in His hands reminded Him of the bitterness in His soul. And as He thought of it, it was more than He could bear, and this cry, involuntarily almost, broke from His lips, "Verily I say unto you, One of you shall betray Me, even he that eateth with Me."

The Sorrow of Lost Opportunities

And that is the first thing I find in this bitter cry. I find in it a hint of the *measureless sorrows of the Lord*. You can find other things in it I know. Read it like this: "One of *you* shall betray Me," and I think I could preach a sermon from it upon *opportunities lost and privileges abused*. "One of *you*!" It was not one of Christ's foes who was to do this thing! It was not one of the Scribes or Pharisees with whom He had been so often in conflict. It was not one of the priests whose anger He had incurred by His exposure of their evil deeds. It was not one of the indiscriminate multitude who had only seen Christ from afar and had never felt the compelling power of His goodness or the charm of His love. It was "one of *you*!" One of the Twelve men who had been chosen to be Christ's intimates, who had seen Him at close quarters, who knew best how good and holy and gracious He was! "One of you!" Judas spent two years in close company with Christ and turned traitor at the finish! Privileges will save no man. Opportunities and privileges were wasted upon Judas. "One of *you* shall betray Me."

The Sorrow of Willful Sin

Read it again like this, "One of you shall betray *Me*," and from that text I think I could preach a sermon upon the awful and unspeakable lengths to which human wickedness can go! "Shall betray *Me!*" It was not some man of evil life that Judas was selling to the priests; it was not some one whose influence was a blight; it was not a political malefactor; it was not a disturber of the nation's peace. "One of you shall betray *Me!*" Me! the Man Who had never done an evil deed, or spoken an evil word! The Man Who had gone about doing good! The Man Who had carried a blessing with Him whithersoever He had gone! The Man Who had given cleansing to the leper, and sight to the blind, and hearing to the deaf, and power to the palsied, and life to the dead! The Man Who had blessed innumerable homes, and brought new hope and courage into innumerable lives! Sin a light thing? This is the length of wickedness to which sin can go. It can sell and scourge, and kill the Christ! But it is neither of these things that I see primarily and chiefly in this startling and tragic announcement.

The Sorrow of the Lord

I see in it—above everything else—the *sorrow of the Lord*. The vision of that overwhelming sorrow allows me to see scarcely anything else in this bitter cry. You remember the old prophetic word in which Jeremiah bids the people turn aside and see if there was any sorrow like unto his sorrow. Well, the sorrow of Jeremiah, no doubt, was deep and bitter, for he too was rejected and despised by his own; but the deep unfathomable sorrow of the world is not the sorrow of Jeremiah but the sorrow of Christ. There was not a single ingredient of bitterness left out of His bitter cup. It was not, as Dr. Chadwick says in his commentary, the physical sufferings of our Lord that constituted His immeasurable Passion. We have thought too much perhaps of the scourging, and the thorn crown, and the nails, and the agonizing thirst. What hurt Christ most—the really unfathomable sufferings of our Lord— were His sufferings of soul. And amongst those sufferings of soul was that inflicted by the treachery of one of His chosen friends. It bit deep. It wounded to the quick. "One of you shall betray Me, even he that eateth with Me." Our Lord passed through that bitter experience of the Psalmist, "Mine own familiar friend, in whom I trusted, which did eat of My bread, hath lifted up his heel against me" (Psalm 41:9). There are two passages in Shakespeare's great play of "Julius Caesar" which illustrate by contrast the bitterness of being betrayed by a friend. The first is a sentence Shakespeare puts

into the mouth of Brutus himself. Brutus had seen his cause overwhelmed with disaster and he was just upon the point of falling
upon his sword. But with ruin overtaking him and death staring
him in the face he had one deep source of joy. "Countrymen," he
said,

> "My heart doth joy that yet in all my life,
> I found no man but he was true to me."

Now turn by way of contrast to the scene in which Shakespeare
describes the assassination of great Caesar himself. You remember
how, under pretense of presenting a petition, the conspirators
crowded round Caesar's seat. Decius, Cassius, Casca—they were
all there. When the petition was refused, Casca gave the sign for
attack by saying, "Speak, hands, for me." He aimed his dagger at
Caesar's breast; and at once Decius and Cassius, and Cinna had
their daggers out too. Caesar resisted for a time until he saw
Brutus—one of the most cherished of his friends—also with his
dagger raised to strike. But when he saw Brutus—his friend—he
ceased to struggle. "*Et tu*, Brute," he cried, "And thou, Brutus.—
Then fall Caesar." And through that bitter experience our Lord had
to pass. He had not the joy of feeling that however much his enemies might rage, his *friends* had been true to Him. It was a friend
who betrayed Him: it was a friend who sold Him. It was one who
ate His bread who lifted his heel against Him. The very thought of
it wrung Christ's heart with anguish, and provoked this cry from
His lips. "One of you shall betray Me, even he that eateth with
Me." "Behold, and see, if there be any sorrow like unto My sorrow" (Lam. 1:12).

Does Judas Stand Alone?

I am tempted, before I pass on, to ask a question like this—"Is
Judas the only friend who has ever betrayed the Lord?" Is he the
only one who has eaten the Lord's bread, and then lifted up his
heel against Him? Of course I know that there is a sense in which
the crime of Judas can never be again committed. Never again can
Christ be betrayed into the hands of men. Never again can He be
sold to the shame of the whipping-post and the tree. And yet, from
another point of view, He is not beyond the reach of wounds and
treachery and shame. Why, one of the sacred writers declares that
it is in our power to "crucify Christ afresh." And we do it. Yes, we
often do it; we, His so-called friends crucify Him afresh and put
Him to an open shame. What Christ suffers from most, is not the

attacks of His foes. There are certain miserable people in the world
who make it their business to attack Christ. They fight against Him
and His cause. They stand at street corners and vilify Him. They
write in the papers, and caricature and blaspheme Him. But these
are not the people who do Christ harm. The blasphemies of Hyde
Park orators, the coarse caricatures of the Free-thinker—these are
not the things that impede the progress of Christianity. We can
afford to laugh at them. They do not count. They are beneath contempt. But I will tell you what it is that injures Christ and
impedes His cause—not the attacks of His foes but the failures of
His friends. We profess to belong to the circle of His disciples, and
there out in the world yonder we deny Him, and sell Him, and
betray Him. We call Him Lord, and then we turn our backs upon
Him. We come to His table and eat His bread, and then we lift up
our heel against Him. Christ suffers still from treachery and betrayal. The most grievous wounds which He ever endures, are the
wounds which He receives in the house of His friends.

The Fear of the Disciples

And now let me ask you to notice the effect of this solemn
announcement upon the disciples. "And they began to be sorrowful," says Mark. Up to that moment they had been a glad and
happy company—but upon this announcement their sunshine
went out in dark and bodeful gloom. Their hearts were filled with
a chilly sense of fear and dread. And one by one with blanched lips
and tremulous voices they began to say to Christ, "Is it I? Is it I?"
Now it seems almost callous to analyze this heart-breaking question. But I see two things in it that are infinitely to the credit of
these disciples. I see first of all *their trust and hope for one another*,
and I see in the second place *their fear and distrust of themselves*. I
see, first of all, *their trust and hope for one another*. Not a man apparently suspected Judas! I know it speaks volumes for the
circumspectness and prudence with which Judas must have
conducted himself. But it speaks volumes for those disciples too.
They never suspected Judas. They thought Judas every whit as
good a disciple as themselves. They never suspected any one of
their little band. We have often had occasion to notice faults and
failings in these disciples of our Lord. We shall have to notice many
a fault and failure still. They were indeed full of faults and failings.
But here is something that must be set down to the credit side of
their account. They had a splendid faith in one another. They
believed the best of one another. Not a man of them had dreamed
that another could turn traitor. These disciples blundered often—

they were proud, they were self-seeking, they were materialistic in their notions; but when I hear them cry, "Lord, is it I?" suspecting no one but themselves, I am quite sure they had caught from their Lord some of that "love which suffereth long and is kind; which is not easily provoked and thinketh no evil; which rejoiceth not in iniquity but which rejoiceth in the truth, which beareth, believeth, hopeth and endureth all things."

Their Fear of Themselves

I see, secondly, in this question *their fear and distrust of themselves*. When the Master said, "One of you shall betray Me," these disciples did not cast their eyes round their little company to try and discover who of their number looked most like a traitor. They did not listen—as we often do—for somebody else. They did not try to fit the cap on to somebody else's head. They listened for themselves. They took the warning home to their own souls. When Christ said, "One of you shall betray Me," every man of them looked into his own heart. And it was what they saw there, that brought this cry to their lips, "Lord, can it be I?" For when they looked within, they saw the prince of this world had something in every one of them—there was weakness there and timidity there and cowardice there, and love of the world and of life there! And the sight struck terror to their souls. "Lord," they cried in broken accents, "Can it be I?" And this distrust of themselves is also to be set down to the disciples' credit. I like them better distrusting themselves like this, than when boasting that neither prison nor death can daunt them. I have more hope for them when taking this humble estimate of themselves than when bragging of their courage and their constancy. He that humbleth himself shall be exalted; he that exalteth himself shall be abased. Mr. Fearing wins his way at last to the Heavenly City but the last sight we get of Presumption is lying fast by the heels in a hollow far from the journey's end.

A Question for All

"Lord, is it I?" It is a question that often leaps to the lips of a man who has looked into his own heart. Who really knows the enormities of which he may be guilty? Who knows what possibilities of evil lie latent within? This much I know; we find it easy still to sell Christ; we sell Him in order to succeed in business; we sell Him for pleasure; we sell Him for social position. We crucify Him afresh and put Him to an open shame by forgetting Him, repudiating His authority, bringing disgrace upon His name. "One

of you," He says to us in these latter days "shall betray Me." I cannot treat that warning as if it did not concern me. Like the
disciples, knowing my own weakness, I know that one may be
myself. All I can do is to give myself and this treacherous heart of
mine into the keeping of Almighty Love, and say with the
Psalmist, "Keep back thy servant also from presumptuous sins; let
them not have dominion over me; then shall I be upright and I
shall be innocent from the great transgression" (Psalm 19:13).

90
The Last Supper—I

"And as they did eat, Jesus took bread, and blessed, and brake it, and gave to them, and said, Take, eat; this is My body. And He took the cup, and when He had given thanks, He gave it to them: and they all drank of it. And He said unto them, This is My blood of the new testament, which is shed for many. Verily I say unto you, I will drink no more of the fruit of the vine, until that day that I drink it new in the kingdom of God." —Mark 14:22-25.

Two Subjects Out of Many
BEFORE CONSIDERING THESE verses, which tell us in Mark's brief but vivid way of the institution of the Lord's Supper, I want to call attention to this fact, that, of all that happened in the Upper Room, *the announcement of the Betrayal* and the *institution of the Supper* are the only two things which Mark troubles to record. Now these were by no means the only things that happened. Luke devotes twenty-four verses, while John occupies five whole chapters in telling us the story of that memorable evening, which Mark here concentrates into eight brief verses. The incident of the feet-washing, the varied questions the disciples asked, those marvelous talks of our Lord which John has recorded for us—all these Mark passes over in silence. He just fastens our attention on the announcement of the Betrayal, and the institution of the Lord's Supper; and the former in a way leads up to the latter. Christ knew that His hour was come; He knew that the hand of the traitor was with Him on the table; He knew that soon the ways of earth would know Him no more; it was in view of His approaching death, because treachery was soon to do its deadly work, that He instituted this simple feast to His abiding and perpetual memorial. So that, taking all the circumstances into account, I am not misrepresenting Mark's view, when I say, that for him, the great happening of that night in the Upper Room was *the institution of the Supper.*

A Theory and the Gospel Narratives
Now I think it is worth while emphasizing this point in view of the fact that many scholars of our day would have us believe that

the Lord's Supper as we know it, is largely the creation of Paul. They tell us that Jesus had no intention of instituting an ordinance which was to be perpetually observed in His church and that all that Jesus did or meant to do was just to break bread and drink wine for the last time with His disciples; that it was Paul who transfigured and exalted this simple act of our Lord's into a Sacrament which should be the Lord's abiding memorial. But the whole tenor of the Gospel narrative is absolutely fatal to such a suggestion. It is perfectly true that in Mark's version the Lord does not say, "This do in remembrance of Me." But even if we had nothing but Mark's brief version to go upon, we should still conclude that when Christ broke the bread and drank the cup, He did something which had significance not simply for the eleven who reclined at the table with Him, but for all His disciples of after days. I should gather that from the very words He used, and especially from His word about the "new covenant." No one can read such a word with open and candid mind, remembering that it was spoken at that feast at which a lamb was slain and eaten in token of God's covenant of mercy with the Israelites, without feeling that this simple rite of the Lord's institution was meant to be for His people what the Passover was to the Israelites, a perpetual reminder of a mightier deliverance, and of a better covenant of grace sealed with the blood of Christ Himself. But I should argue my point not simply from the words, but from the fact that this is the one incident picked out for recording. If this rite was meant for none but the eleven men reclining with Him, then there were other things which would have been far better worth recording, as e.g. our Lord's teaching about greatness, His announcement of the coming of the Comforter, His parable of the Vine and the Branches. These great teachings of our Lord have at any rate universal and abiding validity. But Mark passes all these things over in silence. It was his habit, as I said in the last chapter, to seize only upon the salient points, the outstanding points, and to let many lesser things pass without notice. And as far as the events of the Upper Room were concerned, the salient outstanding vital occurrence was the institution of the Supper.

Mark and the Testimony of Peter

You will remember that though in speaking of the Gospel we know it as Mark's, universal tradition says that Mark was "the interpreter or secretary" of Peter—that what Mark records conveys to us the remmiscences of the Primate of the Twelve. If that be so, we have here Peter's view. I do not suppose Peter would ever for-

get the incident of the feet-washing and the quarrel about precedence. I do not suppose Peter any more than John would ever
forget that sacred and intimate talk about the Father's house—the
prepared place. Yet looking back he feels that the one supreme
event of that never-to-be-forgotten night was that Jesus instituted
this simple feast.

The Practice of the Church

In a way, this little paragraph accounts for the practice of the
church. Right away from the beginning of things the disciples met
to break bread. They met together on the Lord's Day and did it.
They broke bread and drank the cup after their meals in their own
homes. And the reason for it was that on the night on which He
was betrayed, Jesus said to His disciples, "This is My body. Take
ye. This is my blood of the covenant which is shed for many." This
is no rite which the immense influence of St Paul has imposed
upon the Church. Paul and Peter on this point (as on all the essential points) are agreed. They observed this feast because on that
awful night Christ bade them break the bread and drink the cup in
remembrance of Him. So we do well to perpetuate the rite. The fact
that by many the simplicity of it has been overlaid, is no reason
why we should think lightly of it or neglect it. This is the Lord's
Supper, i.e. it is Jesus Himself Who instituted the feast, it is Jesus
Who still provides it and invites us to it, and presides at it. No! it
is not Paul's Supper! Paul, when He became a Christian, found it
already in existence, found it indeed to be the central sacred act of
worship and devotion of the Christian Church. It was the way in
which the Lord Himself had bidden His disciples keep His
memory fresh and green.

The Time of the Institution

Now, turning to the narrative, let me call your attention to what
Mark says, about the point in the proceedings at which Jesus instituted this beautiful and sacred rite. It was "as they were eating."
It was sometime during the course of the Passover meal. Now, as
I said in the last chapter, the observance of Passover had come to
be attended with a certain amount of ritual. There was a kind of
"order of service." First a hymn was sung, and a cup of wine was
drunk. Then the bitter herbs were placed on the table and eaten
with thanksgiving. Then the unleavened bread and the flesh of the
lamb were presented and a second cup of wine was mixed. Then
the bread was broken, the flesh of the lamb was eaten and
prayer was again offered and the third cup was drunk. It is diffi-

cult of course to say exactly at what part of the Passover Feast
Christ broke away from the established order and instituted this
new Passover. But most commentators think it was after the flesh
of the lamb had been eaten and the third cup had been drunk so
the Paschal meal proper was finished. That is indeed the expression that Luke and Paul use—"after supper." But the precise
point at which the supper was instituted matters little or nothing,
and I do not know that I should have stayed to refer to it at all—
but for one thing, and that is the stress that is laid in some quarters
upon the time at which it is fitting to celebrate the Communion.

The Bond of Union Marred

It is a strange and lamentable thing that there is scarcely an
aspect of this feast that is not associated with controversy. This
feast that ought to have been the bond of union between
Christians has become the occasion of strife. It divides Romanists
and Protestants. It divides even Protestants themselves. Luther and
Zwinglius in Germany and Switzerland respectively were both
engaged in the blessed work of Reformation. They ought to have
joined hands. It was on the rock of the Supper they split. That this
feast, which Christ meant to be a bond of union, and which seems
as if it might so easily become a visible sign of our essential unity
(for whatever our name or sign we can all unite in remembering
the Lord Who bought us with thanksgiving), that this feast
should have become a source of division and strife and bitter controversy is surely one of the ironies of history. Everything
connected with it, its meaning, its efficacy, the manner of its observance, who have a right to administer it, who have a right to
receive it, all these things have been matters of angry recrimination
and debate.

Reversing Christ's Order

Amongst other things men have wrangled as to the time of its
observance. There is a tendency amongst certain of our fellow-
Christians to insist upon fasting communion. Now, I am quite
prepared to admit that some may find it helpful to think of their
Lord in the early hours of the day. Just as I find it easier to preach
in the evening, some people find their souls fresher and more alert
in the morning. "In the morning," said the Psalmist, "will I order
my prayer unto Thee and will keep watch." Very well, let them,
if that be so, remember their Lord in the morn's virgin hours. But
when "fasting communion" is imposed on the Church as a rule,
I will not yield by way of subjection, no, not for an hour. I do not

myself think the time matters; that is one of those things indifferent which may be left to the convenience of those who are meeting together to remember the Lord's dying. But the one method that has absolutely no warrant for it in the Scripture is this method of "fasting communion." I am not going to enquire into the origin of the practice. As a matter of fact it originates in a materialistic and superstitious view of the Supper itself. It allies itself to the belief in Transubstantiation. All I care for now is to point out to you that at least this much is true, it is a complete repudiation of Apostolic practice; it is an almost complete reversal of our Lord's method when He instituted the Supper; for when I turn to the evangelists and read what they have to say, I find that it was "as they were eating," that it was "after supper," that the Lord brake the bread and distributed the cup.

The Remembrance of Christ's Death

Now I pass on to the fact that this feast of our Lord's institution was not only meant to be a memorial feast, but it was specially meant to be a memorial of His death. The desire to be remembered is a natural and almost universal desire. When men are about to leave for another land, they give little presents to their friends as mementos of their friendship. Our Lord was just about to leave His friends. In bodily form He would no longer walk with them along the streets of Jerusalem, or the lanes of Galilee. And so He gave them this simple feast as a memorial. It was the Lord's *forget-me-not.* "Do this," He said, "in remembrance of Me." But the significant point about the feast is, that it is not a memorial of Christ's life in general, shall I say. It is a memorial of a particular act in it. The bread He gave to His disciples was broken bread. The wine He gave was out-poured wine. They were meant to symbolize His broken body, and His shed blood. In other words, the memorial feast which Christ instituted was a memorial of His death. That was the thing Christ wished to be remembered by—His death: that was the thing He wished His disciples to retain in perpetual remembrance—His dying. "As often as ye eat this bread and drink the cup," said Paul, "ye do shew the Lord's death till He come."

Remembrance of Victory through Death

Now here surely we come across a striking and significant thing—Jesus wished to be remembered by His death. I have noticed that there are certain anniversaries which men delight to observe. But I have never heard of their meeting to celebrate a day of darkness and disaster and overthrow. It is not defeat men cel-

ebrate, but victory. And yet here Jesus institutes a feast to com-
memorate His death. Here is a feast to keep fresh and vivid in the
mind of His people that Cross of ignominy and shame on which
He died. He will not allow us to forget His torn and mangled body
and His pierced side. That is how He wants to be remembered.
Not as He spoke on the hill-side with an eager throng all about
Him; not as He stood up in the boat bidding wind and wave be
still; not as the Mighty Healer curing leprosy with a touch, and
blindness and deafness with a word; not as the Master of Death
bidding Lazarus in a loud voice come forth: He wants to be
remembered as He hung upon the tree, the sport and derision of
Jerusalem, the apparently forsaken of God. He wants to be
remembered not as the Great Preacher; not as the Master of
Nature; not as the Miracle Worker; but as the Sufferer, the Victim,
the Dying Lamb. Is not that strange? Is not that an amazing thing?
"It is," as Dr. Chadwick says, "as if your nation exulted in
Trafalgar, not in spite of the death of our great Admiral, but solely because he died; as if the shot which slew Nelson had itself been
the overthrow of hostile navies." And that is exactly what it does
mean. The Cross was not a defeat but a victory, deliverance.

A Life Laid Down for Us

People talk of Christ's death as a martyrdom. They say He was
martyred by the priests for His loyalty to the truth of God. Well,
the priests and all who took a part in the crime of the crucifixion
will bear their punishment and doom. Of Judas, Christ said, it
would be good for him if he had never been born. From the standpoint of the priests and Pilate the death of Christ was a crime, the
crime of history. But to represent Christ's death as a martyrdom, a
death which He could not escape, to put Him on a level with
Socrates, and Paul, and Latimer, and other men who were hounded to death by their foes is entirely to misrepresent the Gospel
narrative. It is to fly in the face of all the facts of our Lord's life. It
is to construct an absolutely new account of Him.

The Purpose of the Incarnation

I believe that Jesus came into the world to die. No! I do not
absolve the agents of the crime, but nevertheless Jesus had to die. It
was the condition of winning deliverance and redemption for men.
Had there been no Judas, no priests, no Pilate, Christ would still
have died. Death, with the rest of us, is something we cannot help.
It is simply the close of life. But Jesus chose to die. Had He not chosen to die, not all the nails in the world could have fastened Him to

the tree. No one took His life away from Him, He laid it down of Himself. And He did not look upon His death as defeat and disaster. He looked upon it as the means of His triumph. We may admire the courage of the martyrs. But nevertheless we deplore their death. To that extent it meant the defeat of their cause. But we do not deplore the death of Christ. He did not deplore it Himself. It was not defeat, but triumph. By His death He was to accomplish a deliverance. Death was not something Christ suffered. It was something which He did. It was the mightiest act of His life. And of all things that is what He wishes us to remember. We are to remember His death. For His death was His triumph and His sacrifice was our life.

Christ Not a Teacher Only, but a Savior

On this I have one other word to say. Those who would shift the emphasis from the Cross of Christ to His teaching, from Calvary to the Sermon on the Mount are flying in the face of the teaching of this Sacrament. It is not too much to say that they are flying in the face of the mind and will of Christ Himself. It was not there He Himself placed the emphasis, not on His teaching but on His dying. Not on the sermon on the hill, but on the Cross. For Christ came not simply to teach men, but to redeem them. Not simply to illumine their darkness, but to deliver them from sin. And when it comes to redemption, it was on the Cross that the mighty deliverance was won. I am not now going to discuss it. Let it suffice to say that His blood was shed for many; that He died the just for the unjust, that because He died we are free from the law of sin and death. That is what happened on the Cross. He won release for us. He redeemed men from the power and pain of sin. And when He bids us remember Him that is how He would have us do it—*on the Cross* with body broken, and blood shed. And that is how I for one delight to remember Him. I listen to Him on the hill and I too am filled with astonishment, for He teaches with authority. But His words are so profound, His ideas so lofty, His demands so vast, that they fill me with despair. "Who shall ascend into the hill of the Lord?" Not I, if these be His demands. They are high, and I cannot attain to them. But I go to another Hill and I see Him hanging there for love of me, sealing a new covenant of love and grace with His blood, bearing my pain and shame and reproach, and I hear the old word, "The blood of Jesus Christ cleanseth from all sin." My burden is lifted as I look, and I go on my way rejoicing. That is how I would remember Christ as this feast bids me remember Him, as the Lamb of God Who taketh away the sin of the world.

91
The Last Supper—II

"And as they did eat, Jesus took bread, and blessed, and brake it, and gave to them, and said, Take, eat: this is My body. And He took the cup, and when He had given thanks, He gave it to them: and they all drank of it. And He said unto them, This is My blood of the new testament, which is shed for many. Verily I say unto you, I will drink no more of the fruit of the vine, until that day that I drink it new in the kingdom of God." —Mark 14:22-25.

THE LORD'S SUPPER IS primarily, as His words show, a memorial of Christ's dying; but it is also something more, and it is with that something more I want to occupy myself in this chapter. What is it more than a memorial feast?

The Sacrament of Friendship

I answer first it is the sacrament of friendship. Dr. David Smith reminds us in his *Life of Christ* of the sacredness attached in the East to the common meal. It constitutes, he says, a solemn and indissoluble bond. He tells a story of the lengths to which the Arabs carry this idea that when men have broken bread with one another, they become perpetual friends. "Zail-al-khail, a famous warrior in the days of Mohammad," so the legend runs, "refused to slay a vagabond who carried off his camels because the chief had surreptitiously drunk from his father's milk-bowls before committing the theft." We have a little of that feeling even in these more prosaic Northern regions. If we accept the hospitality of another, we feel bound at any rate to keep within the conventional obligation of friendship. "A breach of hospitality" is regarded as an ugly and hateful thing even here in England.

Now, the supper was a common meal. Jesus invited these men to accept His hospitality. They broke the bread and shared the cup with Him. It was a sacrament of friendship. The one disciple who was no friend but a traitor in disguise, had probably gone out to do his nefarious deed, but the eleven who remained, whatever their faults, were brave and loyal souls, and when they shared this meal with their Master, He declared Himself their friend, and they declared themselves His friends, and pledged themselves, that, come weal come woe, He should always have the love of their devoted and loyal hearts. Do you know what I have been reminded of as I thought of Christ and that little company of eleven sharing this meal together? I have been reminded of King Arthur and his Knights of the Round Table. The presence of the Knights at that table was the outward sign and symbol that they had pledged allegiance to Arthur. You remember how Tennyson makes them sing,

> "The King will follow Christ and we the King
> In whom high God hath breathed a sacred thing,
> Fall battleaxe and flash brand! Let the King reign!"

And these eleven disciples were to Jesus what his Knights were to Arthur. When they sat at His table they pledged themselves to His service.

A Double Tie

It was a beautiful sacrament of friendship. And that is what the Supper is still. It is only for the friends of Christ. In it Christ offers us His hospitality, and when we accept it, we proclaim ourselves His friends and pledge ourselves to His cause. It is an ugly thing to sit at the Lord's table, and then to deny Him. It is a base thing to accept His hospitality and then betray Him! Better never eat the bread and drink the cup at all, than eat and drink and then by our life repudiate our Lord. That is why Paul says that every man ought to examine himself, and so eat of the bread and drink of the cup. For this common meal is a sacrament of friendship, of Christ's friendship for us, and our friendship for Him, and only the friends of the Lord have a right to participate in it. And let me add this word, this common meal is not only a sacrament of friendship between Christ and those who share in it, but it is a sacrament of friendship between one disciple and another. When we sit down to this meal together it means that we are not only all of us friends of the Lord, it means also that we are friends of one another. We all eat of the same bread and drink of the same cup in token that we all share in the same life. We "commune" not simply with our Lord, but also with one another. I wonder whether this aspect of the Supper is not often forgotten or ignored by us.

The Supper is the family meal, the perpetually recurring reminder that we are all members of one great household. It always strikes me as a strange and pitiable thing that men and women can sit down together at the table of the Lord and clean forget one another outside; that there is so much distance, lack of sympathy, absence of friendship between members of the same Church. It would alter the climate of many a Church, and bring cheer into many a lonely heart if we only remembered that this blessed feast is a sacrament of friendship with one another. Shall we try to remember? Shall we try henceforth to enter into one another's joys and sorrows? To bear one another's burdens? And to show special love to them that are of the household of faith? You will remember the Supper is a "communion of Saints" as well as a communion of the body and blood of Christ. It is a sacrament of friendship with one another as well as with Him. The man who sits down to the Supper and then neglects his brother has denied the faith.

Christ, the Giver of the Feast

I pass on next to say that this is a feast of which Christ is the giver and we are the recipients. There is a beautiful and significant sequence of verses in one of the most familiar of Psalms that runs like this, "What shall I render unto the Lord for all His benefits towards me?" asks the Psalmist. And he answers his own question by saying, "I will take the cup of salvation and call on the name of the Lord." I had read those two verses scores and hundreds of times and not noticed their point. It was my friend, Mr. Elvet Lewis, who first called my attention to the beauty of the sequence. Here is a Psalmist overwhelmed by a sense of God's infinite goodness, and as he thinks of it, in a perfect transport of gratitude he cries, "What shall I render to the Lord? What shall I give to Him? What shall I pay back to Him for all His benefits?" And in the answer he gives to his own question, I find nothing about paying back, giving, rendering to God. He talks of taking once again. "What shall I render? . . . I will take the cup of salvation."

Man Receives and Repays

Taking yet again is the only way of rendering to God. Receiving once again is the only way of *paying back* to God. Opening the heart still wider to the reception of His blessings is the only way of thanking Him for blessings already given. And this is all illustrated in the Supper. No one can think of the mighty sacrifice of Christ, of the Exodus He accomplished, of the deliverance He won, without being constrained to say, "What shall I render?" You remember how Isaac Watts, facing the Cross, bursts out into that impassioned verse,

"Were the whole realm of Nature mine,
That were a present far too small.
Love so amazing, so Divine,
Demands my life, my soul, my all."

We all feel like that when we stand before the Cross and realize its meaning. What shall we give is our dominating thought. And instead of giving we are asked to take once again. "What shall I render unto the Lord," we cry, "for all His benefits toward me?" And the Lord Himself answers us and says, "Take ye, this is My body." And He hands to us the cup saying, "This is My blood of the covenant, which is shed for many." Instead of paying back we are asked to receive once again. Indeed the only payment the Lord asks of us is that we should be willing to receive the yet larger grace He is willing to bestow. "As they were eating He took bread, and when He had blessed it, He brake it and gave to them and said, 'Take ye, this is My body.' And He took a cup and when He had given thanks, He gave to them. And they all drank of it. And He said unto them, 'This is My blood of the new Covenant which is shed for many.'" "Take ye," He says. Christ in this feast is the Giver. We are the recipients.

The Giver of Himself

What is it He gives? His body and blood under the symbols of bread and wine. Now, I dislike even glancing at controversial topics in connection with a theme so sacred as this. And yet I should be scarcely a faithful minister, I should not be declaring the whole counsel of God, if I did not refer to certain misunderstandings of these words which have had disastrous consequences for the Christian Church. The doctrine of Transubstantiation is based upon a literal interpretation of the words, "This is My body," and "This is My blood." Now, if this were the time I think I could prove that the doctrine of Transubstantiation has been the source of much harm. It has externalized the Sacrament. It has converted it from a spiritual Communion with a living Christ, into a magical rite. It has made the virtue of the Sacrament to depend upon the act of participation, quite apart from the spiritual condition of the receiver. It has, as a result, been inimical, not to say fatal, to deep, earnest, serious religious life. But I am not concerned at the moment with its evil results. What I want to emphasize just now is that there is absolutely no Scriptural or rational ground for the doctrine.

Christ's Language

To understand this phrase, "This is My body," literally, is to forget that the words were spoken by Christ Himself to eleven men who were sitting at table with Him. The eleven never for one moment imagined that the bread was changed into Christ's body or the wine into His blood, for there their Lord was living, breathing, talking to them. Then, to take these words literally is to forget the Eastern fondness for vivid, figurative language. Christ was in the habit of speaking in this bold and vivid way. He said among other things, "I am the Door." "I am the True Vine." There is as little reason for interpreting the phrase, "This is My body," literally, as there would be for interpreting, "I am the Door," literally. And then, finally, as if specially to guard against this from a materialistic interpretation of His words, our Lord uttered an express warning against it. All commentators are agreed that for the interpretation of what Christ means by "taking His body," and "drinking His blood," we must turn to that great chapter in St John's Gospel in which He speaks of Himself as the Bread of Life. The "bread," He proceeds to explain, is His own flesh which He is to give for the life of the world. The Jews like the Romanists made the mistake of taking Him literally, and asked, "How can this Man give us His flesh to eat?" Then Jesus, seeing the mistake which the Jews and some of His own disciples were making, after asserting once again that His flesh was meat indeed, and His blood was drink indeed, adds this word, "It is the Spirit that quickeneth, the flesh profiteth nothing." It is as if the Lord foresaw the mistake so many in His Church have made and forewarned them against it. The mere physical participation in the bread and the wine of itself profits nothing; we gain no benefit from the Supper until we enter into spiritual communion with the Christ, and especially, the suffering and dying Christ of Whom the bread and the wine speak.

Spiritual Feeding on Christ

But if on the one hand the Romanists are guilty of asserting about this feast more than is true, I think sometimes we Protestant folk, and especially Free Church folk, are apt to assert of it less than is true. I mean that so many are content to regard the Supper as a memorial feast and nothing more. The bread and the wine help us to remember how on Calvary's Hill Christ gave His body to be broken and His blood to be shed for our redemption. But the feast is more than that. We do not simply remember Christ. He gives Himself to us. We impoverish the meaning of the feast if we forget this truth. He gives, we receive, at this feast. He gives Himself to us for our sustenance and support. The bread and the wine signify, He says, His body and blood. Body and blood again together signify His life—His human life. And the meaning of the Sacrament is that Christ's life is to us, what bread and wine are to the physical existence. Bread and wine are the emblem, as Dr. Chadwick says, of food in its most nourishing and its most stimulating form. And in the same way—such is the teaching of the Sacrament—the life of Christ, the body and blood of Christ, the sacrificed and distributed life of Christ, nourishes and sustains the soul. And He gives Himself to us at this feast.

The Double Aspect of the Rite

"If," says St Paul (Rom. 5:10), "while we were the enemies, we were reconciled to God through the death of His Son, how much more, being reconciled, shall we be saved by His life?" That great verse always seems to me to throw light upon the double aspect of the Supper. In the first limb of the verse there is the remembrance of Calvary. The sacrifice of Calvary was an act, accomplished and done. By that act something was effected. The reconciliation was won. The redemption of the race was achieved. Forgiveness was made open and free for the race. From that point of view, it is true to say that Calvary is the ground of man's acceptance with God. But that mighty act in the past does not in and by itself save a man. It clears the way for his salvation. It wipes out his guilt. As Paul would say, it justifies him. But then I believe Christ's death did that for every one. As far as God is concerned, redemption, forgiveness, reconciliation have been won for every one. But every one is not saved. Saving man means more than cancelling his debt, absolving him from guilt, blotting out his past sin. Saving a man means delivering him not only from the *penalty* but also from the *power of sin*, emancipating him from the dominion of lust and passion, and helping him to a clean, sober, righteous manhood. And what does that is *the power and presence and life of Christ in a man*. Christ in us is the hope of glory. We are reconciled to God by Christ's death, but we are saved, enabled to triumph over lust and passion and sin, by His life. And this feast does more than remind us of the death by which we were reconciled. Christ here bestows upon us Himself, offers to us His life by means of which we are saved. Christ is a giver at this feast. He gives *Himself* to us for our sustenance and support and salvation.

I find it difficult to explain; perhaps because it is a thing to be felt rather than demonstrated. But I imagine the experience of many is like mine, when I say that when I have come to the Table of the

Lord and humbly and gratefully eaten of the bread and drunk of
the cup, somehow or other the Master seems specially near. I clasp
Him here with firmer faith. I feel He gives Himself to me as I par-
take of the emblem. New tides of hope and power seem to flood
my soul. I rise from the Table refreshed with might in my inner
man. I go forth better able to stand in the evil day. I thank God
humbly for the Cross on which atonement was made for my sin.
But I thank God more that Christ did not leave it there; that having died for my reconciliation, Christ now gives me this life for my
salvation.

Man, the Recipient

Christ is the Giver. Man is the Receiver at the feast. But before
the feast profits us in the least we must consciously, deliberately co-
operate in the Sacrament. "Take ye," said the Lord. And the bread
and the wine will profit us not at all unless we take. Christ's offer
of His life to strengthen and save us will profit us not at all unless
we appropriate it and receive it. This feast does not profit all and
sundry. The mere partaking of it does not ensure for any one the
blessing of it. "All the wicked and profane in the land were admitted to the Communion," was the complaint the first Separatists
made against the Church of their day. The "wicked and profane"
went to the Sacrament in the vain hope that mere participation in
it would save them from the results of sin and win them all the
benefits of the death of Christ. But it was a futile hope. This feast
is not a bit of pagan magic transferred into the Christian Church.
The benefit of it depends upon the state of the Recipient. It profits
nobody unless received with faith. If a man discriminate not the
body of the Lord, says St Paul, he simply eateth and drinketh judgment to himself. If we are to receive the benefits of the Supper,
there is a preparation of the soul through which we need to pass.
Prayer, desire, an expectant faith, an open heart—these are the conditions of blessing. If we come to the Table and receive no
blessing it is not because Christ has been unwilling to give, it is
because we have been unfit to receive. But if we come in faith, with
hearts opened to receive Him we shall never come in vain. We
shall always "see the Lord." He will give us Himself. We shall be
saved by His life.

The Anticipated Triumph

Verily, He said to His disciples, when the Supper was over, "I
will no more drink of the fruit of the vine, until that day when I
drink it new in the Kingdom of God." He ended the Supper which

commemorated His dying with a confident anticipation of His triumph. The morrow, when the Cross was reared, looked like the triumph of evil. But with calm and unruffled confidence Christ looked beyond the black tomorrow and foresaw the triumph of the Kingdom of God. And in that Kingdom of God He would drink another and a better sort of cup with His disciples to celebrate His complete and final victory. And the feast remains still a prophecy of the better things to come. However dark today is and tomorrow promises to be, there is glory ahead. Our Lord must reign till He has put all His enemies under His feet. This is the prayer we ought all to offer, that we who sit at His table here below may be amongst those, who, having loved Him loyally and served Him faithfully, may sit down at the marriage Supper of the Lamb, and drink of the new cup in the Kingdom of God.

92
Sin and the Sin-Bearer

"And they came to a place which was named Gethsemane: and He saith to His disciples, Sit ye here, while I shall pray. And He taketh with Him Peter and James and John, and began to be sore amazed, and to be very heavy; And saith unto them, My soul is exceeding sorrowful unto death: tarry ye here, and watch. And He went forward a little, and fell on the ground, and prayed that, if it were possible, the hour might pass from Him. And He said, Abba, Father, all things are possible unto Thee; take away this cup from Me: nevertheless not what I will, but what Thou wilt. And He cometh, and findeth them sleeping, and saith unto Peter, Simon, sleepest thou? couldest not thou watch one hour? Watch ye and pray, lest ye enter into temptation. The spirit truly is ready, but the flesh is weak. And again He went away, and prayed, and spake the same words. And when He returned, He found them asleep again (for their eyes were heavy), neither wist they what to answer Him. And He cometh the third time, and saith unto them, Sleep on now, and take your rest: it is enough, the hour is come; behold, the Son of man is betrayed into the hands of sinners. Rise up, let us go; lo, he that betrayeth Me is at hand." —Mark 14:32-42.

The Lord's Sorrow

THERE IS NO paragraph in the whole of Scripture which I more shrink from handling than I do this. These brief verses take us into the Inner Sanctuary of our Lord's sorrow. Sometimes I feel that the best and only way of reading them is to read them in silence upon our knees. It seems something like sacrilege to criticize and discuss the Lord's sorrow. And yet I would have you turn aside for a moment and see this great sight and notice how "the Lord of all, above, beneath, was bowed with sorrow unto death." We will enter Gethsemane with bared head and unshod feet, remembering that the place whereon we stand is holy ground; but still we will enter and gaze on this subduing sight and seek to understand something of its meaning. Possibly, as we watch and wonder, there may steal into our souls a fuller realization of

> "All our redemption cost,
> All our redemption won;
> All it has won for us the lost,
> All it cost Him, the Son."

"Greatly Amazed"

Let me begin by calling attention to the fact of Christ's sorrow. All the evangelists bear testimony to it. Look at the description Mark gives in these verses. "And taking with Him Peter and James and John, He began to be greatly amazed and sore troubled." To be "greatly amazed!" The word in the original Greek is an exceedingly strong one. It is peculiar to Mark. He uses it in one place to express the effect upon the crowd when Jesus came down from the Holy Mount. "All the multitude, when they saw Him, were greatly amazed." The evangelist uses it again to describe the effect produced upon the women, when, on the morning of the Resurrection, they found Christ's tomb opened, and, instead of the dead body of the Lord, found in it a white-robed angel. "They were amazed!" says Mark. They were startled, staggered, bewildered, affrighted. And it is the same strong word Mark employs here to describe our Lord's condition in the Garden. Not only "greatly amazed"; He was "sore troubled."

"Sore Troubled"

And this again is a most expressive word. It expresses, one commentator says, "the distress which follows a great shock." Judging it by the derivation suggested by some authorities, the word would seem to mean, "out of one's usual surroundings," "homeless." "He began to be greatly amazed and homeless." Treading the winepress alone, He felt the solitariness, the distress of the homeless. Now listen to the expression of our Lord's own feeling. "My soul is exceeding sorrowful even unto death." "Exceeding sorrowful," or, as the Greek might be rendered, to convey the exact meaning of the word, "My soul is sorrowful all round and round." Christ found Himself in the Garden in a weltering sea of trouble. "My soul is sorrowful all round and round—even unto death." It was a killing sorrow. It was literally crushing out the Savior's life. For our Lord died, as the thrust of the Roman spear revealed, not as the result of the nails which were driven into His hands and feet; He died of a broken heart. His soul was sorrowful all round and round even unto death. There is no need for me to quote what the other evangelists say about Christ's sorrow in the Garden; there is no need for me to remind you of the agony and bloody sweat of which Luke (22:44) speaks, and of the "strong crying and tears" of which the writer to the Hebrews (5:7) speaks. What Mark tells us is sufficient in itself to show us that here we are in the presence of some deep, mysterious, unutterable woe. "Behold, and see," says the Prophet, "if there be any sorrow like unto My sorrow" (Lam. 1:12). And it is in the Garden that incomparable sorrow is to be witnessed. He was a Man of Sorrows all His life through. Right away from His early years He had grief to carry and burdens to bear. But it all came to a climax and a head in the Garden. There was never sorrow in the world like this.

> "Deep waters have come in, O Lord!
> All darkly on Thy human soul;
> And clouds of supernatural gloom,
> Around Thee are allowed to roll.
> And Thou hast shuddered at each act,
> And shrunk with an astonished fear,
> As if Thou couldst not bear to see,
> The loathsomeness of sin so near."

The Springs of Christ's Sorrow

I pass on from the fact of Christ's sorrow to the sources of it. Why was our Lord so "stunned" in the Garden, and what was this "cup" which He prayed His Father to take away from Him? Several answers have been given. Some have said that in Gethsemane our Lord was overwhelmed with the fear of death, and that "death" was the cup which He begged the Father to take away from Him. And on the strength of this explanation, sceptics have reveled in pointing out that many ordinary and everyday men have been braver than Christ. They would have us believe that, however noble His life may have been, there was something timid and craven about His death. They tell us that, in the matter of courage, many of Christ's followers—those frail women who faced the beasts in the Roman amphitheater, or who served as living torches in Nero's garden, a girl like Margaret Wilson who was drowned in the waters of the Solway singing with her latest breath the twenty-fifth Psalm—they say that these were braver than the Master.

No Fear of Death

I confess that if their representations of things were correct, I should feel sore troubled, for courage is an element in the perfect character, and a Christ Who lacked courage would be something less than a perfect Christ. But when men say that it was from the mere physical pain of dying Christ shrank in the Garden, they do greatly err. Christ had faced death before, as in the wild storm on the sea, with perfect calm. When the morrow came and the awful suffering of the Cross had to be endured, He bore Himself like a king!

The thought of death, the physical act of dying, never troubled Jesus Christ. He often talked of it. He could have avoided it if He had been really afraid of it. But instead of seeking to avoid it, He steadfastly set His face to go to Jerusalem. No, it was not the act of dying that made Him feel amazed and homeless. Had there been nothing but death in His purview, He would have carried into the Garden the triumphant and exultant spirit with which He left the Upper Room. It was something else, not dying, something far more awful than death, that brought desolation and anguish to our Lord.

Human Sin

What was that something? I answer, it was human sin. Now in seeking to understand the connection between human sin and the suffering of the Lord, notice this truth, which Dr. Fairbairn admirably emphasizes; Christ being Who He was, was bound to suffer in this sinful world. His very purity and sinlessness made suffering inevitable. There is a sort of adaptation, Dr. Fairbairn says, between a sinful man and a sinful earth. They suit each other. He has never known any home but this; he has never been accustomed to anything better; and so he does not realize its essential misery and woe. But Christ had had another home. He came down to earth from a heaven, where all is holiness and obedience and perfect happiness and health. And the result was our Lord felt the disorder and unhappiness of earth as no man could possibly feel them. A child brought up among the lepers at Molokai would get accustomed to the sight of festering limbs and rotting stumps, and would never realize the horror of them. The loathsomeness of it all would be a matter of course to him. But a visitor like Stevenson, knowing that all the world was not a lazar-house, coming from a place where men lived happy lives immune from this dread disease, saw Molokai in all its naked ghastliness, and his brief visit there was unmitigated pain and sorrow to him. In just the same way it was Christ, the visitor from another and happier sphere, who realized most the misery and woe of this disordered and sin-stricken world.

The Pure Soul and the Awfulness of Sin

Then, again, Jesus was not only familiar with a better and happier life and so saw the misery of the the world by contrast, but His very purity made Him *exquisitely sensitive* to the pain and shame of sin. The finer the nature, the greater the exposure to pain. Take a simple illustration: the finer the ear, the greater the sensitiveness to discord. A violin slightly out of tune inflicts no

discomfort on a man with a dull and unmusical ear; it is sheer torment to a man whose ear is fine and sensitive. And it is with the
soul as it is with the ear. The purer the soul the keener its sense of
the awfulness of sin. It is not the sinner who feels the horror and
shame of sin most keenly, but the saint. That is why the most
poignant confessions of sin come, not from the lips of the worst of
men, but from the lips of the noblest and best. Now the Man Christ
Jesus was an absolutely pure soul—a soul whose sensitiveness had
never been dulled or blurred by sin. And so He felt sin, the shame
of it, the awfulness of it, as no one else in the world ever did. Take
one illustration. A brutal crowd once dragged into His presence a
woman who had forgotten her womanliness. They were
untouched apparently by the awfulness of the sin; they were
unmoved by any sense of pity for the fallen woman; all they
thought about was the opportunity of putting Christ into a corner.
But the Lord Himself, when the woman was brought into His presence, hung His head. The pity of it, the tragedy of it, the vision of
that woman's defiled soul filled Him with horror. The brutal crowd
thought nothing of the sin except in its legal aspect; it blistered and
scorched the pure soul of Christ.

The Shame and Ruin of Sin

Again, Christ saw the extent of sin and the ruin it caused, as no
one else did or could. "He knew," we are told, "what was in man."
Sometimes perhaps we wish we had the power of reading character. But if all the hidden wickednesses of the hearts of men and
women were revealed to us, faith would fail, reason would well
nigh totter, and we should cry out to God to take away from us a
faculty that inflicted upon us such heart-breaking pain. You
remember the story about Drummond? The students in Edinburgh
used to make him their father confessor. They used to tell him of
their failures and sins. But the revelation of human wickedness thus
made to him was almost more than he could stand. He was found
one Sunday night with haggard and drawn face, leaning on the
mantelpiece, unable to take bite or sup. And when invited to eat, he
broke out into a cry of sheer pain, "Oh, the sins of these men, I wonder how God can stand it!" Well, Jesus knew what was in man. He
saw the sin and evil of the human heart. It was spread before Him
like an open book. What pain it caused Him, who can tell?

The Sorrow of the Sin-Bearer

Now all this has its pertinency, but it scarcely gives us the key to
the special horror of Gethsemane. We can, however, find that key

in Christ's realization of what being the world's sin-bearer meant and involved. Christ's agony in the Garden was caused not simply by the thought of the wickedness of those who were going to be involved in His death; it was caused even more by the realization of what was to happen to Himself. For He was to lose the touch of His Father's hand and the sight of His Father's face. The clue to the mysterious agony of the Garden is in that terrible cry, "My God, My God, why hast Thou forsaken Me?" The spitting, the scourging, the piercing pain of the nails, these were nothing. But the hiding of His Father's face! That was the "cup" He prayed to have been spared. But that was the cup which He drank. "He Who knew no sin became sin for us." Or, as Paul puts it in another tremendous word, "He hath redeemed us from the curse of the Law having become a curse for us." And because Christ drank that bitter cup in the Garden, you and I are able to take the cup of Salvation; and because He tasted death, you and I shall never see death; and because He became "homeless," you and I have an eternal home in the Father's house of many mansions.

93
Christic in the Garden

"And they came to a place which was named Gethsemane and He saith to His disciples, Sit ye here, while I shall pray. And He taketh with Him Peter and James and John, and began to be sore amazed, and to be very heavy; and saith unto them, My soul is exceeding sorrowful unto death: tarry ye here, and watch. And He went forward a little, and fell on the ground and prayed that, if it were possible, the hour might pass from Him. And He said, Abba, Father, all things are possible unto Thee; take away this cup from Me: nevertheless not what I will, but what Thou wilt. And He cometh, and findeth them sleeping, and saith unto Peter, Simon, sleepst thou? couldest not thou watch one hour? Watch ye and pray, lest ye enter into temptation. The spirit truly is ready, but the flesh is weak. And again He went away, and prayed, and spake the same words. And when He returned, He found them asleep again (for their eyes were heavy), neither wist they what to answer Him. And He cometh the third time, and saith unto them, Sleep on now, and take your rest: it is enough, the hour is come; behold, the Son of man is betrayed into the hands of sinners. Rise up, let us go; lo, he that betrayeth Me is at hand."
—Mark 14:32-42.

THE DISCUSSION OF the central significance of the Agony by no means exhausts the lessons this paragraph has to teach. First of all, let us study reverently the conduct of our Lord in the Garden.

Christ and Solitude

And herein notice our Lord's use of solitude. This was in accord with His custom. He often resorted to secret and solitary prayer. "When thou prayest," such was His counsel to His disciples, "enter into thine inner chamber and pray to thy Father Who seeth in secret." And this counsel He gave to others He practiced Himself. Night after night He would steal away to the mountain to pray. During the whole of Passion Week He had sought out Gethsemane. "Judas knew the place," the Fourth Evangelist says, "for He oft resorted thither with His disciples." So that, from one point of view, it was in accordance with His usual habit that, on the night in which He was betrayed, He should resort to the Garden to seek strength in private prayer. But I do not think I am fanciful in thinking that there was a special solitariness about Christ in the Garden. He took the eleven with Him to Gethsemane. But He left eight of them somewhere near the gate. He took Peter and James and John, the three who came nearest to Him, a little further on; but even them He had to leave. "He went forward a little," says Mark. "He parted from them about a stone's cast," says Luke. Even the three chosen disciples could not share in His prayer, could not sympathize with His purposes, could not bear the least little bit of His burden. Jesus was absolutely solitary in His trial. He trod the winepress alone and of the peoples there was no man with Him.

The Loneliness of the Great

The great are of necessity lonely. Their greatness carries a certain amount of loneliness along with it. The mountain that flings its peak high up above the surrounding hills, pays for its exaltation with a certain solemn and terrifying solitude. The man who in character, vision and ideal, surpasses his fellows, pays for his pre-eminence in the same way. He cannot find, in the same degree as others, companions, associates, sympathizers, friends. There is no one on his level; he is of necessity a lonely man. But there was none who towered over men as Jesus did. What Wordsworth says of Milton could be applied with ten-fold truth to Jesus. "His soul was like a star and dwelt apart." He was lonely in His own home, for His own brothers did not believe in Him. He was lonely even when the crowds were thronging Him and pressing Him, for the multitude had absolutely no sympathy with Him and followed Him only for what they could get. He was lonely even in the circle of the chosen Twelve. They continually misunderstood Him, and upon the things that lay nearest His heart, He could not even speak. The loneliness became intensified as the Cross drew near. When Jesus talked about dying, Peter took Him and began to rebuke Him. He was "homeless" in the Garden. Even Peter and James and John could not help Him. There was only One in the wide universe Who understood Him and that was His Father. And to that Father in the Garden He betook Himself. "Abba, Father," He cried, "all things are possible unto Thee; remove this cup from Me; howbeit not what I will, but what Thou wilt."

Christ's Prayer

I pass now from our Lord's loneliness to His prayer. It is almost too sacred to discuss, and I shall only dwell on one feature of it. It is the filial submissiveness of it all that impresses me. Filial confidence is revealed even in the petition that the bitter cup might pass. Christ had no secrets from the Father. He told every desire of the soul to His Father. If there were some other way of accomplishing the Divine purpose other than by the Cross, Christ would have welcomed it; but there is nothing that detracts from His perfection in this. His frank and unreserved utterance of the feelings of His soul, only shows how entirely filial was His relationship with His Father. For that is the perfect relationship between Father and child when perfect confidence obtains between them; and the innermost desires of the soul are laid bare. Our Lord would have been less than perfect only if He had peremptorily refused the cup; if He had set up His own will in opposition to His Father's. But there is nothing of that here in our Lord's prayer.

Filial Submission

The very spirit of filial submission breathes through it. He knows God's will is good, and God's way is best. "Father, all things are possible with Thee; remove this cup from Me; howbeit not what I will, but what Thou wilt." "The cup which the Father hath given Me to drink," He said when Peter impulsively pulled out his sword and tried to save Him by force from the impending doom, "the cup that the Father hath given Me to drink, shall I not drink it?" That is the last word in our Lord's prayer, simple trust in God's goodness, unreserved acceptance of His will.

Our Example in Prayer

In all this, this prayer of our Lord's Agony is a model prayer. Prayer should be entirely frank and unreserved. The tendency in these days is to emasculate and impoverish prayer. Someone wrote to the papers the other day suggesting that the only prayer we have really any right to offer is the prayer that we may be willing to accept the will of God. But prayer must not be limited and circumscribed in that way. Prayer is speech between Father and child. A perfect confidence, an unreserved confidence is the mark of the perfect prayer. I am not ashamed or afraid to tell my Father about all my anxieties and cares, yes, even about my temporal anxieties. I know that what concerns me, concerns Him! I know that nothing is too small for His regard. But while prayer to be filial must be unreserved and frank, prayer also to be filial must be trustful and submissive. It is right to tell God everything; but the real mark of the filial spirit is this, that when we have spread our petitions before Him and told Him our own desires we should add, "Howbeit not what I will, but what Thou wilt."

The Reward of Prayer

Observe also the reward of prayer as illustrated by our Lord's experience in the Garden. He was a sorrowful, troubled Christ at the beginning of His hour of agonizing prayer; He was a calm and majestic Christ at the finish. Compare His first word to His disciples and His last. "Simon," He said the first time, "sleepest thou? Couldest thou not watch one hour?" That is the appeal of the sorrowful. "Sleep on now and take your rest," He said, when He came the last time. And that is the word of One Who has conquered, and has gained a strength which lifts Him above all need of human succor.

Power and Peace

And that was the result of Christ's prayer in the Garden. I do not know that the fashion of His countenance became altered and His raiment became white and glistening as on the Holy Mount. But I believe that there was some wonderful glory about Him that made the soldiers when they advanced to seize Him, go backward and fall to the ground. But the transformation was not so much outward as inward. The mighty change was not in our Lord's appearance but in His spirit. When He came forth from the olive trees, He came "Content with death and shame." "They that wait upon the Lord," says the Prophet, "shall renew their strength." That is what happened in the Garden. Our Lord renewed His strength. He received from God a new baptism of power. That is how Luke expresses it—"there appeared unto Him an angel from heaven, strengthening Him." Power was given Him for His mighty task. And that is the reward of all earnest and believing prayer still— we renew our strength. We find ourselves made equal to tasks and duties from which we shrink. Victorious strength comes to us as we touch the hand of God. We are called to tread rough ways, steep ways, forbidding ways still. But if we wait upon the Lord, we shall renew our strength and shall walk and not faint.

Suffering and Perfection

There is a relation between this dread experience in the Garden and the perfected character of our Lord. The writer of the Epistle to the Hebrews speaking of our Lord's Agony in the Garden, says, "He learned obedience by the things which He suffered." He learned some of the cost of obedience in the temptations of the Wilderness; He learned its uttermost cost in the Agony of the Garden. When He awoke His disciples, saying to them, "Behold He that betrayeth Me is at hand," and advanced with majestic step to meet Judas and his traitor band, the last lesson in obedience had been learned. And "obedience" was not the only lesson that He learned! In another place that same writer says that He was made "perfect through sufferings." We love Him all the better that He suffered thus. He suffered being tempted. It cost Him something to obey. And it is this that makes Him perfect—as a friend, a sympathizer, a high priest for sinful men. When temptations come and the fight goes hard; when duty points one way and inclination pulls in another—we may comfort ourselves with this assurance, He knows! He suffered being tempted. He learned obedience. He knows all about the struggle and the cost. And if sometimes we falter and fail, He knows! He has been through it. This experience has enriched Him. It has made Him the perfect Friend. "Wherefore it behoved Him in all things to be made like unto His brethren, that He might be a merciful and faithful high priest in things pertaining to God, to make propitiation for the sins of the people. For in that He Himself hath suffered being tempted, He is able to succor them that are tempted."

94
The Arrest

"And immediately, while He yet spake, Judas cometh, one of the twelve, and with him a great multitude with swords and staves, from the chief priests and the scribes and the elders. And he that betrayed Him had given them a token, saying, Whomsoever I shall kiss, that same is He; take Him, and lead Him away safely. And as soon as He was come, he goeth straightway to Him, and saith, Master, master; and kissed Him. And they laid their hands on Him, and took Him. And one of them that stood by drew a sword, and smote a servant of the high priest, and cut off his ear. And Jesus answered and said unto them, Are ye come out, as against a thief, with swords and with staves to take Me? I was daily with you in the temple teaching, and ye took Me not: but the scriptures must be fulfilled. And they all forsook Him and fled."

—Mark 14:43-50.

The Traitor

ALL THE DISCIPLES had not followed Christ to the Garden. His little circle of chosen associates numbered twelve, but there were only eleven with Him in the hour of His desolation and sorrow. One had left the Upper Room some time before Jesus and the rest sang their hymn and set their faces towards the Mount of Olives. At a certain stage in the proceedings in the Upper Room Judas Iscariot had left the little company. Nobody save Jesus knew why or whither he had gone. They had heard Christ say to him, "That thou doest, do quickly," and they had inferred that as Treasurer of the Apostolic band Judas had some purchases to make for the feast, or some charities to distribute to the poor. But it was upon no such kindly errand that Judas was bent when he left the Upper Room. There was treachery and a deadly purpose in his soul. Avarice and ambition had played havoc with Judas. Whatever enthusiasm or love he had had for Jesus at the start had died out of his heart and had given place to sullen and embittered resentment. Already in this bitter resentment he had made a bargain with the priests to betray Jesus to them. And when he left the Upper Room it was to go to the priests to tell them that he was prepared to carry out his bargain that very night. So, while Jesus was speaking to the eleven disciples who were left those matchless words of love and comfort which we find in the fourteenth and subsequent chapters of St John's Gospel, we must think of Judas as in conspiracy with the priests and elders planning the arrest of Christ.

The Plot

First of all, they arranged the force that was to seize Christ in the Garden. It consisted for the most part of the Temple Guard, with servants of the priests. And these were armed with cudgels and small swords. But, partly because they were conscious that Christ possessed some mysterious power, and partly because they wished to conciliate Pilate, who would have resented resort to force by followers of Jesus in Passion week, they asked for reinforcements in the shape of a detachment of garrison soldiers. The negotiations with Pilate probably took some little time, but at length a detachment was sent and everything was ready for the arrest. One thing only remained to arrange, and that was a sign by which the soldiers should know whom to seize. For it is not at all probable that the soldiers were acquainted with the appearance of Jesus; and there were eleven other men with Him at the Garden. With only the light of the moon, and under the dark shadows of the olive trees, it would have been easy to make a mistake, and to arrest the wrong man. So the sign Judas arranged with his following was this (and there was a refinement of cruelty and a depth of baseness in it almost beyond words), "Whomsoever I shall kiss, that is He; take Him and lead Him away safely."

Its Execution

And so at length the traitor's band, with Judas himself at its head, set forth. Altogether it was a huge company, for in addition to the soldiers, there was a "multitude from the chief priests and the scribes and the elders," and (judging from what the other evangelists say), even some of the high priests and temple captains and elders, in their eagerness to see Christ taken, followed in the wake of the throng. They carried lanterns in their hands and so marched through the streets of Jerusalem. Many a sleeper must have awakened as he heard the tramp of the soldiers' feet, and like the young man of whom the next verses speak rushed out to see what it all meant. When they came near to the Garden, Jesus Himself was the first to notice their approach. When He came back to His disciples the third time He said, "The hour is come; behold the Son of Man is being betrayed into the hands of sinners.

Arise, let us be going: behold he that betrayeth Me is at hand." For He had seen the flash of the lanterns through the trees, and heard the tramp of approaching feet, before His disciples, heavy with sleep, had noticed either.

Christ, it is clear, did not wait till His foes, after search, discovered Him; He strode forth to meet them. He anticipated His fate. "Arise, let us be going," He said to the three who were with Him in the inner recesses of the Garden; not "Let us go into the farthest corner, let us hide, let us seek to escape"; but "Let us be going to meet them." There was no need of the lanterns, no need for zealous search. It was not the traitor and his band that found Jesus, it was Jesus Who found them.

Mark's account of our Lord's arrest is not complete. If you want to know everything that happened in the Garden, you must compare his narrative with those of the other evangelists, and supply Mark's deficiencies by their additions. What Mark does is to seize upon the salient points and set these down for us. Let us in turn pick out some of the chief lessons which Mark's pregnant and vivid narrative suggests, taking to ourselves the warnings and consolations they convey.

The Sorrow of Treason

"And straightway, while He yet spake, cometh Judas, one of the twelve." "One of the twelve!" That was the peculiar bitterness of the arrest. It was one of the Twelve that led the way! You remember the complaint the Psalmist makes—"It was not an enemy that reproached me; then I could have borne it; neither was it he that hated me that did magnify himself against me; then I would have hid myself from him; but it was thou, a man mine equal, my companion and my familiar friend. We took sweet counsel together, we walked in the house of God with the throng" (Ps. 55:12-14). The sorrows of the Psalmist suggest the sorrows of One still greater. And, even in the presence of the acute physical suffering of our Lord, we can see that this sorrow was a real one. An injury that we can take philosophically when inflicted by a foe wellnigh breaks our heart when inflicted by a friend. Hard words, that would not give us even a twinge if uttered by an opponent, cut to the very quick when spoken by a comrade and colleague. And our Lord suffered that added ignominy and sorrow. He was wounded in the house of His friends; betrayed by one whom He had Himself chosen and called; delivered to His foes by one of His own company.

The Sorrow of a Lost Soul

It was Judas "one of the twelve" that led the traitor band. His
Master was about to die to save men from their sins. And here in
Judas' crime, as Dr. Chadwick puts it, He is confronted with the
very tragedy which He was sacrificing Himself to avert, the loss of
a soul—lost in spite of multiplied privileges, in spite of repeated
pleadings, in spite of all that love could do, in spite of plain and
searching appeals. Do you not think that the sight of Judas, at the
head of the traitor band, would suggest to Christ the thought, the
chilling and almost heart-breaking thought, of the multitudes who
would receive the grace of God in vain, to whom the Cross would
make no appeal, and who would spurn and reject His own dying
love? That was the supreme sorrow of our Lord! That is His
supreme sorrow still. The Lord has died for men! And they go on
their way unmoved, untouched. They pass the Cross by as if it did
not concern them.

The Meekness of Christ

The second thing to notice is the meekness of Christ. It was said
by the Prophet (Isaiah 53:7), speaking by the Spirit of the suffering
of our Lord, that, though He was oppressed yet He would humble
Himself and open not His mouth: that He should be led as a lamb
to the slaughter and as a sheep that before her shearers is dumb, so
He would open not His mouth. And all that was fulfilled in an
amazing and touching way in the Garden. When Judas came up to
Him he called Him Rabbi, and kissed Him. Kissed Him effusive-
ly, the Greek suggests. A man knowing the treachery in Judas'
heart, knowing the kiss was a lying and poisoned kiss, would have
shrunk from it in repugnance and horror. But Jesus submitted even
to that loathsome kiss! He made no attempt to push Judas away.
He flung at him no angry or indignant word. "Betrayest thou the
Son of Man with a kiss?" He said; and that was all! So, too, when
the soldiers seized Him and were handling Him roughly, He had
no harsh speech for them. Only a word of high and solemn remonstrance—"Are ye come out as against a robber with swords and
staves to seize Me?" Here is meekness in its perfect bloom! He had
said Himself in His great sermon, "Resist not him that is evil, but
whosoever smiteth thee on thy right cheek, turn to him the other
also" (Matt. 5:39). It is a hard and difficult precept to obey, but in
the Garden our Lord practiced what He preached. We look at Him
then, submitting to be kissed, "bearing shame and insult rude,"
when He might have summoned twelve legions of angels to His
help had He wished, and we know what meekness is. Those who

witnessed His behavior in the Garden never forgot it. It burned itself into the memory of Peter for example, and in his Epistle, with the Garden in his mind, he recalls how Jesus when He was reviled, reviled not again, when He suffered threatened not, but committed Himself to Him that judgeth righteously (1 Peter 2:23). And in nothing is Jesus more divine than in His meekness. It would have been human to reproach and denounce and resist. It was divine to bear and endure and suffer without a word. If I had to construct an argument for the divinity of Christ, I would base it in part upon His meekness.

The Courage of Christ

Observe, too, the courage of Christ as illustrated in His behavior at the arrest. How calm and collected He was! He was the only calm, collected, unruffled person in the Garden! The traitor having offered his treacherous kiss, slunk into the background and went his way out of the Garden: a tortured soul. Mark says no more about him. But the other Gospels tell us, how Judas never knew what peace was after that night, and how in a brief space of time he put an end to an existence that had become unbearable, and so went to "his own place." The soldiers were flurried and excited. When Jesus calmly asked them whom they sought, and, in answer to their reply, said that He was the object of their search, struck by some mysterious terror they all went backward and fell to the ground. The disciples in their excitement first wanted to fight and then ran away. The one person absolutely calm and serene was Jesus Himself. He takes command of the proceedings. He hands Himself over to the trembling soldiers. He bids His disciples put their swords back into their sheaths. He begs the soldiers as it was Himself they were in search of to let the disciples go away. Calm, serene, absolutely unruffled, our Lord moves through this scene. Now consider the behavior of the disciples.

The Men and the Swords

When the disciples saw their Master in the hands of His foes, they were at first for making a fight of it. Perhaps we have been too hard on these disciples. It is true that the story ends with this shameful sentence, "They all forsook Him and fled." But they were not cowards. I have almost come to the conclusion that it was not fear that prompted their flight, but despair. I believe they would have fought for Christ and died for Him if He had fulfilled their expectation as to the Messiah. But when they saw Jesus meekly surrendering Himself, their faith in Him as Messiah collapsed.

That was the cause of their flight. Their faith was shattered. But they were not cowards, these men. They had only two swords amongst them, but with those two swords they would have faced the soldiers and the Temple mob in defense of their Lord. "Lord," they cried, "shall we smite with the sword?" And before Jesus had had time to reply, Peter's sword was out of its scabbard; he had struck an uncertain and excited blow, and had cut off the high priest's servant's ear. It was done in a moment. But swift upon the blow came the word of Christ. "Put up again thy sword into its place, they that take the sword shall perish with the sword." Violence had no place in Christ's scheme of things. The sword was a useless weapon to further His interests. The weapons of His warfare were not carnal but spiritual.

Compulsion and Faith

Christ's rebuke is for us as well as for Peter, and the Law is as binding upon the Church of today as it was upon the prince of the Apostles. Christ's Kingdom is not to be advanced by the sword. In the affairs of the Kingdom force is no remedy. It is a lesson the Church of Christ has been slow to learn. Again and again the Church has invoked the help of the secular arm. She has again and again used pressure and compulsion to advance her interests. In the early days of the Arian controversy the power of the Roman Empire was used to crush out heresy. In our own England here the conversion of one of the old Saxon kings was signalized by the compulsory conversion of all his people. Again and again the Church has used fire and prison and scaffold. Often, no doubt, it was done honestly and sincerely. But it was all very pitiful and tragic. It was a repudiation of Christ's own teaching. Religion is free, the response of the soul to God. A forced religion is a contradiction in terms.

The Better Way

"Allow me just to move My right hand," said Jesus. And He used it to restore the ear of the injured servant. That was the last miracle Christ performed—a gracious act of mercy to a foe. That is the way to advance Christ's Kingdom, not by imitating the violence of Peter, but by imitating the gentleness, mercy and healing ministry of the Lord.

95

The Young Man in the Linen Cloth

"And there followed Him a certain young man, having a linen cloth cast about his naked body; and the young men laid hold on him: And he left the linen cloth, and fled from them naked." —Mark 14:51, 52.

Why Is He Recalled?

THE INSERTION OF this story of the young man with the linen cloth needs accounting for. Mark omits many important details in the story of Christ's arrest, apparently in the interests of brevity. But this same evangelist, who in his passion for brevity omits items of importance, inserts this story about the young man with the linen cloth, though it is trivial in itself, and in no way affects the course of events. Why did this stern economist of words spare two verses in his brief and pregnant Gospel to tell this irrelevant story about some unknown young man? There must have been some strong reason operating on Mark to induce him to insert it.

A Personal Interest

The usual way of accounting for its insertion is by saying that the little incident must have had some special interest for Mark himself; indeed that he himself was the young man of whom he speaks. If that supposition is right, we can understand how the story came to be inserted. If Mark was the young man in question, the incident was not trivial to him. The act that brought him even into momentary contact with Christ on that dread and bitter night would be one of supreme interest and importance. There are other guesses as to the identity of this young man. Some commentators, for example, think that he was James, the brother of our Lord; others, the son of that unknown friend of Christ's who lent Him the Upper Room; whilst Dean Plumptre and Ian Maclaren make the ingenious guess that he was Lazarus. But all fail to account for the insertion of this trivial incident in the narrative. The one supposition that has real plausibility and likelihood is the one most often adopted, namely, that the young man was Mark himself.

After the Gospel Manner

Let me indicate some of the things that lead me to think this young man was the evangelist himself. (1) I begin with this, that Mark should introduce himself into his narrative in this anonymous way is exactly in keeping with the Gospel manner. Take the Fourth Gospel for illustration. In that Gospel John has to narrate many incidents in which he himself took part, but he never once mentions himself by name. He speaks of himself, half shyly as it were, as "the disciple whom Jesus loved," or "that other disciple." It often happened that artists would introduce their own portraits into the pictures they were painting. But they always put their own portraits in the background. And one had to be familiar with the painters' features to recognize them at all. It was so with the evangelists. If they have to come into the picture, they keep to the background; they stow themselves away in some inconspicuous corner. They introduce themselves anonymously, and for Mark to speak of himself in this way as "a certain young man" is exactly in keeping with evangelic usage.

The Touch of an Eye-Witness

(2) The vivid detail of the narrative seems to suggest the eye-witness. Speaking broadly, this Gospel is Peter's Gospel. The uniform account of tradition is that Mark was Peter's "interpreter," and amanuensis, and that he wrote down the various details of his Gospel as he heard Peter narrate them. Now Peter could not have given him this story. For Peter had taken flight and had not yet recovered from his flight. And even when he did recover, it was "from afar" that he followed, and he was not in a position to know what happened in the near vicinity of Christ Himself. But, if Peter did not give Mark this story, whence did he get it? The almost irresistible conclusion is that Mark puts in here a little bit "on his own." The detail of it, as I say, suggests the personal narrative. And the detail comes out specially in the use of the Greek word which is translated "linen cloth." The evangelist specifies a costly kind of linen cloth, a "sindon," which, according to Edersheim, "no doubt corresponds to the Sadin or Sedina which, in Rabbinic writings, means a linen cloth, or a loose linen wrapper, though, possibly, it may also mean a night-dress." Apparently it had been used as a coverlet for the bed. That the evangelist should specify in this way, should be so minute and exact, and should crowd so

much detail into the account, all points to the conclusion that he was writing of something which happened to himself.

Mark's Circumstances

(3) Once again, all that we know about the evangelist's circumstances favors the idea that the young man was Mark himself. First of all, we know that Mary, Mark's mother, lived in Jerusalem. It is quite possible her house may have been situated in one of the streets through which the procession marched on its way from the Garden to the Judgment Hall. Furthermore, we know that Mary's house was a large house, sufficiently large to accommodate the prayer-meetings of the Church. It was in her house that the Church had met for prayer when Peter lay in his prison, and it was to her house that Peter made his way on his release. We infer that people who live in large houses are possessed of ample means, and so we conclude that Mary, Mark's mother, was a well-to-do woman. This is supported by the fact that one of her connections, Barnabas, was a landed proprietor and a rich man. If Mary was the well-to-do woman we have every reason to think she was, then we can understand how it was that it was a sidon in which her son wrapped himself when he made his hurried rush into the street.

Mark's Character

(4) Moreover, everything that we know of Mark's character fits in exactly with the description of the young man here given. Mark is referred to, as you will remember, more than once in the Acts. He accompanied Paul and Barnabas on their first missionary journey. All went well while they were in Cyprus. But when they crossed over to the mainland of Asia Minor, and were about to face the notorious dangers of the Pamphylian mountains, Mark suddenly deserted the mission and returned to Jerusalem. That is exactly the same kind of person as this young man, who, with headlong enthusiasm championed Christ, but when he found his championship of Christ's cause brought him into trouble, left the linen cloth in the soldier's hands and fled.

Mark, the Stump-fingered

(5) And, finally, I call your attention to the curious epithet by which Mark was distinguished in the early Church. He was called Mark "the Stump-fingered." We are not told why he was so called. But may not the explanation be found, as Dr. David Smith suggests, in this incident? Perhaps the incident, after all, may not have

been quite so trifling as Mark's account would lead us to suppose. Perhaps he lost more that night than his linen cloth. The Roman soldier was in no mood to brook interference, and it may well have been that Mark's interposition on behalf of Christ was rewarded with a sword slash which whipped off his finger.

The Impulse

And now let us just look at Mark's exploit on this dark betrayal night. We must think of Jesus as being led through the streets of Jerusalem from the Garden to the high priest's palace. The passing of the procession caused considerable uproar; the torches the soldiers carried flashed light into many a darkened room and wakened many a sleeper. Some, I have no doubt, got up to see what was astir. Mark was not content simply to get up, he went out, simply casting about him the first article on which he could lay his hands, which happened to be this "linen cloth," this fine linen garment. When he got into the street, he found that a prisoner was being led away for judgment. A second look, as the glare of the torch fell on his face, told him this prisoner was none other than Jesus—the Man about Whom all Jerusalem was talking; the Preacher to Whom he, along with thousands of others, had listened with such keen delight in the Temple: yes, and I can go further, the Jesus in Whom he and his mother had already begun to trust as the promised Messiah, the Man Who had won their souls. Wishing to know what Jesus had done, and why He was being dragged along by the soldiers and the high priest's servants, Mark, undressed as he was, followed with the crowd, keeping as near to Jesus as he could.

The Test

I will believe that, as he walked, love for the Christ and indignation at the treatment meted out to Him, was filling Mark's soul. At a certain stage of the journey something happened, some insult was offered to Christ, some rough and brutal deed was done to Him by the soldiers who held Him on either side, and at last the indignation that was swelling and surging in John Mark's soul became vocal. He made vehement and passionate protest. And upon that, some of the other soldiers in the band promptly proceeded to lay hands on Mark himself, meaning to drag him off along with Jesus. But that was more than Mark had bargained for. At the rough grasp of the soldier's hand and at the flash of his sword, Mark's heat quickly cooled, and concern for Jesus gave way to anxiety for himself. He had no intention of standing in the dock as a prisoner side by side with the Lord. So by a sudden wrench he extricated himself from the soldier's grip, and leaving behind his "linen cloth," and possibly his finger, he fled naked.

That is the story. And from that story we may gather a lesson or two for life today. Mr. Spurgeon has, I believe, a sermon on this incident, which he divides into two heads. (1) Here is Hasty Following. (2) Here is Hasty Running Away. Those are the two thoughts which the story inevitably suggests.

Hasty Following

Here is hasty following. Everything about Mark in this midnight adventure betokens impetuousness and haste. If he had thought for a moment, if he had meant to follow Christ to the bitter end, he would not have been content with the linen cloth about his naked body. That was no garb in which to face danger and peril for the Lord's sake. The "linen cloth" in a sense is symbolic and characteristic of a merely temporary discipleship. For that headlong zeal that made Mark "follow with Christ," when He was in the hands of the soldiers, and all His disciples had fled, I have nothing but admiration. There is something generous, unselfish, noble about it. I only wish we had more of it in our Christian life and our Christian service today, for nobody can say that the modern Church suffers from excess of zeal. What I criticize is not the enthusiasm but the hastiness of it. It was not a reasoned, considered, steady enthusiasm. The "linen cloth" which was his only garment carries "temporariness" stamped upon it. And a Temporary, at the time, Mark turned out to be. At the touch of the soldier's hand and the sight of the naked sword, Mark's enthusiasm fizzled out. "He left the linen cloth and fled naked."

Its Peril

What does Tennyson say about "haste"? Is not it this? "Raw haste, half-sister to delay." Raw haste is half-sister to delay, and unthinking enthusiasm is half-sister to desertion. As I read the Gospels I am almost driven to believe that Christ feared haste as much as anything. He knew the Christian service and the Christian life were not lightly to be embarked upon. He knew there were difficulties to be encountered, and hardships to be endured, and perils to be faced. He knew that the difficulties and the hardships and the perils lasted the whole way. The Christian life was a long and arduous campaign. A mere fit of enthusiasm would carry no man through it. It would need courage, not simply dash, but steady courage, a fixed and resolute will to enable a man to endure to the end. And so our Lord would have no man become a disciple in a hurry. He was constantly bidding would-be disciples to stop and think. He bids men sit down first and count the cost. For in the Christian life it is not the first step only which costs, it costs all the way through. And it is only he who can endure to the end who gets saved. And because Christ is anxious that no follower of His should turn deserter, He bids us still stop and think before we embark upon His service. It is not to ease Christ calls us, but to labor. It is not peace He sends, but a sword. It is not to comfort He invites us, but to a campaign. A "linen cloth" is no equipment for this business. No, if we mean to see it through, we shall have to take to ourselves the whole armor of God, the breastplate of Righteousness, the shield of Faith, the helmet of Salvation, and the sword of the Spirit. For the men Christ wants are not the men who follow Him today and desert Him tomorrow, but men who will be faithful unto death and so receive the Crown of Life.

Hasty Desertion

Hasty following in John Mark's case issued in hasty running away. It may be, as Dr. Watson suggests, that the thought of the appearance he would make arrayed before the Jewish Court with only this linen cloth about him, had something to do with his flight. That makes no difference to the truth I am now trying to enforce. Even if it were modesty and not fear that lay at the root of his desertion, it remains true that it was his haste in following, that led to his haste in running away. And the one generally ends in the other. Our Lord in His parable of the seed warned us of this tragic and disappointing sequence. The seed sown on the rock, He said, represented those who, when they heard the word, straightway with joy received it. But when tribulation or persecution arises because of the word straightway they are offended. They were in a hurry to begin, they were in a hurry to give up. There is not a Church in the land, there is not a Christian minister in the land who does not know of men and women who began but were not able to finish, who did run well but who are not on the course today. What of ourselves, have we faltered? Are we of them that draw back?

The Changed Man

I have talked of Mark's hasty following and his equally hasty running away. But that was not the end of Mark's Christian career. Had it been so this Gospel that bears his name would never have been written. I am not going to trace his history, but to remind you of one little fact about Mark. Venice boasts of Mark as its patron saint, and there, close to the Grand Canal, you can see the pillar dedicated to his name. And on the top of the pillar a lion. The lion of St Mark! That is Mark's symbol in Art—the lion! He does not shape much like a lion in this incident. The timid hare would seem to us a fitter symbol of this man who ran away at the first onset of danger. But the Church is right. The lion is Mark's legitimate symbol. For this man got the better of his timidities and fears, and developed into a brave and dauntless soldier of the Cross. Christ changed him, Christ transformed him, and Mark, the runaway, at Alexandria laid down his life for his Lord.

96
The Ecclesiastical Trial

"And they led Jesus away to the high priest: and with Him were assembled all the chief priests and the elders and the scribes. And Peter followed Him afar off, even into the palace of the high priest: and he sat with the servants, and warmed himself at the fire. And the chief priests and all the council sought for witness against Jesus to put Him to death; and found none. For many bare false witness against Him, but their witness agreed not together. And there arose certain, and bare false witness against Him, saying, we heard Him say, I will destroy this temple that is made with hands, and within three days I will build another made without hands. But neither so did their witness agree together. And the high priest stood up in the midst, and asked Jesus, saying, Answerest Thou nothing? what is it which these witness against Thee? But He held His peace, and answered nothing. Again the high priest asked Him, and said unto Him, Art Thou the Christ, the Son of the Blessed? And Jesus said, I am: and ye shall see the Son of man sitting on the right hand of power, and coming in the clouds of heaven. Then the high priest rent his clothes, and saith, What need we any further witnesses? Ye have heard the blasphemy: what think ye? And they all condemned Him to be guilty of death. And some began to spit on Him, and to cover His face, and to buffet Him, and to say unto Him, Prophesy: and the servants did strike Him with the palms of their hands." —Mark 14:53-65.

THERE ARE A GREAT many omissions in Mark's account of the trial of our Lord. Those details mattered little to the people to whom Mark originally addressed His Gospel; but every little detail in the story matters to us, and we like to follow our Lord step by step along the sorrowful way that led from Gethsemane to the bitter Cross. And so I propose, before beginning the exposition of this paragraph, to trace what seems to have been the actual course of events after Jesus was arrested in the Garden.

The Two Trials

One broad fact stands out plain and clear as we read and compare the various Gospel narratives, namely that there were two stages in the trial of Jesus. There was an ecclesiastical trial when His judges were the priests and the elders; and there was a civil trial when His judge was Pilate. The reason for the double trial was

this. Rome dealt very leniently, not to say generously, with conquered and subject nations. She allowed them a very large
measure of what we should call "Home Rule." And especially was
Rome generous in the matter of religion. She never attempted to
interfere with any local religion so long as the religion in no way
menaced her imperial power. The consequence was that Rome did
not interfere with Judaism, nor did she attempt to destroy the
Sanhedrin—the supreme Jewish court. The Sanhedrin was allowed
to try and to punish religious offenders; only, if the offense was a
capital one, the case had again to be tried before the Roman
Governor, for the capital sentence could only be inflicted by the
supreme authority of all. The chief priests and elders would gladly have settled the whole matter in their own court, but they would
be satisfied with nothing save the death punishment, and to get
that they had to secure the assent of Pilate.

The Two Charges
That is why, too, the ground of accusation in the civil trial differs
so much from the ground of accusation in the ecclesiastical trial. In
the ecclesiastical trial, as we shall shortly see, the offenses charged
against Jesus were religious offenses. He was charged with
threatening the Temple; He was charged with making divine
claims for Himself. But if His accusers had come with such accusations into Pilate's court he would probably have brushed them
aside, as Gallio did subsequently at Corinth, saying that it was
none of his business to interfere in their religious disputes. So
when they appear before Pilate they shift their ground and
charge Him with a State offense, namely, that of conspiring
against Caesar. Or, to express it slightly differently, the ground on
which the Sanhedrin condemned Him was blasphemy; the actual
charge for which He was sentenced to the Cross was high treason.
Pilate crucified the Lord, not because He said He was the Son of
God, but because He said (or rather they said that He said) that He
was King of the Jews.

The Ecclesiastical Trial: First Stage
Of these two trials, of course, the ecclesiastical trial took place
first. It was as a result of the Sanhedrin's condemnation of Him that
our Lord was brought before Pilate at all. The next thing to be
noticed is, that in the ecclesiastical trial there were three distinct
stages. It is in tracing these successive stages of the trial that we need
to supplement Mark's account by the accounts of the other evangelists. After our Lord's arrest, He seems to have been taken first of

all to Annas. Annas was father-in-law to Caiaphas the high priest. Some years previously he had been high priest himself, and he enjoyed this unique distinction, that, after his own deposition from that high office, four of his sons and his son-in-law held it. All of which is sufficient to show that Annas was a man of enormous power and prestige. Caiaphas was the titular head of the Sanhedrin, but Annas was the power behind the throne. To him then Jesus was first taken, for a kind of preliminary examination in which the old priest seems to have tried to trick Christ into some kind of damaging confession. But his attempts proved utterly fruitless, and so Jesus was sent on bound to Caiaphas the high-priest.

Second Stage
Then followed the second stage of the trial, namely, the trial before the Sanhedrin—the supreme Jewish court. The members of this Court, who knew what was afoot, had, many of them, in their eagerness, followed the soldiers to the Garden in order to see the arrest take place. They were, therefore, on hand ready to take part in this midnight meeting of the Sanhedrin, and the hour spent by Jesus in Annas' house in that preliminary examination by Annas, gave ample time to summon all the rest. So under cover of night the Sanhedrin met for the trial of Jesus. It was in one sense an "informal" trial, for the legal sittings of the Sanhedrin could not be held till after daybreak. Still, it was at this "informal" sitting that the real business was done. It was then that the witnesses were summoned and their evidence examined; it was then that Christ bore witness to His own Messiahship; it was then that He was pronounced to be worthy of death. It is this second stage of the trial that Mark gives us in this paragraph, for this was the critical and vital stage.

The Third Stage
The third stage in the trial took place immediately after daybreak, when the Sanhedrin became a legal and regularly constituted court. But the proceedings at that legal session were brief and purely formal. Mark dismisses it all in one verse, at the beginning of the next chapter. All the Sanhedrin did at its legal sitting was to confirm the decision already arrived at in the more prolonged, but informal, investigation held during the small hours of the morning. It was, however, the second trial which really settled Christ's doom. Let us look for a minute or two at Mark's account of what happened.

The Denial of Justice

I have called it a trial. Perhaps I ought to withdraw that word. A "trial" suggests gravity, dignity, the careful weighing of evidence, a strict and rigid impartiality. But there is no suggestion of impartiality about this trial. This was no case of doing justice; it was a case of making a mock of justice. The judges were themselves the prosecutors. Instead of carefully weighing the evidence they themselves procured it. "The chief priests and the whole council sought witness against Jesus to put Him to death." Indeed, in their determination to make an end of Jesus, they flung to the winds the very show of legality. They disregarded and violated the forms of their own court. With a keen sense of the value of human life the Jewish Law had laid down certain stringent regulations as to the conduct of capital trials. These men, thirsting for the blood of Christ, ignored and outraged every one of them. For instance, the Law laid it down that the witnesses for the defense should be summoned first, and that the witnesses for the prosecution before they gave evidence should be warned of the solemnity of their position and enjoined to speak nothing but what were matters of certain knowledge. Instead of that these bloodthirsty and cruel men themselves hunted up fake witnesses against Christ, and called never a one to speak a word on His behalf. They further indulged in interrogation of the accused which the Law declined to sanction, and they ended with a demand for a confession which the doctors of the Law expressly forbade; and then for a climax to their wickedness, they disregarded the rule which interposed delay between an accusation and a sentence, and huddled trial and sentence all into a few brief hours. "Such a process," says Mr. Taylor Innes, the great Scotch jurist, "had neither the form nor the fairness of a judicial trial."

The Sin of the Judges

"By oppression and judgment was He taken away," says the prophet, that is to say, by a judgment which was itself an oppression, a travesty and denial of justice. They condemned Him not because He had done anything worthy of death, not because any charge had been proved against Him. They condemned Him because, like Mr. Malice in the trial of Faithful in the *Pilgrim's Progress*, they hated the very look of Him, and because, as Mr. Live-loose confessed, He was always condemning their way. What a revelation of human wickedness this is, these men sitting in judgment on the Holy One and the Just, and sticking at nothing, not even at perjury, in their resolve to have Him put to death! "The heart of man," says the old Book, "is deceitful above all things, and desperately wicked." If you want commentary upon that view and confirmation of its truth, think of these priests and elders at their dastardly and devilish work in the dark hours of this particular morning. "There are depths in human nature into which it is scarcely safe to look," says Stalker. "It was by the very perfection of Christ that the evil of His enemies was brought out."

Savorless Salt

Those enemies were an illustration of corrupt religion. Religion is the best thing a man can have; it is the thing that binds him to God, and makes him a partaker of the divine nature; but a corrupt religion is the worst of all things. A religion which has degenerated into a formalism is worse than no religion. For the form of religion has a way of searing the conscience and deadening the soul. The crime of history has to be laid to the account, not of the men who were openly and notoriously bad, but of men who observed the forms of Godliness and denied the power thereof, of men who paid tithes and said prayers but neglected mercy and truth. Let us never forget that solemn word which declares that while religion when real and true is the savor of life unto life, the same religion when nothing but a cloak and an empty form becomes the savor of death unto death!

The Majesty of Christ

Now consider the conduct and behavior of Christ while He stood before the Sanhedrin. He observed throughout the proceedings a grave and majestic silence. I will not have it, that, as some suggest, it was a silence of "proud disdain." His silence was rather the silence of obvious and unchallengable innocence. There was no need to speak. The accusations these suborned witnesses conjured up fell harmless to the ground. They destroyed each other. Even the garbled account of what He had said about destroying the Temple and raising it again in three days came to nothing. There was no evidence against Him. He stood there in the midst obviously harmless, holy, undefiled, separate from sinners. There was no need to speak. His appearance and record spoke for Him.

The Claim of Christ

At last in despair the high priest put Him on His oath, and challenged Him to give him a plain answer— "Art Thou the Christ, the Son of the Blessed?" And thus challenged, Christ answered plainly. He kept His Messiahship veiled in the days of His popularity, when to reveal it might have meant an attempt to set Him on the throne; but now that He was in the hands of His foes, and the confession of His Messiahship would mean death, He made no concealment at all. Jesus replied, "I am." Silence at such a moment would have been, as the commentators say, a dereliction of all His claims and a betrayal of His mission. "I am," He said, and then looking round about upon them, dressed in their little brief authority, He said, "And ye shall see the Son of Man sitting at the right hand of power and coming with the clouds of heaven." The high priest had his answer, and in a simulated frenzy of indignation he rent his clothes and said, "What further need have we of witnesses, ye have heard the blasphemy: what think ye?" And they all condemned Him to be worthy of death.

Why Christ Was Condemned

There are two other points which call for notice.

(1) If there is one thing absolutely certain it is this—Jesus was condemned to death by the Sanhedrin for claiming to be the Son of God. People in these days try to eliminate all Christ's great claims for Himself. They try to reduce Him to the limits of a mere man. They speak of Him as the Carpenter of Nazareth, the meek and lowly Jesus. They would have us believe that Christ's self-consciousness was merely a human self-consciousness. They rule out all the mighty assertions of the Fourth Gospel as being the product of a later age, the result of a process of deification which set in after Jesus had left the earth. But this view of Jesus entirely fails to account for the facts. Even supposing for the moment we leave the Fourth Gospel out of our view, it entirely fails to account for the claims Christ made for Himself in the Synoptics. And amongst other things it entirely fails to account for His death. If anything is certain it is this, that Christ died because of the assertion of His Messiahship. He was condemned by the Sanhedrin because He claimed to be the Son of God.

The Triumph of the Cross

(2) The second thing is this: Jesus in the shadow of His Cross foresaw His triumph. "Be of good cheer," He said to His disciples just before His betrayal when the clouds were looming up darkly in His sky, and strange forebodings and fears were filling the hearts of the Twelve. "I have overcome the world." And the same spirit is His now, as He faces these men who had sunk the judge in the accuser. It was the hour of their seeming triumph. They had Him in

their hands. And yet He knew the victory was not to rest with them. "Ye shall see," He said to Caiaphas and the exultant priests, "the Son of Man sitting at the right hand of power and coming with the clouds of heaven." The hate and fury of men avail nothing against the purposes of God. "The kings of the earth set themselves and their princes take counsel together against the Lord and against His anointed." "He that sitteth in the heaven shall laugh, the Lord shall have them in derision." They may put His Son to death on the cruel tree, and yet, in spite of them, God will set Him as King upon His Holy hill of Zion. How true this is we can in part already see. Caiaphas and the priests availed nothing. They could not put an end to Christ. His Cross became His throne, and as we gaze upon the Son of Man today that is how we see Him—"sitting at the right hand of power." And from the past triumph of the Cross of Christ let us take heart and hope. We have our reactions and setbacks no doubt. But nothing can avail against Christ, or frustrate the purposes of God. Christ must reign till He has put all enemies under His feet. Christ's words to His judges were both a warning and appeal. They passed unnoticed by them. Are they to pass unnoticed by us? In a fashion Christ stands before us for judgment today. But never forget that we must all stand before the judgment seat of Christ, and then the question will be what Christ will do with us. And what He will do with us depends on what we do with Him. May we have grace to receive Him and to accept Him and to confess Him, that we may be amongst those who love His appearing.

97

The Great Denial

"And Jesus saith unto them, All ye shall be offended because of Me this night: for it is written, I will smite the shepherd, and the sheep shall be scattered. But after that I am risen, I will go before you into Galilee. But Peter said unto Him, Although all shall be offended, yet will not I. And Jesus saith unto him, Verily I say unto thee, That this day, even in this night, before the cock crow twice, thou shalt deny Me thrice. But He spake the more vehemently, If I should die with Thee, I will not deny Thee in any wise. Likewise also said they all. . . . And Peter followed Him afar off, even into the palace of the high priest: and he sat with the servants, and warmed himself at the fire. And as Peter was beneath in the palace, there cometh one of the maids of the high priest: And when she saw Peter warming himself, she looked upon him, and said, And thou also wast with Jesus of Nazareth. But he denied, saying, I know not, neither understand I what thou sayest. And he went out into the porch; and the cock crew. And a maid saw him again, and began to say to them that stood by, This is one of them. And he denied it again. And a little after, they that stood by said again to Peter, Surely thou art one of them: for thou art a Galilean, and thy speech agreeth thereto. But he began to curse and to swear, saying, I know not this man of whom ye speak. And the second time the cock crew. And Peter called to mind the word that Jesus said unto him, Before the cock crow twice, thou shalt deny Me thrice. And when he thought thereon, he wept." —Mark 14:27-31, 54, 66-72.

THE FIRST THING to be done in studying the pitiful account of Peter's fall is to reconstruct the actual story. For there are considerable differences in the Gospel narratives; though when sceptical writers try, by magnifying these differences, to cast doubt upon the whole episode, they clean over-reach themselves.

The Story of the Fall

There is perhaps no event in the whole of the Gospel story which is more clearly and fully attested. The evangelists tell the story from their own special points of view, and with slight variations; but upon the fact that, in the high priest's palace, Peter did three times deny his Lord they are all agreed. The variations can practically all be harmonized, and in any case they detract nothing from the reliability of the narrative, they rather add to it. They only show how widespread and familiar the story was in the very earliest days of the Christian Church.

The Boldness of Peter and John

Comparing Gospel with Gospel, the course of events seems to have been something like this. First there is the Lord's solemn announcement, "All ye shall be offended because of Me this night," followed by Peter's confident assurance of his own loyalty. Then the prophecy of Peter's fall, and his vehement protest. The Agony in the Garden of Gethsemane is swiftly followed by the arrest. After this, sudden panic seems to have seized the disciples. "They all left Him and fled." But in the case of at any rate two out of the eleven, the panic does not seem to have lasted very long. Peter and John seem to have recovered some measure of courage, and instead of running away, they followed the procession as it made its way to the house of Annas. They followed "afar off" says Mark, no doubt keeping themselves in the shadow of the houses and the trees in order to avoid detection. When the procession arrived at the house of Annas (where many hold that the denial took place) John passed in with Jesus and the soldiers into the high priest's hall. John was in some way or other known to the high priest and had the entree into his house. But Peter had no such privilege, and when the procession passed through the gateway, he remained without. John, Peter's inseparable comrade, did not like to think of his friend being left outside there in the darkness. So he went and spoke to the portress and persuaded her to open the door and let him in. It was done with the best motives in the world, but John, unthinkingly, did a disservice to Peter that night. He introduced his friend without knowing it into a perfect furnace of temptation. "The best of friends," says Dr. Stalker, "may do this sometimes to one another, for the situation into which one man may enter without peril may be dangerous to another." John saw no risks in the high priest's palace; Peter wellnigh lost his soul.

The Danger Zone

In order to understand the sequence of events, observe the arrangement of a great house such as that into which Peter entered. The houses of the rich in the East are built quadrangular fashion, and the windows all look in upon the courtyard in the middle. Facing the road there is often just a blank wall, with a great gate in it, through which admission is gained. The gate opens upon a passage leading to the courtyard which is open to the sky. Round the courtyard, and raised a little above it, are the reception rooms and the living rooms. When Jesus was brought in by the traitor band, He was taken promptly to one of these rooms off the court-yard, there to be examined by Annas. But the soldiers and the servants who had been the instruments of the arrest, stayed in the open courtyard, and as the night seems to have been bitterly cold, for their greater comfort they kindled a fire. Now that was the dis-position of things when John begged the portress to admit Peter. Jesus was in one of the private rooms undergoing examination, the soldiers and servants were gathered in a noisy group about the fire.

Suspicion Aroused

When the portress let Peter in she scrutinized him, and some-thing in his manner made her a trifle suspicious. However, the probability is, she said nothing at the moment, but allowed Peter to pass unchallenged. He at once made for the group sitting round the fire, partly because he, too, wanted to share in the grate-ful warmth, and partly because he thought that by mingling with the crowd he would be less likely to bring suspicion upon himself. John seems to have passed on immediately to the room in which Jesus was undergoing examination.

The First Challenge

But the place which Peter imagined promised him safety, proved his undoing. As I said, something in Peter's manner had aroused the suspicion of the girl at the gate as he passed. But it was not till the light of the fire fell full upon Peter's face that her sus-picion was changed into something like certainty. Leaving the gate for a moment and running to the group around the fire, she chal-lenged Peter and said, "Thou also wast with the Nazarene Jesus." The challenge took him clean by surprise. He felt himself in a trap. Besides, he had compromised himself. For while he had been sitting there at the fire he had tried to pass himself off as one of the crowd. I daresay they had been jesting about Jesus, making coarse jokes about Him, and Peter had listened to it all without protest, and perhaps affected to laugh with the rest. What could he do now he was thus challenged? What could he do but try to keep up the deception? And so he pretended that he did not under-stand. The agitation, the sheer terror of the man is reproduced in his answer, as it is rendered in the margin of the R.V. "I neither know, nor understand; thou, what sayest thou?"

The Second Challenge

At the moment Peter does not seem to have been pressed any further. But he came to the conclusion that the glare of the fire was a thing he ought to avoid. And so he took the first opportunity of withdrawing into the shade of the porch, perhaps intending to slip out as soon as ever the great door should open. But in the porchway, the same maid, or another maid to whom she had communicated her suspicions, or possibly both together, returned to the charge and said to the servants lounging near, "This man is one of them." And again Peter denied, and to escape the attention of the maid, sought once more to hide himself in the crowd at the fireside.

The Final Challenge

But the whole company was now on the alert, and Peter's agitation and distress were obvious. He had no sooner taken his place amongst the servants by the fire, than a man took up the work of baiting the Apostle. He had plunged into the conversation in order to give an impression of ease, and to divert suspicion. But it only made matters worse. "Of a truth," said this man, "without doubt thou art one of them, for thou art a Galilean." Peter's rough accent betrayed his Galilean origin. And what should a Galilean be doing there in that company if he was not one of the Galilean followers of Jesus! And then to bring things to a climax, another of the servants, a kinsman of Malchus, scrutinizing Peter's face, remembered he had beneath the flash of torches seen those features in the Garden. "Did I not see thee in the Garden with Him?" he said.

The Denial and the Reminder

Peter was now really in trouble, and, frantic with fright, he began to curse and to swear that "he knew not the Man of Whom" they spake. And possibly this final denial had its effect—for these soldiers and servants knew at any rate as much as this about the servants of Jesus, that profane speech never issued out of their mouths. They did not believe Peter's assertion, as Dr. Stalker puts it, but they could not help believing his sins. This cursing and blaspheming man could be no disciple of Him Who was holy, harmless, undefiled, separate from sinners. The "swearing" was probably only the resurrection of a bad old habit that had lain dormant for the last two or three years. But it silenced Peter's accusers, and they made no attempt to stop him when he rose to go. Then at that moment something happened, or rather two

things happened. "Straightway the second time the cock crew."
And Peter remembered! Remembered his own proud and foolish
boasting; remembered the Lord's tender and solemn warning. And
the remembrance filled him with contrition and shame.

Conviction and Remorse

And then something else happened. It chanced that at that very
moment Jesus was being conducted, with hands pinioned behind
His back, through the courtyard on His way to the judgment hall
of Caiaphas. Perhaps He had heard these wild and frantic curses
with which Peter accompanied his last denial. Anyhow, He
knew what had happened, knew the depths of shame and apostasy to which His chosen Apostle had sunk—knew it all. And as
He was led through the courtyard He turned round and looked
full in the face of His conscience-stricken Apostle. The cock-crowing had made him realize his sin; the Lord's look broke his heart.
"When he thought thereon," when he remembered his Lord's
warning, and realized the meaning in that look, "he began to
weep." Or, as the Greek might be translated to bring out its exact
force, "he wept and he wept," "he kept on weeping." He wept as
if he could never stop. Peter as he flung himself shame-stricken
and heartbroken out of the house of Annas in the early dawn of
that tragic day could have taken those familiar lines of Toplady's
hymn into his lips and they would have expressed the feelings of
his guilt-laden soul.

> "Could my zeal no respite know,
> Could my tears forever flow,
> All for sin could not atone,
> Thou must save and Thou alone."

Lessons of the Story

Now sceptics and cynics have poured floods of cheap scorn over
what they are pleased to call the cowardice of Peter. But I agree
entirely with Bishop Chadwick—this is not the story of the
breakdown of a coward. We miss its significance if we do not realize this is the story of the breakdown of one of the bravest and the
best. This story is a warning, not to the weak, but to the strong.

A Warning to the Strong

It is addressed not simply to the Fearings, but to the Greathearts of the Christian host. For in spite of this calamitous
failure, Peter was a brave man. His boast that he was ready to die

with Christ was no vain and empty brag. Remember how he drew sword in the Garden, and would have defended his Lord, one man against a multitude! If Peter had had his way in the Garden, the soldiers would only have laid hands on Jesus over his own dead body. This is not the story of the failure of the coward; it is a story of the breakdown of the brave. And the solemn warning it sounds across the centuries is this: "Let him that thinketh he standeth take heed lest he fall."

And Against Self-Confidence

Now the initial mistake that Peter made, the *fons et origo* of all these calamitous denials was this, he was absolutely sure of his own steadfastness and strength. Self-confidence is always the peril of the strong man. It was Peter's peril. You remember how he boasted of it, only a few hours before. He could conceive of all his fellow disciples turning traitor, but he could not imagine himself turning coward. "Though all should deny Thee, yet will not I." He was so absolutely sure of himself that he had felt no need of watching and praying in the Garden. And that self-confidence led directly to his fall. For it was self-confidence that made him enter the high priest's hall in the first instance. He deliberately thrust himself into temptation. He ventured into the danger-zone and he fell. There is one verse in Peter's first Epistle which always seems to me to be written not with common ink but with the Apostle's own life-blood, for it embodies the lesson learned from the most humbling and shameful experience of his life. It is this, "Be sober, be watchful, your adversary the devil, as a roaring lion, walketh about seeking whom he may devour." It is the warning of a strong man who fell through over-confidence to other strong men against committing the same fatal mistake.

The Danger of Compromise

Now, notice what a series of calamitous blunders Peter committed since he put himself in the way of temptation by entering Annas' house. He made his first blunder when he went and joined the group by the fire and tried to pass himself off as one of them. It was fear that made him do it. He sought to divert suspicion from himself by pretending to be just one of the crowd that had joined in the arrest of Christ. But instead of diverting suspicion he fatally compromised himself. For as I suggested a moment ago, the talk around the fireside had all been about Jesus. It had very likely been coarse and scurrilous talk. And Peter had made no protest of any sort. On the other hand he tried to look as like one of the scorners himself as he could. So doing, he put himself between the devil and the deep sea. Either he had openly to confess himself a cheat, or else he had to maintain the deception by denying all knowledge of Jesus. The one safe course for Christian folk to take is boldly to avow themselves as Christ's followers. The man who begins by being ashamed of Christ is almost sure to end by betraying Him. There is only one way of being a Christian—be strong and very courageous.

98
The Civil Trial

"And straightway in the morning the chief priests held a consultation with the elders and scribes and the whole council, and bound Jesus, and carried Him away, and delivered Him to Pilate. And Pilate asked Him, Art Thou the King of the Jews? And He answering said unto him, Thou sayest it. And the chief priests accused Him of many things: but He answered nothing. And Pilate asked Him again, saying, Answerest Thou nothing? behold how many things they witness against Thee. But Jesus yet answered nothing; so that Pilate marvelled." —Mark 15:1-5.

The Sport of the Persecutors

THE ASSEMBLY OF the Sanhedrin at which Jesus had been examined and sentenced, the account of which Mark has given us in the previous chapter, was really an informal, not to say illegal, assembly. For this meeting was obviously held in the early hours after midnight, and the Sanhedrin could not hold a legal sitting until daybreak. So, to regularize their proceedings, they seem to have met again in a formal way as soon as day had dawned, and then ratified the decisions they had come to in the small hours of the morning. Probably the meeting did not last many minutes. And if you want to know how these men spent the time that intervened, you have the story told you in 14:65. "And some began to spit on Him, and to cover His face and to buffet Him and to say unto Him, Prophesy; and the officers received Him with blows of their hands."

Priests and elders began the sickening sport and the servants joined in. Here is an abyss of horror into which we shudder even to look. Do you remember the story Froude tells about the preaching of Newman at Oxford? Froude says that Newman was once describing closely some of the incidents of our Lord's Passion, the insults and indignities that were heaped upon Him. He then paused. For a few moments there was a breathless silence. Then in a low, clear voice, of which the faintest vibration was audible in the farthest corner of St Mary's, he said, "Now, I bid you recollect that He to Whom these things were done was Almighty God." "It was," says Froude, "as if an electric stroke had gone through the building." And if we, too, would realize the shame and horror of that verse 65, which says how some began to spit on Him, and to cover His face and to buffet Him, and how the officers received Him with blows of their hands, we too must recollect that He to Whom these brutal things were done was Almighty God.

The Resort to Pilate

But daybreak brought the cruel sport to an end. "Straightway in the morning the chief priests with the elders and scribes and the whole council held a consultation, and bound Jesus and carried Him away and delivered Him up to Pilate." The formal session of the Sanhedrin was held; the solemn farce was soon over, and a few minutes after daybreak Jesus with arms bound behind Him was on His way, attended by priests and elders en masse, to the palace of Pilate the Governor. The Priests and elders would like to have dispensed with the necessity of submitting the case to Pilate at all. They had pronounced Jesus guilty of blasphemy and therefore worthy of death, and they would like to have put an end to Him off-hand. But to Pilate the Governor, much against their will, they had to make their appeal. So with verse 2 in this chapter begins Mark's account of what we may call the civil trial of Jesus.

The Civil Trial

Like his account of the ecclesiastical trial, Mark's account of the civil trial is incomplete. When we compare Gospel with Gospel, we find that in the civil trial, as in the ecclesiastical trial, there were three distinct stages. (1) First of all Christ was taken to Pilate and briefly examined by him, the result being a declaration on Pilate's part of Christ's innocence. (2) Then, He seems to have been taken to Herod and tried before him, on the ground that being a Galilean, He belonged to Herod's jurisdiction. (3) Then, finally, He was brought back to Pilate for another examination. The upshot of it all was that He was condemned to death, not because He was guilty, but to appease the murderous hate of the Jews. Now of these three stages in Christ's trial, Mark says nothing at all about the second. He satisfies himself with an epitomized account of the two trials before Pilate. It is with the first of these trials the paragraph of the text deals. And even this account is, as I have said, epitomized. If you want to have the full account of what happened at Christ's first appearance before Pilate, you must supplement what Mark says by what the other evangelists—and especially the fourth—have to say.

The Accusers and the Governor

The course of events seems to have been something like this. The whole Sanhedrin escorted Jesus to Pilate's palace. They knew their man. Pilate was a person who could be coerced and frightened. And the size of the deputation was deliberately meant to compel Pilate to yield to their will. They foresaw there would be difficulty in securing the condemnation of Christ. They knew that legally they had no case. By going all together they wanted to make Pilate feel that the demand for the death of Jesus was a national demand, and that, if he refused to yield to it, he would have the entire nation to reckon with. Pilate lived, during his stay in Jerusalem, in the Praetorium, a gorgeous palace, once the residence of Herod the Great. Towards that palace then the crowd tumultuously made its way. But when they reached the palace, they rigidly refused to enter. By entering the palace they might have incurred ceremonial defilement and so excluded themselves from the solemnities of the festal season. What a revelation of perverse religion! What a revelation of a twisted moral sense! These men were afraid, as Dr. Glover says, of a little leaven, but they were not afraid of innocent blood; they were scrupulous about entering an unswept room, but they were unscrupulously bent upon the murder of the Holy and the Just; they were punctilious in the observance of religious ritual, but their hearts were aflame with the fires of hell. When religion degenerates into mere ritual it becomes full of deadly peril to the soul. There is something deadening, hardening, morally stupefying in religion, when it ceases to be a spirit, and becomes a set of rules.

The Accusers and Their Purpose

But, to return to the story. Seeing that they refused to enter the palace, Pilate had, however, unwillingly to come out to them. He took his seat beneath one of the porticoes, and Jesus bound was set before him. "What accusation bring ye against this Man?" he asked the mob of priests and elders. Perhaps this was more than they expected. Perhaps they had hoped that Pilate would be content without enquiry just to confirm their sentence. But Pilate, with all his faults, had the Roman sense of justice in him, and if he had to sign the death-warrant he insisted on knowing the crime; he declined to be executioner unless first he had been judge. The priests reply that unless Christ had been a malefactor they would not have brought Him to Pilate. "Very well," Pilate answers, "take Him and judge Him." They would gladly have done so; they had indeed already done so but what they could do to Jesus would not satisfy their hate. They blurted out the truth, saying, "It is not lawful for us to put any man to death." Death! Nothing less would satisfy their hate. That being so, Pilate insists again upon knowing Christ's crime. The crime of which the Sanhedrin found Christ guilty was the crime of blasphemy. They sentenced Him to death because He said that He was the Son of God. But that was not the charge they brought forward now. They knew Pilate would have brushed such a charge contemptuously aside. So, in accusing Jesus to Pilate, the priests and elders changed their ground. With brazen impudence they charged Him, not with blasphemy, but with treason. They made practically a three-fold charge (judging from Luke's account). They accused Him first of perverting the nation, secondly, of forbidding the payment of taxes to Caesar, and thirdly, of stating that He Himself was an anointed king.

The Accusers and Their Charges

All this argues almost incredible baseness, for to begin with the charges were outrageously false. Fancy charging Jesus with forbidding to pay tribute to the Emperor in face of that word of His, "Render to Caesar the things that are Caesar's." And they were not only false, but on the lips of the men who made them, they were impudent as well. Pilate knew that, in their heart of hearts, every man in this crowd was a rebel against Rome. Yet now in order to hound Jesus to death they affected an enthusiastic loyalty. In their thirst for the blood of Christ they were ready to trample upon their religious and their national hope. But Pilate was not deceived by this sudden access of enthusiasm for Rome. He knew that for envy they had delivered Him. Now that is the point at which the proceedings had arrived when Mark takes up the story. The priests and elders had just hurled their accusations against Christ, including as the crowning accusation of all, the charge that He made Himself a king. Pilate thereupon withdrew within the palace and took Jesus with him, that he might examine Him quietly as to these charges they brought against Him.

The Kingship of Christ

And that was the first question he asked, "Art Thou the King of the Jews?" The form of the question expresses blank incredulity. The Greek brings out the tone of the question much better than our English rendering. "Thou!" so the Greek reads. "Thou! art Thou the King of the Jews?" Thou! He looked at the Christ, and he knew that the charge of treason was absurd. The person he saw before him was poor and worn; He was friendless and alone; He was clothed in peasant garb; His face bore the traces of the foul usage He had endured in the judgment hall. Pilate looked at Him and he knew that here was no rebel against Rome. The charge of aspiring to kingship was, in Pilate's eyes, plainly absurd. Judge therefore of the surprise he felt when in answer to his question, "Thou, art Thou the King of the Jews?" Jesus replied, "Thou sayest," or as it might be translated to bring out its full meaning, "It is exactly as you say." Just exactly as He had avowed Himself the Son of God to Jewish priests and elders, so He avows Himself a king to the Roman Governor. Pilate was to be left without excuse. He was to be under no delusion as to the person with whom he was dealing. Here was no ordinary prisoner, no common malefactor. Here was One Who made the most stupendous claims for Himself. And there was something in the Lord's bearing that ratified and confirmed His claim. "It is exactly as you say," said Jesus, and Pilate knew it to be true. It was not in ignorance Pilate crucified the Prince of Life. He knew what He was doing. Christ confessed Himself a king, and Pilate in his heart of hearts admitted the claim to be true. It left his crime without excuse.

No Threat to Rome

But while Christ confessed His kingship and so left Pilate in no mistake as to the person with whom he was dealing, He at the same time revealed to him the character of His kingship, so as to make it clear that He in no way threatened Caesar's rule. His kingdom, He went on to say to Pilate, was not of this world. He was no rival to Tiberius. Had He been a rival to Caesar He would have commanded His servants to fight; instead of that, He had ordered Peter to put his sword back into its sheath. His kingdom was not of this world. Caesar reigned over men's bodies. Christ wanted to reign in their hearts. Christ was no rival to Caesar, but by this claim He set Himself far above Caesar and every other earthly potentate! He claimed to be King in the realm of the eternal and the spiritual! He claimed to be the supreme Lord of conscience! He claimed to be the final answer of God to the enquiring spirit of man! The Truth! The truth about God, the truth about man, the truth about life and death and the hereafter, it is all in Christ! There may have been other pioneers in the kingdom of truth, other seekers and enquirers—there were prophets and psalmists and philosophers and seers before His day—but in the kingdom of truth He is sole and undisputed King! And the honest soul gladly acknowledges His kingship; the man of sincere and guileless heart does homage to Him; the man who is true and wants to be true bows down to Jesus. "Everyone that is of the truth heareth My voice."

The Failure of Pilate

"Everyone that is of the truth heareth My voice," He said, and in that word there was an appeal to Pilate. The Lord was fighting for the soul of Pilate. Pilate saw the truth, but he was not of it. And so, instead of responding to the Lord's appeal and manfully taking his stand on the side of truth, he sneered, "What is truth?" and never waited for an answer. That was the moment of Pilate's collapse, that is the real condemnation of Pilate. He saw the truth and refused to obey it. He saw the gleam and refused to follow it. The truth still confronts us in Christ and claims our allegiance. What do we do with Him? Do we listen to Him? Do we obey Him? Do we follow Him? Christ is still the test of character. He reveals the bias of men's hearts. If the heart is honest it cannot help but love Him. "Jesus," it cries, "the very thought of Thee with sweetness fills my breast." But if the heart repudiates Him, disowns Him, rejects Him, it can only be because the heart is evil. Our attitude towards Christ fixes our place. "Everyone that is of the truth heareth My voice."

The Silence of Christ

Pilate's failure to respond to Christ's appeal may account for Christ's subsequent unbroken silence. When Pilate turned on his heel with that sneer on his lips, "What is truth?" and faced the mob outside, it was to tell them bluntly that he found no fault in the prisoner. With his Roman sense of justice, he brought in a verdict, "Not guilty," and if left to himself would have acquitted Christ on the spot. But the priests and elders did not mean to be denied their prey. They began to clamor out one charge after another. "The chief priests accused Him of many things." And in the midst of the clamor and the tumult Jesus stood there calm, unmoved, silent. Never a word did He attempt to say in reply. Pilate wondered at it. He had never known a prisoner like this. "Answerest Thou nothing?" he asked, "Behold, how many things they accuse Thee of." But Jesus declined to break His peace. "He no more answered anything, insomuch that Pilate marvelled." This silence of Jesus, what are we to make out of it?

The Silence of Innocence

(1) It was the silence of conscious innocence and holiness.

"Answerest Thou nothing?" asked Pilate in astonishment. There was no need to answer. The accusations fell harmless. Christ stood there clothed in the garb of a holy character, and let the charges refute themselves. Men had but to look at Him, and they knew these charges were absurd, ridiculous, lying. "If you throw plenty of mud," said Newman when replying to Kingsley, "some of it will stick. Stick," he said, "yes, but it will not stain." The mud the priests flung at Christ could not stain Him, did not even stick to Him. His very presence gave the lie to every accusation, He was obviously holy, harmless, undefiled. And not only does His silence testify to His innocence, but also to the calm serenity of spirit. "There are few tests of a man's spiritual condition more searching and decisive," says Cotter Morison, "than the temper with which he bears unmerited insult and railing speech." Christ passed through that searching test in perfect triumph.

The Silence of Judgment

(2) But it was more than a silence of conscious innocence. I cannot help feeling there was an element of judgment in it. "Jesus no more answered anything." No more! There had been a time when He had been willing to speak to priests and elders. But a few minutes before He had gladly spoken to Pilate! But high priests and elders had received His declaration of His Messiahship with shouts of "blasphemy," and Pilate had turned aside His appeal with a sneer. "And Jesus no more answered anything." They had hardened their hearts, and He ceased to speak. They had refused to listen, and so He became silent. He refused to give that which is holy to the dogs and to cast His pearls before swine.

The Warning

The silent Christ! The incident is full of solemn teaching and warning. Man is in sore plight when the Lord becomes silent to him! Does He ever become silent? There is a solemn Bible word which says, "My Spirit shall not strive with men forever," and it is a tragic fact of experience that men may so harden themselves in sin that conscience shall cease to speak and they shall become impervious to all holy appeals. It is at our peril we neglect and reject the Gospel appeal. For that is when Christ becomes silent, when we refuse to listen. To the listening and responsive soul Christ is never the silent Christ. Before we call He will answer, and while we are yet speaking, He will hear.

99
Barabbas or Christ?

"Now at that feast he released unto them one prisoner, whomsoever they desired. And there was one named Barabbas, which lay bound with them that had made insurrection with him, who had committed murder in the insurrection. And the multitude crying aloud began to desire him to do as he had ever done unto them. But Pilate answered them, saying, Will ye that I release unto you the King of the Jews? For he knew that the chief priests had delivered Him for envy. But the chief priests moved the people, that he should rather release Barabbas unto them. And Pilate answered and said again unto them, What will ye then that I shall do unto Him Whom ye call the King of the Jews? And they cried out again, Crucify Him. Then Pilate said unto them, Why, what evil hath He done? And they cried out the more exceedingly, Crucify Him. And so Pilate, willing to content the people, released Barabbas unto them, and delivered Jesus, when he had scourged Him, to be crucified." —Mark 15:6-15.

The Final Stage of the Trial

THE THIRD AND final stage in our Lord's trial was the most protracted of the three. Mark does not tell the whole story here. Pilate tried one device after another to escape from the necessity of condemning an innocent man, and yet to avoid coming into open conflict with the priests and the Jerusalem mob. His struggles were as hopeless and as pitiable as those of a bird caught in a net. I need not rehearse the story of his shifts and evasions. You can read it for yourself in the pages of the other Gospels. Mark contents himself with noting just one of the stratagems to which Pilate resorted. He records this particular one because it really marks the crisis of the trial. When this failed Pilate had no expedient left. He knew himself doomed to defeat. He realized that he could not stand against the relentless hate of priests and people. The end of the story has all the tragic inevitability of a fate when you know the actors in it. Here is the pitiful heartbreaking end, "And Pilate wishing to content the multitude released unto them Barabbas, and delivered Jesus, when he had scourged Him, to be crucified."

603

The Passover Prisoner

And now for the particular episode that Mark here narrates. It appears that it was the custom of the Roman Governor at Passover time to release a prisoner, and to allow the people to choose the prisoner to be so released. Some think that this was a custom that had come down from Maccabean times, but most probably it was introduced by the Romans themselves to conciliate the goodwill of the Jewish people. Just exactly as European monarchs celebrate their marriage day or their coronation day by remitting sentences and extending free pardons, so the Roman Governors honored the great feast day of the Jews by making it the occasion of extending the imperial pardon to some one prisoner whom the people were allowed to select. While Pilate was on the judgment seat, telling the accusing priests that he could find no fault in Jesus, and proposing to chastise Him (as a sop to his accusers) and then to release Him, the crowd came up to the palace gates begging Pilate to grant them the usual Passover boon. Pilate welcomed the interruption, it opened to him another door of escape from the odious necessity of condemning Jesus.

Barabbas

There happened to be lying in prison at the time a criminal named Barabbas, or to give him his full name (as tradition records it) Jesus Barabba. Now Barabba means simply "Son of the Father." And "father" was a title in those days given to the Rabbis, as today it is given to the Roman priests. He was, therefore, a man of good family who had fallen into ways of crime. The probability is that he belonged to one of those fanatical parties which swarmed in Judaea at this time, and were continually stirring up revolt against the Roman power. In one of these insurrections this Jesus, the son of the Rabbi, had committed murder, and has been caught red-handed in the crime. He has been flung into prison to await the arrival of the Governor for judgment. For such a crime there could be but one penalty, and that was death. It is very likely that a desperado of this kind could enjoy a certain popularity with the crowd, who would think of him not as a murderer but as one who was doomed to die for his devotion to his country's cause. But while willing to admit that Barabbas may have enjoyed a certain undeserved popularity, I question very much whether they had decided to ask for Barabbas' release when they surged up to Pilate's gates. What they clamored for was that the usual boon should be granted them.

Pilate's Offer and Its Reception

Pilate at once fell in with the crowd's humor and suggested that Jesus, "the King of the Jews," as he called Him, should be the prisoner to be released. That would be killing two birds with one stone—granting a favor to the crowd and at the same time escaping the necessity of condemning Jesus. And against the idea of condemning Jesus Pilate's whole soul rebelled. "He perceived that for envy the chief priests had delivered Him up." But the chief priests were not to be denied of their prey in this fashion. They stirred up the crowd to demand Barabbas. Possibly they painted him as a kind of national hero. Note again the hypocrisy of the whole proceeding. What was the accusation the priests brought against Jesus? The accusation of treason. But Barabbas had been guilty of the very crime of which they had falsely accused Jesus. Barabbas had committed insurrection and involved himself in the crime of murder in the process.

Pilate's Struggle

Pilate was staggered by the demand for Barabbas. He imagined that given the choice between Jesus the son of the Rabbi and Jesus the King of the Jews, they would not have hesitated an instant. "What then," he asked in remonstrance, "shall I do with Him Whom ye call the King of the Jews?" And the cry rang out, "Crucify Him!"—give to Him the punishment intended for Jesus the son of the Rabbi. Pilate was shocked. His moral sense was outraged. "Why," he asked, "what evil hath He done?" But the only answer to his "Why?" was another angry shout, "Crucify Him!"

Pilate's Surrender

To that menacing and bloodthirsty crowd, Pilate made a weak surrender. No apologies can wipe out the stain of that crime. The chief priests and scribes must bear their burden; but their cruelty is no excuse for Pilate's cowardice. He washed his hands before the crowd, as if to repudiate all responsibility for the crime. But the formality of washing his hands before the multitude has not washed out the bloodstains. You remember Macbeth's pitiful cry after the murder of Duncan—

> "Will all great Neptune's ocean wash this blood
> Clean from my hand? No, this my hand will rather
> The multitudinous seas incarnadine, making the
> green one red."

It is so with Pilate. The whole sea would avail nothing to wash out his bloodstains. His name and his crime are inseparably associated together, "Crucified under Pontius Pilate."

Perhaps the easiest and clearest way of summarizing the lessons of this tragic episode is to consider briefly the conduct of the actors in the scene: Pilate, the chief priests, and the Jerusalem mob.

The Priests and Their Crimes

First, consider the conduct of the priests. No one can read the story of the Passion without feeling that it is at their door and not at that of the Roman Governor that the responsibility for the murder of the Christ primarily lies. On them Peter, at the first appearance before the Sanhedrin, lays the blame. He never mentions Pilate. The men whom he saw before him were the real murderers. "Jesus Christ of Nazareth Whom ye crucified." *Ye!* The word is emphatic. Perhaps he recalled the scene (for if he had not witnessed it, he had heard about it); how these people, when Pilate washed his hands, had cried, "His blood be upon us and upon our children." In their rage and fury, they were willing to take the responsibility and the blame. Later they sought to shift the blame on to Pilate's shoulders. The high priest, when Peter appeared before the Sanhedrin the second time, made it a ground of complaint that the Apostles were holding himself and his colleagues responsible for the death of Christ. "Ye have filled Jerusalem," he said, "with your teaching, and intend to bring this Man's blood upon us." But it was no case of intending. His blood *was* upon them. Peter bluntly repeated the charge. "The God of our Fathers," he replied, "raised up Jesus, Whom ye slew hanging Him on a tree."

The Root of Their Crime

What was it moved these men to this black deed of blood? Probably many things combined. Possibly they never forgave Christ for the public rebuke He inflicted when He swept the Temple clean of the mob of traffickers in whose gains they shared; they hated Him because He threatened their "vested interests." No doubt they smarted under the humiliation of repeated defeats, when they came to Him seeking to catch Him with their questions. But Mark mentions none of these things; he fastens upon one motive which perhaps was the mightiest and most potent motive of all. He says that Pilate perceived it was for envy the chief priests had delivered Him up. Trace this crime to its root and you find it sprang from envy. These men, the nominally religious leaders of the people, were envious of Christ's power and popularity with the people, they were envious of His obvious and unchallengeable goodness. "A man that has no virtue in himself, ever envieth virtue in others," says Bacon. And these men, where piety was a cloak, who were like whited sepulchres, envied Jesus because of His very goodness and purity and truth.

The Power of Envy

Do you imagine that in tracing the crime back to envy we are assigning an insufficient motive? That is because you have not really thought upon the malignity of this evil passion. "It is also the vilest affection and the most depraved," says Bacon, once again, "for which cause it is the proper attribute of the devil himself." There is no crime to which envy will not resort. It is as cruel as the grave. Do you remember how envy and murder are coupled together in Scripture? In Romans, Paul describing the people of reprobate mind describes them as full of "envy, murder." Envy . . . murder, they are akin, and there is but a step from the one to the other. I do not know that we are as afraid of envy as we should be. It finds a lodging in most of our hearts more or less. I know of no surer evidence of depravity of human nature than this, that we can scarcely hear even of a friend's success without a pang! At the back of all our slandering and detracting, and backbiting, lies this evil spirit. Fear it! It is the very spirit of murder! Let us ask for the love which envieth not.

The Crowd

And now for a minute let me turn from the priests to consider the conduct of the crowd. The commentators tell us that we are not to identify this crowd with the throngs which escorted Christ into Jerusalem in lowly triumph a few days before, crying, "Hosanna to the Son of David." The applauding crowd of the Sunday, they say, was a Galilean crowd; the mob that clamored for His death on the Friday was a Jerusalem mob, and upon the mob in Jerusalem Jesus had but little influence. That may be so. And yet I am not sure. The fickleness of crowds is proverbial. The hero of one day is the object of their fury the next. The London mob went frantic over Wellington when he came home after Waterloo; a few years later they were thirsting for his blood. So there would be nothing incredible in the assertion often made in popular sermons that it was the same crowd who shouted, "Hosanna" on the Sunday that cried, "Crucify Him" on the Friday. But for the credit of human nature let us accept the commentators' verdict and believe that this was another and a different crowd. This was the Jerusalem proletariat let us say.

Democracy Fallible

What a hint, then, we get here as to the tragic mistakes a democracy may commit. Pilate set Jesus of Nazareth, and Jesus the son of the Rabbi, a robber and a murderer, side by side, and the Jerusalem mob chose Barabbas! There is an old Latin phrase, very popular in these days, "Vox populi, vox Dei," "The voice of the people is the voice of God." But, popular though the phrase may be, is it true? There is an old story told of John Wesley and his sister (a woman of intellectual gifts not unworthy of her two great brothers), who were discussing this very point. John Wesley, to bring the discussion to an end, laid the law down rather imperatively by saying, "I tell you, sister, the voice of the people is the voice of God." "Yes," replied his sister, "it cried, 'Crucify Him, crucify Him.'" In these democratic days, when in our own land the people are rising to a sense of their power, it is well we should be reminded that the democracy may make the most tragic mistakes. I do not say this by way of disparagement of the democracy. I do not say this with any intention of criticizing the democratic form of Government. As a matter of fact, as far as the crucifixion of Christ is concerned, the aristocracy of Judaea stand in exactly the same condemnation with the democracy. I say it only to guard against the fallacy that democratic government necessarily means the beginning of the millenium. The mob may go as fatally wrong as a monarch. Here is the staggering proof of it, they chose Barabbas rather than Christ. No! there is no divine right in democracy as such. Crowds may be blinded by prejudice and passion just as easily as kings.

Contrasted Ideals

Barabbas and Christ! They stood for different ideals. Both had a kingdom in their minds—but the kingdoms differed in nature. Barabbas dreamed of a temporal kingdom to be established by violence; Christ aimed at a kingdom of righteousness and peace and joy to be established by a change of heart. Barabbas stood for faith in the sword, Christ stood for faith in character and goodness. And the Jerusalem crowd said, "Not this Man but Barabbas." Get down to the essential meaning of the choice and it means this, they believed more in violence than they did in love, they had more faith in the sword than they had in character. They thought their kingdom was likely to be advanced by Barabbas' method rather than by Christ's. Every nation, and every class within a nation, is confronted with the same choice. It may say, "might is right" or it may say, "right is might." There is a God who judges in the earth, and the only way in the long run for a nation to be strong is for it to be strong in Him.

The Abiding Choice

Barabbas or Christ? Pilate offered the crowd the option, and they chose Barabbas and rejected Christ. In a different form the same option is presented to every one of us. It is true we have not to choose between some red-handed robber and the Lord. Something else takes Barabbas' place. But in every case there is a choice. That is always how Christ presents Himself to us—as an alternative. We have to choose between Him and the world, in one or other of the many forms it assumes— between Him and a life of pleasure, between Him and Mammon, between Him and self. And the choice is as critical for us as it was for this Jerusalem crowd. Our eternity depends upon it. Do not think that none have said, "Not this Man but Barabbas," since that fatal Friday. They are saying it continually, for they are choosing self and sin and the world, and saying of Christ, "We will not have this Man to reign over us." The choice presents itself to us. Barabbas or Christ? God help us to choose the better part, which shall not be taken away from us; to go outside the camp with Christ bearing His reproach, to be willing to suffer with Him that we may hereafter be glorified together.

100
Pilate

And so Pilate, willing to content the people, released Barabbas unto them, and delivered Jesus, when he had scourged Him, to be crucified."
—Mark 15:15.

HAVING TRACED THE trial of Christ to its end, we are now in a position to form some kind of judgment upon the character and conduct of Pilate himself. His is a pitiful story. He was an unwilling participator in this deed of blood. Left to himself, he would have liberated Christ. He struggled to secure His release. But at length he was coerced into committing the wickedness which his soul abhorred. He is not the man on whom the chief guilt of the crime of history rests. Christ Himself said, "He that delivered Me unto thee hath greater sin." Caiaphas, the chief priest, is the one on whom the greater guilt principally rests. But every man must bear his own burden, and Pilate must bear his.

Pilate as Procurator

Now in coming to discuss Pilate's character and his conduct, something must be said about his antecedent career, for that antecedent career of his had a mighty influence upon his action in connection with our Lord's trial. Nothing is known about his family or his origin. He appears upon the pages of history when he assumes office as procurator of Judaea. The Roman procurator was a kind of subordinate governor. He occupied the same kind of relationship to the Governor of the Roman province of Syria, as, say, the Lieutenant-Governor of Bombay or Madras does to the Viceroy of India. But within the limits of his province, which included Judaea, Samaria, and Galilee, the Procurator exercised practically unlimited and almost despotic power. Pilate held this office for about ten years. He came to Judaea just about the time when John the Baptist began to preach, and so his rule covered the period of our Lord's ministry, and of the first establishment of Christianity in Judaea.

His Blunders

What sort of a man was this Pontius Pilate? Philo, the Jewish author, describes him as "inflexible, merciless, and obstinate." No doubt, as Dr. Purves says, this is a one-sided representation. But it has this value for us; it shows the kind of esteem in which Pilate was held amongst the people over whom he ruled. His administration in Judaea had been marked by a series of calamitous mistakes. Rome, as I have already said in one of my previous studies, was generous and liberal in her treatment of subject nations. She allowed them as large a measure of home rule as was consistent with the maintenance of her own imperial supremacy. And she was especially considerate and tolerant in matters of religion. She had followed her usual policy in Judaea. She had allowed the Jewish court or Sanhedrin to retain a large measure of power. And she had respected the religious prejudices of the Jews. Out of regard, e.g. for their feelings, the display of images on the part of the Roman soldiers had been forbidden in Jerusalem. But Pilate either through ignorance, or more probably out of contempt for the Jews, had willfully offended their prejudices. Josephus tells us of two or three actions of his which irritated the Jews to something like madness.

The Figures on the Standards

Here is one. His predecessors, as I have said, had respected the Jewish prejudice against images. It seems that the standards of the legions were adorned with an image of the Emperor. Previous procurators had taken care, when marching their soldiers into Jerusalem, to remove these images. But Pilate disdained to humor what, no doubt, he regarded as a contemptible prejudice. So he ordered the troops to enter the Holy City with the Emperor's effigy in its usual place upon the standard. The troops entered by night, but in the morning the standards were seen upon the citadel crowned by what, to the Jews, were idolatrous images. Forthwith, multitudes hastened to Caesarea to beg Pilate to remove the figures. For five days Pilate scorned to listen to them. On the sixth day he bade them gather on the racecourse, and when they again renewed their appeal, a band of soldiers, placed in ambush, suddenly rushed out and with drawn swords threatened to kill them if they did not desist from their clamor and return home. But Pilate had not reckoned with the fanaticism and obstinacy of the Jewish character. To his amazement, instead of ceasing their cries, they flung themselves on the ground, bared their necks, and declared they would rather die than endure the violation of their laws.

Pilate had met his match in this stubborn people. Sorely against his will, he had to order the images to be removed.

The Raid on the Temple Treasury

Another story Josephus tells about him is this. He took in hand the business of building an aqueduct in order to provide Jerusalem with a water supply. And he seized the money paid in to the Temple treasury to help in the payment for the work. Once again the Jews were up in arms. It was perverting sacred money to profane and secular purposes. When Pilate visited Jerusalem, an abusive and threatening mob—tens of thousands of them, says Josephus—came clamoring that he should not persist in his design. Pilate who seems to have foreseen trouble had introduced some of his legionaries disguised into the crowd. When the Jews refused to go away, he gave these disguised soldiers the signal, and they at once attacked the crowd with their bludgeons. They used more force than Pilate had intended, with the result that they scattered the crowd indeed and quelled the disturbance, but not without wounding many and beating some even to death.

The Case of the Galileans

We have a reference to another unfortunate incident in Pilate's career in the Gospels. He mingled the blood of some unhappy Galileans with their sacrifices. No doubt, they had been concerned in some riot or tumult, but so little regard had Pilate for any of the Jewish notions of sacredness, that he slaughtered them in one of the Temple courts. Incidents like these reveal something of Pilate's character. He was a typical Roman in his contempt and scorn for the Jews—"the horde of the circumcised," as one Latin writer calls them. But they are still more illuminating as to the relationship between Pilate and the people over whom he ruled. They cordially detested one another. Pilate detested the Jews because more than once they had foiled him and beaten him. And the Jews detested Pilate because he had deliberately offended them, insulted them, and outraged them.

The Burden of the Past

Now, notice how Pilate's conduct at the trial of Christ was affected by his past career. What was the consideration that most powerfully influenced Pilate in his conduct of the trial of Jesus? Not regard for justice. Had that been the case, he would instantaneously have acquitted Him. With trained mind he saw through the farce from the first moment. He knew that "for envy" they had delivered Him unto him. But justice really counted for nothing in the trial of Jesus. What really did count, what dictated all Pilate's actions was fear of the people. That was why he resorted to the various tricks and stratagems of which the evangelists tell us. He wanted to release Jesus and retain the favor of the mob at the same time. When he found he could not do both, he elected to retain the favor of the mob. Mark tracks the crime to its real and ultimate root in this verse 15, in which he describes the issue of the trial, "Pilate wishing to content the multitude, delivered Jesus to be crucified." That is why Pilate became the legal executioner of Jesus; he sought to curry favor with the crowd. Why? Because of the mistakes and crimes which marked his past administration.

Caesar's Way

The master of the Roman empire at this time was that cruel and suspicious tyrant, Tiberius. There were two things, apparently, that Tiberius cared about, the due receipt of the taxes and the maintenance of peace. So long as his Governors in various parts of the world saw to these two things, Tiberius was well content. But a Governor who failed to exact the necessary tribute, one who by blundering actions created unrest and disaffection, fell under Tiberius' displeasure. Now one complaint with reference to Pilate's administration had already been made to Tiberius and had brought forth a sharp reprimand from him. A second complaint might prove his ruin. These crimes of his were just weapons in his opponents' hands. And that was the threat that finally brought Pilate to his knees. Philo, speaking of another occasion on which the Jews threatened to report him to Tiberius, says, "The threat exasperated Pilate to the greatest possible degree, as he feared lest they might go on an embassy to the Emperor, and might impeach with respect to other particulars of his government, his corruption, his acts of insolence, his rapine, and his habit of insulting people, his cruelty, and his continual murders of people untried and uncondemned, and his never-ending, gratuitous and most grievous inhumanity." Thus Pilate knew that he had given only too much ground for complaint, and that he could not afford to let these priests and elders complain to Caesar. Here was a man burdened by his own past.

The Past and the Present

A past of sin is a terrific hindrance to a present of virtue. This is a commonplace that scarcely needs enforcement. Peter's first lie to the maid, for instance, almost drove him to the blasphemous denial before the officers round the fire. When the men challenged him, Peter's courage might have come back and he might have bravely owned his Lord. But he had already given himself away by lying to the maid, and he had to keep up the deception. A young fellow away from home accompanies foolish and wicked companions to some evil haunt of pleasure. By so doing he delivers himself into their hands. Later, he may want to turn over a new leaf. He may want to live pure and speak true. But evil companions can always quote against him his own past. "Why," they will say to him, "you saw no wrong in it on such and such a time." And so the sin of yesterday becomes a hindrance in the way of uprightness today. All this teaches the old and familiar lesson— beware of the first beginnings of sin. For sin is not done with when it is committed. Do you remember that tragic confession of Sir Percivale in Tennyson's Idylls? With other knights he had been inspired to engage in the quest of the Holy Grail, which is only a mystical way of saying that he was moved to give himself to the holy and dedicated life. But his past proved an insuperable obstacle:

> "Then every evil word I had spoken once,
> And every evil thought I had thought of old,
> And every evil deed I ever did,
> Awoke and cried, 'This quest is not for thee.'
> And lifting up mine eyes I found myself
> Alone and in a land of sand and thorns,
> And I was thirsty even unto death;
> And I too cried, 'This quest is not for thee.'"

Pilate was like Percivale. He was crippled for the duty of today by the wrong of yesterday.

Scepticism and Weakness

That was one cause of Pilate's breakdown. The second main cause of his failure was his scepticism. When Jesus talked about every one "who was of the truth," hearing His voice, Pilate asked in reply, "What is truth?" Now there are all sorts of ways of saying, "What is truth?" A man may say it with desperate and almost heart-broken earnestness. He may be lost in the mazes of perplexity and doubt, and he may feel that his very happiness and life depend on knowing what is truth. "O that I knew where I might find Him that I might come even to His seat," cries one of the patriarchs. His heart was in the cry; for the truth about God was a matter of life and death to him. A man may ask, "What is truth?" in the spirit of intellectual curiosity. He may be interested in the truth as a problem. That perhaps is the prevailing temper of our own day. But Pilate did not ask the question, "What is truth?" in the spirit of the man who is intellectually interested in the search for truth. Still less did he ask it with the passionate eagerness of the man who feels he must know the truth or die. He asked it in the sneering temper of the sceptic. "Jesting Pilate!" Bacon calls him. But "jesting" is not the right adjective. Jesting carries with it a suggestion of geniality and sunshine. But there was nothing genial about this question of Pilate. It was bitter, scornful, cynical. It was sceptical, unbelieving Pilate who asked that question. Pilate did not believe there was such a thing as truth. You remember Gibbon's epigrammatic description of the Roman attitude towards religion. "The various modes of worship which prevailed in the Roman world, were all considered by the people as equally true, by the philosopher as equally false, and by the magistrates as equally useful." Pilate as an educated Roman reproduced the sceptical temper of his day.

Pilate, Weak, Unprincipled

Now the main criticisms passed upon Pilate in his conduct of Christ's trial are these: (1) He showed himself a weakling. He allowed himself to be driven into the crime of sentencing to death a person who was not only innocent, but who impressed him as the noblest and holiest person in whose presence he had ever stood. "I find no fault in Him," that was Pilate's verdict. He delivered Him to be crucified, that was Pilate's sentence. For all his Roman pride, Pilate showed himself a moral weakling. (2) And the second criticism is this, he tried to secure by policy and stratagem what he ought to have stood out for on principle. Christ was innocent and he knew it. But instead of acquitting Him as a matter of justice, he tried to secure His acquittal by policy.

Because Without Faith

These criticisms are amply justified, but they only deal with surface symptoms and not with the real disease. His weakness and his stratagem are the evidences of a deeper mischief. And that deeper mischief was this: he was a man without faith, without any outlook to the spiritual and the eternal. Pilate's scepticism was the secret of his moral collapse. Pilate's universe was bounded by the world he could touch and hear and see. The factors he had to deal with were Tiberius away in Rome, and these menacing priests and the howling mob before his eyes. God never entered into his calculations. That is why Pilate proved a weakling. For to be courageous a man must have faith in God. If there is no God vindicating right and punishing wrong, if there is no judgment beyond the human judgment, then to the clamorous demands of the people, to the will of society men will inevitably bow. It is only in the fear of God men can brave the wrath of their fellows.

The Lesson for Us

The lesson of it all is obvious. Scepticism in the long run spells weakness and disaster. A great deal has been written and said in praise of "honest doubt." I frankly admit there may be "honest doubt"; with the honest doubter I have every sympathy. But the state of doubt even when honest is not a state to be cultivated. According to our faith it shall be unto us. Faith is the positive quality in life. Without faith, morality is not safe. The ethical life stands but a poor chance apart from religion. The man who has no fixed stars in his sky, in the shape of faith in God, and in right, and in a judgment to come, makes shipwreck. If we are to do right at all costs, to live pure, to speak true, we must have faith in God.

Here is a prayer for us, living as we do in a world crowded with temptation, lest we sin as Pilate sinned and fall as Pilate fell, "Lord, increase our faith."

101

The Scourging and the Crowning

"And the soldiers led Him away into the hall, called Praetorium; and they call together the whole band. And they clothed Him with purple, and platted a crown of thorns, and put it about His head, And began to salute Him, Hail, King of the Jews! And they smote Him on the head with a reed, and did spit upon Him, and bowing their knees worshipped Him. And when they had mocked Him, they took off the purple from Him, and put His own clothes on Him, and led Him out to crucify Him."   —Mark 15:16-20.

THIS IS A terrible paragraph, one of the most awful paragraphs in the whole of Holy Writ. Dr. Stalker points out a great change that has come over the feelings of Christian people with reference to the physical sufferings of Christ. A century or two ago, Christian folk almost revelled in the contemplation of these sufferings. The German mystic, Tauler, for example (as he points out) enlarges and exaggerates every detail until his pages seem to reek with blood, and the mind of the reader grows almost sick with horror. We incline, on the contrary, to fling a veil of reserve over the details of our Lord's death and passion. The reaction, while in some cases it is carried to an extreme, is on the whole a healthy one. It argues a certain coarseness and almost brutality of mind to be able to peer into and discuss the details of the outrages inflicted upon our Lord's sensitive flesh. I confess to having that feeling strong within me as I approach this paragraph which tells the sickening story of the scourging and the crowning. With the briefest possible word, by way of explanation, I pass on to the lessons the paragraph has to teach.

The Scourging

It seems it was the practice amongst the Romans to scourge a criminal before they crucified him. Pilate did not depart from the usual custom in the case of Christ. On the other hand, he had a definite object in view in ordering the scourging to take place as usual. He intended when the scourging was over, to make one final appeal to the people; he meant to show them the Christ after the soldiers had done their brutal work upon Him—pale, exhausted, bleeding—in the hope that the sight of Him in that condition might appeal to their pity. As a matter of fact, he did so, as you remember; he brought out the tortured Christ, and said to the Jews, "Behold the Man." But even that appeal failed to touch the bloodthirsty mob. Their answer to Pilate's last pleading was, "Crucify Him, crucify Him." Of Pilate's motive in ordering the scourging and of his appeal at the end of it, Mark, however, says nothing. They in no way affected the course of events and so were not essential to his narrative. He contents himself with recording the bare fact of the scourging and the subsequent brutal mockery.

The Mock Coronation

Not content with the brutality of the scourging, the soldiers took Him into the Praetorium, and there set themselves to mock and ridicule and insult Him. Very likely these soldiers thought that it was already finally decided that Jesus should die. They knew nothing of the plan that Pilate had in his mind; and so they proceeded to take these liberties with Christ which seem to have been not uncommon in the treatment of condemned criminals. They called together the whole band (probably about five or six hundred of them) and proceeded to make cruel sport of Jesus. They had gathered that the charge on which He stood accused was that of aspiring to be a king, and the game they played was that of a mock coronation.

Jesus had been stripped of His clothing when He had been led forth to be scourged. Now, after they had led Him inside the Praetorium, they flung over His torn and excoriated back a "purple" cloak, probably some officer's cast off garment, "a faded rag," as Dr. Swete says, "but with enough color left in it to suggest the royal purple." And then some one suggested that being a king He ought to have not simply a purple cloak upon His shoulders, but a crown upon His head. And so some one ran out and from the shrubs in the palace garden gathered a few twigs which he twisted into a wreath in derisive imitation of that wreath of victory which the Roman Emperors wore on the days of their triumphal processions. That the twigs happened to carry on them sharp and jagged thorns only added to the humor of the situation. This crown of thorns they pressed upon the Lord's meek brow. Then a king must have a scepter, and Matthew says they put, for scepter, a reed into His hand. And having thus fitted Him up with a travesty of the regalia of royalty, each of them advanced and did mock homage to Him, crying, "Hail, King of the Jews!" And then to show that the whole thing was meant for deadly insult, every man of them, as he rose from his knees, seems to have snatched for a moment the reed Christ held in His hand, smitten His head with it, and then spat in His face. There is the story in its bare simplicity.

The Dignity of the Lord

And now let me turn from the contemplation of the brutality of the soldiers to the consideration of the Christ Who endured such brutality at their hands. It is a relief so to turn. For if the conduct of the soldiers is a revelation of iniquity and wickedness, the conduct of the sufferer is a subduing revelation of meekness and moral majesty. I think sometimes that He never appears greater than when enduring these indignities at the hands of the soldiers. Was there ever patience and meekness like this? "He was led like a lamb to the slaughter and as a sheep before her shearers is dumb, so He opened not His mouth," says the prophet (Isa. 53:7). It was all fulfilled in the Praetorium that morning. "When reviled," says Peter, "He reviled not again, when He suffered He threatened not" (1 Pet. 2:23). He might have summoned legions of angels to His aid. Instead of that, He submits to these accumulated indignities without a murmur or a protest. Here is meekness more than human! It would have been human to flare up into indignation and wrath, but meekly and silently to bear it all was nothing less than divine.

The Crown

I pass from the consideration of the majesty and dignity of the Lord to speak a word or two about the crown and scepter the soldiers gave Him. It seemed absurd to these Roman soldiers that one so poor and friendless and weak as Jesus was should aspire to kingship. And their brutal sport was meant from first to last to be a mockery of that claim. And yet God in His Providence made the wrath of these men to praise Him. More than once, things that were meant for insults to our Lord were transfigured into testimonies. When they called him "friend of publicans and sinners," they meant it for derision and contempt, but time has transfigured it into the Lord's most splendid title. And so exactly these rude soldiers meaning to mock Christ, unconsciously and involuntarily bore witness to Him. They could not more perfectly have expressed the nature of His kingship than by putting a crown of thorns upon His head, and a reed for scepter in His hand. For think, first, of the crown they put upon His head and all that it implies. His crown is a crown of thorns, for His kingship is based upon His sufferings. "He humbled Himself and became obedient unto death even the death of the Cross," says St Paul, "wherefore God highly exalted Him and gave Him the name which is above every name." Wherefore! His sufferings were the cause of His exaltation. His disciples thought that all was over with Christ when they saw Him beaten, bound, scourged, crucified. As a matter of fact, these unspeakable sufferings of His have given Him His power over the hearts of men. And why have our Lord's sufferings done all this for Him? Because they stand for love. That is why the thorn-crown is the most fitting crown that Christ could wear. A crown of gold stands for pomp and power—a crown of thorns stands for love—for strong, uttermost, self-sacrificing love. And love after all is the mightiest power on earth.

The Scepter

I think, now, of the scepter they placed in our Lord's hand. It was a reed, says St Matthew, and a reed is a frail, weak thing. It is easy to break and bruise a reed. A reed—not a mace, or an axe, or a sword, but a reed! Christ rules not by force, but by meekness and gentleness. If the crown sets forth the ground of His kingship, the scepter sets forth the nature of His rule. Christ does not constrain men by force, He woos them by His gentle and gracious love. How gentle He was in all His dealings when here on earth. How exquisitely tender He was with the woman who was a sinner, and that other woman who came behind Him in the press and "healing virtue stole." And how exquisitely gentle He was to fallen Peter. He did not smite Peter with the sword of His wrath. "The Lord turned and looked upon Peter." And when He rose from the dead He sent a special message to this erring disciple. "Go, tell His disciples and Peter." Gentleness is the very spirit of Christ's rule.

The King Indeed

They called Him king, did these rough soldiers in mockery. But He is King indeed and of a truth. The kings of the earth set themselves and the princes took counsel together against the Lord and against His anointed in Jerusalem long ago. They heaped every ignominy and insult upon God's anointed. And yet, in spite of them, God has set His King upon His holy hill of Zion. Yes, God has made His Son the King! He rules and reigns today. What are we going to do with Him? I present Him to you with the thorn of crowns on His head and the reed in His hand, and I say to you, "Behold your King!" Will you bow down and worship Him? Will you serve Him and obey Him? Will you in daily life do His will? For my own part when I see Him thus with that crown upon His head, I am in the mood to say,

> "All hail, Redeemer, hail,
> For Thou hast died for me,
> Thy praise shall never fail,
> Throughout eternity."

102
Simon of Cyrene

"And they compel one Simon a Cyrenian, who passed by, coming out of the country, the father of Alexander and Rufus, to bear His cross."
—Mark 15:21.

WE COME NOW to the touching and beautiful story of how Simon of Cyrene carried the Lord's cross. I have noticed, in consulting my authorities, that this incident stirs even the most prosaic of them to something like poetry. Of course, one expects poetry from a man like Dr. John Watson, and the chapter in which he treats of Simon in his *Companions of the Sorrowful Way* is idyllic in its simple and moving pathos. But Dr. Stalker is a severely sober and restrained writer, and yet even his pages glow with imagination and throb with feeling as he speaks of this man, who for a brief space stood substitute for Christ and bore His Cross. But it is the plain prose of the affair I want to give you, though indeed the plain prose of it, without any imaginative adornment is in itself poetic enough.

On the Way to the Cross
In our country when sentence of death is passed, usually some time is allowed for the condemned prisoner to prepare himself for the last dread change, but in the case of our Blessed Lord the execution followed swiftly upon the sentence. Immediately after the failure of Pilate's last appeal, the soldiers led away Christ to crucify Him. In these days of ours we take care not to add to the bitterness of the condemned prisoner's lot. It is punishment enough to have to die, without surrounding death with unnecessary horrors and pains.

The Open Shame
But, in the hard and cruel world in which Jesus lived, everything was done to make the death of the criminal more bitter. Executions were always in public, and the prisoner was marched through streets lined by curious and jeering spectators to the place of doom. And in the case of those condemned to die by crucifixion (the most

degrading and shameful death of all) this added ignominy was inflicted upon the victim that he had to carry his own cross. Now both these indignities they inflicted on Jesus. It was in the Governor's palace that the trial had taken place. When sentence was finally pronounced the soldiers proceeded to lead Jesus through the streets of Jerusalem to a place called Golgotha, which was the appointed place of execution. Where exactly Golgotha was it is impossible to say. Apparently it was so-called because of its shape; it is, as Dr. David Smith says, "a skull-shaped knoll" just outside the city. Whether the Via Dolorosa that is still pointed out to pilgrims is the actual way that Christ took is very questionable, but at any rate this is certain, that He had to walk through the streets of Jerusalem while brutal crowds scoffed and jeered at Him as He passed. And not only had He to walk to His place of execution through jeering crowds, but He had to walk bearing His own Cross. We must, a little, correct our notions of the kind of cross on which Christ died. It was not the heavy and massive thing we usually see depicted. "It was," says Dr. Stalker, "not much above the height of a man and there was just enough wood to support the body."

The Burden of the Cross

No doubt such a cross was not too heavy for the usual sort of criminal to carry. But with Jesus it was otherwise. Recall the experiences of the previous few hours. First of all He had passed through the mysterious and exhausting agony of the Garden. Then had come all the tense excitement of the various trials, first before Annas, then before the Sanhedrin, then before Pilate, then before Herod, and finally before Pilate again. And then to crown everything there had come the scourging, a cruel punishment beneath which often the sufferer died. When the soldiers, therefore, came to put His Cross upon His shoulders, they were placing upon Him a burden greater than He could bear. As Dr. Watson says, "He was willing to die upon the Cross, but it seemed likely that He would not be able to carry it to Calvary." John's account makes it clear that faint and spent as He was, He carried the awful burden for some distance, probably through the Jerusalem streets, but when He reached the city gate, the little strength He had gave out, and He staggered and fell beneath His load.

Simon the Substitute

It is at this very point that Simon comes into the story. The soldiers, realizing that Christ was helpless, looked around for someone whom they could press into the service. It was an ignominious service this carrying of the cross, and as Roman soldiers they scorned to do it themselves. Their choice fell upon Simon. He was a man of Cyrene, a prosperous North African town. That is not to say that he was an Ethiopian, as some people think. Cyrene had a large colony of Jews. In fact the Jews of Cyrene were so populous that there was a special synagogue set apart for their use in Jerusalem. And the probability is that Simon was just a Jew from Cyrene who had come to Jerusalem for the Passover feast. He was lodging not in Jerusalem itself, but in one or other of the little villages outside. And he happened to be making his way into Jerusalem just as the procession to Golgotha was issuing out of the gate. And it was this man, Simon of Cyrene, the soldiers impressed into the ignominious service of carrying the cross.

Why Chosen?

Why was Simon the soldiers' choice? Dr. Watson apparently thinks that it was Simon's strength and size that attracted the attention of the soldiers. He speaks of him as a "sturdily-built country man." "His prominence and his bulk," he adds in another place, "perhaps an unconscious sympathy growing on his face, attracted their eye. Here was a fellow nature had intended to be a carrier of loads, a common man who could make no complaint, a simpleton who had pity on an outcast." But all this is pure imagination. No hint is given us in Holy Writ of his stature or condition. For myself, I prefer to account for Simon's choice in another way. It is possible that Simon in some way showed sympathy with Jesus. Coming in from the country and seeing this crowd surging out of the gates, curiosity may have impelled him to try to discover what the excitement was about. Edging his way through the crowd he would find himself face to face with Christ. It may be that just at that moment Christ fainted and fell beneath His burden, and some brutal act of the soldiers may have extorted from Simon some evident sign of sympathy. It was this, I suggest, that attracted the attention of the soldiers to Simon. They revenged themselves for Simon's indignant remonstrance by taking the Cross from Christ's shoulders and placing it upon his. And so it came to pass that Simon walked with Jesus to His place of execution carrying His Cross.

Let me gather up two or three of the most obvious truths this touching little incident has to teach.

How Christ Crossed Simon's Path

First of all, observe how Christ crossed Simon's path. Simon was coming in out of the country, Christ was going out of the city to Golgotha, and they met at the gate. It looks, as we say, like an accidental meeting. But there was nothing accidental about it. It was divinely ordained of God that Simon should meet with His Savior there, and that he should go outside the camp with Him, bearing His reproach. Many have deleted those mighty words— foreknow, foreordain, predestinate, from religious speech. But they stand for eternal verities nevertheless.

A Divinely Ordered Meeting

Accident, luck and chance, are pagan words. In a world which God rules there can be no accident or luck or chance. "Nothing walks with aimless feet." "The steps of a good man are ordered by the Lord." It was by the Lord's ordering that Henry Barrow's steps were led to the Separatist conventicle; it was by the Lord's ordering that John Angell James' steps were led to a house where for one brief night he shared a room with a praying youth; it was by the Lord's ordering that Charles Spurgeon's steps were led to that little Primitive Methodist Chapel where he found his Savior. God besets us behind and before and lays His hands upon us. And it was by the Lord's ordering that Simon and His Savior met at the gate leading out of the city.

Decisive for Simon

Again, Christ crossed Simon's path in an unwelcome fashion, but the meeting probably marked a crisis in the life of Simon. His first introduction to Christ must always in his mind have been associated with that painful and humbling experience. Yet the quarter of an hour he spent with Christ's cross upon his back may have been the most sacred and blessed time in his life to Simon. From what we know of him, it seems possible that Christ so spoke to his soul by the way that before its end Simon knew he had found his Savior. And today, as then, Christ crosses men's paths as He crossed Simon's. Our first introduction to Him is often associated with painful and humbling experiences. He has met with many a man before today upon a bed of sickness; He has met with many a man in the shadow of bereavement; He has met with many another by the side of the open grave. The pain, the sorrow, the grave, how we shrink from them! And yet, looking back, we know that our chastisement has yielded to us the peaceable fruit of righteousness.

The Lord's Helpers

The story of Christ's end is not altogether a story of coarseness and brutality and murderous hate. You can make an ugly picture gallery out of Judas and the priests and Pilate, and Herod and the brutal soldiers. But let us not forget those who were kind to Christ. The darkness is not unrelieved. Let us not forget that in this last terrible and awful week Martha and Mary had made Him a feast. One unknown friend had lent Him an ass's colt; another had given Him his Upper Room; yet another had made Him free of his Garden; and when the day of His death came, Pilate's wife put in a word for Him, the women of Jerusalem wept over Him, Joseph of Arimathea begged His body, and Nicodemus brought an hundredweight of spices. And amongst those who did kindness to Christ, was Simon the Cyrenian who carried His Cross. And whoever would be a disciple of the Lord, must still bear His Cross. We must enter into the fellowship of His sufferings, we must become conformed unto His death.

What Christ Did for Simon

And now, let me set down in a sentence or two some of the things Christ did for Simon. First He immortalized his name. It may seem a little matter, but it is worth bearing in mind that the righteous shall be held in everlasting remembrance. Of more importance is this, that the Lord saved Simon's soul. I make no doubt at all that Simon was a Christian man after that brief walk in the company of Christ. There is no need to identify him with that Christian preacher in Antioch, Simeon who was called Niger. Just let it suffice to say that in Christ Simon found Him of Whom Moses in the Law and the Prophets did write, the King of Israel, the Redeemer of His soul. He gave him the souls of his sons as well. You notice that Mark describes him as "the father of Alexander and Rufus." That can only mean that at the time Mark wrote his Gospel, Alexander and Rufus were prominent and honored members of the Christian Church. There is a Rufus mentioned in Paul's Epistle to the Romans (16:13), and he may have been the Rufus here referred to. But in any case the fact remains that Simon's two sons grew up to be honored Christian men and Christian workers. And he saw the desire of his soul. And I do not know whether in later days Simon was prouder of the deed he himself had done for Jesus, or of his holy fame as the father of Alexander and Rufus.

Christ's Rewards

What a rich reward for a simple kindness! And that is how
Christ rewards men still. The way to be eternally rich is to put
Christ in your debt. For here is the great and glorious promise,
signed by Him Whose word never faileth, countersigned by the
experience of innumerable saints, "There is no man that hath left
house or brethren or sisters, or mother, or father, or children, or
lands, for My sake and for the Gospel's sake, but he shall receive
a hundredfold now in this time, houses, and brethren, and sisters,
and mothers and children, and lands . . . and in the world to come
eternal life" (Mark 10:29, 30).

103

The Crucifixion

"And they bring Him unto the place Golgotha, which is, being interpreted, The place of a skull. And they gave Him to drink wine mingled with myrrh but He received it not. And when they had crucified Him, they parted His garments, casting lots upon them, what every man should take. And it was the third hour, and they crucified Him. And the superscription of His accusation was written over, THE KING OF THE JEWS. And with Him they crucify two thieves; the one on His right hand, and the other on His left. And the scripture was fulfilled, which saith, And He was numbered with the transgressors. And they that passed by railed on Him, wagging their heads, and saying, Ah, Thou that destroyest the temple, and buildest it in three days, Save Thyself, and come down from the cross. Likewise also the chief priests mocking said among themselves with the scribes, He saved others; Himself He cannot save. Let Christ the King of Israel descend now from the cross, that we may see and believe. And they that were crucified with Him reviled Him." —Mark 15:22-32.

The Cross and Its Significance

Zophar, one of the friends of Job, speaking of the character of Almighty God says to the rebellious patriarch, "It is high as heaven, what canst thou do? Deeper than Sheol, what canst thou know?" (Job. 11:8). That verse can be applied with perfect fitness to the dying of our Lord. Who can hope to find out its meaning to perfection? It is as high as heaven; it is deeper than hell. It is as high as heaven, for all the grace of God is in it. It is as deep as hell, for all the hate and fury of wickedness is in it. It is a subduing revelation of love; it is a shuddering exhibition of sin. It is at once glorious and shameful, humbling and exalting, radiant with the light of heaven, and dark with all the darkness of the pit. The Cross of Christ is the meeting-place of the ages. It is the great watershed of history. To it all preceding ages pointed; from it all subsequent history takes its trend and shape. To that Cross millions of men and women look back today as the ground of all their hopes and the source of all their joys.

Golgotha

Golgotha has become the most sacred place in the world because Christ died upon it. Before Christ died there it was a place of shame and contempt—just the place where criminals died. If people thought of it at all, it was with shuddering and loathing. But Christ died upon it, and the place has become holy ground. With what tenderness of heart Christian people think of the "green hill far away!" How the flood gates of the heart are opened when they think that "He hung and suffered there!" Most nations have some spot invested with special interest for them because of its association with some event of national importance. But Calvary is of interest not to a nation but to a world. On it the mightiest deliverance was wrought. On it the greatest emancipation of all was accomplished. On it, the Lord, by dying, won for all who believe in Him the forgiveness of their sins. And, just as Christ by His dying on Golgotha has converted that awful place into a veritable gate of heaven, so has He converted the Cross, that instrument of insult and of shame, into a thing of glory.

The Cross Itself

I have no mind to dwell upon the horrors of the crucifixion; and yet we must follow Christ to Golgotha, and with awed and humbled hearts listen to what they did to Him when He hung and suffered there. And, first of all, of the Cross itself. There were three types of cross. One was shaped like an X and is popularly known as St Andrew's Cross, from the tradition that the Apostle was put to death on a cross of that kind. Another was shaped exactly like a T, that is, it consisted of an upright beam and a crossbeam at the top of it. But in the Roman Cross the upright projected above the cross-beam, and it was upon this kind of cross that Jesus died, as is evident from the fact that there was room above the cross-bar for a superscription to be written indicating the charge on account of which Jesus was put to death. Usually the victim was fastened to his cross before it was fixed in its socket. He was laid upon this instrument of torture after being stripped of his raiment, and first of all his hands were fastened to the transom by nails driven through the palms. The arms, too, were usually bound to the beam by means of cords lest the weight of the body should tear the hands away from the nails that fastened them. For the same reason, there was in the middle of the upright beam a peg or narrow shelf on which the body was made to rest. Finally, the feet were either tied or nailed to the base of the upright. And then the cross with its quivering load was lifted up and the victim was left to die a lingering death. Sometimes his sufferings lasted for two or three days. The death of the cross was, in fact, the cruellest, the most agonizing form of death ingenuity could devise. "And they crucified Him."

"They Parted His Garments among Them"

But Christ was not even allowed to die in peace. His last hours were marked by accumulated insult and reviling. First of all, and nearest to the Cross, were the Roman soldiers in charge of the crucifixion. As soon as their brutal work was done, they had no more concern for their victim. All they cared about was their share of his property. It appears that the garments of the suffering were always regarded as the perquisites of the executioners. Christ had not much in the way of personal apparel to leave. He was not one of those who were clothed in purple and fine linen. But there was His cloak for one of them, and His girdle for another, and His sandals for the third, and His turban for the fourth. There was just one other garment, the tunic, which tradition says, that Mary His mother had woven for Him with her own hands. They were about to tear this into four equal portions when the fact that it was seamless arrested their notice. And one of them proposed that instead of tearing it up and so rendering it worthless they should cast lots for it. So the dice-box with which the Roman soldier was only too familiar was speedily forthcoming. And with a callousness that is beyond speech these soldiers gambled for the Lord's seamless cloak at the very Cross's foot.

The Title on the Cross

Pilate, too, had a hand in making Christ's death more bitter. It was the Roman fashion to placard above the criminal the crime on account of which he was suffering. Pilate ordered this to be written over Christ's head, "The King of the Jews." No doubt the insult embodied in that superscription was levelled primarily at the Jewish leaders. Pilate was repaying them for the humiliation they had inflicted upon him. And from that point of view it answered its purpose, for it stung the Jews to something like madness. But in insulting the Jews, Pilate insulted Jesus too. For that inscription meant the repudiation of Christ's kingship, it meant that this Man Who claimed to be a king deserved to be treated only as a criminal and a slave.

The "Busy Mockers"

But what embittered Christ's death most of all was the mockery of His own people and their leaders. "Those that passed by," the indiscriminate crowd, "railed on Him and wagged their heads and said, 'Ha! Thou that destroyest the Temple and buildest it in three days, save Thyself and come down from the Cross.'" And the chief priests and scribes, while refraining from the open jeering of the common people, yet mocked Him among themselves in tones loud enough for Him to hear. "He saved others, Himself He cannot save." "Let the Christ the King of Israel now come down from the Cross that we may see and believe." The very brigands who were suffering with Him joined in the chorus of insult. "They that were crucified with Him reproached Him."

Human Depravity Revealed

What a commentary this all is upon the evil possibilities of our human nature. The human nature I see revealed in the soldiers and the priests and the scribes and the people is not so much divine as devilish. That men should be able to make a jest and joke of the suffering of anyone would have been bad enough. But that they should turn the dying Christ into an object of mockery argues a wickedness almost beyond speech. For this Christ Whom they mocked was One Who had never done an evil deed. He had gone about doing good. He had healed the sick; He had cleansed the leper; He had turned houses of mourning into houses of rejoicing. He had carried joy and blessing with Him wherever He went. He was absolutely good, utterly loving, entirely holy. And they mocked at Him. They turned His dying into a jest. They hanged the Incarnate Goodness, and the Incarnate Love, and the Incarnate Holiness to a tree, and reviled Him as He suffered there.

The Last Temptation

The very taunts they levelled at Christ made His dying more difficult, because they thrust upon Him once again the temptation He had fought in the Wilderness and in the Garden. They said, "Come down from the Cross!" They said, "Save Thyself!" They said that if He came down from the Cross they would believe. In a word they invited Christ to take another and an easier way to the throne than the way of the Cross. That was the temptation that had dogged His steps all the way through. It faced Him first in the Wilderness when the devil offered Him all the kingdoms of the world and the glory of them if He would but fall down and worship him. It assailed Him again when Peter at the mention of the Cross took Him and began to rebuke Him saying, "This shall never be unto Thee." It assailed Him once more in the Garden. It was the fight against the temptation to take an easier way that made His sweat as it were great drops of blood falling to the ground. And through the taunts of the people and the priests it assailed Him once again on the very Cross itself. "The devil," says Luke in his account of the Temptation in the Wilderness, "departed from Him for a season." Yes, it was only "for a season." The attack was again and again renewed. The final victory was won only when that cry, "It is finished," broke forth from the lips of the dying but triumphant Lord. When He chose to hang there, bearing all the pain and shame, there was no more that Satan could do. Then was fulfilled that saying of our Master's, "I beheld Satan fallen as lightning from heaven." But it all added to the pains and sufferings of Christ.

The Cup He Refused

And now I turn from the contemplation of the wickedness of men to consider the glory of the Christ as we see it revealed in this paragraph. And first notice the courage of Christ. It seems to have been the custom amongst the wealthy and charitable ladies of Jerusalem to provide a portion of medicated wine for such as were condemned to die by the slow agony of the cross in order to make them less sensible to the pain. It was a humane practice, and in accordance with their custom they handed to Christ a vessel containing wine mingled with myrrh or gall. Our Lord seems to have put this drink to His lips, for the exhaustion of the scourging had left Him parched and faint; but when He realized what it was, He refused the drink. "He received it not." Why was it that Christ refused to avail Himself of this merciful provision? Martyrs in the Marian persecution did not hesitate to accept the bags of powder provided for them by the kindness of friends, in order to escape the slow agony of the flames. Why did Christ refuse this stupefying draught? Two or three reasons have been suggested and I think there is something in all of them.

The Cup He Drained

He did it because He would not omit one bitter drop in the cup the Father held to His lips. That is a significant phrase the writer to the Hebrews uses, "He tasted death for every man." He tasted death—all there was in death. He did not want, shall I say, to slip through death without knowing what it was. He tasted death in all its darkness and horror. For a refutation of the charge of cowardice you need go no further than this. When they offered Christ an opiate, He refused to take it. You remember the story of Dr. Johnson's passing. One day he asked his doctor to tell him plainly whether he could recover. "Give me," said he, "a direct answer." The doctor, having first asked him if he could bear the whole truth, which way soever it might lead, and being answered that he could, declared that he could not recover without a miracle. "Then," said the brave old moralist, "I will take no more physic, not even my opiates: but I have prayed that I may render up my soul to God unclouded." That was splendid courage, but it pales before Christ's courage on the Cross. There was an agony of physical pain, there was a depth of spiritual horror in His death which leaves us speechless and appalled, and yet with open eye and mind unclouded, He faced it all. "They offered Him wine mingled with myrrh, but He received it not."

The Meekness of Christ

And secondly, notice the meekness of Christ. I have read somewhere that oftentimes the victims of this awful punishment would rend the air with their curses. Hanging there, bound and helpless, speech was left to them. And maddened by the fiery torture they would assail the agents of their death with all manner of insult and abuse and furious maledictions. But our Lord bore all with patience and majestic meekness. "As a sheep before her shearers is dumb so He opened not His mouth." I believe it was the meekness and patience of Christ on the Cross that Peter had in his mind when he wrote, "Who, when He was reviled, reviled not again; when He suffered, threatened not" (1 Pet. 2:23). I sometimes fancy that we are still inclined to look for proofs of the Lord's divinity in the wrong place. We are in danger today of the error of which these priests and scribes were guilty long ago. Power is our proof of Deity. If Christ would only display His power in some striking way so that we might see it, we would believe. But to me the meekness of the Lord seems always more impressive even than His mighty works. Here is meekness nothing less than divine, amid all the tortures of the Crucifixion, overwhelmed as He was with insult and abuse "no ungentle murmuring word escaped His silent tongue." His only reply to His tormentors was to pray for them. Surely this was the Son of God.

The Self-Sacrifice of Christ

Finally, what an illustration we have here of the self-sacrifice of Christ. "He saved others," they jeered at Him, "Himself He cannot save." The taunt has been converted into a tribute. It is quite true. Just because He wanted to save others, He could not save Himself.

But the "cannot" was not the cannot of physical impossibility. The chief priests and scribes thought He could not come down because the executioners had done their work too well, because of the nails driven through His hands and His feet, and the ropes around His arms. But not all the nails and ropes in Jerusalem could have held Christ there had He wished to come down. What were nails and ropes to One Who could still the tempest with a word, Who had legions of angels at His command? No, it was not the nails and ropes that held Him there—but His own mighty and sacrificial love. No one took His life from Him, He laid it down of Himself. And He laid it down because that was the only way of gaining redemption for the world.

He could not save Himself because He was intent upon saving others. I was in Salisbury Cathedral recently, and I saw there a tablet to a doctor who in a visitation of cholera had given himself with unstinted devotion to the task of ministering to the stricken and especially the poor; who as a result caught the deadly sickness himself, and died at thirty-two. It reminded me of my Master. There was great and self-sacrificing love in both cases. Only the love of the Lord was infinitely nobler and more beautiful. The young doctor perhaps hoped that he might escape. Jesus knew that He must die. And He died willingly. To save others He sacrificed Himself; "Who for the joy that was set before Him endured the Cross, despising shame, and hath sat down at the right hand of the throne of God" (Heb. 12:2).

104
The Death

"And when the sixth hour was come, there was darkness over the whole land until the ninth hour. And at the ninth hour Jesus cried with a loud voice, saying, Eloi, Eloi, lama sabachthani? which is, being interpreted, My God, My God, why hast Thou forsaken Me? And some of them that stood by, when they heard it, said, Behold, He calleth Elias. And one ran and filled a sponge full of vinegar, and put it on a reed, and gave Him to drink, saying, Let alone; let us see whether Elias will come to take Him down. And Jesus cried with a loud voice, and gave up the ghost. And the veil of the temple was rent in twain from the top to the bottom. And when the centurion, which stood over against Him, saw that He so cried out, and gave up the ghost, he said, Truly this man was the Son of God."
—Mark 15:33-39.

MARK REMAINS FAITHFUL to his habit of conciseness and brevity even in his account of the Lord's dying. There were several things of moving and pathetic interest which happened in the interval between the third hour when they nailed Jesus to the Cross and the sixth hour with which this paragraph begins. But Mark passes them over in silence. The one thing he is concerned about is that men should contemplate the actual dying of the Lord, and that in that death they should see not a martyrdom, but the atoning sacrifice of the Son of God's love. And so without staying to notice the events that happened by the way, he passes swiftly to that tremendous hour of crisis when having borne our sin and the curse of it, the Lord gave up the ghost.

The Darkness
"When the sixth hour was come," he says, that is when it was broad noon by the time of day, instead of being broad noon, it was more like midnight, for "there was darkness over the whole land until the ninth hour." It was not the darkness of eclipse. It may have been nothing more than the darkness of a brooding storm, as Dr. David Smith suggests. There is nothing in the narrative to suggest it was miraculous or supernatural. The evangelists make no suggestion as to how the darkness was caused, they simply record the

fact, that for three long hours Jerusalem and the whole land as far as eye could see was enveloped in murky gloom. But the fact that they record the darkness at all shows this, that they felt there was some relation between the darkness of nature and the dark deed that was being perpetrated upon the Cross. It was as if nature went into mourning for the death of Christ. Milton giving the reins to his poetic fancy pictures the earth as hushed and still and expectant when Jesus was born. That is mere imagination. But it is simple historic fact that nature dressed herself in habiliments of woe when Jesus died. The people mocked at the victim, the priests taunted Him and jeered at Him, but nature hid her very face for shame. Nature sympathized with God; shared in the sorrow of God, "There was darkness over the whole land until the ninth hour."

Darkness and the Man of Sorrows

The darkness was not only in nature. There was darkness also in the soul of Christ. For at the ninth hour the Lord cried with a loud voice saying, "Eloi, Eloi, lama sabachthani?" which is being interpreted, "My God, My God, why hast Thou forsaken Me?" Now this darkness that overwhelmed the soul of Christ is an infinitely more amazing and awful thing than the darkness which covered the face of the land. For usually our Lord lived in the sunshine. Outwardly it is true Jesus' life was hard and rough and troubled enough. He had few of what we call the comforts of life. He was born into a poor home. At an early age He had to address Himself to the hard and wearing toil of the carpenter's shop. He earned His bread in the sweat of His face. As a man His poverty clung to Him. He had not where to lay His head; He was dependent upon the kindness of friends for His support. And He had other trials to bear beside those which are incidental to poverty. He was a lonely man because He was a misunderstood man. The people at large misunderstood Him, at one time in mistaken enthusiasm wanting to take Him and make Him King, and at another in their fury wanting to kill Him out of hand. His disciples misinterpreted Him, and with the deeper purposes of His soul showed scant sympathy; His own kinsfolk thought Him mad; while as for the leaders of the nation—the priests, the scribes, the elders—they had pursued Him almost from the first with malignant and relentless hatred.

Who Was Also the Man of Joy

I agree that, as far as its external conditions went, it is hard to conceive a stormier and more troubled life than that of Jesus. And yet, to say that Christ's was an unhappy life would be to give an entirely false impression. He was not simply the Man of Sorrows. He was also the Man of Joy. He lived in the sunshine. He rarely or never talked of His sorrow. What He talked about was His joy. "His joy" was the bequest He wished to leave to His disciples. When "His joy" was in them there would be nothing left to wish for; perfect satisfaction and content would be theirs, their joy would be fulfilled. And the secret of our Lord's happiness, the source of this deep and abiding joy was His consciousness of the Father's presence and smile. Between Him and the Father there was constant and unbroken communion. You remember how the sense of this uninterrupted fellowship finds expression again and again in His speech. "I am not alone, the Father is with Me." "Believe Me that I am in the Father and the Father in Me." "I and My Father are one." No matter what our Lord's outward circumstances might be, He knew that the Father's smile was resting upon Him. No matter though the priests and people reviled Him, He could always hear His Father say, "Thou art My beloved Son."

"Why Hast Thou?"

But now, on the Cross, at this sixth hour, His soul was overwhelmed with deep night. He felt Himself bereft of His Father's fellowship. He missed the shining of His Father's face. He bore the pain of the nails, and the mockery of the people, and the taunts of the priests without a murmur. But when for a moment God's face was hidden from Him He broke out into this lamentable and heartbroken cry, "My God, My God, why hast Thou forsaken Me?"

The Cry on the Cross

Now, this brokenhearted cry of our dying Lord is almost too sacred a thing to discuss and analyze. And discuss and analyze it as we may we shall never perhaps fully understand the desolation of soul that called it forth. The mystery of the Cross is in this cry. And while we may get glimpses into the meaning of the Cross, we are constrained to confess that there are heights and depths in it that are still beyond our knowledge. If I dwell on our Lord's bitter cry, it is not because I think I can completely explain it. It will suffice to point out some of the elements of the deep and measureless sorrow which evoked it, and to repudiate some fake and cruel theories which have been built on the foundation of this cry.

Not a Cry of Bodily Weakness

The words themselves, as you all know, are quoted from the first verse of the twenty-second Psalm. On the lips of the Psalmist they form little more than the complaint of a lonely and deserted man. But there is a depth of meaning in them as Christ used them, that the Psalmist who first uttered them knew nothing about. What did they mean on the lips of Christ? First of all, we can dismiss absolutely the idea that the cry was wrung from Him by fear of death. Christ never feared the physical fact of death. As a matter of history, the victims of this cruel punishment of crucifixion longed and cried and prayed for death. Death to them was not a foe but a friend, bringing them relief from intolerable agony and pain. Nor was it a case of a soul clouded by bodily weakness. In the extremity of weakness and pain faith sometimes faints and fails. But Christ was not in the extremity of bodily weakness. His mind was not clouded. He was in the possession not only of all His faculties but of a large amount of physical strength when He actually died. Christ's death was not the death of one whose vitality was exhausted. He cried with "a loud voice" just before He gave up the ghost. The people could not believe that He really was dead. Pilate could not believe it when they told him. The fact is, Christ did not die as other men die. While vitality was strong within Him He laid down His life of Himself.

Nor of Remorse

Again, I entirely repudiate the suggestion that this is the cry of "infinite remorse which Christ suffered as being the chief Sinner in the universe, all the sins of mankind being upon Him." To speak of Christ, even when we think of Him as the representative Man, as being the "chief Sinner in the universe" is perilously near blasphemy. And to attribute remorse to Christ is to attribute to Him a feeling of which He knew absolutely nothing. How could One Who knew no sin, neither was guile found in His mouth, know "remorse"? Moreover, the very form of the cry in itself puts this explanation clean out of court. This is not the cry of One Who felt Himself the chief of sinners, this is the cry of One conscious of His own innocence. Christ was unconscious of any reason for desertion. That is what overwhelmed and astonished Him. "My God, My God, why hast Thou forsaken Me?"

Nor Drawn out by "The Wrath of God"

I will have just as little to say to that other explanation which declares that Christ on the Cross was enduring the "wrath of God" even though it comes to us backed by the authority of the Shorter Catechism. Accepting this explanation, certain theologians have spoken of God as hating Christ to the uttermost. But this too is something like blasphemy. It was in obedience to the Father's will that He hung and suffered there. To say that God was angry with Christ because He gave this final proof of His obedience, because He became obedient unto death, even the death of the Cross, is to sacrifice the character of God. As a matter of fact, "God was in Christ reconciling the world unto Himself" (2 Cor. 5:19). Christ was His beloved Son at the Baptism when He took up His redeeming mission, He was His beloved Son at the Transfiguration when He faced and accepted the Cross, but He was most truly God's beloved Son when He actually hung upon the Cross and in obedience to the Father's will, and to further His Father's redeeming purpose, made that last and final and uttermost sacrifice of Himself. "For this," He said Himself, "doth the Father love Me, because I lay down My life."

But as the Cry of the Sin-Bearer

What then is the explanation of this exceeding bitter cry? I find my clue to its meaning in the way in which Christ identified Himself with men. He became bone of our bone, flesh of our flesh. He took hold upon the seed of Abraham. He was made in all things like unto His brethren. He entered our family and became our Elder Brother. But it was a sinful family He entered, and He, the one pure member of it, took the sin of the whole family upon His own heart as if it were His own. He bore our griefs and carried our sorrows, and the Lord laid upon Him the iniquity of us all. The Elder Brother did no sin, but He felt the shame and pain of His brother's sins. They sinned, and in His own pure soul He felt the guilt. As Paul puts it, " Him Who knew no sin He made to be sin on our behalf" (2 Cor. 5:21). Now one bitter and inevitable result of sin is this, it separates between a man and God. The sinner feels like Cain, "cast out from the presence of the Lord." Sin like a black and threatening cloud hides from man the shining of God's face.

Now, Christ so realized our sin that for the time He shared in that awful doom of sin and His fellowship with the Father was arrested. So long as He had His Father, nothing mattered. But to be robbed of His Father's fellowship was very death to Christ. And yet He submitted to it, because it was thus that redemption was to be won. It was not that God had withdrawn His face or was angry with the Son Who was doing His will. It was that these crowding sins of ours hid the vision of God's face. "It needed not," as Dr.

David Smith says, "the Father's displeasure that He might lose the sense of the Father's presence."

But God Is Near in the Darkness

I find a blessed and helpful truth suggested in this. God may be near to us when we seem to have lost sight of Him. We have our occasional bright and sunny days when we can say, " The Lord is at my right hand, I shall not be moved." But there come to us also days of darkness when our enemies mock at us and say, "Where is now thy God?" when we ourselves are tempted to think that God has clean cast us off, and to cry with our Lord, "My God, my God, why hast Thou forsaken me?" Our prayers seem to go unanswered, and the heavens are as brass to our appeal. At such times it will comfort us to remember our Lord on the Cross. He too felt homeless and forsaken, and yet the Father knew and was at hand. It may be just like that with us. In the darkest hour He may be near. When we fear that He has forgotten us, He may be thinking upon us for our good. He can never forsake those who trust in Him.

After the Anguish the Triumph

But note that though apparently forsaken, though enveloped in darkness, Christ says, "My God, My God." Here is superb and subduing trust. He trusted God in the deep night. When He could not see Him, He still clung to Him. He was "my God" through it all. Here is the veritable triumph and climax of faith, to believe in God when we cannot see Him: to trust where we cannot trace. No soul is ever lost that out of its darkness and despair can still cry, "my God." Follow our Lord's story. Anguish gave place to triumph. "It is finished," is the Lord's cry. "Father," He said, "into Thy hands I commend My spirit." And so it will be with us. If in the night we still cling to Him and say, "My God," the joy of assurance and recovered vision will come in the morning. Only a short time elapsed, when Jesus "crying with a loud voice" (showing that death was not due to exhausted vitality) gave up the ghost.

No Death Like This

Other men die because their hour is come and they cannot help it. But Jesus, while life still beat strongly within Him, gave up the ghost. He of His own free will laid His life down. There was never dying in the world's history like this. "Truly," said the Centurion, "this Man was the Son of God." It was not the mere suddenness of the dying at the last that impressed him, but the whole circumstances of it—His answer to the dying thief, His prayer for His enemies, His meekness, His moral majesty. This pagan soldier had seen nothing like it. "If the death of Socrates was that of a sage," Rousseau said, "that of Jesus was the death of a God." Can we say less than that? At the foot of the Cross, let us make our confession, "Truly this was the Son of God." And believing that Jesus was none other than the Son of God, let us rejoicingly believe that He offered for sin the "one full perfect and sufficient sacrifice, oblation and satisfaction for the sins of the whole world."

105

The Faithful Women

"There were also women looking on afar off: among whom was Mary Magdalene, and Mary the mother of James the less and of Joses, and Salome; (Who also, when He was in Galilee, followed Him, and ministered unto Him;) and many other women which came up with Him unto Jerusalem."
—Mark 15:40, 41.

The Sorrow-Stricken Group

HATE AND SCORN and furious and savage contempt surged up to the very Cross of Christ, but sympathy and love were not wholly lacking. "There were also women beholding from afar." "There were also women." Your picture of the people gathered round the Cross is not complete unless you see this little group of sorrowing women. They hung upon the outskirts of the crowd. They dared not venture near. Perhaps it was that they did not care to venture into the thick of that mocking, brutal crowd. Perhaps it was that they were afraid; it was scarcely safe for anyone to identify himself or herself with Christ that day. But there they were beholding! And there was a tumult of sorrow in their hearts. For like the rest of the Lord's disciples these women had trusted that it was He Who should redeem Israel. And here He was dying before their very eyes in defeat and shame. They did not know what to think. Their hopes were all in ruins about them. Their faith was broken and shattered. But, amid the ruins of their faith, love still survived. Though He was dying there, the despised and rejected of men, their hearts still clung to Him, they still loved Him, He was to them still the chiefest among ten thousand and the altogether lovely. It was that love of theirs which brought them to that dreadful place. It was torture to them to gaze at Christ suffering, and to listen to the insults heaped upon His sacred head, but love kept them rooted to the spot. Love gave them boldness. Love lent them courage. Their perfect love cast out fear.

The Women

The disciples all forsook Him and fled. Peter, Thomas, Philip,

642

Matthew, they were nowhere to be seen. But there were certain women beholding from afar. Prominent among them were the three whom Mark mentions by name. First and foremost, Mary of Magdala, out of whom, the evangelist tells us, Jesus had cast seven devils. It was a passion of adoring gratitude which brought Mary there. She owed everything worth having to the Lord. She had been redeemed from the lowest hell by His power. The priests and scribes might heap what insult and scorn they pleased upon His head, but nothing could dethrone Him from the supreme place in Mary's affections, for all she was and hoped to be she owed to Him Who hung and suffered there. And near her was Mary, the mother of James the Less and Joses—James the Less being the second Apostle of that name in the little circle of Twelve. And near her again was Salome, the mother of James and John. Two mothers of Apostles and a woman who was herself an embodiment and illustration of Christ's saving power, these were the most prominent persons in the little group. This was not the first time on which they showed their devotion to the Lord, for they, says Mark, "when He was in Galilee followed Him and ministered unto Him." Our English translation scarcely reproduces the exact force of the Greek. The Twentieth Century Testament is nearer the mark where it renders the words, "all of whom used to accompany Jesus when He was in Galilee and attend on Him."

Their Work

What a vivid light this throws upon the conditions under which Christ exercised His Galilean ministry. It is not altogether easy for us to reconstruct the historic conditions. Supposing that we had been privileged to watch Christ in His journeying through Galilee—we should have seen Him, as other Jewish rabbis had been, accompanied by a little group of chosen disciples. But the twelve Apostles were not the only people in the entourage of Christ. There were also some humble, devoted women in it too. And what was the special function or office of these women? They "ministered unto Him." "There were humbler points in His personality," says Dr. Morison, "in which He touched the conditions of ordinary mortals, numerous little wants to which they were capable of ministering and by their attention to which they could leave Him disembarrassed for His higher engagements." Let me put that in slightly simpler and plainer language. When Jesus took up the work of preaching, He gave up His home and His livelihood. From the material point of view He was worse off than the birds and the beasts, for, as He Himself put it, while foxes had holes and the birds of the air had nests, the Son of Man had not where to lay His head. During the whole period of His public ministry Jesus was entirely dependent upon the kindness of His friends for sustenance and support. And that was the special duty these faithful women took upon themselves. They "ministered" to Him. They took care of His physical comfort. They prepared a home for Him. They looked after His rest and refreshment. Jesus was so absorbed in His work that He was neglectful of Himself. He had no leisure so much as to eat. I picture to myself these devoted women with gentle firmness pressing food upon Him, taking care of Him as a mother would take care of her son.

The Ministry of Women

And all this suggests certain thoughts about the services women have rendered to Christ and His cause all down the centuries. This is the first little group of ministering women, but they have never lacked their successors. Women have always been prominent amongst those who follow Christ and minister to Him. I wonder sometimes what the Church would have been like, what indeed the Church of Christ would have done, but for its saintly, devoted, godly women. In every age they have been the Church's strength; they are the Church's strength at this very hour. In a way, I am not at all surprised to find that women are foremost in the service of Christ, for they owe Him a vast and incalculable debt. From one point of view, it is almost true to say that Christ has done for the whole of womankind what He did for Mary of Magdala in particular. He found womankind in the horrible pit and the miry clay, in a state of degradation and dishonor, treated as mere chattels or things. From that pit of dishonor and shame it was Christ's hand that lifted woman up and set her on that pinnacle of respect and dignity on which she stands today. Even men, like Comte, who reject Christ's Gospel, admit frankly that He immeasurably raised the status of women. Thus, it is not surprising that women should be foremost in the service of Christ. They are simply discharging a vast and infinite debt.

Its Breadth Today

"They ministered" unto Him! And what an enlarged conception of ministry a little phrase like that suggests! Mary of Magdala and Mary the mother of James and Salome, "ministered" to Christ by just attending to the needs of our Lord and His disciples. Have we not, in our time, unduly narrowed that word "ministry"? The public preaching of the Word is not the only ministry Christians can render. The point has been raised afresh, and in a very definite form, whether women ought not to be allowed to preach and speak in churches. I do not say that women have no right to take part in public services. They have most right. But let us not make the tragic mistake of thinking that the only "ministry" of Christ is a public ministry. Christ has some of His most faithful and useful "ministers" amongst timid and shrinking women who never dare make their voices heard in the public worship of the sanctuary. I think of my own mother. I never heard her voice lifted up in one service. I never heard her even offer a word of prayer in public. But I know that she was a devoted "minister" of the Lord. And what was true of my own mother is true of those multitudes of godly mothers who are the saving of our homes and the strength of our land. And not only of mothers, but of those other women like Mary of Magdala, who have no children of their own, but lavish the affection of their souls upon the sick and the helpless and the forlorn of whom this world of ours is so full. These are the Salomes and Marys of our modern Christian life, and they are as true "ministers" of Christ, as those others whose calling it is to stand in our pulpits.

An Office for All the Faithful

But it is not only in the case of women, but with regard to all Christian folk that we need this wider conception of ministry. Every Christian is or ought to be a minister. There is a striking passage in St Paul's Epistle to the Ephesians about the function which pastors and preachers have to fill, the force of which I do not think the average Christian has grasped. Paul says that God gave the Church Apostles, evangelists, pastors and teachers, for the perfecting of the saints, "unto the work of ministering" (Eph. 4:12). Now that is an ambiguous rendering. Although this view is not accepted by some scholars, I prefer to follow the rendering given in the Twentieth Century Testament, "He gave His Church Apostles, evangelists, pastors and teachers, to fit His people for the work of the ministry." It is, then, to the work of ministry that we are all called; and this work is within the reach of every one of us. We want our preachers and pastors and teachers of course. But they are not the only ministers; and theirs is not the only form of ministry. There is a gracious ministry that can be exercised in the home; there is a ministry that can be exercised in the office and the shop; there is the ministry of the personal word which is within the reach of every one of us; there is the ministry of prayer. And there is the ministry of simple kindness and beneficence. We can still "attend" to Christ as these women did. We can still minister to His necessities. For He walks our ways still in the shape of the poor and lonely and sick who need our help. May God give us grace—like these holy women—to do what we can, to render our service.

106
Joseph of Arimathea

"And now when the even was come, because it was the preparation, that is, the day before the sabbath, Joseph of Arimathea, an honorable counsellor, which also waited for the kingdom of God, came, and went in boldly unto Pilate, and craved the body of Jesus. And Pilate marvelled if He were already dead: and calling unto him the centurion, he asked him whether He had been any while dead. And when he knew it of the centurion, he gave the body to Joseph. And he bought fine linen, and took Him down and wrapped Him in the linen, and laid Him in a sepulchre which was hewn out of a rock, and rolled a stone unto the door of the sepulchre." —Mark 15:42-46.

An Unsuspected Friend

ALL HIS LIFE through Christ had more friends than the world dreamed of. Had you asked one of the leaders of His day, what friends and followers Jesus had, he might have replied scornfully and contemptuously, "Just a handful of ignorant Galileans of no account." The Jerusalem Pharisees noted the fact, that none of the rulers or the Pharisees believed on Him. They tried to create prejudice against Christ by making it out that no person of intelligence or standing accepted His claims; that it was only amongst the ignorant, uncultivated, credulous people of the North that He found followers. Yet all the time Christ had His followers even in Jerusalem, and numbered friends amongst people of culture and station. In the days of Christ's popularity they did not obtrude themselves very much. They kept modestly, or, if you prefer so to put it, timidly, in the background. But when troubles came and the day of the Lord's distress dawned, they came out of their hiding places, stood by His side and comforted Him with their devotion and love. They were like the stars, they only revealed themselves when the darkness fell. Here in the paragraph we read of an "unknown friend" who charged himself with the care of the last tender offices of respect and love; it was Joseph of Arimathea, an honorable counselor, but a secret disciple, who provided the Lord with a grave. But before we concentrate our attention on Joseph, let us run through the story.

The Death of the Crucified

It was a Friday on which our Lord was sacrificed, that is, it was
the Preparation or the day before the Jewish Sabbath; and the
Sabbath that followed the day of our Lord's death was one of espe-
cial sanctity because it was the Paschal Sabbath. Now it was the
cruel Roman custom to leave the bodies of the crucified hanging
on their crosses for a length of time, exposed to sun and rain and
to the attacks of carrion birds and beasts of prey. But the more
humane Jewish Law commanded (as you will see from the concluding paragraph of Deut. 23) that the bodies of executed
people should not remain a night upon the tree, but should be
taken down and buried the same day. I do not know whether the
Romans always respected the Jewish prejudice in this respect: I do
not even know whether the Jews asked them in ordinary cases to
make this concession to their prejudices. But this was not an ordinary case. It was the Eve of the Passover. And they did not want
their city on the day of the great Feast to be defiled by the vision of
those three corpses hanging on their crosses. So they went to Pilate
and begged that the legs of the crucified might be broken in order
to hasten death (for death by crucifixion was a slow and even prolonged agony), and that their bodies might be taken away. In the
case of the two robbers this was done; but in the case of Christ it
was unnecessary, for death had taken place already, though the soldier to make assurance doubly sure thrust his sword into the
Lord's side, and so drew out that stream of blood and water which
by some has been taken as evidence that our Lord died literally of
a broken heart.

The Intervention of Joseph

Now Joseph knew full well what happened to the bodies of crucified criminals, unless friends came forward and by gifts of money
to the authorities purchased the privilege of affording them
decent burial; he knew that they were cast out as refuse to be
devoured by pariah dogs or indecent birds. And so he plucked up
courage to intervene just at this point. "When even was now come,"
that is, in the space between afternoon and sunset, Joseph took his
courage in both hands, went boldly in unto Pilate and asked for the
body of Jesus. The "boldness" came in here, for his preferment of
this request meant the open avowal to Pilate and probably also to
the Jews, that he was a friend and disciple of Jesus. And that was an
avowal which required some pluck for a man in Joseph's position
to make. But he made it. He risked everything and made his
request to Pilate.

Pilate's Compliance

Pilate was surprised to hear that Jesus was already dead. He could not believe it was true until he had called the Centurion who was in charge of the execution, and had verified the fact. But when he knew it was even so, "he granted the corpse to Joseph." The words in this phrase are arresting. The verb translated "grant" means "gave as a free gift." The word I render "corpse" is also significant. Though used in the New Testament much as we use "body," it here seems definitely to imply a dead body. Looking at these two words, commentators give two completely opposite accounts of Pilate's conduct. Fastening on that word corpse Dr. Chadwick sees in this another illustration of Pilate's incurable frivolity. "He gave away the corpse as if it was a worthless thing." "Take it, I make you a free gift of it." On the other hand, commentators, emphasizing the word "gave freely," see here again another proof of the deep impression Christ had made upon Pilate. Everything was extraordinary about this Person. His bearing at the trial had been extraordinary. His character was extraordinary. Now the manner of death was extraordinary. Pilate was so deeply impressed that for once in a way he forgot to be avaricious; he declined to take the money which it was usual for Governors to demand, and probably was offered by Joseph for the right of taking Christ's body down and burying it. On the whole I incline to this second explanation. Pilate had been impressed by Christ all the way through. It would be strictly in line with his conduct throughout the trial that he should show this much respect for the dead body of the Man, the like of Whom his eyes had never beheld before, to grant it freely without bribe or price to this honorable counselor when he asked for it. At any rate, Pilate granted the petition of Joseph who immediately hurried back to Calvary, and with reverent hands took the body of Jesus down from the Cross.

The Burial

Joseph was joined in the sad task, according to St John's account, by Nicodemus. Together they wrap the Lord's body in a clean linen cloth, placing the spices, which Nicodemus had brought, in the folds of the linen, as they wrapped it round. There was need for haste, as the Sabbath was swiftly drawing on (for Sabbath, as you remember, always began at sunset on the preceding day). But happily Joseph had a garden near at hand, and in that garden a tomb hewn out of the solid rock, in which Joseph intended that one day his own body should lie. To that garden they hurry with the sacred body; in Joseph's new tomb they reverently lay it, and then they roll a great stone into the mouth of the tomb.

Now look at the character of Joseph as here revealed.

Joseph Looking for a Kingdom

There are two facts about Joseph upon which the evangelist lays emphasis. He was himself looking for the Kingdom of God; and he was a counselor of honorable estate, that is to say, he was a man of rank and standing in the councils of the nation. Now those two facts in themselves suffice to explain Joseph's spiritual history. The first explains how he came to be a disciple of Christ at all, and the second explains why it was that for a long time Joseph feared to declare himself, and was content to remain a secret disciple for fear of the Jews. Let us take the first fact to begin with. "He was himself also looking for the Kingdom of God." In other words Joseph was one of those faithful souls in Palestine who longed for the coming of Messiah and expected His speedy advent. There were in Jerusalem many who belonged to this noble order of expectant souls. While, perhaps, the majority of the people allowed themselves to be absorbed in the business and pleasures of this life, the eyes of these people were always on the watch for the first sign of Messiah's approach. They watched for Him more eagerly than they who watch for the morning. Now there is a promise that everyone that seeketh findeth. The man who waits and watches for the Lord does not wait and watch in vain. The vision he has watched for comes at length to gladden his eyes and bring peace to his soul. And how did it fare with Joseph? When the first reports about Jesus got noised abroad, they may have stirred strange feelings in Joseph's soul. I believe, nay, I will go further and say, I am absolutely certain that Joseph journeyed north to see and hear for himself. I am quite sure that he was one in those crowds that hung on His words; that he was amongst the wondering multitude who beheld His works of mercy upon the blind and lame and the leprous and the possessed; that he was one of those who held that no one could do the works that Jesus did unless God was with Him. Yes, in his soul, Joseph said, "I have found Him of Whom Moses in the Law and the Prophets did write."

But Unwilling to Leave All for Christ

But how was it, if what I have been saying is true, that Joseph is not mentioned in the list of Christ's disciples? How was it that the rulers in Jerusalem were obviously unaware that he had become a friend and disciple of Christ? The answer to these questions is to be found in the second fact about Joseph which the evangelist emphasizes. He was one who looked for the Kingdom of God, but he was also a counselor of honorable estate, a man of rank and position, and as Matthew adds, rich into the bargain. All this explains why, though Joseph was sure in his soul that Jesus was the Messiah, he was not to be found in the circle of His disciples, and openly, at any rate, he was not seen in the Lord's company.

Secret Discipleship

You remember how Christ, commenting on the departure of the rich young ruler, says, "How hardly," that is, with what difficulty, "shall they that have riches enter into the Kingdom of God" (10:23). Joseph's conduct will serve as a commentary on that word! Had Joseph been a poor man, he would, I believe, have been among Christ's open and avowed disciples. He might perhaps have been a member of the glorious company of the Apostles. But he was an honorable counselor: he was rich, and he was not willing to pay the price of open discipleship. The Jews had agreed that if any one confessed Christ, he should be put out of the Synagogue; excommunicated, treated as an outcast. And Joseph, the honorable counselor, was not prepared to make that sacrifice. He had not reached the point when he was ready to count all things but loss for Christ. And so he was a disciple, but secretly, for fear of the Jews.

Its Failure

Can a man be a secret disciple? They try to be. There are plenty of timid, trembling souls who really love the Lord, and yet are afraid to declare their love. But in the long run, no man can be a secret disciple. A man came to his minister once and asked him, "Can I be a disciple of Jesus without anybody knowing it?" "No," replied his minister, "whoever wants to be in partnership with Christ, must write his name upon the sign-board." The attempt to be a secret disciple is trying to get the Crown without the Cross, to get the reward of discipleship without paying the price. As a matter of fact, it cannot be done, for at least two reasons. If a man is a disciple, the fact will reveal itself. The Christian character does not need a label to make it known. "How can a man be concealed?" cries Emerson. Character evermore declares itself. No, it is impossible for a man to conceal himself. And it is certainly impossible for a Christian man to conceal himself. If the love of Christ is in a man's heart, it will reveal itself in word and act and life.

"They took knowledge of them that they had been with Jesus," it is said of Peter and John. And if we have really been with Jesus, all the world will know. Discipleship, if it is real, simply cannot be kept secret. Moreover, Jesus refuses to acknowledge the secret disciple. He knows that discipleship means suffering and sacrifice. He knows that a big price has to be paid. And He summons men to pay the price, and make the sacrifice. You remember Mazzini's cry to young Italy, "Come and suffer." And Christ's call to man took a similar tone. Christ never for a moment disguised the fact that discipleship was a costly business. But He never hesitated to ask men to pay the cost. But Joseph was not willing to pay the cost. And as I think of him, believing in Christ in his soul and yet clinging to his riches and his honorable position, I begin to tremble for Joseph. For there is another solemn and almost menacing word of the Lord. "Whosoever shall be ashamed of Me and of My words . . . the Son of Man also shall be ashamed of him when He cometh in the glory of His Father with the holy angels" (8:38).

Joseph, the Brave Confessor

But happily for Joseph, if, at the beginning, his fear overcame his love, in the end his love cast out his fear. And strangely enough it was in the day of our Lord's shame and defeat that Joseph declared himself. It was when the disciples forsook Him and fled that Joseph came and stood by His side. Upon fine natures danger acts like a call to courage and high resolve. Men who on ordinary days seem hesitant and timid, in days of crisis get nerved to a pitch of daring that knows no shred of fear. When Christ hung on the Cross scorned and dead, Joseph went in boldly unto Pilate and asked for the body of Jesus. "He ventured to go in," for it took courage to do what Joseph did. It took courage to face Pilate, sore as he was after his defeat in the morning. It took courage to concern himself with a dead body at that particular time, for it meant that Joseph would incur defilement and would, therefore, be allowed no participation in the great Paschal celebration. And above everything, it took courage to declare to his fellow-countrymen, to all the members of the council with whom he had been accustomed to associate, in the very hour of their insolence and triumph, that he was a follower and a friend of the Jesus Whom they had crucified.

The Call for Courage

And still it requires courage to become a disciple of Jesus. Not courage of the sort Joseph showed. It is not the opposition and hate of the outside world we have to fear. Our difficulty comes in dealing with our own appetites and lusts and passions, in crucifying our flesh, in deliberately laying self upon the altar. But even this difficulty can be overcome. We shall have courage even to lay self on the altar if we have Joseph's passionate and whole-hearted love.

107
The Visit to the Sepulchre

"And when the sabbath was past, Mary Magdalene, and Mary the mother of James, and Salome, had bought sweet spices, that they might come and anoint Him. And very early in the morning the first day of the week, they came unto the sepulchre at the rising of the sun. And they said among themselves, Who shall roll us away the stone from the door of the sepulchre? And when they looked, they saw that the stone was rolled away: for it was very great."
—Mark 16:1-4

Love in Action

THE GREATEST THING in the Christian Religion, at any rate on its practical side, is love. Our Lord Himself summed up all the Commandments in the commandment to love God and love one's neighbor. The Apostle Paul declared that love was the fulfilling of the Law. Now there is, as it seems to me, a theory and a practice of Christian love. When it comes to the theory, it is all set out for us in that matchless, exquisite hymn on love in 1 Cor. 13. There is no more familiar passage in the whole of sacred writing. We are quite aware of what Christian love is like; it never fails; it hopes, believes, endures all things; it rejoices not with iniquity but rejoices with the truth; it outlasts prophecy and tongues; it is greater than either faith or hope. That is the theory of Christian love. But where shall we look for illustration of the practice of it? We have all of us sadly to confess we are better at the theory than we are at the practice of love. But if I were asked to give an example of Christian love in action, I should point to these holy women who ministered to Christ in Galilee; who watched Him die upon the Cross; who followed Him to the tomb and beheld where Joseph and Nicodemus laid Him; who very early on the first day of the week came with the spices they had prepared to anoint His dead body.

The Endurance of Love

Here, for example, is love in its patient endurance. "An angel declareth the Resurrection of Christ to three women"—so the para-

graph is summed up in our A.V. But as far as the women themselves are concerned, "Love never faileth," is the aptest title.
"Many waters cannot quench love," says the writer of the Song of
Songs, "neither can the floods drown it." No! If floods could
drown it and many waters could quench it, the love of these
women would have been quenched and drowned clean out of
existence. For what deep waters of affliction they had been
through; and what floods of sorrow had surged up against
them! They had seen Christ made a gazing stock. They had seen
Him branded as a criminal. They had seen Him die a slave's death.
And they had hoped it was He Who should redeem Israel! They
had hoped that it was He Who was to sit on David's throne! The
Cross therefore shattered all their expectations. But amid the
wreckage and ruin only one thing remained unshaken and unim-
paired, and that was love. Faith had gone, hope had gone, but love
endured. "When the Sabbath was past, Mary Madgalene, and
Mary the mother of James, and Salome bought spices that they
might come and anoint Him." They did all that for a dead Jesus, a
Jesus Who by dying had falsified every hope and expectation.
"Love never faileth."

Love in Its Lavishness

And here is love in its lavishness. "Love is kind," says the
Apostle. A commentator suggests that the word indicates the self-
abandonment of kindness. Love is always lavish, uncounting in
the deeds of kindness which it does. And that characteristic of love
I find illustrated in the action of these holy women. You will notice
that two out of the three who are mentioned as paying this early
visit to the sepulchre are also mentioned in the last verse of the preceding chapter as having beheld where Christ was laid. That is to
say, they watched His burial. They were there watching and weeping when Joseph and Nicodemus paid the last tender rites of
reverence and affection to His body. And therefore they must have
noticed Nicodemus' lavish offering of spices. He brought, John
says, a mixture of myrrh and aloes, about a hundred pounds'
weight—enough, says one of the commentators, to cover the
whole body and the floor of the tomb. "More," says another, "than
was used in the funerals of the richest men." And yet, though they
had seen all that, I read here that "Mary Magdalene, and Mary the
mother of James, and Salome bought spices." "Bought spices!"—
although Nicodemus had already lavished a hundred pounds'
weight upon the Lord's body. They had gone beyond duty.
Judas would have said of the action of these women, what he said

of the action of Mary at the Bethany feast, "Whereunto is this waste?" But "Love is kind." Love is literally "self-abandoned" in its kindness. Love never calculates, love never economizes: love never bargains. Love is open-handed, free, generous, lavish. Love never asks what other people have done; love always wants to know how much it can do itself. "What shall I render unto the Lord for all benefits towards me?" is its cry. And that was the kind of love these women showed when they bought spices to add to Nicodemus' bounteous provision.

Love in Its Eagerness

And here also is love in its eagerness. These women seized the first available opportunity of rendering their offices of reverent love to the body of the Lord. They were awake while the rest of the world slept. It was "very early" on the first day of the week, says St Mark, that they set out for the tomb. It was at "early dawn," says St Luke. It was "yet dark," says St John. The probability is that the first signs of the approach of the sun lit up the sky as they neared the tomb, but it was dark when they sallied forth. They could not wait for daylight to come, such was their loving haste to reach the grave. The Greeks did well to picture Love as a boy with wings. For that is the characteristic of love: it is swift, speedy, eager. Do you know what it is to have been absent for a week and to have traveled far from your loved ones? Then you know this also, that when you have set your face homewards, ocean greyhounds and express trains do not travel swift enough for your love. Love is a winged creature—swift, eager, impatient. And so it was with these women. Had they been professional anointers, had it been a mere matter of business with them, they would have waited for business hours, they would have waited till the day had fairly come. But love pays no attention to hours. Love is always hasting. "How am I straitened," said the Lord of His work, "till it be accomplished." And the same pressure and constraint were on these women. "Very early on the first day of the week," while it was yet dark they were on the way to the tomb. It was the winged eagerness of love.

Love in Its Disinterestedness

And here, too, is love in its disinterestedness. "Love," says the Apostle once more, "seeketh not its own." That is a mark of real love, it lavishes itself expecting to get nothing back. There is no such thing as a selfish love. It is a contradiction in terms. You might as well talk of a white black, or a sunny night. Love is the antithesis of selfishness. Selfishness looks in; love looks out. Selfishness thinks only of its own things; love thinks of the things of others. Selfishness asks, "What shall I get?" Love asks, " What can I give?" We talk in our familiar speech of what we call "cupboard love." And by "cupboard love," we mean the show of affection where we stand to gain by it. Such a thing is not unknown. People will sometimes pay a great deal of attention to other people by whom they expect to profit. The fuss folk make of rich relations, for example, has passed into a proverb. But "cupboard love" is not love at all. It is selfishness masquerading as love. It is Satan appearing as an angel of light. For this is the mark of genuine love, it is disinterested, unselfish, "it seeketh not its own." Do you remember our Lord's advice as to the people to be invited to our feasts? "When thou makest a feast," said Jesus, "call the poor, the lame, the maimed, the halt, the blind." There would be genuine love and kindness in such an invitation; it would reveal a really unselfish desire to make the world a happier and brighter place, "for they cannot recompense thee." And that is the mark of love, it never expects to be paid back. We do not really love Christ until we love Him for Himself. We do not love Him until we love Him not with the thought of gaining aught, or seeking a reward. Supposing there were no heaven to gain or hell to shun, how should we feel to Christ then? Do you remember that little poem of Richard Watson Gilder, called *The Song of a Heathen*?

> "If Jesus Christ is a Man,
> And only a Man, I say
> That of all mankind I will cleave to Him,
> And to Him will I cleave alway.
>
> If Jesus Christ is a God,
> And the only God—I swear,
> I will follow Him through heaven and hell,
> The earth, the sea, and the air."

Jesus Christ anyhow, anywhere, everywhere, through good report or evil report, whether for loss or gain, Jesus Christ for His own sake, that is the only real, genuine love. Now, the love of these women was exactly of that unselfish and disinterested kind. They brought the spices which they had prepared, to anoint a dead Jesus. They did this kindly service to One from Whom there could be no prospect of a return, not a word of thanks, not even a smile. They did it not with the hope of reward, but just because they loved Him, with a pure, devoted and unselfish love.

Self-Examination as to Endurance in Love

Here, I say, we get the love of that chapter, 1 Cor. 13, in action.
The beautiful theory is here reduced to still more beautiful and glorious practice. And in the light of all this, I have been putting
questions to my own soul as to the nature and quality of the love
which I profess to have. And as I put them to my own soul so
would I also address them now to those who shall read this chapter. (1) First of all, then, as to this matter of endurance. "Love never
faileth." What about my love? What about yours? Has it never
failed? Is it burning as strongly and brightly as it did on the day on
which its flame was first kindled? "I have this against thee," was
the message of the angel to the Church at Ephesus, "that thou didst
leave thy first love." "Because iniquity shall be multiplied, the love
of many shall wax cold," said our Lord Himself. "The love of
many shall wax cold." That solemn word has been fulfilled in the
experience of multitudes of people. The glow and ardor and enthusiasm of their early devotion have died down. "Demas has
forsaken me." "Ye did run well!" They had lost their first love.
Disappointment, delay, hardship, difficulty had weakened it,
smothered it, almost entirely destroyed it. But the mark of a real,
vital, heart-felt love is this, it holds on. Through delay, difficulty,
hardship, temptation, it holds on: through shame and insult and
rejection, through the Cross and the Grave it holds on. Our love is
often sorely tried, does it hold on? For that is the mark of a genuine
love—it never faileth, it hopeth, believeth, endureth all things.

As to Love's Lavishness

(2) And then what about the matter of love's lavishness?
Giving is of the very nature of love, and the giving is always without stint or measure. It scorns the love of a nicely calculated less or
more. "Love is kind," it is self-abandoned in its kindness. Well,
what about our love? Our love to Christ, I mean. Is it lavish? Is it
without stint? Is it self-abandoned? I do not want to judge harshly or to speak unkindly, but I ask myself sometime whether there
is very much sign of an abandoned love in a fact like this, that we
spend more on Christmas cards than all the Churches put together spend on the work of extending the Kingdom of Christ. That is
to say, we spend more on wishing our friends the greetings of the
season than we do on helping our Lord to see of the travail of His
soul. And that is typical of our general attitude. We are free in
spending on our own pleasures; we grudge the money we give to
Christ. But money is not the only, or even the best, gift we can offer
Him. What about our personal service? How much of that have we

given Him? You know, when a person loves a man or a cause he never thinks any trouble too great to advance that man's or that cause's interest. Think, for example, of the zeal men will show and the labor they will undertake to win success for their candidate and party at election times! Most Christians scarcely show that kind of abandoned zeal, do they? Yet surely the cause of Christ is better worthy of labor and sacrifice than the cause of a party. Have we made sacrifices? Have we been lavish of time and money and labor in the holy cause of Christ?

As to Love in Its Disinterestedness

(3) And then what of that quality of disinterestedness? Our religion has a good deal to say about rewards and punishment. It is perfectly true that the man who in the enthusiasm of his love leaves all and follows Christ is no loser. The Christian life is not impoverishment, but enrichment. The disciple gets a hundred-fold even in this life, and in the world to come life everlasting. And it is perfectly true that the man who turns his back on Christ and lives for self and sin, dooms himself to eternal loss. And yet, we can scarcely call ourselves Christian at all, if we only follow Christ for the sake of avoiding punishment or winning the reward. We are only genuine Christians when we follow Christ for love. Love is never prudent, love is passionate. Love "seeketh not its own." Here is the root of all genuine discipleship and service, "The love of Christ constraineth me."

I have been inviting you to look within, to examine your own hearts to see whether this lavish, unfailing, self-sacrificing love dwells within them. The examination is bound to be a humbling one. But it is well to be humbled and ashamed, if it leads us to make this our daily and hourly prayer:

> "More love, O Christ to Thee, more love to Thee,
> This is the prayer I make on bended knee,
> More love, O Christ, to Thee, more love to Thee."

108
The Stone and the Grave

"And they said among themselves, Who shall roll us away the stone from the door of the sepulchre? And when they looked, they saw that the stone was rolled away: for it was very great. And entering into the sepulchre, they saw a young man sitting on the right side, clothed in a long white garment; and they were affrighted." —Mark 16:3-5.

The Stone at the Tomb

IN CONTINUING THE story of the holy women I feel almost constrained to do so in terms of love; for it is love that I still find illustrated in their conduct. When they set out in the darkness of that early morning for the tomb, all their thoughts were of their buried Lord, and the honor they meant to pay Him. But they had inadvertently left out of their calculations one most important factor. Apparently they had never heard that to make assurance doubly sure the priests had sealed the stone with the official seal, and had also set a guard to prevent any intruders from coming near. All they knew about was the great stone which they had seen Joseph and Nicodemus roll up to the entrance of the grave on the Friday. As they stole through the silent streets on their kindly and gracious errand, the remembrance of that struck a sort of chill to their souls. It seemed to doom their errand to failure; it seemed to make absolutely impossible the fulfillment of their loving purpose. For the stone was "very great," far beyond the power of a few weak women to roll away. The consternation the remembrance of this "very great" stone caused them is suggested by the form of the Greek verb. "They were saying among themselves," our R.V. translates, and that is an improvement upon the A.V. with its "they said," as it does suggest continuance. "They kept saying," would have brought out the idea which the Greek tense suggests. This one difficulty absorbed their thought. They "kept saying to one another, who shall roll us away the stone?" But though they remembered that a great stone lay across the mouth of the tomb, they never seem to have dreamed of turning back. Not one of them seems to have said, "It's of no use, we might just as well go home."

Constraining Love

They realized all about the seemingly insuperable difficulty that confronted them, they could not get that great stone out of their minds. They kept saying to one another, "Who shall roll us away the stone?" and yet, in spite of it all, they held on their way. And if you ask me why, I can only answer that love constrained them. I do not know what they expected when they got there. Possibly, as some rather prosaic commentators suggest, they thought they might find some laborers on their way to work, or Joseph's own gardener who would help them to open the tomb. Possibly, I say, but I do not know. What I do know is, that love constrained them to press on.

The Recklessness of Love

And here I get another quality of a real and genuine love for the Lord—there is an element of holy recklessness about it. "Love hopeth all things," says the Apostle. "Hopeth all things," hopes in spite of difficulties, and obstacles, and impossibilities. Hopeth all things, hopeth always, hopeth everywhere. There is a sort of reckless and abandoned courage about love. "Magnificent," said Napoleon about a charge the British cavalry made upon the serried ranks of the French infantry, "magnificent, but not war." If I may use the illustration (though it is obviously imperfect), love flings itself in the same splendid and reckless way into what look like hopeless enterprises and impossible tasks. It never turns back in face of a difficulty; it may not see how the "great stone" confronting it is to be removed, but it marches on, it makes the attempt nevertheless. That is one of the unfailing marks of a deep and devoted love, it "hopeth all things," it makes ventures, it takes risks, it attempts the impossible, it is reckless and quixotic in the abandonment of its courage. That is how love worked in the case of these holy women. They had a mighty love for their crucified and buried Lord; and their love developed in them a mighty faith, the kind of faith that can remove mountains and laughs at impossibilities.

How Love Works

That is how love always works. Love is always driving men to do the apparently impossible. Look at Paul, making the world his parish, laying evangelistic plans that embraced not Palestine and Syria merely, but Asia and Greece and Italy and even distant Spain. There was something reckless in the daring of it. What was the impulse that drove him to it? The love of Christ constrained him. Think of William Carey of Northampton, the "consecrated cobbler," as Sidney Smith sneeringly called him, going out to attack the ancient religion of India. It seemed an absurdly reckless enterprise upon which to embark. So indeed it was. But he went, in the holy recklessness of love. Think of Robert Morison and his mission to China. Men openly scoffed at him. They said that the idea of one man being able to affect that mighty and stolid empire was absurd. And so it was, but it was the kind of absurdity in which love ever delights. For that is the very mark of love, it never counts difficulties.

Does It Work So in Us?

This reckless and daring love, this love which issues in a faith that removes mountains, is it a characteristic of ours? Is it an outstanding quality of the Church of today? Do we astonish the world by the recklessness of our courage, by the dash and abandon with which we fling ourselves into apparently impossible enterprises? That is not my reading of the situation. There is not much recklessness about the modern Church. Her policy is a calculating, prudential kind of policy. We make sure that a job is compassable and manageable before we tackle it. We cut our coat according to our cloth. We do not say, "Here is a world to be evangelized—let us go forth and evangelize it." We say rather, "Here is so much money, and here are so many men, we will confine our efforts to this little corner." You would not say there was much "recklessness," much daring about our missionary policy. We are lethargic, limited in our view, tepid in our temper. We hear of no great and daring schemes; of no mighty challenges to our faith. There is no imperious summons to attempt the seemingly impossible. We only do what we think we can easily accomplish. There is an absence of the heroic temper. And that again is the result of coldness of heart and lack of love. Religion is a propriety with us and not a passion. What men will do when a mighty passion takes hold of them!

Love in Action

G. K. Chesterton tells this story. St. Francis of Assi was terrified of leprosy. And one day, right in the middle of the narrow path he was traveling, he saw, horribly white in the sunshine, a leper! Instinctively he recoiled from the contamination of that loathsome disease. But then he rallied; and ashamed of himself, he ran and put his arm about the sufferer's neck and kissed him and passed on. A moment later he looked back, and there was no one there, only the empty road in the hot sunlight. All his days thereafter he was sure it was no leper, but Christ Himself whom he had met.

This story may or may not be true, but it illustrates the meaning of love in action. Love lay behind his action. And Francis was willing to risk contamination of the horibble disease to show his compassion. In that he reminds us of the attitude of our Lord Himself toward the lepers who crossed his path. He loved them so much that He touched them to heal them! What a model of love for us to emulate!

The Victory of Love

Commentators find in all this a truth of great comfort, as we think of the difficulties confronting us, namely this, that difficulties disappear if we march boldly up to them. There is an old Indian legend which tells how a traveler once came to what seemed an impassable river, and on the other side of the river, a thicket of thorns through which he could see the eyes of fierce beasts glaring at him. But when, undaunted, the traveler pressed on, the impassable river turned out to be nothing but a mirage, and he walked on solid ground; and the thorn thicket a phantom thicket, so that he passed through it without hindrance; and the wild beasts were mere imaginings. John Bunyan teaches much the same lesson when he says that Christian for a time was hard put to it, and dare not move because he saw fierce lions on the path. But when he plucked up heart to continue his journey, he found the lions could do him no harm for they were chained. The obstacles disappeared when boldly and courageously confronted. And while I do not wish to imply that our difficulties are shadowy and unreal, I do believe this, that if we march up to them with the courage born of a great love, we shall be able to overcome them all. The difficulty is more in our own hearts than in the tasks confronting us. We have our big problems here at home, the indifference of the masses of the people, the tremendous power of drink and lust and sin of every form; we have our vast problem abroad, with large numbers of the world to win for Christ, but I believe if we had that kind of blazing love which is not afraid to tackle big tasks, and undertake mighty enterprises, we should find ourselves able to solve these problems, and overcome these colossal difficulties. Love that is adventurous and daring, soon becomes love triumphant and victorious. For when love marches up to these great stones that seem to obstruct the path of Christ, she finds that other and mightier hands than her own are busy in the work; she finds the mightiest difficulties removed, the most impossible tasks accomplished by that God Who is able to do exceeding abundantly above all we can ask or even think.

The Angel in the Tomb

"And entering into the tomb, they saw a young man sitting on the right side, arrayed in a white robe; and they were amazed." And this was why they found no "great stone" across the mouth of the tomb to bar their entrance. God had been there before with them. He had prepared the way for them. I turn to Matthew's account: "And, behold, there was a great earthquake; for an angel of the Lord descended from heaven, and came and rolled away the stone, and sat upon it" (Matt. 28:2). On their way to the tomb, they had kept saying to one another, Who shall roll us away the stone? And already God had sent one of those immortal spirits who ever do Him service to remove every difficulty out of their path, so that when they came to the grave, they found not a "great stone" but an "open door." And they were "amazed." They had never thought of the angel. They had never lifted up their eyes above the earth; they had never once thought that heaven might intervene for them. And so when they saw this radiant being sitting there, they were "amazed."

Forgetting the Angels

We are continually making the mistake these women made, leaving the angel out of account. We contemplate the "great stones" we have to remove, and then we reckon up our own scanty resources and we cry, "Who is sufficient for these things?" We forget that God is in business. We forget that this world of ours is the scene of vast and incalculable spiritual ministries. We greatly err when we confine God and His holy angels to some far-off and inaccessible heaven. God is here: the angels are all about us. "The angel of the Lord encampeth round about them that fear Him and delivereth them." "Behold," was God's promise to Israel, "I send an angel before thee, to keep thee by the way and to bring thee into the place which I have prepared." And still the angels go before us and fight for us. And that is why difficulties that seemed to us so insurmountable often clean vanish from our path when we advance boldly upon them. God has gone before us and His angel has rolled away the stone. It will be a great day for us when we catch the vision of the angel: when we see the mountain of the Lord full of horses and chariots of fire. The day when we get that vision will be a day of amazement, but it will also be a day when pessimism and despair will forever flee away; we shall shrink from no task, we shall tremble before no "great stone," for the task is not ours only but God's.

Life, Not Death

No wonder they were amazed. They came expecting to find a dead body, and they found a white-robed angel. They saw an "angel" in the tomb; triumphant life in the place of death; a representative of eternity in the place of mortality; immortal youth in the place of weakness and decay. And that is what believing men and women have seen in the grave ever since that first Easter morning; they have seen the angel. Before that Easter morning men and women saw in the grave little but corruption, decay, dissolution. Even in these days people who turn their backs on Christ see little else. But we who know that Jesus died and rose again are always able to see the sheen of the angel's robe and to hear the beating of the angel's wing when we gather round the grave. And to us, about our own dear ones he says, as did this angel about the Lord, "He is not here, He is risen." And the vision of the angel in the tomb enables us to rejoice even at the grave with "joy unspeakable and full of glory," for we know now that if the earthly house of this our tabernacle be dissolved, "we have a building of God, a house not made with hands, eternal in the heavens."

109
The Empty Grave

"And he saith unto them, Be not affrighted: Ye seek Jesus of Nazareth, Which was crucified: He is risen; He is not here: behold the place where they laid Him." —Mark 16:6.

The Fourfold Testimony

WE COME NOW to the consideration of that stupendous event which created Christian faith, and which has been, ever since, the foundation stone of the Christian Church. Much has been made of the differences and inconsistencies of the various evangelists' accounts. And, for my own part, I am not in the least disposed to deny that it is very hard to fit the various details supplied to us by the four evangelists into a connected and consistent story. It was a day of confusion and excitement. And something of the excitement and subsequent confusion seems to have crept into the narrative. It is impossible, therefore, to be sure of every detail. It is impossible to be sure as to the exact order in which the events of the day occurred. But the difficulty of reconciling the various stories as to the happenings of the first Easter morning in no way affects the truth of the Resurrection. It rather helps to establish and confirm it. For the differences go to prove this, that we have in the four Gospels the stories of independent witnesses. It is not a fourfold reproduction of the same story. It is a case of four independent accounts. And while there are differences in detail (as there always are in accounts of one and the same event written from varying viewpoints) the significant thing about them is that they are in emphatic and complete agreement about the essential facts, that on the first Easter morning the grave was found empty, and that Jesus Himself appeared to certain of His disciples alive!

The Angel's Message

"They entered into the tomb," the chamber quarried out of the rock, "and saw a young man sitting on the right side, arrayed in a white robe." And they were amazed. But their astonishment was soon changed to another feeling.

"Be not amazed," said the angel to the women, "ye seek Jesus the Nazarene, Who has been crucified." Notice how careful the angel is in his identification. "Jesus the Nazarene, Who has been crucified." It was to dispel any doubt that might lurk in the women's mind, as to whether they were thinking and he was speaking of one and the same person. "He is risen; He is not here: behold the place where they laid Him." He is risen! That was the tremendous announcement the angel had to make. They could see His body was not there. But the reason for its absence was not that anyone (whether friends or foe) had stolen it. He had " risen again." He had taken His body with Him. It was not a case of spiritual survival. It was a Resurrection. Christ in the totality of His personality—soul and body—had risen again. The women had come to anoint a corpse, and instead of that they were told of a living Christ. But when the angel uttered these three simple words, "He is risen," he set men in a larger universe, he altered the current of human history, he changed the face of the entire world. Let us consider for a moment or two some of the wealth of its significance. "He is risen." What did that imply?

The Messiahship of Jesus

First of all, the Messiahship of Jesus. If my account of the condition of the disciples is correct, the Cross, while it had been powerless to kill their love for Jesus, had shattered their hopes. "We *hoped*," said the two disciples, speaking in the past tense which as good as implies that the hope was dead and gone, "we hoped that it was He Who should redeem Israel." The Cross laid any such faith in ruins, and out of the wreck only personal affection still remained. They could not help loving Jesus, in spite of the disappointment of their expectation, but the shameful death of the Cross finally disposed of all claims to Messiahship. Friday and Saturday these people were bewailing a lost leader and a discredited cause. But this simple announcement, "He is risen," changed the entire outlook, totally altered their point of view. It was not Jesus only Who rose again from the grave. Faith, *faith* which had been buried in the same grave, rose again, buoyant, confident, exultant. The Jewish rulers by nailing Christ to the cursed Cross, had tried to brand Him as a slave, but by the Resurrection God proclaimed Him as His glorious Son. "He was declared to be the Son of God with power," says St Paul, "by the Resurrection from the dead."

I fancy those great and splendid words of the second Psalm must have come back to the minds of the disciples when it really came home to them that Christ was alive. "The kings of the earth set themselves and the rulers take counsel together against the Lord and against His anointed . . . He that sitteth in the heaven shall laugh, the Lord shall have them in derision." On the Friday Pilate and Herod and the priests had conspired against the Lord's anointed. Conspired, as it seemed, with success when Jesus hung dead upon the tree. But on the morning of the first day of the week the disciples knew they had conspired in vain. "Yet," said God, by the Resurrection of His Son, "have I set My King upon My holy hill of Zion." "My King," God's Holy One, that was what Christ really was!

God's Testimony

The Resurrection was God's testimony to Jesus. The rejected of men was the accepted and the honored of God. They knew Jesus for what He really was as the result of the Resurrection. Their faith in His Messiahship revived. They were "begotten again" as Peter puts it, "unto a living hope by the Resurrection of Jesus Christ from the dead." The hope that died in the Cross and was buried with Jesus in His grave, sprang up into new and imperishable life at the Resurrection. Priests and people might heap up what scorn and contempt they pleased upon Jesus. Easter morning proved Him to be "God's King."

And the second thing the Resurrection did was this, it set the Cross in an entirely new light. In the popular conception of Messiah the idea of death had no place. He was to be a conquering Prince, and the deliverance He was to effect was deliverance from political oppressors and conquerors. In that conception of Messiah's work the disciples shared, and therefore Christ's death was the death-blow to their hopes, because it seemed fatal to Christ's Messiahship. But in the light of Easter morning they felt they had to give a new interpretation of the Cross. After all, the person who died on the Cross was the Messiah, He was declared to be God's Son with power. The Resurrection showed that death was in Messiah's destiny. It was no mishap, it was no evil chance. It was part of Messiah's work. The Resurrection was God's seal of approval upon Christ's dying. It was, as someone has said, " The Amen " of the Father, to the " It is finished" of the Son. And so, not all at once, perhaps, but gradually, the disciples came to understand that the Cross was not a martyrdom but a sacrifice. They began to realize that what Messiah came to deliver people from was not the Roman yoke but sin. And He delivered them from sin, by bearing it Himself, by enduring the death which was its punishment, by exhausting all the curse of it in His Cross. And so, in course of time, the Cross, which when they saw it reared had broken their hearts, became the ground of their confidence and hope. Instead of being the disproof of Christ's Messiahship, they came to feel that it was in the Cross He fulfilled His Messianic mission. "God forbid that I should glory," cries the greatest of them all, "save in the Cross of our Lord Jesus Christ." It was the Resurrection that had transfigured it from a shame to a splendor.

Sin and Sacrifice

And still it is only in the light of Easter morning that we can understand the Cross! The instinct for sacrifice is bedded deep in the human soul. Sin has to be paid for, atoned for. And the payment cannot be a light one. Every sacrifice offered on Jewish or pagan altars bears witness to the sort of feeling men everywhere possess that life has to be given for life if sin is to be atoned for and forgiven. And that instinct of the soul is met and satisfied in the Cross. At the Cross men believe in the forgiveness of sin. They feel that in it atonement has been made. They actually receive the reconciliation. The Cross is to them the one full and perfect oblation and sacrifice, to which every other sacrifice in the world pointed. And what makes them believe it was a sacrifice is the glorious triumph of Easter morning. Had Jesus never risen again, men would never have triumphed in the Cross; they would never have received forgiveness and peace at the Cross; they would never have sung, "In the Cross of Christ I glory, towering o'er the wrecks of time." Had there been no Easter morning, Christ's death would have been just one more martyrdom and nothing more; and though He might have been the first and noblest of the martyrs, men would as soon have thought of looking to Socrates' hemlock cup for salvation as to the Cross of Jesus, if He was a martyr to truth and nothing more. It is Easter that illumines Good Friday. It is the empty grave that flings back glory on the Cross. If Christ did not rise, no sacrifice has been offered; no atonement has been made; no redemption has been won—we should be still in our sins. But with the empty grave before our eyes we can and do joyfully believe that He was delivered up for our trespasses and was raised for our justification.

The Living Christ

And thirdly, it meant this, that Jesus was alive and with His disciples still. Now it cannot be too emphatically stated that union with the living Christ is the ultimate proof of our faith. That is how we live the Christian life, by living union with a living Lord. Christ Himself illustrated it by the figure of the vine and the branch. The branch lives only by vital union with the vine; the Christian lives only by a similar vital union with Christ. That is not only how we live the Christian life, that is the Christian life itself. "I live yet not I, but Christ liveth in me." He Himself had said, "Apart from Me, ye can do nothing." He had comforted them then by telling them He would come back again. It was the Resurrection that ratified and fulfilled that promise. The disciples knew that Jesus was alive and with them still. And in fellowship with that living Christ they found themselves able to live the life and do the work. That is the secret of the brave and heroic lives they lived, that is the secret of the work they did—they were conscious of union with the living Christ.

The Message of the Empty Tomb

That is what the empty grave does still, it assures us of the living Christ; and the living Christ is the spring both of our Christian life and service. It cannot be too often asserted, that the Christian life is not the attempt today to imitate the life of somebody who lived and worked in Palestine nineteen centuries ago. The Christian life is the life which we live as a result of our union with a living Lord. The *imitatio Christi* might easily degenerate into a very hard and exacting legalism; but there is nothing hard, or constrained, or legalistic about the Christian life. It is free, joyous, spontaneous, for it is just Christ living over again in us. "He was raised," says Paul, "for our justification." And that does not mean simply that only in the light of the Resurrection can we believe that His death was an atoning sacrifice which "justifies" us in the sight of God. It means that it was only the risen and living Christ Who could become the new life-principle for mankind. That is what the Resurrection has done—given us not a Christ without us as an example, but a Christ within us as a power. And it is that Christ within us Who is the hope of glory.

The Source of Our Power for Service

Moreover, not only does the Resurrection give us a living Christ Who is our power for Christian life, it gives us a Christ Who is our helper in Christian service. These disciples would never have flung themselves upon a world had Jesus remained in Joseph's grave. But when they knew He was alive and with them in the fight, they felt nothing was impossible to them. There is a significant sequence at the close of this chapter. "So then the Lord Jesus was

received up into heaven and sat down at the right hand of God—
and they went forth and preached everywhere." The vision of the
Lord, and then the missionary enterprise; the certainty that
Christ was alive, and then the abolition of fears. "They went forth
and preached everywhere." The world was against them! but what
did that matter? A living Lord was with them! Up to Easter morning they had kept themselves locked in the Upper Room for fear.
As soon as they knew Jesus was alive, they flung the doors open
and preached Him without trace of apology or timidity to the men
who had crucified Him. "The doors were shut for fear of the
Jews"—that is one picture. "When they saw the boldness of Peter
and John"—that is the other, and it was the living Christ Who
made the difference. And He makes all the difference still. The
tasks that confront us are vast, stupendous, appalling. But if we are
quite sure of the living Christ we shall be strangers to fear. We shall
fling ourselves with undaunted courage upon the most difficult of
tasks saying with the Apostle, "We can do all things through Christ
Who strengtheneth us."

The Victory of Right
Finally, that empty grave means this, that Right rules. There is
much that is tangled and bewildering and perplexing in the events
of this world of ours. Amidst all the perplexity and bewilderment
the empty grave is a mighty comfort. There in symbol and type
you get the result of the conflict between truth and falsehood, right
and wrong, God and the devil. On the Friday it looked as if
wickedness was triumphant, as if the only right was might; for
Jesus, Who did no Sin, in Whom no fault could be found, was
dead, and the priests were congratulating themselves on their victory. But the empty grave put another complexion on things.
Victory lay not with Pilate and the plotting priests, but with Jesus.
Right was might! Let us go back to the empty grave when we are
disheartened and discouraged. Right is might! Truth shall prevail!
God must reign. We may seem to be living sometimes in truth's
Good Friday. But

> "Truth pressed to earth shall rise again,
> The eternal years of God are hers,
> But Error wounded, writhes in pain,
> And dies among her worshippers."

110
The Same Jesus

"But go your way; tell His disciples and Peter that He goeth before you into Galilee: there shall ye see Him, as He said unto you. And they went out quickly, and fled from the sepulchre; for they trembled and were amazed: neither said they any thing to any man; for they were afraid. Now when Jesus was risen early the first day of the week, He appeared first to Mary Magdalene, out of whom He had cast seven devils." —Mark 16:7-9.

The Women and the Angel's Message

IT MAY BE that, if we wanted to reproduce with exactitude the happenings at the graveside on that first Easter morning, we should have to insert asterisks at various points in the evangelic narrative. Asterisks in a narrative imply the lapse of time, and I am quite sure that such lapses took place on Easter morning. And I am doubly sure of this when I come to Mark's account, for of all the evangelists Mark is the most concise and compressed. I do not think, for example, that the angelic speech to the women went on without pause or break as Mary records it here. I believe that between verses 6 and 7 you ought to put the asterisks. "He is risen, He is not here, behold the place where they laid Him," the angel said. And then he paused. He gave the women time to take that in. He gave them time to try to realize the tremendous fact that their dead Master was alive again. It needed time, for Resurrection was not in all their thoughts. I picture these women in the moments that followed that tremendous angelic word. I picture to myself the feelings that expressed themselves on their faces. For one mood followed another as sunshine and shadow chase one another on an April day. First there was mere and sheer fright at the sight of the empty grave and the vision of the angel. And then there was wonder, incredulous wonder almost. And then as the meaning of it all began really to come home to their souls, the wonder gave place to an expression of ecstasy and rapture. And then once again the sunshine gave way to shadow, and the rapture was replaced by something like doubt and fear.

A Dawning Fear

The fear was caused by this—the women began to wonder whether the risen Jesus would be like the Jesus Who had companied with them in Galilee. Differences in rank and station have before today proved almost fatal to friendship. Here are two lads, bosom friends at school. They go forth into life. One remains all his days poor and obscure. The other, blessed with more shining gifts, wins for himself name and fame and wealth. And it has happened before today that the man who has so advanced in wealth and position has forgotten his friendship for the poor man who was the school mate of his boyhood. Now the Resurrection, the women must have felt instinctively, must have made a difference to Christ. It revealed Him as a greater person than they had taken Him for. He was declared to be the Son of God with power by the Resurrection from the dead. He had lived humbly enough in the days of His flesh. Fishermen and humble women might dare to be on terms of friendship with One Who was Himself by trade a village carpenter—though even during those days of His lowliness they had been surprised now and again by flashes of glory. But by the Resurrection God had highly exalted Him and given Him a name which was above every name. It was one thing being on terms of friendship with Him Who was so poor that He had not where to lay His head; it was quite another thing being on terms of friendship with One Whom God had exalted to be a Prince and a Savior. Perhaps a cold and chilling doubt crept into the souls of these women and brought a shadow into their faces, doubt as to whether this exalted Lord would still count them His friends and show them the old affection and love.

A Fear Removed

And it was to meet that doubt, and chase it clean away out of these women's hearts that the angel spoke as he did. I do not think he spoke it in the same breath as the previous verse. You must put asterisks between the sixth verse and this one. He made the great announcement of Christ's Resurrection to chase away the fear caused by the sight of the empty grave. He added this further word to chase away the fear that the Resurrection might have made a difference in Christ's affection and love. For this is the effect of this further word which the angel spoke, it reveals Jesus as the same Jesus. The Resurrection had revealed as by a flash His divine glory, but the Resurrection had made not a whit of difference in His feelings towards the men and women who had companied with Him, and loved Him and served Him in the days of His flesh. The Resurrection has changed His form, it had not changed His heart.

Vision and Duty

Now, let us look at this verse which shows us that Jesus was the same Jesus. "Go your way," said the angel, "tell His disciples and Peter." A place where angels are to be seen, is the kind of place that tempts one to linger. The disciples did not want to leave the Holy Mount where they saw their Lord in His glory. "Let us make three tabernacles," they said, "one for Thee and one for Moses and one for Elijah." They wanted to continue living in the enjoyment of that beatific vision. And possibly these women showed signs of remaining rooted to the spot, rapt in contemplation of the empty tomb and the living angel. Small blame to them if they did! I can understand and sympathize with them. To be able to converse with an angel, to hear the angel bear his testimony to their Master was a rare and wondrous privilege. But just exactly as our Lord brought the season on the Holy Mount to a close, and led His disciples back again to the business waiting for them in the plain below, so now it is the angel that brings the moment of vision and rapture to a close. "Go your way, tell His disciples," he said. Vision was to end in duty. Rapture was to be interrupted because there was business to be done. Away in Jerusalem, in the Upper Room, there was a little company of men plunged in a gulf of deep despair because they thought that Jesus was dead. Their hopes were all shattered, their hearts were wellnigh broken, and their future was all dark, because they believed that Jesus was dead. And Jesus was alive. The women were not to remain at the grave in solitary enjoyment of the gladness. They were to remember those people in the Upper Room for whom the announcement that Jesus was alive would change winter into spring. "Go your way," said the angel, "tell His disciples." Rapture was to give way to duty. Their good news was to be shared!

Good News to Be Shared

The good news about Christ is always to be shared. Here is the reason for all missionary and evangelistic work; the joy of salvation was never meant to be a selfish and solitary possession; it was meant to be diffused, spread abroad, shared. The news of God's love in Christ makes a difference. Wherever it goes, it makes a difference. It changes gloom to gladness, and fear to confidence and joy. And so long as there is in the wide world a solitary person sitting in doubt and fear, to whom the news about Christ would bring comfort and freedom and joy, we are bound to tell it to him. "Go thy way, tell!" that is the command still laid upon us. Life is not all rapture, it is service, ministry. It is not selfish enjoyment, it is a blessed sharing. The vision ends always in a duty. "We cannot at the shrine remain." When we have heard the good news about Christ, we must straightway go our way and tell.

The Considerateness of the Lord

But it is not for the light it throws upon the duty of the Christian disciple, but for the light it throws upon the risen Lord that I chiefly value this verse. The angel dispersed the fears that were beginning to arise in the hearts of the women when he gave them this message for it showed this, that despite the glory of His risen state, He was still the same Jesus. Notice, to begin with, the considerateness of Christ as illustrated in this message. That was one of His great characteristics when He was alive. He was so considerate, considerate I mean of the comfort and happiness of others.

As at Cana

Take the marriage at Cana for illustration. Possibly, as some of the commentators suggest, it was the unexpected arrival of Jesus and His disciples that brought about the shortage of wine which threatened to bring the rejoicings to a premature conclusion. After all, the addition of half-a-dozen unexpected guests is enough to upset the calculations of any housekeeper. But whether that be so or not, I am sure that when Jesus heard His mother whisper to Him, "They have no wine," He felt for the predicament in which the host and hostess found themselves. He knew the humiliation that would come upon them if their hospitality failed. And so without a word to any one as to what He was doing, He replenished the exhausted store with that water which His grace had converted into the wine of the finest vintage. None but the servants knew what had happened. The master of the feast did not know, the bride and bridegroom did not know, the assembled guests did not know. Our Lord had the fine instinct of the perfect gentleman. He spared the hosts the shame of a public announcement. He spared them even the anxiety of knowing that the supply ran short! It was all beautifully and exquisitely considerate!

And with His Own

Or think of His treatment of the disciples themselves when they came back after their first preaching tour. They were tired from their labors, they were excited with their success. "Come ye apart

by yourselves and rest awhile," He said to them. He was beautifully considerate always of their needs and welfare. Or think of His
behavior on the Holy Mount. Peter wanted to stay. Jesus Himself
led the way down. The fact was, His own glory and happiness
always came second to the needs and wants of others. Up on the
holy hill, I think He could in His soul hear the shrieks of the
demented lad, and the vain appeals of the heartbroken father; and
in pure and beautiful considerateness for human need He left the
scene of His glory and hurried to their help. And this verse makes
it plain that this trait in the Lord's character had no whit changed.
His first thought on rising again was of His troubled disciples; His
first message on rising was a message which was meant to dispel
their sorrow. In a sense, you may say that the whole of the post-
Resurrection appearances illustrate the considerateness of Jesus.
When He rose again from the dead, Heaven was open to Him. But
for forty days He lingered about the familiar scenes of His earthly ministry. The fact is there were humble friends of His who
needed comfort and assurance.

And not until He had clean dispelled their sorrow, and filled
them with triumphant hope and gladness, did Jesus finally leave
them to take possession of His glory. It was ever "others first" with
Jesus. He was always delicately, beautifully considerate of the
needs and wants of others. And the Resurrection had not changed
Him in this respect. His first thought was of the sorrow and grief
of His disciples. "Go your way," was the angel's first command
after His rising, "tell His disciples and Peter, He goeth before you
into Galilee."

The Forgiving Love of the Lord

Not only was He the same in His considerateness, but this message shows this too, that He was exactly the same in His love. In a
sense this is implied in what I have already said, for considerateness is one of the beautiful fruits of love. It is only the loving soul
that is a really considerate soul. It was because Jesus loved His disciples so well that He was eager at the first possible moment to
relieve them of their sorrow and grief. But it is not love in the general sense of a kindly and affectionate feeling that I am thinking of
just now, but love in the particular sense of love that stoops, and
lavishes itself on the unworthy, and forgives unto seventy times
seven. Now that was a great, if not the outstanding, characteristic
of Jesus in the days of His flesh. It differentiated Him from every
other teacher of His time. He had a love which reached out to
those who had gone farthest astray, and stooped to those who had

fallen into the deepest depths. Enemies made it indeed the foundation of a slander. They called Him "the friend of publicans and sinners." They said that He found His proper company amongst the outcasts and moral derelicts of Palestine. But the slander has long since lost its sting and been converted into a glory. That is Christ's crowning grace, He was the mighty Lover of Souls. He loved not only kind and lovable people like Martha and Mary and Lazarus, but He loved a cheating publican like Zacchaeus, He loved the woman who was a sinner, He loved the dying thief. It was a love from whose blessings not even the vilest and the worst was outcast. And that was what drew the hearts of the sinful and the fallen with such passionate devotion to Christ. "The publicans and sinners drew near unto Him for to hear Him." The people of whom every one else despaired turned with eager and thankful hope to Jesus. He had a Gospel for them. He loved them out of their sin and despair into newness of life.

A Continuous Love

But it was one thing for the Nazarene to be the "friend of publicans and sinners," it was quite another for the exalted and glorified Son of God. Did the chilling doubt invade the souls of these women as to whether His love had survived the mighty change? Did Mary Magdalene wonder whether the Mighty Prince and Savior would give her a place in His heart? In the days of His flesh, He had stooped to her help when she was a poor, demented, derelict, unclean woman; He had cast seven devils out of her; but would the risen Lord give a thought to such a poor and humble creature? Well, again, if such fears did arise, they were dispelled by the angel's message. "Go, tell His disciples and Peter." It was the special mention of Peter that removed all doubt. It was the special singling out of Peter that made them sure there was no difference in the love. It was as if Jesus said, "I want them all to come, but specially I want Peter to come." And I look back in my Gospel, and the last notice of Peter which I come across is this. "But he began to curse and to swear, I know not this man of whom ye speak." I put the two verses side by side. "But he began to curse and to swear, I know not the man." "Go, tell His disciples and Peter, He goeth before you into Galilee," and one thing becomes abundantly plain to me, and that is this, death has made no difference to the lavish, stooping love of Christ. After the Resurrection as before, it was a love that forgave until seventy times seven.

The Restoration of Peter

It is a significant fact that it is only Mark who records the special invitation to the fallen Apostle. Now Mark was, as we know, Peter's "interpreter." He got his account of the Gospel story mainly from the Apostle's own lips. When the Gospels came to be written, Matthew had forgotten about this special mention of Peter, Luke's informants had forgotten it, indeed the Christian people as a whole had forgotten it; but Peter himself had never forgotten it. It was the turning point in his life. But for that special word "and Peter" he might have made his bed in hell. For I will believe, that the wide world contained no more unhappy man than Simon Peter during the two days that intervened between his shameful denial in the judgment hall, and the receipt of this special invitation, unless indeed it might be Judas Iscariot who had betrayed innocent blood, and who found his misery so intolerable that he went out and hanged himself. But the special invitation was like the bursting of the sun into Peter's tempest darkened sky; it scattered his despair. It was his Lord's assurance to him that he still had a place in His heart, that his great and terrible sin had made no difference to the strength and tenderness of his Lord's love. I say this special invitation was the beginning of Peter's restoration. But its permanent significance, and its gracious assurance to you and me is this, that Resurrection has made no difference to the love of Christ. The love of the Lord is a love that survives in spite of sin. "Many waters cannot quench love, neither can the floods drown it," says the old Book. And we may adapt that and say, "Many sins cannot quench love, neither can our iniquities drown it." The love of the Lord is a love that persists and endures and holds on. The love that gave an invitation to the blasphemer, invites and welcomes the world. There is not one outcast from it. He can save to the uttermost those who come to God through Him.

"This Same Jesus"

"He goeth before you into Galilee," said the angel, "there shall ye see Him, as He said unto you." And this again only gives further evidence that He was still the same Jesus. For why was Galilee appointed the meeting-place? Surely to make the disciples feel that between them and their Lord there could be the old feelings of happy friendship and fellowship.

And the Meeting-place

I do not think that it was in our Lord's plan to appear in Jerusalem at all. If the disciples had really believed His words, and had a simple faith in Him, immediately the Crucifixion was over they would have hurried northwards and waited there for the reappearing of their Lord. It was fear and faithlessness that chained them to Jerusalem and constrained our Lord to show Himself first to them there. But Jerusalem was a place of bitter memories and painful associations. There was everything in Jerusalem to fill the disciples with shame and humiliation. It was in Jerusalem Peter had denied Him, it was in Jerusalem they had all forsaken Him and fled. The memories of Jerusalem would impose restraints and constraints upon their fellowship. But no bitter memories attached to Galilee. That was the place of their first enthusiasm, of the rapture of their early devotion. That was the place where their companionship with Jesus had been free and happy, and altogether beautiful. And it was there Jesus would meet with them. It was like telling them that He had no place in His memory for treachery and wrong and desertion. It was inviting them to resume the old and happy relationship of their first love.

> "Unwearied in forgiveness still,
> His heart could only love."

The same Jesus! And what a Jesus! The hope of the world lies here, that Jesus has not changed. He is the same seeking and compassionate Lord! There is a length and breadth and height and depth in His mighty love which passeth knowledge.

111
Love and Vision

"Now when Jesus was risen early the first day of the week, He appeared first to Mary Magdalene, out of whom He had cast seven devils. And she went and told them that had been with Him, as they mourned and wept. And they, when they had heard that He was alive, and had been seen of her, believed not." —Mark 16:9-11.

The Last Twelve Verses

IN A COMMENTARY of this character it is not necessary for one to go into the critical questions connected with the last twelve verses of the Gospel according to St Mark. The R.V., as you know, makes a break, and interposes a space between verses 8 and 9. It explains in the following note the reason why it detaches this concluding paragraph from the main body of the Gospel —"The two oldest Greek manuscripts and some other authorities omit from verse 9 to the end. Some other authorities have a different ending to the Gospel." For our present purpose it will suffice to say that, by whomsoever they were written, these verses were attached to the Gospel from its very earliest days. In the second century they were already recognized as part of the Gospel; and even if they are not Mark's own workmanship they do not on that account lose their authority and force. We may confidently accept the passage as an "exceedingly ancient and authentic record of the words and deeds narrated in it." The paragraph itself gives a kind of synopsis of Christ's post-Resurrection appearances. It would have been a truncated and woefully imperfect Gospel if it had ended simply with the vision of the empty grave, and the angelic announcement that Jesus was alive. To complete the story it was necessary to add, not simply that some of the women had seen angels, but that this one and the other, now singly and now in companies, had seen the risen Lord Himself, and that ultimately the victory of the Resurrection had been crowned by the triumph of His Ascension into glory. And that is exactly what we get in these concluding verses.

The First Appearance of the Risen Lord

First of all, notice that though our paragraph does not follow naturally and easily upon what has gone before, it does mark an advance in the story. The first eight verses of the chapter tell us of the empty tomb and the announcement of the Resurrection; these verses tell us of the actual appearances of Christ to His disciples. The first of His disciples to whom He appeared was Mary Magdalene. But once again, we are compelled to confess that it is not easy to form a clear and definite judgment as to the sequence of events on the Resurrection morning. Apparently it was something like this. Very early in the morning, while it was yet dark, the holy women came with their spices to the tomb, found the grave empty and heard the angelic announcement. Then, as is stated in verse 8, they fled from the tomb, ran back to where the other disciples were gathered, and stammered out their startling news. Whereupon Peter and John ran to the tomb and found for themselves that the women's report about the grave at any rate was quite true. Peter and John had been followed by Mary Magdalene. And when they went away again, she lingered near the tomb, rooted to the spot by love and sorrow. And it was to this weeping woman that Christ first revealed Himself. "He appeared first to Mary Magdalene out of whom He had cast seven devils."

Not as Man Would Have Chosen

Now this is not the kind of first appearance that we might have expected. The appropriate thing we might have thought would have been such an appearance as would have confounded all His foes and put them to an open shame. If we had had the arranging of Christ's Resurrection appearances, we should, as Dr. Glover says, have waked all Jerusalem with a blast of the angelic trumpet, and have bidden the people, who had shouted "Crucify Him," come and look at His empty grave. Or we should have confronted Pilate and the priests and elders who had sentenced Him to death with a vision of the glorious, majestic Lord. An appearance that would have been striking, dramatic, and that should overwhelm His foes with confusion—that is the kind of first appearance we should have arranged for Him. Instead of that He appeared first to Mary Magdalene from whom He had cast out seven devils. It was to this humble (and as far as the great world outside was concerned, unknown) woman that Christ first showed Himself alive after His passion.

But after Our Lord's Manner

All this is quite typical of our Lord's actions. He consistently set aside the temptation to startle men into some sort of faith in Him by spectacular displays of power. That is the real meaning of Christ's rejection of the devil's suggestion that He should cast Himself down from the pinnacle of the Temple, and by such a display of power practically compel the people to accept Him as divine. That is why He flatly declined to give the people a sign from heaven though they repeatedly asked for it. It was faith that Christ wanted. And a compulsory belief is not faith. There is a moral element in faith. A man has to choose; he has to give his vote. But if Christ had overwhelmed men's minds with tremendous displays of power there would be no room for choice. Men would simply be constrained to believe; in which case, again, belief would be absolutely no test of character. If there is to be a real faith, it seems as if there must be room left for doubt. Men must have an option; they must be able to believe or disbelieve. So the Lord was quiet, and unostentatious, in His working. The kingdom of God, as personified in His risen self, did not come with observation.

Why Mary Was Chosen

But, while Mary was not the person we should have chosen to be the happy recipient of the first revelation of the risen Lord, yet when we think a little more deeply, and look at things a little more closely, we shall see that of all people she was the most fitted to receive the first revelation. For there is always a question of fitness in this matter of seeing Christ. It is not to every one He reveals Himself. "Thus saith the Lord, to this man will I look, even to him that is poor and of a contrite spirit, and that trembleth at My word" (Isa. 66:2). There must be a certain moral preparedness if the Lord is to show Himself. The pure in heart shall see God, but the evil-hearted would not recognize God even if they saw Him.

A Woman Now of Faith and Love

I notice two things about Mary, which are suggested even by the bare narrative of my text. She was a woman of persevering faith; and she was a woman of a loving heart. First of all, she was a woman of persevering faith. She had run with the other women to bring the disciples word of the empty grave and the vision of angels. But she did then what the other women apparently did not do, she returned in the wake of Peter and John to the grave. And when Peter and John had finished examining the grave, and had gone back again home, Mary still lingered in the Garden. Now why did she linger there? Possibly, as some commentators suggest, because, after her own experience of the Lord's redeeming power, she had a mightier faith in His divinity than the rest of His disciples. "She was more capable of a belief in Christ's Resurrection than even John was," says Dr. Glover. That may be so. But without dogmatizing on that point, one thing I know, that after Peter and John had gone home because they felt there was nothing more to be heard or seen, Mary lingered on. Perhaps it was only gratitude and love that rooted her to the spot; but anyhow she lingered on. And to this woman who lingered on, there was given first a vision of angels, and then the sight of the risen Lord Himself. All of which suggests that it is the people who hold on and persevere and endure who get the blessing. Peter and John gave up too soon. They concluded too soon there was nothing to be gained by remaining at the grave. But the woman who lingered on saw the Lord. Do you not think we often give up too soon? In the matter of prayer, for example? Are we not all too ready to say, "The heavens are as brass, there is nothing"? It is the lingerers, the people who hold on, the people who endure, who get the blessing. That is what we want in these days, "Courage to wait and watch and weep, though mercy long delay." Persevering faith is in the long run always rewarded faith. If we hold on, and do not grow faint or weary, our eyes too will be gladdened with the vision of the Lord. The first appearance to Mary implies the reward of persevering faith.

Love and Vision

And in the second place, it was the reward of a devoted and whole-hearted love. That little touch "from whom He had cast out seven devils" explains much. It explains why Mary was foremost in the work of preparing spices; it explains why she was very early at the grave; it explains why, when the other women remained in the Upper Room, she returned to the Garden; it explains why, when Peter and John went back again home, she still lingered near the grave. The other women and Peter and John and the rest of the disciples, loved the Lord. But perhaps none loved Him as Mary did. For none had received such unspeakable blessings at His hand as she had done. She had been lifted up out of the pit of degradation and shame and despair. "To whom much is forgiven," said Jesus, "the same loveth much," and we can vary it and say, "to whom mighty blessings are given, the same loveth much." And Mary had received mighty blessings at the hand of Christ, and so she loved him best. Those are the people who see Christ still—the people who love Him best and long for Him most. People say that love is blind. They never made a greater mistake. Love is vision, love is sight. There are no eyes so keen as a mother's eyes.

The Insight of Love

How is it that mothers are able to detect things about their children—signs of illness or mental distress, for example—which had passed quite unnoticed by ordinary folk? It is simply because of the insight of love. "While he was yet a long way off, his father saw . . ." the prodigal son. No one else saw him; the elder brother with his narrow and jealous spirit did not see him. But his father saw him. Love caught sight of him. And it is love that sees the Lord; not intellect, not cleverness, but love. That is Christ's own promise. "If any man love Me, I will come unto him and will manifest Myself to him." And perhaps that is our greatest need today. More even than faith we need love; more even than the illumined mind, we need the devoted heart. We are living in dull days; there is no open vision. "Return, O Lord, how long?" we cry. But the fault is not in Him, but in ourselves. Our love is so cold and poor. We have no sense of the debt we owe to Him. If only our hearts got warmed, this sentence would have to be written of us, "Then were the disciples glad because they saw the Lord."

112
"In Another Form"

"After that He appeared in another form unto two of them, as they walked, and went into the country. And they went and told it unto the residue: neither believed they them." —Mark 16:12, 13.

IN THE PREVIOUS chapter I said that this concluding paragraph gives a kind of synopsis of our Lord's post-Resurrection appearances.

The Appearance to the Two Disciples

We have an illustration of what I meant in these two verses. The appearance to the two disciples as they walked on their way into the country is no doubt the appearance to the two disciples on the way to Emmaus. As Luke tells it for us it is one of the most exquisite of the Resurrection stories. How Cleopas and his unknown friend set out on that eight mile walk to Emmaus; how a Stranger joined them and entered into conversation with them; how He gave them the most moving and delightful Bible lesson they had ever received in their lives, proving to them that far from making Messiahship impossible, suffering and sacrifice were its very badge and signs; how in the interest of the conversation Emmaus was reached before they were aware; how the Stranger whose talk had so fascinated and warmed their hearts made as though He would go further; how the two disciples, eager to hear more of His wonderful speech, pressed Him to stay with them; how He had sat down with them at their simple meal; and how at length He was known to them in the breaking of bread, and they recognized that the marvelous Stranger was none other than their beloved Lord Himself, come to life again. How all this happened Luke tells us in one of those passages to which we continually turn, finding in it a spring of inexhaustible instruction and delight. But here the story is compressed into two verses, giving us the bare fact, that Christ did so appear unto two disciples as they walked into the country. And yet even in this brief statement there are one or two arresting things, that open up great avenues for thought and speculation.

"Another Form," but the Same Lord

I have been struck and arrested by that phrase "in another form," "in a different form," "altered in appearance." For the phrase calls attention to one characteristic of our risen Lord. His Resurrection had made a difference to Him; He was altered in "appearance." But He had not altered a bit in spirit. His love had not altered. His exaltation did not make Him distant with His friends. This is obvious from what we are told of what He said and did after His Passion. He never could look upon distressed and sorrowing people in the days of His flesh without wishing to help them. So, when He saw Mary sobbing her heart out at the tomb, His word, "Mary," transfigured sorrow into triumph.

His Compassion

He never could look even upon physical want in the days of His flesh without wishing to minister to it. "I have compassion on the multitude, they have been with Me three days and have nothing to eat." And so He provided for them that bountiful meal out in the wilderness. And in just the same way His heart was moved with sympathy for those men who had toiled all night and caught nothing, and who were drawing near to the shore disappointed, cold and hungry. And so when they stepped out, they found a fire of coals burning and fish laid thereon and bread. He was compassionate towards those who had sin on their souls. He was eager above all things to lift that load, to bring peace to the troubled conscience. "Son, be of good cheer, thy sins are forgiven thee," He said to the paralytic who had been brought into His presence. To the woman who was sobbing out her shame at His feet He said, "Thy sins are forgiven thee, go in peace." And so, exactly, He was quick and eager to bring peace to the soul of that disciple who had lived in an agony of remorse and shame ever since his denial in the judgment hall. His first message was one that conveyed the assurance of pardon and abiding love, "Go, tell His disciples and Peter." There was no change in the spirit of the risen Lord. And this likeness extended even to His personal ways. I am not going to etherealize Jesus, to de-personalize Him, so to spiritualize Him as to spiritualize Him clean away. Personality abides, and Jesus is a person. Even beyond death He retained certain personal characteristics. Mary knew Him by His voice. He was known by these two disciples "in the breaking of bread."

"Altered in Appearance"

But though the same He was different; not in essential things, but in outward guise. That is as unmistakably proved by the Resurrection stories, as the other fact that He was essentially the same. There is one striking and significant feature about our Lord's various Resurrection appearances. Scarcely any of those to whom He revealed Himself recognized Him at the first. Recall what the Gospels tell us. When He appeared to Mary, Mary did not recognize Him; she supposed Him to be the gardener. When He appeared to the two disciples on the way to Emmaus, they walked the whole distance to the village without even guessing Who He was. They took Him to be some pilgrim-stranger who had come to Jerusalem for the feast. When He showed Himself to the Eleven on the first Easter evening, they did not recognize Him; not until He showed them His hands and His side did they come to believe it was their Lord Himself. When He appeared to the five disciples fishing on the Lake they seem to have taken Him for a passing traveler. It was only when the nets enclosed a great multitude of fish that the truth flashed upon John's soul, and he said to Peter, "It is the Lord." When He appeared to above five hundred brethren at once on that mountain in Galilee, the mount on which He had preached the great Sermon, and to which He was accustomed to retire and pray, He was so different that not all who saw Him believed that He was Jesus, for "some doubted."

Faith and Sight

It needs a certain preparation of soul and spirit to be able to see Jesus. Before sight can be established, there must be not only an objective and external world to be seen, but also an eye to see it. A man may say, "I can see nothing." It does not follow that there is nothing to be seen. "I never see such sunsets," said a lady to Turner. "Don't you wish you could, madam?" was the reply. The lady wished to imply that there were no such sunsets to be seen. Turner's plain hint was that the sunsets were there, but that she had not the power to see them. And just as there are dimsighted, short-sighted, and blind people, as far as physical vision is concerned, so there are people whose spiritual vision is defective. They are dimsighted, short-sighted, blind souls. Because some people see "no beauty in Him that they should desire Him," it does not follow that Christ is not the chiefest among ten thousand and the altogether lovely. The defect is not in Christ, but in these who look at Him. The chief priests crucified Christ because He said He was the Son of God. They called Him a blasphemer. It does not follow that He was not the Son of God. It was the priests who were spiritually blind. "These things are spiritually discerned." You must have an eye, and the clearness of the spiritual eye depends upon the purity of the heart. That is why some people, when they heard a voice from heaven, said that it thundered; and others who came into contact with the risen Christ did not recognize their Lord.

"Another Form"

"Another form." Has this no bearing upon our own condition in the life beyond? There are some things which death cannot change. It cannot touch character; it cannot change personality. We shall be essentially the same people on the other side of the grave as we are on this. Life is continuous. We shall retain our identity; and yet we shall be "altered in appearance." Our "forms" will be changed. But it is not this gross material body that we shall possess in the life beyond. We shall possess then a body which shall be a fitting sheath for the soul; which shall be the visible expression, so to speak, of the soul. In that sense, as Paul says, "we shall all be changed." As to the nature of that heavenly "form" which we shall then wear, it is idle to speculate. We can see that our Lord's Resurrection body was not subject to the laws of time and space. It was wholly different from the "body" He wore while a workman in Nazareth, and a preacher in Galilee and Jerusalem. But wherein the difference consisted it is impossible for us to say. Let us be content with the great words of the Apostle Paul. "It is sown in corruption; it is raised in incorruption; it is sown in dishonor; it is raised in glory; it is sown in weakness; it is raised in power; it is sown a natural body; it is raised a spiritual body" (1 Cor. 15:42-44).

Christ Revealing Himself to Many

But the phrase "in another form," suggests what appears to me to be an abiding feature in the ministry of Christ. Is He not continually appearing to men in "another form"? The old Greeks had a legend about an old man of the sea called Proteus, that he had the power of appearing in many shapes and disguises. People used to wish to consult him because he was supposed to have the power of prophecy. But now Proteus would appear as a fish, and now as a horse, and so on. Those who did not know his secret were apt to miss him; but those who held on to him, no matter the guise he assumed, were always rewarded, for to them Proteus would reveal himself in his true shape, and tell them what they wanted to know. That is simply legend; but, in what the Greeks used to say of the fabled Proteus, there is a suggestion of what really occurs in the case of our Lord. He comes to men in different forms. He does not walk the earth today in visible presence. But nevertheless He has not left it. He is with us always to the end of the world.

In Many Ways

He comes to us today in the person of His Spirit. The Spirit pleads with men today, by the voice of conscience, by the influence of holy parents, by the words of this old Book, by the appeals of the Christian preacher. And when conscience is thus stirred, and the heart is thus touched, Christ has come to our house as surely as He went to Zacchaeus' long ago; He is calling us just as clearly as He called Matthew from his toll-booth. Looked at from another point of view, He comes to us in the varied experiences of life. He comes to us sometimes in the shape of a great joy. And He comes to us, sometimes, perhaps oftener, in the shape of a great sorrow. He comes to us, again, in the persons of His people. "Saul, Saul, why persecutest thou Me?" Saul had been haling humble men and women and casting them into prison. And all unthinking he had been doing over again what the priests and the soldiers had done to Jesus. He had been persecuting Him, scourging Him, crucifying Him afresh. "I am Jesus Whom thou persecutest," said the voice to him. Jesus was on the earth still in the person of His persecuted and suffering people. He comes in the shape of that lonely person who needs friendship, or that bereaved person who needs comfort; He comes in the shape of the sick who need healing, and the weak who need help, and the hungry who cry for bread. That is the "different form" in which Christ presents Himself to men and women today. Let us beware of missing Him.

Not in the Same Form to All

Does not the phrase also suggest this, that different ages and different people may view Christ rather differently? There is no one definite, stereotyped, unalterable conception of Christ. You cannot find it even in the New Testament. You know how varied and different are the faces of Christ which the artists put on their canvases. There are no two pictures of Christ the same. The fact is each artist depicts his own Christ, the Christ of his own imagination and affection, the Christ as He appears to him. And He appears to no two in exactly the same form. The difference in the artistic representation of Christ is but symbolic of the difference in men's thoughts about Him. There are differences, as I have already said, even in the New Testament pictures of Him. Peter's Christ, and John's Christ, and Paul's Christ, they are all at bottom the same Christ, the Christ Who loved men's souls, and died for their sins, and rose again in triumph on the third day. But in each Apostolic picture there is a difference in the point of view. He appears to James perhaps mainly as the Lord of Conduct, and to John as the Illumination of the Soul, and to Paul as the mighty Savior from Sin. I do not think we ought to expect all men to construe the person of Christ in exactly the same way. Augustine after a life of sensuality and sin will think of Christ in one way; the great Greek father Origen will think of Him in another; a man who has been rescued from the lowest depths of vice will emphasize Christ's redeeming love; a man like Emerson who kept through life an almost stainless soul, will think of Him mainly as the revelation of God's love and life. But it is the "same Jesus." Just because He is so rich and full, He appears to the infinite varieties of men in different forms, according to their several needs, and is able to satisfy the wants of all.

And as it has been with individuals, so is it with the ages. Every age needs a new Christ, and finds a new Christ. As the years pass, men grow in knowledge. And as they grow in knowledge, old intellectual statements become obsolete and impossible. And so we must expect views of Christ to alter. They have altered, but we need have no fear that Christ is going to be superseded or discarded. There is such infinite fulness in Him that every age finds its satisfaction in Him. He appears to every new age, as it is born, "in another form."

But Still the Same Jesus

And yet the same Jesus. Amid the almost infinite changes, He remains essentially the same. We have advanced far since Augustine's or Luther's or John Wesley's days. But still to us, as to them, He is the Revelation of God, our Redeemer from sin. The divine sacrificial love of Christ, that is the central and essential thing. And that abides. It is not "another form" of Jesus we get if the Cross is neglected. It is another Jesus Who is not another. "And He showed them His hands and His side," that is how the disciples knew Jesus. "Show me the nail-print," said an old saint in the cell to a being who pretended to be the Christ. It is the infallible sign. There may be changes in men's views of Christ, changes that sometimes perplex us, but if it is the Christ with the nail-prints in His hands we see, we can be content. "It is the Lord."

113
The Disciples' Unbelief

"And they, when they had heard that He was alive, and been seen of her, believed not.... And they went and told it unto the residue: neither believed they them. Afterward He appeared unto the eleven as they sat at meat, and upbraided them with their unbelief and hardness of heart, because they believed not them which had seen Him after He was risen."
—Mark 16:11, 13-14.

THERE WERE ONLY two things at which Christ in the days of His flesh expressed astonishment—the faith of the Roman centurion and the unbelief of the Nazarenes. But of His own people after the Resurrection we read in verse 14 that "He upbraided them with their unbelief and hardness of heart." And I am sure it filled the heart of the writer of this paragraph with wonder too. Notice how he recurs to it again and again. He cannot get it out of his mind. Next to the wonder of the Resurrection itself, the most wonderful thing was the stubborn and persistent refusal of the disciples to believe it had really occurred. Follow the story as he summarizes it. The first to bring the disciples the good news was Mary Magdalene.

The Great News
She came upon them as they mourned and wept with the gladdening announcement that she had not only seen the Lord, but had spoken with Him, and was the bearer of a message from Him to them. And instead of receiving the news with joy, the disciples chilled Mary to the marrow by the blank incredulity with which they listened to her. Notice what the evangelist says. "They, when they heard that He was alive, and had been seen of her, disbelieved."

Discredited and Denied
They disbelieved. It was not simply that they could not persuade themselves that what Mary said was true, they scornfully and contemptuously rejected her story. It was a case of positive

and summary repudiation. They said that Mary's story was an idle tale. There was something almost aggressive in their attitude. It was not doubt; it was denial. Then later in the day, came the incident of the two disciples who had set out to Emmaus, but who had immediately returned to Jerusalem when they had discovered Who their wonderful Companion was. And once again instead of breaking into Thanksgivings and Hallelujahs, the disciples received the news in chilling silence. "They went away and told it unto the rest: neither believed they them."

Doubted

"Neither believed they them." The expression, you will notice, is not so emphatic as that which is used in Mary's case. Here it is, "they did not believe"; in Mary's case it is, "they disbelieved." They had abruptly rejected Mary's tale. But certain things had happened since then. It had been rumored, for example, that Peter had seen the Lord. At any rate, they did not feel that they could reject the story of the two disciples off-hand. And yet they could not bring themselves to accept it as true. The stage of blank denial had passed, but they were in the stage of doubt and difficulty still; "Neither believed they them."

Doubt Passing into Faith

And then Jesus came and stood in the midst and said, "Peace be unto you." And so obstinately unbelieving were they, that they could not believe the evidence of their own senses. They were terrified and affrighted, Luke says, and supposed that they beheld a spirit. With their Lord there before them, they debated in their hearts whether it was He or not. And not until Jesus said to them, "See My hands and My feet that it is I Myself; handle Me and see," did their stubborn unbelief give way to a timid and trembling faith. And even after that first Sabbath evening, Thomas refused to believe. It was in vain his fellow disciples told him that they had seen Him, and rehearsed to him the words which Jesus had said. Thomas, I suppose, put all his fellow-disciples in the same category with Mary. They had taken to believing and repeating idle tales; nothing they said carried weight with Thomas. He was stubbornly, obstinately unbelieving. "Except I shall see in His hands the prints of the nails," he said, "and put my finger into the print of the nails and put my hand into His side, I will not believe." "I will not believe," that was the sort of temper in which the disciples met the news of the Resurrection.

The Value of the Disciples' Unbelief

Now, as I have already said, from the point of view of apologetics it is better that the disciples should have been thus stubbornly and obstinately incredulous. It adds enormously to the value of their testimony. It knocks the bottom out of the vision-theory which is the theory of the Resurrection most favored by sceptic writers. These "appearances" of the Lord, they say, were all the work of the imagination of the disciples. They wanted to see Him and so they thought they saw Him. It all began with the excited imagination of Mary, and the other disciples followed suit.

The Vision Theory Disproved

But before people see visions, they must expect the vision and believe it possible. Even the advocates of the theory admit as much as that. They concede the point, when they say the disciples wanted to see, and so they saw. Visions only come where there is expectancy, anticipation, enthusiasm. Had there been amongst the disciples an exultant belief in the Resurrection, we can understand how they should have taken to seeing visions. But there was no such expectation, no such anticipation, no such enthusiasm. When the disciples saw Christ laid in Joseph's rocky tomb, they thought they had seen the last of Him. Their temper was one of desolation, dismay, despair. Anything more grotesquely unlike the facts than Renan's picture of the disciples as a group of imaginative and enthusiastic and ecstatic people, cannot well be imagined. Far from expecting the Resurrection, it required proof after proof to convince them it had taken place. They were not excited people ready to accept any story, they were sceptical, incredulous, slow to believe. Mr. Latham in his *Pastor Pastorum* has a very interesting passage on the character of the Apostles as witnesses. He contends that by the very nature of their upbringing, education, and occupation, they were admirably fitted to be plain, straightfoward, matter-of-fact witnesses. Well, whatever we may think of Mr. Latham's general contention (and I for one quite agree with it), at any rate we can say that the witness of the Apostles to the Resurrection carries special weight and conviction, for it is the witness of cool, critical, and almost sceptical men.

But the Doubt Sinful

But while from the apologetic point of view we may almost be grateful that the Apostles were thus persistently and obstinately incredulous, from the moral point of view, their doubt was unreasonable, indefensible, sinful. That was evidently how it appeared to our Lord Himself, "He upbraided them with their unbelief and hardness of heart." He reproached them with it. In our Lord's eyes, their stubborn unbelief was blameworthy. Now let me remind you once again that there was a certain kind of doubt and unbelief that our Lord treated very gently and tenderly. How gently, for example, He dealt with the doubt of that agonized father who could only cry, "Lord, I believe, help Thou mine unbelief." Doubt arising from ignorance, from honest difficulty—our Lord never "reproached" men for that. A bruised reed He never broke and smoking flax He never quenched. The only doubt Christ ever "reproached" was the doubt that had a moral or rather an immoral root, the doubt that had its rise, not in the perplexed intellect, but in the evil heart. And that is exactly why He upbraided these disciples of His with their unbelief. Their unbelief rooted itself in moral defect. He upbraided them with their unbelief and hardness of heart. If they had only kept their hearts open and guileless, they would have been on the lookout for the Resurrection instead of scornfully disbelieving it, even when it actually occurred. For consider how many intimations of their Lord's Resurrection had been given to them.

A Sin against Light

First of all, there was their own Jewish Scripture. If they had only read their Scripture with open and unprejudiced minds the Cross and the Grave would not have filled them with despair. They would have known that it was through the Cross and the Grave that Messiah was to march to His triumph. "Ye know not the Scriptures, neither the power of God," said Jesus to those Sadducees who denied the Resurrection of man. He might have brought exactly the same charge against His own disciples. They had read the Scriptures through the spectacles of Jewish prejudice. If they had read the Scriptures with open and unprejudiced minds, they would not have despaired because of the Cross, but they would have been waiting with eager hope for the dawn of the Resurrection morning.

A Sin against Experience and Christ's Character

Then, again, they had been privileged to come into close touch with Jesus Himself. It was this that really made their unbelief so inexcusable and blameworthy. As they had companied with the Lord, they had been privileged to see in Jesus an absolutely holy person. He was unlike every one else who ever lived in this respect. He did no sin neither was guile found in His mouth. He was holy, harmless, undefiled, and separate from sinners. These men felt that His holiness was so perfect, His purity so dazzling, that sometimes it filled them with an overwhelming sense of their own sin and shame, and they were almost ready to leave Him because that sense of shame was almost more than they could bear. Now, if they had had open and guileless hearts, it ought to have been no surprise to them that such a person should have escaped the bonds of death. One of the Psalmists ventured long before the assertion that while death might be the wages of sin, death could not conquer and overcome perfect holiness. "Thou wilt not leave Thine Holy One," he cried, "to see corruption" (Ps. 16:1a). And Paul afterwards finds, shall I say, the key to the Resurrection in the same stupendous fact of our Lord's sinlessness. He was "declared to be the Son of God with power, according to the spirit of holiness, by the Resurrection of the dead" (Rom. 1:4). They ought to have known that death and corruption could never be the portion of One Who was without spot or stain of sin. And they would have known, had it not been that their hearts were hardened.

And of His Works

In addition to the wonder of our Lord's person, there were the wonders of His deeds. These very disciples had seen the most amazing evidences of His power. They had seen His power over disease. He had given sight to the blind, hearing to the deaf, cleansing to the leper, power to the paralyzed. He had even shown Himself to be Lord over death itself. He had summoned back the breath of the little daughter of Jairus the Ruler of the Synagogue. He had stopped a funeral procession outside the gates of Nain and restored the young man, whom they were carrying out to burial, to his weeping and broken-hearted mother. He had, most amazing wonder of all, summoned Lazarus back to life though he had been in the grave four days. In these wonderful ways He had shown Himself Lord and Master of death. And was it likely that He Who had snatched this one and the other from the jaws of death, was Himself at the last to become death's helpless victim? They might have known, they ought to have known, in face of what they had seen, that here was One Who had the keys of Death and of Hades. They would have known, had it not been that their hearts were hardened.

And Forgetfulness of His Predictions

And then finally, there were the plain and definite predictions of our Lord Himself. He had spoken of "His Resurrection" by symbol and parable. He had said that in three days He would build the Temple of His body up again. He had said that the only sign that would be given His generation was the sign of Jonah the Prophet. But He had also spoken of it in set terms. He had done it again and again, "Behold, we go up to Jerusalem, and the Son of Man shall be delivered unto the chief priests; and they shall condemn Him to death, shall deliver Him unto the Gentiles, and they shall kill Him, and the third day He shall rise again." Nothing could have been more specific or definite. But the disciples took no heed. The words fell on deaf ears. They refused to believe that Jesus would die, and therefore were deaf to any speech about Resurrection.

The Results of Prejudice

And so it came to pass that when the third day came it found them absolutely unexpectant, skeptical, unbelieving. They disbelieved Mary; they did not believe Cleopas and his friend; they could scarcely believe the evidence of their own senses. And if you ask what it was that had thus made their hearts hard and impenetrable, I reply it was prejudice. They had been brought up in the Jewish conception of Messiah. They expected the conquering prince of the popular imagination. Death had no place in their ideas of God's anointed. When the Lord spoke therefore about death, He was confronted with deaf ears and absolutely impenetrable hearts. You remember what John Bunyan in his *Holy War* says about the defense of Ear Gate? When Immanuel set out to capture Man Soul he addressed his summons first to the Captain in charge of Ear Gate, which of course is only Bunyan's way of saying that the Gospel is announced to most men and makes its appeal to most men by means of human speech. But my Lord Willbewill, Diabolus' Commander-in-Chief, had taken precautions to meet the attack, for he had stationed one, old Mr. Prejudice (an angry and ill-conditioned fellow) as Captain of the Ward at that Gate, and put under his power sixty men, called Deaf-men, men advantageous for that service, for as much as they muttered no words of the captains nor of their soldiers. And that is exactly what had taken place in the case of these disciples: they had put old Mr. Prejudice in charge of Ear Gate, so that all that their Master said to them fell on deaf and unheeding ears. For when prejudice is in possession of the heart, truth finds no admission. And that is why Christ blamed and reproached His disciples for their unbelief.

Warning for us

Now, in all this there is a rather solemn warning for us. First of all, let us plainly recognize this, that there are certain kinds of doubt for which our Lord has not pity, but blame. I think that needs to be said, and perhaps emphatically said, in these days, for we have exalted doubt into a kind of virtue. Perhaps that hackneyed line of Tennyson's, about their being more faith in honest doubt than in half the creeds, is in part responsible for it. Now there are two things we ought to be clear about and those are these.

Against Doubt

Doubt, even when honest, is a condition to be deplored. We talk in these days as if the condition of "honest doubt" was really the kind of ideal condition, and as if the "honest doubter" was a very superior person. What we have to recognize is that doubt is not a thing to be bragged about or admired, even when honest, it is to be deplored. For doubt always means weakness, indecision, misery of soul. In fact, I will go further, and say that doubt when it is really honest, is always in an agony. That is the mark of honest doubt. Like the man in the story it cries out with tears, "Help mine unbelief." Braggart doubt, flippant doubt, is by those very characteristics revealed to be not honest doubt at all.

Especially Doubt When a Cloak for Sin

And the second thing is this; much that parades as honest doubt, is not honest doubt at all, but doubt that springs from an evil heart. Yes, I will believe that Christ will deal very gently with the honest seeker, the man who longs for the light but finds himself still in the dark; but for the parade of doubt that covers an evil heart, that is really nothing but a cloak for sin, the Lord has not pity but indignation. It is a terrible thing to say, but it is nevertheless true, many men do not believe, because they do not want to believe. There is a close and intimate connection between scepticism and moral wrong. Men reject Christ not because they have examined His claims and found them wanting, but because they love their sin. Such a doubt, it is as well to be plain, does not receive the pity of Christ, but is exposed to the wrath of the Lamb.

And Appeal

"He reproached them with their unbelief and hardness of heart." And do you not think our Lord has similar cause for upbraiding this generation? What multitudes of people are absolutely indifferent to Him and to all intents and purposes reject Him! And it is not for lack of evidence of His grace and power. Here in the Gospels we have the story of His life, the one perfect and sinless life; here in His Church we have the evidence of His continuous life; here in saved and regenerated lives we have the evidence of His divine power! And still men go on their way unheeding. It is unbelief for which there is no excuse. It springs from "hardness of heart." And do you not think He has ground of complaint against His Church? For we do not take Him at His word, and we are incredulous of His power, and we fail to exercise the mighty privileges that are ours in Him. Like the disciples, we are not able to cast the evil spirits of our age out and it is all because of our unbelief. And our unbelief again springs from hardness of heart. What is our great need? Simple, guileless, believing hearts; hearts freed from prejudice; hearts that will take God at His word; hearts purged of all secret reservations. "A humble, lowly, contrite heart, Believing, true and clean."

114
The Great Commission

"And He said unto them, Go ye into all the world, and Preach the gospel to every creature." —Mark 16:15.

The Commission: When Given

I DO NOT think that Christ uttered these words and laid this commission upon His disciples on the occasion of His first visit to them on the evening of Resurrection Day. It is true the verse follows immediately upon the verse which tells us of that particular appearance. But then these nine verses do not profess to be detailed history. As much as that can be inferred from the bare fact that the nine verses are made to cover ground that occupies whole chapters in the other evangels. The writer has compressed and welded a good many things together without strict regard to chronological order. He has picked out of the happenings of the forty days just enough to make it plain that Jesus had really risen, and that the missionary activity of the Church in the days in which he was writing was the result of the specific direction and plain command of the Lord Himself. So we must not conclude that, because the writer seems to attach the "Great Commission" to the first appearance, therefore it was given on that occasion. I do not think it was. I should argue for my view in the first place on general grounds.

Not Immediately

The disciples on that first evening were not prepared to receive a command like this. They were not in a fit spiritual condition to think of missionary work. On that first evening the disciples needed to have their own faith quickened. "He upbraided them," I read above, "with their unbelief and hardness of heart." It would have been of no use giving a command like this to unbelieving or half-hearted men. Before these humble men would venture out to preach to all the world, they themselves would have to be possessed of a triumphant and enthusiastic faith. And it was to the quickening of faith in the disciples themselves that Christ devoted Himself on the first Easter evening. "He showed them His hands and His side." "Handle Me," He said, "and see that it is I Myself." And in addition he tried to bring home to them the realization of their power. He breathed on them and said, "Receive ye the Holy Ghost." Further than that our Lord did not go on that first Easter evening. His whole concern that night was with the disciples themselves. His one desire was to quicken faith in His own Resurrection, and as a result to beget within them a sense of power.

But to Men Prepared

It was later, when doubt had clean gone, and an enthusiastic faith and the courage born of it had taken its place, that our Lord spoke the great words of my text. It was to men convinced that Jesus was the Son of God, because of the Resurrection from the dead, and ready therefore to dare anything for Him, that Christ said, "Go ye into all the world and preach the Gospel to the whole creation." When He said it, we are not told, but probably towards the end of His earthly sojourn. They would scarcely have been prepared to hear it sooner, for these disciples had much to learn before they were ready even to understand a command like this. There is a suggestive verse in the opening chapter of the Acts of the Apostles which is not without its bearing on this. Luke is summing up the events and conversations of the forty days, and says: "He shewed Himself alive after His passion by many proofs, appearing unto them by the space of forty days, and speaking the things concerning the Kingdom of God." It is that last phrase which is the important and significant one. The recurring theme of conversation between the risen Master and His disciples was the Kingdom of God, the topic upon which they most needed instruction and guidance. Even though chosen as the men through whom the Kingdom was to be established, they were in the meantime ignorant of the true nature of the Kingdom. Nothing is more striking than the disciples' perverse misunderstanding of the nature of the Kingdom which Christ had come to found. They were so entirely possessed by their Jewish prejudices that the true view of Christ's Kingdom never really became lodged in their minds.

In Understanding of His Kingdom

For example, take these three points. First of all, their conception of a Kingdom was that of a temporal Kingdom. Messiah's Empire, as they thought of it, was a kind of counterpart of Caesar's. In the second place, they thought this Kingdom was to be established by worldly weapons. They wanted to call down fire from heaven.

They wanted to smite with the sword. Their idea was that nations were to be conquered by the sword, and so vast tracts were to be added to the Kingdom at a single stroke. And thirdly, their idea of the Kingdom was not universal but national. The Kingdom they thought of was a Jewish Kingdom. It represented the triumph of the Jew. And only the Jew and those who became Jews had part or lot in it. Now on each of these three points Christ's Kingdom was diametrically opposed to their thoughts of it. The Kingdom of God which He had come to establish was a spiritual Kingdom; it was no earthly empire, it was the reign of God in the souls of men; it was to be established not by force but by love, and all men were to find a place in it, Jew and Gentile on equal terms.

The Command and the Message

Notice the nature of the messages to be given: "Go ye into all the world," He said, "and preach the Gospel to the whole creation." What was this Gospel which they were to preach? It was the news about Himself; the story of His life and death and Resurrection. It is implied that in some way His life and death and Resurrection affected the whole world of men. The tragedy and triumph both took place in Jerusalem. But though they took place in Jerusalem, it was not Jerusalem and Palestine only that were concerned. What happened in Jerusalem in those days, had what the theologians call "a cosmic significance." Distant lands were concerned, peoples and tribes who had never heard of Jesus were concerned; generations yet unborn were concerned. What happened to Him was of infinite moment to the universe. "Go," He said, "and preach this Gospel of My dying and rising again—go into all the Kosmos and preach it to the whole creation."

A Message of Glad Tidings

Nor was it only that what happened to Him concerned the world, it is also implied that it would be good news to the world. It was an evangel they had to preach. The world's happiness and hope were bound up with the knowledge of what had happened to Him. In some wonderful way the story of His living, dying, and rising again would bring light and joy and comfort and peace to the manifold peoples of the earth.

The Witness of the Message

Now if Christ said this, it demolishes the theory of those who tell us that all the emphasis laid on the person of Christ, and the mighty place assigned to Him, is the result of a process of idealization and deification that set in after His death. For you cannot reduce the person of Christ to the dimensions of a simple, lowly Galilean teacher without tearing the Gospels to rags and tatters. The impoverished Christ of so-called liberal theology is impossible; He never had any existence. There is no escape from the supernatural Christ, unless you deny His existence altogether. See what you have here—a Person Who thought so highly of Himself, that He thought Himself essential to the world, that He claimed the world as His own, that He declared Himself indispensable to the Hope and Happiness of the World. And who was this Person Who made these claims for Himself? Unless we are to be shut up to the answer that Christ was not even a good man, but was the most colossal egoist the world ever saw, we are bound to give the answer the Church has always given, "Thou art the King of Glory, O Christ."

Christ's Faith in the Disciples

Observe, now, Christ's faith in His disciples. "Go ye," He said, "into all the Kosmos and preach the Gospel to the whole creation." Christ committed His cause and Kingdom to the keeping of these disciples of His. He laid upon them the gigantic task of evangelizing the world. It was a tremendous task to which He summoned them. For consider the kind of people they were—for this commission was not given to the Apostles only, it was given to the whole body of His disciples.

Their Inexperience

They were men and women, most of them, who had never been out of Palestine. The only little bit of experience of evangelizing work they had had, had been gained within the limits of Palestine and probably of Galilee. They knew no language save their own Aramaic dialect and possibly commercial Greek. And to these people, who were all perhaps without experience of the great world outside Palestine, Christ gave this commission, "Go into all the world and preach the Gospel to the whole creation." With their meagre, and as it seemed, hopelessly inadequate equipment, they were to set about the gigantic task of evangelizing the world.

Their Humble Station

In the second place, not only were they untraveled men and women, but they were humble and socially insignificant into the bargain. There was not a wealthy man, or a man of rank or learning amongst them. "Not many wise, not many noble, not many mighty were called." But God chose the weak things, and the base things, and the despised things of the world to do His work. When during the great war Britain wished to set our case before their American cousins they sent their very best men— Mr. Balfour, the Archbishop of York, Sir G. A. Smith—to do it. But Christ chose for His ambassadors fisher folk and publicans. To them He committed the task of preaching His Gospel. And His trust was not misplaced. These weak men went everywhere, they appeared before governors and kings, they turned the world upside down, they were able to do all things through Christ who strengthened them.

The Present Duty

Now this was not a command laid upon the first disciples only, this is the permanent commission of the Church. Here is the great end for which she exists. There are various reasons which can be urged for zeal in missionary work. With our fathers, it was mainly concern for the future state of the unevangelized heathen. With the majority of people today it is perhaps pity for their present wretchedness and misery. The motive that inspired our fathers to such desperate earnestness in the cause of missions has lost much of its old power amongst us. But I am persuaded that the motive which we find in the thought of the present distress of the heathen is inadequate. Missions will limp and lag and fail if we depend upon that for our driving force. We must get back a mightier and more potent inspiration. And that mightier inspiration we get in the call and command of Christ. Here is the final and sufficient reason for missions. Christ commands them: "Go into all the world." A Christian is just a man who obeys Christ. It is open to question whether a man who says he does not believe in missions and who refuses to help missions is a Christian at all.

A Duty to All the World

"Go ye into all the world!" You notice the uncompromising demand. The news about Christ was not to be confined to Palestine in those early days; the whole world had a right to hear it. The good news is not to be confined to Europe and the West in these latter days; every nook and corner of the world has a right to hear it. We have not to pick and choose. Some lands are difficult. Mohammedanism in Africa, Hinduism in India seem to oppose almost impenetrable barriers. But the Christian Church must not neglect India and North Africa because of their difficulty. Some lands are dangerous. But danger must not daunt us. It never has daunted the Church. The Gospel has entered into possession of nearly every land by a living way. Palestine by the blood of James and Stephen; Europe by the blood of Paul and Peter; the South Seas by the blood of John Williams; Africa by the blood of Bishop Hannington; New Guinea by the blood of James Chalmers. And still we must go in spite of danger. To the barbarians of Central Africa, and the untamed savages of New Guinea we must "go and preach."

And a Duty of All

"Go ye into all the world." This is the business not of some but of all. This was not a commission given to the Apostles but to the whole Church. We must all take our share. We must all bear a hand. It matters not how poor and insignificant we may be, we have all a part to play. By gifts and prayers, if not by personal service, we must participate in this task. The first business of the saved man is the salvation of souls, says Andrew Murray. What we need to realize is that this is our first and chief concern, the spread of the Kingdom. Behind the command there lies the faith, that the news about Christ is the news the wide world needs; that the story of Christ, living, dying, rising again is a Gospel to all who hear it. It is a faith which is confirmed by all the facts. When the Apostles first set out on their missionary journeys, it was a mighty venture of faith, it was, shall I say, an experiment. They undertook their missionary labors on the bare word of their Master. But in our case, we know by actual experience, that the news about Christ is a Gospel to all who hear it and receive it; that wherever it is proclaimed it carries with it joy and peace and freedom; that it emancipates and saves men when everything else has failed. There is a multitude which no man can number of all nations and kindreds and peoples and tongues who have washed their robes and made them white in the blood of the Lamb. The world needs Christ. He meets its wants. He can save it from its sin. And no one else can. "Give us your Christ," said the people of Japan to Drummond as he sailed back to England. It is the appeal of the world. Shall it appeal in vain?

115
Belief and Unbelief: and Their Results

"He that believeth and is baptized shall be saved; but he that believeth not shall he damned. And these signs shall follow them that believe; In My name shall they cast out devils; they shall speak with new tongues; They shall take up serpents; and if they drink any deadly thing, it shall not hurt them; they shall lay hands on the sick, and they shall recover." —Mark 16:16-18.

The Place of Baptism

HERE, NO DOUBT, is a résumé of the last command and commission given by Christ to His disciples. Two subjects emerge: belief and baptism. In a work of this character, I avoid here all points of contention as to the rite of baptism, and deal only with some of its main aspects. For His Church the rite of baptism is a rite of our Lord's own institution. But it was not a rite He was the first to use. It had long been familiar to the Jews, and submission to baptism was one of the demands John made of all who repented of their sins. And now, in His great commission, Christ told His disciples to baptize all those who believed through their word. The rite of baptism was to be the outward badge and sign of their discipleship. It was beautifully fitted to be the symbol of the great change, for it typified that cleansing of the entire nature which only God could impart. It was the outward sign of an inward grace— the visible expression of the cleansing by the Spirit of God of the very springs of a man's being. And to this rite men who believed the Word were requested to submit as an open confession of their faith and new allegiance.

Saving Belief

I now ask your attention to the great antithesis of this text, "He that believeth shall be saved; he that disbelieveth shall be condemned." This is one of the most tremendous statements in the Bible. And as salvation and condemnation are in the issue, it is vital we should know exactly what the statement means. Let me take the first limb of the antithesis to begin with. "He that believeth shall be saved." Now the first question that suggests itself is this, what exactly are we to understand by believing? And whom or what are we to believe? It is obvious that what we are to believe is the Gospel referred to in the previous verse. And that Gospel centers in the proclamation of Jesus living, dying, rising again. It is in that living, dying, risen Lord that we are to believe.

Its Nature

By believing is meant not a mere intellectual assent to facts. We believe that two and two make four. We believe that there have been such men in existence as Simon de Montfort and Oliver Cromwell, and that they played a great part in English life in their day. And so we may believe that nineteen hundred years ago there lived in Palestine a Man, Christ Jesus, Who went about doing good, Who was Himself a holy Person, Who was put to death on a Cross under Pontius Pilate, and Who rose again on the third day. We may believe it all as a matter of history. But that is not the belief which is here meant. In so far as belief is a mere belief in facts, the devils believe and tremble. Nor is believing to be interpreted as acceptance of a creed. To know all about the "plan of salvation," to believe in the great doctrines of the Incarnation and Atonement, is not the "saving faith" of which Christ here speaks. As a matter of fact, a man may be an expert theologian without being a Christian. It was of a great statesman in the early part of Queen Victoria's reign that it was said that he combined the theological learning of a divine with the morals of a rake. In the New Testament the phrase is usually employed to describe faith in Christ; it is not, "Believe the Lord Jesus Christ," but, "Believe on the Lord Jesus Christ." There is a great difference between the two phrases. "Believe the Lord Jesus Christ," would mean "Believe His words, believe that what He says is true." But "Believe on the Lord Jesus Christ," means "Trust yourself to Him, rely upon Him, surrender yourself to Him."

Trust in a Person

That is what saving faith really is, not believing Christ's words, but so trusting Him as to be willing to commit ourselves to Him for time and eternity; is not simply belief in certain statements but trust in a person. The man who believes to the saving of his soul is the man who trusts Christ; trusts what He has done; trusts His sacrifice; trusts His intercession; trusts in Christ and His work, in opposition to any trust in himself and his attainments; who commits himself to Christ and bases all his hopes on this great truth, "The Son of God loved me and gave Himself for me."

Salvation

The man who so believes shall be saved! And what again do we mean by "saved"? "Saved" in the first place from the pains and penalties of sin. Saved from that "death" which is the penalty of sin; "saved" in the sense of being pardoned and justified and set right with God. It is only a vain fool like Rousseau who will frantically brag about appearing before God with the record of his life in his hands and claiming acquittal as a matter of right. Most of us know we have done wrong; most of us know that in the course of justice none of us should see salvation. My hope of acceptance is that I shall be found in Christ. When I commit myself to Christ I make His life of obedience in faith and intention my own, and I am accepted in the Beloved. There is no condemnation to them that are in Christ Jesus.

And Power

But "saved" not only from the penalties of sin, but saved also from sin itself. When a man so believes in Christ as to commit himself to Him, new power is imparted to him; he renews or rather exchanges his strength, and he is able to fight and overcome sins that had previously been too strong for him. I have just been reading an article by William James in the very last volume of essays and addresses published after his death, in which he says this, that we habitually exert less than our maximum of power. There are stores of power available which we never use. There are higher levels of living possible to us but which we never reach. We "live at a poor dying rate," as Cowper puts it. And he illustrates what he means by the phenomenon of what is called "the second wind." In a game, at a certain stage, players get fatigued and winded, but if, instead of giving up, they keep on, all of a sudden the fatigue seems to vanish, exertion becomes easy, they seem to have tapped a new source of power, they have got their "second wind." And there are levels of moral and spiritual power waiting to be tapped, he says, but men usually need some great emotion, some mighty excitement, to make them tap them. And one of the mighty experiences that make men tap this new source of power, he says, is conversion.

Conversion and Power

Somehow when men are in Christ they find themselves possessed of a strength undreamed of before. In the power of it old

habits are broken, old sins are clean put away. Zacchaeus the
miser becomes a philanthropist; the woman who was a sinner
becomes a saint; John Bunyan the blasphemer becomes a writer
of holy books; J. B. Cough the drunkard becomes a mighty temperance orator. When men commit themselves to Christ, they rise
to new levels of living. They exchange their strength. Undreamed
of drafts of power flow into them. They are clean emancipated
from the bondage and lust of sin. They put away the evil uses of
a life. They can do all things through Christ Who strengthens
them. And all that is involved in salvation. Release from the
pains and penalties of sin in and of itself would be a small thing.
But victory over sin itself is a great thing. And that is what Christ
does for a man. When a man commits himself to Him, He saves
him, for "He breaks the power of cancelled sin and sets the prisoner free."

Disbelief and Condemnation

"He that believeth shall be saved . . . he that disbelieveth shall
be condemned." And in turning to consider the second limb of the
antithesis I want to begin by saying how inexpressibly grateful I
am for the change the revisers have made in my text. The A.V. runs
like this. "He that believeth not shall be damned." Now we could
scarcely have had a more misleading translation. I am glad the
revisers have changed "He that believeth not" into "He who disbelieveth," for the plain implication of the Greek is, that it is not
every one who does not believe who is going to be condemned,
but he who, having the chance of believing, deliberately refuses
and rejects and repudiates the Lord. But I am gladder still they
have altered that word "damned." Originally perhaps it meant
pretty much what "condemned" means now, but in the course of
the years certain theological ideas have become inseparably
associated with the word. When we speak of the "damned" we
mean "lost souls," souls for ever separated from the mercy of God.
But the Greek word carries with it no such ideas. It does not say
that the people of whom it speaks are hopelessly and eternally lost.
What it says is serious enough, but there is no need to deepen and
darken the colors. The simple, solemn statement of my text is this:
"He that disbelieveth shall be condemned." It is the unbelief of one
who had the chance of belief. It is the unbelief of one who has seen
the good and has deliberately chosen its opposite saying, "Evil be
thou my good."

A Warning to Ourselves

It is to men and women like ourselves this solemn word addresses itself. It is impossible to take up a neutral attitude towards Christ. There is no middle course. There is no neutral area. He is set either for our rise or fall. We must either accept Him or reject Him, we must either believe or disbelieve. The one thing we cannot do with Christ is either to neglect or ignore Him. And "He that disbelieveth shall be condemned." There is nothing said here about the character or the duration of the punishment. The reserved and reticent character of all the Bible references to the future marks this reference also. All that is said is this: he that disbelieveth shall be condemned. But let not the reserve and reticence of the reference make any one think lightly of it. Its very simplicity and reserve make it all the more awe-inspiring to me. "Shall be condemned." We say little of the stern side of the Gospel in these days. We have subscribed to a rather sloppy and sentimental kind of optimism, and comfort ourselves with thinking everything is coming out all right in the end. What foundation have we for our optimism? What the Scripture says, what our Master says, is: "He that disbelieveth shall be condemned."

Not to Be Neglected

How foolish it is to shut our eyes to the austere side of the Gospel! We do not get rid of the judgments of the Lord, and the wrath of the Lamb, by refusing to think or speak of them. The man who comforts himself amid a life of folly and sin with the thought that everything will come right in the end is putting his soul to the hazard. I do not know what will happen in the end. What I do know is that Scripture is urgent, that in the making of the great decision not a day should be lost. "Now is the accepted time." The man who can willfully reject Christ when he has seen Him, needs no Judge from a great white throne to pronounce his condemnation, he has pronounced his own.

It was a curator in one of the great art galleries of Italy, where some of the masterpieces of Italian painting were preserved, who declared that it was not the spectators who criticized the pictures, it was the pictures that judged the spectators. By their appreciation or otherwise of the pictures, the spectators revealed themselves as possessed or devoid of the artistic sense. And in exactly the same way by their attitude to Christ, men reveal whether they have or have not the love of goodness in their souls. "We needs must love the highest when we see it." Yes, if we have good and honest hearts; but if we reject the highest, it is because our hearts are evil. That is why it remains eternally true, "He that disbelieveth shall be condemned." He is condemned already, he has condemned himself.

Upon the signs that should follow belief I will not dwell: let it suffice for us to think on the great alternative set before us in our Lord's commission to His people.

116
The Ascension

"So then after the Lord had spoken unto them, He was received up into heaven, and sat on the right hand of God." —Mark 16:19.

A New Title

THE LORD JESUS! Here in St Mark is a new appellation for the Master. Its occurrence here does not mean that something had happened which had "ennobled" Christ; but that something had happened which enabled the disciples to see the glory that had been His all along. That something was the Resurrection. That had opened the eyes of the disciples to the real glory of their Master; the empty grave told them Who He really was; and recognition of the Master's dignity finds expression in the new title. There is a new note of reverence and worship in their reference to Him. He was "Jesus" simply before the Cross; He was "the Lord Jesus" after the empty grave. It was not a human Jesus the early Christians preached to the world, but an exalted Lord. There never would have been a Christian Church if there had been only a human Jesus to proclaim. The early disciples went everywhere because they were absolutely sure of this, that the Jesus they had companied with was the exalted Lord. So when people say, Let us get back to the plain, simple, human Jesus of the early days, I say that is not getting back to Him at all, that is getting away from Him. The Jesus of the early days and the first disciples was not a plain, simple, human Jesus, He was "the Lord Jesus." We are true to the primitive faith, to the belief of the men who saw Christ and companied with Him, only when we acknowledge His unique and solitary majesty.

The Fact of the Ascension

Now in these concluding verses the writer seems to be rounding off his Gospel; and so, very briefly, the Ascension is recorded. The direct evidence for the event is meagre. It occupies a very small place in the Gospel records. Matthew and John give no distinct report of it; Mark and Luke are the only two who mention it directly; and in this Gospel, as you notice, it is referred to in this brief and simple way. The only circumstantial account we get of the Ascension is in Acts 1. But it is quite natural that we should get the most detailed account in that particular book. As Dr. Salmond puts it, "the Gospels report the story of our Lord's ministry on earth. The Book of the Acts reports the story of His ministry in heaven discharged through His Apostles, and it begins appropriately with the Ascension." But it would be a great mistake to think that our belief in our Lord's Ascension depends only upon the two-fold mention by Luke, and this brief reference in Mark. No one can read the Epistles without seeing that it occupies quite a prominent place in the Apostles' testimony. It is not directly proved; it is assumed, presupposed, taken for granted. It is very much with the Ascension as it is with the Incarnation. The great doctrine of the Incarnation is nowhere in the Epistles formally stated and proved. It is taken for granted; it is the background of all the Apostolic thinking. It is much like that with the Ascension. It is axiomatic in the Apostles' thinking. When they think of the Lord Jesus they think of Him as One Who has passed within the heavens. It was from heaven Christ appeared to Paul on the way to Damascus; it is from heaven, according to the same Apostle, that Christ will come to judge both the quick and dead. Peter speaks of Christ as having gone into heaven and being on the right hand of God, angels and authorities and powers being subject unto Him. John declares that he saw in the midst of the New Jerusalem, One like unto the Son of Man Whose eyes were as a flame of fire and His voice as the sound of many waters, and Who said to him, "I am the first and the last, and the Living One, and I was dead and behold, I am alive for evermore, and I have the keys of death and of Hades." No one can read the New Testament without seeing, then, that the Ascension forms the background of the Apostolic thought. "The conviction of our Lord's Ascension," says one writer, "fills the mind of the Apostolic age."

The Completion of the Resurrection

The Ascension was the natural completion of the Resurrection. People in these days affect to find difficulties in the story on the ground of natural law. They say that a body should ascend is a contravention to the law of gravity. It is just the kind of objection one might expect from a materialistic age. For it leaves out of account the mighty power of God. I will set no limits to that power. Believe in God, and you see no difficulty whatever in believing that He exalted Jesus to His own right hand. Far indeed from seeing difficulty in the Ascension, it appears to me to be pre-eminently natural and fitting. When Jesus rose again from the dead, it was not to resume the old life, it was not to spend a few more years like those He had spent in Galilee and then again fall a victim to death. Death had no more dominion over Him. He had risen into a state over which death had no power. Earth, with mortality as its distinguishing characteristic, was no home for such a person. He belonged to the spiritual and eternal world, and that He should pass into it is not surprising but supremely natural and fitting and indeed inevitable. The Ascension, I expect, was the completion of the Resurrection. The Lord delayed His departure for forty days in the interests of the disciples. As soon as their training and teaching was completed, He was seen no more on the ways of earth. He resumed His glory. "So then, the Lord Jesus, after He had spoken unto them, was received up into heaven."

The Benefits of the Ascension to Men

And the Ascension was more than the return of Christ to His glory: if this Book is to be believed it became a source of blessing to men. "He was received up into heaven." At first sight that seems to stand for loss; as a matter of fact it stands for gain. That was the first feeling of the disciples when their Lord was parted from them. The world seemed a poor place. They stood gazing up into heaven. All they had treasured and loved seemed to have vanished into the skies.

Not Loss but Gain

As a matter of fact, Christ's departure meant not impoverishment but enrichment. How shall I put it? They gained their Lord by losing Him. They lost Him in visible form, to have Him with them as a Spiritual Presence forever. "It is expedient for you that I go away," He had said. It was a hard saying at the time. I can imagine it was a hard saying to them on the day of the Ascension itself. And yet it was abundantly true. It was only by losing their Lord they could hope to keep Him. "Lo, I am with you all the days," He had said to them. And to be able to fulfil that promise, it was essential He should go away. Christ could only become the universal Christ by becoming the heavenly Christ. Supposing the disciples had been able to do what Mary in her eager but mistaken love sought to do, supposing they had been able to keep Him with them, Jesus would have become a local Presence. He would have been in Judaea, and men would have felt He was nowhere else. And then what Henry Drummond speaks of would actually have taken place, everybody who believed the Gospel would try to get within sight and touch and hearing of Jesus. Supposing He still walked in bodily form in Palestine today, we should all be making pilgrimages to the Holy Land, and so many millions of us would go that not only would the ordinary business of life be dislocated, but years and years might pass, indeed a whole lifetime might be spent without our being able to come near enough to Him to gaze upon His face or hear His voice. But He went away that He might come near to us all. There is no need to journey to Palestine or anywhere else. He is spiritually near to us always and everywhere. In the shop, in the office, in the home, in our pleasures, in our sorrows, in our temptations, the Lord is spiritually near. A localized Christ would have been to multitudes an absent Christ. But the Christ Who has passed within the heavens is by His Spirit present with us always even unto the end of the world.

Christ's Reign

"He was received up into heaven, and sat down at the right hand of God." Now the "right hand of God" is in Scripture a synonym for the omnipotent energy of God. Recall such phrases as these. "The right hand of the Lord is exalted, the right hand of the Lord doeth valiantly." "I will uphold thee with the right hand of My righteousness." "He will answer Him from heaven with the saving strength of His right hand." To sit down at the right hand of God means, therefore, to be clothed with all the energy and power of omnipotence. So the Lord Jesus when He left the earth assumed the place of supreme power. He is in the place of absolute power and dominion. "He sat down at the right hand of God." The Jesus Who died on the Cross is now the Jesus Who reigns. Is there not inspiration and encouragement in that thought? In these days of anxiety and turmoil there is nothing we need more than this, to realize that Jesus is at the right hand of God. That is what we need for our comfort in the midst of the perplexities and harassments of our own time. We see various forces at work in society, forces that menace and threaten our well-being—greed, hate, lust, envy. But the destinies of men are not at the mercy of these things after all. Let us comfort our hearts with this assurance—Jesus has sat down at the right hand of God. And that, too, is what we need for our encouragement in our Christian work.

The Strengthening Vision

The slow progress of the work has filled the hearts of Christian people with doubt and depression, and the doubt and depression in turn have paralyzed our energies. What we want to see is Jesus at the right hand of God. This is a vision that will banish despair. Our Lord has already won His victory and taken His seat on the throne. He only waits now for the fruit of His victory to be gathered. "When He had offered one sacrifice for sins forever, He sat down at the right hand of God, from henceforth expecting till His enemies be made the footstool of His feet." No matter how discouraging the work or how slow the progress, we shall be quite sure the Kingdoms of this world are to become the Kingdoms of our God and of His Christ, for already the Lord Jesus has been received up into heaven and has sat down at the right hand of God.

117
The Labor of the Disciples

"And they went forth, and preached every where, the Lord working with them, and confirming the word with signs following. Amen." —Mark 16:20.

THE GOSPEL STORY, so far as the evangelist is concerned, really ended with the Resurrection of Jesus Christ. But he adds these two sentences to let us know what happened to the Lord and to His disciples afterwards.

The Afterwards

What happened to the Lord was this, "He was received up into heaven and sat down at the right hand of God." What happened to the disciples was this, "They went forth and preached everywhere." But while the two sentences thus tell us the "afterwards" of our Lord and His disciples, we must not conceive of them as independent statements. They are rather two limbs of our statement. The one stands over against and balances the other. If we are to bring out the full force of the original we should have to render it something like this: "So then the Lord Jesus, on His part, was received up into heaven and sat down at the right hand of God, and the disciples, on their part, went forth and preached everywhere." The one action balances the other, follows upon the other, is the consequence and result of the other. It is a case of action and reaction. It was because Jesus was received up into heaven that the disciples went everywhere. It was the exaltation of the Lord that kindled the missionary fervor of the disciples. As Dr. Glover says, these two concluding verses tell the story of two ascensions, first the ascension of the Lord to glory, and then the ascension of the Church out of its gloom and sorrow and doubt and despair into courage and hope and triumphant zeal. And the one ascension was the consequence and result of the other. There would have been no Missionary Church, there would have been no Church at all, had it not been for this assurance in the hearts of Christian men and women, that "their Jesus had gone up on high."

716

Can we see why the one ascension should have issued in the other? Can we see why the fact that Jesus should have been received up into heaven inspired the disciples to go forth and preach everywhere? I think we can. I am going to suggest two reasons.

The Exalted Christ and the Gospel

First of all, it was the fact of the exaltation of Christ that gave them a Gospel to preach. I mean this, the Christ these men preached was the glorious and only Son of the Most High God. It was because He was the glorious and only Son of the Most High God, that they felt it worth their while to go everywhere and preach about Him. And it was the Resurrection and the Ascension (for the one was simply the completion of the other) which put Christ's glory and divinity beyond dispute. So that in a very deep and real sense it was the Resurrection and Ascension that gave them their Gospel to preach. We may be quite sure that, had our Lord's life ended in Joseph's rocky grave, the disciples would never have "gone forth everywhere and preached." They would have stolen away back to their Galilean homes and tried in absorption in work to forget the shattering of all their hopes in the Cross. But the Resurrection and Ascension made them quite sure their Master was the Son of God. It was in the light of the Resurrection and Ascension that they saw Jesus had a "cosmic significance." It was the exaltation of Jesus which gave them a Gospel which not only they could preach to the world, but which they felt they must preach to the world. It was the fact that Jesus was set down at the right hand of God that sent them forth everywhere.

The Apostolic Theme

For does any one imagine that these men would have gone everywhere preaching, and suffering untold things in the process, if they had only a good and brave man to speak about? The Greeks had, from their own point of view, a great and good man in Socrates, but I never heard of the Greeks going everywhere to preach Socrates. Does any one imagine—if Jesus had been only a kind of Jewish Socrates—that these disciples would have gone everywhere? The mere asking of such questions demonstrates the absurdity of the assertion that if we could only get far back enough we should find just Jesus the good Man. It was not Jesus the good Man these Apostles traveled far and wide to preach, but Jesus the mighty Son of God. They traveled far and wide to preach Him because it was of vital importance everybody should know of

Him, because men's redemption and eternal life depended on Him, because in Him God Himself had come down for the rescue of the world. That is why Paul traveled all the way from Antioch to Rome, because "there was no condemnation for men in Christ Jesus." That was why Peter toiled and dared and suffered because "there was no other name given under heaven amongst men wherein they must be saved." At the back of this missionary zeal of theirs was this mighty Gospel of theirs that Jesus was the only begotten Son of God, demonstrated as such by this fact, that He had been received up into heaven and had sat down at the right hand of God.

The World's Hope Today

There is no Gospel for the world in any faith less than that. If Jesus was the divine Son, if in Him God came down to this world for the redemption and rescue of man, there is a Gospel in that worth carrying to the ends of the earth, there is a Gospel in that which men will feel they must carry to the ends of the earth. But if Jesus was only a good Man and nothing more, what is the use of troubling about missions to the heathen? There have been other good men in the world, and if Jesus was nothing but a good Man He would be on the same level with Buddha, and Socrates, and Confucius, and it would be as profitable to preach one as the other. If that is all you can say about Him there is no sense in sending people to India and China and Africa to "preach Christ." In fact when men get to that point they do not trouble to preach Christ. Unitarianism does not as a rule issue in foreign missions, it shows no enthusiasm for the evangelizing of the world. Let me put it in a nutshell: you cannot impoverish your Christology without emptying your Gospel, and you cannot empty your Gospel without cutting the nerve of your foreign missionary enterprise. This is the only thing that will send men forth to preach everywhere, the belief that Jesus is the only Savior, the only begotten Son of God, demonstrated as such by the fact that He has been received up into heaven and has sat down at the right hand of God.

The Exalted Christ and Courage to Preach

But the fact of the exaltation of Christ not only gave the disciples a Gospel to preach, it also furnished them with the strength and courage that enabled them to preach it. Let us again try to put ourselves in these disciples' place. Look at the men and then think of the task; there seems a ridiculous disproportion between the one and the other. Apart from any opposition to be encountered, the work in mere extent appears absolutely impossible for such a handful of men. But it was not simply the extent of the work, there was also the difficulty of it. It was not simply that the world was a big place, it was a hostile place. Fancy flinging a little handful of men like this upon such a task when the wealth and learning and power of the world were all hostile to them! Fancy putting this little company of Galileans against the rulers and kings of the known world! If ever it seemed as if people had embarked upon a forlorn hope it was surely these disciples when they confronted the peoples, rulers, princes, kings of this world with their story of a crucified Christ. But they did it!

Undaunted Endeavor

With magnificent and subduing courage they did it! And they did not think they were engaged in a hopeless enterprise either. They flung themselves into the attack with a sort of joyous zest. They knew they were bound to win. Discouragements and disappointments did not daunt them. They were imprisoned, they were tempted, they were stoned, they were sawn asunder, they were slain with the sword; they wandered about in deserts and mountains and caves and the holes of the earth, they were destitute, afflicted, evil entreated, but they never for a moment lost heart. The Jewish Sanhedrin, the mob, the Roman magistrates, great Caesar himself, stirred themselves up to oppose and destroy them, but they never flinched or faltered. They knew that the power was not in the hands of the Jewish Sanhedrin, or the Roman magistrates, or even the so-called Master of the world; they knew that the Jesus Whom they preached had been received up into heaven and had sat down at the right hand of God. They were in the service of a victorious Lord. One ascension explains the other. The Lord arose into heaven, and they at the same moment arose out of all cowardice and fear. The Lord sat at the right hand of God, and they went everywhere preaching the Word.

And Courage for Us

And let me add again as I pass, it is the vision of that glorified and exalted Lord that will give us courage and strength for our task today. Stupendous tasks still confront us both at home and abroad. Think of the mighty problem of the vice and sin and religious indifference of our great cities; think of the world shaken and shattered by war; think of the vast unevangelized lands of heathendom. If we look at the task and then simply look at our own resources we shall despair. What we need to do is to look at our exalted Lord. You remember how Dr. Dale used to say that when thoughts of Christ's tenderness and love failed to bring him the comfort he wanted, the thought of Christ's Lordship steadied and strengthened him. That is the thought we need to recover, the thought of Christ's Lordship, the remembrance of His victory. He is already at the right hand of God. We see Jesus crowned. All things are in His hands. He will not faint nor be weary. He will not fail nor be discouraged. Let us think of Him. Let our eyes gaze upon Him. Let us see Him there in the place of supreme power. Then doubt will flee. If we see Jesus at the right hand of God, we too shall be ready to go everywhere, preaching the Word.

The Blessed Partnership
"They went forth and preached everywhere, the Lord (that is, Christ) working with them." Their Lord had been received up into heaven, but He had not left them to toil alone. He worked with them. They were encouraged in their toil not simply by the thought of their Lord's triumph, but by His actual presence and help. It was not a case of the Lord smiling upon them from a distance, it was a case of the Lord clasping their hands and making them sufficient for the fight. You remember what Paul says when the most critical hour of his life was come and he was set before Caesar. His friends had practically all deserted him, but he says, "The Lord stood by me and strengthened me and delivered me out of the lion's mouth." That is it, exactly, "The Lord stood by me and strengthened me." And He stood by and strengthened all His disciples. He did not leave them to toil alone. Their work was done in a blessed partnership. In and of themselves they could have accomplished little. But when you read this sentence, "the Lord working with them," it changes the entire outlook. "With five shillings Teresa can do nothing," said the great Spanish mystic when her friends smiled at her idea of building an orphanage when funds seemed to be almost wholly absent, "but with five shillings and God there is nothing Teresa cannot do." And it is so still. All Christian work is done in this happy partnership. They talk of the Pope as the Vicar of Christ. But vicar means one who takes the place of another because that other is absent. But Christ needs no vicar. Because Christ is not absent. He is with us always even to the end of the world. And therein lies our sufficiency. It is not we who are engaged in the work. It is Christ and we. "The Lord working with us." We have known it sometimes. When we have been tired and dispirited we have had Paul's blessed experience, the Lord has stood by us and strengthened us.

"We touch Him in life's throng and press, and we are whole again."

The Signs that Follow

"And confirming the word by the signs that followed." Confirming the word, ratifying it, demonstrating the truth of it, by the signs that followed. The signs that followed are no doubt the signs referred to in verses 17 and 18. The world was not able to dismiss the Gospel the Christian preachers brought with a shrug of the shoulders, because of the signs that were wrought by their hands. Men felt that the mighty power of God was working through them, and that these mighty works were God's testimony that the words which they spoke were true. They were the divine seal to the message. The Lord confirmed the word by the signs that followed. But we need not, and indeed we ought not, to confine these signs to such wonders as the raising of Dorcas to life by Peter, or the healing of the lame man at Lystra by Paul, or the deliverance of the demented girl in Philippi by the same great Apostle. The conversion of evil men was a still more notable sign and that sign was continually following the Word. Take what happened in Corinth as an example. Corinth was in some respects the most notorious city of the ancient world. Vice there was exalted not simply into a fashion but into a religion. These were the kind of people Paul found in Corinth, "drunkards, adulterers, fornicators, revilers, effeminate and such like." But the great miracle happened, "Ye were washed, ye were justified, ye were sanctified in the name of the Lord Jesus and in the Spirit of our God." And that was the mightiest sign that followed the Word. That was what demonstrated its divinity and truth. That was what impressed the world to which it was preached. By it bad men were made good; foul men were made clean; drunken men were made sober; hard men were made kind. By it men entered into possession of eternal life. And it was that which impressed the world. "The Lord confirmed the Word by the signs that followed."

And still Follow

And these signs still follow. We are still privileged to behold confirmation of the Word in the transformation of human lives. We see the miracle here at home; the missionaries are privileged to see it abroad. Wherever the Gospel is preached it produces the same amazing transfiguration of human life. There are a multitude around the throne of all tribes and nations and peoples and tongues who have washed their robes and made them white in the blood of the Lamb. They are the signs that confirm the Word. There may be many things about the doctrines of our faith that puzzle us, but this thing we know, the preaching of Christ and Him crucified, changes, converts, transforms, transfigures men. It accomplishes this miracle where everything else has failed. What further need have we of witness? The best evidence of the truth of Christianity is that it is a converting religion. There is in our Christ cleansing, healing, saving power. Let us go forth and preach Him everywhere! He will work with us and confirm the Word by the signs which follow.

Other Expositions of Mark

J (oseph) A (ddison) Alexander, *Commentary on Mark* (Grand Rapids: Kregel Publications, 1980).

A (lexander) B (almain) Bruce, *The Training of the Twelve* (Grand Rapids: Kregel Publications, 1971).

James Morison, *The Gospel According to Mark* (Grand Rapids: Kregel Publications, 1981).

H (enry) B (arclay) Swete, *Commentary on Mark* (Grand Rapids: Kregel Publications, 1977),